FOR the PEOPLE

1,608 Ways to Get Your

Share of the Little-Known Bargains

the Government Offers

Edited by
KEVIN IRELAND

RODALE

Cover photographs by Kurt Wilson/Rodale Images (currency) and PhotoDisc (flag)
Illustrations by Eve Steccati (shields) and Alan Baseden (sidebar icons)

Library of Congress Cataloging-in-Publication Data

For the people : 1,608 ways to get your share of the little-known bargains the
government offers / edited by Kevin Ireland.
        p.   cm.
Includes index.
ISBN 1–57954–094–5 hardcover
ISBN 1–57954–296–4 paperback
1. Administrative agencies—United States—Handbooks, manuals, etc.   2. Grants-
in-aid—United States—Handbooks, manuals, etc.   3. State governments—United
States—Handbooks, manuals, etc.   4. Local government—United States—Handbooks,
manuals, etc.   I. Ireland, Kevin, 1952–
        JK421 .F59 2000
    352.7—dc21   00–023831

Distributed to the book trade by St. Martin's Press

2   4   6   8   10   9   7   5   3   1   hardcover
2   4   6   8   10   9   7   5   3   1   paperback

Visit us on the Web at www.rodalebooks.com, or call us toll-free at (800) 848-4735.

RODALE

WE **INSPIRE** AND **ENABLE** PEOPLE TO IMPROVE
THEIR LIVES AND THE WORLD AROUND THEM

FOR THE PEOPLE STAFF

MANAGING EDITOR: Kevin Ireland

WRITERS: Ronald Campbell, Sara J. Henry, Dean King, Erik Kolbell, Jordan Matus, Nick Morrow, Jan Norman, Susan Paterno, Charlie Slack, Kim Caldwell Steffen, Rob Walker, Logan Ward, Judy West, Bernard Wolfson, Roger Yepsen

ASSOCIATE ART DIRECTOR: Charles Beasley

COVER AND INTERIOR DESIGNER: Tanja Lipinski Cole

ASSOCIATE RESEARCH MANAGER: Jane Unger Hahn

PRIMARY RESEARCH COORDINATOR: Anita C. Small

BOOK PROJECT RESEARCHER: Jan Eickmeier

EDITORIAL RESEARCHERS: Leah Flickinger, Karen Jacobs, Jennifer S. Kushnier, Mary S. Mesaros, Elizabeth B. Price, Anita A. Small, Terry Sutton-Kravitz, Teresa A. Yeykal, Nancy Zelko

SENIOR COPY EDITOR: Jane Sherman

EDITORIAL PRODUCTION MANAGER: Marilyn Hauptly

LAYOUT DESIGNER: Pat Mast

MANUFACTURING COORDINATORS: Brenda Miller, Jodi Schaffer, Patrick T. Smith

RODALE ACTIVE LIVING BOOKS

VICE PRESIDENT AND PUBLISHER: Neil Wertheimer

EXECUTIVE EDITOR: Susan Clarey

EDITORIAL DIRECTOR: Michael Ward

MARKETING DIRECTOR: Janine Slaughter

PRODUCT MARKETING MANAGER: Sindy Berner

BOOK MANUFACTURING DIRECTOR: Helen Clogston

MANUFACTURING MANAGERS: Eileen Bauder, Mark Krahforst

RESEARCH MANAGER: Ann Gossy Yermish

COPY MANAGER: Lisa D. Andruscavage

DIGITAL PROCESSING MANAGER: Leslie M. Keefe

PRODUCTION MANAGER: Robert V. Anderson Jr.

OFFICE MANAGER: Jacqueline Dornblaser

OFFICE STAFF: Julie Kehs, Mary Lou Stephen, Catherine E. Strouse

CONTENTS

INTRODUCTION

Government for the people.

That's a phrase you probably ran across in grade school when you memorized Lincoln's Gettysburg Address. But does it apply in the real world today? Or more important, beyond paving the roads, beyond building parks and policing the streets, does government actually work for people like you?

The answer is yes—emphatically yes.

At the local, state, and national levels, the government and its more than 19 million employees can offer you thousands of dollars worth of goods, services, and advice to help improve your life. Add what's offered by schools and nonprofit groups—most of which are supported directly or indirectly by the government and your taxes—and you have access to the equivalent of a tidy second income. And it's all yours simply for the asking.

So why aren't you taking advantage of what's available? Often, it's because you—and most other people—don't know that these amazing programs exist. Or if you do, you haven't figured out how to access them.

For the People will change that.

This book will take you to the heart of the government and show you exactly how to get what it has to offer. And we do mean exactly. To produce this book, we spent more than a year searching for the government's hidden riches. Our 15 savvy writers investigated official records, explored the Internet, and wrote dozens of letters. Then they made nearly 2,000 phone calls to people who really know the ins and outs of government—from government insiders and influential lobbyists to shrewd political activists and the most effective civic leaders. The result is this road map to hundreds of extraordinary opportunities, some buried so deep that few people other than government employees even know they exist.

For example, this book will show you how the government can:

> ...beyond paving the roads, beyond building parks and policing the streets, does government actually work for people like you? The answer is yes —emphatically yes.

✓ Help you can vacation beachside in the U.S. Virgin Islands for $20 a night

✓ Cut through red tape to get you exceptional service, whether you want a special tour of the White House, a last-minute passport, or some political pressure to get your mom's Social Security check delivered on time

✓ Help you write a résumé and improve your interview skills so you can get a better-paying job

✓ Provide training, advice, and loans to help you start your own business

✓ Help you trim your health care costs, plan your retirement, and burglarproof your home

✓ Offer you a wealth of free and low-cost goods—from videotapes, photos, and books to plants, rare foods, and firewood.

SAVVY WAYS TO WORK THE SYSTEM

But *For the People* is much more than an incredible listing of goods and services. It also explains how the "system" works and teaches you the skills you need to truly make government respond to your needs.

If you're struggling to get your town to clean the trashy lot next door or fighting to get the police to curb speeders on your block, this book will show you five ways to get results instead of a polite brush-off. If you want your school district to build a new playground or your city to save the last piece of open land in your area, the insiders in this book will explain how you can make a powerful case and muster community support for the project.

With the expert advice and shrewd tips and insider contacts this book provides, you'll be able to handle problems in virtually every area of your life.

Think of *For the People* as an operating manual for running the government machine. With its help, you'll see that government truly is here to do your bidding, to meet your needs—to work for the people.

Now read this book and let government work for you.

HOW to USE THIS BOOK

Early in researching this book, we learned one clear fact: The government is a moving target.

Area codes and telephone numbers change. The names of specific programs shift. Even the level of government that administers a program can change. That means that some of the contact information we've offered here may not be accurate by the time the book reaches your hands.

Recognizing this, we've suggested several ways to gain access to the goods, services, and advice we've mentioned. First, we've provided mailing addresses, since these are least likely to be revised. Next, we've directed you to local sources with the most current telephone numbers for the programs we cite. Finally, we've pointed you to Web sites, which are one of the best ways to reach government these days.

If these don't lead you to the service you want, look in the government pages of your local phone book for officials who conduct much of the government's day-to-day business. This means people such as your town clerk or the caseworker in your state legislator's or congressmember's office. They are in touch with agencies at many levels of government, and if they can't help you directly, they should be able to point you to someone who can.

> The Internet has had a dramatic impact on most of America, and nowhere is that impact more apparent than in improving your access to the government.

THE INTERNET: YOUR KEY TO GOVERNMENT'S DOOR

The Internet has had a dramatic impact on most of America, and nowhere is that more apparent than in improving your access to the government. Once, you might have phoned a government agency and been stymied by busy signals or passed from person to person without getting the answer you wanted. Now, using a computer at home or at your local library or college campus, you can quickly get in touch with a government agency's World Wide Web site. There you'll find virtually anything you need, from answers to tax questions and health advice to information on jobs, scholarships, and plant care.

Keep in mind, though, that Web site designs change frequently, so you may not find the name of the specific publication, program, or service we mention when you get to the home page we've referred you to. If that's the case, click on the home page's search button (almost all government home pages have one) and type in the name we've cited. That will usually lead you to a link to the correct Web page as well as to pages on related subjects.

ONE

Putting Government in Perspective

CHAPTER 1

GETTING GOVERNMENT to WORK for YOU

Two hundred years ago, you wouldn't have needed this book. One hundred years ago, you would have needed three or four paragraphs. Fifty years ago, a couple of chapters would have sufficed.

Today, you need all of it.

The top-down, faceless government of the past is morphing, evolving at high speed into something that's more responsive and potentially more generous, especially to people who learn the secrets of operating in the new system. To make the new government work for you, though, you need to understand two things.

✓ The trends that are changing it

✓ The techniques for making government more responsive to your needs

Let's start with the trends.

> The way government operates has changed dramatically, opening up a wide array of new benefits and services that the average American has never heard of. Here's how you can take advantage of these changes.

THE CHANGING FACE OF GOVERNMENT

The founders of the country had a strong belief in a minimalist government after living through the tyranny of the British monarchy. Thomas Jefferson, for example, felt that government should stay out of the way and let the natural workings of society make it prosperous.

"We don't believe that any more," says Gordon S. Wood, Ph.D., professor of history at Brown University in Providence, Rhode Island. Now, government is considered the key to the economy and a major player in nearly every aspect of our lives. "Neither Jefferson nor even Lincoln could have anticipated the kind of government we have now," says Dr. Wood. "This country's first 100 years were spent

FACTOID

EACH YEAR, THE FEDERAL GOVERNMENT ALONE SPENDS ABOUT $1.5 *TRILLION*, OR MORE THAN $5,000 PER PERSON ON AVERAGE. THROW IN STATE AND LOCAL GOVERNMENT SPENDING, AND THE AVERAGE RISES ABOVE $11,000.

dismantling the government. The next 100 years were spent bringing it back in."

Consider government as employer. Today, the federal government, the 50 states, and myriad cities, counties, and other local governments together employ nearly 17 million people. That's one of every eight American workers. And that total doesn't include the millions of people who work for public schools, hospitals, and relief groups, all dedicated to the public interest.

Government clearly has a huge impact on your life, but its role is changing in ways that can make it even more responsive to your particular needs.

Service at the Speed of Light

Looking over the past 2 centuries, you can see that if there has been one constant to government, it's been change. That's even more true today, says Thomas J. Bergin, Ph.D., professor of computer science and information systems at American University in Washington, D.C.

Two of the driving forces behind today's changes are relatively new pieces of technology: the personal computer and the Internet—and it's not only the face of government that now has a digital appearance.

"The Internet will become the major backbone of our entire culture," predicts Dr. Bergin. Already, it has revolutionized the way government interacts with its citizens. As an example, Dr. Bergin tells how, not so long ago, he needed a tax form.

"I called the feds, and I was on the phone for 45 minutes," he recalls. "After that, it took a full 3 weeks to get the form in the mail." Today, you can download that form from the Internet and print it out in a matter of minutes.

That's just one small way that the government's Internet connection is making it more responsive to the average person's needs. If you live in Boston, you can pay your traffic tickets online. If you're a contractor in Seattle, you can check on the progress of your building permit via computer. If you own a company in Washington state, you can pay your taxes on the Internet.

In addition, the more removed you are from a major city, the more valuable this connection can be. "Some poor guy out in the hinterlands, for example, can now put together a federal loan application in days instead of months," says Dr. Bergin. Over the next 10 years, governments at all levels hope to put nearly all of their services online, he says.

The Evolution of Devolution

There's an even more exciting concept being embraced by government officials these days. It's called devolution. Basically, it means shifting responsibility—and money—from the federal level to the states and from the states to the local governments.

Devolution has been gathering speed for two decades, since the first presidential term of Ronald Reagan, says Frank T. Colon, Ph.D., professor of political science at Lehigh University in Bethlehem, Pennsylvania, who also serves as an elected official in nearby Hanover Township.

In the early 1980s, for example, the federal government stopped building its own subsidized housing for the poor; instead, it gave the states grants to provide a variety of social services, including housing. Another example: In 1996, Congress and the president enacted welfare reform, giving states control of the welfare system.

But you're not on welfare, and you don't live in subsidized housing. How can devolution affect you?

Try money, accountability, and accessibility.

When programs are passed down to the local level, it means that the people in charge of them— your state, county, city, and town representatives— are closer to you and hence more accessible and accountable.

This kind of accessibility is going to be increasingly important, says Dr. Colon, as more programs and services are devolved. Expect to see fewer state

GETTING CONNECTED

The government is a storehouse for a wealth of valuable information. Until recently, however, accessing that knowledge meant following pretty much the same steps that Americans used 200 years ago: writing or visiting an office in person, requesting information, and hoping that the workers there had time to get you the files you wanted.

The Internet has changed all that forever.

The federal government, all 50 states, and many cities and counties have posted valuable facts on the Internet. They're putting the *public* back in *public information.* All you need in order to harvest this cornucopia is a computer, a Web browser, and some patience.

Finding your state's Web site is a breeze. Just type in www.state.*(insert the two-letter state abbreviation)*.us. This will take you to your state's home page. From there, you can click on popular sites like "Tourism," or search for specific information. Many states offer links to city and county sites as well.

Unfortunately, cities and counties don't use a standard form for their Web addresses. If your local government is on the Web, the city or county clerk or your city council member's office can give you the address. Expect to find nuggets such as building permit information and city budgets there.

If you're planning a long vacation, be sure to check the Web sites of the states that you want to visit. Each state Web site offers tourist information. A handful of states, such as North and South Dakota, even offer updates on local road conditions and weather.

Many state Web sites contain links to legislators and to departments that you may need to deal with. A handful go far beyond these basic services, giving their citizens easy access to information that would normally require days of digging. Others, with a little kick from the public now and then, are sure to follow.

For example, many parents of young children struggle to find good child care. If you live in Ohio, you need look no fur-

ther than the state Web site. For a quick, easy guide to licensed child care facilities near your home or work, all you have to do is click on "Previously Featured Sites." The child care search service even lets you zero in on facilities that care for infants or provide after-school care.

If you have elderly parents living in Florida, visit the Florida Web site and check the Agency for Health Care Administration Guide to Nursing Homes in Florida. This site can help you choose a nursing home and warn you away from homes that give substandard care.

At the New York state site, careful donors nationwide can find useful financial information on most of the big national charities. Click on the link for the state attorney general, then search for "charity." The attorney general posts annual reports for every sizable charity that solicits money from New Yorkers. You can look there for your favorite charity's annual income and expenditures, as well as for a breakdown of its spending on programs, overhead, and fund-raising.

police and more regional police forces in the future. Expect more environmental programs to move from the state to the local level. The same is likely to be true of many other services, such as employment programs, park management, and land use—all things that will directly affect you.

GETTING YOUR SHARE

Yes, government has changed, potentially opening up a world of benefits, goods, and services to you. As Dr. Wood says, "There are expectations that you wouldn't have dreamed of years ago, when the only contact with government you had was when it delivered the mail."

To get what you want, you need to know whom to contact at the local level and then how to get them to respond to your needs. Here are six ways to find the right people.

Read the Local Newspapers

"Ask 10 people where they get their news, and 9 of them will say TV and major newspapers," says David Hershey-Webb, community advocate for New York State Assemblyman Edward Sullivan. But the major media concentrate on the big names. The small names—the elected officials, volunteer commissioners, and full-time bureaucrats who run your town or city—rarely appear in print outside of small-town and giveaway newspapers.

WHAT ONE TOWN OFFERS

Think government has nothing more than the basics to offer you? Think again. Government serves a rich buffet of goodies to the public, most of them cheap, and many of them free. Just ask the 7,130 residents of Rochester, Michigan.

Rochester's citizens get basic services from the city, but the services don't stop with the ABCs, like police protection. And they don't stop with the city government, either. Residents of Rochester can take advantage of services offered by the city, Oakland County, and the state, as well as local schools and parks.

"In the summer, the downtown development authority stages a 2-day concert," says city manager Ken Johnson. "The greater Rochester area also has a variety of programs for our older citizens. Some years ago, Rochester purchased an old school and converted it into a senior center, where Rochester, Rochester Hills, and Oakland Township offer recreation, woodworking, ceramics, and the like. The Older Persons Commission also offers a free shuttle service to the center, as well as to local shopping districts and, when necessary, doctors' offices."

Tennis, anyone? The local schools operate lighted courts, which are available to the public. And golfers can putter around nearby public courses. If practicing your tee shots during a Michigan winter seems unappealing, don't worry: The Oakland County parks department operates a dome-covered driving range. The parks department also operates a water park and a refrigerated toboggan run.

Two nearby state-supported colleges, Oakland University and Oakland Community College, "offer a variety of cultural programs, exhibits, symposia, and lectures, many of which are free to the public," city clerk Nancy Hill says.

"There are hidden treasures of information in small newspapers that only the savvy know to look for," Hershey-Webb says. For example, stories about local boards will tell you who chairs each meeting, who runs the staff—in short, who really makes the decisions.

These newspapers also will tell you over time which agencies get a lot done and which ones merely talk. As an added benefit, small-town papers are crammed with features such as comprehensive listings of elected officials' offices.

Check Out the Local Library

"It may seem kind of tame, but most public libraries have tremendous amounts of information about services at a local level," says Bill Schechter, director of the Program for Community Problem Solving at the National Civic League, an organization based in Washington, D.C., that promotes citizen participation. "Librarians can point you in the right direction, but few people ever think to look there."

Ask your librarian for written materials listing the top officials in local governments; the local, state, and federal programs that serve your region; and how you can use those services.

Visit the Local Historical Society

Historical societies "are seldom-used reservoirs of information about how things work," Hershey-

"In addition," Hill says, "Rochester supports a superb library program that includes summer reading programs for kids and book groups and chat groups for people of all ages."

Rochester and Rochester Hills sponsor a recreation program for children, including such activities as a "breakfast with Santa Claus," "teddy bear picnic," and "nursery school olympics" for younger kids, as well as instructional sports camps for older ones, according to director John Andersen. They even have a dance program that draws more than 1,000 children each year, and a 9-week day camp for which they will subsidize the cost if a child cannot pay full tuition. Adult sports programs, including volleyball and soccer, are also available for a team fee.

One of the best examples of the city's support is something that most residents see only indirectly: Government has kept the town flourishing by investing in the downtown commercial district. Johnson says that through the efforts of the downtown development authority, the city has put in parking lots and pedestrian amenities such as sidewalk benches and trees to make the downtown appealing. And Oakland County has offered help through its economic development experts.

In addition, the county provides an annual economic forecast, giving business-people expert insights into financial trends. Entrepreneurs looking for new opportunities can find ideas in county-published community profiles of Rochester and the other towns and cities in the county. The profiles list major employers, demographic trends, education levels, tax rates, and other information of interest to businesses hunting for a good location.

Also, the state of Michigan offers an array of incentives, including assistance in recruiting employees and finding sites, to businesses that want to make a home in Rochester.

Webb says. "Curators are often oral historians who can tell you exactly how your government operates and who's in charge."

Also, historical societies may interview prominent local citizens to get perspective on past controversies. Sometimes, the people they interview are still active in local affairs, and what they say about past doings can give you insight into who really runs your town and how they think and act.

Look for a Community Organization

"Community organizations are often well-kept secrets," Hershey-Webb says, "but the good ones have a keen knowledge of whom to bring pressure on in order to get certain things done."

Highly visible community organizations will get regular mentions in the community newspaper. But don't stop there. Hershey-Webb also suggests calling local clergy to see if they can point you to a good community organization. You should attend at least one meeting, introduce yourself to the group's coordinator, and ask for literature about their issues and work.

Meet a Caseworker

Every member of Congress, many state legislators, and even county and city elected officials hire caseworkers, whose job is to make government work for voters.

Casework is a big deal to elected officials because it helps them be reelected. Former U.S. Senator Alfonse D'Amato of New York was so famous for his attention to constituent service that he was known as "Pothole Al."

Schechter suggests making an appointment with a caseworker in the office of one of your local officials. Tell the caseworker that you want to know what he does, how he might help you, and how to contact him.

Caseworkers are valuable allies. They know how the system works, they can tell you where to find the answers you need, and they can make that vital first call to get you in the right door. If that isn't enough, they can intercede, using the clout of their boss on your behalf.

"Usually, when people need assistance, they'll ask their congressmember or assemblymember, because that's what they're there for," explains Schechter. "But the real grassroots work is done by caseworkers, the local foot soldiers who work in the offices of these officials and whose responsibility it is to troubleshoot specific problems for individual constituents."

Meet Your Neighbors

If a neighborhood problem concerns you, there's a good chance that it concerns some of your neighbors as well. Neighborhood associations exist to deal with the gritty problems that are too small for community groups or city councils but too big for one or two discontented residents. Neighborhood associations are great vehicles for lobbying for traffic lights, fighting unsightly developments, and generally making the neighborhood heard at city hall.

In Los Angeles, for example, the nation's second largest city, neighborhood groups routinely have a say in big developments. Local groups demanded and achieved preservation of some wetlands near the site of Steven Spielberg's proposed DreamWorks studio. Other neighborhood groups won parking restrictions near the billion-dollar Getty Center and made sure that the vast arts campus was painted pale tan, not bright white as architect Richard Meier had intended.

WAYS TO GET WHAT YOU WANT

So, now you know whom to ask for help. That still leaves a big question: How can you make sure that you, of all the thousands of folks seeking help, are heard? Keep these four simple rules in mind.

Be Polite

Say you're a government worker, and you get calls from two citizens. The first one is demanding and obnoxious; the second is friendly and reasonable. Which person would you go out of your way to help?

"The more pleasant you are to government workers, the more approachable they'll be," says Bob Kalian, co-author of *The Best Free Things in America*.

➜ WHAT INSIDERS SAY:

Harold Rubin, a professional mediator with more than 20 years of experience, suggests three steps that

---

LIVING NEXT DOOR TO "CITY HALL"

Why fight city hall when you can invite it over for a quiet chat instead?

The newest and most pervasive form of government is the homeowners' association. In suburbs and planned communities across the country, homeowners' associations set speed limits and curfews, repair streets and roofs, and act as middlemen between residents and local governments.

"In a city or town, a homeowners' association will probably be responsible for little more than cosmetic issues—agreements that you can't put aluminum siding on your house or have a pickup truck in a driveway, that sort of thing," says Bill Schechter, director of the Program for Community Problem Solving at the National Civic League, an organization based in Washington, D.C., that promotes citizen participation. "But in unincorporated areas

such as Columbia, Maryland, or Highlands Ranch, Colorado, that don't fall under the jurisdiction of a town or village, they can be quite potent. There they can assess property, establish rules, elect a board of directors, and adjudicate disputes between residents. In effect, they don't augment local government. They often *are* local government."

One of their most critical roles is representing neighborhood interests to larger governments, just as a city pleads its residents' case to the state.

Listen to Nancy Morrison, a board member of the River at North Campbell Homeowners' Association in Tucson.

"Our neighborhood was erected with very narrow streets," she says, "and some time after it was completed, the fire department came through and informed us that

we had neglected to identify one of these streets as a fire lane, which meant that a series of signs had to be posted along the length of the street.

"Some homeowners didn't want the signs because they felt that they would detract from the beauty of the street, and they wanted us to fight it. But the fire department was not only within its rights to force us to erect the signs, it was also prepared to levy a substantial fine on us.

"On behalf of the members, the association board entered into negotiations with the fire department and was able to reach a compromise. We agreed to the signs, they agreed to place the signs in such a way that they would not detract from the beauty of the street, and they agreed to waive any and all fines. Everybody won something," she says.

you can take to put a government official in your corner. "First, acknowledge that you're grateful that this person is there to help you and that you respect his ability and appreciate his willingness to help," he says. "Second, make it clear that you don't see him as the problem; you're coming to him because he has the skill to take care of you. And third, sympathize with him and acknowledge how difficult it must be to have to listen to people's complaints all day. This puts you both on the same side of the fence instead of on opposing sides."

Be Prepared

Before you ask for help, be sure you have answers to the obvious questions. How deep is the pothole that you want filled? Where exactly is it? How long has it been there? Is it isolated or part of a major road problem?

"Try to prepare ahead of time for any questions the government worker might ask you," says Kalian. "By making his work a little easier, you stand a better chance of getting swift action on your request."

Be Clear

Don't ask to have your street repaved when you simply need a pothole filled. Figure out exactly what you want before you ask. You probably will get only a few minutes of an official's time, so don't waste it on side issues.

Be Assertive

Don't let someone stonewall you. If you're not getting satisfaction from the "assistant director of pothole repair," politely ask to speak to the director. If you can't find an employee who will give you satisfaction, take your case to the elected official who oversees the department.

If the first person you call doesn't have the authority to help you, ask him to recommend

someone who does have it. Ask the first person to help you get your foot in the next guy's door. And be sure to mention your first contact's name when you call the next person in the chain. That should convince him that you're serious and prevent him from bouncing you back to the person you first called.

"It never hurts to create a careful 'paper trail' of your complaints and how you've gone about trying to solve them," Hershey-Webb says. "Letters, photographs (where applicable), and even phone logs serve to keep the issue clear to you and can serve as evidence of your efforts to solve the problem if you have to appeal to a higher authority."

●◆ *WHAT INSIDERS SAY:*

Watch the calendar. There are days when even the friendliest government agency won't have the time to help you.

"In general, few government workers are going to be able to do much for you if you call them on a Friday afternoon or the day before a long weekend," Kalian says.

Other times to avoid? "The end of the fiscal year (September 30 for the federal government and June 30 for most state and local governments) can be bad because agencies are trying to close their books," Kalian says.

"The start of a newly elected administration means a lot of new people in new offices, so they won't necessarily have a grasp of their agency. Also, depending upon the agency, governments usually have their fewest workers on staff in the summer months."

THE INSIDE TRACK

Suppose that you want to get to know a family who just moved in down the street. You probably would stop by, introduce yourself, and get to know them on a personal basis. Well, the same principle holds true for getting what you want from government. Here's how to make yourself and your wishes known.

THE SAVING OF STRAUS PARK

Developing relationships with government officials, attending local meetings, and pleading your case again and again: It sounds like a lot of work to get what you want, but the payoff can be great when everything clicks. Ask Leon Auerbach, a New York City resident who, with his neighbors, decided to save Straus Park, a ¼-acre "vest-pocket park" that had been abandoned to vandals.

Auerbach, who lives near the park, says that its revival began with a small step. "Three families wanted to see some trees planted on our block, and through private solicitation and city funds, we managed to do so," he says. "The trees were an impetus for us to create a block association that encouraged our neighbors to care for the new trees, hire an evening security force, and eventually, begin spending Saturdays in the park on cleanup and spruce-up detail."

Auerbach and his neighbors wanted the city to back their efforts, so they contacted the parks department and got the cooperation of officials in what they wanted to do. They also contacted the local police precinct. Eventually, they forged a relationship with the community patrol officer, who agreed to maintain an occasional police presence in the park.

"Over time, we became something of a known entity in the neighborhood and approached our community board for money to renovate the park," Auerbach says. The board, together with the office of the borough president, agreed to put some funds into the park. Later, the city parks department put more money in the till. The parks department also supervised the redesign and reconstruction of the park, welcoming the neighbors' input.

"We even fell into some additional funding for a fountain restoration when descendants of the Straus family came forward and agreed to set up a trust fund for the fountain," Auerbach said.

Today, the group, known as Friends of Straus Park, continues to work with the borough president, the parks department, the police precinct, the sanitation department, and neighboring block associations to keep the park vital and beautiful, he says.

What advice does Auerbach have for fellow activists? "Make sure you have enough people involved in your cause. With so many two-income households, free time is short, so you have to have many hands to do your work. Also, make sure your cause is shared by other volunteers. The hard work of neighbors, particularly the individual who tends the flower gardens, contributed to the fact that people clearly saw the park as a place to come and relax and a place for their kids to come," he says.

"Also," says Auerbach, "this was a success because the community worked together to identify a problem, came up with an action plan, and worked with local officials."

Be a Familiar Face

You get mail every day. You probably get several phone messages at home and at work. If you have Internet access, you may get dozens of e-mails daily. You have all of this communication, and you're a private citizen. Now suppose that you're trying to reach the person in charge of repairing your city's streets. Imagine the volume of letters, phone messages, and e-mails that he gets every day. Yours will be just one more on the pile, unless you make yourself stand out.

How can you do that? By meeting your public servants face-to-face.

Hershey-Webb offers a specific example. "I get maybe 20 or 30 calls a day just from constituents who are having some sort of problem with their landlords. Many of them are simply voices at the end of a phone line. And we do what we can for them.

"Not long ago, though, an elderly woman came into our office with a typical complaint—a landlord who wasn't turning on the heat. We sat together, talked a while, and I got a better feel for what she wanted and how I could help," he says. "I think I naturally cared for her more, too, because there's something about a face-to-face encounter that makes strangers become, if not friends, at least allies. Eventually, our office turned up the heat on the landlord, and he did the same in her apartment building."

◗◆ *WHAT INSIDERS SAY:*

Want to improve your chances of getting help from your local rep? Take the time to develop a relationship before you need assistance. "If I'm a public servant, and I've shaken the hand of a constituent at a traffic commission meeting, and we've exchanged pleasant words, I'm going to care more about that constituent when he calls me about installing a stop sign on his corner than I would if we'd never met," Kalian says.

Join a Board

Elected officials in local government are almost always part-time, says Lehigh University political science professor Dr. Frank Colon. Because of that, there's no way they have the time to keep track of everything that goes on in their governments, so they form volunteer advisory boards. There are numerous examples: parks and recreation boards, zoning boards, hospital boards, library boards, and police boards. The boards are staffed by unpaid volunteers, nominated by members of local government. They usually meet once or twice a month for a couple of hours.

If you volunteer for one of these boards, says Dr. Colon, "you get to be an insider and see how things function. You get to know who the players are. You have access."

Let's say that you have a beef about your new property tax assessment. If you're on a board, chances are good that you'll know the assessor's name and the elected official who oversees that department. And if you don't know it, you'll know someone who does. "Best of all, you're in a position where somebody is more likely to listen to you," says Dr. Colon.

Getting on a board is usually pretty easy. Simply write or call the local town or county official who represents your area. Ask for a list of board vacancies and look for one that might interest you, then ask the official to nominate you for the position.

In many areas, local governments are starved for board members, says Dr. Colon, and they'll be glad for your involvement. In other areas, it might be a bit tougher. If that's the case, you may be put on a waiting list.

CHAPTER 2

The SECRETS of GETTING YOUR WAY

When you need a permit for your company's annual picnic, advice on what to plant in your backyard, or access to any of the dozens of other standard services that local government provides, chances are you'll get what you want without a hitch. But if you're making a special, large-scale appeal, such as asking your town to build a nature trail or lobbying a city department to fund a seniors program, getting the answer you want may be a little tougher.

That's when you need to apply some pressure. "Figure out what's necessary to make government officials do what you've asked them to do, what they were hired to do," says Bob Kalian, co-author of *The Best Free Things in America*.

How do you go about it? With persistence and strategies like those in this chapter.

> Sometimes government just won't work for you, no matter who you ask, no matter how skillfully you push the buttons. That's when you need to get people's attention by turning things up a notch.

WORKING AROUND THE ROADBLOCKS

Say that you've asked your parks department to create a nature trail on the outskirts of town, and, for whatever reason, the department has turned you down. Don't get frustrated. Don't shout and point fingers. And don't give up. Success may be just a matter of making one more phone call or finding a bit more backing. The trick is figuring out where and how to apply your effort, so first you need to do a little digging.

Ask the Right Questions

Request a meeting with the official who made the decision and ask why it was made. You may find

FACTOID

WHEN YOU'RE LOBBYING GOVERNMENT, IT PAYS TO KEEP THE FOCUS LOCAL. ACCORDING TO A NATIONWIDE STUDY OF CITIZENS' GROUPS, PEOPLE HAVE THE MOST IMPACT ON GOVERNMENT WHEN THEY CONCENTRATE ON THEIR OWN NEIGHBORHOODS AND STICK TO LAND POLICIES, WATER QUALITY, AND OTHER ENVIRONMENTAL ISSUES.

that the department doesn't have enough money in the budget to grant your request. Or you may learn that the head of the department doesn't have enough staff to oversee the project. Whatever the reason, once you know why the answer was no, you can work on the underlying problems.

Look for Financial Collaborators

Is a lack of money holding up your request? Try spreading the cost by getting officials in other layers of government to do what they should, advises Gabriel Miller, leader of Harlem Initiatives Together, a broad-based organization of churches and schools in New York City that is dedicated to building power in Harlem.

This tactic worked successfully when an inner-city public school wanted to have a playground built, says the Reverend Erik Kolbell, minister for social justice at Riverside Church in New York City and a long-time community activist. The school principal wanted the playground, but her district superintendent couldn't find the necessary $50,000. "So the principal worked her way up the ladder, first by garnering support from her local city councilman," Rev. Kolbell says. "His willingness to back the project and generate some funds led to the Manhattan borough president's endorsement and a designation of additional funds, which in turn eventually led to the state school construction authority overseeing the entire project.

"She succeeded in part because she was able to identify and recruit those governmental offices that had both the power and the willingness to come together, work collaboratively, and accomplish what any one office probably couldn't," he says.

Suggest Alternatives

If you're stalled because government doesn't want to administer a new program, offer to take on part of the responsibility. For instance, you and a group of your friends might volunteer to create the na-

ture trail and maintain it if the town parks department sets aside the land and provides signs and benches.

The key is to provide options that take away some of the risk or responsibility for what you're requesting, says Carol Sonnenschein, Ph.D., associate director of the Liberty Prairie Foundation in Grayslake, Illinois.

Seek Allies

So you want a police patrol in front of your child's school, and the police chief has said no. Chances are, he'll take a second look if you enlist the principal and a couple of school board members in your cause. Seek out influential people—clergymen, elected and appointed officials, or business and union leaders—who might see things the same way you do. Then meet with them one-on-one and ask for their support.

Take It to the Top

In chapter 1, you learned how legislative caseworkers cut red tape. But big problems demand big firepower: If you can't get the local bureaucrats to work with you despite your best efforts, bypass the caseworkers and speak to their boss: your city council member, state legislator, or congressmember. These elected officials depend on your continued support.

George Hochbrueckner, a lobbyist from Long Island who served five terms in the New York State Assembly and four terms in Congress, suggests four steps for putting your legislator to work.

First, make sure you're asking the right guy. Don't ask a state legislator to solve a city problem. Don't ask your councilman to intercede with federal bureaucrats.

Second, "don't be shy. When you want your representative to invest some time and attention in your problem," Hochbrueckner says, "you're smart to make an appointment and go directly to them for a face-to-face meeting."

Third, "be concise and clear in your request, and ask when you can expect results."

Finally, be respectful. "You want your representative to want to help you," he says.

➡◆ WHAT INSIDERS SAY:

When you get the goods or services that you want from an elected official, send a thank-you note. "Other than Santa Claus, elected officials are the least-thanked people in America," Hochbrueckner says. "If I'm in Congress and I receive thanks from a constituent I've helped, I'm going to remember that constituent the next time he calls me, if only because so few people take the time to do that."

ORGANIZING A GROUP

When quiet persuasion fails, it's time to go public. Small groups of people change public policies literally every day. The key is to find like-minded people and organize effectively around a clear and common goal.

"What savvy organizers understand," says Gabriel Miller of Harlem Initiatives Together, "is that the principle or issue is *shared*." If you can organize people who share your cause, government is more likely to pay attention. Numbers bring clout, he says. Here's how you can do it.

Start Small

Your organization can begin with a sideline conversation at your kid's soccer game or at a block party. "You need to start with the neighbor next door and then maybe the neighbor down the street," says Leon Townsend, project director for the National Association of Neighborhoods, a group that comprises 2,400 neighborhood organizations.

"A lot of our groups are 20 to 30 people," Townsend says. "You need to start small. It gets bigger, but it's the issues that bring people together."

Miller agrees. "Organizers are often anxious to get a lot of people together at one time to tackle an issue, but if you're smart, you begin by talking to one person at a time," he says.

"Find out who in your neighborhood might care as much as you do about your issue, sit down, talk about it, listen to one another, and see if you both agree that you want to take it on," he advises. "Begin to build a relationship with that person, and then agree to conduct other one-on-ones. Begin to expand your circle in this way."

Widen the Circle

Throw a potluck barbecue in your backyard or a coffee in your living room for your little group—"something to bring them all together," Townsend says. Ask each member to bring a neighbor. "What a lot of our members do is just knock on doors," he says.

➡◆ WHAT INSIDERS SAY:

Contrary to what most people think, "organizing is not fundamentally about agitating or protesting, it's about building relationships," says Miller.

Develop Clear Goals

Sure, you're sick of the speeding cars in your neighborhood. But what do you and your neighbors—your new allies—want to be done about it? Do you want a sign saying "Children at Play," a few additional police patrols, or speed bumps? Gather everyone together to define your issue and your objectives.

"People want real, immediate, and concrete improvements in their lives," says Kim Bobo, a community organizer for 20 years and executive director of the Chicago-based National Interfaith Committee for Worker Justice, an advocacy group for U.S. workers. "A savvy organizer will lead a group in defining a campaign that's clear, worthwhile, and winnable and that can be executed in a specific time frame."

Name Your Group

By yourselves, you and your neighbors are just disgruntled citizens. Naming your group gives you a collective identity, something to rally around. A catchy name gives the public, the press, and the government something to focus on. Use your group's name every chance you get—at your meetings, in correspondence, at government hearings, and with the media—to build public recognition.

Build Coalitions

Look for opportunities to link your group with other groups. Perhaps the block association in another neighborhood is also concerned about speeders. Perhaps the PTA at another school is also lobbying for police patrols. A coalition "increases the urgency," Townsend says. "That's where they get a lot of stuff done."

Appeal to Nonmembers' Interests

"The smartest way to appeal to other groups for support is to show them that it is in their self-interest to get involved in your campaign," says the Reverend David Ostendorf, a longtime organizer and community activist and director of the Center for New Community, a faith-based Chicago organization committed to revitalizing communities for social, political, and economic democracy. "Let them know in real dollars what the cost of inactivity will be to them and why it's valuable for them to join you."

➡◆ *WHAT INSIDERS SAY:*

Whenever you meet with another organization or hold a rally or other gathering, ask the people who

---

THE THRILL OF VICTORY

It's not easy to fight government and money—but the rewards can be immense. The reward for a group of Maryland residents was 477 acres of wetlands. Their 4-year fight to save Franklin Point from bulldozers teaches important lessons in community organizing.

The fight began when the wetlands' owner, a prominent Washington, D.C., developer, announced plans to build luxury homes on the property on Chesapeake Bay. The waters off Franklin Point harbor one of the largest Chesapeake Bay blue

crab nurseries in that part of the bay. The area is also a critical breeding ground and wintering place for many species of ducks, whistling swans, and other birds, including the threatened black rail.

"Housing and commercial development are the biggest threats the bay faces," says Amanda Spake, acting president of the South Arundel Citizens for Responsible Development (SACReD), a citizen activist group that was born in opposition to the project.

"Most of the time, valuable

nature is also valuable real estate," says Joe Browder, a nationally known environmental leader who became involved in SACReD's fight. "People have to organize and fight to create a political environment in which land can be saved."

At first glance, SACReD's members looked outgunned. They're middle-class working folks without much money or social clout. Usually, says Browder, the people who save land from development are wealthy and socially promi-

attend to provide their names and phone numbers. This makes them easy to contact if you need their help again.

Treat Fellow Volunteers with Respect

"Simple gestures can go a long way," says Miller. "If you have a program or a meeting, ask everyone when they will have to leave. Don't assign work to someone who can't do it. Make it clear how important each person's work is to the overall picture. And give public recognition for people's efforts."

◆● *WHAT INSIDERS SAY:*

To improve participation at a rally or teach-in, be sure to offer services that your group's members may need, such as transportation and child care. Also, start events on time and keep them brief. That will encourage people to come back the next time.

TELLING THE WORLD

Once you've developed a cause and built a group, you need to make the rest of the world aware that you exist. How? By attracting publicity and media attention through every possible avenue. Here are some specific suggestions.

Take Your Story to the Press

Newspapers, radio, and TV are the megaphones of modern society. If you need to make noise or shed

---

nent. They can put up their own money to save the land, and they can call friends in high places, like the governor's office.

Lacking those advantages, SACReD made up for them with a strong organization. Its leaders treated the effort to save the wetlands as if it were a political campaign.

SACReD decided to wage a publicity war to stop the project. Spake, a journalist, took the assignment. It also attracted specialists—lawyers, environmental scientists, and political professionals like Browder—who could marshal

evidence for policy-makers.

Key to the struggle was a road sign campaign about the importance of Franklin Point and the need to preserve it. The sign campaign galvanized the community.

The dispute frequently turned testy and heated. At one point, the developer sued SACReD for defamation, asking for $50.2 million in damages. But SACReD won the suit, pushing the dispute toward a settlement.

After meeting with SACReD, the developer became convinced that they should work together to persuade the state

and county to buy the ecologically sensitive area. He was willing to sell the land for $5.7 million—"enough to make him 'whole,' and that's all," Browder says.

Ultimately, the state and Anne Arundel County agreed to split the bill for buying and preserving the wetlands. County officials had favored the development, but they came to realize, Spake says, that preserving Franklin Point actually would save money, since taxpayers wouldn't have to pay to pave roads, expand schools, and install new water and sewer lines.

a lot of light in a dark corner, you need the media's help. The secret here is to understand that the media is always looking for a good story (see "Media Savvy").

Hold a Hearing

Some groups have staged community hearings to gather complaints or created sites on the World Wide Web where people can register their concerns on an issue, according to Liam O'Connor, program officer for Partners for Livable Communities, a Washington, D.C., group that promotes livable communities through public-private partnerships. Both Web sites and community hearings are great ways of documenting that you and your group are not the only people who are upset about a particular issue. Also, the more publicity you can gain for your cause, the more likely people in public office are to resolve the matter in your favor.

MEDIA SAVVY

The media is the outlet that allows the audience for your story to increase from 30 to 3,000, but to attract coverage, you have to win and hold their attention. Here are eight sure-fire methods.

Make your story compelling
Matthew Lombardi, a news producer for NBC News in New York City, says that a story needs two elements to generate interest: clearly defined conflict and interesting characters.

"Let's say a group wants to protest the fact that a government building without handicapped access is being built in their town," Lombardi says. "The group should write a press release citing the federal law that the building would be violating. That makes it contro-

versial. Then, one of the spokesmen identified in the release should be a sympathetic figure—maybe an ex-government employee—whose access to the building will be impeded. In addition, the group should be able to identify and name the government official who okayed the plans in the first place. Now you have your characters to go along with your conflict. That's going to catch someone's eye."

Make yourself accessible
Choose someone from your group who understands the media, perhaps a journalist or a public relations specialist, to serve as spokesman.

Plan something memorable
Even the smallest newspapers get dozens of pleas for coverage every day. You have to

stand out from the rest. Humor is a great way to draw media attention.

"People often think that if their cause is good, the coverage will be good, but it doesn't work that way," says Kim Bobo, a community organizer for 20 years and executive director of the Chicago-based National Interfaith Committee for Worker Justice, an advocacy group for U.S. workers. "You need to be clever as well," she says. "A few years back, when a citizens' organization wanted to dramatize how the rising costs of automobile insurance were forcing people to choose between buying the insurance and paying their rent, they built a home into a car, complete with a toilet in the trunk. The media loved it."

Write a Few Well-Chosen Words

Some of the most powerful, best-read messages that you can deliver for your cause begin with the words "Dear Editor." Letters to the editor are popular, well-read features in newspapers around the world. To get them printed and read, you need to keep three points in mind.

First, keep your letter brief. Chances are that your local newspaper prints only short letters so that it can get more opinions onto each letters page. Don't expect the editors to make an exception in your case. A wordy letter invites editing or, worse, rejection.

Second, keep it well-reasoned. Your goal isn't to write an emotional argument that speaks only to people who are already converted to your cause. You want to reach folks who don't care as much or know as much about an issue as you do.

Tell the media what you're going to do

A week or so before a media-worthy event, send a concise, one-page press release to local newspapers, radio, and TV. You can get the name of the appropriate editor by calling the paper or station. Be sure to put your spokesman's name and phone number on the release.

Say something memorable

No, they're not going to broadcast your entire 30-minute event or print every word of your 15-page report. Give the press sound bites—short, clever statements that their audiences will remember. Design them ahead of time.

WHAT INSIDERS SAY:
To increase the chance of getting positive television coverage, hold your event in a setting that will look good on camera. If you're holding a rally in a hall, have lots of colorful banners and placards, and choose a hall just large enough to accommodate your expected turnout, so the place looks jammed. Also, have the name of your organization both on the podium and behind it so the cameras will pick it up.

Prepare press packets

When the press arrives to cover your event, a press liaison should hand each reporter a packet of information that explains who you are, why your issue is important, what will happen, and any other pertinent data that you wish them to have. Be sure to include the name, address, and phone number of your spokesman as well as relevant photographs.

Cultivate relationships

You can improve your chances of coverage by meeting with the editors of local newspapers and radio and TV stations.

"It's not necessarily difficult to meet with an editor," says Pamela Dinsmore, assistant managing editor for news for the *Sacramento Bee* in California. "What editors want to see is a clear, brief statement of the controversy and news clips of previous coverage, sent in written form to the attention of the editor whose area of editorial responsibility overlaps that of your group. And a follow-up phone call never hurts."

Find other ways to reach the public

"Letters to the editor, public service announcements, and postings on public bulletin boards all count as ways of communicating with large groups of people and shouldn't be minimized," Bobo says.

Third, respect your opponents. Newspapers may occasionally print caustic letters, but you will do your cause no favors with slash-and-burn rhetoric. Let the other guy act mean.

Sign on the Dotted Line

Petitions are dramatic ways to demonstrate popular support for an issue—but you need to know their limits.

"Petitions are of limited use when sent to an elected or appointed official because the officials understand that not everyone who signs their name to a petition is committed to whatever the petition is trying to achieve," says Chicago community activist Rev. David Ostendorf. "The key thing is not just getting signatures on paper but what to do with those signatures."

Experts say there are a few secrets to making sure that your petition grabs attention.

First, says Gabriel Miller of Harlem Initiatives Together, if you're going to send a politician a petition, make sure he also gets plenty of personal mail on the subject. "Politicians respect the time

---

Amazing Stories

MUCH ADO ABOUT COUNTRY

On one side stands Paul Thompson, a long-established pig farmer who plays country music to soothe his animals. On the other is the high-powered legal machine of the Florida Club, a new golf course and housing subdivision whose members object to the crooning of Garth Brooks as they tee off on the 15th hole. The country club has filed a lawsuit in an effort to make this the day the music dies.

"It's amazing," says Thompson. "I've lived here on this farm for 42 years. This country club was built 3 years ago, and I'm the one who has to change the way I live?"

Thompson is determined to put up a fight, and he's turning to the media to generate attention for his cause. He has created a Web site where people can contribute to the Paul Thompson Pigfarmer Legal Defense Fund and has hung a large banner with his Web address on the front of his barn. There's no word on how much money the site has raised, but it is gener-

ating publicity. Reporters, including one from the *New York Times*, who have heard of his site have stopped by to cover the case.

Thompson has another powerful ally, a law called the Florida Right to Farm Act, designed to protect long-standing farms from being forced out by burgeoning development. According to the law, "No farm operation which has been in operation for 1 year or more since its established date of operation and which was not a nuisance at [that time] shall be a public or private nuisance if the farm operation conforms to generally accepted agricultural and management practices."

Of course, the country club may have a point in suggesting that loud country music isn't a generally accepted agricultural or management practice.

Will Thompson win? No one's certain, but one can only hope that the pigs will hold up through all this strain.

someone puts into writing a letter," Miller says. "They see it as a more committed expression of opinion on a given topic." If you can, he suggests, collect the letters and send them all at once, and if you have pictures of the problem, send those, too. A politician "can't refute irrefutable evidence," he says.

Second, keep your petition clear and concise. "Too often, people turn petitions into manifestos, which no one will take the time to read," says Miller. "Experienced organizers know to confine their statement to one or two simple lines."

Third, ask petition signers for their names, addresses, and telephone numbers. "If nothing else," says Rev. Ostendorf, "this provides a way of adding to your group's mailing list."

Finally, present your petition with flair. If it's done right, the simple act of handing a politician a sheaf of paper can get media attention, and that will magnify the petition's effect.

"A number of years ago, a community organization in Connecticut gathered thousands of signatures in protest of a rate hike proposed by a utility," says Miller. "Instead of simply mailing them to the state senator whose committee would consider the hike, they wound thousands of pages of completed petitions onto a large wooden spool owned by the utility, with the company's name stenciled on its side, and rolled them into the senate chamber. It was a great visual!"

Good visuals are just a small part of making government work for you. They rarely make a bad case compelling or a weak organization strong. But a strong case, strong allies, and a strong message can work wonders with balky officials.

As Miller puts it, "If you're clear about what you want, if others also want it, if you work in concert with one another, and if you're wily about how to make your demands felt, at day's end, you will prevail."

●◆ *WHAT INSIDERS SAY:*

Want to increase the chances that people will write letters supporting your cause? Set up a letter-writing table right next to your petition table so supporters can do everything in one stop. Display a few sample letters, and be sure to stock plenty of paper, pens, and envelopes, plus stamps for sale.

CHAPTER 3

WHAT'S in STORE if YOU PERSIST

As you read through this book and discover the keys to getting government to work for you, you'll begin to realize that they will open a storehouse of advice, goods, and services that's rich beyond belief.

Whether you need help with your job, your education, your health, the safety of your street, or the plants in your backyard, government can help. Whether your goal is to cut costs on daily expenses like food and transportation or to build your savings for the future, government is there. In fact, it's there for virtually every aspect of your life, from the serious to the sublime, and maybe even a bit of the fun and silly.

This chapter celebrates that last category. Here you'll find some of the more unusual ways that government can be of benefit to you, from providing the unique to offering unparalleled bargains.

> Satellite photos, bargain horses, a signed picture of the president— the list of items that government can offer you is both eclectic and amazing. Here's a taste of some of the more fun items available.

GOVERNMENT GIFTS

When it comes to presents, there are few who can match the generosity of the government. At any given time, Uncle Sam has literally millions of items in his catalog that are available to you for free or at a discount. It's quite a smorgasbord, too— from flags to photos to films. Here's a taste of what you'll find.

A Flag Flown over the Capitol

For a nominal fee, you can purchase an American flag that was flown over the U.S. Capitol Building in Washington, D.C, says Janice Siegel, manager of New York congressman Jerry Nadler's Washington office. You pay less than $25, depending on the size flag you choose, plus $4.05 to have it

! FACTOID

IN ALASKA, THE GOVERNMENT IS SO FLUSH WITH MONEY FROM THE OIL PIPELINE THAT NOT ONLY IS THERE NO STATE INCOME TAX OR SALES TAX, BUT EACH CITIZEN RECEIVES WHAT'S CALLED THE ALASKA PERMANENT FUND DIVIDEND. IN RECENT YEARS, THE DIVIDEND HAS BEEN AS HIGH AS $1,500 A YEAR.

hoisted aloft and postage to have it sent to you. In addition to the flag, you receive an official certificate with your name and the date your flag was flown. You can even request that it be flown on a specific date—maybe an anniversary, a birthday, or a graduation. To obtain a flag, call the office of your local senator or representative. The number is listed in the government pages of your phone book.

Greetings from the White House

Care to have the president of the United States acknowledge a special occasion? You can get a presidential citation to honor such events as a couple's 50th (or more) wedding anniversary, a Girl Scout's Gold award, a Boy Scout's Eagle Scout rank, or the birth of a child. To request a citation, write to the White House Correspondence Department, Room 39, 1600 Pennsylvania Avenue NW, Washington, DC 20500. Be sure to include the recipient's name and mailing address, the date of the occasion, and your phone number.

●◆ WHAT INSIDERS SAY:

If you want to present a greeting at a special occasion, plan ahead. Send your request 4 to 6 weeks before the event.

A Citation from City Hall

No good deed should go unnoticed, in the government's opinion. And most levels of government are more than willing to provide a citation recognizing the work of your local PTA, Rotary Club, volunteer fire department, or what have you. "Getting a handsome, personalized document of recognition from city or town hall usually takes little more than a phone call or visit to your local representative," says David Hershey-Webb, community advocate for New York State Assemblyman Edward Sullivan. "Most governments are eager to acknowledge local civic organizations. And it can really boost the morale of your members and the visibility and credibility of your group."

To request a citation, contact a caseworker in the office of your city, town, or county officials or your state or congressional representative. (The number is listed in the government pages of your phone book.) This person can meet with you, take down the information about your group, and put your request in motion in very little time and at no cost to you.

An Autographed Photo from the White House

If a photo is more to your liking, the White House Greeting Office is willing to fulfill your request. Color photographs of either the president or vice president, with facsimile autographs, are available. Again, make your request 4 to 6 weeks in advance, because the pictures are subject to availability. To get a picture, address your request to the president or vice president, White House, 1600 Pennsylvania Avenue NW, Washington, DC 20500.

Your Family's Immigration Records

If your ancestors came to America by boat, there's a good chance that the National Archives and Records Administration (NARA) can supply you with a copy of the log from the ship that delivered them to our shores.

The agency's written records go back as far as 1820, says Constance Potter, archivist with the National Archives. In most cases, if you can supply the person's name and port of entry and the approximate date of arrival, the agency should be able to find the passenger list and copy it for you. Note, however, that there are no indexed entries from 1847 to June 1897 for ships that came into New York Harbor, so if you want a passenger list from that era, you'll need to know the exact date that it entered port. There is a $10 fee per search, but it's applicable only if NARA finds your ancestor's name.

To request a list, write to the National Archives and Records Administration, Attn: NWCTB, 700 Pennsylvania Avenue NW, Washington, DC 20408, and request Form 81, "Order for Copies of Ship Passenger Arrival Records." In addition, if you have access to the Internet, you can get more information about the archives and how to obtain genealogical records (including ships' passenger lists) by visiting the agency's Web site at www.nara.gov/genealogy/genindex.html.

Photos of Military Events

You can remember the Alamo, or the *Maine*, or any other military engagement, for that matter. Another service that the NARA provides is access to photographs of any war for which photos were taken as well as images and lithograph reproductions of events from any war, from the most recent all the way back to the American Revolution.

The images are for sale at reasonable costs, with the price depending on several factors, including the size of the picture, whether it's black-and-white or color, what kind of shape it's in, and which of the nine vendors that contract with NARA to reproduce pictures actually does the work (the vendors set their own prices). According to Mary Ilario, archive specialist, the average price for an 8-by-10 black-and-white photo is around $20.

To locate an image, start by telling the agency specifically what you're after. So, "instead of saying 'I'd like a picture of World War II,' which is kind of broad, people should be able to identify a specific battle or commander or range of dates," suggests Ilario. The NARA will then search for appropriate images, photocopy them, and send you the photocopies so you can pick which ones you'd like to have turned into prints.

For more information, write to the NARA Special Media Division—Still Pictures, Room 5360, 8601 Adelphi Road, College Park, MD 20740-6001. You can also find information about the photo archives on the Internet at www.nara.gov.

Voices from the Past

Do you want to hear one of FDR's Fireside Chats from the Depression? How about a description of future uses for electricity from the man who made it famous, Thomas Edison? Recordings of these people and many more are available from the National Archives.

The collection includes more than 160,000 recordings, including presidential speeches, NASA communications, and comments from famous citizens like Amelia Earhart. You can visit the archives to listen to and make your own recordings for free or find out about hiring a contractor to do the work for you.

For more information, write to the Motion Picture, Sound, and Video Branch, National Archives, 8601 Adelphi Road, College Park, MD 20740-6001.

Newsreels of Famous Events

Would you like to give someone a special birthday treat? How about a first-hand look at what happened in the world in the year that person was born? Those events and many more are available through the National Archives newsreel collection.

First shown in movie theaters, the newsreels cover major events from the late 1920s to the mid-1960s. Most are about 10 minutes long. You can view the reels at the National Archives and make a copy using your own equipment for free, rent a dubbing station for $20, or hire a contractor to make a copy for you for a fee.

For more information, write to the Motion Picture, Sound, and Video Branch, National Archives, 8601 Adelphi Road, College Park, MD 20740-6001.

Low-Cost Art Education

If the visual arts are what interest you, the National Gallery of Art can fill your eyes with images. The agency's department of education resources lends videos and slides covering a number of subjects and periods. All you have to pay is return postage.

You can get an introduction to the world of art, study artistic styles such as cubism and impressionism, or view representative art from this and other countries. Or you can look into specific topics such as the birds painted by naturalist John James Audubon.

To learn more about the program, write to the Department of Education Resources, Education Division, National Gallery of Art, Fourth Street and Constitution Avenue NW, Washington, DC 20565.

Watch a Rocket in Flight

You and your family and friends can get a feel for life on top of a rocket by witnessing a space shuttle launch at the Kennedy Space Center. There are two public viewing sites (one about 6½ miles away from the launch pad, the other just under 8 miles away). You can get a free pass by writing to Car Passes, PAPASS, Kennedy Space Center, FL 32899. Due to tremendous demand for these passes, however, they may be snapped up more than a year before a launch, so plan ahead.

A limited number of bus tickets to view the launch from an area 8 miles from the launch pad are available. They go on sale 5 days before the launch on a first come, first served basis. You have to pick them up in person, the cost is $10 per ticket, and there is a limit of six tickets per family.

For more information about car and bus passes and launch schedules, write to Delaware North Park Services, Mail Code DNPS, Kennedy Space Center, FL 32899, or check out the NASA Web site at www.nasa.gov and click on "See a Launch."

●✦ WHAT INSIDERS SAY:

If the heavy demand for tickets prevents you from getting into a government viewing site, try watching a launch from a public location. The best places for public viewing are along U.S. Highway 1 near Titusville and on the beaches in Cape Canaveral and Cocoa Beach. All of these sites are free.

UNCLE SAM'S BARGAINS

Think of the government's stockpile of surplus items as your grandmother's attic multiplied by about 2 million. Need new drapes or a dozen pairs of dancing shoes? Want to buy a mule, a speedboat, or some carpeting for the hallway? Uncle Sam's bargain bazaar is open for business.

The thing you need to keep in mind, however, is that unlike Granny's attic, this stuff is all over the place—at different departments, different agencies, and even different regions throughout the country, so your best bet is to get a clear picture of what you're in the market for and where best to find it.

Horses and Burros at a Discount

How'd you like to own a low-cost Trigger? The U.S. Department of Interior's Bureau of Land Management (BLM) may be able to help. Several times a year, it thins out herds of wild horses and burros that live on federal land in the West and puts some of the animals up for adoption. "We have about 9,000 adoptees a year," says Sharon Exarhos, a wild horse and burro specialist with the Milwaukee office of the BLM. And while the days of the $5 horse are gone, the current prices of the animals can be quite reasonable. Prices start at $125 for a single horse or burro and $250 for a mare with a foal.

What you get for that price depends on what came in with the latest roundup. But, says Exarhos, "if you adopt a healthy palomino, you could be walking off with a $2,000 horse for $125."

To find out more, write to the Adopt a Wild Horse or Burro Program, Bureau of Land Management, P.O. Box 631, Milwaukee, WI 53201. If you have access to the Internet, you can also visit the department's special Web site at www. adoptahorse.blm.gov.

●✦ WHAT INSIDERS SAY:

To adopt a horse or burro, you must show that you have the space and shelter to properly care for the animal. Also, while the animals available for adoption have been held for at least 30 days to adjust to life in a corral, they are likely to still require some taming. The BLM office suggests that you visit an adoption site before getting caught up in the bidding. "You're more or less a foster parent," says

Exarhos, "and you might want to see the animals for yourself."

Prisoner-Trained Horses

In several western states, the BLM runs a remarkable program to tame wild horses for you, with

Amazing Stories

A HORSE CALLED DRAGONFIRE

Connie Gleckler is determined one day to win Oklahoma City's International Finals Rodeo, the Super Bowl of rodeos. And if she does it, chances are that she'll do it on a cavalry horse.

At 14, Connie's already riding the pro circuit, having won 45 trophies and 18 belt buckles as an amateur. Her specialty is barrel racing, in which horse and rider race the clock around three barrels set in a large triangle. The event requires a strong, agile horse with lightning-fast response time. For Connie, that horse is Dragonfire, which her father, Doug Gleckler, bought for $700 at the Defense Reutilization and Marketing Service (DRMS for short) auction at Fort Hood, Texas, south of Waco.

"When they are racing, Connie and Dragonfire become one," says Doug, who lives with his family in Joshua, just south of Fort Worth. "When she applies a little leg pressure, he knows just what to do."

A registered quarter horse, Dragonfire once belonged to the First Cavalry Division horse platoon, which marches in parades and stages monthly re-creations of historic cavalry charges, complete with mule-driven chuckwagons, dogs, and cannons. There was one problem: Dragonfire was afraid of gunfire. Every time the cannons

boomed, he would break formation and bolt for the exit.

On the day of the DRMS auction, Doug remembers, there were two horses for sale, one of which was Dragonfire. He was 10 years old and, at 1,200 pounds and 17 hands high, was closer in size to a thoroughbred than most quarter horses, which usually stand 14 or 15 hands high.

"Connie took a liking to Dragonfire," he remembers. "He kept poking his nose down to her." The youngster looked up at her father and said, "Daddy, he's mine." When the horse came up for auction, he says, "I just stuck my number in the air and didn't take it down until I had him."

The price, it turns out, was a bargain, considering that many registered quarter horses fetch between $1,200 and $2,000. A few years earlier, Doug had paid about the same price for another cavalry horse, Parker, at a Fort Hood auction.

Connie had begun training Parker when she was only 6 years old. Now, after working with Dragonfire for 5 years, she has transformed the once-skittish cavalry horse into a real rodeo pro. Only one reminder remains of Dragonfire's military career: a big "US" brand on his left shoulder.

prisoners acting as cowboys. This federal agency gives inmates the opportunity to learn the delicate yet demanding skill of taking the wildness out of a horse. Once trained, the animals are available for adoption in California and Wyoming. For more information, write to:

✓ Bureau of Land Management, Eagle Lake Field Office, 2950 Riverside Drive, Susanville, CA 96130

✓ Bureau of Land Management, Wyoming State Office, 5353 Yellowstone, Cheyenne, WY 82003

The agency also has a cooperative agreement with the Colorado Department of Corrections Facility at Canon City, in which horses are fully saddle-trained. This requires more time and effort, and those horses are available for adoption for about $840. For more information, contact the Bureau of Land Management, Royal Gorge Field Office, 1370 East Main Street, Canon City, CO 81212.

Sunglasses, Hand Towels, Hacksaws

"Excuse me, but can I get 100 pairs of sunglasses to go?" Of course you can, if the U.S. Postal Service happens to have them in one of their three mail recovery centers, where damaged and unclaimed mail is gathered and then auctioned off throughout the year. "Anything that is mailed can end up undeliverable, either because it's damaged or because there's a problem with the address. That's when we step in," says Michael Miles, communications programs specialist with the Postal Service in Atlanta.

In the past, the collection has included some unique items, like the sun-baked skull of a Longhorn steer and a set of gold teeth. And while it's hard to gauge exactly how much you might save on any particular item you bid on, you can rest assured that "our selections are huge and our prices exceedingly reasonable," says Miles.

The auctions are held throughout the year at three mail recovery centers. You can learn more

about the next auction by writing to one of the following addresses.

✓ Atlanta Mail Recovery Center, P.O. Box 4416, Atlanta, GA 30336-9590

✓ San Francisco Mail Recovery Center, P.O. Box 7872, San Francisco, CA 94120-7872

✓ St. Paul Mail Recovery Center, 443 Fillmore Avenue E., St. Paul, MN 55107-9607

You also can visit the Postal Service Web site at www.usps.gov or www.usps.com.

●◆ WHAT INSIDERS SAY:

Most items are sold in lots, so be prepared to bid on large amounts and then divvy up the items among friends and family. Also, it's good to get to the auction site early, before the auction actually starts, so that you can inspect the merchandise before bidding on it.

A UFO's View of Your Home

Do you want to see what your little patch of Earth looks like from outer space? Both the U.S. Geological Survey (USGS) and NASA have hundreds of pictures that might interest you.

The USGS can provide you with a view of your hometown from 20,000 feet above the surface of the Earth. Their national aerial photography program has black-and-white and color infrared photos of all states except Alaska and Hawaii. If you supply the agency with your zip code or the name of your town, it can try to match it.

If you are more interested in declassified spy photos or seeing how deforestation is changing the face of the Earth, check out the USGS Special Image Gallery.

The cost for an image ranges from about $10 to $75, depending upon the size and quality of the final picture, and color photos cost more than black-and-whites. For more information on these photos, write Customer Services, U.S. Geological Survey, EROS Data Center, Sioux Falls, SD 57198, or visit the agency's Web site on the Internet at http://edcwww.cr.usgs.gov.

Similarly, you can get copies of NASA's photographs of the Earth as well as of space. Because of the huge demand for the photos, the agency sells them through vendors around the country. Prices range from about $15 to over $70.

The NASA educational division also makes available a limited number of free lithographs of the Earth and space, each accompanied by explanations of the picture. While this program is intended for teachers, nonteachers can get them as well.

For more information on how to obtain NASA images, visit www.nasa.gov. Click on the "Educational Resources" button for photographs and lithographs.

Heavy-Duty Deals

Need some machine tools, electronic equipment, radios, or heavy vehicles? The U.S. Department of Defense is open for business. At any one time, the Defense Department has more than 600,000

items for sale through auction, bids, retail, or negotiated sales.

No, you can't buy any weapons or intelligence equipment. "If you're looking to purchase that missile launcher you've always wanted to use against your noisy neighbor, what you'll end up with is a good four-wheel-drive truck with the launcher removed and melted down for scrap," says one insider.

But there are still good bargains. At one auction, slightly used high-powered computers sold for as little as $800. At other sales, bidders have picked up fire hoses, aircraft parts, typewriters, microwave ovens, and radar equipment. "People need to keep in mind, though, that while we still operate some retail stores, we generally sell items at auction, where they're usually in lots," says Tim Hoyle, public affairs specialist with the Defense Reutilization and Marketing Service (DRMS), the group that conducts the sales for the Defense Department.

The sales take place throughout the year at the DRMS's field offices and local military bases. You also can write to DRMS, National Sales Office, 74

DREAM JOBS FOR THE CREATIVE OR THE CRYPTIC

You want some unusual examples of how government can benefit you? Here is a handful of the big-ticket freebies offered by federal and state governments.

✓ The National Security Agency pays salary, travel costs, and more to mathematicians who study the kind of mathematics most useful in cryptography, the science of breaking codes.

✓ The state of Illinois provides $10,000 grants to support photographers, writers, artists, and poets.

✓ The American Library Association pays $34,000 to librarians who are willing to spend a year working in a library overseas, helping to promote international sharing of resources.

✓ The National Institute of Standards and Technology

and the U.S. Department of Energy offer an average of $83,000 to inventors working on new, non-nuclear energy sources.

✓ The federal government donates or lends obsolete military equipment (even Navy ships!) for historical or ceremonial displays.

✓ The U.S. Postal Service pays artists up to $3,000 to design a single stamp.

North Washington Avenue, Suite 6, Battle Creek, MI 49017-3092 for sale information. Better yet, go to its Web site at www.drms.dla.mil. You can find out what is available in the entire system rather than just locally, as well as browse catalogs and place bids.

●◆ *WHAT INSIDERS SAY:*

Whenever you go to an auction, have a fixed price that you're willing to pay for any item and don't go beyond it. For example, if you're buying a computer, find out its market value from ads in the newspaper. And get to the auction early so you can talk to veterans of the auction circuit to learn how to inspect items and how to bid.

From Headstones to Guitars

If your taste runs to the eclectic in large amounts, the U.S. Department of the Treasury has your number. It sells items that have been confiscated either because of criminal investigation or because the property was abandoned at Customs.

What might you find? How about 82 crates of headstones for $13,000, 49 vintage guitars for $48,700, or, more moderately, a low-mileage, 6-year-old Toyota for $2,900?

Treasury auctions are held about every 9 weeks in the main sales centers in Miami/Fort Lauderdale; Los Angeles; El Paso, Texas; Nogales, Arizona; Edison, New Jersey; and elsewhere as needed. For information on the sales, write EG&G Services, U.S. Customs Service Support, 3702 Pender Drive, Fairfax, VA 22030. Or, for more information on the times and places of upcoming auctions and the items to be offered, visit the Treasury Department's Web site at www.treas.gov/auctions/customs.

TWO

Daily Essentials

CHAPTER 4

CUTTING COSTS on the BASICS of LIFE

Regardless of personal tastes or lifestyles, there are some things that you just can't do without. Things like food, fuel, furniture, and, unless you want trouble with the law, clothes to put on your back (and elsewhere).

Fortunately, government agencies and nonprofit organizations are loaded for bear with ways to make acquiring these daily essentials easier and less costly—provided you know where to look. And as you'll see, "government" and "nonprofit" don't translate into "dull."

In this chapter, you'll learn how to get a gourmet natural feast in the Big Apple for a song. How to fill your woodshed with the best hardwoods for next to nothing. Even how to plant your tomatoes on government-owned land, then get a taxpayer-paid expert to advise you on growing them right.

> Spend a fortune on the good life? No need! With help from the government and nonprofit groups, you can sample gourmet meals for a song, harvest luxury foods for free, and buy designer clothing at a discount.

You'll also learn how to make friends and save big on groceries by starting a buying club. In addition, we'll show you how to garner an old-fashioned Steelcase desk for a buck. There are even ways to get the government to help you cut your fuel bills. Here are the specifics.

FOOD

If you're an average American, you spend $2,671 for each person in your family for a year's worth of groceries and restaurant meals, according to the USDA. For a family of four, that translates into a whopping $10,700 a year just to keep everyone's stomach from growling.

When that expense proves to be too much of a burden, the federal government provides a safety net in the form of billions of dollars in assistance to

FACTOID

IT'S ESTIMATED THAT 48 MILLION TONS OF FOOD ARE WASTED IN THE UNITED STATES EACH YEAR, MUCH OF IT SIMPLY BECAUSE THE FOOD ISN'T USED BY ITS DESIGNATED SALE DATE.

needy families. But even if you're not a candidate for government aid, there are plenty of opportunities—through food cooperatives, buying clubs, or even dining at cooking schools—to take a bite out of your food bill and have fun doing it.

Reaping the USDA's Bounty

The USDA Food and Nutrition Service spends $40 billion a year to feed Americans through more than a dozen separate assistance programs. All told, one in six Americans uses one or more of the programs.

Some programs, such as school breakfasts and lunches and meals for senior citizens, are open to everyone, regardless of family income. The amount the government kicks in for you depends on your level of need.

Most of the programs are for those truly in need, however. "The Food and Nutrition Service really focuses on nutrition assistance for low-income people," says Phil Shanholtzer, acting director of public information for the service in Alexandria, Virginia.

If you think that you may qualify for some sort of assistance, but you aren't sure, it's worth your time to investigate. Some people never get their benefits simply because they don't know that they qualify, Shanholtzer says.

Since all USDA food programs are administered at the state and local level, the best way to obtain applications or information is to call the local government social services agency in your area. The Food and Nutrition Service offers detailed descriptions of all of its programs on the Internet at www.usda.gov/fns. Or write to the Food and Nutrition Service, 3101 Park Center Drive, Alexandria, VA 22302.

Here are the USDA food programs that are open to all.

THE PEOPLE'S DEPARTMENT

It was President Abraham Lincoln who started the U.S. Department of Agriculture (USDA) in 1862. He dubbed it "the people's department."

Back then, "the people" meant farmers; 90 percent of Americans were farmers. The USDA was established to provide seed and information on crops.

Today, just 2 percent of Americans live on farms, but the term *people's department* might still apply to the department. With 109,000 employees and an annual budget of $55 billion, President Lincoln's baby covers a vast range of services and activities that touch just about every American's life.

In addition to its better-known duties, such as distributing $40 billion worth of food stamps and other assistance per year to the needy or inspecting 7 billion poultry birds and 136 million head of livestock headed for American dinner tables, did you know that the USDA also:

✓ Runs the Beagle Brigade—teams of dogs at 21 major airports, trained to detect prohibited food and produce in passengers' baggage from overseas?

✓ Manages the nation's 192 million acres of national forests and range lands—an area larger than Texas?

✓ Operates the world's largest agricultural research libraries, located in Beltsville, Maryland, with 48 miles of bookshelves?

School Meals

Regardless of your income, your child is eligible to be one of the 26 million schoolchildren nationwide who eat balanced lunches subsidized by the USDA. "Even well-to-do kids can participate and get a low-cost meal through the school lunch program," Shanholtzer says.

Although prices vary from school to school, lunches generally cost under $2. Low-income children get their lunches free. Even children who pay full price are being subsidized by the USDA to the tune of 18 cents per meal. The meals are healthy, too. "The USDA requires that the schools meet certain nutrition standards," Shanholtzer says.

Similar to the lunch program, the USDA's school breakfast program—with a budget of $1.2 billion—serves about 7 million children a day. It's also open to all children, with discounts varying according to need.

For Senior Citizens

Hey, you're only as old as you feel. But even though you're young at heart, if your birth certificate says you're 60 or over, or if you are married to someone who is, you can get meals at senior centers or through meals on wheels programs around the country. It's part of a joint program of the USDA and the U.S. Department of Health and Human Services, called the Nutrition Program for the Elderly. There's no income requirement. Participants who are unable to contribute get their meals for free.

Getting Help Growing Your Own

Growing your own produce won't just lighten your grocery bills; it will also give you a feeling of accomplishment and put healthy food on the table. Some of the best advice you'll find anywhere is free for the asking at hundreds of cooperative extension offices around the country, staffed and paid for by your tax dollars. Don't be shy about asking—you're paying for the services, whether you use them or not.

Public land-grant universities (schools that specialize in research and education on farming, horticulture, and forestry) in each state, under the direction of the USDA, operate extension offices in most counties in America. They are vast storehouses of agricultural and horticultural information. Knowledgeable extension agents and volunteers are ready to answer questions, and most offices are stocked with free or low-priced booklets, pamphlets, and flyers on everything from growing the tastiest sugar snap beans to ridding your garden of pests.

Best of all, the information is often geared to the growing conditions in your area, offering tips that you might not get from a standardized gardening book. Thinking of planting pear trees in central Minnesota, for example? An extension agent in that region will tell you that Golden Spice, Gourmet, and Summercrisp varieties should do fine, but Parker, Patten, and Luscious may not be hardy enough for the cold.

Agencies vary from state to state and from county to county in the programs they offer. Most are happy to answer any gardening questions they can, either in person or by sending you printed information. The best way to find out what's available near you is to call or drop by your local extension office. Check the county government listings in your phone book.

Below are some examples of services at extension offices around the country. Check with your local office to see if it offers something similar.

❧ WHAT INSIDERS SAY:

When you pose a gardening question to an extension agent, be as specific as possible. Letting the agent know exactly what you need will save time and help ensure that you get the most helpful information. For instance, don't just say, "Please send me information about tomatoes" when what you really want to know is how to care for the plants once the growing season is over. There's likely to be a detailed flyer on just that subject.

Take a Class in Sunny Arizona

Residents of Pima County, Arizona, around Tucson, can learn anything and everything they need to grow a vegetable garden. All they need to do is visit the Pima County Cooperative Extension, says John P. Begeman, horticulture agent. Agents and Master Gardener volunteers specialize in helping gardeners grow things in the desert climate.

Here's one local tip: Raising tomatoes in the desert? Try cutting the plants back severely in August, and by September, you'll be gathering your second crop, thanks to the hot climate.

One of the more popular offerings is free, weekly Wednesday morning classes on constantly changing gardening topics, such as preparing your garden for spring. "We'll take as many people as show up," Begeman says. The office is open Monday through Friday from 9:30 A.M. to 3:30 P.M. Check the bulletin board for flyers with seasonal growing tips. The office also stocks a wide range of pamphlets and brochures published by the University of Arizona, the land-grant university with which it is affiliated.

If you live in Pima County and have a gardening question or want more information on programs, write to the Pima County Cooperative Extension, 4210 North Campbell Avenue, Tucson, AZ 85719.

Garden Calls in Minnesota

House calls by physicians may be largely a thing of the past, but gardeners in Morrison County, Minnesota, about 75 miles northwest of Minneapolis, can summon government-trained Master Gardeners to their homes at no cost. These gardening gurus act as troubleshooters, helping to determine why a resident's cucumbers are wilting or why the corn won't grow.

The county's six active Master Gardener volunteers have each received intensive horticultural training provided by the University of Minnesota Extension Service. The program is similar to those run by other land-grant colleges around the country. In return for the training, graduates are required to volunteer their time, says Jim Carlson, extension educator with the Morrison County Extension Office. The volunteers help staff the extension office and will visit homes or farms to consult on horticultural problems.

Before asking for a home visit, you should call the office or drop by. Often, Carlson or one of the volunteers can offer a solution on the spot. It helps if you can take along a sample of a diseased plant. Morrison County residents may write the office at 213 First Avenue SE, Little Falls, MN 56345-3100. Elsewhere, check with your local county extension office to see if they offer a similar service.

Information from Indiana

If you can't get the information you need from a local extension office, send for a free catalog from Indiana's Purdue University Cooperative Extension Service. The catalog lists hundreds of brochures and flyers on everything from "Onions and their Relatives" to "Growing Beans in the Home Vegetable Garden." There is a charge (usually less than $2) for some of the publications, but most are free. And you don't have to be a resident of Indiana to take advantage of the service.

For a copy of the catalog, write to the Media Distribution Center, 301 South Second Street, Lafayette, IN 47901-1232. If you have access to the Internet, you can call up the catalog at www.hort.purdue.edu/ext. Click on "Purdue Gardening Publications." Many of the individual publications are available online at the same Web site.

Joining a Community Garden

You don't need a backyard to grow your own fruits and vegetables, and you don't have to balance your tomatoes in window boxes. All over the country, Americans regularly put their green thumbs to use in community gardens located on taxpayer-owned land.

Gardeners who join a community garden usually pay a fee for a designated plot on which they may grow fruits and vegetables or flowers. Fees and rules vary from garden to garden and town to town. Some are publicly funded and operated, some are run by private, nonprofit foundations, and still others are run by small groups of private citizens.

Some cities with large numbers of vacant lots actively encourage residents to establish gardens on lots owned by the city as a way of transforming eyesores and increasing community pride. "It's good for everybody," says Sally McCabe, a board member of the American Community Gardening Association (ACGA), a nonprofit group based in Philadelphia.

To find out where community gardens are located in your area, write to the American Community Garden Association at 100 North 20th Street, 5th Floor, Philadelphia, PA 19103-1495.

If there are no community gardens in your area, the ACGA can provide free basic information to help you start one. Your county extension office is also a good place to check for information on local community gardens and for help in organizing one. Check the government listings in your phone book.

In the meantime, here are some established, government-supported community gardening programs around the country.

The Seattle P-Hawks

The P-Patch Program in Seattle is the largest and most extensive city-run, taxpayer-funded community gardening program in the country. The program operates 39 gardens throughout the city, attracting some 4,500 gardeners from all economic backgrounds.

"A lot of our residents live in places where they have no private space to garden," says Julie L. Bryan, community garden coordinator for the program. "This provides a sense of community, a way for people to talk with one another."

The whole thing started in the early 1970s when a local farmer named Rainie Picardo donated land to the city (hence the *P* in P-Patch). Today, the gardens range in size from 281 plots at the original Picardo P-Patch in northeast Seattle to the 7-plot Admiral Garden, located behind a warehouse in west Seattle. Twelve of the gardens are on land owned by the city. Most of the rest are leased from private owners.

Fees range from $21 a year for a 10-by-10-foot plot to $34 for a 10-by-20-foot plot to $53 for a 10-by-40-foot plot. But no one is turned away because they are unable to pay the fee, Bryan says. New gardens are added periodically, but the program is so popular that many have waiting lists. All the gardening is organic, meaning that no chemical fertilizers or pesticides are permitted. Residents grow a wide variety of fruits and vegetables; raspberries are a local staple.

Write to the P-Patch Program for a free information packet containing maps and brochures. The address is 700 Third Avenue, Fourth Floor, Seattle, WA 98104-1848. If you have access to the Internet, look up the P-Patch Program at www.ci.seattle.wa.us/don/ppatch.

●❖ *WHAT INSIDERS SAY:*

Veteran P-Patchers say that you stand a better chance of getting a plot quickly if you don't have your heart set on one particular garden. You may place your name on up to three waiting lists. Keep in mind that waits tend to be shorter at larger gardens and at those in outlying parts of the city.

Within the Austin City Limits

Hundreds of gardeners in Austin, Texas, grow their own okra, black-eyed peas, and hot peppers on land owned by the state. Austin Community Gardens, Inc., an independent, nonprofit organization funded in part by the city, operates a 6-acre spread provided by the Texas School for the Blind and Visually Impaired.

The organization has subdivided the garden into 230 plots, each 20 feet by 20 feet, that are available to any resident for $70 dollars per plot per year. That's fairly high compared with some other community gardens in the United States, but the fee covers a year-round growing season, use of communal tools, compost, and water.

"This is a semi-arid region, so water is expensive," says Terri Buchanan, executive director of Austin Community Gardens.

The organization also runs several smaller gardens and youth and senior programs in low-income neighborhoods, where members pay what they can afford. To join, you must visit the garden in person, but the organization will send you a free informational brochure. Send a self-addressed, stamped envelope to Austin Community Gardens, Inc., 4814 Sunshine Drive, Austin, TX 78756.

◐◑ WHAT INSIDERS SAY:

Many newcomers to fast-growing Austin come from the north and don't think of gardening until springtime. By that time, many of the plots are taken. Instead, consider joining during the excellent fall growing season, when plots are more plentiful.

Filling Vacant Lots in Philly

To help beautify and revitalize its inner city neighborhoods, the city of Philadelphia permits residents to garden free of charge on vacant lots owned by the city. Today, several thousand Philadelphians till and toil on some 1,500 city-owned lots. "It puts vacant real estate to use, offering an alternative to people littering on it," says Kenneth A. Sipos, a real estate specialist with the city's Department of Public Property.

If you have a likely-looking lot in mind, you must apply in writing to the city's Vacant Property Review Committee, which meets monthly. Approved gardeners must sign an "urban gardening agreement," pledging to fence, clean, and maintain the lot. In ex-change, they receive a free license, which must be re-newed each year. To request an application, write to the Department of Public Property, City of Philadelphia, 1401 JFK Boulevard, Room 1000, Philadelphia, PA 19102-1677. You may also request an application electronically by sending e-mail to kenneth.sipos @phila.gov.

◐◑ WHAT INSIDERS SAY:

No matter where you live, community garden experts strongly warn against simply "squatting" on a vacant lot near your home, even if the lot seems abandoned. The owner may reclaim the property at any time, thus ending your garden. Also, make sure that the lot was never home to a gas station or other chemical site before planting food crops.

Check with the department of public property in your city or town to find out about local policies on gardening on vacant lots. If you write to the American Community Gardening Association at 100 North 20th Street, 5th Floor, Philadelphia, PA 19103-1495, they will send you detailed, step-by-step procedures for starting a community garden.

Indianapolis in the Summertime

Indiana's capital city will rent residents a place to grow their own vegetables and even till the soil for them. Plots at the Mayor's Garden Plot in the city-

THE STORY OF COMMUNITY GARDENING

Community gardening in the United States dates back to the world wars, when Americans on the home front relied on their own labors for fresh food. In World War I, they were called War Gardens. During World War II, they went by the name Victory Gardens.

"Folks in the United States were growing more than a quarter of their own fresh vegetables back then," says Sally McCabe, a board member of the American Community Gardening Association, a non-profit group based in Philadelphia.

The trend died down after World War II but surged again in the 1970s as a result of re-newed interest in both organic gardening and revitalizing cities. Today, the American Community Gardening Association estimates that 1.5 million Americans till the soil of 150,000 community gardens, located in big cities and small towns nationwide.

owned Eagle Creek Park range from $14 for a 25-by-25-foot plot to $42 for a 50-by-50-foot plot. Residents ages 55 and older pay half-price.

The growing season runs from April 1 until November 1. Just before the season opens, city workers till the soil and stake out the plots. To apply for a plot, write to the Mayor's Garden Plot in late March, say you want to join, and include your phone number. A parks representative will call you to let you know about availability. The address is Eagle Creek Park Office, 7840 West 56th Street, Indianapolis, IN 46254.

There's a second, smaller garden on the corner of 21st Street and Luette Street in downtown Indianapolis on property that is the headquarters for city maintenance workers. Plots at this garden, open April through November, cost $15 to $30, depending on size. Write to the Indianapolis Depart-ment of Parks at 1502 West 16th Street, Indianapolis, IN 46202.

Foraging in the Forest

The squirrels, birds, and bears do it, so why not you? At national and state forests and parks, you are permitted and even encouraged to harvest nature's bounty of berries, nuts, and mushrooms.

In some cases, you are required to visit a ranger's office and fill out a form before getting out there under the trees and foraging. But if you aren't harvesting commercially, you may be able to skip the paperwork. In the USDA Forest Service's Northern Region, you are allowed to pick up to 30 gallons of huckleberries for family use without a permit. (That's a pretty generous

FREE SEEDS FOR INDY GARDENERS

You might call Ginny Roberts a modern-day Johnny Appleseed. But you'd have to change the title to Johnny Cucumber–Tomato–Green Pepper–Herb–Seed. Each year, Roberts, program assistant for the federally funded Capital City Garden Project in Indianapolis, distributes thousands of packets of free, donated seeds to community gardeners in the city.

The Garden Project, funded by the USDA and administered by the Purdue University Cooperative Extension Service, helps city residents set up and run successful community gardens.

Most of the free seeds come from private companies that donate them following an annual hardware convention in Indianapolis. Some years, up to 20,000 packets are donated, including seeds for a wide variety of fruits, vegetables, and flowers. Garden centers also donate. Often, the seeds are at or past their stamped "sell by" date but remain perfectly good, Roberts says. "Seeds are guaranteed to germinate for a year."

Roberts divides the seeds by type and mails them on request to leaders of community gardens around Indianapolis. In addition to two city-run gardens, there are nearly 80 privately run community gardens in the city. If you would like free seeds for your community garden in Indianapolis, write to the Capital City Garden Project, 9245 North Meridian Street, Suite 118, Indianapolis, IN 46260-1874. If you live elsewhere, call your county extension office (listed in the government pages of your phone book) and ask if it has a free seed program.

offer; the region's going commercial rate is $14 a gallon for wild berries, meaning that you can pick $420 worth before having to bother with a permit.)

In New York's state forests, it is understood that visitors may gather hickory nuts, beechnuts, and all sorts of berries without a permit. But it's a good idea to check with the ranger in charge at any park, either in person or by calling ahead. If you have to pay a fee, it will be modest.

As for mushrooms, you can find more than 30 species in northwestern parks alone. Foragers turn out by the thousands for boletes, morels, white and yellow chanterelles, Oregon black truffles, cauliflower mushrooms, spreading hedgehogs, and matsutakes, among others. Gathering is often regulated by permits. Many guidelines are posted on the World Wide Web; the Forest Service Web address is www.fs.fed.us/recreation. The National Park Service is at www.nps.gov. For each state, the starting point is www.state.*(insert the two-letter state abbreviation)*.us or www.parks.state.*(insert the two-letter state abbreviation)*.us.

●◆ *WHAT INSIDERS SAY:*

Mushroom hunting can be a lethal hobby if you have trouble distinguishing delicacies from deadly poisonous species. It's best to forage with an expert, using a field guide, until you are confident. At some parks, rangers will have a look at your gleanings to check for any that should not be eaten. Even touching certain toxic species can be harmful, so wear gloves when foraging, and don't involve young children in this activity.

Joining a Cooperative

The federal government gives a tax break to food cooperatives, which, as nonprofit organizations,

Amazing Stories

THE FUNGUS AMONG US

Foraging for wild edibles is usually a low-stress pastime—unless you're searching for the matsutake mushroom, that is. The matsutake, found primarily in the forests in and around Oregon's Crater Lake National Park, is a highly sought-after delicacy in Japan. It's nicknamed "white gold," which makes sense considering that during its glory days, a single matsutake sold for $1,500.

Does this mean that you should chuck your law career and head out to become a mushroom picker? Not so fast. Once people realized how much the matsutakes were worth, a virtual war erupted between groups trying to control the harvest. Although the Forest Service has implemented rules that have diminished violent outbursts, it's still not uncommon for mushroom pickers to carry semiautomatic weapons and guard their prime harvest areas. Rumors of gambling, prostitution, gangs, extortion, gunplay, and other frontier-type high jinks also abound.

Also, unfortunately, the price of matsutakes has dropped sharply lately (it's now down to around $12 a pound), so it's unlikely that this is your best way to strike it rich.

pay no income taxes. Join a cooperative, and you'll reap the rewards in the form of low prices, rebates, and dividends on the shares that you buy to join.

Of course, consumer prices vary from store to store and city to city, but cooperatives can frequently offer savings of 20 percent or more, based on comparable items in a mainstream grocery store. "Because the business is organized for the members and by the members, its purpose is not to make a profit for outside stockholders," says Leta Mach, spokeswoman for the National Cooperative Business Association, a nonprofit organization based in Washington, D.C.

Nonmembers may also shop at cooperatives, but the benefits really roll in when you join. As a member, you save money either through an upfront discount or a rebate at the end of the year that's based on how much food you have bought. Rebates vary from store to store and year to year (they may be lower if the elected board decides to pour more money into capital improvements, for example), but an average shopper can expect enough of a rebate to buy about a week's worth of groceries, Mach says.

As added benefits, members often get special discounts and subscriptions to a co-op newspaper (offering coupons, recipes, nutritional articles, and so on). Membership shares usually cost around $5 to $10 each, and the number you are required to have depends on the policies of that co-op. Your investment is generally refundable with limited interest if you quit.

There are more than 325 nonprofit retail food cooperatives around the country. Though some U.S. cooperatives date back to the Great Depression, many started during the late 1960s and early 1970s, when large numbers of consumers began seeking natural, organic foods that were difficult or impossible to find in conventional grocery stores.

Today, even mainstream grocers have caught on to the trend toward healthier eating, and many offer their own natural and/or organic food departments. But that hasn't taken the steam out of cooperatives. In addition to saving money, members of cooperatives get to vote for the boards that run them, and thus have at least an indirect say in what is offered.

"There's an important community element, a feeling of being part of something," says Dave Gutknecht, editor and publisher of *Cooperative Grocer* magazine in Athens, Ohio. Below are some examples of the types of cooperatives that you might find in your own city or town.

●◆ *WHAT INSIDERS SAY:*

A good way to locate cooperatives near your home is through one of the large regional cooperative warehouses that supply co-ops and buying clubs (see "Starting a Buying Club" on page 43). Or write to Editor, Cooperative Grocer *magazine, P.O. Box 597, Athens, OH 45701.*

Co-op in the Windy City

One of the oldest and largest retail food cooperatives in the United States, the Hyde Park Cooperative Society in Chicago offers just about anything you can find in a mainstream supermarket, plus a wide array of natural foods. The main store, at 1526 East 55th Street, features a bakery, video rentals, an in-store café, and a liquor store. There are now two additional stores, at 1226 East 53rd Street and at 1300 East 47th Street and Lake Park Avenue.

Hyde Park Co-op was started as an informal group in 1932, at the height of the Great Depression, and incorporated a year later.

"It's a community institution," says John K. Wilson, editor of *Evergreen*, the co-op newspaper sent out monthly to members. You can join by visiting one of the stores and purchasing at least one share for $10. The stores are open to nonmembers, too, but members enjoy special discount days and discount coupons. For more information, write to the Hyde Park Cooperative Society at 1526 East 55th Street, Chicago, IL 60615.

Food and Gas in Old New England

The Hanover Cooperative Society in New Hampshire has been serving this small town, best known as the home of Dartmouth College, since 1936.

"The original purpose was to get things that weren't available in northern New England at the time, such as fresh citrus from Florida," says Terry Appleby, general manager. Today, the society serves its 20,000 members at two locations (the second is in nearby Lebanon). In addition to great food at great prices, benefits include access to a consumer and nutrition lending library, savings on seeds and garden supplies, check-cashing privileges, and free notary public services.

The society even runs a pair of auto service sta-tions in Hanover that, like the food stores, are open to members and nonmembers. Membership in the society requires the purchase of 10 $5 shares ($50), either at the time you apply or through deductions from your rebate. Write to the Hanover Cooperative Society at P.O. Box 633, Hanover, NH 03755.

Going Healthy in Seattle

One of the largest retail food cooperatives in the nation, Puget Consumers Co-op has seven stores

THE WAREHOUSE CONNECTION

If you're thinking of starting a buying club, call the warehouse that serves your state. They're listed below, and they should be able to provide you with plenty of details to get started.

✓ Hudson Valley Federation of Co-ops, 6 Noxon Road, Poughkeepsie, NY 12603. Serves Connecticut, New Jersey, New York, and Pennsylvania.

✓ Northeast Cooperatives, Inc., P.O. Box 8188, 49 Ben-nett Drive, Brattleboro, VT 05304. Serves Connecticut, Massachusetts, New Hamp-shire, New York, Rhode Island, and Vermont.

✓ Blooming Prairie Ware-house, Inc., 2340 Heinz Road, Iowa City, IA 52240, and Blooming Prairie Nat-ural Foods, 510 Kasota Avenue SE, Minneapolis, MN 55414. Together they serve Iowa, Illinois, Kansas, Michigan, Minnesota, Missouri, Nebraska, North Dakota, South Dakota, and Wisconsin.

✓ Federation of Ohio River Cooperatives, 320-E Outer-belt, Suite E, Columbus, OH 43213. Serves Indiana, Kentucky, Maryland, Michigan, North Carolina, Ohio, Pennsylvania, South Carolina, Virginia, and West Virginia.

✓ North Farm Co-op Ware-house, 204 Regas Road, Madison, WI 53714. A second location is at 1505 North Eighth Street, Supe-rior, WI 54880. Together they serve Illinois, Indiana, Michigan, Minnesota, Mis-souri, Ohio, and Wisconsin.

✓ Ozark Co-operative Warehouse, Box 1528, Fayetteville, AR 72702. Serves Alabama, Arkansas, Florida, Georgia, Kansas, Louisiana, Missouri, Missis-sippi, Oklahoma, Tennessee, and Texas.

✓ Mountain Peoples Ware-house, 4005 Sixth Avenue S, Seattle, WA 98108. Serves Alaska, Idaho, Montana, and Washington state.

✓ Tucson Cooperative Ware-house, 3505 Toole, Tucson, AZ 85701. Serves Arizona, southern California, Col-orado, New Mexico, Nevada, Texas, and Utah.

✓ Frontier Natural Products Co-op, Box 299, Norway, IA 52318. Serves the entire country with herbs and spices.

and more than 35,000 members throughout the Seattle area. Started during the 1960s, the cooperative specializes in natural and organic foods, recycled paper products, and environmentally friendly household cleaning products.

Joining requires investing $60 (good for a lifetime membership), payable all at once or in installments of $6 each. Members receive cards that entitle them to discounts on a wide variety of items. The co-op also holds regular cooking and nutrition classes, with special discounts for members. New members get a tour of the co-op's kitchen. If you are 65 or older, have a disability, or receive federal food stamps or Women, Infants, and Children vouchers, you may receive member discounts without actually joining by purchasing a $2 shopping pass. The pass is good for as many return visits as you like. For more information, write to the Puget Consumers Co-Op at 4201 Roosevelt Way NE, Seattle, WA 98105.

Starting a Buying Club

If you can't find a good retail food cooperative near your home, you want natural food items that no store seems to carry, or you're just a born organizer, consider starting your own food-buying club. Like retail cooperatives, food-buying clubs are nonprofit and thus enjoy the same government exemption from corporate income taxes.

Buying clubs are informal cooperatives that differ from their retail counterparts in that there is no physical store and no paid staff. Each month, a designated member of the club takes orders from each member, by mail, phone, fax, and so on, then places a large order with the warehouse. Most warehouses require a minimum order of $500 from each club.

Once the order has been processed, the warehouse dispatches a truck that arrives with the food at a given location, such as a church parking lot, and time. Some items are purchased in bulk (a 50-pound bag of flour, for instance) and divided among several members, but members may also buy items individually.

The National Cooperative Business Association estimates that there are more than 4,000 buying clubs in the United States. "A buying club is an informal association of neighbors or people in a church organization," says Robert J. Pickford, chief executive officer of the Federation of Ohio River Cooperatives, an Ohio-based food warehouse that distributes natural and organic food to cooperatives and buying clubs in nine states. "We service buying clubs with as few as 4 or 5 families and as many as 150 families."

Lee Sexton, buying club coordinator for the Ozark Co-op Warehouse in Fayetteville, Arkansas, says, "The first reason people do it is that you can save 20 to 40 percent when you do the work for yourselves," compared with buying at the retail level.

Buying clubs usually start with the initiative of one or two interested, enthusiastic people who are able to encourage neighbors, friends, or fellow parishioners to join them.

"You have to be a planner," says Nan L. Erbaugh, founder and coordinator of the Twin Creek Co-op, a buying club in West Alexandria, Ohio. Erbaugh runs the buying club in addition to working as an independent insurance agent. She says, "You have to have a key person who has organizational skills and the ability to inspire others to come to the cause."

The National Cooperative Business Association offers a $19.95 video, "How to Run a Co-op Food-Buying Club." Also, ask them to send you a free, handy flyer, "Food-Buying Clubs," that explains some of the basics. Write to the association at 1401 New York Avenue NW, Suite 1100, Washington, DC 20005-2160.

◗◆ *WHAT INSIDERS SAY:*
Buying clubs succeed or fail based on the participation of their members. No matter how energetic the founder is, the club is doomed if one or two people do all the work. Here are some tips for success from experienced buying club organizers.

Require members to contribute a set amount of work per month or year (taking orders, writing the newsletter, alerting members to deliveries, and so on) and/or require members to pay a small fee to cover club expenses. Computerize your buying club. Use a laptop so that several members can share the book-keeping and ordering. "Our laptop makes the rounds," says Sue Murphy, founder of the Milk and Honey Buying Club in Starkville, Mississippi.

Food for Good Deeds

Why not cut your food bills in half while doing something for your community? Private, nonprofit World SHARE, Inc. will sell you a food package containing $28 to $30 worth of groceries for $14 to $15, provided that you perform 2 hours of community service.

Paint over graffiti, help adults learn to read, join a highway clean-up program. It's up to you. All you need is a voucher from a charitable or volunteer organization explaining what you did to help out. "We don't like to prescribe for people what to do," says Michele Medugno, a World SHARE spokeswoman in San Diego.

Some 300,000 people in 30 states participate each month. The food is distributed through local nonprofit organizations such as churches. It is not donated; World SHARE buys in bulk from the same suppliers and manufacturers that stock grocery store

DOUBLE THE FUN

Sue Murphy's interest in starting a buying club began with a simple desire to feed her family the natural foods that she believed would provide a healthier diet. Unfortunately, such items could be difficult to come by near her home in Starkville, Mississippi.

"I wanted unrefined whole grains, unrefined oils and sweeteners, whole-grain flours, and alternatives to dairy products," she says.

Murphy had been a member of a buying club before moving to Starkville, and, although new to the area, she knew a few people well enough to ask them to join her in starting a new one.

The original handful of members placed their first order with the Ozark Co-operative Warehouse in Fayetteville, Arkansas (the warehouse serving Deep South states), for about $500 worth of food. That was in 1993.

Today, the club has burgeoned to 70 members who order up to $6,500 worth of groceries a month and save roughly 30 percent off retail prices, Murphy estimates. Regular purchases range from frozen tortillas to frozen prepared organic dinners, baby food, baking supplies such as vanilla extract, powdered milk, and bulk items such as flour and dried beans.

Although members don't have to order in person, each month, Murphy opens her house for an "ordering party" preceded by a potluck supper. "I really believe that the social aspect is greater than the food," she says. "The food is what brings you together. It's almost like a little town square where you can meet and talk."

Murphy's experience was so positive that she formed a second buying club to purchase fresh fruits and vegetables from a local produce vendor. That club's 140 members pay $10 to $12 every 2 weeks for a mixed bag of seasonal fruits and vegetables worth about $30 retail. Today, Murphy estimates that she does 95 percent of her food shopping through her two buying clubs.

Department of Commerce's *Commerce Business Daily*. This paper, published Monday through Friday, is available at federal depository libraries and on the Web at www.cbdnet.access.gpo.gov. You can subscribe to the print version at a cost of $275 a year by writing to the Superintendent of Documents, U.S. Government Printing Office, P.O. Box 371954, Pittsburgh, PA 15250-7954.

The National Sales Center

Because of the concentration of federal government in Washington, the Federal Supply Service operates a national sales center in suburban Springfield, Virginia, with regularly scheduled sales and auctions of furniture, vehicles, and other items. For information on upcoming sales, write to the Federal Supply Service National Sales Center at 6808 Loisdale Road (3FP-W), Springfield, VA 22150.

Other Regional GSA Offices

✓ For Connecticut, Maine, Massachusetts, New Hampshire, Rhode Island, and Vermont: 10 Causeway Street, Third Floor, Room 347 (2FBP-1), Boston, MA 02222-1076.

✓ For New Jersey, New York, Puerto Rico, and Virgin Islands: Room 20-112, Box 10 (2FBP), 26 Federal Plaza, New York, NY 10278.

✓ For Delaware, Maryland, Pennsylvania, Virginia, and West Virginia: Wanamaker Building (3FPD), 100 Penn Square East, Philadelphia, PA 19107-3396.

✓ For Arkansas, Louisiana, New Mexico, Oklahoma, and Texas: 819 Taylor Street (7FMP), Fort Worth, TX 76102-6105.

✓ For Alabama, Florida, Georgia, Kentucky, Mississippi, North Carolina, South Carolina, and Tennessee: Peachtree Summit Building, 401 West Peachtree Street (4FD), Atlanta, GA 30365-2550.

✓ For Illinois, Indiana, Iowa, Kansas, Michigan, Minnesota, Missouri, Nebraska, Ohio, and Wisconsin: *Vehicles only:* 230 South Dearborn Street (5FBF), Chicago, IL 60604. *Other items:* 1500 East Bannister Road (6FBP), Room 1102, Kansas City, MO 64131.

✓ For Colorado, Montana, North Dakota, South Dakota, Utah, and Wyoming: P.O. Box 25506, Denver Federal Center, Building 41 (7FP-8), Denver, CO 80225-0506.

✓ For Alaska, Idaho, Oregon, and Washington: 400 15th Street SW (10FZP-S), Auburn, WA 98001-6599.

✓ For Arizona, California, Hawaii, and Nevada: 450 Golden Gate Avenue Fourth Floor West (9FBP), San Francisco, CA 94102-3434.

Seized Furniture

On the flip side of surplus goods are items that federal law enforcement agencies have seized from criminals, customs violators, and so forth. This is where the flashy stuff—Rolex watches, souped-up sports cars, and valuable antique furniture—comes in.

Each year, the U.S. Marshals Service, part of the U.S. Department of Justice, sells about $75 million worth of items that have been seized by its investigative agencies, including the Drug Enforcement Administration, the Immigration and Naturalization Service, and the FBI.

Bargains from the Marshals

The Marshals Service doesn't conduct auctions and sales itself. Instead, it sells some items through the GSA and contracts out to a wide range of professional auctioneers and brokers around the country.

One of the larger contractors is Atlanta-based Manheim Auctions, Inc., which handles luxury cars, jewelry, fine antiques, and many other items and conducts auctions around the country on behalf of the Marshals Service.

As Manheim's director of government services, Dean Echols has auctioned off everything from a warehouse full of antiques that were once owned by a group busted for selling drug paraphernalia to the desk once used by convicted spy Aldrich Ames.

Furniture seized from drug dealers and other criminals runs "the entire gamut from the gaudiest to some very, very nice furniture," Echols says. "Some of them should be arrested for having no taste at all."

To avoid paying too much, bidders at government auctions should have a set price in mind for a given item before the bidding starts, Echols advises. "They should not exceed that."

For information on locations, dates, and items for sale at upcoming Manheim auctions of government goods, write to Manheim Auctions, Inc., 1400 Lake Hearn Drive, Atlanta, GA 30315.

Other auctions of items collected by the Marshals Service are run by private auctioneers and brokers. The Marshals Service does not maintain a mailing list to let buyers know when sales are taking place, but the sales are usually advertised in the classified sections of newspapers where they are to be held.

Also, you can find out about upcoming sales by contacting private sellers directly. A list of all of the private auctioneers and brokers who contract with the Marshals Service, as well as the federal agencies that sell property for it, is available on the Internet

Amazing Stories

TREASURE IN AN OLD BOX

If you haven't been to Salvation Army or Goodwill retail stores in recent years, you may not know what you're missing. Both of the venerable charitable groups have upgraded, with improved merchandise, brighter stores, and better locations. And with retro clothing in full style, the stores are increasingly attracting young, fashion-conscious shoppers. Besides, you never know when you might find a true treasure in one of these bargain stores.

A self-proclaimed "thrift shop diva," Melissa Baltchilder has been prowling church basements and charity warehouses since she was a child growing up in Canada.

"I found out that I could get a whole bunch of good clothes for the same price I was paying for one pair of Vidal Sassoon jeans," says Baltchilder, a former staff writer for *NonProfit*

Times, a magazine based in New Jersey.

Several years ago, at a church basement thrift shop in Canada, Baltchilder paid $1 for a box full of random goods that had failed to sell individually. She wasn't expecting much; indeed, the box seemed to contain nothing but old scraps and worthless bric-a-brac.

After letting a good friend and another woman rummage through the box and extract what they wanted, Baltchilder fished around and found a pair of costume earrings at the bottom. Then she noticed that the fasteners screwed on rather than snapping on, a sign that they might be valuable. She took the earrings to an appraiser, who informed her that the "costume" earrings were in fact authentic pearls set on solid gold posts. Estimated value: $500.

shelves. Typical packages include ground beef, chicken, fish, processed foods such as pasta sauce, pasta, frozen breakfast items, and fresh fruits and vegetables—enough for five meals for a family of four.

World SHARE is open to anyone, regardless of income, so don't worry that you'll be taking food out of the mouths of the needy. In fact, getting people from different backgrounds together is the whole point. "By inviting everyone to participate, we're putting together people who might otherwise never have the opportunity to interact," Medugno says.

To find the affiliate that's closest to your home, write World SHARE at 6950 Friars Road, San Diego, CA 92108, or visit the Web site at www.worldshare.org.

●◆ *WHAT INSIDERS SAY:*

Stock your freezer with meat. Purchase at least one regular food package and you may buy a separate package containing only meat for the same price or at a discounted price. SHARE has no age limit for participants and no limit on the number of food packages you may buy, so get the whole family involved in volunteering. Packages are distributed monthly. Participants pay for them 2 weeks before delivery, so don't just show up and expect to take home food the same day. Contact your local affiliate for specific times and dates.

Splurging on a Budget at Cooking Schools

Dining out, once an infrequent treat for many Americans, has become a way of life. According to the USDA, the average American now spends $1,197 a year on restaurant meals, compared with $1,474 on groceries.

But you don't have to pay full fare for great fare. True to the old adage "There's no practice like doing," cooking schools across the country, many subsidized by the government, operate restaurants where student chefs practice their art on a willing public.

"It gives those students a real-world education,"

says Caitlin Storhaug, director of communications for the National Restaurant Association Educational Foundation in Chicago. "They are no longer just learning about being in the restaurant business. Now they are in the restaurant business," Storhaug says.

So what's in it for you? Gastronomical bargains, for one thing. Prices vary according to the type of restaurant and what you order, and eating at a cooking school will still set you back more than a Big Mac and fries. For an evening-out splurge, though, you'll save at least 20 percent compared with a similar meal at a regular restaurant.

"Since our restaurants are actually classrooms, it is important for us to have people in the seats so our students can have a real-world experience of interacting with patrons," says Thomas E. Peer, a certified master chef who serves as director of food and beverage operations for the Culinary Institute of America in Hyde Park, New York.

In addition to good prices, diners get a chance to experience great chefs in the making. Students are closely monitored by pros, and any rough edges in cooking and service are likely to be compensated for by the exuberance of the staff.

"You're being served by very enthusiastic people who are excited about what they're doing and about embarking on a new career," says Dorlene V. Kaplan of New York City, editor of *The Guide to Cooking Schools*, an annual guide for prospective chefs who are looking to enter a school. "They're eager to please."

With a recent growth of interest in cooking as a vocation, new cooking schools and restaurants are opening all the time. "It's sort of a growing trend," Kaplan says.

The best way to find one in your area is to look in the phone book under "Culinary Schools," Storhaug says. "Even if they don't have a full restaurant, they may well do something like beer tastings." Or check with local colleges to see if any have a cooking school with a restaurant.

Eating at the Institute

About 90 minutes outside Manhattan, in New York state's leafy Hudson Valley, the famed Culinary Institute of America serves up gourmet fare in four award-winning restaurants. Prices range from about $30 per person (including wine) at Caterina de Medici, an Italian restaurant, to around $50 at the Escoffier Restaurant, which serves French fare on fine china amid linen and crystal. Students are supervised by decidedly finicky teachers, who monitor every step in the process.

"We have some of the greatest chefs in the world working here. They scrutinize the food very, very closely to make sure that we get the best ingredients," says Peer. "We are proud to be able to provide fine cuisine and outstanding service, and our restaurants have been recognized with many industry awards."

In addition to the regular restaurant menus, the college offers a special "Culinary Institute of America dining series" each year from November to May that includes special wine tastings and theme dinners that start in a modern amphitheater and end in one of the restaurants. At the time of the *Titanic* movie craze, the college offered an exact duplication of the first-class fare served on the night the big boat sank—except these passengers stayed dry and paid just $45 per person.

For information, write to the Culinary Institute of America at 433 Albany Post Road, Hyde Park, NY 12538-1499.

●◆ *WHAT INSIDERS SAY:*

Reservations, which are recommended year-round, are especially important during the autumn foliage season.

Au Naturel in the Big Apple

If health food's your thing or you're simply open to new culinary experiences, consider the Natural Gourmet Cookery School the next time business or pleasure calls you to New York City for the weekend. On Friday nights, the school opens its doors to the public for a one-price, five-course, candlelit vegetarian feast for $25 per person—a true bargain by New York standards.

And don't expect a lump of tasteless tofu on a pile of seaweed. The fare more likely will include such delicacies as roasted chili pepper soup with basil coulis or wild rice pilaf served in a baby pumpkin. The staple beverage served with meals is kukicha, a Japanese tea made from roasted twigs. If your tastes run to beer or wine, bring your own.

"The idea is beautiful, sophisticated food that's on a par with mainstream food in terms of presentation and flavor," says Jenny Matthau, director of the chefs' training program and co-president of the school. "We don't believe that healthy food should taste bad." The school, located at 48 West 21st Street, between 5th and 6th Avenues, takes reservations (required) up until the Wednesday before a dinner. Seating for all meals is at 6:30 P.M. Write the Natural Gourmet at 48 West 21st Street, 2nd Floor, New York, NY 10010.

West Coast Victuals

The California Culinary Academy offers two restaurants in the heart of one of America's most beautiful cities, San Francisco. The academy is on Polk Street, a short walk from the theater district, Symphony Hall, the Civic Center, and City Hall.

Carême, described as "the jewel around which the school revolves," offers contemporary cuisine in a formal dining room that dates to 1912. The restaurant is open for lunch and dinner Monday through Friday, with a lavish buffet on Friday night. Dinners average about $30 per person, not including wine.

Tavern on the Tenderloin, a San Francisco–style steak house and grill, is somewhat less formal and averages around $25 per person. The culinary academy offers public tours weekdays at 11:00 A.M. and 5:00 P.M. For reservations at the restaurants or for tour information, write to the California Culinary Academy, 625 Polk Street, San Francisco, CA 94102.

International Dining, Chicago-Style

You can sample the menus from some of the finest restaurants in Chicago without actually entering the city limits. Just north of Chicago, in the suburb of Evanston, Kendall College, the School of Culinary Arts, puts on banquets featuring various ethnic cuisines. Head chefs from various restaurants oversee the students as they prepare the food. The banquets, served at 6:30 P.M. on selected Monday evenings, costs $24.50 for four or five courses.

The school's regular student-run restaurant, called the Dining Room, serves French cuisine for lunch Monday through Friday from noon to 1:30 P.M. for $14.95. Dinner is American fare, served Tuesday through Saturday from 6:00 to 8:00 P.M. (8:30 on Saturday) at an average cost of $25 to $30 per person.

"The quality of the food is extremely high," says Steve Grand Pré, dining room instructor. "With that said, the price is very reasonable." The school has no liquor license, so patrons are encouraged to bring their own wine. For information, write to the Dining Room, 2408 Orrington Avenue, Evanston, IL 60201.

FUEL

Americans spend a staggering $115 billion each year on fuel and electricity for their homes. Your family's share, assuming that you consume an average amount of energy, comes to nearly $1,300. Almost half of that goes toward just maintaining a comfortable air temperature.

Some fuel expense is unavoidable, of course. Still, the U.S. Department of Energy says that Americans waste millions of dollars a year because of drafty windows and doors, insufficient insulation, and any number of other energy missteps.

Fortunately, government agencies are well-equipped to help with strategies for cutting your fuel bills, not to mention easing our national consumption of natural resources.

Getting Good Advice

Follow a few well-established guidelines on insulation, caulking, and so forth, and you may cut 10 to 50 percent off your home energy bills, just like that. It's not only good for your pocketbook, it's good for the environment. The Energy Department estimates that poorly insulated doors and windows alone squander as much energy as is supplied by the Alaska pipeline each year. So if you're looking for the best tips on fuel savings and efficiency, the natural place to start is the Energy Department itself.

Check with the Information Clearinghouse

The Department of Energy distributes much of its information to the public through the Energy Efficiency and Renewable Energy Clearinghouse, which is based in northern Virginia, just outside of Washington. The clearinghouse offers dozens of free, useful DOE booklets and fact sheets on saving energy in the home.

One of the most popular publications is a 36-page booklet called "Energy Savers: Tips on Saving Energy and Money in the Home." The booklet is clearly written, well-organized, and bursting with tips on everything from insulating doors and windows to conducting your own home energy audit.

Other titles include topics such as "Cooling Your Home Naturally: A Guide to Making Energy-Smart Purchases" and "Energy-Efficient Water Heating." To order any of these free publications or to get a list of others, write to the Energy Efficiency and Renewable Energy Clearinghouse, P.O. Box 3048, Merrifield, VA 22116. If you have access to the Web, you can read many of these publications at www.eren.doe.gov.

Ask an Energy Expert

If the publications don't answer your questions, or if your problem is just too tricky to find in a booklet, you can plug into a staff of experts at the clearinghouse. They'll answer just about any home energy question you may have, in writing, at no charge.

Try to make your questions specific and detailed. Send them to "Ask an Energy Expert" at P.O. Box 3048, Merrifield, VA 22116; you should allow 2 to 4 weeks for a response. You can save time and postage if you file your question electronically by filling out a form on the Web at www.eren.doe.gov.

Free Energy Checkups

Some states, in an effort to encourage residents to decrease energy consumption, will give a free home energy inspection and may even help pay for modifications to make your house more snug. If you live in Oregon and heat your home with oil or propane, for example, you can get a free home inspection under the State Home Oil Weatherization Program (SHOW). An inspector, working for a private firm under a contract from the state, will examine your abode from attic to basement, looking for trouble spots.

"They check your insulation and your vents, they check underneath the house for pipe wrapping, they look for duct insulation, and they check around the windows," says Sylvia de la Rosa, energy coordinator for the Oregon Office of Energy in Salem. "If you have an oil furnace, they'll do an efficiency test to see what capacity it's running at."

The inspection takes about an hour. If you de-

What Is It?

"COOPERATIVE"

As the term implies, cooperatives ("co-ops," for short) are organizations in which people pool their resources in order to satisfy some mutual need. It's a strength-in-numbers thing. Independent farmers, for example, often form co-operatives to share information or equipment and to get their crops to market more efficiently.

Retail co-ops operate under a similar principle. Unlike for-profit stores, co-ops are owned by the people who shop there. They use their collective buying power to purchase items at a bulk rate, and everybody shares in the savings. Any earnings are distributed back to the members in the form of rebates.

"The business is organized for the members and by the members. Its purpose is not to make a profit for outside stockholders," says Leta Mach, spokeswoman for the National Cooperative Business Association, based in Washington, D.C.

The modern cooperative movement dates to mid-nineteenth-century England and a bunch of cotton weavers who were fed up with their low wages and the high prices they had to pay for food and household goods. They decided to start their own store. The Rochdale Equitable Pioneers Society opened in December 1844 and offered just four staples—flour, oatmeal, sugar, and butter. Each member controlled one share and one vote. The store was so successful that it expanded its time open from two nights a week to five.

"That's considered to be the first successful cooperative," Mach says. The idea spread across England. By 1900, some 1.7 million people in England had joined cooperatives, and the idea was spreading to other countries.

Today, the International Co-operative Alliance, founded in 1895, has members in more than 100 countries, including the National Cooperative Business Association in the United States.

cide to proceed with improvements, the state will rebate 25 percent of the cost (up to $400) for insulation, caulking, or weather-stripping. You may also be eligible for a special 6.5 percent loan from participating banks for up to $5,000 toward improvements.

The program is not open to people who heat with electricity or gas, since those privately run utilities offer their own energy incentive programs. For more information, write to the SHOW program at the Office of Energy, 625 Marion Street NE, Suite 1, Salem, OR 97301-3742.

To check for similar programs in your state, consult the government listings in your phone book. Some states operate weatherization programs through the energy department; in others, it's the housing department. If you reach a dead end, phone the governor's office and ask which department handles home weatherization programs.

Heating Oil Cooperatives

Although they're not operated by government agencies, fuel cooperatives, as nonprofit organizations, enjoy an exemption from paying corporate income taxes—and these savings are passed along to their members. But the real savings come through negotiating long-term contracts with heating oil companies to deliver oil at low prices.

"When prices go up on the wholesale market, oil dealers certainly take advantage of it," says Matthew C. Patrick, executive director of Self-Reliance Corp., a cooperative serving southeastern Massachusetts and Cape Cod. "We act as a buyers' cooperative. The staff and I negotiate with local oil dealers to arrive at a fixed profit over their wholesale price. That prevents them from arbitrarily increasing their prices to take advantage of cold weather and shortages."

Although savings depend on the going retail rate for heating oil, Patrick estimates that the cooperative's 3,500 members average a 5 to 30 percent savings over buying individually from an oil company. Membership costs $15 per year, or $7 per year for senior citizens or those receiving state fuel assistance. Members are also eligible for low-interest loans for energy-related home improvements as well as a number of other money-saving benefits, and they receive a quarterly newsletter full of energy-saving tips. You can write to Self-Reliance Corp. at P.O. Box 3203, Waquoit, MA 02536-3203.

➡️ WHAT INSIDERS SAY:
Finding a fuel cooperative in your own area may take a little digging. Unlike food cooperatives, which have a strong national network of suppliers and organizations, fuel cooperatives tend to be highly localized. Public Citizen, a nonprofit consumer advocacy group based in Washington, surveyed fuel cooperatives based in the Mid-Atlantic states and the Northeast. If you live in Connecticut, Delaware, the District of Columbia, Maryland, Virginia, Massachusetts, New Jersey, New York, Pennsylvania, or Rhode Island, write to Public Citizen at 1600 20th Street NW, Washington, DC 20009-1001 for a list. The group operates its own cooperative, Buyer's Up, with about 4,000 members in Washington and its suburbs, which you can contact at the same address.

If you live in another state, Garland Auton, program manager for Buyer's Up, suggests calling heating oil companies (listed in the yellow pages) and asking if they participate in a cooperative.

Firewood

The USDA Forest Service operates 155 national forests in 42 states, with a combined 191 million acres of woodlands. That adds up to a lot of trees owned by you, the taxpayer. Snow, wind, ice, and other natural elements claim their fair share of those trees each year. For wood burners with some time, energy, and a sense of adventure, those dead trees can provide a long-lasting supply of firewood for a song.

Firewood permits vary from forest to forest, but the cost is generally less than $10 per cord, with a maximum number of cords allowed per person. Regulations also vary from forest to forest, as do the seasons in which gathering is allowed.

Most forests require that you bring along some fire prevention equipment, such as an extinguisher and a pail and shovel. You will also need a pickup truck, a chain saw, and protective clothing. Harvesting firewood is hard work.

Knowing the local regulations and the layout of the forest before you start out is essential. At some forests, you will be limited to gathering only in certain areas. Rangers at other forests will allow you to choose the spot, but they will want to know in advance where you plan to be. That means checking in at the district ranger's office (where you can buy the permit) before you start.

The Forest Service in Washington will send you some general guidelines for gathering firewood as well as the addresses and phone numbers of district rangers in your area. Write to USDA Forest Service\Attention Forest Management, P.O. Box 96090, Washington, DC 20090-6090. You can also find information and contacts for individual forests on the Internet at www.fs.fed.us. Click on "National Forests," then "The Outdoors." You can select national forests by region or name.

●◆ WHAT INSIDERS SAY:

The Forest Service sees its relationship with wood gatherers as a symbiotic one. Gatherers get a plentiful supply of cheap wood, and they help the forest by clearing away dead wood. As a result, rangers tend to give gatherers leeway. "We sort of operate on the honor system," says one ranger. But don't mistake that friendly attitude for an invitation to simply show up and start sawing away. If a ranger drops by your site and you can't produce a permit, you will be fined.

In the Great Northwest

The Ochoco National Forest covers more than 850,000 acres of central Oregon, swelling with lodgepole pines, ponderosa pines, and tamaracks. The severe winters down enough trees to provide a gold mine for energetic firewood collectors. The firewood season runs from April 1 through the end of November. Permits, good for the whole season, are $10 a cord, with a maximum of eight cords to a household.

The forest is divided into four districts. You'll find good wood in each, but check your map for the Big Summit District. That's where you'll find the heaviest concentration of tamaracks. "The tamarack is a deciduous evergreen that drops its needles," says Linda D. Rock, an information assistant for Ochoco National Forest. "It's the preferred wood to cut. The grain is very tight, so it's a hard wood and burns well."

What Is It?

"A CORD OF WOOD"

A cord of firewood is a stack measuring 4 feet high by 4 feet wide by 8 feet long, for a total of 128 cubic feet. That's the official measurement, but it's unlikely that any ranger is going to pull up and whip out the tape measure.

Out in the forest, the definition becomes a bit looser. There's a lot of give and take between rangers and firewood gatherers—namely, if you don't take too much, they're not likely to give you a hard time. One state forest ranger says that a good estimate for a cord of wood is two loads for a large pickup truck or three loads for a compact pickup.

Many firewood collectors make the mistake of heading to the Ochoco in late summer or fall. By then, "the woods are going to be picked over," Rock says, with much of the best wood gone. The best time is just after they open in April, she says. Not only is the weather mild, but you'll have the best selection of trees downed during recent winter storms.

Good Wood for a Pittance

Dead, fallen trees are fair game year-round in Vermont's Green Mountain National Forest, which covers 350,000 acres and runs a vertical path through the heart of the state. Firewood permits cost $6 per cord and are good through December 31 of the year in which they are purchased. You must buy permits for at least 2 cords, with a maximum of 10.

The most popular firewood in the forest is the dense sugar maple. Beech and ash are also coveted. If you have difficulty telling one species from the next, forester Robert J. Clark suggests cutting with an experienced partner. "Firewood gathering is a great outdoor activity, and cutting with a partner makes good safety sense," he says.

For information, write to Manchester District, Green Mountain National Forest, 2538 Depot Street, Manchester Center, VT 05255.

Private businesses are periodically permitted to cut down live trees in specific areas of the forest for commercial use, such as logs for home construction. The tops of downed trees, which are left behind, are a bonanza for firewood collectors. Not only is a good portion of the cutting already done for you, but the wood is guaranteed not to be rotten, and you won't have to hunt all over the forest to find it. When you purchase your permit, ask about upcoming dates for commercial timber harvests.

Wood from Your State

Federal property isn't the only place to fill up your woodshed. State forests provide another bountiful source. Visitors to the Bald Eagle State Forest in Pennsylvania come not just for the fishing, camping, and hunting but also for the generous supplies of red oak, chestnut oak, and other hardwoods that make for perfect burning. Even without their leaves, oaks are identifiable by their deeply fissured bark.

The 196,000-acre forest, located amid the Appalachian Mountains northwest of Harrisburg, is open to firewood gatherers year-round except for March and April. Permits cost $10 per cord and are good for 30 days. "Most people do it in the fall. It's not as buggy then," says Amy G. Griffith, district forester for Bald Eagle State Forest. Permit holders may cut either fallen or dead standing trees. Before collecting, you need to let the rangers know where you plan to go. For a map and guidelines, write to Bald Eagle State Forest, Box 147, Laurelton, PA 17835.

Firewood policies at state forests vary from forest to forest and from state to state. The Savage River State Forest in western Maryland, for example, is open year-round for firewood collection, but permits, costing $8 per cord, are good only for 2 weeks. To check policies at state forests in your area, call your state forestry services department. Check the government listings in your phone book.

CLOTHING

Think "government property," and what leaps to mind? Trucks? Granite buildings in Washington? Aircraft carriers? Chances are, clothing wasn't one of your first choices. Think again. From surplus Navy pea coats to dungarees lost in the mail and collected by the Postal Service, to boatloads of blouses seized by customs agents, the federal government generates lots and lots of excess threads. In sales held by numerous agencies all over the country, the government regularly encourages members of the public to take the shirt off its back.

Government Sales

Clothing and other goods sold to the public by the federal government come from two general sources. First are surplus items that the government no longer needs. Second are items that have been seized by a government law enforcement agency.

Items are sold by a variety of agencies through a complex network of open auctions, sealed-bid auctions, and fixed-price sales. However you buy your stuff, you can expect to pay a reasonable price. Stories of $1 yachts and $5 minks are pure myth, government sales experts warn. In fact, government auctioneers reserve the right to reject any bid deemed too low.

The U.S. General Services Administration (GSA) has a comprehensive, well-organized guidebook called "The U.S. General Services Administration Guide to Federal Government Sales" that explains just which agencies sell what items and how the sales are handled. To order the booklet by mail, send $2 to R. Woods, Consumer Information Center, P.O. Box 100, Pueblo, CO 81009. You can save time and money by calling up the complete booklet on the GSA's Consumer Information Center Web site at www.pueblo.gsa.gov.

➡◆ WHAT INSIDERS SAY:

Most government goods are sold "as is," and most sales are final. This means that you should inspect items carefully before placing a bid. Policies vary from agency to agency and from sale to sale, but just about all auctions are preceded by public viewing periods, allowing would-be buyers to inspect the merchandise. If you haven't attended a sale or auction before, experts suggest that you observe the proceedings for a while before jumping in. Pay attention to the prices that people are paying for items similar to those you're interested in. When in doubt, don't be afraid to ask a staff salesclerk what price a given type of item has traditionally sold for.

From the Military

The branches of the U.S. military generate thousands of surplus items, including clothing. You can find items ranging from pea coats to tennis shoes and from fatigues to winter hats. Some items are brand new; others are used. After the items have been offered within the U.S. Department of Defense, then to other federal agencies, state and local governments, or charitable organizations, what's left is put out for public sale by the Defense Reutilization and Marketing Service (DRMS).

The service's national sales office in Battle Creek, Michigan, handles sales of high-value items such as aircraft parts or ships. But clothing, household goods, and other smaller goods are sold through more than 100 local marketing offices, usually located at or near military installations. These sales are advertised in local newspapers and radio, but your best bet is to get a catalog. The most frequent sale method is spot-bid auctions, and items are often sold in bulk lots. But some offices hold retail sales in which items are sold individually.

To find the DRMS office nearest you, write Defense Reutilization and Marketing Service, 74 Washington Avenue N, Suite 6, Battle Creek, MI 49017. They'll send you a free sales information kit listing locations of local offices and types of items sold. The kit also includes applications to sign up for free catalogs that list various types of goods. To save time and paper, you can get the same information at the DRMS Web site at www.drms.dla.mil.

Clothing Seized in Illegal Deals

The U.S. Department of the Treasury regularly sells to the public a wide variety of items seized by four agencies: the Bureau of Alcohol, Tobacco, and Firearms; the U.S. Customs Service; the Secret Service; and the IRS. Reasons for seizures range from drug violations to failure to pay taxes or customs duties.

"Our property ranges from Iranian carpets to false teeth to furniture to Ferraris to property. Also a lot of wearing apparel," says Kerry Cooper, public relations coordinator for EG&G Services, a private company that handles all Treasury Department sales under a contract with the government. Clothing often comes from seizures by the Customs Service of large bulk shipments. This could mean cases of identical men's suits or baby outfits, which are usually bought by clothing dealers. But frequently, EG&G will break out items for sale to individual shoppers. "We're never really sure until we have the sale what we're going to have," Cooper says.

General auctions are held every 9 weeks at five locations around the country: Edison, New Jersey; Miami/Ft. Lauderdale; El Paso, Texas; Los Angeles; and Nogales, Arizona. They are also held elsewhere as needed. Each auction usually attracts several hundred people. In Edison, which holds the largest auctions, crowds can number nearly 1,500 people.

Items are available for public inspection prior to each sale. For information and dates of specific auctions, write to EG&G Services at 3702 Pender Drive, Suite 400, Fairfax, VA 22030. Or check out the Web site at www.treas.gov/auctions/customs. Serious buyers may want to subscribe to a flyer service that will keep them updated on items for sale at upcoming auctions. Subscriptions are $25 per year for info on eastern or western U.S sales or $50 for a national subscription. Contact the above address or the Internet site for more information.

The Post Office

Need $800 worth of T-shirts? How about $900 worth of blue jeans?

"We sell only in big lots," says Robert R. Adams, manager of the mail recovery program for the U.S. Postal Service. "Shoes, socks, panty hose, shirts, undergarments, jeans, coats, caps, hats, just about every article you can think of."

The Postal Service collects huge numbers of lost, damaged, and unclaimed items, including clothing, every year. Some of them are simply lost in the mail. Others are items that shoppers returned to the post office box of a company that has gone out of business. After a grace period of at least 90 days, these items are classified as mail recovery and eventually make their way to one of three sale sites around the country: San Francisco, Atlanta, or St. Paul, Minnesota. The items are sold through periodic auctions, sealed bids, and fixed-price sales.

Because of the volume of goods, clothing is usually divided into lots in large, metal containers usu-

ally used for hauling mail in postal trucks. You can't expect to attend a mail recovery auction and pick up a pair of blue jeans. But if you operate a flea market or have some other pressing need for large quantities of clothes at a good price, mail recovery sales may be just the thing.

You can write to any of the three sites to be placed on a mailing list for notices of upcoming auctions. Write to the U.S. Postal Service, Mail Recovery Center, at any of these locations:

✓ P.O. Box 7872, San Francisco, CA 94120-7872

✓ 443 Fillmore Avenue East, St. Paul, MN 55107-9607

✓ P.O. Box 44161, Atlanta, GA 30336-9590

●◆ WHAT INSIDERS SAY:
All merchandise, whether new or used, is sold "as is," so be sure to get a look at the stuff you're thinking of buying. The goods are open for inspection for 1 hour before a sale begins.

FURNITURE

Furniture routinely sold by government agencies across the country runs the gamut from plain but serviceable desks and chairs used by government employees to gaudy antique tables and cabinets confiscated from drug dealers. No matter what your needs, whether you want to furnish your office with bargain items or add to your collection of fine antiques, the chances are good that some government agency has what you're looking for.

The trick, of course, is knowing where to find the stuff. Given the number of agencies and the incredible variety of goods, the choices can seem overwhelming. In addition to the contacts and numbers listed below, consider spending $2 for a handy booklet called the "The U. S. General Services Administration Guide to Federal Government Sales." To order the booklet by mail, send $2 to R. Woods, Consumer Information Center, P.O. Box 100, Pueblo, CO 81009. You can save time and money by calling up the complete booklet on the General Services Administration's Consumer Information Center Web site at www.pueblo.gsa.gov.

Surplus from the GSA

In recent years, large quantities of free-standing desks, bookcases, file cabinets, and similar items have been coming up for sale as more and more federal offices convert to modular furniture and workstations.

The General Services Administration (GSA), which is in charge of buying the things the federal government needs to operate, is also responsible for selling a lion's share of what the government no longer needs. The GSA's Federal Supply Service sells used furniture and many other goods through several regional offices around the country, plus a national sales center located in Springfield, Virginia, near Washington. Sales methods include sealed-bid auctions, live auctions, spot-bid auctions, and fixed-price sales.

◗❖ WHAT INSIDERS SAY:

Auctions attract sizable crowds, including many experienced furniture dealers looking for items to resell in their stores. Don't be intimidated, advises a GSA representative. Instead, use the dealers' expertise to your own advantage. Observe the bids for a while to find the prevailing prices for the types of items that you are interested in. "Mr. John Q. Public would be smart to show up," says the GSA rep. "Go a dollar or two over [the going price], and you can make yourself a good buy at a good price."

Getting the Scoop on GSA Sales

Call or write the sales office in your region (listed opposite) and ask to be put on the free mailing list for upcoming sales. Address your inquiry to "Personal Property Sales." While you're at it, ask for the free brochure, "How You Can Buy Used Federal Personal Property," with lots of good information and contacts.

You can also get information on upcoming sales dates from the GSA Web site on the Internet. Go to http://pub.fss.gsa.gov/property. Or read the U.S.

HOW THEY SELL IT

What's the difference between a sealed bid and a spot bid? Glad you asked. Here are the methods that the General Services Administration uses to sell surplus property.

Sealed bid

Sealed-bid sales are used when items are in widely scattered locations. Once you ask to be placed on a GSA mailing list, you will periodically receive something called an invitation

for bid, which lists items for sale, terms and conditions of the sale, when the items may be inspected, and other information. To bid, you complete a form included in the invitation. Only bids received by the day of the opening are accepted.

Auction

Live auctions are held when there is a large number of items up for sale in one location. Buyers have an opportu-

nity to inspect the items before the auction. GSA auctions are frequently conducted under contract by private auction companies.

Spot bid

Spot bids are written down rather than voiced, and bidders may bid only once per item.

Fixed-price sales

Just as in a store, each item has a set price and is sold on a first-come, first-served basis.

Department of Commerce's *Commerce Business Daily*. This paper, published Monday through Friday, is available at federal depository libraries and on the Web at www.cbdnet.access.gpo.gov. You can subscribe to the print version at a cost of $275 a year by writing to the Superintendent of Documents, U.S. Government Printing Office, P.O. Box 371954, Pittsburgh, PA 15250-7954.

The National Sales Center

Because of the concentration of federal government in Washington, the Federal Supply Service operates a national sales center in suburban Springfield, Virginia, with regularly scheduled sales and auctions of furniture, vehicles, and other items. For information on upcoming sales, write to the Federal Supply Service National Sales Center at 6808 Loisdale Road (3FP-W), Springfield, VA 22150.

Other Regional GSA Offices

✓ For Connecticut, Maine, Massachusetts, New Hampshire, Rhode Island, and Vermont: 10 Causeway Street, Third Floor, Room 347 (2FBP-1), Boston, MA 02222-1076.

✓ For New Jersey, New York, Puerto Rico, and Virgin Islands: Room 20-112, Box 10 (2FBP), 26 Federal Plaza, New York, NY 10278.

✓ For Delaware, Maryland, Pennsylvania, Virginia, and West Virginia: Wanamaker Building (3FPD), 100 Penn Square East, Philadelphia, PA 19107-3396.

✓ For Arkansas, Louisiana, New Mexico, Oklahoma, and Texas: 819 Taylor Street (7FMP), Fort Worth, TX 76102-6105.

✓ For Alabama, Florida, Georgia, Kentucky, Mississippi, North Carolina, South Carolina, and Tennessee: Peachtree Summit Building, 401 West Peachtree Street (4FD), Atlanta, GA 30365-2550.

✓ For Illinois, Indiana, Iowa, Kansas, Michigan, Minnesota, Missouri, Nebraska, Ohio, and

Wisconsin: *Vehicles only:* 230 South Dearborn Street (5FBF), Chicago, IL 60604. *Other items:* 1500 East Bannister Road (6FBP), Room 1102, Kansas City, MO 64131.

✓ For Colorado, Montana, North Dakota, South Dakota, Utah, and Wyoming: P.O. Box 25506, Denver Federal Center, Building 41 (7FP-8), Denver, CO 80225-0506.

✓ For Alaska, Idaho, Oregon, and Washington: 400 15th Street SW (10FZP-S), Auburn, WA 98001-6599.

✓ For Arizona, California, Hawaii, and Nevada: 450 Golden Gate Avenue Fourth Floor West (9FBP), San Francisco, CA 94102-3434.

Seized Furniture

On the flip side of surplus goods are items that federal law enforcement agencies have seized from criminals, customs violators, and so forth. This is where the flashy stuff—Rolex watches, souped-up sports cars, and valuable antique furniture—comes in.

Each year, the U.S. Marshals Service, part of the U.S. Department of Justice, sells about $75 million worth of items that have been seized by its investigative agencies, including the Drug Enforcement Administration, the Immigration and Naturalization Service, and the FBI.

Bargains from the Marshals

The Marshals Service doesn't conduct auctions and sales itself. Instead, it sells some of its property through the GSA and contracts out to professional auctioneers around the country.

One of the largest, the Atlanta-based Manheim Auction handles luxury cars, jewelry, and many other items and collector items around the country on behalf of the director of government services, has auctioned off everything from a warehouse full of antiques that were once owned by a group busted for selling drug paraphernalia to the desk once used by convicted spy Aldrich Ames.

Furniture seized from drug dealers and other criminals runs "the entire gamut from the gaudiest to some very, very nice furniture," Echols says. "Some of them should be arrested for having no taste at all."

To avoid paying too much, bidders at government auctions should have a set price in mind for a given item before the bidding starts, Echols advises. "They should not exceed that."

For information on locations, dates, and items for sale at upcoming Manheim auctions of government goods, write to Manheim Auctions, Inc., 1400 Lake Hearn Drive, Atlanta, GA 30315.

Other auctions of items collected by the Marshals Service are run by private auctioneers and brokers. The Marshals Service does not maintain a mailing list to let buyers know when sales are taking place, but the sales are usually advertised in the classified sections of newspapers where they are to be held.

Also, you can find out about upcoming sales by contacting private sellers directly. A list of all of the private auctioneers and brokers who contract with the Marshals Service, as well as the federal agencies that sell property for it, is available on the Internet

Amazing Stories

TREASURE IN AN OLD BOX

If you haven't been to Salvation Army or Goodwill retail stores in recent years, you may not know what you're missing. Both of the venerable charitable groups have upgraded, with improved merchandise, brighter stores, and better locations. And with retro clothing in full style, the stores are increasingly attracting young, fashion-conscious shoppers. Besides, you never know — you might find a true treasure in one of bargain stores.

Baltc—claimed "thrift shop diva," Melissa and cl— been prowling church basements growing—uses since she was a child "I foun—of good clot—for one pair o—d get a whole bunch Baltchilder, a fo—e price I was paying —ans," says —NonProfit

Times, a magazine based in New Jersey.

Several years ago, at a church basement thrift shop in Canada, Baltchilder paid $1 for a box full of random goods that had failed to sell individually. She wasn't expecting much; indeed, the box seemed to contain nothing but old scraps and worthless bric-a-brac.

After letting a good friend and another woman rummage through the box and extract what they wanted, Baltchilder fished around and found a pair of costume earrings at the bottom. Then she noticed that the fasteners screwed on rather than snapping on, a sign that they might be valuable. She took the earrings to an appraiser, who informed her that the "costume" earrings were in fact authentic pearls set on solid gold posts. Estimated value: $500.

at www.usdoj.gov/marshals (click on "Seized Assets") or at www.pueblo.gsa.gov (use the search function to look for "national sellers list"). You can also get the list by mail, but that means sending a check or money order for 50 cents to the Consumer Information Center, Department 386E, Pueblo, CO 81009.

The Treasury Department

The U.S. Department of the Treasury sells about $46 million in goods and property seized by the Bureau of Alcohol, Tobacco, and Firearms; the U.S. Customs Service; the Secret Service; and the IRS. Reasons for seizures range from drug violations to failure to pay taxes or customs duties. Sales are handled exclusively by a private company called EG&G Services.

Furniture often comes from seizures by the Customs Service of large bulk shipments. These are usually bought by furniture dealers, but EG&G frequently breaks out items for sale to individual shoppers.

When customs seized and then put up for sale a large shipment of wrought iron patio furniture, for example, "we broke out two sets for individual sales," says Kerry Cooper, public relations coordinator for EG&G.

General auctions are held every 9 weeks at five locations around the country: Edison, New Jersey; Miami/Ft. Lauderdale; El Paso, Texas; Los Angeles; and Nogales, Arizona. They are held elsewhere as needed. The auctions usually attract several hundred people. In Edison, which holds the largest auctions, crowds can number well over 1,000.

For information and dates on specific auctions, write to EG&G Services at 3702 Pender Drive, Suite 400, Fairfax, VA 22030, or check out the Web site at www.treas.gov/auctions/customs. EG&G also publishes flyers on upcoming sales. The annual subscription is $25 per year for info on eastern or western U.S sales or $50 for a national subscription. Contact the above address or Web site for more information.

School Furniture

With their constant turnover of students, teachers, and staff, schools and colleges find themselves with loads of surplus furniture, much of which finds its way to the public through sales and auctions.

If you need an inexpensive desk that your child can spill paint on without causing a disaster or a serviceable desk or bookshelf for your own office, these sales can be the answer. The best place to find out about surplus sales in your area is to call your local school district headquarters and ask for the purchasing department.

"Purchasing departments almost always handle surplus disposal," says Terry Schueler, purchasing director for the Thompson School District in Loveland, Colorado.

Twice each year, the Thompson School District teams up with two other districts in this semirural area north of Denver, along with three cities, two counties, and the University of Northern Colorado, for a grand auction featuring everything from vehicles, printers, and fax machines to student desks and chairs, file cabinets, bookshelves, storage cabinets, and tables. Desks can be had for as little as $2 to $10, depending on wear and tear.

College Surplus

Where can you find a used mattress and a roll-top desk? An old stove and a walnut drafting table? These and hundreds of other items make their way each month through the surplus warehouse at Oregon State University in Corvallis.

"We sell 800 items a month, at least 300 of which are furniture—desks, filing cabinets, bookcases, chairs, conference tables, mattresses, and couches," says Bil Burton, user support analyst for the warehouse.

Prices vary according to the amount of wear, but whatever you pay, it's bound to be less than you'd pay in a retail store. Wooden desks, for example, cost anywhere from $35 to $75. Some items sell for unbelievably low prices. The warehouse once unloaded

50 Steelcase desks for a grand total of $50. The reason few people want these sturdy old clunkers? "They weigh as much as a car," Burton says.

Once a month, the warehouse staff unfolds a set of collapsible bleachers and invites the public in for an auction. Two evenings a month, the ware-house opens its doors for a fixed-price sale, with each item tagged.

To find campus sales in your area, Burton suggests calling a local university and asking for the surplus property department. If the school doesn't have one, ask for the property department.

Best Bets

SURPLUS STARS
(AND DUDS) ON CAMPUS

Bil Burton, user support analyst for the surplus goods warehouse at Oregon State University in Corvallis, has seen the good, the bad, and the ugly when it comes to surplus office equipment and furniture. Here are his top five popular resale items, along with five items that no one seems to want. The top five are listed with the average selling price at the warehouse's bi-weekly sales and monthly auctions. The bottom five aren't priced because, well, they'll take just about anything you offer. And don't get Burton going on the subject of orange furniture. You see, that's one of OSU's colors, and . . .

STARS	DUDS
Computers ($75 to $125)	Steelcase desks
Wooden desks ($35 to $75)	Irregularly shaped tables
Tables ($20)	Furniture painted OSU orange
Straight-back wooden chairs ($5)	Old refrigerators from student housing
Printers ($5 for dot matrix to $75 for laser)	Old stoves from student housing

CHAPTER 5

QUICK WAYS to UPGRADE YOUR CASTLE

America may still be the land of rugged individualism and pioneer spirit, but when it comes to establishing and caring for your homestead, you need not be on your own. Whether you're building your own home, buying an existing one, or sprucing up one you already own with energy-efficient solar heat, you can tap into a vast array of government and nonprofit services and expertise. And if your ailing house threatens to make you and your family sick, Uncle (make that Dr.) Sam can provide crucial information and contacts to heal your home.

Why is the government so interested in helping you out on the home front? Think of it as a mutually beneficial relationship in many ways. First, while owning your own home may fulfill your personal dream, home ownership also helps the country by creating a steady, stable workforce and tax base. Because of this, federal and state agencies have devised an array of mortgage insurance and loan programs to aid Americans who are trying to buy their first homes.

Second, while cutting your home energy use lowers your fuel bills, it also helps to chip away at our national dependence on foreign oil, which is good for national security. That's one reason the government subsidizes such measures as installing solar energy equipment in your home.

Third, while getting rid of hazards around your home will help protect your family and your investment, it may also save the government from the expense and risk of saving you after a problem develops.

Okay, the reasons that Uncle Sam and his relatives want to help are clear. Now let's look at the

> In a land where home ownership abounds, few things excite Americans more than the idea of having a beautiful home of their own. Here's how the government can make this dream a reality for you.

FACTOID

IN ADDITION TO HOME LOANS, THE FEDERAL GOVERNMENT PROVIDES FLOOD INSURANCE FOR PROPERTIES THAT ARE SO CLOSE TO WATER THAT THEIR OWNERS MIGHT NOT OTHERWISE BE ABLE TO INSURE THEM. AS OF 1999, THE GOVERNMENT WAS INSURING $485 BILLION WORTH OF PROPERTY.

specifics of how they can improve your home and your life.

BUILDING A HOME

So you've decided to build your dream house, or to make your current house dreamier through a remodeling project. Unless you're creating a lean-to on a desert isle, you can count on intimate government involvement from the time you draw up the plans until the moment you toss down a welcome mat. That's not necessarily a bad thing, either.

The government employees who review your plans and inspect the construction done by you or your contractors are there to ensure that your home will be a safe place to live. They want to know that beams won't crash down on your head in a strong wind, that sparks won't fly when you turn on the lights, and that your new rec room and deck addition won't collapse the first time you invite the neighbors over for a barbecue. View their participation in this way, and you may see them as helpful partners rather than intrusive busybodies.

To get government approval for your project, you'll need to go through three phases of oversight.

1. **Plan approval.** You'll need to draft plans for all aspects of the job and have them certified by your local planning department.

2. **Permit approval.** You'll need to get permits for construction and other parts of the project from your local building department.

3. **Work approval.** Government inspectors will need to review and approve every major step of the construction.

Here's how insiders say you can smooth the process at every stage.

The Planning Phase

Long before you think about pouring a foundation and driving nails, your local planning department will want to see a general plan, called a site plan, showing your proposed house or addition, along with the lot on which it will be built. Planners are mainly concerned with making sure the work will meet local zoning requirements governing the size and height of the house; the grading of the lot; any architectural restrictions, if these apply in your community; and so forth. Among the zoning issues they'll review are setback and unit density requirements.

Setback refers to the minimum distance that must remain between the house and the given property lines. For both aesthetic and fire safety reasons, most localities impose setback requirements to prevent people from building homes right up to their property lines.

Unit density stipulates the maximum percentage of lot space that the house may occupy. Pico Rivera, California, a city of 63,000 residents just north of Los Angeles, has a density limit of 40 percent for single-family homes. That means that if the lot is 10,000 square feet, the house may take up no more than 4,000 square feet of the lot.

Before moving on to the construction phase, you may also have to submit plans to various agencies to make sure that your new house will have access to adequate power, water, and sewers, and will meet any state or local environmental regulations. More on this later.

The planning review is relatively straightforward and shouldn't take long or cost you an arm and a leg.

"We're pretty quick about it," says Marco Cuevas, an assistant planner with the Pico Rivera Department of Community Development, which oversees home building. That city charges $50 for a site plan review, which is usually completed within 1 to 3 days. Still, there are steps you can take to smooth the process.

Do Your Research

"The biggest mistake that people make is drawing up plans before checking the requirements," says Cuevas. That leads to unnecessary anguish as people find that they must alter plans that they've already fallen in love with. Design within the guidelines from the start, and this won't happen.

Very early in the process, visit the local government office that oversees building projects and ask for a complete list of procedures and requirements. Usually, this office is part of the department of building or planning. You can find the number in the government pages of your telephone book.

Ask, Ask, Ask

There's no shame in visiting your town building inspector early and asking a basic question such as, "What do I need to do to make you happy?" says Rick Schwolsky, former senior editor of *Builder* magazine, the official publication of the National Association of Homebuilders, and current editor of *Tools of the Trade* magazine in Washington, D.C. More than likely, he says, the inspector will take that as a sign that you are eager to follow all of the rules.

●◆ WHAT INSIDERS SAY:

Don't get so caught up in satisfying government regulations that you forget to check the deed to your lot (preferably before buying it, of course) for possible restrictions agreed to by the previous owner. Restrictions might affect what you can and can't build.

"Anyone who sells the land can impose any deed restrictions he wants," says Wasfi Youssef, Ph.D., of Mamaroneck, New York, author of Building Your Own Home: A Step-by-Step Guide *and* All You Need to Know Before Buying a Home. *"Even if the zoning laws tell you your house is okay, if you disregard deed restrictions, you may be in trouble," he explains. "The title insurance company will not insure the mortgage."*

The Permit Process

Once you've passed the planning phase, the next step is to acquire permits that will allow you to begin construction. Here's where the nitty gritty really starts. You'll need to apply for several permits, some of which you may need when you file your plans. For example, if you plan to use a well or septic system instead of a municipal water supply and sewer system, special permits may be required, which you need to present with your plans.

"If you are going to get the water from a well, you need to get a certificate to show that the water's been tested," says Dr. Youssef. Rules and regulations for these and other permits vary widely, so ask your local planning office for a detailed list of permit requirements.

Your main requirement, though, is a building permit from the building department, giving you a green light to start construction. The department will review your house plans in close detail. They'll want to make sure, for example, that you plan to install windows that are large enough to provide an escape route during a fire, that your house will be properly ventilated, and that your chimney won't be so tall that it might be unstable.

The plans you submit should be legible and well-organized. Not only will this save time, it will also indicate to inspectors that you are serious and professional. Before applying, visit the building department office. Ask for any brochures or guidelines that they have on how to turn in the best possible set of plans. Establish a rapport. Don't be afraid to ask questions. All of this will help identify you as someone who is eager to comply with the codes.

●◆ WHAT INSIDERS SAY:

Just how deeply you involve yourself in permits depends on how much work you plan to do yourself. If you hire a competent architect and an experienced general contractor, these pros will guide your house through the process as part of their work. If you design the house yourself or work from preset plans and then act as your own general contractor during construction, the responsibility for meeting review requirements shifts to you.

The Inspection Process

Once you've received the permit and construction begins, you can count on a government inspector beating a path to your door during each phase of construction. The number of required inspections varies according to the locality, but an average home may undergo 20 inspections from the time the trenches are dug for the foundation footings until the final check for electrical work and finish, according to Dave D. Hertzing, director of community development for the City of Pico Rivera.

The relationship between you and your building inspector is going to last for the life of your construction project, so you want to make it as comfortable as possible from the outset. Home builders and inspectors alike say that creating a bond of trust and communication is the key. Here are some specific tips.

Don't Cut Corners

"You can't pull any fast ones. It doesn't pay," says Schwolsky. Attempts to circumvent regulations by cutting corners, ignoring codes, or hiding mistakes from an inspector will only result in costly delays, work that must be torn up and redone, and, possibly, stiff fines.

Be Organized

If you're acting as general contractor, understand that this job "takes more organizational skill than building skill," says Schwolsky. Be aware from the

---

What Is It?

"ZONING VARIANCE"

If local zoning laws make it impossible for you to build your house on the lot you own, you may apply for a zoning variance, which, if approved, will allow you to build in spite of the prevailing zoning code. Zoning laws govern such features as the height of the house, whether multifamily housing is permitted, and so forth.

In Pico Rivera, California, a minor zoning variance request costs $350 and involves submitting a standard form to the planning department. Be forewarned, though, that variances are not handed out lightly and typically are granted only if something about your lot or project makes it impossible to meet the established zoning laws.

In other words, don't waste your time and money asking for a variance simply because you want a roomier house than your rectangular lot permits. "If you have a square or rectangular lot, there are basically no variances allowed," says Marco Cuevas, an assistant planner with the Pico Rivera Department of Community Development. If, on the other hand, your lot is shaped like a slice of pepperoni pizza, and the only way to meet the zoning requirements would be to build a triangular house, you may well be eligible for a variance.

●◆ *WHAT INSIDERS SAY:*

If you're not sure whether your plans might qualify for a variance, by all means visit your building department (check the government pages of the phone book for the number and address) before paying the variance application fee. Take your plans along and ask for advice. If your variance request doesn't stand a prayer, at least you'll find out painlessly. "We don't encourage people to submit applications that wouldn't be approved," Cuevas says.

start which inspections are required and in what order. Also, find out whether the inspector will come to your site right away when you call or if there is a wait of several days. Your goal is to have the inspector arrive as soon as possible after a given portion of the work is finished. Otherwise, your project may face lengthy delays and your workforce may drift away. Subcontractors make their livings by staying busy, Schwolsky says, and will quickly move on to other projects if yours is hung up in red tape.

Keep the Construction Site Clean

This is more than just cosmetics, so keep things tidy, and insist that your subcontractors do the same. A clean, well-maintained site is a sign to an inspector that chances are, you're doing a good job on the actual construction, says Hertzing. A sloppy site, with tools, litter, and materials strewn haphazardly about, will raise suspicions of sloppy workmanship.

Get Help

Even if you're doing your own general contracting, your subcontractors may agree, for a modest additional fee, to show up for inspections to answer any questions regarding their work. This is a good idea, especially if you are unfamiliar with the inspection process. "They'll help make sure the process goes smoothly," Schwolsky says.

Treat the Inspectors as Human Beings

"It helps if you stroke their feathers a little," says Carl Heldmann, a longtime building contractor in Grand Rapids, Michigan, and author of *Be Your Own House Contractor*. No, we're not talking about bribery here. But if you treat inspectors rudely or give them reason to suspect that you are cutting corners, you're bound to raise suspicions that can delay your project and drive up the cost.

BUYING A HOME

Owning a home. It's a dream many people harbor. But how can you make it happen if you can't save enough of a down payment to qualify for a mortgage? Ask a wealthy relative to step in and co-sign

that loan. The relative? Why, your Uncle Sam or one of his friends, of course.

Between programs offered by the federal government and those available from individual states, there are several ways that the government can take some of the pain out of buying a house.

Most of these programs are geared toward low- to middle-income citizens who are buying their first homes, but help is available for veterans and others who meet special criteria, regardless of income. What's more, you may be surprised at how broadly the government defines *first home* and *low income*. In other words, those definitions may include you.

Mortgage Help from Uncle Sam

The federal government doesn't want to be in the mortgage loan business, so with the exception of one program for rural residents, it doesn't lend money directly. Instead, the feds will back, or insure, a loan that you receive from an outside lender.

Such backing guarantees that the lender will be paid interest and principal if you default. This gives private lenders the confidence to approve border- line mortgage applications that they might other- wise deny. Here are several loan programs that the federal government offers.

FHA-Backed Loans

The Federal Housing Administration (FHA) was started during the 1930s as a way to increase the number of Americans able to buy their first homes. Since then, the FHA, part of the U.S. Department of Housing and Urban Development (HUD), has insured home loans for about 24 million Americans. In 1996, 10 percent of all homes purchased in the United States were backed by the FHA.

FHA-backed loans offer several advantages over conventional mortgages, particularly for buyers without a lot of working capital. The most obvious is the low down payment—as little as 3 percent of the cost of the house. And, unlike conventional mortgage lenders, the FHA will allow you to use a gift from a family member or nonprofit organiza- tion as your down payment. Another advantage is that recipients may borrow the closing costs as part of their mortgage, something that many private insurers will not allow. Finally, the FHA is likely to be more lenient in granting loan applications for people who have credit problems on their records.

FHA-insured mortgages are open to everyone, regardless of income. Still, the FHA targets low- and middle-income home buyers by capping the amount of the mortgage. The cap varies from city to city and from county to county; it's higher in places where real estate is more costly and lower where homes are cheaper. In 1998, the maximum FHA-backed mortgage for a single-family home in regions with high real estate prices was $170,362, but the limit nationwide averaged $86,317. There's also a higher limit for multifamily homes. (You can use an FHA loan to purchase up to a four-family home, as long as you plan to be one of the occupants.)

Rather than going straight to the FHA, you apply for an FHA-backed loan through a standard lender. If you want information on FHA mortgages, the best place to start is with a lender approved by the FHA or with your real estate agent. Any good agent should be able to tell you which lenders in your area are FHA-approved. If they can't, find another real estate agent.

●◆ WHAT INSIDERS SAY:

The home that you want to buy must pass an FHA inspection before the agency will agree to back your loan. "There must be a lack of peeling paint, and windows need to be in good condition. They're going to look for loose hand rails, broken glass, and frayed wiring," says Kay Stolsonburg, a Middleville, Michigan, a real estate broker whose firm, Miller Real Estate, deals with many buyers using FHA loans.

Even if the FHA inspector finds a problem with the house you want to buy, and neither you nor the seller have the cash to pay for repairs, all is not necessarily lost. Assuming the problem is relatively minor, Stolsonburg suggests bartering with the seller by offering your labor in exchange for materials. Say that peeling interior paint is holding up the deal. You might offer to do the painting yourself if the seller will buy the paint

and brushes. After all, you both have an interest in seeing the deal go through.

Loans for Veterans

If you have served in the military in peace or in war, you or your spouse may be eligible for a U.S. Department of Veterans Affairs (VA) mortgage loan. As with the FHA, the VA does not actually lend money to home buyers but insures the loan in case borrowers default.

The primary advantage of a VA-backed loan is that borrowers may not be required to put any money down. The FHA requires at least 3 percent. Also, unlike the FHA, the VA has no cap on the amount you can borrow. At this time, though, there is a practical limit of $203,000 because that is the maximum that most private lenders will lend on a VA-backed mortgage.

Eligible veterans include those with at least 90 days of active service during a time when the nation was at war or 181 days during a time of peace. In exchange for backing the loan, the VA charges a funding fee equal to 2 percent of the value of the loan. To avoid paying that lump sum up front, you can fold the funding fee into the loan and pay it off with the loan.

As with FHA loans, you apply for a VA-backed loan through an outside lender. A good real estate agent should be able to tell you which lenders in your area are VA-approved and have the most experience dealing with VA loans. Or call your local Veterans Affairs office; the number is with other federal listings in the government pages of your phone book.

●◆ WHAT INSIDERS SAY:

The VA tends to be tougher than the FHA when it comes to assessing credit risks, so you'll want to eliminate any credit problems well before you apply for a loan. How to do it? Start paying off debt 2 to 3 years before you expect to apply for a loan, and make sure you pay all of your credit card bills right on time. "With the FHA, you need pretty clean credit for a year. With VA, it needs to be 2 years, and you'd better have a good reason for anything that happened before that," says Stolsonburg.

Loan Support for Rural Residents

The USDA's Rural Housing Service (formerly called the Farmers Home Administration) provides Guaranteed Rural Housing Loans (formerly FmHA Loans) for people of low or moderate income who live in rural areas. The USDA uses a complex formula for determining just what constitutes a rural area, but any good real estate agent or lender should be able to tell you whether your area is on the USDA list.

Borrowers must have a good credit history and a steady source of income at or below 115 percent of the median income in the area in which they live. If you live in an area where the median income is $40,000, for example, you must earn $46,000 or less to qualify for a Rural Housing Loan. These loans are good options for people with little or no savings. As with VA loans, borrowers may buy a home with no money down, and they must apply for the loan through an approved lender. A good real estate agent should be able to tell you which lenders in the area are approved for these types of loans. Or check the federal government listings in your phone book for "USDA Rural Development."

●◆ WHAT INSIDERS SAY:

A Rural Housing Loan is similar in terms and advantages to a VA loan. If you qualify for both types, you may want to choose the former. The VA charges a fee of 2 percent of the mortgage cost, but a Rural Housing Loan comes with a 1 percent fee. Also, the Rural Housing Service will probably be a little more lenient in reviewing your credit history.

Direct Loans for Rural Homes

In addition to its mortgage-backing program, the Rural Housing Service lends money directly to some home buyers. It's one of the rare instances in which the federal government actually provides mortgage money to individual buyers. These direct single-family housing loans are limited to lower-income people who live in rural

---

What Is It?

WHO QUALIFIES AS A FIRST-TIME BUYER?

The Federal Housing Administration (FHA) restricts its mortgage program to people who are buying their first homes. Most state-run mortgage lenders follow the same guidelines. Does that mean that unless you've rented homes or lived with your parents all your life, you're out of luck? Not exactly. The FHA's definition of "first-time buyer" is sufficiently elastic to include many individuals who have owned or co-owned homes in the past.

According to the FHA, you qualify as a first-time buyer if you:

✓ Haven't owned your principal residence for the past 3 years

✓ Are a displaced homemaker who has only owned a home with a spouse

✓ Are a single parent who has only owned a home with a former spouse

✓ Have owned only homes not affixed to a permanent foundation, such as mobile homes

✓ Own a home that doesn't meet government safety codes and can't be fixed for less than the cost of a new house

areas and are turning to the government as a last resort. "The program is intended for those who cannot obtain financing elsewhere," says Edith Lank, a syndicated real estate columnist in Rochester, New York, and author of *The Home-buyer's Kit.*

Because the government is actually lending the money, direct loans come with more strings attached than do regular government-insured loans. For instance, when you sell the house, the Rural Housing Service will "recapture" a portion of the proceeds as payment for the loan. The amount is based on a formula that factors in how many years you've been in the home, the amount of the subsidy, and the interest you've paid. Although the recapture amount varies from case to case, the charge frequently equals half of the equity you've built in the house. If you've built $20,000 equity in the house by the time you sell, for example, the government may require you to repay $10,000.

●◆ *WHAT INSIDERS SAY:*

The best time of year to apply for a direct Rural Housing Loan is in September and October. The USDA receives only a fixed amount of money each year for the program. Since the federal budget runs from October to October, the program is relatively flush with cash starting around November 1. Although in some years the service spreads its money evenly over the four quarters of the year, in other years the money is spent on a first-come, first-served basis. By early spring, the allotment for an entire year could be gone.

Winning a Loan from Your State

Although the feds, except in rare cases, won't lend you money to buy a house, your state just might. Several states have established housing authorities specifically to lend money to low- and middle-income buyers. The primary advantage of state loans is that they come with lower interest rates than those offered by private lenders.

The Virginia Housing Development Authority, the nation's largest state housing finance agency, "can give borrowers the advantage of an interest rate 0.75 to 1 percent below market," says Michele G. Watson, the authority's assistant director of single-family development in Richmond.

Although founded and monitored by state government, the authority is an independent agency that finances its loans not through taxes but through the sale of tax-exempt bonds. Bond sales allow the authority to tie interest rates to the bonds rather than to prevailing private home mortgage rates.

Another advantage of state loans is that state housing agencies tend to charge less in terms of points and other fees at closing than do private lenders. "What we can charge for fees is restricted," Watson says. "Our fees and points and interest rates are all very closely monitored."

The maximum loan available from the Virginia authority depends on where in the state you live. Limits range from $171,800 ($173,200 if you're building a house) in pricey northern Virginia, which borders Washington D.C., to $113,200 in less costly portions of the state. Income limits range from $79,500 for a family of three in northern Virginia to $54,900 elsewhere. Loans are available to first-time buyers or those who haven't owned a home in at least 3 years.

If you live in Virginia, you may apply for a state loan through a private approved lender or directly through the authority. Your real estate agent should know which lenders in your area are approved.

If you live in another state, call your state housing development authority to find out if it offers home mortgage loans. The number should be in the state government listings in your phone book. Agency names vary from state to state. If you have trouble locating yours, the National Council of State Housing Agencies will send you the name, address, and phone number. Write to them at 444 North Capitol Street NW, Suite 438, Washington, DC 20001.

Want to cut your home-buying expenses to a minimum? Apply for a state loan that also is backed by the FHA, VA, or Rural Housing Service (see above). You get the best of both worlds: a low interest rate and little or no down payment required.

Low-Cost Mortgage Advice

The federal government doesn't just throw loans and loan subsidies your way when you're ready to buy a house. It also offers money-saving advice and tips on handling the many issues involved in purchasing a home.

All of this good information comes from the Consumer Information Center in Pueblo, Colorado, the federal government's clearinghouse for hundreds of informational booklets, pamphlets, and brochures. The center has dozens of publications on buying and maintaining a home. Most cost less than $2, and many are free.

If you have access to the Internet, by far the easiest and cheapest way to get the publications is by visiting the center's Web site at www. pueblo.gsa.gov. Once you're at the site, click on "Housing." The documents are available in full, and you can read all of them for free. If you prefer hard copies or don't have access to the Internet, you can get a free catalog listing the publications by writing to the Consumer Information Center, Pueblo, CO 81009. Here is a sample of the publications that are available (any costs listed apply only if you order hard copies).

What Is It?

LOAN TERMS

If you think points are for basketball games, a title is what they call you at work, and the principal is someone your grade school teacher sent you to see when you misbehaved, you may need to brush up on your home loan terminology.

Like any specialty, the mortgage business has its own language, which can be confusing to outsiders. The U.S. Department of Housing and Urban Development has produced a handy booklet called the "Home Buyer's Vocabulary" to help dispel that confusion. Here are some sample definitions.

Appraisal: An estimate, done by an expert, of the dollar value of a real estate property as of a given date.

Closing costs: A blanket term for the various expenses that buyers and sellers routinely must pay in order to complete a real estate sale, including attorney's fees, inspections, title insurance, and others.

Points: A point is equal to 1 percent of the value of the mortgage loan. With a $100,000 mortgage, for example, a point is $1,000. Lenders frequently charge points during closing. These can be paid by the buyer or the seller, or split between them.

Principal: The total amount of your mortgage that you have left to repay, not counting interest and mortgage insurance premiums.

Title: The right of ownership to a particular property.

You can find the complete A-to-Z booklet on the Internet at www.pueblo.gsa.gov. Once you get to the Web site, click on "Housing."

✓ "How to Buy a Home with a Low Down Payment" is a free, nine-page brochure that covers all the basics. It includes advice on figuring out how much you can afford as a down payment, overcoming obstacles to home ownership, and qualifying for a loan with a low down payment. It also provides a guide to various government loan programs. It was prepared by the Mortgage Insurance Companies of America in cooperation with the USDA Extension Service.

✓ "The HUD Home-Buying Guide" is a free, 11-page brochure that details the ins and outs of buying a home from HUD, the agency that oversees FHA loans. HUD resells homes that the FHA takes over when borrowers default on loans. The brochure details the best ways to find HUD homes for sale in your area, how to choose a mortgage lender and find the best type of financing, how to bid on a HUD home, and many other tips.

✓ Check out "Twelve Ways to Lower Your Homeowners Insurance Costs." Did you know that quitting smoking won't just improve your health—it could bring down your homeowners insurance costs, too? Smoking accounts for 23,000 residential fires each year, and insurance companies take that into account when deciding how much you should pay for insurance. That's just one tip in this four-page brochure that sells for 50 cents. The brochure includes information on shopping around for insurance policies, lowering costs by raising your deductible, and beefing up home security.

✓ "Buying Your Home: Settlement Costs and Helpful Information" is a comprehensive guide to paying for a house. This 35-page booklet, priced at $1.75, covers such areas as the role of the real estate broker, selecting an attorney, shopping for a loan, securing title services, settlement costs, and your right to file complaints.

An Education in Home Buying

Many state housing development agencies provide plenty of pamphlets and brochures on buying a home and getting a mortgage; some go a lot further than that. Virginia, for example, offers comprehensive classroom training in the art of home buying.

The Virginia Housing Development Authority runs a two-part, 6-hour class taught by real estate agents, loan officers, credit counselors, home inspectors, and attorneys. As the range of teachers indicates, this course is designed to familiarize home buyers with every aspect of the home-buying process. It's taught periodically in 14 locations around the state.

The class is free and open to all, regardless of income. Even those who are buying their second or third home, using solely private lenders and insurers, can benefit from the class, says Watson. "It's a public service," she says. "We get the satisfaction of knowing that we have an informed home buyer."

If you live in Virginia and would like to take the class, write to the Virginia Housing Development Authority at 601 South Belvidere Street, Richmond, VA 23220.

If you live in another state, call your state housing development authority to find out whether it offers a similar program. Check the state government listings in your phone book. Agency names vary from state to state. If you have trouble locating your state agency, write to the National Council of State Housing Agencies at 444 North Capitol Street NW, Suite 438, Washington, DC 20001, for the name, address, and phone number.

●◆ *WHAT INSIDERS SAY:*

Everyone who completes the Virginia course (or a similar one offered by another state) receives a certificate. If you present your certificate when applying for an FHA-backed loan, you will receive a 0.25 percent discount off the fee that the FHA charges to back your mortgage loan.

UPGRADING YOUR HOME

The government wants to get inside your house and look around. Hey, relax, we're not talking about searches and seizures here. We're talking about government agencies providing tips and tax breaks for making your home more efficient and safer. Who could argue with that?

If you want to tap into the government's vast array of resources, you'll have to know where to look and whom to ask. Rest assured, though, whether it's remodeling to draw power from the sun or taking control of a radon problem, there's plenty of help available.

Loans for Solar Conversions

During the oil crisis of the 1970s, it was easy to get government tax breaks and advice on installing solar water heaters and other devices that would reduce your reliance on foreign oil. Want to know a secret? Many of those programs are still in effect; they're just less publicized these days.

"There are a lot of good programs that people aren't aware of," says Susan LeFever, communication director for the American Solar Energy Society in Boulder, Colorado. Here are some opportunities.

Federal Energy Programs

If you are buying or renovating a home with a loan insured by a federal backer such as the FHA or the VA, you may be eligible for financial breaks when you make the home more energy-efficient. The FHA, for example, offers the Energy-Efficient Mortgage Program, which allows borrowers to exceed the FHA-established loan limits for their area if the money will go toward energy-efficiency improvements such as solar energy. The renovations can cost up to $8,000 or 5 percent of the value of the property, whichever is greater.

That's just one of the programs listed in "The Borrower's Guide to Financing Solar Energy Systems," a booklet compiled by the U.S. Department

of Energy's National Renewable Energy Laboratory (NREL), in Golden, Colorado.

With such programs, "you save money on your mortgage, and you save money on your utility bills as well," says Patrina Eiffert, Ph.D., NREL's solar project leader and author of the booklet. Plus, the Energy Department estimates that every $1 reduction in annual heating bills adds $11 to $25 to the value of your home. To request a free copy of the booklet, write to the National Technical Information Service, 5285 Post Royal Road, Springfield, VA 22161.

●◆ WHAT INSIDERS SAY:

If you think that you may be eligible for one of the solar programs listed in the booklet, Dr. Eiffert suggests taking it with you when you visit your lender to apply for your home loan. Many lenders are unaware of solar provisions, so "you have to go in armed with the book," she says.

State Energy Programs

In addition to the federal programs, some 35 states offer incentives ranging from income tax credits to sales tax exemptions for people who buy and install solar energy equipment in their homes.

Residents of Arizona, for example, receive a state income tax credit worth 25 percent of the price of buying and installing solar equipment in their homes. The maximum credit is $1,000. For more information on Arizona's policies, write to the Arizona Solar Energy Industries Association, 2034 North 13th Street, Phoenix, AZ 85006.

●◆ WHAT INSIDERS SAY:

Want quick advice on your state's incentive programs? The North Carolina Solar Center at North Carolina State University in Raleigh monitors and updates a list of programs offered by individual states. The information is available on the Internet at www.ncsc.ncsu.edu/dsire.htm.

Curing a Sick House

Your home is your joy, your haven, your sanctuary from a hectic world. But even the coziest of abodes may be susceptible to hidden problems, such as radon contamination and bad air quality, that could harm you and your family if left unchecked. Fortunately, state and federal agencies are on call to help you solve problems. Why not take advantage? After all, you're paying for these services through your taxes whether you use them or not.

Air Quality

Since they began studying indoor air pollution during the 1960s, scientists have identified innumerable causes, including poor ventilation, inefficient heaters, asbestos, new carpets, and household cleaning products, to name just a few. The effects, depending on the type of pollutant and the length of exposure, can range from irritated eyes and coldlike symptoms to respiratory conditions, heart disease, and cancer.

Fortunately, specialists at the Environmental Protection Agency (EPA) and state health departments are loaded with free information and advice to help keep your home happy and healthy. If you have concerns about the quality of air in your home or simply want more information, a great place to start is "The Inside Story: A Guide to Indoor Air Quality." This comprehensive booklet has detailed sections on the causes of indoor air pollution, its health effects, and practical steps that you can take to eradicate the problem. Sections on asbestos, lead paint, biological contaminants, and other pollutants include a load of contacts for further information, as well as tips on hiring the most qualified inspectors and contractors to get rid of the problem.

You can read the guide for free on the Internet at www.epa.gov/iaq/homes.html. If you prefer a hard copy or don't have Internet access, write to the EPA's Indoor Air Quality Information Clearinghouse, P.O. Box 37133, Washington, DC 20013-7133. They'll send you a single copy for free.

➡◆ WHAT INSIDERS SAY:

If the booklet doesn't answer your questions, you can write to the clearinghouse at the above address with a specific question or problem. They'll provide written information, answer questions if they can, and offer referrals to government and nonprofit agencies specializing in your problem.

Hotline Advice

One level below the feds, each state operates a telephone hotline, usually maintained by the state health department, to answer indoor air-quality questions. In most states, the indoor

What Is It?

HWÄT ĬZ ĬT?

"RADON"

Radon is an odorless, colorless gas that is produced naturally when uranium in soil and rocks breaks down. It can seep into your house through cracks in the foundation, floor and wall joints, mortar joints, or the water supply. Once inside, radon can concentrate to potentially harmful levels.

An estimated 6 million Americàn homes have significant levels of radon. Radon leads to some 14,000 lung cancer deaths per year, second only to those caused by smoking. It exists throughout the United States, and no state or region is immune.

The good news is that once discovered, radon problems are fairly easy to eradicate. Radon-trained contractors can seal cracks and install an exhaust system to suck radon-tainted air from beneath your home's foundation.

air-quality specialist is the same person who runs the state radon hotline. Check the state government section of your telephone book for the listing "Radon Hotline." If you can't find it there, look under "Health Department" and contact that agency for help. Or you can find the contacts for each state, with addresses and phone numbers, on the Internet at www.epa.gov/iaq/contacts.html.

Radon Advice

Each state government has a radon hotline, usually operated by the health department. The experts who man these hotlines can answer questions about radon and radon testing, and they will send you written information.

"I get calls from the general public, schools, and businesses," says Kara Bishop, manager of the Idaho Indoor Environment Program in Boise. "Anybody who's interested in radon can contact me."

In addition to lots of written information, Bishop can provide residents with average radon levels, listed by zip code and county throughout the state. This can give people an idea of whether their neighborhoods have had problems. Since radon can't be seen or smelled, you need a mechanical testing kit rather than an inspector to tell if your level is too high. Commercial kits are widely available and inexpensive, ranging from $12 for a short-term do-it-yourself kit that provides results in about 2 days to $25 for more precise and in-depth readings over the course of 3 months to 1 year.

If tests indicate a radon problem, Bishop and her counterparts in other states can provide a list of local contractors that have been certified by the National Environmental Health Association as being specially trained in dealing with radon problems. To find the number of your local radon hotline, look for "Radon Hotline" in the state government listings in your phone book, or contact your state health department, which also will be listed in this section of the phone book. You can find a state-by-state list of radon hotlines on the Internet at www.epa.gov/iaq/contacts.html.

RESTORING A HOUSE

Others see a heap of weathered old boards; you see a proud old house. Others see an eyesore; you see an architectural treasure in need of a little TLC.

If this describes your feelings for old homes, you're not alone. Preservationists say that more and more Americans are tapping into our architectural past by purchasing and rehabilitating historic homes. Indeed, Barbara Wishy, director of the revolving fund for Historic Preservation Foundation of North Carolina, Inc., in Raleigh, says that she knows of people who are able to live anywhere because of telecommuting but who choose locations based on where they find the best old houses. "They will go anywhere they find the house of their dreams," she says.

Whatever the draw, if you have the itch to restore an old home, the federal and state governments and nonprofit foundations may be willing to give it a scratch. Whether your goal is to garner prestige by being listed on the National Register of Historic Places or to secure financial aid through tax credits and low-interest loans, there is a variety of ways that these groups can help.

The National Register of Historic Places

Think of it as the nation's A-list of old buildings. Since 1966, when Congress passed the National Historic Preservation Act, some 70,000 historic districts, sites, and individual buildings and homes around the country have been honored by inclusion on the National Register. Meet the criteria, and your house could join this exclusive club, which is administered by the U.S. Department of Interior's National Park Service.

Among the individual homes on the register, some were sites of major historical events, while others gained admission because a major historical figure lived there. But it isn't necessary that your house have had such a brush with greatness to qualify. In fact, most homes are on the list simply because their architecture, materials, and/or

THE FIVE WORST FIRE-SAFETY MISTAKES

After doing hundreds of inspections of homes in Sugar Land, Texas, outside Houston, Lieutenant Troy Holby and his inspectors on the Sugar Land Fire Department have seen all sorts of fire-safety mistakes. Here, Lt. Holby, who is public education specialist for the department, offers five of the worst and most frequent mistakes, along with solutions.

1. Smoke alarms
that are old or don't work

Replace them. It's not enough to simply keep changing batteries. After 10 years, the failure rate for smoke alarms increases greatly. Not only that, but smoke alarm technology, like everything else, has improved. You want the latest technology protecting your home and family. Make each Tuesday your test day, and test your alarms without fail. Change batteries regularly. As a reminder, change them every time you set your clocks forward or back for Daylight Saving Time.

2. No prearranged
family fire escape plan

Devise one, and involve everybody. Focus first on the bedrooms. Each bedroom should have two escape routes. If the door is blocked by smoke or fire, a window is the second choice. Be sure that windows can be opened easily from the inside. Don't install burglar bars over windows unless it's absolutely necessary. If you must have bars, make sure that they can be opened from the inside without a key.

Decide on a family meeting place outside where you will be able to tell immediately if everyone has gotten out. Don't assume that you will be able to get to your children's rooms. Begin talking about fire safety when they are about 3 1/2 years old. By age 6 or 7, they should be able to evacuate the house with no help.

3. Extension cords
used as permanent wiring

Homeowners, especially in older homes with few electrical outlets, all too frequently run extension cords under carpets in order to reach some distant appliance. This keeps the cords from "breathing," and in time, they can overheat. Also, constant traffic over the carpet can fray the cord's coating, posing an additional fire hazard. The solution is to have an electrician install more electrical outlets. The one-time expense is more than worth the added safety.

4. Multiple plugs
used in a single outlet

You've seen 'em. Maybe you even use 'em. These handy gadgets allow you to plug two, four, or even eight appliances into a single outlet. Firefighters hate them. "The outlets are designed to carry a certain amount of energy," Lt. Holby says. "When you overload them, you can cause the wiring to heat up." The remedy is the same as for number three.

5. House numbers
that are difficult
to see from the street

Numbers should be at least 4 inches high, reflective for better nighttime visibility, and posted prominently on the house. Numbers posted on the curb are fine but are not sufficient on their own. If a car is parked in front of them, a fire truck may waste precious seconds looking for your house.

craftsmanship represent an important architectural period.

A listing on the National Register offers no guaranteed protections, but it can help save your house from the wrecker's ball should it stand in the way of a proposed highway or other government construction project.

"It's the best you can get in the United States in terms of protecting property from state and federal projects," says Mark Wagner, National Register manager for the Virginia Department of Historic Resources in Richmond. "You have more perceived clout."

Beyond that, the advantages are largely symbolic. Inclusion on the list makes your house part of an exclusive fraternity of designated treasures. You get to buy an official plaque (price: $70 to $500, depending on the style you choose) that proclaims the importance of your site. The house could be included on historic tours of your city or town. "You stand out in the community," Wagner says.

Making the List

Actually finding your way onto the National Register is no easy task. The application process is complex, and the standards are tough and exacting. The actual application can run for more than 20 pages and require footnoted historical documentation, supporting photographs, and a bibliography. "It is a fairly formidable document," says Wagner.

Also, before convincing the feds, you will have to persuade your state's historic preservation office that your property is an authentic gem. The vast majority of sites that are approved by the feds are referred to them by states.

Some states help ease the process. Virginia, for example, which is home to some 1,800 National Register sites, sends all would-be applicants in that state a free starter kit with informational pamphlets and a preliminary form to fill out. This form is much less onerous than the actual National Register application, and it helps weed out unlikely applicants. Your state's historic preservation office can tell you whether the state offers similar help.

Once you've convinced state staffers of the value of your property, they can be your best friends and strongest advocates. They will answer questions as you fill out the federal application, advise you on writing it, and present your case to the federal government. Plus, some states, including Virginia, maintain their own registers of historic places. If the state's historic preservation department thinks that your property is worth presenting to the National Register, you'll almost certainly be included on the state register as well.

If you think that your home may be significant enough to be on the National Register, contact your state's historic preservation office. These offices are affiliated with different departments in different states, but most often with the state department of environmental protection, so you can start by calling this agency. The number is in the state government pages of your phone book. If the agency can't help you directly, it should be able to refer you to the right number. You also can write to the National Conference of State Historic Preservation Officers, Hall of the States, 444 North Capitol Street NW, Suite 332, Washington, DC 20001 for the number and address of your state office. Or, if you have access to the Internet, you can visit the Heritage Preservation Web site at http://grants.cr.nps.gov/shpos/shpo_search.cfm.

! FACTOID

BEFORE 1976, THE FEDERAL TAX CODE ACTUALLY REWARDED PEOPLE FOR DEMOLISHING RATHER THAN PROTECTING HISTORIC PROPERTIES. SINCE THE TAX CODE WAS CHANGED, MORE THAN 27,000 HISTORIC BUILDINGS HAVE BEEN SAVED.

Tips on Reviving Your Home

Unless you have special training and skills, restoring a historic home is not a go-it-alone proposition. You will want to work closely with both an architect and a contractor who specialize in historic properties. But that doesn't mean that you shouldn't learn as much as you can on your own. The National Trust For Historic Preservation, a private, nonprofit organization that works closely with federal, state, and local government preservation agencies, has many low-priced booklets on every aspect of the preservation process.

For beginners, the best bet is the "Starter Kit." It includes information on researching the history of a house and hiring competent pros to do the work, guides on architectural and landscaping styles, and other tips and info. Among dozens of other titles are "Appraising Historic Properties," "Buyer's Guide to Older and Historic Houses," and "Coping with Contamination: A Primer for Preservationists." The booklets cost $6 each.

If you have a specific question on a restoration project, you may write to the trust's resource center. Staff members will answer your question directly, for free, or will refer you to an expert in your area. To contact the resource center, to order a booklet, or to request a catalog listing the publications, write to the National Trust for Historic Preservation Resource Center, 1785 Massachusetts Avenue NW, Washington, DC 20036-2117.

Federal Financial Assistance

Looking for a way to trim the cost of renovating your older home? Check with the federal government. You may qualify for a tax credit if your building is considered historically significant and you put the property to commercial, industrial, agricultural, or residential rental use. That can mean something as simple as turning it into a bed-and-breakfast or rental housing.

THE 10 COMMANDMENTS OF REHABILITATING HISTORIC PROPERTIES

As a rule, properties must be at least 50 years old and represent some important piece of social or architectural history to be listed on the National Register of Historic Places. Nevertheless, the integrity of the building is just as important as its age. Your house may be a 200-year-old colonial, but if you stripped the original exterior and slapped up vinyl siding, you're probably out of luck.

The U.S. Department of the Interior, which administers the National Register through its National Park Service, has established 10 standards for rehabilitating historic properties. These standards are not only crucial guidelines for the National Register, they have come to be seen by preservationists as a sort of 10 commandments for rehabilitating historic properties in general. The Secretary of the Interior's standards for rehabilitation say that you should:

1. Use a property for its historic purpose, or else in a way that changes little about the building and its environment.

2. Preserve the historic character and features of a building.

Depending on the historical value of your home, you may be eligible for a 10 to 20 percent rehabilitation tax credit. The credit comes from the Federal Historic Preservation Tax Incentives Program, which is jointly run by the National Park Service and the IRS and administered in partnership with the historic preservation officer in each state. If you qualify for a credit, you can deduct part of the cost of the restoration from your federal income taxes. For example, if you're eligible for a 20 percent credit and you spend $10,000 on renovations, the government will let you deduct $2,000 from your taxes.

To be accepted for the program, you must apply to the state historic preservation officer and meet certain criteria, including:

✓ Spending at least $5,000 on renovations

✓ Agreeing to keep the building for at least 5 years after you get the tax credit

✓ Agreeing to refrain from making unapproved alterations during that time

●◆ *WHAT INSIDERS SAY:*

In order for you to get the 20 percent tax credit, the National Park Service must approve your project to be sure it suits the historical character of your property. Don't start any renovations until get your application approved, because you could threaten your chance for approval.

For a quick read on construction do's and don'ts, get copies of the "The Secretary of the Interior's Standards for Rehabilitation" and "Guidelines for Rehabilitating Historic Buildings." The standards booklet is available from Federal Historic Preservation Tax Incentives, Heritage Preservation Services, National Park Service, 1849 C Street NW, Washington, DC 20240 or at the Heritage Preservation Web site, www2.cr.nps.gov. The guidelines are available on the Internet as well. Go to the above site and click on "Historic Buildings" to get to the guidelines link. You can also order the book through the U.S. Govern-

3. Never add features that create a false sense of history.

4. Retain changes that have occurred over time and have become part of the building.

5. Preserve distinctive features, finishes, and construction techniques that characterize the property.

6. Repair rather than replace deteriorated historic features. If they must be replaced, new features should match the old in design, color, texture, and, whenever possible, materials.

7. Avoid chemical or physical treatments, such as sandblasting, that can damage materials. Cleaning should be done as gently as possible.

8. Protect significant archeological resources around the building.

9. Make sure that new additions and exterior alterations don't destroy historic materials that characterize the property. They must be distinct from the historical sections and compatible in terms of size and features.

10. Make sure that new additions can be removed without harming the original building.

ment Printing Office by writing to Superintendent of Documents, P.O. Box 371954, Pittsburgh, PA 15250-7954.

Other Financial Incentives

Even if the federal government turns you down for a grant, you may be able to receive renovation help from state and local governments and hundreds of local nonprofit organizations that offer a wide variety of tax breaks and low-interest loans. In searching for assistance, the best place to start is with your state preservation office. Staffers there will be able to tell you about state tax incentives, and they are also excellent sources of general information about private nonprofit groups and the restoration community.

To find your state preservation office, look in the government pages of your phone book, write to the National Conference of State Historic Preservation Officers, Hall of States, 444 North Capitol Street NW, Suite 332, Washington, DC 20001, or check the Heritage Preservation Web site at http://grants.cr.nps.gov/shpos/shpo_search.cfm.

State Tax Breaks

Unlike federal incentives, tax credits offered by many states are available for private homes as well as homes used for businesses. In Virginia, owners of historically significant homes may deduct 25 percent of the cost of rehabilitation from their state income tax in the year in which the improvement is made.

To receive the tax credit, properties must be eligible for the Virginia Landmarks Register, which closely parallels the National Register of Historic Places. "Generally, a property eligible for listing is at least 50 years of age and has some significance," says Susan E. Smead, architectural historian for the Virginia Department of Historic Resources in Richmond. "It can be either nationally important or more local."

If your application is approved, you receive a certificate that you include with your state tax return. You claim the credit for the year in which the project is completed.

For an application or more information on the Virginia program, write to the Virginia Department of Historic Resources, 2801 Kensington Avenue, Richmond, VA 23221. If you live elsewhere, contact your state's department of historic preservation. Check the government pages of your phone book for a number, or write to the National Conference of State Historic Preservation Officers, Hall of States, 444 North Capitol Street NW, Suite 332, Washington, DC 20001. A list is also available at the Heritage Preservation Web site at www2.cr.nps.gov/shpo.

➥ WHAT INSIDERS SAY:

Don't wait until you've started or finished the project to apply for the tax credit. Virginia and other states closely follow the Department of Interior's guidelines for restoring historic properties and will demand that you follow them. "It can be problematic if someone undertakes the work before submitting the applications, because they may do work that is not in keeping with the standards," Smead says. If you have already finished the work, expect to be asked for detailed records, including photographs of the work at various stages.

Low-Interest Loans

Dozens of private, nonprofit preservation organizations around the country are dedicated to preserving and restoring historic buildings and houses. Many of these groups work closely with state historic resource departments to identify and save important sites. Many of them also offer financial incentives, such as low-interest loans, to individuals or businesses that want to restore a historic property.

The Utah Heritage Foundation, based in Salt Lake City, offers intermediate-term loans from a revolving fund, with interest rates at half the current prime rate. The prime rate, a benchmark in the loan industry, is the interest rate that banks offer to their most favored customers.

Loans from the foundation average $45,000

and may be used for a wide variety of restoration projects, according to Dina W. Blaes, the foundation's assistant director. The owner's debt can be no greater than 95 percent of the value of the building.

The historical standards for such loans tend to be far less stringent than those for getting on the National Register. The Utah Heritage Foundation demands that properties be at least 50 years old, but they don't have to be one-of-a-kind. "Very few of the buildings that we make loans for are really significant architecturally or historically," Blaes says.

Like state and federal agencies, though, private foundations are adamant that the integrity of the building be maintained. The time to contact the

Amazing Stories

YOU *CAN* GO HOME AGAIN

Thanks to a low-interest loan from the non-profit Utah Heritage Foundation, Lynda L. Henderson was able to save her ancestral home (and a piece of history) from the wrecker's ball.

Long the home of her great-grandparents, Andrew and Jenssine Thompson, the house in Spring City, Utah, was occupied by members of the Thompson family for more than 100 years. Andrew Thompson had arrived in the 1870s after leaving his wife and children behind in his native Denmark to cross ocean, prairies, and mountains to start a new life among followers of the Mormon Church.

He expanded a small adobe home begun by his parents, who had immigrated before him to this town 75 miles south of Salt Lake City. Then he sent for his wife and children. He and Jenssine raised 10 children in the house, but when the couple's last surviving child died in the 1970s, the house fell into neglect. By the mid-1990s, it was slated for demolition by Sanpete County.

Lynda Henderson had kept her eye on the place through the years, however. Although she lived about 150 miles north in Ogden, she returned to Spring City frequently to honor family members who were buried there.

In 1996, she bought the old house for $15,000 from a young couple who had purchased it and then found the prospect of renovating it too awesome. Henderson, too, was almost bowled over. The place needed a new roof, a new north wall, and new flooring in three of the five main rooms. And that was just for starters.

She almost gave in to the temptation to tear the place down. Then a friend suggested that she contact the Utah Heritage Foundation, a nonprofit preservation group that offers low-interest loans to borrowers who want to restore historic homes. The $49,000 loan that she received through the foundation paid for a new wall, roof, and flooring as well as many other renovations. "It would have been impossible to get a regular bank loan on a home like that," Henderson says.

Today, she says simply, "The house is beautiful. People can't believe what it looks like." She stays there once a month, and on Memorial Day, it's the site of extended family gatherings. "It's a miracle house," she says. "It's like a dream come true."

foundation is before you've even signed on with a contractor. The foundation will want to know specifically what materials and procedures are going to be used.

"We require that applicants submit bids from contractors," Blaes says. "That enables us to track the project. We don't want anything done that's going to damage the property."

If you live in Utah, contact the Utah Heritage Foundation at P.O. Box 28, Salt Lake City, UT 84110. Elsewhere, contact your state historic preservation office and ask about private foundations in your area that offer loans.

➥ WHAT INSIDERS SAY:

Even if you don't want or don't qualify for a loan, private foundations can be wonderful sources of information and advice on historic home restoration. Most can tell you about contractors who specialize in historic restoration projects and can offer loads of additional advice to help you avoid mistakes.

CHAPTER 6

LOW-COST CURES for WHAT AILS YOU

There are only two certain things in life, said Ben Franklin: death and taxes. But if Ben were alive today, he might add a third item to that list: rising health care costs.

In the last decade alone, the annual cost of health care has jumped 100 percent, with the average family of four now spending roughly $14,000 a year in direct and hidden expenses, says Charles Inlander, president of the People's Medical Society, America's largest nonprofit consumer health advocacy organization, in Allentown, Pennsylvania. This includes out-of-pocket payments to doctors and hospitals, insurance premiums, medical equipment purchases, the amount of federal and state tax money that is devoted to health care, and the costs of health care benefits that are built into the goods and services you buy, he says.

Clearly, even if you're well-insured, every backache, toothache, muscle strain, and cold can be a major pain in the wallet—if you let it. But there are ways to hold down health care bills with the help of the government, universities, and nonprofit groups.

If you're tired of dipping into your wallet to pay the difference every time the deductible on your dental insurance rises, you can turn to a university dental school. The care there may be available for a fraction of what you're paying now. If you need emotional counseling or medical care that your HMO won't cover, you can get help from several nonprofit groups. And the government can offer guidance and maybe even financial sup-

> Health care costs may be on the rise, but don't let that faze you. The government, nonprofit groups, and universities can help you pare your bills and keep more money in your wallet.

FACTOID

THERE ARE MORE PLASTIC SURGEONS PER CAPITA IN WASHINGTON, D.C., THAN ANYWHERE ELSE IN THE UNITED STATES.

port to help you care for an aging parent or spouse. You can even get free advice that will help keep you healthy in the first place, thus saving you money on doctors' visits and hospital stays.

Interested? Read on.

DENTAL CARE

People who look at portraits of George Washington are often struck by his tight-lipped, sober expression, and even in his day, he was known as a man of few but powerful words. You can write all of this off to aloof brilliance or the weight of the role he played as our government's first commander-in-chief. The answer, though, according to some historians, could be much simpler: His false teeth may have fit so badly that he was reluctant to open his mouth.

Thankfully, dental care has improved 1,000 percent since the days when the best cure for bad teeth was to have a hand-carved block of hickory pressed onto your gums. But so have costs. Today, the price of crowning a cracked tooth can top $750, and regular cleanings and checkups can run from $50 to $100. What can you do? Take advantage of these helping hands that the government and others provide.

Dental School Discounts

You bite into an ice cube, and—ouch!—you crack a tooth. Don't worry. The cure may be no farther away than a nearby dental school. At more than 50 dental schools around the nation, dental students, working under faculty supervision, offer care at a fraction of a dentist's customary fees.

The students provide all the services a licensed dentist does, but the cost "may be considerably less than what a dentist in private practice charges," says Lawrence Warner, associate dean for clinical affairs at the School of Dentistry at the University of Southern California in Los Angeles. To find a school near you, contact the American Dental Association Commission on Dental Accreditation, 211 East Chicago Avenue, Chicago, IL 60611.

Braces for Less

If you or your child needs braces, but you have no desire to pay the thousands of dollars it might cost to make the necessary repairs, look into treatment at a dental school: You'll save from one-third to one-half the cost of work offered by orthodontists in private practice, says Peter Sinclair, D.D.S., professor and chairman of the department of orthodontics of the School of Dentistry at the University of Southern California in Los Angeles.

Dentists studying for their orthodontic specialty certification perform the work under the supervision of professors who are certified orthodontists. And patients are chosen without regard to income. That said, your case does need to meet certain criteria, says Dr. Sinclair. To find out about orthodontic services, call a dental school near you, ask for the orthodontic clinic, and inquire about becoming a patient. The American Dental Association's Commission on Dental Accreditation, 211 East Chicago Avenue, Chicago, IL 60611, can point you to a school.

●◆ *WHAT INSIDERS SAY:*
The key to being chosen for low-cost orthodontic work is having a moderately difficult problem that an orthodontic student can fix, says Dr. Sinclair. If your teeth need very little work, the dental school is unlikely to choose you because the work won't be challenging enough for the student. But the opposite is also true: If the problem is too complex, the orthodontic students may not yet be qualified to fix it.

Lend Your Mouth to Research

Want to get the most modern dental care possible and save some money to boot? Look for a dental school that does research. Often, these schools receive hefty government research grants for projects requiring patient volunteers. If you're one of the lucky ones to be chosen, you can receive treatment at a reduced cost, or even for free. For example, you can get permanent tooth implants to replace false teeth. You can have an impacted molar removed using new techniques. You can receive treatment for facial pain, taste disorders, and herpes simplex. And not only is treatment sometimes free, it may also include the drugs, ice packs, and any supplies that you'll need to recover.

The National Institutes of Health (NIH) in Bethesda, Maryland, also conducts research. Being selected for one of their studies is easy—if you fit the profile for the sort of person that the researchers need to conduct their study, says Sally

Power to the People

DEALING WITH OVERPRICED DRUGS

If you are really struggling to cover the cost of much-needed prescriptions, you may be eligible to get them for free directly from the companies that manufacture them. Be forewarned, though, that this service is usually reserved for the poor and the elderly on fixed incomes.

Your doctor can tell you if you qualify. Or, if you have access to the Internet, you can visit the Pharmaceutical Research and Manufacturers of America (PhRMA) Web site at www.phrma.org and look for its "Directory of Prescription Drug Patient Assistance Programs." This will provide you with a list of the manufacturers that participate. To find it, click on "Publications" in the Web site's directory, then click on the name of the publication. You can also write to PhRMA at 1100 15th Street NW, Suite 900, Washington, DC 20005.

For those who don't qualify for government-subsidized assistance, Neil Shulman, M.D., associate professor of medicine at Emory University School of Medicine in Atlanta and author of *Better Health Care for Less* offers the following tips for finding the best price deals on drugs.

1. Ask your doctor if there is an equally effective drug that costs less.

2. Buy generic instead of name-brand drugs.

3. Take advantage of money-back offers or other guarantees and promotional deals from drug companies. "Don't hesitate to call the company's customer service number or the local manufacturers representative—whose number your doctor or pharmacist will know—to ask a drug company what incentives they can give you," says Dr. Shulman.

4. Take drugstores up on their promises to "match any price," especially if driving to a far-away store for a better price is inconvenient or not possible for you. Call around to find the best price on the drug you need, then go to the nearest pharmacy that offers to match the price. "You'll save money and a trip across town," Dr. Shulman says.

5. If you're older than 60, ask for a senior discount, which is usually good for 20 or 30 percent off the list price.

6. Make sure that your doctor fills out a prescription for any supplies, over-the-counter drugs, equipment, or home modifications that you need to care for an aging adult at home. Then you can deduct the costs from your income tax.

Wilberding, a specialist with the National Institute of Dental and Craniofacial Research, which conducts research on oral disease.

One project there, for instance, studied the effect of dental implants on patients with diabetes, so "if you were a diabetic in need of a dental implant, you'd be chosen to come for a screening. If you wanted to participate, you could. It's that easy," says Wilberding. The studies are safe for volunteers, she adds, and she can think of no time when a volunteer has had to endure unexpected side effects or problems. To ensure the safety of patient volunteers, "the researchers go through all kinds of studies before clinical treatments begin," she says.

To find out whether you're a candidate for research at the NIH, write to the Patient Recruitment and Public Liaison Office, Warren Grant Magnuson Clinical Center, National Institutes of Health, 10 Cloister Court, Building 61, Bethesda, MD 20892-4754. The clinical center also has a Web site at www.cc.nih.gov. Just click on "Current Clinical Research Studies" for a list of the types of studies that are under way.

●◆ WHAT INSIDERS SAY:
Being chosen for a study usually boils down to whether or not the patient fits the study's parameters. It's up to the physician who's doing the study to decide if the patient's problem and medical history will fit.

Dental Q&A

Have a question or concern about a particular oral disease? Contact the National Institute of Dental and Craniofacial Research, whose staff will send you free information. To query them about an ailment, write to the National Institute of Dental and Craniofacial Research, Public Information and Liaison Branch, 45 Center Drive, Bethesda, MD 20892-2290.

Tips on Caring for Your Teeth

One of the best ways to lower costs is to prevent dental disease from occurring in the first place. The National Institute of Dental and Craniofacial

Research provides free single copies of publications on how to keep your teeth and gums healthy, including "Seal Out Dental Decay," which explains how plastic coverings on children's molars can prevent tooth decay; "A Healthy Mouth for Your Baby," aimed at teaching parents how to care for their young children's incoming teeth; and "Snack Smart," a nutrition guide for kids. Write to the National Institute of Dental and Craniofacial Research, 45 Center Drive, Bethesda, MD 20892-2290. Or, if you have access to the Internet, check out their Web site at www.nidcr.nih.gov and click on "News and Health Information," then "Health Care and Patient Information."

Low-Cost Programs for Some Seniors

Often, dentists donate their time to make sure that the elderly are taken care of, says Matthew Lesko, founder of Information USA, Inc., a consulting service in Rockville, Maryland, that helps businesses draw on the resources available from the government and nonprofit groups. Many of the programs, adds Lesko, who is also the author of books on the goods and services the government offers, are reserved for those with low incomes or are open to people who can prove that financial hardship prevents them from affording the needed care. Some other programs are state-funded and open to seniors on fixed incomes or limited budgets.

Since each state has its own program, the eligibility requirements vary. Some states, like California and Maine, have Senior-Dent programs that offer free and reduced-cost dental care to those older than 60 who earn less than $20,000 annually.

For information on government offerings and eligibility requirements in your state, contact your state's dental association. The number may be in the government pages in your phone book, or you can try calling your county office of health and human services (listed in the government pages) for assistance.

Dental Care for the Disabled

Some state and local governments sponsor low-cost treatment for people with mental or physical disabilities or for children born with cleft palates. In Colorado, for instance, the government-sponsored Handicapped Children and Cleft Palate Program provides services to children, with charges based on the family's ability to pay. A family of four with an income of $21,347 would pay nothing for services, says Sandra Jacquez, a provider coordinator for the Health Care Program for Children in Denver, and those with larger incomes may apply for discounts. Eligibility is based on an evaluation of each family's financial situation.

Colorado also runs Dental Care for the Handicapped, a program that provides free or low-cost dental care for mentally or physically disabled people who are on a limited income due to their handicaps.

Since programs for the disabled are usually run by state or local governments, you'll have to contact your state's dental association to find out what's available near you. The number may be in the government pages in your phone book, or you can try calling your county office of health and human services (listed in the government pages) for assistance.

●◆ *WHAT INSIDERS SAY:*

Even if you have a middle-class income, you may qualify for a program that offers lower-cost dental work for the disabled, but you'll need to prove that paying full price for the care represents a financial hardship. Most discounts and free treatment programs are reserved for the truly needy.

Teeth on Sale!

You can get big savings on false teeth through your state's denture program, which is usually available to anyone who needs dentures, regardless of age. Kentucky, for instance, has the Denture Access Program, which provides dentures at reduced rates depending on your ability to pay.

Although there are no firm income limits for those who wish to receive services, the aim is to help those who can prove that financial hardship prevents them from affording dentures, says Melissa Nathanson, director of communications with the Kentucky Dental Association in Louisville, the group that administers the Denture Access Program. Dentists who volunteer to participate in the program evaluate the finances of the families they agree to serve, then charge them accordingly, explains Nathanson.

To see what's available in your state, contact your state's dental association. The number may be in the government pages in your phone book, or you can try calling your county office of health and human services (listed in the government pages) for assistance.

EMOTIONAL CARE

It might be due to a problem in your relationship with your spouse or child. It might be the result of losing a loved one or even a job. Whatever the cause, there are likely to be difficult emotional periods in your life when you could profit from counseling.

Unfortunately, many insurance policies either exclude mental health counseling and marital mediation or expect patients to bear a large portion of the bills. There are ways to keep the costs down, though. Dozens of nonprofit agencies provide free information on mental health and marital problems. And for no fee or a reduced fee, they can help you find and choose a counselor or mediator. In addition, many nonprofit support groups offer free brochures that might give you the help you need to weather a minor problem.

●◆ *WHAT INSIDERS SAY:*

Even if your insurance provider does cover mental health services, it may refuse to pay if you fail to follow the insurance company's rules to the letter. Be sure to check with your provider before visiting a counselor.

Marital Advice

Perhaps the best source of information on marital and emotional counseling is the nonprofit American Association for Marriage and Family Therapy. The organization offers free publications and advice on a wide range of topics, from divorce, family mediation, and custody arrangements to broader issues, such as finding a qualified marriage and family therapist.

To request free copies of any of its publications, write to the American Association for Marriage and Family Therapy, 1133 15th Street NW, Suite 300, Washington, DC 20005. Also, if you have access to the Internet, you can get information from the association's Web site at www.aamft.org.

Help for Children with Disabilities

Free publications are available through the National Institute of Mental Health on a variety of topics, including how to diagnose and help children with learning disabilities, attention deficit hyperactivity disorder, autism, depression, and schizophrenia. Write to the National Institute of Mental Health, Public Inquiries, National Institutes of Health, 6001 Executive Boulevard, Room 8184, MSC-9663, Bethesda, MD 20892-9663. Or go to the group's Web site at www.nimh.nih.gov and click on "For the Public."

Relieving Anxiety

For free and low-cost information on identifying anxiety disorders and finding treatment, contact the Anxiety Disorders Association of America. This nonprofit group serves as a clearinghouse, providing advice on phobias, panic attacks, and obsessive-compulsive disorders, among other conditions. Write 11900 Park-

YOUR RIGHTS AS A PATIENT

Although a host of federal legislators and consumer health care advocates have passed laws to guarantee a patient's rights to medical care, at this point, there aren't any uniform rules in effect.

However, the American Hospital Association has produced its own patient's bill of rights, outlining the level of care that it expects from the nation's hospital and medical personnel in federally supported managed care settings. Compliance is voluntary, but the bill of rights provides broad outlines of what you can expect from health care professionals.

The following is an abridged version of the bill. For a copy of the full document, write the American Hospital Association, 1 North Franklin, Chicago, IL 60606.

1. You have the right to considerate and respectful care.

2. You have the right to be well-informed about your illness, possible treatments, and likely outcomes and to discuss this information with your doctor.

3. You have the right to know the names and roles of people treating you.

4. You have the right to consent to or to refuse a treatment, as permitted by law, throughout your hospital stay. If you refuse a recommended treatment, you will receive other needed and available care.

5. You have the right to have an advance directive, such as a living will or health care proxy. These documents express your choices about your future care or name someone to decide if you cannot speak for yourself. If you have a written advance directive,

lawn Drive, Suite 100, Rockville, MD 20852, or look for this information on the Internet at www.adaa.org.

Beating Eating Disorders

For free advice on treating eating disorders, for physician referrals, or for information on joining support groups in your area, contact the nonprofit National Association of Anorexia Nervosa and Associated Disorders. The association helps people organize self-help groups, provides speakers for self-help and community groups, and distributes free publications. Also, it will serve as your advocate if you're having trouble getting your insurance company to cover treatment for these conditions. Write to the association at P.O. Box 7, Highland

Park, IL 60035. You can also find this information on their Web site at www.anad.org.

Finding Low-Cost Clinics

Medical schools that operate in conjunction with government-funded community health centers often provide low-cost outpatient mental health services. Doctors usually base their fees on your ability to pay. To find a clinic, check with the public affairs departments of nearby medical schools or look in the government pages under listings such as "Community Health Center," "Public Health," or "Health."

●◆ *WHAT INSIDERS SAY:*

Want to save up to 80 percent on emotional counseling? Take a class at a local college or university that

---

you should provide a copy to the hospital, your family, and your doctor.

6. You have the right to privacy. The hospital, your doctor, and others caring for you will protect your privacy as much as possible.

7. You have the right to expect that treatment records are confidential unless you have given permission to release information or reporting is required or permitted by law. When the hospital releases records to others, such as insurers, it emphasizes that the records are confidential.

8. You have the right to review your medical records and to have the information explained, except when restricted by law.

9. You have the right to expect that the hospital will give you necessary health services to the best of its ability. Treatment, referral, or transfer may be recommended. If transfer is recommended or requested, you will be informed of risks, benefits, and alternatives. You will not be transferred until the other institution agrees to accept you.

10. You have the right to consent or decline to take

part in research affecting your care. If you choose not to take part, you will receive the most effective care the hospital otherwise provides.

11. You have the right to be told of realistic care alternatives when hospital care is no longer appropriate.

12. You have the right to know about hospital resources, such as patient representatives or ethics committees, that can help you resolve problems and questions about your hospital stay and care.

offers free counseling services to students, says Dr. Shulman. If you are a student, even part-time, you often become eligible for services. If the coursework costs a couple of hundred dollars, your savings is still significant: You use the counseling service once a week for 15 weeks. To get the same service in the private sector could cost upward of $1,000.

MEDICAL CARE

When it comes to medical care, as you'd expect, the main role of government and nonprofit groups is as a safety net. They provide regular care for those with low incomes who are unable to pay on their own.

This doesn't mean, however, that you'll be shut out of government help if you live above the poverty line. Government-funded low-cost and free programs exist for people—rich or poor—who need help paying for health care. Also, you can get free care if you're willing to be part of a research project. And, of course, as one of the biggest disseminators of information, the government offers lots of free advice to help you deal with your own small problems.

●◆ WHAT INSIDERS SAY:

Too many people mistakenly believe that health insurance is an unnecessary expense, forgetting that one hospital stay could clean out their bank accounts and leave them with second mortgages. Even if you can barely afford it, take out a health insurance policy.

One of the least expensive forms of health insurance is a high-deductible catastrophic policy, which usually covers major medical expenses and serious, long-term illnesses. But, say experts, these plans are usually best

---

Best Bets

TOP BOOKS ON HEALTH CARE

There are a number of valuable books that can help you identify ways to reduce your health care costs. Below are 10 of the best. Since many of these books are hard to find or expensive, your best bet is to locate them in the reference section of your local library. Otherwise, try a bookstore that has a comprehensive medical and health care section.

✓ *Health Care Choices for Today's Consumer* by Marc S. Miller

✓ *Better Health Care for Less* by Letitia Sweitzer and Neil B. Shulman

✓ *150 Ways to Be a Savvy Medical Consumer* by Charles Inlander

✓ *Free Health Care!* by Matthew Lesko

✓ *Free or Low-Cost Health Information* by Carol Smallwood

✓ *Does Your Doctor Charge Too Much?* by James B. Davis

✓ *Free Money for Health Care* by Laurie Blum

✓ *Free Money for Children's Medical and Dental Care* by Laurie Blum

✓ *Free Money for Diseases of Aging* by Laurie Blum

✓ *Free Money for Treating Infertility* by Laurie Blum

for relatively healthy families with low to average med-ical expenses. J. Robert Hunter, director of insurance at the Consumer Federation of America in Washington, D.C., advises, "Don't opt for this coverage if you have a family member who is chronically ill or if you can't meet your deductible in an emergency."

Getting Help Paying the Bills

One good way to reduce your out-of-pocket med-ical costs is by dipping into Uncle Sam's pocket. The government allows you to deduct money from your paycheck on a pretax basis to pay for most medical or dental expenses that aren't reim-bursed by your insurance company. Your em-ployer has to participate in this program for you to take advantage of it, but if it does, you pay a certain amount from each paycheck—say, $100—into a medical spending account. Then, every time you receive a bill that's not covered by in-surance, you submit it to the account for reim-bursement.

Not only will this force you to save money to defray medical expenses, it lowers your taxable in-come and can therefore help you save on taxes. (Just how much you'll save depends on myriad fac-tors, such as your income and deductions.) Ask your company's human resources representative if this is an option available to employees. If not, you may want to encourage your company to begin of-fering it.

●◆ *WHAT INSIDERS SAY:*

If you want to start a medical spending account, think carefully about how much you put into it. The government's rules say that you must forfeit any money that is left in the account at the end of the year. You may want to be conservative in estimating the first year.

Free and Low-Cost Advice

While there is no substitute for a doctor's care, why should you spend hundreds of dollars for informa-tion on health care when you can get the best, up-to-date information on a wide range of topics at no cost? The government and nonprofit organizations provide free or low-cost publications on everything from baby care to cancer. Here are some of the best of the offerings.

Baby Basics

The National Maternal and Child Health Clearing-house, a government-supported, nonprofit agency, provides a number of free publications for mothers-to-be, including "Nutrition during Pregnancy and Lactation: An Implementation Guide" and "Health Diary: Myself—My Baby." It also offers a quarterly magazine called *Parents Expecting.* Write to Na-tional Maternal and Child Health Clearinghouse, 2070 Chain Bridge Road, Suite 450, Vienna, VA 22182. Some of the publications are available to download from the Internet at www.nmchc.org. Click on "Full-Text Publications."

Pregnancy Questions

If your doctor says that you have developed a com-plication of pregnancy called gestational diabetes, the National Institute of Child Health and Human Development, a division of the National Institutes of Health, can help you cope with it. The agency publishes a booklet about this short-term condition called "Understanding Gestational Diabetes: A Practical Guide to a Healthy Pregnancy." To get a copy, write to the National Institute of Child Health and Human Development Clearinghouse, P.O. Box 3006, Rockville, MD 20847. It's also available online at www.nichd.nih.gov. Click on "Publications/Clearinghouse."

Dealing with Your Diet

Do you need help getting your cholesterol and blood pressure under control? The National Heart, Lung, and Blood Institute, which is part of the National In-stitutes of Health, offers a number of free and low-cost publications, including "Check Your Weight and Heart Disease IQ," "Facts about Blood Choles-terol," "Healthy Heart Handbook for Women," "How to Prevent High Blood Pressure," and "Step-by-Step: Eating to Lower Your High Blood Cholesterol." For more information, write to the National Heart, Lung, and Blood Institute Information Center, P.O. Box 30105, Bethesda, MD 20824-0105. Or, go to their Web site at www.nhlbi.nih.gov and click on "Health Information," then "List of Publications."

Aid for Alzheimer's Caregivers

The Alzheimer's Disease Education and Referral Center, a service of the National Institute on Aging, offers free information to help you detect and cope with Alzheimer's disease, along with a series of free publications on a wide variety of medical, ethical, and societal issues relating to Alzheimer's disease. One of the key fact sheets is "Alzheimer's Disease: Unraveling the Mystery." For more information, write the Alzheimer's Disease Education and Referral Center, P.O. Box 8250, Silver Spring, MD 20907-8250. Or visit their Web site at www.alzheimers.org and click on "Alzheimer's Disease Publications."

Free Care for Rich or Poor

Another way to help defray expensive medical costs—especially for chronic illnesses—is to volunteer to participate in medical experiments or studies. Large research universities around the country conduct privately funded and government-sponsored studies and experiments, and they frequently advertise for volunteers. Not only do you receive free treatment, but the project's organizers may pay for your meals and sometimes your lodging. Some healthy people (sometimes called professional guinea pigs) make a decent living by volunteering to participate in studies.

To find a study being conducted in your area, scan newspaper advertisements or contact the public affairs offices or clinical research departments of nearby medical schools or medical research universities.

●❯ WHAT INSIDERS SAY:

Research topics can be as common as testing new treatments for allergies or as exotic as finding volunteers who are willing to overeat by 1,000 calories a day for 8 weeks to determine why some people get fatter than

others. Remember, though, that the studies are usually experimental, so there may be some very real risks. Before you volunteer, ask the researchers about the pros and cons and consult another health care professional if the answers you get aren't satisfactory.

Care for an Aging Parent

While the government-sponsored Medicare program pays for a large chunk of health care costs for people 65 and older, it won't pay for long-term or home care unless the person meets strict low-income requirements. Many seniors have to draw on health insurance, then dip into savings and assets or seek their children's help to defray expenses not covered by Medicare.

If your family needs assistance in paying for long-term care, look to the following special government and nonprofit programs for help.

Planning Long-Term Treatment

Your county or state department of social services can help you develop a plan of care for a parent who needs long-term treatment, then help you find people to carry it out. (The advice is often free or very low cost.) The same agency will help you monitor how successful the program is in meeting your parent's needs, and also help you review the costs and your ability to pay them. Look under the county or state heading in the phone book, then look for a specific listing for the social services department or office on aging.

From Meals to Wheels to Beds

Volunteers of America, a nonprofit group, can help you find low-cost nursing facilities and therapeutic and medical services, home-delivered meals, home health care, and homemaker and home repair services. They also can advise you on low-cost options for transportation to medical appointments and grocery shopping, affordable senior housing, volunteer in-home caregivers, and adult day care. To find out what's available in your area, contact your local affiliate of Volunteers of America, listed in the white pages of your phone book. Or write to the national office at Volunteers of America National Services, 110 South Union Street, Alexandria, VA 22314.

Advice on Services for the Elderly

The Eldercare Locator is a national toll-free directory that is a public service of the U.S. Administration on Aging. It can help you find local community services for seniors, including home-delivered meals, adult day care, transportation assistance, and home care. Look in the government pages of your phone directory for the local Area Agency on Aging, or write the National Association of Area Agencies on Aging, 927 15th Street NW, 6th Floor, Washington, DC 20005. The phone number is also usually available from the local office of the United Way.

●◆ *WHAT INSIDERS SAY:*

Still concerned about how you or your parents will cover the cost of long-term care? "How to Pay for Nursing Facility Care," published by the American Health Care Association, provides tips on finding the highest-quality, least expensive care available. To get a copy of the free booklet, write to the American Health Care Association, 1201 L Street NW, Washington, DC 20005, or go to their Web site at www.ahca.org and click on "Consumer Information."

Amazing Stories

THE PROFESSIONAL GUINEA PIG

Bob Helms is a professional guinea pig. He makes good money at it, too. He is one of thousands of people in the country who lend their bodies and minds to scientific studies— and are paid for their time.

Helms estimates that he earns anywhere from $10,000 to $15,000 a year as a healthy subject who participates in drug and treatment research projects. He uses the money he earns as a guinea pig to supplement his income from his other jobs, including movie consultant, house painter, counselor for the mentally disabled, and construction worker.

He also publishes a newsletter of sorts in Philadelphia called "Guinea Pig Zero: A Journal for Human Research Subjects," aimed at people who volunteer as medical or pharmaceutical research subjects. Basically, says Helms, 41, a former union organizer, "I do it for the money." The pay can be as high as $300 a day for those willing to lend themselves to testing experimental drugs, he says.

Helms's best-paying gig, he says, earned him $2,500 for a 2-week drug study. So far, he reports having no serious side effects during his 3-year career as a guinea pig, just a fainting spell or two and some "grouchy" episodes as reactions to the drugs. But that doesn't mean it's a perfectly safe way to make a living, he warns. A few people whom he's come into contact with have been seriously injured, he says. And some studies pay so poorly, "it's like parceling your life out for pennies."

With "Guinea Pig Zero," Helms says that he hopes to lay bare the good and the bad of volunteering for drug and medical studies and to help people feel "proud of the occupation of being a guinea pig," he says. The little profit he makes from his publication "gets plowed back into research."

Stay Home and Save

One of the more common ways that Americans are reducing the costs of caring for the elderly is by keeping them at home: Nearly 23 million U.S. households are caring for an elderly relative or friend, according to a 1997 national caregivers survey conducted by the National Alliance for Caregiving and the American Association of Retired Persons.

Experts warn, however, that going this route can take both an emotional and a physical toll on the caregiver. Recognizing this, government and several nonprofit agencies offer help finding and maintaining low-cost home health care and day care for your elderly loved one. To find the best fit for your family, consider the following.

Discover Day Care

Adult day care operates along the same lines as day care for children: You find a home or a center that provides care, meals, and stimulation for your elderly loved one during the day. To find low-cost, high-quality programs in your area, ask for recommendations from your Area Agency on Aging, usually listed in the government pages of the phone book under city, county, or state listings. Or write to the National Association of Area Agencies on Aging, 927 15th Street NW, 6th Floor, Washington, DC 20005. In addition, the phone number is usually available from the local office of the United Way.

Let Them Come to You

If you or your loved one feels uncomfortable about leaving home for care, you can hire an in-home day caregiver. The National Association for Home Care, a nonprofit association representing home care providers, can refer you to people in your community who can come to your home and provide a wide variety of services, from personal grooming to administering medication.

The association's extensive directory of home care providers lists thousands of organizations and hospices nationwide. You can find the directory at libraries and hospitals. For a free copy of the organization's consumer guide "How to Choose a Home Care Provider," write the National Association for Home Care, 228 Seventh Street SE, Washington, DC 20003. Or go to www.nahc.org and click on "Consumers."

To locate other home care providers in your area, look in the phone book under United Way; Area Agency on Aging; the county or state department of health, family services, or social services; Visiting Nurse Association; Catholic Charities; or Jewish Family Services. These organizations offer various free or low-cost home care services and can provide you with information on how to secure them.

Therapy at Home

Local nonprofit Visiting Nurse Associations provide quality home care to anyone who needs it, regardless of ability to pay. Services include nursing; home health aide services; personal care; physical, speech, and occupational therapy; nutritional counseling; adult day care; wellness clinics; hospice care; and home-delivered meals. For information on what's available in your area, write the Visiting Nurse Associations of America, 11 Beacon Street, Suite 910, Boston, MA 02108. Or you can check their Web site at www.vnaa.org.

Help for the Disabled

If you have a loved one who is disabled or handicapped and needs help becoming more independent, there are hundreds of sources of free help and money from federal, state, local, private, and nonprofit organizations, says author and consultant Matthew Lesko of Information USA, Inc.

The government may provide low-interest loans to help physically disabled people buy medical equipment or modify their homes and give financial or other assistance to disabled people who can prove that home modifications will allow them to return to work and prevent future hospitalizations. Here are some examples of the programs available.

Dollars for Handicapped Vets

If you or a loved one is a veteran who was disabled while on duty, the U.S. Department of Veterans Affairs provides grants to help you modify homes and automobiles to accommodate wheelchairs. Grants can cover up to 100 percent of the cost of the improvement, and they're available to anyone who's eligible, regardless of income.

Two programs administered by regional Veterans Affairs offices provide for disabled veterans: the Housing Grant for Catastrophically Disabled Veterans and the Auto Adaptive Grant. For information, call the Department of Veterans Affairs national number, listed in the government pages of the phone book.

Another program, the Home Improvement and Structural Alteration Grant, is administered through your local Veterans Affairs medical center. Look for its number in the government pages.

Money for Retraining

In many states, the Office of Vocational Rehabilitation will help you secure free money for education and training if your disability gets in the way of keeping or finding a full-time job. The office will also help you find a job. If you already have a job, and you need special equipment or transportation in order to keep it, officials will provide you with the goods and services that you'll need to continue working. For information, call the Office of Vocational Rehabilitation in your state. The number is listed in the government pages of the phone book.

Advice and Information

The federal Department of Education Clearinghouse on Disability Information offers several free publications, including "The Pocket Guide to Federal Help for Individuals with Disabilities," a general reference guidebook. Also, the clearinghouse can answer specific questions and provide information about free and low-cost services for the disabled that are available through national, state, and local government programs. Write to the Clearinghouse on Disability Information, Office of Special Education and Rehabilitative Services, Communication and Media Support Services, U.S. Department of Education, 330 C Street SW, Room 3132, Washington, DC 20202.

Help with Medical Bills

If you have a family of four and an annual income of $16,700 or less, you qualify for free or greatly reduced medical care through the government sponsored Hill-Burton Free Medical Care Program. Hill-Burton funds are available to anyone—foreign-born or U.S. native—who has resided in the United States for a minimum of 3 months.

If you think you might qualify for free or low-cost health services through the Hill-Burton program, you must first find a certified, government-designated Hill-Burton medical facility in your region. If you have access to the Internet, the easiest way to locate a facility is to connect with the government's Health Resources and Services Administration Office of Special Programs. It has a Web page at www.hrsa.gov/osp/dfcr. Once you connect to the site, click on "Obtaining Free Care." Or you can write for a booklet that lists the clinics nearest to you. Contact the Office of Communications, Health Resources and Services Administration, 5600 Fishers Lane, Room 14-45, Rockville, MD 20857. You can also find income eligibility requirements at the Web site.

Free Money for Costly Care

Do you live in Oregon? Are you a woman looking for financial assistance for health care for yourself or your children? Do you work for the U.S. Customs Service? If you can answer yes to any of these questions, you may be eligible for up to $10,000 in free financial assistance to help defray medical expenses. Most of these grants have no specific income eligibility limits, although in some cases the awarding foundation will assess each candidate's financial circumstances to determine the amount of the grant. Hundreds of private foundations and nonprofit corporate agencies offer grants to help reduce or pay medical bills, although they usually carry restrictions of some sort, such as a requirement to live in a particular state or region or work for a specific company. To find out what grants are available to you, check first with the human resources department of the company where you work, then go to the library and ask a reference librarian to find one of the many directories of private foundations operating in the United States. The directories often list the nature of the awards available, the eligibility requirements, and contact addresses and phone numbers. Here are some examples of the types of grants available.

Assistance for Artists

The nonprofit Adolph and Esther Gottlieb Foundation, Inc., provides grants of up to $10,000 to help visual artists who have suffered catastrophic illnesses and need help defraying medical expenses. The average grant is $4,000, and eligibility is limited to sculptors, painters, and print makers who have 10 years of experience. For more information, write the foundation at 380 West Broadway, New York, NY 10012.

Relief for Oregon Residents

The nonprofit Elizabeth Church Clarke Testamentary Trust Fund Foundation offers awards of up to $10,000 to Oregon residents in need of money for medical care. Average grants vary from a few hundred to a few thousand dollars. For more information, write the trust fund in care of the Scottish Rite Temple, 709 Southwest 15th Avenue, Portland, OR 97205.

Free Care for Customs Workers

The Roger L. Von Amelunxen Foundation, Inc., provides funding for medical expenses not reimbursed by health insurance for families of U.S. Customs Service employees who demonstrate need. The foundation puts no limit on the amount of funds that you can receive, but it determines the amount depending on each individual's financial circumstances. For more information, write the foundation at 83-21 Edgerton Boulevard, Jamaica, NY 11432.

GETTING POT FOR MEDICAL PURPOSES

Marijuana is a relatively cheap drug that contains the active ingredient THC, which offers some sick people serious pain relief. Even as a handful of states and municipalities have passed laws protecting citizens' rights to use marijuana for medical purposes, the federal government continues to consider it a crime for doctors to prescribe marijuana and for pharmacies to possess and dispense marijuana for use of any kind. It also remains a federal offense to smoke pot.

Federal prohibition "severely limits states in their ability to protect patients from criminal prosecution or provide medical marijuana to those who need it," says Paul Armentano, with the Washington, D.C.–based National Organization for the Reform of Marijuana Laws. In addition, federal officials have threatened to sanction physicians who recommend or prescribe marijuana in compliance with local law, he said.

So where does that leave you, the consumer? Buy at your own risk. In states like California, where laws have been passed making it legal to use marijuana for medicinal purposes, private clubs allow patients to purchase the drug for legitimate medical needs. That means that you'll need a doctor's signed recommendation, a detailed health questionnaire, and follow-up visits to your doctor. To find out where the clubs are located and to receive a description of your state's medical marijuana laws, write to the National Organization for the Reform of Marijuana Laws, 1001 Connecticut Avenue NW, Suite 710, Washington, DC 20036.

CHAPTER 7

KEEPING PROBLEMS off YOUR BLOCK

When Matt Peskin and his neighbors learned that residential burglaries were a big problem in their Philadelphia suburb of 60,000 residents, they decided to do something about it. They founded the Lower Merion Community Watch, a mobile patrol, and after being trained by the police, they launched daytime and nighttime patrols, using two-way radios to call in anything that looked suspicious to them.

It was quick, easy, and amazingly effective. Residential burglaries in the area dropped from a high of 900 annually to around 180, Peskin says, largely because of the community watch program. He is now executive director of the National Association of Town Watch, an umbrella organization of crime-watch groups.

What made the neighbors so successful?

Simple—they educated themselves and they got involved. And those things, say police and other crime experts, are the keys to curbing any type of neighborhood problem, whether it's burglaries, vandalism, phone fraud, trash dumping, or speeding cars.

Knowing this, police and other crime-prevention groups have established dozens of programs to help people like you control neighborhood crime. You can get advice on discouraging burglars. You can learn how to make your community less attractive to speeding cars and other nuisance crimes. You even can get tips on handling door-to-door sales scams. In fact, no matter what type of problem you face on your block, the government and nonprofit groups can offer help—usually free for the asking.

> What's the best protection against crime? It's not more police or a burglarproof home that can withstand an attack of the Huns; it's *you*—provided that you practice the skills of safe, secure living.

FACTOID

THE AVERAGE HOME BURGLARY OCCURS DURING THE DAY, WHEN HOMEOWNERS ARE MOST LIKELY TO BE AT WORK OR SCHOOL. THE BURGLAR ENTERS THROUGH THE LEAST CONSPICUOUS DOOR, STAYS JUST 4 MINUTES, AND TAKES LESS THAN $1,000 WORTH OF MERCHANDISE.

HOME SECURITY

You may live in a great neighborhood where you figure that the chances of being burglarized are just about nil, but the fact is that about every 13 seconds, a burglar breaks into a home in the United States. With a bit of preparation, you can reduce the odds of it being your home that's hit. Even taking simple, inexpensive steps such as trimming back your hedges can dramatically reduce the chance that a burglar will try to visit, says Jeff Fryrear, director of the National Crime Prevention Institute in Louisville, Kentucky.

The goal with steps like this, say crime-prevention experts, is not to burglarproof your home—that's not possible. Instead, you want to do what police call target hardening, says Robert E. Lassahn, crime-prevention specialist with the Maryland Community Crime Prevention Institute in Woodstock. This means making it tougher for burglars to break in and easier for a neighbor to see them if they do.

Before you can harden the target, though, you need to take a critical look at how well-prepared you are now. Here's how your government can help you do that.

Free Home-Safety Survey

Maybe you've installed a few light timers and deadbolts, and you figure you've done about all you can to protect your home from crime. Not quite. Now it's time to check every room, every door, and every window. In many areas, the police or sheriff's department will survey your home, room by room, for free—all you need to do is call and ask.

"Most districts have a person assigned who will come to your home, walk through, and discuss things with you," says Fryrear. The officer will go through a checklist item by item with you, making valuable suggestions on how to make your home safer. And that doesn't necessarily mean costly improvements. "All homes don't need wrought-iron bars," Fryrear says. "If the officer is at all aware of

FORTIFYING YOUR HOME

Here are six quick steps that you can take to make your home safer.

✓ Trim shrubbery away from windows. Look at your house from the street to see if there's a good line of vision. "You don't want to provide hiding places where a bad guy can work on a window or a door," says Robert E. Lassahn, crime-prevention specialist with the Maryland Community Crime Prevention Institute in Woodstock.

✓ Install outdoor lighting, or turn on what outdoor lights you do have. Your goal should be to have enough lighting that a burglar cannot work on a door or window without being seen.

✓ Think "safety" before you open the door. "When the doorbell rings, instead of checking to see who's there, people will open it to almost anybody," says Lassahn. They shouldn't. If someone says he's from the gas or electric company, don't automatically believe him. Ask him to hold his ID up to your peephole. (If you don't have a peephole in your door, buy one at a hardware store and install it.) "If you offend them, so what? Put your priorities in the right order," he advises.

the type of crime that's prevalent in the area, he can lead you to inexpensive changes."

These can include such things as basic motion detectors and lights. "A lot of it is also strengthening existing equipment," explains Lassahn (see "Fortifying Your Home" for specific suggestions). The officer also may discuss alarm systems and explain what to look for if you decide to invest in one. To find out if your local police department offers this service, call the department's general number, which you can find in the government pages of your phone book.

●◆ WHAT INSIDERS SAY:

Some of the best defenses are the simplest, says Lassahn. For example, one of the most common home weaknesses is the latch plate that your door locks into. "Most of the time, it's installed with the screws that came with the lock," he says. "They're maybe 1 inch long and just reach to the trim portion of the door." A burglar can put a foot or shoulder to a door like that and easily break the wood holding the latch plate in place. What you want to do is replace the short screws with longer ones that run through the trim and into the two-by-four behind it, he advises.

The Do-It-Yourself Check

In some communities, rather than doing a survey for you, the police will furnish a reader-friendly safety checklist that you can complete. It may also include line drawings showing why some locks are more secure than others or how to keep someone from breaking in through your windows, explains Fryrear. "The diagrams are clear and concise. The self-administered surveys are pretty short and pretty easy to use." Call the general police or sheriff's department number listed in the government pages of your phone book to learn whether your town offers such checklists.

Test Your Safety Electronically

Think your home is safe enough that you don't need to bother with precautions? If you have ac-

✓ If you have a shed detached from your house, be sure it's locked at all times.

✓ Don't leave your garage door opener in your vehicle in plain sight. It's tempting for a thief, who knows that plenty of people don't bother to lock the doors between their houses and garages—and the few who do probably have plenty of valuables in their garages. The odds are great that somewhere in your car, perhaps on your vehicle registration, is your home address. So for the amount of effort and the few seconds it takes to punch out a lock on your car door, you've essentially handed a burglar an invitation to help himself at your home.

✓ Always lock the door leading from your house into the garage. You never know when someone has a garage door opener that's set to the same frequency as yours or has a gadget that scans radio frequencies to find the one that opens your door.

●◆ WHAT INSIDERS SAY:

In general, anything that will make a would-be burglar make more noise is good. This means tougher doors and windows, which take effort and noise to kick open or break out. "Most people will not break a large double-paned glass door, for instance, because it would make a lot of noise," says Shawn Parris, crime-prevention officer with the Nashville Police Department. "They want to get in, get out quickly, and not be heard."

cess to the Internet, you can find out if you're right in about 5 minutes by taking a free "Rate Your Risk" test created by Captain Ken Pence of the Nashville Police Department. Just type in www.nashville.net/~police, then click on the "Rate Your Risk" button to connect to this interactive quiz. You'll be instructed to check off answers to about 75 questions about the perimeter of your home, conditions on your street, and so forth.

Once you've completed the quiz, you'll get an instant result that ranks your home's risk for being burglarized as low, moderate, high, or extremely high. You'll also receive specific suggestions for making your home safer. Here are some of the more unusual survey questions and Capt. Pence's rationale for asking them.

✓ Are your phone lines buried? If not, a thief can cut them to prevent you from calling for help or to disable your alarm system.

✓ Have you answered a detailed telephone survey or completed a phone credit application in the past year? If so, people know how much you earn, where you live, and where you work, and they can probably make a pretty good guess as to when you'll be at work and what kinds of valuables you have in your house. Also, people can use this information to

WHEN CRIME HITS BEFORE YOU MOVE IN

When Bonnie and Norton Edwards started building a new home near Nashville, the quiet neighborhood seemed to be crime-free. But about a month before the house was completed, they had a rude shock. Thieves vandalized the house and stole everything that could be taken, including cabinets and appliances.

Often, a house under construction is a crime waiting to happen, says Robert Lassahn, crime-prevention specialist with the Maryland Community Crime Prevention Institute in Woodstock. There are multiple workers coming and going—roofers, electricians, phone company employees, people delivering appliances—and

often, a truck is parked overnight on-site. No one in the neighborhood thinks anything is amiss when they see strangers coming and going. Your workers may be honest, but every time they mention to a friend or neighbor, "Hey, I'm busy working on that new house over on Wilson Street," they've widened the web of people who know that there's a house full of goodies waiting to be robbed. What can you do? Here's what the experts recommend.

Contact neighbors before anything happens
Introduce yourself, in person or by a note or flyer, and provide a phone number to call if they see any thing suspicious.

Know who's working for you
Select a contractor who uses employees that he knows or who have references rather than workers hired off the street.

Lock it up
Usually, a finished door with a lock is one of the last things installed, but that doesn't have to be the case. You can insist that your contractor lock up the house after workers leave and disperse only a limited number of keys. Then you can have the lock rekeyed before you move in. As a last resort, after your appliances and other expensive fixtures have been delivered, hire a guard for the evenings.

fill out a credit card application and order another card in your name, says Capt. Pence.

✓ Do you leave mail in your car with the address visible? This alerts a would-be burglar where you live and that you're not at home. If you also keep your garage door opener in the car, a burglar can help himself and waltz into your garage.

✓ Are your name and home address printed in a company directory, church directory, or other publication? Names in a church directory are often used as a source of homes to burglarize while people are in church, says Capt. Pence. Other directories can be used in similar ways, such as targeting your home during the annual company picnic, for instance.

Play Burglar for a Day

Want to find out how safe your house really is? Try this simple self-test: "Go home tonight, pretend that you've been locked out of your house, and see how hard or how easy it is to get in," advises Shawn Parris, crime-prevention officer with the Nashville Police Department. Can you slip the lock on the back door with your credit card? Can you reach in and pop open the chain lock? Is there a screen that you can slip out and a window that you can force up? Are there secluded, poorly lit doors and windows where you could take your time to break in? Bear in mind, of course, that you're trying to "break in" without actually damaging your house, while a burglar will have no such compunctions.

◗◆ *WHAT INSIDERS SAY:*

Want to get a quick read on whether your house looks tempting to burglars? "Walk around outside and observe," says Michael C. Modrak, resident agent in charge of the criminal investigation division of the U.S. Customs Service in Nashville. "Can you see inside the windows, and if so, what do you see? Expensive stereo equipment, cameras, jewelry?" Valuables like this in plain sight can be magnets for a thief.

Prove That TV Is Yours

Your VCR and small color television have disappeared from your basement rec room, and you spy them in the backseat of a car down the street. But the car owner says the equipment just looks like yours, even down to the long scratch that you recognize on the side of the VCR. What does this mean? You're out of luck, because a scratch isn't proof.

But if the property were engraved with your personal identifying numbers, and you had a list of the serial numbers, the thief would be the one out of luck.

Many police departments and crime-prevention organizations offer a program called Operation ID, which helps you mark your property so that you can identify it if it's recovered after a theft. They'll lend you an engraving tool and include directions for marking your items, tips on recording a description of each piece, and stickers that warn a prospective thief that all items in the house are marked.

Some libraries also lend engraving tools. In Nashville, says Parris, "we have 10 libraries where you can check out engravers, plus four police sectors." To find out if your community offers this service, call your police department's general information number or ask at your local library.

◗◆ *WHAT INSIDERS SAY:*

"It's a good idea to mark an item where it's noticeable and in a second place where it's hidden," suggests Parris. That way, if a thief obliterates one marking, the second will still be there to prove the item is yours.

Protect Your House while You're Away

When does your home look most tempting to a burglar? When it's empty for an extended period, such as when you're on vacation or a business trip, says Fryrear. This gives the burglar plenty of time to make sure that no one's around and to figure out when he's least likely to be seen by neighbors if he breaks in. But police say that your empty home won't invite theft if you follow these tips.

Give It the Complete Lived-In Look

Of course, you'll stop mail, newspaper, or other deliveries and ask a neighbor to cut the grass or shovel your snow and such. But don't stop there. If you think that you're likely to get a delivery from a mail-order company while you're away, call the delivery company in advance so you won't end up with a yellow "attempted-to-deliver" ticket fluttering on your front door. This just proclaims to all that you're not at home. If you'd prefer not to tell company workers that you'll be away, you can ask a neighbor to check your front door daily.

Don't Advertise Your Absence

Do you proclaim your holiday plans on your calendar, marking through the days you'll be gone and writing "Trip to Disneyland!" in big letters? It's not a good idea, says Lassahn. You may trust everyone who comes into your home or workplace, but all it takes is one repairman, house cleaner, or friend of a friend who happens to mention to the wrong person that you'll be out of town that week, and you've issued an invitation for burglary.

➥ WHAT INSIDERS SAY:

Many police departments or sheriffs' departments will, if requested, send a patrol car by your house when you're out of town. But you may want to think twice about asking for this, say crime experts. Requesting a drive-by means that a number of people will know that you're away. "It's better to rely on a neighbor to check the residence and look out for strange vehicles," says Modrak. Another option, of course, is getting a house-sitter.

Safeguarding Your Mail

You may not think of your mailbox as an invitation to thieves, but it can be a tempting box of goodies for the unscrupulous.

Diane Strange of Oak Ridge, Tennessee, had

KEEPING THIEVES OUT OF YOUR MAILBOX

If you suspect that your mail is being stolen, you need to call the postal authorities as well as the police. But don't stop there. There are things that you can do on your own to help safeguard your mail from thieves, says Stephen M. Cheuvront, a team leader with the U.S. Postal Inspection Service, Southeast Division, in Nashville.

Drop it off

Instead of sticking your outgoing mail into the box and putting the flag up (which says to a thief, "Come help yourself!") drop it off at any blue postal box or at the post office.

Pick it up quickly

"Don't leave your mail sitting in your box," advises Cheuvront. If you're home, pick it up soon after the mail carrier stops. If you can't see the mailbox from your house, buy a gadget that alerts you when your mail arrives. (Some hardware stores and mail-order companies sell them.) If you're going to be out of town, have a trusted neighbor pick up your mail, or have it held at the post office until your return.

Get a locking box

If, like most of us, you work during the day and can't pick up your mail until you return home, you may want to buy a mailbox with a key lock. You can find several different varieties at building supply stores. Or you can rent a box at your local post office.

Choose direct deposit

Instead of having paychecks mailed to your house, have

no idea that someone was stealing her mail until a neighbor came by to feed her dog. The neighbor noticed that the mailbox was full when she entered the house and empty when she left a short time later. The next day, another neighbor, a retired man who lived across the street, sat on his front porch and watched Strange's mailbox all afternoon. He saw the paperboy leave the paper and then stuff something into his paper bag.

Sometimes, as in this case, mail theft is just a kid making mischief. Other times, thieves are looking for checks, money, airline tickets, tickets to the theater or a sporting event, or music CDs, says Stephen Cheuvront, team leader of the U.S. Postal Inspection Service, Southeast Division, in Nashville. Even your bank statements can provide valuable information, such as account numbers, that a thief can use to try to access your money.

If you suspect that someone is stealing your mail, call the local police department, says Cheuvront. Give whatever description you can of a person you suspect, a vehicle you may have seen—whatever you think may help. If your information leads to the arrest and conviction of someone who's been stealing mail, you could get a reward of up to $5,000. The police should forward a copy of the police report to the postal inspector, but you may want to call your local post office as well. You'll be asked to fill out PS Form 1510, "Mail Loss and Rifling Report," or PS Form 2016, "Mail Theft and Vandalism Complaint."

●◆ *WHAT INSIDERS SAY:*

Neighborhood kids may not be aware that tampering with mail or mailboxes is a federal crime, and sometimes a gentle warning is enough to dissuade them. The Postal Inspection Service can furnish Label 33, a sticker that warns that damaging mailboxes or stealing mail is a crime.

---

them deposited directly into your bank account, advises Cheuvront. You can also choose to have some bills paid directly from your checking account or pay them over the Internet rather than putting checks in the mail.

Let neighbors know there's a thief in the area

If your mail is being tampered with or your mailbox battered, start a telephone notification chain or drop notes off at everyone's house. Other people may be having problems that they haven't bothered to report, or parents may suddenly realize that Junior has a bunch of new CDs that he can't account for, says Cheuvront.

Choose a different envelope

It's fun to pick out or to receive big, brightly colored envelopes containing cards for birthdays, anniversaries, or other special occasions. But to a thief, those big, colored envelopes spell money! "That envelope can be an invitation," says Cheuvront. This type of thievery, unfortunately, can happen in mailrooms as well as after the envelope lands in your mailbox. One smart rule: Never send cash through the mail, he says.

Dispose of mail carefully

Realize, too, that problems can happen with your mail after you've received it. An unscrupulous trash collector can find unused credit card checks, credit card receipts, bank statements, and other valuable papers that you've tossed into the trash. If you have a shredder (available at all office supply stores and many big discount stores), shred these items; if not, rip them up.

NEIGHBORHOOD DEFENSE

Protective measures are great, but there's nothing that can compare with the alert eyes of residents. They know better than police who's normally in their neighborhood and who isn't, and what behaviors are out of the ordinary. "We try to tell communities the importance of watching out for each other," says Lassahn. "It's neighbors looking out for one another."

There are a number of groups that can help you set up neighborhood programs to deter crime. Here are some of the best, say crime-prevention experts.

Hands-On Help from the Police

In many communities, police will help you organize crime-watch groups, such as Neighborhood Watch, Block Watch, or Apartment Watch—what Nashville police crime-prevention officer Shawn Parris calls "a free alarm system." The police will show members how to set up a group and run it.

"They make sure you understand that you're out there as extra eyes and ears," explains Matt Peskin of the National Association of Town Watch. "They teach you what to look for, what's suspicious, what might raise the hair on the back of your neck, and how to report it."

If you'd like to create a watch program, call your local police department or sheriff's department and ask to speak to a crime-prevention officer. The officer will likely suggest that you poll the area to find out how many people are interested and will send you a planning guide with information or advice.

There's no set minimum number for starting a group, although Parris says that roughly 30 percent of the people in a neighborhood need to participate for the program to be effective. He advises perseverance when you're starting a group: "It can take up to a year to get a good Neighborhood Watch established," he says.

If you want to give your watch group some clout, invite your local councilperson to one of your meetings. "Even if everything's going fine, it's good to get to know that person, who's often a great asset to the community and police as well," says Parris.

Crime-Watch Start-Up Kits

The National Sheriffs' Association provides materials for the Neighborhood Watch program, offering brochures, warning signs, bumper stickers, and a video called "Joining Forces" that explains how Neighborhood Watch works and how to set it up. The items aren't free, but the cost is reasonable—100 brochures, for example, cost just $6. Write to the National Neighborhood Watch Program, National Sheriffs' Association, 1450 Duke Street, Alexandria, VA 22314.

Crime-Prevention Pamphlets

For lots of great tips on how to make your neighborhood safer, turn to the National Crime Prevention Council, which, among other things, coordinates the McGruff the Crime Dog program. You can order the following free pamphlets by writing to National Crime Prevention Council Fulfillment Center, P.O. Box 1, 100 Church Street, Amsterdam, NY 12010. You can also order these and other publications from the group's Web site at www.ncpc.org.

✓ "Not Alone, Not Afraid"

✓ "Getting Together to Fight Crime"

✓ "Stop the Violence, Start Something"

The group also offers the following useful, low-cost publications (add 10 percent for shipping costs).

✓ "Maintaining Neighborhood Watch" ($3.95)

✓ "Helping Communities Mobilize Against Crime, Drugs, and Other Problems" ($5.95)

Amazing Stories

ON A ROLL
TO BATTLE CRIME

If you're out and about in the evening hours in Philadelphia, you may catch sight of a couple of skaters cruising past on in-line skates, wearing matching T-shirts and reflective shorts and toting walkie-talkies, cell phones, and whistles.

They may resemble cruising police officers—in fact, they're sometimes mistaken for police—but these are civilian members of the In-line Town Watch, an offshoot of the Landskaters In-line Skate Club, who patrol the sixth and ninth districts of the city each weeknight from 8:00 P.M. to midnight.

Club member Rick Short started the group in 1995, when he skated into an area police station and asked if there was anything he could do to help out. Thus, the nation's first skating town watch was born. Skaters signed up and attended a 3-week training session, and now there are about 50 on the roster.

They wear matching garb of city-supplied blue shirts and black shorts with reflective trim, plus helmets and other protective gear: elbow, knee, and wrist pads. They meet at the police station, then cover about 10 miles a night, as long as it's not raining. Their goal: to act as eyes and ears for the police force, calling in to report crimes or suspicious situations. To participate, members must be at least 18 and be at least intermediate skaters.

For Short, the patrols have been educational: He's learned that criminals often travel in pairs, so one can watch out while the other commits the crime; that people carrying gym bags may be planning to do a "smash and grab" theft; and that a tow truck may be on its way to steal a car. Also, "you learn not to come up to a situation too fast," he notes. "You learn to always have a place to take cover."

Once, he caught sight of a man threatening a taxi driver with a knife and blew his whistle from half a block away. "The guy just took off running," says Short. He followed at a discreet distance until the man ran through a pizza restaurant and was nabbed by police on the other side. On other nights, he's reported fires, and he once found a stolen pocketbook after an assault.

The downside is that sometimes people act belligerent or make snide comments. "Occasionally, people hassle you and say nasty things. It's 90 percent good and maybe 10 percent bad," he says. "But I think it's safer than walking." The skaters have a big advantage—they're quite mobile and very fast. About the only thing they can't do is climb fences.

Helping to catch the knife-wielding taxi passenger was exciting, but what Short finds more rewarding are the small, helpful things he does: escorting people to cars, notifying drivers when they've left their headlights on, tracking down a husband who's lost his way after a wine-tasting party. One of Short's most rewarding shifts was the night a woman who was visiting from Texas lost the diamond from her engagement ring. He eventually found it, and "she was so happy, she was crying," he says.

✓ "Creating a Climate of Hope: 10 Neighbor-hoods Tackle the Drug Crisis" ($14.95)

✓ "Uniting Communities through Crime Prevention" ($14.95)

Crime-Prevention Handbook

The nonprofit National Association of Town Watch sells a low-cost block captain's handbook that explains how to start a community watch group and includes forms and announcements that you'll need to organize your group and notify neighbors who may be interested in joining. The association also sponsors a National Night Out event on the first Tuesday each August, with block parties and parades—"a night to promote crime prevention," explains Peskin.

For more information, write to the association at P.O. Box 303, Wynnewood, PA 19096. Or, if you access to the Internet, visit the group's Web site at www.natw.org.

●◆ WHAT INSIDERS SAY:

Regardless of whether you create a watch group, don't underestimate the importance of communicating with your neighbors.

"A lot of people think they are in 'safe' areas, while stuff is happening all around them. I've had people say at meetings, 'We don't have a problem,' and then hands fly up with people reporting that their cars were broken into or other things that have happened," says Parris.

Keep in mind that burglars often return to hit the same area three or four times, says Parris, and your best protection is knowing that they're around so you can be on the alert. How can you keep track? Set up a communication chain. You can drop a newsletter or flyer at neighbors' front doors to tell them when crimes occur, or you can make a phone chain in which each neighbor calls the next person on a list. Let your neighbors know what time of day the burglary occurred, how the burglar gained entry, and what types of things were stolen.

Best Bets

THE CITIES
BURGLARS SHUN

Burglaries can happen anywhere, but some cities have fewer than others. Among cities with populations of around 100,000, these 10 had the fewest burglaries in the first half of 1998–the most recent year for which statistics were available–according to uniform crime report statistics from the FBI.

TOWN	BURGLARIES	POPULATION (1990)	BURGLARIES PER 10,000 RESIDENTS
Amherst Town, NY	80	111,711	7
Sterling Heights, MI	188	117,810	16
Naperville, IL	199	85,351	23
Burbank, CA	225	98,545	23
Thousand Oaks, CA	225	104,352	22
Simi Valley, CA	239	100,217	24
Stamford, CT	253	108,056	23
Sunnyvale, CA	274	117,229	23
Norwalk, CA	283	92,279	36
Mesquite, TX	294	101,484	30

WHAT TO DO IF A BURGLAR'S IN YOUR HOME

Early in his career, Dustin Hoffman did a movie called *Straw Dogs* in which he had to fend off a half-dozen local bullies who were trying to break into his home. The crazed fear on his face was almost palpable.

That's the way most people would react if a burglar tried to enter while they were at home. But being scared doesn't mean that you have to give in. Crime-prevention experts say there are several steps that you can take to keep that burglar at bay. Here's what they recommend for specific situations.

If you hear a knock on the door:
Most burglars want to work on an empty house, so they start by knocking on doors to see if anyone answers. "If you're at home, go to the door, but don't open it," suggests Shawn Parris, crime-prevention officer with the Nashville Police Department. "Ask who it is and let the person know you're at home. If you don't, the intruder may go to the back door and try to kick it in."

If someone is breaking in:
"Most burglars want to operate in a stealth mode," says Robert E. Lassahn, crime-prevention specialist with the Maryland Community Crime Prevention Institute in Woodstock. "If someone who's contemplating breaking in realizes that there are people inside who are aware of his presence, he's lost his edge." So while calling the police, turn the lights off and on to alert the burglar that you know he's there. Chances are good that he'll move on in search of an easier target.

If someone is in the house:
If you become aware that there's a burglar in your house, seek a safe retreat, advises Lassahn. "Keep distance and a barrier between yourself and that person," he says. Go to an area of security, like a bathroom or bedroom, and take a cordless phone—or better yet, a cell phone. Your hiding place should have a window to the outside and a lock that you can secure.

Call 911 once you're locked away. If you have an alarm system with an emergency mode, key in the code that tells your alarm company to send the police. If the burglar tries to break into your hiding place, tell him calmly but firmly to take anything he wants and leave, and that the police are on the way. Never try to confront a burglar or defend your possessions, says Lassahn.

If an intruder is in your bedroom:
What if you wake up and discover a burglar in your bedroom? There's no easy correct answer. "Every situation is different," says Parris, "but at this point, if you move or shout, you could turn a nonviolent situation into a violent one." This may be a good time to play possum, but if the intruder's aware that you're awake, make it clear that you're not going to try to stop him, says Lassahn.

What if he threatens harm or assaults you? Again, there's no clear answer. If you do fight back, move fast and decisively, says Lassahn, and don't stop fighting until you get away.

Protecting Your Car

It happens to all of us at one time or another: You rush into the mall to make a purchase, and when you come out, you can't find your car. For most people, that sinking feeling passes quickly, and the car turns up. For an unfortunate few, however, it's an introduction to the world of car theft.

Cars can disappear at any time, from any place. Thieves may prefer unlocked cars, but it only takes moments to punch out the lock on most cars and start the car with a screwdriver jammed into the ignition switch, says U.S. Customs agent Michael Modrak. A "club" locking device will slow thieves down, but nothing is fail-safe.

This said, you can take steps to protect your car and improve the chances that you'll get it back if it is stolen. Many police departments offer a low-cost program called Combat Auto Theft. When you sign up, you're given a sticker for your car that gives the police the legal right to pull your car over if it's seen out between certain hours, such as 1:00 and 5:00 A.M., explains Parris. If you're driving your own car, there's no problem, but if not, you've just helped the police stop the thief who took it. The time period during which cars can be stopped varies in different areas.

SCAMS

You can be the victim of crime while sitting comfortably in your own home, by way of the telephone, mail, or door-to-door sales. But you're far from helpless when someone tries to draw you into a fraudulent deal. There are several ways that the police, government, and nonprofit groups can help protect you from these types of scams. Here are your best resources.

Stopping Fraud at the Door

It's spring, and you're starting to think about all the work you need to do outside when you hear a knock on the door. The guy standing there says that he's a skilled yardman and he's willing to give you a great price on landscaping if you act quickly. The catch: He needs your money up-front so he can buy the mulch and trees. What should you do?

First, trust your instincts and say no: If something doesn't seem right, it probably isn't, says Lassahn. Your next step should be to call the police or sheriff's department and report that there's a suspicious salesperson in your neighborhood. The police should know if the person or organization is accredited or has a permit for door-to-door sales, and they'll know, too, if other people have already complained. Even if the salesperson was just belligerent and made you uncomfortable, call the police. They may want to send an officer out to make a report of the incident and possibly to talk to the salesperson.

Scam-Prevention Pamphlets

The nonprofit American Association of Retired Persons (AARP) offers free publications that can help you avoid sales fraud. You can write AARP Fulfillment, 601 E Street NW, Washington, DC 20049, and request current publications on salespeople or home repair problems. Or, if you have access to the Internet, view the publications free online. Go to www.aarp.org and use the Quick Search button to search for the phrase "sales fraud."

Canceling Bad Deals

If you buy something from a door-to-door salesperson or sign a contract to have work done, but then you have second thoughts about whether you made a good move, the government can help you. The Federal Trade Commission has enacted a 3-day cooling-off period that gives you 3 business days from the date a sale is made to change your mind, cancel the deal, and get back any money you may have paid. This cooling-off period applies to any service or object that costs $25 or more and is sold to you at your home or workplace or in a temporary facility like a restaurant or hotel.

When you make the deal, the salesperson should give you two copies of a cancellation form. To kill the deal, you must notify the person or company that you dealt with by signing, dating, and sending in one copy of the cancellation form. And it's best to send it by certified mail. Then the person or company must refund your money within 10 days.

When a Sale Goes Bad

When you return a product or cancel a deal, you expect to get your money back. If you don't, or you otherwise feel that you've been cheated, put your complaint in writing and send the letter certified, return-receipt-requested to the other party. If you still get no satisfaction, the Federal Trade Commission would like to hear from you. The commission can't settle your individual dispute, but if enough people have problems with a certain organization, it may be able to take action. Write to the Federal Trade Commission, CRC-240, Washington, DC 20580. If you have access to the Internet, you also can reach the commission by connecting to its Web site at www.ftc.gov, and you can find a complaint form by clicking on "Complaint Form."

Fraud by Mail and Phone

If you think that you've been the victim of a telephone or door-to-door scam, call the police as well as your regional branch of the Better Business Bureau, the state attorney general, and the local district attorney.

There are 130 Better Business Bureaus in the United States. You can locate your regional office in the white pages of your phone book under Better Business Bureau, or you can visit its Web site at www.bbb.org. Once on the site, just click on "Online Complaint Forms" to find a form, "Resource Library" for publications, or "Find Your Local BBB" to find the office serving your area. The main office is Council of Better Business Bureaus, Inc., 4200 Wilson Boulevard, Suite 800, Arlington, VA 22203-1804.

If you don't know who your attorney general is, you can write to the National Association of Attorneys General, 750 First Street NE, Suite 1100, Washington, DC 20002.

Making Them Play by the Rules

There are strict rules about what telemarketers can and can't do, and the Federal Communications Commission can explain them to you. For the free publication "What You Can Do about Unsolicited Telephone Marketing Calls and Faxes," write to 445 12th Street SW, Washington, DC 20554. You can also find this and other electronic publications at the agency's Web site at www.fcc.gov. To get to the publications, click on "Consumer Info."

If you believe that rules have been broken and you want to file a complaint, write all details to the Federal Communications Commission, Consumer Complaints, at the same address, or visit the Web site for more information.

Bring In the Postman

If you have a complaint about fraud through the mail, failure to deliver merchandise, or scams such as supposedly "free" prizes or people pretending to solicit money for charities, the U.S. Postal Service is your white knight.

If you think you've been the victim of mail fraud, you'll need to complete Form 8165, which is available at all post offices. When completed, return the form to your local post office or mail it to Chief Postal Inspector, U.S. Postal Service, 475 L'Enfant Plaza SW, Room 3021, Washington, DC 20260-2100. There's also a toll-free mail fraud complaint center hotline that you can call (you can get the number from your local post office).

Don't assume that this is a useless exercise. The Postal Service pursues offenders and seizes assets. In 1998, for example, it seized $8 million from a man convicted of breaking federal anti-gambling laws for soliciting contributors to foreign lotteries by illegal mailings. The $8 million was split among his victims.

The Postal Service also offers useful information and pamphlets that are available free on its Web site at www.usps.gov or www.usps.com.

Cancel That Bill

If you used a credit card for a transaction that you believe may have been fraudulent or just an error, the government offers you some protection. The federal Fair Credit Billing Act requires credit card companies to "freeze" any disputed amount and not charge interest while a dispute is being investigated.

To take advantage of this service, write to your credit card company within 60 days, stating that you are disputing the purchase and why, and giving your name, address, and credit card number. Look at your most recent bill for instructions on where to write; there may be a form on the back of your bill.

NEIGHBORHOOD NUISANCES

Living around people requires some compromises, whether it's dealing with the endless thump of the neighbor kid's basketball, enduring the sounds of the garage rock band practicing every weekend, or having to look at the knee-high weeds next door.

Some of these "problems" you may want to overlook or learn to cope with. For example, the

A CRIME-RESISTANT COMMUNITY

Wouldn't it be great if there were a design for crimeproof houses? Unfortunately, there's no such thing, but law enforcement agencies and town planners are working together to produce the next best thing: crime-resistant communities.

New communities or neighborhoods are being designed—and older ones retrofitted—to discourage crime through a process called Crime Prevention through Environmental Design (CPTED).

"The plan might cover open space, traffic patterns, the flow of people, and use of land," explains Robert E. Lassahn, crime-prevention specialist with the Maryland Community Crime Prevention Institute in Woodstock. Some areas now mandate such an assessment, and the local law enforcement body must sign off on plans. Recommendations for existing communities could include moving trees, altering paths to change where people walk, planting shrubs, or installing lighting. Basically, Lassahn says, the designs make it easier for law-abiding residents to monitor the area, and they eliminate likely spots where muggers could lie in wait, for instance.

If you're building a new home, ask your builder to ensure that your plans meet CPTED standards. If you have a neighborhood association that has a fund earmarked for making changes and that is interested in adopting these standards, call your local police or sheriff's department and ask to speak to a crime-prevention officer, or call your zoning or codes department. If the department doesn't have anyone trained in CPTED, ask someone there to direct you to the right place.

kids playing basketball may be noisy, but they're kids who aren't getting into trouble. "Plus, a group of teens hanging out may even deter criminals from coming into the neighborhood," says U.S. Customs agent Michael Modrak.

For other problems, such as abandoned cars, empty or seriously damaged houses, or trash dumped on the ground, you need to act, and act fast.

"We call it the broken window theory," explains Nashville crime-prevention officer Shawn Parris. "If you have a building with one window broken out, if it isn't repaired quickly, it makes it that much easier for someone to knock another one out. The same thing is true of trash in your neighborhood: If someone throws a can or a bottle or a whole sack of trash alongside the road, people think, 'Oh, these people will tolerate this,' and they'll feel a little better about tossing things out there than they would in a clean environment."

Here's how the experts suggest that you handle six of the most annoying neighborhood problems.

Dealing With Dumpers

Jane Morrison of Franklin, Tennessee, was walking her dog down her dead-end street when a pickup truck went past. She heard the truck zoom around the end of the street and then a loud thud. Moments later, the truck passed her again. When she reached the end of the street, she noticed a big metal table and several pieces of broken lawn equipment. It was trash, dumped by someone who didn't want to bother to visit a landfill.

If something like this happens in your neighborhood and you spot the license number of the trash dumper's car, call your local police. If you're too late to catch the dumper, call the public works department or the health or sanitation department. They'll send an inspector to search through the trash, looking for names to identify the guilty party, says Henry Richard Gordon, chief housing inspector at the Department of Codes Administration in Nashville. And they'll arrange for its disposal as well.

Tackling Derelict Homes

It doesn't take much imagination to see that an abandoned house can attract trouble, whether it's from a neighbor kid sneaking some puffs or squatters taking up residence. If you believe that a nearby home has been deserted or is neglected, call your local housing or codes administration department. If you can't find a listing, call the county clerk or town clerk and ask whom you should notify.

Be realistic, though. "You're not going to call about an abandoned house and have a bulldozer there the next day," says Parris. In a best-case scenario, the problem house will be gone within a month or two. In a worst-case scenario, it could drag on for years, especially if the owner refuses to cooperate. What can you do in the meantime? Keep making pleasant phone calls to the department to which you reported the house until it's at least boarded up, and report any evidence of crime to the police.

Slowing Speeders

Cars zooming down your street are a police issue, says Gordon. Call and give all the details you can, such as whether the problem occurs all the time or at a certain time of day and whether it's neighbors or commuters who are using your street as a shortcut. If it's a persistent problem, ask the police to come out with a radar gun to nab the guilty parties.

Do you believe your street needs a speed limit sign? Ask the police or call the town traffic division. Think the present speed limit needs to be changed? Your best bet is to call your councilperson, who will know where to present your request.

Getting Rid Of Junked Cars

Derelict cars can be eyesores, and they can also encourage vandalism. So what do you do if a neighbor has an unsightly junker sitting in the side yard, or if someone has parked a derelict vehicle on the street? First, you have to determine if the car really is a derelict. The definition of "abandoned" can vary; in Gordon's area, it refers to a car that is in disrepair and cannot be moved under its own power, whether or not it's registered.

Where you call to report a junked car varies from area to area. For a derelict car in someone's yard, you might call a housing department. If the car is in the street, you'd likely need a zoning department. (These numbers are listed in the government pages of your phone book.) You'll need to report where the car is, and it can't hurt to report its condition—headlights broken, flat tires—and how long it's been sitting there.

Stalling Wheeled Nuisances

If you live in a housing development or apartment building, your community may have rules that cover people roller skating, skateboarding, or bicycling where they shouldn't. Check the rules and take your complaint to the neighborhood representative or apartment manager, or pass out flyers or newsletters gently reminding people of the rules. If these steps don't work, you can call the police. For problems such as dirt bikes being ridden on the road or other violations, you can ask the offenders to stop, but if the problem continues or you're not comfortable talking to them, contact the police. It can help if you make note of the times the problem occurs and give a brief description of the lawbreakers if you don't know their names.

Quieting Noise Problems

Most areas have ordinances that cover the level of noise permitted in neighborhoods, whether from cars or boom boxes or parties. You can try approaching neighbors yourself, but if you can't resolve the problem, report it to the police. How loud is too loud? "As a general rule, if we ride by and can hear it from the street in our car with the windows rolled up, it's too loud," says Parris. Usually, the police give a warning the first time and a citation the second time.

CHAPTER 8

HOME MANAGEMENT 101

Three hundred or so years ago, the writer Samuel Johnson said, "No money is better spent than what is laid out on domestic satisfaction." If anything, his words are even more true today than when he wrote them.

We Americans spend more than 55 percent of our days in our homes. And with the proliferation of videocassette recorders, home entertainment centers, home computers, and telecommuting, that figure is on the rise.

Fortunately, the government and several major nonprofit groups share our love affair with home living, and they've devoted a fair portion of their money to researching ways to make life around the house easier, safer, and less expensive.

Whether your concern is cooking or credit cards, food, fuel, or anything in between, you can bet that Uncle Sam or his friends stand ready to offer excellent advice. They can show you how to organize your house better. They can help you find the best phone rates. They can protect you from tainted food and allergy-producing dust. And they may even throw a little money your way, in the form of subsidies, rebates, and loans, to buy more energy-efficient appliances.

Follow their advice, and the government and nonprofit groups will make you feel right at home.

> Uncle Sam as Suzy Homemaker? Yes, the government does know a thing or two about domestic life, and if you follow the advice it offers, you can run a cleaner, safer, more efficient, and more economical home.

RUNNING YOUR HOME

Want to know how to manage your home finances? Organize your desk drawers? How about canning peaches? Safeguarding your food? Cleaning your home efficiently and cheaply?

FACTOID

MANY EXPERTS BELIEVE THAT THE KITCHEN IS HOME TO MORE POTENTIALLY DANGEROUS BACTERIA THAN ANY OTHER ROOM IN THE HOUSE, INCLUDING THE BATHROOM.

Whether you're a newlywed or a single person setting up a first home or an experienced home-maker looking for new tips, there's great advice available from the government and your local schools—most of it free or at a low cost. Here are the best sources.

Classes in the Art of Homemaking

Along with courses on computers and biology, many high schools and colleges throughout the United States offer inexpensive adult education classes to help you improve other aspects of your life, including home life. The Portland School District in Maine, for example, teaches homemaking classes in its adult education program. One 2½-hour, one-evening course was "Never Apologize for a Messy House." There, you could learn systems to help you organize and simplify your home life, all for just $18.

At Jacksonville University in Florida, you can learn a host of home skills, from decorating cakes to decorating your home.

To locate adult education classes in your area, call the general number for your high school, junior college, or nearby university or college. It will be listed in the white pages of your phone book.

Home Advice from the Cooperative Extension

Back in 1914, the Smith-Lever Act mandated that land-grant universities, which specialize in research and education on farming, horticulture, and forestry, share their research results and information with the people in the state where each university is located. From this grew a na-

HOW TO AVOID FOOD POISONING

Ever been felled by a bout of nausea, a touch of diarrhea, an episode of vomiting? You may have shrugged it off as a virus, but the truth is, it may have been food poisoning.

Usually, the body can handle the bacteria that cause food poisoning, but people with weakened immune systems may become seriously ill. Those who are infected with HIV, the virus that causes AIDS, or who have AIDS itself, are particularly susceptible. Also, people with cancer or diabetes, those who have liver disease or stomach problems, pregnant women, babies, and elderly people should be particularly careful to avoid food poisoning.

Here are some food safety guidelines, supplied by the Food and Drug Administration, that can help you avoid food poisoning.

✓ Choose pasteurized milk and cheese products; avoid products that contain raw meat or raw dairy products. Also, bypass the bargain cart that contains products that have passed their "sell by" dates. Don't buy anything with damaged packaging.

✓ When you buy meat or fish, put it in a plastic bag and tie it shut before putting it in your cart with other foods.

✓ If it takes you more than an hour to get home from the market, equip your car with a large cooler to store chilled or frozen foods. When the temperature of food rises, bacteria may begin to grow.

tionwide network of offices known as cooperative extensions. Although these extensions are best known for providing good gardening advice (see chapter 17), they also can offer brochures, tips, classes, and personal answers to questions on home life.

The University of Nebraska Cooperative Extension in Lincoln, for example, offers free or low-cost publications on cleaning your home, managing your time and money, setting up a household budget, even creating a well-organized sewing center. A little farther west, the extension at Washington State University in Pullman provides printed advice on developing a better diet for your family, canning all types of food, curing and drying foods, and freezing foods.

But that's not all. Need to know the most efficient way to sanitize dishes or how to make your own furniture polish or floor wax remover?

The cooperative extension can tell you these things, too.

You can contact your local cooperative extension office by calling the number listed in the phone book. It may be listed in the white pages under the name of your state's land-grant university; in Pennsylvania, for example, you would look for Penn State Cooperative Extension. Or it may be in the government pages, listed as "Agricultural Extension" or "Cooperative Extension" under the state department of agriculture or the USDA.

If you have access to the Internet, you also can track down extension information on the Web. Use your Internet browser's search function to look for "cooperative extension." This will take you to a list of a wide variety of sites around the nation, many of which have publications that are available free for printing or downloading.

✔ After you handle one type of food, wash your hands with hot water and soap before handling another to prevent cross-contamination.

✔ Use plastic cutting boards for raw meat or fish and wash them thoroughly in the dishwasher or in hot water after using.

✔ Wash fruits and vegetables thoroughly and keep them in the refrigerator in covered containers. (Your fridge should be set at or below 40°F.)

✔ Pay attention to cooking times and temperatures, as heat kills bacteria. Red meat should be cooked until well-done; the juice from well-cooked poultry will be clear. Heat leftovers to at least 165°F.

✔ Don't eat raw eggs or foods made with them, such as Caesar salad dressing. Use pasteurized eggs in recipes for ice cream, mayonnaise, or eggnog. Cook eggs until both white and yolk are firm.

✔ Follow microwave cooking instructions closely. If they say to let food stand 5 minutes after cooking, do so; this lets it heat all the way through. Also, stir food midway through cooking if instructed to do so.

✔ When eating out, order food well-done. If your meat is pink or bloody, send it back. Fish should be flaky. Don't eat runny scrambled eggs or sunny-side-up eggs. Ask about ingredients in prepared dishes to ensure that you don't eat raw eggs.

✔ Forget about eating raw seafood or shellfish or lightly steamed seafood such as snails and mussels.

Test Your Food-Safety Savvy

Every year, 80 million Americans become ill from food poisoning. Some illnesses are caused by contamination or by undercooking meat and poultry, but the major culprit is mishandled food. These illnesses are almost 100 percent preventable if you take simple safety steps, such as storing food properly and keeping the area where you prepare food clean.

To check whether you're taking the proper precautions, the Food and Drug Administration created "Can Your Kitchen Pass the Food Safety Test?" This 12-question quiz checks your knowledge of food storage, handling, and cooking. It covers questions such as the proper temperature for a refrigerator, how you should handle leftover meat, chicken, or fish, and whether your kitchen sink drain and disposal are sanitary.

You can order this test for free from the Consumer Information Center, Pueblo, CO 81009, or find it on the Internet at the group's Web site, www.fda.gov/fdac/features/895_kitchen.html.

Four Keys to Safe Food

Experts say that there are four basic principles to preventing food poisoning at home: keep surfaces clean, keep meat separate from other foods, cook to proper temperatures, and keep foods as cold as required. You can get the specifics on meeting each of these standards by reading these free pamphlets:

✓ "Critical Steps toward Safer Seafood"

✓ "Fight BAC!: Four Simple Steps to Food Safety"

✓ "Fresh Look at Food Preservatives"

✓ "How to Help Avoid Foodborne Illness in the Home"

To order the pamphlets, write the Consumer Information Center, Pueblo, CO 81009. If you have access to the Internet, they're also available on the group's Web site at www.pueblo.gsa.gov/food.htm.

Updates on Food Scares

Are you worried that some of the food in your home might be part of a food-safety alert that you recently heard? The federal Center for Food Safety and Applied Nutrition in Washington, D.C., offers the latest information on food problems 24 hours a day on a special free hotline. You can get information on current health concerns, such as unpasteurized juices, oysters or other seafood, dietary supplements, nutritional labeling and other food-safety-related issues, and food recalls. Through this number you can also order any of 75 free publications and have them sent to you by mail or fax.

To get the number, call the 800 operator listed in the front of your phone book and ask for the toll-free number for the Food and Drug Administration Consumer Inquiry Information Line.

What to Do With Faulty Food

Maybe you found a rock in your can of soup or a bug in your cornflakes. Perhaps you think that the pepperoni pizza you had delivered last night is what made your family ill.

You can turn to the USDA or the Food and Drug Administration (FDA) for help and information on any of these issues. The experts there will explain what's safe and what's not, and in some cases, they will test your food for problems. Here are the specifics.

Problems with Meat and Poultry

If you have concerns about meat, poultry, or egg products, the USDA can help. (For eggs in the shell, you have to contact the FDA.) The staff can tell you how to safely handle these foods to avoid foodborne illness. Plus, they can act on complaints about products that may have caused illness. If necessary, they'll even send someone to your home to pick up a suspicious product, then test to see if it is contaminated.

To act on a food complaint, the agency needs the food's original container, any uneaten portion of the food (you can freeze it), and, if you think there was something inappropriate in the food, the foreign object you found.

For information on these services, contact the USDA, Food Safety and Inspection Service, 1400 Independence Avenue SW, Washington, DC 20250.

Meat and Poultry Hotline

For quick answers to your questions, the USDA maintains a toll-free meat and poultry hotline. You can get information on recalls of food products, the suspected problem with recalled food, and the symptoms of the illness that the food is suspected to cause. You also can file a complaint about tainted food.

To make a complaint, you'll need to know the brand name and manufacturer of the product, the size of the package, the can or package codes from the wrapper, the EST number (which identifies the plant where the food was processed), and the place and date that you bought the item.

To contact the hotline, call the 800 operator listed in your phone book and ask for the USDA number. Someone there can give you the number of the hotline.

Problems with Other Foods

For other food products that make you ill or appear to have been tampered with, contact the federal FDA. You can find the listing for the district office for your area in your phone book under "U.S. Government, Health and Human Services."

You also can find detailed instructions on reporting food poisoning or contamination on the agency's Web site at www.fda.gov. Click on "Foods," then on "How to Report Problems to FDA." To report a problem by mail, write the FDA at 5600 Fishers Lane, Rockville, MD 20857.

CUTTING COSTS

"An ounce of prevention is worth a pound of cure."

This old adage is usually used in reference to health care, but it can be applicable to keeping down costs around the house as well. With a little attention and forethought, you can slice utility bills, credit card rates, and a host of other monthly expenses. Choosing the right washing machine, for instance, can save you a bundle on your electric bill. And picking the best credit card for your buying pattern could trim the interest you pay by $100 or more annually.

Many government agencies and utility companies offer advice that can help you make the right decisions about these and other costs. In some cases, such as energy efficiency, they may even provide rebates and subsidies if those decisions lead you to buy more efficient appliances and lights.

Selecting the Best Credit Card

Through direct-mail offers and telemarketing, you're inundated with credit card offers. Each one claims its interest rate, "free" gifts, and member services are better than the next. The truth is that there are some good deals available—and some bad ones, too. And while deciphering the small print and terminology used in these offers takes a little time, it can result in great savings in interest, late fees, and annual fees, says the Federal Reserve Board.

To help you make the best choice, the board has published a booklet called "Shop . . . The Card You Pick Can Save You Money." It provides a concise explanation of credit card rates and terms. For 50 cents, you can order the publication by writing to Consumer Information Center, Pueblo, CO 81009. You can also find the publication for free at the center's Web site at www.pueblo.gsa.gov by clicking on "Money."

◆● WHAT INSIDERS SAY:

Many people don't realize it, but credit card interest rates aren't cast in stone. In these days of highly competitive cards, often all it takes is a phone call to your credit card company to ask for a reduced rate. When a Las Vegas woman's father died suddenly, leaving credit card debts with 19.9 and 15 percent interest rates, she made two phone calls to the companies and suddenly had much more manageable 12 and 10 percent rates. If the company seems reluctant, mention that you plan to switch to another card if your rate isn't changed. That may motivate them to lower your rate.

FIVE TIPS FOR PICKING THE BEST CREDIT CARD

If you've chosen a credit card simply because it's affiliated with your local bank or it was the first offer to arrive in the mail, you may be shortchanging yourself, says the Federal Reserve Board. Here are five ways to make sure you get the best deal.

Pick the right card for your lifestyle

Do you carry a balance from month to month or pay off the charges each time a bill arrives? If you fit the first profile, you need a card with a low interest rate. For the second, the interest rate doesn't matter, so you can search for other benefits, such as no annual fee or a low one.

Also, look at your buying pattern when choosing a card. Would you benefit most from a card that offers frequent flier discounts, free or reduced-rate minutes on your phone bill, cash back at the end of the year, or coupons for your favorite retailers? Some of these perks can be attractive. The L.L. Bean card, for example, offers free L.L. Bean shipping and coupons for L.L. Bean merchandise, while Southwest Airlines cards offer credits that can be used for free flights.

Carefully study the interest rate

If you're offered a low introductory rate on a card, look at the fine print. See if the rate will zoom to 18 or 20 percent after 3 to 6 months or if you send a payment late during the introductory period. Also, see if the low initial rate applies to the life of any balance that you transfer to the new card. If so, and you have a large balance on another card, it may be worthwhile to switch.

Negotiate the annual fee

If you have an account in good standing with your current credit card company, ask it to waive the annual fee.

Most issuers will waive the fee for good customers, or offer some "goodies" to keep you.

Check how finance charges are calculated

The most common methods are "average daily balance," "previous balance," and "adjusted balance." Of the three, the adjusted balance is usually the least expensive and the average daily balance the most costly.

Use your power as the customer

The credit card market is extremely competitive, and you can use this to your advantage. Call your credit card issuer to negotiate interest rates, late fees, and annual fees. If you almost always pay your bill on time, for example, but are charged a late fee after making one late payment, call the company. Most customer service representatives can waive such fees for good account holders.

Finding the Best Phone Rates

Television commercials tout 10-cents-a-minute rates or 5-cent Sundays. Celebrities rattle off 10-10 "dial-around" numbers that claim to save you money by letting you bypass the long-distance service you're signed up for. If you're confused by all these offers, you're not alone.

Thankfully, the Telecommunications Research and Action Center (TRAC) can provide some answers. This nonprofit organization offers a series of helpful low-cost pamphlets, including:

✓ "TRAC's Residential Long Distance Comparison Chart" ($5). This booklet compares the rates, services, and features of seven major long-distance companies.

✓ "TRAC's Small Business Long Distance Comparison Chart" ($7). This compares the rates and plans that eight long-distance providers offer to small businesses.

✓ "TRAC's Consumer's Guide to Dial Arounds (10-10-xxx Numbers)" ($1). This pamphlet compares the costs of dial-around services, explaining which plans are money savers, which aren't, and the do's and don'ts of using a dial-around service.

✓ "A Consumer's Guide to Cellular Telephone Service" ($7.95 plus $1.50 postage). This booklet compares the rates of cellular phone companies and explains the difference between technologies such as analog and digital services.

✓ "A Consumer's Guide to Long Distance and Local Directory Assistance Calling" ($1). This booklet compares the rates that long distance and directory services charge for directory assistance.

To order any of these pamphlets, send the name of the publication, a check or money order for payment, and a long, self-addressed, stamped envelope to Telecommunications Research and Action Center, P.O. Box 27279, Washington, DC 20005. (For "TRAC's Residential Long Distance Comparison Chart," your self-addressed envelope will need two stamps.)

You can also find some information and order the booklets from the group's Web site, www.trac.org.

●◆ *WHAT INSIDERS SAY:*

The phone company, like anything else, can make mistakes. If there are calls on your bill that you didn't make, call your long-distance provider. Some, including AT&T, offer a phone menu selection that lets you simply punch in the amount of the call in question; you'll get an automatic credit for that amount.

Also, if you find that you've run up an abnormally large number of long-distance calls on an expensive plan, call your long-distance provider. The company may let you switch retroactively to another calling plan that better fits your calling patterns and refigure your bill.

Saving Bucks On Your Water Bill

You may never give your water consumption a thought, but if your rate rises or water shortages in the hot summer months require cutbacks in water use, you'll probably be looking for ways to reduce your usage.

There are two good sources for information: your local cooperative extension bureau and your state consumer protection office. Washington State University's Cooperative Extension office, for example, produces a free publication on "Conserving Water Indoors," while the Ohio Consumers' Counsel provides information on reducing water use and finding leaks. One good tip from the Ohio agency: If you can read your water meter (call your water company if you need instructions), you can become an energy detective and determine whether you have a serious leak. Turn off all water inside and outside your house, mark down the current meter reading, and wait 15 to 20 minutes. If the reading has changed, you have a leak.

You can contact your local cooperative extension office by calling the number listed in the phone book. It may be in the white pages under the name of your state's land-grant college; in Pennsylvania, you would look for Penn State Cooperative Extension. Or it may be in the government pages, listed as the agricultural or cooperative extension under the state department of agriculture or the USDA. If none of these options pans out, call your state legislator's office, listed in the government pages.

To reach your state consumer protection agency, look in the government pages of the phone book.

Trimming Home Energy Use

Ever watch your electric meter turn—around and around and around—and wonder just where all that energy is going? Often it's going into energy-guzzling appliances that waste your money. How can you stop it? Turn to your government experts. They can show you how to change your energy consumption habits, help you locate more energy-efficient appliances, and possibly subsidize the cost of buying them.

How to Reduce Electric Leaks

Maybe you've noticed how cats like to curl up on top of a cable television box. That's because it's nice and warm. And how about those power converter packs that you use to plug your answering machine, computer scanner, or other devices into wall outlets? If you touch them, you'll see that they're warm, too. In each case, that means that the device is using electricity even when it's not turned on.

Electricity that leaks from these devices—as well as televisions, VCRs, and cordless phones—wastes more than $1 billion annually, according to the American Council for an Energy-Efficient Economy. This nonprofit research group's aim is to reverse that trend. It works with the U.S. Department of Energy, U.S. Environmental Protection Agency, and other federal agencies to educate the

GETTING HELP PAYING YOUR PHONE BILLS

A telephone isn't a luxury. You need it to call for assistance if you're ill, for example, or to call the fire department if a neighbor's house is on fire, or to call the police if you see a crime taking place.

Realizing this, many state governments have set up programs for people who can't afford to pay for their own phones.

In Tennessee, a program called Link-up will pay half of the installation charges for phone service, up to $30, and ask the phone company to split the remainder of the charge over several months. Then, a second program, the Lifeline Telephone Assistance Program, will subsidize the cost of local phone service, saving up to $10.50 a month.

People who are receiving Supplemental Security Income, Temporary Assistance for Needy Families, food stamps, or Medicaid automatically qualify and can sign up for this program by calling their local telephone service. People whose monthly income is no more than 125 percent of the federal poverty level also qualify. If you think you or a family member might qualify, call your state regulatory authority. The number is in the state government pages of your phone book, under listings such as "Public Utilities Commission," "Public Service Commission," "State Commission," or "Regulatory Authority."

public on waste and encourage manufacturers to redesign machines that draw energy even when the power is off.

One of the easiest cures: Unplug devices that you won't be using soon. Doing this with your cable box alone can reduce electricity use by 10 to 15 watts per hour, points out Jennifer Thorne, research associate with the council and co-author of *Leaking Electricity: Standby and Off-Mode Power Consumption in Consumer Electronics and Household Appliances.*

Another option is replacing the bulky wall packs that power your answering machine, computer scanner, and other small home appliances with "tiny switch" adapters. These new switches—about the size of the plug on the end of a regular electric cord—are not only handier to use and more attractive, but they use far less power than the standard wall packs, says Thorne.

You can find more useful tips like these in *Leaking Electricity*, available for $14. Order it from American Council for an Energy-Efficient Economy, 1001 Connecticut Avenue NW, Suite 801, Washington, DC 20036, or from the group's Web site at www.aceee.org.

Your Personal Energy Advisor

Sure, you'd like to trim your energy use, but how do you do it? Simple: Turn to the Energy Advisor. This Web site is a joint project of the Department of Energy, the Environmental Protection Agency, and the Lawrence Berkeley National Laboratory in Berkeley, California. It will determine the average electric use for a home of your size and type in your region of the country. Then it will guide you through steps you can take to make your equipment more energy-efficient, from the fur-

nace to the air conditioner, refrigerator, and lighting.

The online advisor also will tell you how much each change will save you, then explain what appliances and devices to look for and rank them according to efficiency. You'll even find information on installation and on buying and financing products.

To reach the Web site, just type in http://hes.lbl.gov, then enter your zip code in the box indicated. This lets the program give specific advice according to your region.

Appliances That Are Energy Misers

One of the easiest ways to cut energy use is to buy more efficient appliances in the first place, or so reasons Uncle Sam. So he (actually, the Department of Energy and the Environmental Protection Agency) has partnered with manufacturers and others to create the Energy Star program, which develops products that use significantly less energy than standard ones.

For example, a typical refrigerator made in 1990 uses more than 900 kilowatt hours per year. All Energy Star refrigerators use at least 20 percent less. An Energy Star television requires 3 watts or less of power when turned off, which is just one-quarter as much power as a standard TV.

For an explanation of the program, along with a list of Energy Star products and locations that sell them, write to the U.S. Environmental Protection Agency, Energy Star Programs (6202J), 401 M Street SW, Washington, DC 20460.

At the group's Energy Star Web site at www.energystar.gov, you'll find an explanation of the program and details about specific products as well

FACTOID

IT DOESN'T TAKE MUCH OF A WATER LEAK TO DRIVE UP YOUR BILL. EVEN A LEAK AS SMALL AS A THUMBTACK CAN WASTE MORE THAN 45,000 GALLONS A MONTH.

as a zip-code locator to help you find a store that sells the Energy Star product you're looking for.

●◆ *WHAT INSIDERS SAY:*
Front-loading washing machines can be twice as efficient as the conventional type. These handy machines, which have been popular in Europe for a long time, use one-third as much water as conventional machines. And better yet, studies have shown that front-loading washing machines actually get clothes cleaner.

UNCLE SAM AS YOUR ADVOCATE

When you have a complaint about a utility bill, your first step, of course, is to talk to your utility company. But what if it is unable or unwilling to satisfy you? Then it's time to turn to the government. Several local, state, and federal agencies can provide advice and intercede on your behalf. Here are your best options.

State regulatory agency
Sometimes called public utility commissions, these agencies can do more than just control the rates that a utility charges. In some states, they'll investigate if you complain that a utility has overcharged you, attempted to turn off your service, refused to provide service, or unfairly withheld your security deposit. Also, they can help resolve problems if a long-distance phone company has switched your service without your permission or inaccurately charged you for expensive calls to 900 numbers.

You can find your state agency in the government section of your phone book. It may be listed under the words "Public Utilities Commission," "Public Service Commission," "State Commission," or "Regulatory Authority." You can also find a complete listing of state agencies on the National Association of Regulatory Utility Commissioners Internet site at www.naruc.org. Click on "Resources," then "State PUC."

Consumer protection offices
These agencies investigate complaints and problems with utility companies and offer educational materials and advice.

The Ohio Consumers' Counsel, for example, will walk you through the process of making a formal complaint against a utility. It will even furnish the phone numbers and addresses of contacts for complaints outside its jurisdiction (the agency cannot handle complaints about services provided by municipalities or nonprofit utilities).

To contact your consumer protection agency, look in the government pages of your phone book. Depending on which level of government runs the agency, the number could be under the local, county, or state listings.

Federal Communications Commission
The Federal Communications Commission governs telecommunications and can answer questions about long-distance charges, the practice of "slamming" (unauthorized changing of your phone service), and "cramming" (unauthorized addition of phone services such as call waiting or caller ID).

For information, write to the Federal Communications Commission, Common Carrier Bureau, 1919 M Street NW, Washington, DC 20554. Also, if you have access to the Internet, you can find detailed information sheets by going to the agency's Web site at www.fcc.gov and clicking on "Consumer Info."

Loans, Subsidies, and Free Services

It may seem surprising, but in some areas, the government and utility companies will bend over backward to help you save money on utility bills. In Richland, Washington, the city supplies free reduced-flow showerheads and aerators that will cut water use in the kitchen and bathroom. Also, Richland will make loans of up to $15,000 at interest rates as low as 3 percent so people can buy more energy-efficient appliances.

On the other side of the country, Central Maine Power offers a free "Bundle Up" insulation kit to trim the cost of running a water heater and sells compact fluorescent lightbulbs at reduced prices.

Some utilities also offer incentives to get you to dump an energy-wasting appliance. Southern California Edison passes out $50 U.S. Savings Bonds or $25 checks to folks who buy more efficient refrigerators, and it will even pick up your old unit.

To track down programs like these, call the main office of your city or town (listed in the government pages of the phone book) or call the number listed on a recent electric bill. Ask if either one provides energy audits, loans, or free kits or equipment such as showerheads.

HOME SAFETY

Your home is your castle—and of course, you consider it a cozy, comfortable, and safe place. Without realizing it, though, you could have several hidden hazards that may endanger you and your family.

You may have a dangerous toy, for instance, harmful chemicals that are stored incorrectly, or a refrigerator that's at risk of toppling over if a toddler tugs on it.

What can you do to eliminate the hazards? Plenty. The first step is staying informed, and there are numerous government and nonprofit agencies that are eager to keep you up-to-date.

Warnings on Unsafe Products

Did you hear on television or by word of mouth that a certain toy or home product is unsafe? Or are you just worried about a product that you fear may be dangerous? Check it out!

The U.S. Consumer Product Safety Commission can furnish information on products that have been deemed dangerous as well as take reports from consumers who have concerns about goods. You can write the Consumer Product Safety Commission, Washington, DC 20207 for information or visit the group's Web site at www.cpsc.gov. Once at the Web site, just click on "Recalls."

Hazard and Recall Warnings

The commission also publishes the *Consumer Product Safety Review*, a quarterly publication that reviews home hazards and reports on current product recalls. To subscribe, send a $10 check to Superintendent of Documents, P.O. Box 371954, Pittsburgh, PA 15250-7954. Or you can read the publication on the Internet at www.cpsc.gov. When you reach the site, click on the search button and type in "Consumer Product Safety Review."

Health and Safety Advice

The FDA offers a bimonthly magazine, *FDA Consumer*, that provides health advice, safety warnings, and recall information on everything the FDA regulates, including food, drugs, medical devices, and cosmetics.

FACTOID

MANY PEOPLE BELIEVE THAT CARS ARE THE BIGGEST SOURCE OF AIR POLLUTION IN THEIR PERSONAL LIVES. NOT SO, SAYS THE ENERGY DEPARTMENT. THE FUEL USED TO GENERATE POWER FOR THE AVERAGE HOME CAUSES TWICE AS MUCH POLLUTION AS THE AVERAGE CAR.

To subscribe, send a check for $10 to Superintendent of Documents, P.O. Box 371954, Pittsburgh, PA 15250-7954. You can also read the magazine free on the Internet. Type in www.fda.gov, then click on the search button and look for "FDA consumer magazine." This will give you access to current or past issues. One advantage of online reading is that besides being free, the articles are updated as new information becomes available.

Fire-Safety Inspections

Instead of waiting until your house is on fire to call the fire department, why not call now to arrange an inspection that may prevent that situation from ever arising? Many local fire departments around the country will send experts to your home for free to tell you about obvious (and not-so-obvious) fire hazards.

If you live in Sugar Land, Texas, for example, the fire department will send out an entire engine company crew (that's four firefighters) to inspect your house from top to bottom.

Sugar Land inspectors spend up to an hour examining smoke detectors, making sure your fireplace isn't a fire hazard, and scoping out where you store flammable materials. If your smoke detectors don't make the grade, the inspectors will install new ones for free. The firefighters will also assess things that you may not have thought of, such as making sure that each bedroom window can be opened easily and that the numbers on your house are visible from the street. Such seemingly trivial matters can become crucial during a fire, when a few wasted seconds can make the difference in preventing a tragedy.

To find out if your department offers inspections, call its general number (not 911!). You'll find it listed in the government pages of your telephone book.

➤❖ *WHAT INSIDERS SAY:*

When you call for a fire inspection, resist the temptation to clean your house and yard before inspectors arrive. If you do, you may remove exactly what they're looking for: the potential fire hazards that you usually have around your home. "We like them to just let us come in and see everything as is," says Lieutenant Troy Holby, public education specialist for the Sugar Land Fire Department. "We want to see what the house is like on a normal basis."

Fire-Prevention Checklist

If your local fire department doesn't offer safety inspections, you can locate potential fire hazards yourself, using a detailed survey offered by the Consumer Product Safety Commission.

Called "Your Home Fire Safety Checklist" (#556), the survey is available in printed form by writing to the Consumer Product Safety Commission, Attn: Publications, Office of Information and Public Affairs, Washington, DC 20207. Or, if you have access to the Internet, you can find the survey on the group's Web site at www.cpsc.gov. Just click on the Web site's search button and type in the name of the survey.

Keeping Junior Safe

More than 2 million American children are injured or killed each year by hazards in their homes. Many of these incidents are easily preventable with the use of simple safety devices and knowledge about safety hazards.

Childproofing a home needn't be expensive; even something as simple as emptying a half-filled mop bucket can save a toddler's life. Here's information from the government that will help you spot potential problems and quickly clear them up.

FACTOID

ONE-QUARTER TO ONE-THIRD OF ALL SMOKE DETECTORS DO NOT WORK IN AN ACTUAL FIRE, MOST OFTEN BECAUSE THE BATTERY HAS BEEN REMOVED OR ISN'T WORKING. YOU SHOULD TEST YOUR BATTERY MONTHLY AND REPLACE IT ANNUALLY, PERHAPS WHEN YOU TURN YOUR CLOCKS FORWARD FOR DAYLIGHT SAVING TIME.

THE MOTHER LODE OF CONSUMER ADVICE

Want to know the best type of windows to install? How to prune your trees? The best way to cheer up a depressed friend? The answers await you at the Consumer Information Center in Pueblo, Colorado, a facility the size of a football field that's packed with millions of informative and inexpensive publications.

The center is a clearing-house for consumer information from many federal agencies and departments, explains Carole Collins, senior media specialist at the center. And that work keeps the 82-member staff busy. In 1998, they shipped out a total of 8 million publications.

First on the list? "The Consumer's Resource Handbook." "It tells you how to complain effectively," says Collins. The free handbook suggests ways to resolve disputes and lists thousands of names, consumer contacts, and the addresses, telephone numbers, and e-mail addresses of corporations, trade groups, and state, local, and federal consumer protection offices.

Here are the next four "best-sellers" and their costs.

✓ "Social Security: Understanding the Benefits" (free)

✓ "Guide to Government Sales" ($2)

✓ "Action Guide to Healthy Eating" (free)

✓ "Where to Write for Vital Records" ($2.25)

Another popular publication is the "Parents Guide to the Internet" (50 cents), which provides advice on how to set up your computer so your child can take advantage of the Internet without encountering dangerous or inappropriate material. And the center has slightly more off-kilter stuff as well, such as "The Civil War at a Glance" and "For the Birds" (which has nothing to do with sex, we should emphasize—it's a guide to building bird-houses).

The Consumer Information Center, established in 1970 as a division of the U.S. General Services Administration, advertises itself as a "one-stop shopping center" for federal consumer publications. It constantly reviews publications from the agencies to select material for the catalog and suggests possible topics.

For titles and descriptions of more than 200 publications available free or for a nominal charge, request the "Consumer Information Catalog." It's published quarterly and is divided into sections such as cars, health, housing, children, money, and so on. Twelve million were printed in 1998.

To order publications, write to the Consumer Information Center, Pueblo, CO 81009. If you have access to the Internet, the easiest and fastest way to get documents is to sign on to www.pueblo.gsa.gov. Simply click on the category that interests you or click "Search" to find a specific topic. Once you find a publication you want, you can order it, or you can click the title of the publication to read it, print it, or save it to your computer. In fact, says Collins, the number of printed publications is decreasing because more people are downloading them from the Web site.

12 Ways to Reduce Risks

The Consumer Product Safety Commission (CPSC) has identified a dozen devices that it says will make your small children a whole lot safer. Some are low-cost, such as safety latches for doors and corner bumpers for sharp cabinets. Others are a bit more pricey, such as carbon monoxide detectors and cordless phones (they give you the mobility to keep an eye on toddlers).

You can get the entire list, along with suggested prices for the devices, in the booklet "Childproofing Your Home." Write to the Consumer Product Safety Commission, Attn: Publications, Office of Information and Public Affairs, Washington, DC 20207. Or you can view the entire booklet at the group's Web site at www.cpsc.gov. When you get to the site, click the search button and type in the name of the publication.

➥ WHAT INSIDERS SAY:

Even seemingly harmless objects around the home can be hazards, say experts. For example, the loops formed by the ends of the cords on window blinds can strangle children. The solution is simple: Cut the loops. Ditto for the drawstrings on the hoods of coats or sweatshirts. Either pull the cord out or snip it and sew down the ends.

Preventing Drowning

It's Saturday morning—time to clean house. You've filled your mop bucket, and now you're ready to clean the kitchen floor. Do you know what else you've done? You've just created a potential hazard.

About 50 children a year drown in buckets, and 5-gallon joint compound–type buckets are particularly dangerous because they're tall enough that toddlers cannot free themselves if they fall in headfirst. Home spas, hot tubs, or whirlpools can also be quite dangerous; children's hair can get caught in the drains, and the suction can hold their heads underwater.

Ways to protect your children from these and other drowning hazards are covered in these free brochures.

POSITIVELY KIDPROOF

To Larry and Leslie Stone, the government warnings on child safety at home are more than just good advice; they're concrete rules to live by. The Stones, authors of *The Safe and Sound Child* and owners of Safety Matters, a child-safety business, have developed what may be the ultimate childproof home, equipped top to bottom with safety equipment to protect their three children (ages 6, 4, and 2).

We're not talking simply baby gates and cabinet latches. The Stones have toilet locks that prevent young children from falling in. Plexiglas is installed along stair railings and balconies to eliminate falls and other accidents, and pads cover furniture with sharp corners. A bathtub spout cover prevents kids who fall from chipping teeth, and detachable cords on the blinds avert dangerous tangles.

"Every time we tried to take everything down, I got pregnant again," she says, "so we've had this stuff up for the past 6 years."

Any words of advice from the Stones? "No matter how much childproof equipment you've put up, your baby will try to find a way around it," says Leslie. "Childproofing just gives you an extra minute to foil their schemes."

✓ "How to Plan for the Unexpected—Preventing Child Drownings" (#359)

✓ "Safety Barrier Guidelines for Home Pools" (#362)

✓ "Guidelines for Entrapment Hazards: Making Pools and Spas Safer" (#363)

✓ "Drowning Hazard with Baby 'Supporting Ring' Devices" (#5084)

To order these publications, write to Consumer Product Safety Commission, Attn: Publications, Office of Information and Public Affairs, Washington, DC 20207. Or you can find them on the group's Web site at www.cpsc.gov. Just click on the site's search button and type in the name of the publication you want to see.

◆◆ WHAT INSIDERS SAY:

The CPSC has dozens of child-safety brochures covering everything from poisoning to sleepwear. For a catalog of all publications, write to the address listed above or go the home page of the group's Web site. Click on "Library," then on "CPSC Publications." This will take you to a list of publications that you can read on the spot or print out.

CLEANING THE AIR

Are you or your children bothered by runny or swollen noses? Are you clogged up and wheezy every morning? The problem could be allergies or even asthma attacks that are triggered by various allergy-producing substances. Key among the common sources are droppings of dust mites (tiny insects that you can't even see), animal dander, particles of dead skin, cockroach droppings and saliva, and mold.

The first step in ending your problem is to rid your home of these things. Here are your best sources of information and advice.

Advice on Beating Allergies

Fungi or molds growing in your home can damage the quality of the air you breathe—and they can damage your health as well. To help you identify and eliminate these problems, the Consumer Product Safety Commission and the American Lung Association have produced a publication called "Biological Pollutants in Your Home."

Another useful publication is "Asthma, Air Quality, and Environmental Justice." It discusses

TOP SOURCES OF ALLERGENS IN THE HOME

Home safe home? Not when you're talking about allergies. The floors, walls, and furnishings of your home can host a wide range of allergy triggers. Here are the five major allergens and their sources.

✓ Moisture, molds, mildew, and dust mites. Sources include high humidity, poorly maintained humidifiers and air conditioners, inadequate ventilation, and animal dander.

✓ Formaldehyde. Sources include drapes, furniture and cabinets built from particleboard, and adhesives.

✓ Household products and furnishings. Sources include paints, solvents, air fresheners, dry-cleaned clothing, aerosol sprays, and adhesives and fabric additives in carpeting and furniture.

✓ Airborne particles. Sources include fireplaces, woodstoves, kerosene heaters, unvented gas space heaters, dust, and pollen.

✓ Tobacco smoke.

education and prevention programs to combat asthma and includes tips to reduce asthma triggers such as pollution in your home and the outside environment.

You can order either publication from the National Service Center for Environmental Publications, P.O. Box 42419, Cincinnati, OH 45242, or find them on the Internet at www.epa.gov. Click on the site's search button, then enter the name of the publication you want.

➡◆ WHAT INSIDERS SAY:

The most important step you can take to control your allergies is to make your bed safe, because that's the primary source of contact with allergens. How to do it? Put allergen-proof coverings on pillowcases and mattresses. These are made of tightly woven fabric (not plastic) that keeps the dust mites out while allowing moisture to flow through.

Free Tips from a Nurse

Sometimes you need answers, and quickly. That's what's available from the nonprofit National Jewish Medical and Research Center in Denver. The center has a toll-free 800 number called the Lung Line, where registered nurses can answer your questions about asthma, allergies, or lung diseases and can send you literature. From the Lung Line you also can reach the toll-free Lung Facts, a free automated information service that's available 24 hours a day with information about asthma, emphysema, and other lung diseases.

To locate the Lung Line number, call the 800 operator listed in your phone book. If you have access to the Internet, you can also find the numbers on the National Jewish Web site: Just use the search function on your Internet browser to look for "National Jewish Medical."

➡◆ WHAT INSIDERS SAY:

If you have allergies, have someone else vacuum your house when you're not around. Vacuums launch dust mite leavings, animal dander, and other allergy sources into the air, where you can breathe them in. Dust mite particles will settle down within three-quarters of an hour after vacuuming, although animal dander takes longer. Your best bet is to schedule vacuuming when you'll be gone all day, or to try using a carpet sweeper instead. Also avoid vacuums that filter dust into water; they can emit a fine mist filled with allergens.

CHAPTER 9

GETTING HELP GETTING AROUND

Whether pushing across the prairies in covered wagons or riding rockets to the moon, Americans have always been a people on the go. And it isn't just pioneers and astronauts who are doing the traveling. Americans own more than 130 million cars and motorcycles, which they use to travel across 2.38 million miles of paved roads.

Government workers are no exception. Federal, state, and local agencies use every imaginable vehicle for every imaginable purpose, from the sedans that administrators drive around town to the 18-wheel trucks used to haul large volumes of mail. When the time comes for agencies to trade for newer models, they don't just scrap the old ones. They offer them to the public in sales and auctions held around the country.

> Cars. Trucks. Boats. Bicycles. No matter where your transportation need lies, the government can help you fill it—providing dependable transportation while saving you a good deal of cash.

And when the government isn't traveling itself, it's working toward making your traveling easier. All this means that if you're trying to move from here to there on a budget, the government just may have a way to help you.

Of course, some opportunities are better than others, but after you read the insider advice in this chapter, you'll be well-equipped to do everything from buying the right used vehicle to pleading the case for better public transportation.

Interested? Let's roll.

LOW-COST VEHICLES
Government agencies love to sell their old cars and trucks for one obvious reason: Doing so pours a lot more money back into their budgets

FACTOID

THE U.S. GOVERNMENT GENERAL SERVICES ADMINISTRATION ALONE SELLS NEARLY 50,000 CARS AND TRUCKS EACH YEAR, AND IT IS ONLY ONE OF MANY AGENCIES THAT SELL FEDERAL VEHICLES.

than simply trashing them would. It also reduces the load at local landfills and helps people become mobile in a less expensive way. The thousands of surplus vehicles generated each year create a huge market, and there are plenty of bargain opportunities for shoppers who know where to look.

In addition to surplus vehicles, the government also unloads thousands of vehicles seized by law enforcement agencies each year. Many of these vehicles, unlike surplus items, are virtually brand-new. So, whether you're a weekend mechanic looking for an old heap or a would-be James Bond looking for a fast, sleek set of wheels, chances are good that you can get what you're looking for from a government agency.

Surplus from the GSA

The General Services Administration (GSA), which buys equipment for the federal government, is also responsible for disposing of much of what the government no longer needs. The GSA's Federal Supply Service sells a wide variety of used vehicles through several regional offices around the country. Sales methods include sealed-bid auctions, live auctions, spot-bid auctions, and fixed-price sales.

To find out about upcoming sales, write the sales office in your region (see the list on page 55) and ask to be put on the free mailing list (most of the offices offer this service). When writing, address your request to "Personal Property Sales." While you're at it, ask for the free brochure, "How You Can Buy Used Federal Personal Property," with lots of good information and contacts for the entire realm of things that the agency sells.

Since the GSA sells vehicles and other surplus equipment for a wide variety of government agencies, it follows that the types and conditions of the items vary greatly as well. You can find everything from older, high-mileage sedans that need work to newer vehicles in more pristine condition.

"Relatively new cars, with as little as 10,000 miles on them—cars worth upwards of $20,000 new—might sell for as little as $6,000," says Ray Arnold, automotive equipment specialist for the GSA. These are cars, Arnold adds, that have received "immaculate" care.

For information on upcoming sales dates, check out the GSA's Web site on the Internet at http://pub.fss.gsa.gov/property. Or look for sales information in the U.S. Department of Commerce's *Commerce Business Daily*. This paper, published Monday through Friday, is available at federal depository libraries and on the Internet at www.access.gpo.gov. Click on "Access to Government Information Products." You can subscribe to the print version at a cost of $275 a year by writing to the Superintendent of Documents, U.S. Government Printing Office, P.O. Box 371954, Pittsburgh, PA 15250-7954.

The Postal Service

Looking for a vehicle that "neither snow, nor rain, nor heat, nor gloom of night" can stop? That quote, of course, is from the unofficial motto of the U.S. Postal Service, which sells thousands of surplus vehicles each year. These range from passenger cars used by administrators to local delivery trucks and 18-wheel, long-haul trucks.

While some government agencies sell vehicles only after they've accumulated high mileage, the Postal Service trades in its delivery fleet based on years of service. Since some mail routes in more densely populated areas cover only a few miles, here's your chance to pick up an older vehicle with relatively low mileage at a very reasonable price, according to the Postal Service headquarters in Washington, D.C.

Surplus Postal Service vehicles are sold by vehicle maintenance facilities around the country. Some are sold by auction, others by fixed-price sale.

An added benefit is that the Postal Service has a complete maintenance program that keeps the vehicles in top operating condition. That said, vehicles are sold "as is," and all sales are final. But prospective customers are permitted to take vehicles for a spin around the grounds prior to purchase. Since you're buying the vehicle directly from the maintenance shop, you will be able to read over each vehicle's complete maintenance records before you buy it.

To find out dates of upcoming sales in your area, call or visit your local post office and ask for the number and address of the nearest vehicle maintenance facility. You can also get the local phone number by visiting the Postal Service Web site (www.usps.gov or www. usps.com). Click on "Inside the Postal Service," "Consumer Information," and "Buy Surplus Postal Service Vehicles." The site lists 190 maintenance facilities organized by state and locale. If the facility that you call says that there are no imminent sales planned in your area, ask to be placed on a mailing list to alert you when the next sale comes up.

Seized Vehicles Sold by the Treasury

If your tastes lean more toward the fancy and luxurious than toward the standard-issue vehicles sold as government surplus, then sales of items seized by law enforcement agencies may be for you. It's in these sales that you are likely to find souped-up sports cars, luxury sedans, and so forth.

The Bureau of Alcohol, Tobacco, and Firearms; the U.S. Customs Service; the Secret Service; and the IRS—all of which operate under the U.S. Department of the Treasury—together sell $46 million worth of vehicles and other seized goods per year. The reasons for the seizures range from drug violations to failure to pay taxes or customs duties.

Amazing Stories

THE LONG-DISTANCE DEAL

Anthony Nardino was somewhat nervous in October of 1992 as he bought a car at a General Services Administration auction in Edison, New Jersey.

"I had never been to an auction before in my life, so it was a little unnerving to walk out with a car," he says. The car, a 1989 Chevrolet Celebrity, had 31,000 miles on it, and it fell into his lap for a relatively paltry $4,300.

Seven years later, the car was still going strong, with 149,000 miles on the odometer. "I've had to do the normal maintenance stuff to it, but nothing out of the ordinary," says Nardino. In fact, the auction was such a positive experi-ence for him that he attended another to re-plenish the family fleet. "That time, I found a Chevy Corsica for a great price, as well as a Dodge Daytona for my 17-year-old son," he says. To keep the positive karma going, Nardino do-nated the still-running Celebrity to the Kidney Foundation, where it was re-auctioned.

Nardino's advice for the first time auction-goer? "The auctions take place fairly often, so it's not a bad idea to sit through one and just ob-serve the action, without bidding," he suggests. "Just watching some of the savvy types bid will give you a sense of how the procedures work and what's a fair price."

Sales are handled exclusively by a private company, EG&G Services, which is based in northern Virginia.

Bid prices may range from several hundred dollars for an old, high-mileage car to $70,000 for a fully loaded Mercedes-Benz or more than $100,000 for a Ferrari. Insiders say that while there are bargains to be had—chances are, you'll pay considerably less for a seized vehicle than for one off the showroom floor—don't expect to drive off with a $5 sports car. "You get deals, not steals," says Kerry Cooper, public relations coordinator for EG&G Services.

To give you an idea of what's available, here is a sampling of vehicles offered at one EG&G auction in Edison, New Jersey.

✓ 1998 BMW 528i sedan with 8,925 miles

✓ 1995 Lincoln Town Car limousine, with a TV, VCR, maroon leather interior, and room for eight

✓ 1993 Winnebago motor home with 51,000 miles

✓ 1986 Toyota Corolla with 149,000 miles

✓ 1994 red Harley Davidson "Dynaglide" motorcycle with just 15 miles

General auctions are held every 9 weeks at five locations around the country: Edison, New Jersey; Miami/Ft. Lauderdale; El Paso, Texas; Los Angeles; and Nogales, Arizona. Vehicle auctions are also held approximately every 4 weeks at Chula Vista, California.

Items are open to public inspection prior to each sale. For information and dates on specific auctions, write to EG&G Services at 3702 Pender Drive, Suite 400, Fairfax, VA 22030. Or check out the Treasury Department's Web site at www.treas.gov/auctions/customs.

➡❖ WHAT INSIDERS SAY:

Serious buyers may want to subscribe to a flyer service that will keep them updated on items for sale at upcoming auctions. Subscriptions are $25 per year for information on either eastern or western U.S sales or $50 for a national subscription. Contact the above address or go to the Web site for more information.

Buying from the Marshals

Another good source for seized vehicles is the U.S. Marshals Service. Part of the U.S. Department of Justice, the service includes such agencies as the Drug Enforcement Administration, the Immigration and Naturalization Service, and the FBI. Seized goods come from drug dealers and a wide variety of other offenders.

The Marshals Service doesn't conduct auctions and sales itself but sells some vehicles through the General Services Administration and contracts out to a wide range of professional auctioneers and brokers around the country. One of the larger contractors is Atlanta-based Manheim Auctions, Inc., which handles luxury cars, jewelry, fine antiques, and many other items. For information on locations, dates, and items for sale at upcoming Manheim auctions of government goods, write to Manheim Auctions, Inc., 1400 Lake Hearn Drive, Atlanta, GA 30315.

Other auctions of items collected by the Marshals Service are run by private auctioneers and brokers. The Marshals Service does not maintain a mailing list to let buyers know when sales are taking place, but the sales are usually advertised in the classified sections of newspa-

FACTOID

IF YOU WANT TO BUY A FOUR-WHEEL-DRIVE VEHICLE FROM THE POSTAL SERVICE, YOU'LL HAVE TO TRAVEL TO ALASKA TO GET ONE. THAT'S THE ONLY STATE IN WHICH LETTER CARRIERS USE FOUR-WHEEL-DRIVES.

pers where they are to be held. Also, you can find out about upcoming sales by contacting the private sellers directly. A list of all of the private auctioneers and brokers who contract with the Marshals Service, as well as the federal agencies that sell property for it, is available on the Internet at www.usdoj.gov/marshals (click on "Seized Assets") or at www.pueblo.gsa.gov (use the search function to look for "national sellers list"). You can also get the list by mail, but that means sending a check or money order for 50 cents to the Consumer Information Center, Dept. 386E, Pueblo, CO 81009.

Shopping for Military Vehicles

The branches of the U.S. military generate thousands of types of surplus items, including a vast array of sedans, trucks, and other vehicles. With a few notable exceptions (see "What the Military *Won't* Sell You" on page 134), "everything under the sun" goes to the public through sale or auction, says Chuck J. Beebe, property marketing specialist for the Defense Reutilization and Marketing Service (DRMS). This service, based in Battle Creek, Michigan, sells most of the surplus goods generated by the military.

Such high-value items as ships or airplane parts are sold through the national sales office in Battle Creek. Individual vehicles such as pickup trucks, sedans, and even ambulances and buses are sold at more than 100 local marketing offices, usually located at or near military installations. These sales are advertised in local newspapers and on radio, but your best bet is to get a catalog. The most frequent sale method is spot-bid auctions.

To find the nearest DRMS office, you can write to DRMS, National Sales Office, 74 North Washington Avenue, Suite 6, Battle Creek, MI 49017-3092. You'll receive a free sales information kit that lists locations of local offices and the types of items sold. The kit also includes applications to sign up for free catalogs for various types of goods. DRMS

sales are also advertised in *Commerce Business Daily*, which you can read at the library. The best information source, though, is the service's Web site at www.drms.dla.mil. The site offers a comprehensive catalog of items for sale, listed by category and item.

Surplus Wheels from Your State

Federal agencies aren't the only ones that sell used cars and trucks. State governments also generate surplus vehicles by the thousands, which they offer to you, the public, through periodic auctions. Whether your needs include a subcompact sedan or a tractor for an 18-wheel semi truck, chances are, you can find what you're looking for at a bargain price.

Each state has its own way of collecting and selling vehicles and other surplus goods. In Kentucky, items from virtually all agencies are consolidated and sold by the Division of Surplus Property in Frankfort, the capital. Throughout the year, the division auctions off cruisers formerly used by the state police, Ford Tauruses used by administrators, or heavy trucks used by the transportation department.

Vehicles used by state agencies may be fairly new, and all have received regular maintenance. But don't expect to find one with low mileage. Agencies are bound to get their money's worth out of a car or truck before they sell it as surplus. "Very rarely does the state get rid of a vehicle with less than 100,000 miles on it," says Don Murphy, program coordinator for the Kentucky Division of Surplus Property.

High-mileage (160,000 and up) Chevrolet Caprice or Ford Taurus sedans may sell for as little as $500 to $1,000, Murphy says. Sport utility vehicles command a higher price. During one sale, Ford Broncos nearly a decade old sold for $3,000 to $5,000 apiece. In the market for some really big stuff? A semi tractor in decent running condition, with 300,000 to 500,000 miles on it (trucks are built for higher mileage than cars) might sell for $15,000 to $17,000.

The Division of Surplus Property holds its auctions periodically as items become available. During one period of budget cutbacks, the division curtailed its mailing list informing potential customers of upcoming sales. If you have access to the Internet, though, visit the division's Web site at www.state.ky.us/agencies/purch/auction.htm. The site is well-organized and is regularly updated with news of auctions.

If you live outside Kentucky, call the agency in your state that handles surplus property to find out how and where they conduct sales. Finding the right department may take a call or two, as they go by different names in different states. Some may operate under the finance department, while others are part of the state's general services department. If you don't have any luck finding the right number, most state governments have a general information number listed in the phone book's government pages. Call it and ask who handles surplus property.

●◆ WHAT INSIDERS SAY:

If hunting and fishing are your passions, or you simply like rugged vehicles and gear, the annual Kentucky Department of Fish and Wildlife Resources auction is for you. In addition to high-mileage surplus vehicles used by wildlife rangers, the sale includes vehicles (some nearly brand-new) and equipment seized from illegal hunters and fishermen. In other words, if some joker is caught spotlighting for deer in his late-model cherry red Blazer, that truck (along with whatever gear was in it) could be yours at a bargain.

The Fish and Wildlife sale, run by the state's Divi-

WORKING A GOVERNMENT AUCTION

Just about everyone has heard the myths about walking into a government auction, plunking down $1, and driving off with a fancy sports car or a 50-foot yacht. Well, it doesn't work that way. Government sellers reserve the right to refuse any winning bid if it's too low, and they won't hesitate to do so.

That doesn't mean that you can't find bargain wheels at a government auction, but it helps to be prepared. Here are some tips from the experts on getting the most out of a government auction.

Your first step should be to get a copy of the "The U.S. General Services Administration Guide to Federal Government Sales," a clear, well-written booklet that explains who sells what throughout the federal government.

The opening sections of the booklet offer good, general advice on government sales. The balance traces each federal agency, showing what specific types of items that agency sells, how they are sold, and how to buy them. If you have access to the Internet, the easiest and cheapest way to view this handy document is at the General Services Administration Web site, www.pueblo. gsa.gov. If you don't have access to the Internet, you can order the booklet by mail by sending $2 to R. Woods, Consumer Information Center, P.O. Box 100, Pueblo, CO 81009.

Here are some other tips that insiders recommend for getting a good deal.

Go with a car buff

If all you know about cars is how to turn the ignition key, "my suggestion is to take somebody with you who knows about vehicles, such as a hob-

sion of Surplus Property and held the first Monday in May, is the only state sale that's held on the same day each year. It starts at 9:00 A.M. at the Fish and Wildlife headquarters at Number 1 Game Farm Road, Frankfort, Kentucky. For more information, visit the surplus property Web site at www.state.ky.us/ agencies/purch/auction.htm.

Note: *Surplus goods are available to anyone, but only Kentucky residents may bid on seized items.*

BOATS AT A BARGAIN

If your personal flotilla is short a battleship, you may be out of luck. The government cuts up old warships and sells them for scrap to avoid having them fall into the wrong hands. But if you're looking for a good general-purpose boat, one not

decked out with weaponry, military surplus offers lots to choose from. Beyond these, you'll find opportunities to buy nearly new boats that have been confiscated by federal law enforcement agencies. Here are your best opportunities.

Military Surplus

The Defense Reutilization and Marketing Service (DRMS), based in Battle Creek, Michigan, sells surplus equipment, including boats, for all branches of the military. The boats that are for sale by the DRMS range from inflatable rafts and rowboats to 74-foot landing craft, 50-foot work boats, and 40-foot utility boats.

Of course, you may want to use them for fishing or business, but the uses for these old boats

byist or mechanic," says Don Murphy, program coordinator for the Kentucky Division of Surplus Property in Frankfort. The quality of and amount of wear and tear on surplus vehicles varies widely, and it helps to have someone along who can look under the hood and tell you what you're buying.

Get there early

Even if you can't cajole a car expert into tagging along, just about every government agency holding an auction will have a public inspection period a few days before or on the day of the sale. "Take advantage of the inspection date, and get to the auction site as

early as possible," Murphy says. That way, you won't find yourself assessing and bidding at the same time.

Know the terms of the sale

Most vehicles are sold "as is." Sales agents do their best to accurately describe the condition of the vehicle when they put it out for auction, but there's always the possibility that they'll miss something.

Even after you've successfully bid on a vehicle, it pays to give it a final, close inspection before removing it from the premises. If you notice something amiss, "speak now, or forever hold your peace," says Chuck J. Beebe, property

marketing specialist for the Michigan-based Defense Reutilization and Marketing Service, which sells surplus equipment for the military. This may be your only chance to get a refund. Once you've removed it from the sales lot, the item is yours, and returning it may be difficult or impossible.

Also, find out in advance which payment methods are accepted. Most agencies require a guaranteed payment such as money order, certified check, or cash, although some will accept credit cards. The guide to federal government sales is a good source for such information.

are limited only by your imagination. "We've had people wanting to make houseboats out of them," says Dennis L. Gohl, property disposal specialist for the DRMS.

Boats are sold at local marketing offices around the country, usually located at or near military installations. Boats under 24 feet in length are sold directly by the local office. For anything larger, the sale is handled by the national sales office in Battle Creek, although the boat remains at the local site.

These military surplus boat auctions are by sealed bid. You may place your bid by mail, fax, or e-mail using the DRMS Web site at www.drms.dla.mil.

For information on upcoming sales and to find the nearest local office, write DRMS, National Sales Office, 74 North Washington Avenue, Suite 6, Battle Creek, MI 49017-3092. You'll receive a free sales information kit listing locations of the local offices and the types of items sold. The kit also includes applications to sign up for free catalogs listing various types of goods. DRMS sales are also advertised in *Commerce Business Daily*, which you can read at the library.

The best information source, though, is the agency's Web site (see above). The site offers a comprehensive rundown of sale items, listed by category and item.

Items for sale change constantly. Gohl suggests consulting the Web site weekly to keep abreast of unusual sales. For instance, not too long ago, the

HOW TO BUY A USED (BUT NOT ABUSED) CAR

One of the good things about buying a surplus vehicle from the government, as opposed to a used car from another source, is that you know for sure who the previous owner was. Also, since government agencies follow strict maintenance schedules, you can be reasonably certain that the vehicle was well-maintained.

Still, the fact remains that wherever you buy it, a used car has by definition been around the block a few times, and the risks of getting a dud are inherently greater than with a new car. "Even if you aren't a car expert, you can help minimize your risk by looking for a few trouble spots when inspecting a used car," says Randy Green, manager of public affairs for the American Automobile Association (AAA) Mid-Atlantic division in Richmond, Virginia. AAA offers the following tips to help prevent used-car buyers from being taken for a ride.

✓ Examine the lower edges of the car body, behind the bumpers, and around the rocker panels below the door for rusted-out spots. Also check doorsills, floors, and the inside of the trunk. Cars with large rusted-out areas should be rejected.

✓ Check for badly worn tires, including the spare. Uneven wear on any tire could indicate front-end trouble.

✓ Inspect the inside of the tailpipe. A light gray color indicates proper combustion, while a dark, sooty appearance could mean that the car is burning oil because of excessive piston and ring wear.

✓ Remove the radiator cap to be sure that the coolant is clean and the cap itself

Army declared a load of new, three-person inflatable rafts as surplus, offering a rare opportunity to buy brand-new equipment at a bargain.

Because the types and conditions of boats vary greatly, it's difficult to arrive at a standardized price range, Gohl says. Bids on a used 40-foot utility boat, for example, ranged from a low of $351 to a winning bid of $3,000. The best thing to do is decide on a price you feel comfortable with and submit that as your bid, Gohl says.

Some boats are sea-worthy, with engines intact and in working order. Others may be stripped to the bone and good mainly for spare parts. Sellers will describe the boats as accurately as possible, but it behooves any buyer to inspect a boat carefully before bidding.

When reading the description of a boat for sale, pay special attention to what the buyer's responsibilities are for removing it.

If the boat is sitting out of water in a shipyard, for example, the government in some cases will supply a crane to load the boat onto your truck. If not, renting a crane could cost you several hundred dollars—money that you should factor in when you're deciding on a bid price.

Seized Boats

As with vehicles, the snazzy end of government boat sales comes not from surplus but from seizures by agencies such as the Bureau of Alcohol, Tobacco,

does not have caked-on rust. Check the back of the radiator for obvious leaks.

✓ Step down on the brake pedal, maintaining a steady pressure for at least a minute. If the pedal continues to sink, brake repairs may be in order.

✓ Start the engine, listening for loud or unusual noises. All gauges and warning lights should go on and then go off after the engine starts.

✓ Check headlights, taillights, brake lights, and turn indicators for proper functioning.

During the test drive

Ask if you can test-drive the car. Some government agencies allow this, although perhaps only on their property. Still, that will give you a chance to check for the following conditions.

✓ A wobbly steering wheel and ride could indicate bad ball joints, misalignment of the front wheels, or the need for a balancing job. The automatic transmission (if the car has one) should work smoothly, with no slamming sounds or lurching of the car.

✓ Accelerate quickly from low speed to about 55 miles per hour so that the engine labors. If the car picks up speed smoothly without bucking, missing, or hesitating, the engine is probably in good condition.

✓ Make several sharp turns at low speed. The steering wheel should not stiffen up or become difficult to turn. If the car has power steering, there should be no squeaks or moans.

✓ Make several hard stops, decelerating from about 45 miles per hour. The pedal should remain high and solid. If it becomes spongy or there is a sudden swerving or grabbing, the car may well have brake trouble.

and Firearms; the U.S. Customs Service; the Secret Service; and the IRS.

"We have everything from 15-foot Boston Whalers to 149-foot freighters," says Kerry Cooper of EG&G Services, the private company that sells seized goods for these agencies.

"Most of the boats come from drug smugglers or money launderers," Cooper says, and they command a fair price. A 15-foot Boston Whaler in good condition may go for $8,000 to $15,000 at auction. As for the 149-foot freighter, that brought $78,000. Other boats include Carolina trawler fishing boats and even occasional "cigarette" boats—those, sleek, slender speedsters of the sort seen on the TV show *Miami Vice*.

EG&G auctions most boats at its locations in Miami/Ft. Lauderdale and Los Angeles. Auctions are held every 9 weeks, and items are open to public inspection prior to each sale. For information and dates on specific auctions, write to EG&G Services at 3702 Pender Drive, Suite 400, Fairfax, VA 22030. Or check out the Web site at www.treas.gov/auctions/customs.

Serious buyers may want to subscribe to a flyer service that will keep them updated on items for sale at upcoming auctions. Subscriptions are $25 per year for information on eastern or western U.S sales or $50 for a national subscription. Contact the above address or Web site for more information.

●◆ *WHAT INSIDERS SAY:*

Since EG&G Services sells most of its seized boats in Los Angeles and Miami/Ft. Lauderdale, these auction sites attract the largest concentrations of boat buyers. But some boats are sold at its Edison, New Jersey, lo-

WHAT THE MILITARY *WON'T* SELL YOU

Although various branches of the military offer a huge variety of surplus goods to the public, some of the items for which the military is best known aren't for sale.

A Jeep

It may be the most famous military vehicle of all time, but if you want a Jeep, you'll have to buy one manufactured commercially, specifically for sale to the public. Military Jeeps (called M-151 series vehicles in armed forces lingo) have been classified as off-road vehicles not suitable for highway use since they don't conform to U.S. Department of Transportation safety standards. To be sure that old Jeeps won't be used improperly, the Defense Reutilization and Marketing Service cuts up or crushes the bodies and suspension systems.

A Humvee

You can buy a commercially produced version of this low, wide military vehicle, but don't expect to buy one from defense surplus. The reasons are basically the same as for the military Jeep. Military Humvees haven't met all the highway safety standards required by the Department of Transportation.

A tank

Yes, there are times when it would be nice to be behind the wheel of a tank—when negotiating a jammed highway full of rude drivers at rush hour, for example, or struggling through the muddy slop of some country road during a rainstorm. Unfortunately, that particular fantasy will have to remain a fantasy. Uncle Sam will not sell you a tank at any price. Nor can you buy any vehicle or weapon considered to have offensive (or defensive) capabilities.

cation, so check the Web site for boats coming up for auction there. Edison auctions attract fewer serious boat buyers, so you may be able to snag a real deal. The Web site is also a great place to check on special auctions held elsewhere.

BARGAIN BICYCLES

If your preference is for two-wheeled transportation, the government can offer you several ways to put your seat in a seat cheaply. Depending on where you live, you may find auctions, giveaways, bicycles you can borrow, or even subsidized loans. And if you already have a bike, local government may just make it worth your while to use it to commute to work by offering emergency rides home. Here are some of the best programs available.

Police Auctions

Police departments in many parts of the country auction bicycles along with other goods that have been seized during arrests or recovered as stolen property. As at motor vehicle auctions, your chances of getting something in good condition depend on what's been seized recently, but often, there is a good selection. At one auction held by the Davis, California, Police Department, more than 200 bicycles were for sale. Items are usually sold "as is," so you'll want to check them carefully before bidding.

The timing of auctions varies from department to department. The San Antonio, Texas, Police Department collects enough bikes to hold auctions quarterly. Smaller departments may hold just a single auction each year. To find out about auctions in your area, call your local police department's general information number, listed in the government pages of your phone book.

Two-Wheeled Giveaways

Faced with a warehouse full of bikes, the Lansing Police Department in Michigan decided to take a different disposal approach: Give hundreds of bicycles to nonprofit organizations around the Lansing area.

The department is literally awash in bicycles. The reason: Each spring, as waves of students graduate from mammoth Michigan State University in nearby East Lansing, many simply abandon the bicycles that they have used to tool around campus. Loads of additional bikes are collected from Lansing Community College. And that's not to mention the countless stolen bikes that the police nab each year from criminals.

"The bikes range in quality from ones that are in their final summer to a brand-new racing bike valued in excess of $1,000," says Lieutenant Raymond Hall, public information officer for the Lansing Police Department. Recipients of the free bikes could be a church group that may get more than 100 bicycles or a single resident looking for a few bikes to hand out to underprivileged children in the neighborhood.

Local residents can find out more about the bicycle program by writing to Lt. Raymond Hall, City of Lansing Police Department, 120 West Michigan Avenue, Lansing, MI 48933.

To learn whether your police department has a similar program, call the general police number listed in the government pages of your phone book and ask for the public information officer.

●◆ WHAT INSIDERS SAY:

For the best selection, time your bike pickup for fall, when the largest number become available. Although police departments collect the most bikes in the spring and early summer, as a matter of policy, most departments hold all stolen and abandoned bikes for 3 to 5 months before distributing them.

Bikes You Can Borrow

While some governments sell bikes to raise funds or give them away to good causes, others have put them to use in reducing traffic congestion. More than 30 cities around the country—including St. Paul, Minnesota, and Princeton, New Jersey, have developed loaner programs that allow you to borrow a bicycle, ride it to wherever you need to go, then leave it for the next user. Princeton even offers "in use" signs that you can display if you are running a quick errand and will be off the bicycle for less than 15 minutes.

In most of these programs, the bicycles are donated by police or private citizens. Volunteers then put them in running shape and paint them a bright color—often yellow—so it is easy to spot one when you need it.

Check with your city recreation department to see if it offers a similar program. The number is listed in the government pages of your phone book.

Subsidized Bike Loans

Want to buy a first-class bike, but you're short on funds? That's no problem if you live in Santa Cruz, California, and your employer is a member of the area's Transportation Management Association (TMA). The TMA will lend up to $750, interest-free, to purchase a bicycle for commuting. Then your employer will deduct the monthly payments from your paycheck. Loans can be used for bike accessories as well as the bikes themselves, and some area bike merchants offer discounts to program participants.

Emergency Rides Home

In an equally innovative program, Santa Cruz, California, has established an emergency ride home program for people who commute to work by bicycle. If you or a family member becomes ill or has a crisis, or if your employer asks you to work a longer shift that makes biking home unsafe, you simply call a local cab company and request a free ride. Again, your employer must be a member of the area's Transportation Management Association for you to use this service.

Amazing Stories

A NEIGHBORHOOD BICYCLE "LIBRARY"

For years, kids in Elizabeth and Rudy Barnhill's neighborhood in Lansing, Michigan, could stop by the Barnhills' house and check out a bicycle.

The Barnhills started their informal program after learning of the Lansing Police Department's bicycle giveaways.

"We had a rack in the shed out back," Elizabeth says. "At our peak, we had 20 bicycles out there."

Children were permitted to take out bikes for the day as long as they followed the rules posted on the shed. Among the rules (followed on the honor system): Children had to be doing well in school, they could not ride if they were sup-posed to be in class, and their parents had to know where they were.

When the bicycles became worn, the Barnhills hosted "repair parties" in their yard, during which the kids learned to care for the bikes.

Rudy, who has since joined the Lansing Police Department as a detention officer, says that the neighborhood program slowed not long ago, when the first generation of youngsters grew up and moved away. But the Barnhills are already starting over as the next generation of youngsters moves into the neighborhood. In fact, they have just requested 40 more bikes.

SUBSIDIES FOR ALTERNATIVE VEHICLES

In 1998, Americans used 10 million barrels of oil *per day*, much of it imported from foreign countries. Although in recent years, oil has been plentiful and relatively cheap, the government wants us to be prepared for a time when it may be neither.

That's why the U. S. Department of Energy has set a goal for 2010 of reducing and capping America's oil use at the 1995 level of 9 million barrels per day. As part of that effort, the government is trying to get Americans to consider buying "zero emission" vehicles that run on electricity or vehicles that use cleaner-burning alternatives to gasoline such as propane, liquefied natural gas, compressed natural gas, or ethanol.

Several states, led by California, are demanding that manufacturers who sell gasoline-powered cars in their states offer electric and alternative-fuel vehicles as well. As with any new technology, these vehicles tend to be expensive (average price: $30,000 to $40,000), and not all of the bugs have been worked out. Batteries for electric cars limit the number of miles you can travel before recharging, and refueling spots for alternative fuels are not as convenient or numerous as gas stations.

To make these vehicles more attractive and affordable, federal and state governments have come up with a host of tax deductions, credits, and other perks.

"The main reasons for the government's interest are less reliance on foreign oil and a cleaner environment," says Dana V. O'Hara, program manager for the Department of Energy's Office of Technology Utilization in Washington, D.C. "Our job is outreach. We're educating people, and we're seeding the market."

Federal Tax Breaks

The federal government offers two main tax incentives to individual buyers, one for electric vehicles and the other for alternative fuels. Buyers of

THE ROADS MORE TRAVELED

The U.S. Department of Transportation's Bureau of Transportation Statistics keeps tabs on how Americans move. Here are some highway facts from the bureau's booklet "National Transportation Statistics 1998." (The numbers are for the most recent year available.)

Miles of paved roads in the United States:

✓ 1960: 1.23 million

✓ 1996: 2.38 million

Number of passenger cars and motorcycles:

✓ 1960: 61.7 million

✓ 1996: 133.6 million

Average cost per person, in time and money, of traffic congestion in 10 U.S. cities:

✓ Washington, D.C.: 59 hours, $860

✓ San Bernardino–Riverside, California: 54 hours, $790

✓ Los Angeles: 49 hours, $720

✓ Houston: 46 hours, $680

✓ Atlanta: 44 hours, $640

✓ Dallas, 43 hours, $640

✓ Detroit: 42 hours, $600

✓ Miami: 42 hours, $600

✓ San Jose, California: 39 hours, $580

✓ New York: 32 hours, $460

electric vehicles are eligible for an income tax credit of 10 percent of the cost of the vehicle (up to $4,000), and buyers of alternative-fuel cars are eligible for a tax deduction of up to $2,000. The deduction may also be used to convert a vehicle from gasoline power to alternative fuels. Both the credits and deductions shrink each year until 2005, when each program is scheduled to end.

What's the difference between a deduction and a credit? A deduction is subtracted from your income before you calculate your taxes, while a credit is subtracted directly from the amount of taxes you owe. Both must be taken during the year in which you buy or convert the vehicle.

Alternative Information

Are you interested in an electric or alternative-fuel car, but you have no idea what makes are available? The federal government maintains an Alternative Fuels Data Center Web site that offers a roundup, complete with photos, of the latest vehicles made by Ford, General Motors, Toyota, Honda, and other manufacturers. The Internet address is www.afdc.doe.gov. Click on "Fleet Buyer's Guide" and then on "AF Vehicles." You also can get the number for the agency's telephone hotline from the home page.

The Internet is the best way to go, since you can conduct your own search for exactly the information you need. If you don't have access to the Internet, the Alternative Fuels Data Center will send you information by mail. Write to the National Alternative Fuels Hotline, 9300 Lee Highway, Fairfax, VA 22031-1207.

State Incentives

Individual states augment the federal tax breaks with a wide array of incentives. While some offer incentives mainly for corporations buying fleets of vehicles, others extend them to individual buyers. To help narrow the price gap between clean-fuel vehicles and conventional gas burners, Maine, for example, offers a sales tax exemption on the price difference between the clean-fuel and gasoline versions of the same models. That means that if you buy a clean fuel sedan for $30,000, and the gasoline version of the same sedan costs $22,000, you have to pay sales tax on only $22,000. If there is no identical gasoline vehicle, you receive a 30 percent sales tax exemption for an alternative-fuel vehicle, and 50 percent for an electric one.

Montana offers a 50 percent income tax credit (up to $500 for cars and small trucks and $1,000 for larger vehicles) for converting vehicles from conventional gasoline to alternative fuels.

You can find detailed information on the incentives available in each state by visiting the Department of Energy's Alternative Fuels Data Center Web site at www.afdc.doe.gov. Click on "Fleet Buyer's Guide" and then "Incentives and Laws." You can view federal incentives and search by individual states. The state listings offer loads of state and regional telephone contacts as well as additional incentives offered by local power companies. If you don't have access to the Internet, the Alternative Fuels Data Center will send you information by mail. Address your question to National Alternative Fuels Hotline, 9300 Lee Highway, Fairfax, VA 22031-1207.

THREE

Finances

CHAPTER 10

REMEDIES for the PAIN in YOUR WALLET

Money may not be the root of all evil, but it often is at the center of a lot of problems. Sometimes, the trouble is the result of overspending: Maybe you maxed out your credit cards, and now a collection agency is hounding you. Other times, the problem may involve a specific purchase—one that may have left you feeling unsatisfied or even cheated.

In both cases, government and nonprofit consumer groups can help. Indeed, it's in their own interests to keep you as a healthy, happy consumer. From an economic standpoint, when people fall behind on credit card payments, banks usually tighten credit. That makes it harder for people with good finances to borrow, and it can force troubled borrowers into bankruptcies that hurt business profits and the country's economy. The reason that government and nonprofit groups want you to be a happy consumer is clear: If you're satisfied with your purchases, you're likely to continue spending, and healthy buying drives businesses and the economy.

> Having trouble keeping up with your debts? Feel that you've been ripped off by a company you've dealt with? Don't despair. Here's how the government and nonprofit groups can help you control your spending.

Okay, it's clear that the government and nonprofit groups have a reason to help you. Now the question is, how can they do it? The answer: In several ways.

If you're deep in financial worry—even so deep that the future seems hopeless—you can turn to trained experts in nonprofit public service agencies. They'll work with you to plot out a management plan that will get your debt under control.

If you have trouble with a company that you've done business with, you guessed it: Help is on the horizon in the form of government consumer protection bureaus and nonprofit business associations,

FACTOID

IN THE 3 DECADES SINCE THE FIRST CONSUMER CREDIT CARD CAME INTO BEING, CREDIT CARDS HAVE GROWN FROM OBSCURITY INTO A MAJOR BUYING FORCE. IN 1997, CONSUMERS CHARGED MORE THAN $1 TRILLION WORTH OF GOODS AND SERVICES TO VISA CARDS ALONE.

whose goal it is to ensure your happiness at the end of the shopping day.

That's just a sample of the consumer assistance available. For the rest, read on.

MANAGING DEBT

"Charge it!" is the battle cry of many consumers today. The check comes at a restaurant, and without missing a beat, we reach for our Visas or MasterCards. We charge catalog orders and services on the Internet because that's usually the only acceptable means of payment.

Yet, as cash loses its cachet, the chances increase that people will overcharge, leaving them buckling under the burden of debt. In fact, the average American today has five credit cards and owes $2,900 in unsecured credit (credit not secured by collateral), according to the National Center for Financial Education. And credit cards are just one of the causes of debt problems. Car loans, home mortgages, school loans, and other liabilities plague people as well.

Fortunately, if you fall behind on your bills, there is help in the form of nonprofit debt counselors. They can't make your debt disappear, but they can get bill collectors off your back and offer free advice, putting you on the road to financial recovery. Here's how they work.

Professional Debt Counseling

If you've approached the limits of your credit cards and still pay only the monthly minimum, if you have been threatened with repossession of your car, or if you put off medical or dental visits for financial reasons, you may have a debt problem. If so, one of the first places to turn for guidance is a branch of the nonprofit Consumer Credit Counseling Service.

Diane Wilkman, president of the counseling service's Inland Empire branch in Riverside, California, calls the group the best-kept secret in the country. It may well be, but it is also the most helpful, say experts.

Funded by a variety of community resources—the United Way as well as banks, retailers, credit unions, and other consumer creditors—the counseling service offers professional debt-management advice to people whose unsecured lines of credit—gas cards, department store charge accounts, credit cards, and anything else not guaranteed with collateral—are out of control. (Some branches also receive grant money from the U.S. Department of Housing and Urban Development to advise clients on mortgage problems.)

Counselors can help you plan a workable budget so you don't rack up more debt, and they will help you prioritize bills. In most communities, services are free, and in others, they are available for a reasonable fee. To reach your local branch, check the business pages of the phone book under "Credit and Debt Counseling Services" for the number. If you can't find it there, contact the National Foundation for Consumer Credit, the counseling service's membership association, by writing to the National Foundation for Consumer Credit, 8611 Second Avenue, Suite 100, Silver Spring, MD 20910. Or, if you have access to the Internet, visit its Web site at www.nfcc.org.

◆◇ WHAT INSIDERS SAY:

If your situation is so severe that your income won't cover your monthly expenses, don't rush to declare personal bankruptcy. Experts say that it can wreck your credit for 10 years or more, and it may be unnecessary. Often, after negotiation, your creditors will be willing to reduce your payments to manageable levels. Ask the Consumer Credit Counseling Service for advice.

Starting a Payment Plan

Okay, you've analyzed your debt and your income, and it's clear that even a tight budget won't put you back in the black. What to do? Take advantage of the next step in the Consumer Credit Counseling Service's line: the debt-management plan.

Think of this as a financial crash diet, structured and supervised by your own personal "dietitian": a counseling service counselor. Counselors will analyze how much money you owe each month and how much you make and then negotiate a payment plan with as many of your creditors as possible. They will ask that charges for late payment and interest charges be reduced or dropped altogether. They will call collection agencies off your case. They can eliminate garnishments (the seizure of wages by creditors) and can sometimes even stop foreclosures on your property. In return, you must agree to make a single monthly payment directly to the counseling service office, which in turn pays off your creditors.

Why would creditors agree to these generous terms? It's in their interests, too. Were it not for such programs, many people would be forced to declare personal bankruptcy, which allows them to default on large portions of their debts. Pragmatic creditors are willing to negotiate to avoid getting little or nothing.

"Most of our clients have 10 lines of credit," explains Joy Thormodsgard, senior vice president and chief operating officer of the National Foundation for Consumer Credit. "If every creditor is calling the consumer, the pressure is great, and he is less likely to succeed with repayment. Creditors have seen that it is better if there is one body acting as a mediator."

The counseling service charges a minimal fee to help cover its administrative costs. The fee range is $5 to $65 per month, depending on how much you can pay. In some instances, the agency will waive the fee altogether.

Telephone Counseling

For some people, financial trouble is so shameful that they'd rather avoid help than visit a counseling office. This is especially true for people in upper income brackets, says Wilkman. "There are a lot of consumers in the higher socioeconomic brackets who are not going to walk through the doors of a nonprofit and ask for help," she says. "They assume it's like charity, like a food bank."

For that reason, several Consumer Credit Counseling Service offices offer counseling over the telephone as well as face-to-face. Some have even partnered to create Money Management International (MMI), a strictly confidential telephone service that offers counseling and debt-management programs 24 hours a day, 7 days a week.

You can write to MMI at 9009 West Loop South, Suite 700, Houston, TX 77096 for the phone number, or call your local Consumer Credit Counseling Service. Also, if you have access to the Internet, you can reach MMI's Web site at www.mmintl.org.

➡ *WHAT INSIDERS SAY:*

Beware of bogus credit-repair services that promise to quickly solve your debt problems and remove credit blemishes from your record—often for a high price. These "credit doctors" frequently use names that sound like those of legitimate groups such as the Consumer Credit Counseling Service. "They pretend they're us," says Wilkman. "We can't sue them fast enough." Check to be sure that any credit counselor you deal with is a member of the National Foundation for Consumer Credit, which sets strict standards of accreditation.

There are no quick fixes for bad credit. Says the Federal Trade Commission in a written warning to consumers about these companies, "only time, a deliberate effort, and a personal debt-repayment plan will improve your credit."

If you fall prey to a credit-repair scam, report the incident to your local consumer affairs office or state attorney general. The number is listed in the government pages of your phone book. Or contact the Consumer Response Center, Federal Trade Commission, Washington, DC 20580. You may not get your money back, but you can help put a stop to the company's fraudulent practices.

Getting Free Bankruptcy Advice

Sometimes, even the best credit counselor can't help you get out of debt. For instance, what if the start-up business for which you leveraged everything fails, leaving you jobless and tens of thousands of dollars in the hole? Or what if you fall seriously ill but don't have health insurance? Declaring personal bankruptcy, as harmful as it is to your credit record, might be the best answer. If so, there are ways to get the help of a lawyer without having to pay the high fees they can charge.

Turn to the Government

Every state has a service, partially funded by the government, that offers free legal representation, says Henry Sommer, supervising attorney for Philadelphia's Consumer Bankruptcy Assistance Project, which provides free attorney services to individuals filing personal bankruptcy. Names of this service vary from region to region within the states. In New York City, it is known as the Legal Aid Society; other names are Legal Services Agency and Neighborhood Legal Assistance.

Look for the number of your local office in your telephone directory's white pages or human services pages. Or, for a referral to an agency near you, write to Legal Services Corporation, which keeps a list of the different agencies around the country, at 750 First Street NE, Washington, DC 20002.

Your chances of getting a free lawyer depend on three things: how busy the office is, how much money you make, and how urgent your situation is. "Some people are in danger of having their utilities such as electricity and telephone shut off," Sommer says. Their cases would usually be given priority.

Ask Local Lawyers

There may be a nongovernment pro bono, or free, attorney group in your area that can help you. To find out, talk to someone at the local bar association. Again, the number should be in your phone book's business or white pages.

CLIMBING OUT OF DEBT: ONE COUPLE'S STORY

When Tom Nicholson lost his job as manager of a Houston frame shop, he and his wife, Sharon, were upset but not worried. She still worked as a paralegal at an oil and gas company. The economy was good, and the Nicholsons had money in stocks and other investments.

Then their investments went bad. Her $32,000 annual salary no longer covered their monthly expenses. Bills started piling up, including the monthly balance owed on 10 different credit cards. "A lot of people assume that they're financially indestructible," says Sharon. "We weren't."

As their financial crisis deepened, the Nicholsons realized that they didn't have a Plan B. With collection agencies and credit card companies billing simultaneously, they grew confused about what they owed. The bill collectors started calling—at home and at work. Their stress levels shot up. Finally, the Nicholsons sought the advice of a lawyer. He advised them to consider personal bankruptcy only as a last resort.

Instead, he recommended that they contact a Consumer Credit Counseling Service.

"I was embarrassed," Sharon says, recalling her first appointment with the service's counselor. "I don't think there's anything more closely tied to your sense of self-esteem than being able to pay your monthly bills. I just assumed the worst, that we were going to hand over my income and that we would no longer be in control of our lives."

On the contrary: The counselor explained their rights,

Seek Student Help

Sometimes, university law schools will take on cases. Typically, the school will operate under what are known as student practice rules, which group several law students with a full-fledged attorney who can legally handle the case. To learn whether this service is available to you, contact the nearest university law school and ask if it has any clinical law programs that might take on a personal bankruptcy case.

HANDLING COLLECTION AGENCIES

If you've ever had a collection agency hounding you, you know how unsettling it can be. Maybe you were in debt trouble and were struggling to keep up. Maybe you had another reason for not settling a bill that had nothing to do with your ability to pay—you were in the middle of a dispute with a health insurance company, for instance. Collection agencies don't discriminate.

Nevertheless, even if bill collectors get aggressive—or especially if they do—there are ways of handling them. If you are a debtor, federal law—the Fair Debt Collection Practices Act, to be exact—is on your side. To make the best use of the law, insiders say, you must first understand what it covers, and then you have to know how to use it to your advantage.

How You're Protected

The Fair Debt Collection Practices Act was designed to protect consumers from unfair and deceptive collection practices, says Thomas Kane, an attorney in the Federal Trade Commission's Divi-

---

gave them pointers for getting collection agencies out of their hair, and even joked a bit to make them feel better. Even though he couldn't put the Nicholsons on a debt-management plan—as it stood, their situation was too grim—Sharon says that she walked out of that meeting feeling more positive than she had for months.

Focused and determined, Sharon and Tom got organized. They cut back on their spending and reined in their debt bit by bit, at least enough to make them eligible for a debt-management plan with the counseling service.

Through negotiations, their counselor convinced the credit card companies to cut late fees and stop charging interest on the outstanding balances. Instead of shelling out a combined minimum payment of $500 a month to the various creditors—and remaining in the quicksand-like mire of compounding interest—the Nicholsons agreed to pay the counseling service one monthly sum of $275, which it divvied up among the creditors. The plan worked.

"After your first year on a debt-management plan, you start to breathe a little easier,"

Sharon says. After 4 years, the Nicholsons were debt-free. Tom, who in the meantime earned a degree under the GI bill, landed a well-paying job. Now, they're making more money than ever before. Still, Sharon says their experience with debt changed her life.

"I can promise you I'm a better shopper," she says. "We only have one credit card, despite all those offers of instant credit that we get every week. And I pay off the balance each month. It makes me feel good."

Note: The names of this couple were changed to protect their privacy.

sion of Financial Practices, which regulates the collection act.

Under the act, debt collection agencies cannot threaten to have you arrested if you fail to settle your debt, nor can they threaten a lawsuit unless they intend to pursue one. Further, they can't send you anything that looks like an official document from a court or government agency. "We see collectors use letterhead that looks like it is part of the government," Kane says. "They might put an eagle or 'State Department of Collections' on the letterhead to fool you."

Here are some of the more commonly used tactics that are strictly prohibited under this federal law.

Harassment

Debt collectors may not:

✔ Repeatedly use the telephone to annoy you

✔ Publish your name in a list of people who refuse to pay their debts (except in a list sent to a credit bureau)

✔ Use obscene or profane language

✔ Use threats of violence or harm

False Statements

Debt collectors may not:

✔ Misrepresent the amount of your debt

✔ Indicate that papers sent to you are legal forms when they are not, or vice versa

✔ Imply that they are attorneys or government representatives

✔ Represent themselves as operating or working for a credit bureau

✔ Imply that you have committed a crime

➡◆ *WHAT INSIDERS SAY:*
The Fair Debt Collection Practices Act pertains only to third-party collectors, meaning independent agencies

and attorneys that are contracted to pursue delinquent accounts. It doesn't affect your creditor's in-house collection department. However, some states have laws that help protect consumers from in-house debt collectors as well as third-party collectors. To find out about your state's laws, contact your state attorney general's office. The number is listed in the state government section of your telephone book.

Putting a Stop To the Madness

Knowing your rights under the Fair Debt Collection Practices Act can be empowering, but you have to put the law to use to get debt collectors off your back. That means confronting the agencies in a clear, firm, and professional way, most often in writing. Here's advice for making the law work for you.

Calls at Work

The law states that debt collectors are not allowed to call you at work if they have reason to know that your employer disapproves of such calls. Let the collector know if you can't receive calls at work.

Calls at Home

Likewise, collection agencies are not supposed to call you at home before 8:00 A.M. or after 9:00 P.M. Again, simply tell them to stop.

Calls about Money You Don't Owe

If a collector contacts you about money that you believe you don't owe—there was a billing mistake or you settled your debt—write the collector within 30 days of receiving the written debt notice and state that you do not owe money. By law, the collector must not contact you. If you are sent proof that you actually do owe money, however, the collector is free to contact you again.

➡◆ *WHAT INSIDERS SAY:*
Believe it or not, it's your right by law to ask a collection agency to stop contacting you altogether, even if the

CHECKING YOUR CREDIT RATING

From the moment you signed up for your first credit card, several private companies have been tracking your spending and generating reports on your ability to pay off your debts. That's how banks, insurance companies, and others know whether you're a good risk.

These reports aren't always accurate, though, and mistakes can cost you everything from a new credit card to an insurance policy, or worse. If you're concerned about your report, you can use the Fair Credit Reporting Act to check it.

This act entitles you to a free copy of your credit report if you've been denied credit, insurance, or employment and you request the report within 60 days of the denial notice. You also can receive a report if you can prove that you're unemployed and plan to look for a job within 60 days, that you're on welfare, or that your report is inaccurate because of fraud.

For example, if your application for credit, insurance, or employment is denied because of inaccurate or incomplete credit information, the company you applied to must give you the name and address of the reporting agency. You should follow up by contacting the agency.

If you want to contact any of the three main credit-reporting bureaus in the United States for a copy of your credit report, here are their addresses.

✓ Equifax Credit Services, P.O. Box 105873, Atlanta, GA 30348

✓ Experian, Allen, TX 75002-0949 (write to P.O. Box 949 if you were denied credit and want to see your credit report, P.O. Box 2104 to see your credit report, and P.O. Box 2106 if you are disputing your credit report)

✓ Trans Union, P.O. Box 390, Springfield, PA 19064-0390

When you write to request your credit report, include your full name, complete current address, previous address if you have moved within the last 5 years, Social Security number, full date of birth, your spouse's first name if you are married, and a photocopy of a bill, driver's license, or other document that links your name with the address you have provided. This information is used to ensure your privacy.

There is no charge to dispute mistakes or outdated information on your credit record. Ask the credit-reporting agency for a dispute form and submit it with any supporting documentation. For instance, if the report erroneously shows that you were 30 days past due on a credit card payment, send a copy of your canceled check and a copy of the credit card statement showing that your payment was indeed received on time. If there was a dispute between you and the credit card company, send a copy of any correspondence from the company proving that it settled the dispute in your favor, if that was the case.

debt is legitimate. But you must make the request in writing. "Once the debt collector receives your letter, the agency must stop all traditional collection tactics," says Federal Trade Commission attorney Thomas Kane. You can still be sued by the agency, and the agency can contact you to inform you of a suit, but that's it.

If a Collector Violates the Law

If you have a complaint against a collection agency, file it with the Consumer Response Center, Federal Trade Commission, 600 Pennsylvania Avenue NW, Washington, DC 20580. The commission does not typically intervene in individual disputes, but the complaint will help it find patterns of abuse. You should also contact your state attorney general's office to ask about possible recourse. The number should be in the government pages of your phone book.

You can sue on the grounds that the collection agency violated the Fair Debt Collection Practices Act, as long as you do so within 1 year of the date when you believe the law was broken. If you win,

Power to the People

BUILDING A CASE IN YOUR DEFENSE

If you have a dispute with a company—a retail shop, an auto repair garage, a mail-order company—you obviously want the matter settled in your favor. Whether you're arguing your own case or the situation has been taken up by a third-party mediator, there are certain steps that you can take to strengthen your case. Here's what insiders advise.

Present documentation

Build a paper trail that proves you're right. For example, if you're disputing a bill from your local mechanic because the repairs he made didn't fix your problem, present your warranty, says Bill Johnston-Walsh, director of the public education and information unit for the Pennsylvania Bureau of Consumer Protection. Or if you're disputing an overcharge, "if the company gave you an estimate, take that in along with the bill in order to show a discrepancy between the two." In Pennsylvania, since it's illegal for an auto repair company to do more, unrelated work than was originally estimated, such evidence might win the case for you.

Write everything down

If you're missing any documents, record any pertinent information, such as purchase dates, the purchase price, and reasons for the dispute.

Stick to the facts

Be as professional as possible. Try not to get emotional. You'll only weaken your central argument. Emphasize your worth as a customer. If you are a long-time customer, say so. "Tell the company, 'I've been doing business here for a long time, and you don't want to lose me. Save me as a customer,'" says David Polino, president of the Better Business Bureau of Upstate New York in Buffalo.

Be prepared to compromise

"In 80 percent of our cases, it's not a clear case that the company ripped off the customer. It's a fine line," says Johnston-Walsh. For instance, he says, "a company might agree to refund half of your money." You have to ask yourself if that is better than nothing.

you can recover money for damages, court costs, and attorney fees.

"Put everything you tell a collection agency in writing and send it by certified mail, return receipt requested," says Kane. That way, you'll have an official record if, for example, you tell a collector to stop calling you at work.

RESOLVING BUSINESS COMPLAINTS

Maybe you want to complain about a local clothing store's return policy. Or perhaps you think that a business or public utility intentionally ripped you off. Regardless of how big or small your problem is, you have lots of options for settling a disagreement with a company, starting with the company itself and then working through the several public and nonprofit groups set up to help you.

If you don't get satisfaction from the place where you did business, often your best ally will be a third-party negotiator such as a business association or a mediation center. But there also may be a consumer agency or nonprofit organization with which you can file a complaint. Here are tips on whom to contact and how to proceed.

Start at the Source

If you are unhappy with a company's product or service, the absolutely essential first step is to tell the company, say insiders. Chances are, they'll settle it then and there, sparing you time and hassle.

"Always complain first to the company, and be sure you're complaining to the right person," says David Polino, president of the Better Business Bureau of Upstate New York in Buffalo.

●◆ *WHAT INSIDERS SAY:*

When you're making a complaint, leave your emotions out of it. "Some people use a lot of expletives, thinking that will get someone's attention. Instead, the company may decide that it doesn't care if it loses you as a customer," advises Polino.

Try a Government Watchdog

Most state governments have an office of consumer affairs whose task it is to deal with citizen complaints regarding business fraud and problems with utilities, such as water or power companies. The name of the agency can vary from state to state. In South Carolina, for instance, it's the Department of Consumer Affairs. In Pennsylvania, there are two offices—the Office of Consumer Advocate, which deals strictly with utility complaints, and the Bureau of Consumer Protection, which handles business disputes and scams.

The services that these offices provide vary, too. Often, you must request help by first filling out a complaint form. The office then assigns an agent to the case who will contact the business or utility to try to resolve the problem.

These offices are often set up to mediate or arbitrate cases. "Even if a consumer calls us and says that a business in another state scammed him, we can put the consumer in touch with the right office in that state," says Bill Johnston-Walsh, director of the public education and information unit for the Pennsylvania Bureau of Consumer Protection.

If you would like to contact the agency in your state, look in the government section of your phone book under "Consumer." If you don't see the appropriate agency, call your state attorney general's office, which also should be listed in the government section of your phone book. Consumer protection is often part of the attorney general's domain.

●◆ *WHAT INSIDERS SAY:*

"Even if a business is not required to make an adjustment, we find that a lot of businesses will do so," says a complaint analyst with the South Carolina Department of Consumer Affairs. "A complaint coming through our office puts the business on the alert that the consumer is serious about the matter."

Try a Business Watchdog

If you get into a dispute with a local business over a product or service, the Better Business Bureau (BBB) may be the place to turn. This private, nonprofit group has been around since the early 1900s. One of the bureau's key functions is helping to settle disputes between disgruntled customers and member companies.

For example, a consumer might seek the BBB's help if he believes that a product was not truthfully advertised or that a product he bought doesn't meet reasonable expectations, says Rod Davis, vice president for dispute resolutions for the Council of Better Business Bureaus in Arlington, Virginia. "Sometimes it's a difference of opinion."

HOW TO PROTECT YOUR IDENTITY

It's not hard for marketers and others to get their hands on your personal information—your address and telephone number, annual income, credit history, and other financial details. They use this data in a variety of ways, but mostly to promote products and services to you through mail and telephone solicitations. When that junk mail involves instant credit in the form of preapproved credit cards, bigger problems besides inconvenience can arise.

"Identity theft is a fast-growing area, and it is a direct result of shoddy practices by banks, department stores, and others who make credit available too easily," says Edmund Mierzwinski, consumer program director of the U.S. Public Interest Research Group in Washington, D.C. "I spoke with a woman who had her mailbox broken into. The people applied for credit in her name and said they had moved to a new address." The thieves made more than $10,000 in fraudulent charges in a couple of weeks, says Mierzwinski, and although the victim won't have to pay the charges, the credit card company lost out on the money.

Thanks to laws that help protect consumers, in many instances, you have the power to protect your privacy and subsequently reduce the number of calls and mail solicitations you receive, including those preapproved credit card offers that make you vulnerable to identity theft.

Phone solicitations

Federal law requires all telephone marketers to keep a "do not call" list of people who request not to be bothered. If telemarketers call you, simply tell them you do not want to be called again and ask to be put on their list. By law, they cannot call you in the future. If they do, hang up and report them to your state attorney general's office.

There is also a "do not call" master list, which is made available to many telephone marketing companies. Updated four times a year—in January, April, July, and October—the list is sponsored by the Direct Marketing Association (DMA), a nonprofit organization whose members include companies that market products directly to consumers via the mail, Internet, TV, radio, and telephone. If you want to add your name to the list, send your name, home address, and home telephone number (including area code) and signature to DMA Telephone Preference Service, P.O. Box

The BBB does not take either side in a dispute but will work to facilitate communication between the company and the consumer. In many cases, dispute resolution, including mediation and arbitration, may be available to help resolve the situation.

The BBB recommends that you first attempt to resolve the dispute directly with the company. If that doesn't work, call your nearest Better Business Bureau. Look in the white pages of your phone book or contact the national headquarters to ask which office should handle your case. Write to the Council of Better Business Bureaus, 4200 Wilson Boulevard, Suite 800, Arlington, VA 22203, or visit the group's Web site at www.bbb.org to find out how to file a complaint.

9014, Farmingdale, NY 11735-9014. Your name will remain on the list for 5 years.

●◆ *WHAT INSIDERS SAY:*
While getting on the "do not call" list will stop most major telemarketers from calling, you still may receive phone solicitations from local companies or charities that aren't members of the Direct Marketing Association.

Direct mail

Similar to its telemarketing "do not call" list, the DMA also sponsors the Mail Preference Service, which helps reduce the number of mail solicitations you receive.

If you want to add your name to a list of people who prefer not to receive advertising mail, send your name, home address, and signature to DMA Mail Preference Service, P.O. Box 9008, Farmingdale, NY 11735-9008. The DMA also updates this list four times each year, and your name will remain on the list for 5 years.

When sending your request, be sure to include all versions of your name as they appear on the mail you receive.

●◆ *WHAT INSIDERS SAY:*
While removing your name from mailing lists means that the amount of mail, including unsolicited advertising, that you get will be reduced greatly, you should still get mailings— including catalogs—from companies that you already do business with.

Sexually explicit mail

If you're receiving unwanted sexually oriented mail, there is another step you can take to stop it. The U.S. Postal Service keeps a list of people who don't want sexually provocative mail delivered to their homes. At your local post office, ask for PS Form 1500. When you turn in the signed form to your local post office, it allows the Postal Service to issue an order to a particular company prohibiting it from sending you sexually

provocative advertisements. It also authorizes the post office to add your name to a list of people who don't want to receive such advertising in general.

Credit checks

The banks, department stores, and others who offer preapproved credit cards often get their information from pre-screened lists of eligible consumers provided by a credit reporting bureau. There are three main credit-reporting bureaus—Equifax, Experian, and Trans Union. An "opt-out" service has been established that allows you to have your name removed from lists that these groups sell to credit grantors and marketers. To reduce the number of instant-credit offers that you receive by mail—and to lower your risk of identity theft—call 1-888-5-OPT-OUT and follow the automated instructions. You can have your name removed either for 2 years or permanently.

While resolving disputes after the fact is one of the Better Business Bureau's functions, it also can help head off disputes before they start. The bureau tracks complaints about both member and nonmember businesses and works to ensure that the businesses maintain fair and ethical practices. If you want to know whether you should do business with a company, call the BBB to see whether there have been any complaints against it, and if so, whether the business was responsive.

The BBB's Care Package

In addition to regular services, the BBB offers several specialized dispute resolution programs. The BBB Auto Line assists car owners and companies in resolving problems related to new car warranties. The BBBOnLine program, at www.bbbonline.org, helps consumers and online merchants resolve disputes regarding Internet transactions and privacy violations.

Also, many branches offer a customer assistance program called BBB Care. The more than 58,000 business members of this program have agreed in advance to allow the bureau to settle any disputes that may arise with their customers through binding arbitration.

Under the BBB Care program, the business in dispute pays to settle the disagreement through arbitration (see "What Is It? 'Dispute Resolution'"); the services are free to the customer.

In helping to settle a customer's complaint, the Better Business Bureau will:

✓ Relay offers and write up settlements

✓ Coordinate an arbitration hearing if matters aren't resolved in the early stages

What Is It?

"DISPUTE RESOLUTION"

While there might not be as much at stake, the process for resolving consumer disputes isn't that different from that of international peace negotiations. Here are the three main types of dispute resolution.

Conciliation: The simplest technique used to solve a consumer complaint is conciliation, in which a third party works to encourage communication between the two sides. The conciliator might be a Better Business Bureau representative, who gathers information from each party, presenting the customer's view to the business and the business's view to the customer in a neutral way. Many disputes end quickly and painlessly this way.

Mediation: If conciliation is not effective, this is your next option. Professionally trained mediators help the parties work out their own mutually agreeable solution to the dispute. Effective and confidential, mediation often results in a win-win solution to tricky problems.

Arbitration: The closest thing to a civil court hearing, arbitration, like mediation, involves impartial trained professionals who hear the arguments and view evidence from each side and then reach a decision to end the dispute. Unlike mediation, however, both parties must agree in advance to abide by the arbiter's decision, even if it favors the other party.

✓ Follow up once a settlement is reached to make sure the company has complied

"We help you get your award," says Buffalo BBB president David Polino. "If a business doesn't comply, we'll throw them out of our membership." It works: 80 percent of consumer complaints received by Polino's branch are settled to the consumer's satisfaction, "and I believe that this holds true for most Better Business Bureau offices," he says.

◗◆ WHAT INSIDERS SAY:
Finding out in advance whether a company is a Better Business Bureau member and whether it is precommitted to resolving disputes through the bureau is "like an extra, free insurance policy," says Polino. For instance, "before getting a new roof on your house, call to see what companies are members of the BBB Care program," he says. "Then you know up front what your recourse options are."

Community Mediation Centers

Another option besides the Better Business Bureau for settling disputes is a mediation center. There are more than 500 such centers around the country, many of which belong to the National Association for Community Mediation.

While some mediation centers are partnered with social service agencies, most are nonprofit organizations that help ease the strain on the government legal system. "It's a growing field," says Joanne Hartman, associate director of the National Association for Community Mediation. "Mediation is a lot more efficient than the courts. The turnaround time for us to contact both parties and schedule mediation is faster, and our documentation is kept to a minimum." The emphasis is on results and keeping the costs of dispute resolution reasonable.

While they don't typically handle product complaints, community mediators will get involved with a business over service fees. If you had a complaint about a poorly built patio, for example, you would contact a mediation center. "We have trained intake people who ask questions of you to determine whether mediation is the appropriate course of action," Hartman says. If so, the center in turn contacts the contractor in question. For mediation to begin, the contractor also must agree to a session.

According to Hartman, most sessions are over in a few hours, often with a mutually agreeable decision. "We wouldn't tell the company that it has to fix the patio," she explains, "but that may be what the parties involved agree on."

Some mediation centers offer free services; others charge minimal fees, which are negotiable depending on how much you can pay.

To contact a mediator in your area, look in the business pages of your phone book under "Community Mediation Center," "Dispute Resolution Center," "Dispute Settlement Center," or some other variation. You can also write to the National Association for Community Mediation at 1527 New Hampshire Avenue NW, Washington, DC 20036 for a referral. (For more on the mediation and arbitration processes, see chapter 19.)

Mail-Order and Internet Disputes

The nature of catalog shopping makes liberal merchandise return policies a must. After all, when you buy something based on a catalog picture, there's a chance it won't fit, the color won't look like the color in the photo, or you won't like the feel of the object. Most shop-at-home companies allow you to return the item for a full refund, and some reimburse you for the shipping costs.

Sometimes, though, the system breaks down. A misunderstanding arises, and you don't get your money back. "In some cases, you might just get the wrong person on the phone," says Amy Blankenship, director of the Direct Marketing Association (DMA) Shop-at-Home Information Center. If that happens, she advises, begin by contacting a higher-up at the company, a supervisor to whom you can explain your situation. If that doesn't work, the DMA, a trade association made up of the country's top direct-mail companies, sponsors a free consumer service called the DMA ConsumerLine.

If you want the DMA's help in solving a dispute with a catalog company or Internet shopping site, write a detailed letter explaining the facts to DMA ConsumerLine, Direct Marketing Association, 1111 19th Street NW, Suite 1100, Washington, DC 20036-3603. Include the name and address of the catalog or Internet company involved and photocopies (keep the originals) of any canceled checks, order forms, and other relevant documents. Be as clear, concise, and fair-minded as possible.

A DMA representative will refer the letter to the company on your behalf and ask that it resolve the matter. A referral from the DMA shows the company that you mean business. As a result, the majority of the DMA's mail-order complaints are resolved successfully within 30 days.

THE GARMENT GO-BETWEEN

Have you ever had a dispute with a dry cleaner? Maybe you picked up a pair of white slacks and found purple hues that weren't there when you dropped them off. Or perhaps the gravy stain on your new blouse disappeared, but the blouse shrank to kiddy proportions. If they're at fault, honest cleaners will rectify the problem. But "just like any other business, dry cleaning and laundry service has some bad actors," says David Uchic, vice president of communications for the International Fabricare Institute, a trade association located in Silver Spring, Maryland, that's made up of nearly half of the cleaners in the United States.

The Fabricare Institute can help. Its members can send damaged garments to be analyzed to pinpoint exactly what happened and why, Uchic says. It might be the cleaner's fault, or it might be a problem with the garment, in which case you will be given a copy of the analysis to take to the retailer. "We help our members be the best cleaners they can be, not just in terms of technical service but also in terms of customer service."

What are the most common items that the institute receives? "We do a lot of wedding gowns and pieces that have sentimental value," says Uchic. "We also see a lot of women's blouses and athletic jackets."

Analysis takes 5 days, and the cleaner foots the bill. "Garment analysis is pretty popular with cleaners because they like having a neutral third party," Uchic says. This service is offered by members of the International Fabricare Institute. Cleaners who are members should display the IFI decal.

CHAPTER 11

KEEPING MORE
of YOUR
SHARE of the PIE

*T*he art of taxation consists in so plucking the goose as to get the most feathers with the smallest possible amount of hissing. —*Jean Baptiste Colbert (1619–1684, French minister of finance to Louis XIV)*

As Colbert made clear more than 300 years ago, there are few things as apt to produce a hissing fit as filling out your annual tax forms and watching a portion of your income disappear into some government's coffers. The forms themselves can be difficult to decipher, and the tax burden you face is daunting—just for federal taxes alone, you pay out 15 to 39 percent of your income each year.

The good news is that there are many ways to curb your tax bill, and with the government's help. You can take full advantage of advice and services provided by the IRS, your state tax office,

Paying taxes is like a good game of checkers. You don't need to have a complex strategy to come out on top: you just have to make the right moves. Here's how the government can help you win the tax game.

and other groups to make filing returns less of a headache. Also, you can use legitimate deductions and appeals to reduce your overall tax load to both the IRS and your local community.

As IRS Tax Commissioner Charles Rossotti made clear when he started reforming the agency in 1998, tax agents expect you to contribute your fair share of taxes to keep important services running—you wouldn't expect less. But no one, not even the IRS itself, expects you to pay even one penny extra.

FEDERAL TAXES

When it comes to federal taxes, you and the IRS share a common goal: You both want filing a return to be as painless and simple as possible. For you, the

FACTOID

OF THE 118,362,600 TAX RETURNS FILED IN 1997, THE IRS AUDITED 1,519,243, OR 1.3 PERCENT. THE AVERAGE RECOMMENDED PENALTY WAS $5,505.32.

reason is obvious, but what's in it for the IRS? More money, theoretically. The agency reasons that simplifying the process will reduce taxpayer resentment and attract more filers, thereby increasing its revenue.

To make filing easier, the IRS offers advice in two forms: First, it provides answers to questions that may arise as you complete your return; and second, it provides personal assistance if you need help filling out your 1040 or other forms. Insiders say that these services can help you handle many questions, saving you time and the cost of hiring a professional accountant for basic guidance.

Keep in mind, however, that on the whole, IRS counselors tend to offer more basic and conserva-

tive help. If your goal is to maximize your deductions, you may want to visit a professional CPA who can advise you on aggressive deduction strategies. Here are the particulars of the government's programs.

Tips from the Tax Hotline

The quickest and easiest way to get tax return help is to call the IRS toll-free telephone assistance line, which is listed in the government pages of your phone book. And since January 1999, when the IRS expanded the operation of the help line to 24 hours, 7 days a week as part of its effort to improve taxpayer services, it has been easier than ever.

TAMING THE TAX MONSTER

The Internal Revenue Service once may have been a big, scary monster fueled by baffling forms and unfriendly agents, but ever since 1998, there has been a move afoot to emphasize the *service* in the agency's name.

First, as part of the IRS Restructuring and Reform Act of 1998, the agency dropped the driving force behind its attitude—its old mission statement, which began with a line as warm and fuzzy as a surgeon's scalpel: "The purpose of the Internal Revenue Service is to collect the proper amount of tax revenue at the least cost. . . ." The much

friendlier replacement is "The IRS mission is to provide America's taxpayers top-quality service by helping them understand and meet their tax responsibilities and by applying the tax law with integrity and fairness to all."

Second, the agency has increased the power of the National Taxpayer Advocate to help taxpayers. An ombudsman of sorts, the national advocate's job is to support taxpayers' rights in matters of national tax policy and, through state and regional taxpayer representatives, to assist individuals in specific cases. "The taxpayer advocate is the voice

of the people, and I want to ensure that IRS functions listen to that voice," said IRS commissioner Charles O. Rossotti in a news release announcing the change.

These and other changes have made it easier for you to access tax information from the IRS. They have also improved taxpayers' ability to exercise their rights, including the right to fast and fair problem resolution, the right to appeal a tax audit, the right to tax amnesty in cases where people simply can't pay their taxes and keep food on the table, and the right to maximize tax deductions to lower taxes.

Among other things (many other things), IRS agents can give advice on whether you should itemize; how to report potentially confusing income sources, such as alimony payments or bartering income; and how you can take advantage of credits for the disabled or elderly. It's all free of charge, of course. Consider it your very own tax-time telephone support line.

⇥ WHAT INSIDERS SAY:

Despite the extra hours of operation, you still may be put on hold, especially during peak tax times. To avoid the wait, get an early start on your taxes. The tax season runs from January to April 15, when more than 120 million returns flood the agency. If you're not prepared to ask the bulk of your questions in January, at least avoid calling during the first 2 weeks in April.

Online Help

If you have access to the Internet, you can look to the IRS Web site for advice. The site, at www.irs.ustreas.gov, has quickly become a popular source of tax information, garnering a half-billion visits in the first 3 months of 1999 alone. From the site, you can download tax forms and instructions, the latest tax law changes, and much more.

The IRS also offers an e-mail question-and-answer service. You can't ask about your refund or any other questions involving the status of a particular return, but you can ask specific questions about the current tax laws that pertain to your return, such as the eligibility of a certain itemized deduction or whether you are allowed a certain tax credit. To access the e-mail service, go to www.irs.ustreas.gov/prod/help/newmail/user.html.

Free Walk-In Tax Advice

Before you hire an accountant or stop by a commercial tax preparer, consider visiting one of the government's own counselors. These experts, who are trained in tax matters and are willing to answer questions and advise you on filling out your return, offer their services free of charge during the tax season (January to April 15) at Volunteer Income Tax Assistance sites around the country. While there are no income requirements, the walk-in help offices—found in community centers, public libraries, schools, churches, and shopping malls around the country—are geared to taxpayers who have simple returns. The experts answer questions about federal taxes only.

To find the location and hours of the IRS tax counselor nearest you, call the IRS toll-free telephone assistance line, listed in the government pages of your phone book. You cannot schedule an appointment at many of the sites. The counselors usually see people on a first-come, first-served basis.

⇥ WHAT INSIDERS SAY:

Be sure to take all relevant income and tax materials with you when you visit the counselor, including W-2 forms (wage and tax statements from your employer), 1099 forms (showing interest and dividend income), 1098 forms (which show deductible mortgage or other interest paid out). The more organized you are, the better, since during the tax season, these counselors are pressed for time. Consider having a list of questions handy. Even better, make a copy of your return, then flag or highlight the areas with which you need help.

Free Tax Help for Seniors

In cooperation with private citizens, the IRS offers help to those age 60 and older who need tax advice. The program, Tax Counseling for the Elderly, pairs you with a trained volunteer—often a retired accountant—who works with you for free. The volunteers set up shop in communities around the country, and they travel to retirement homes, senior centers, and even the private homes of the homebound. They provide counseling and some tax return preparation. For information, call the IRS hotline, listed in the government pages of the phone book.

Advice from AARP

Beyond the IRS's direct help, seniors can get tax guidance from the AARP Tax-Aide Program. Run by the American Association of Retired Persons (AARP) in association with Tax Counseling for the Elderly, the program helps seniors at more than 10,000 sites nationwide during the filing season.

"The volunteers are trained and certified by the IRS," says Sabrina Reilly, national communications coordinator of the program. The more than 31,000 AARP counselors can answer all sorts of questions, from the routine to the arcane. "Our volunteers are proficient in typical tax issues that concern senior citizens, such as pensions, retirement benefits, exemptions, Social Security, and earned income tax credits," says Reilly. Find out about the counselor nearest you by writing AARP Tax-Aide Program, 601 E Street NW, Washington, DC 20049. Or, if you have access to the Internet, visit the group's Web site at www.aarp.org/taxaide/home.html.

Have Uncle Sam Do Your Taxes

Yes, you read that right: The IRS will figure out your tax return for you, as long as you follow a few key steps—print your name and address on the return, fill in the lines regarding income and deductions, attach your W-2 forms, and sign and date the return. Then all you have to do is mail the return, and the IRS will do the calculations. You can get more information about this program by requesting publication 967, "The IRS Will Figure Your Tax." To obtain a copy, call the toll-free number for federal tax forms and publications, listed under "Internal Revenue Service" in the government pages of your phone book. You can also visit the IRS Web site at www.irs.ustreas.gov/prod/cover.html and click on "Forms and Pubs."

➥ *WHAT INSIDERS SAY:*

"If your return is very simple, then having the IRS do the math isn't a bad idea," says Edward Karl, taxation director for the American Institute of Certified Public Accountants in Washington, D.C. However, he says, "you wouldn't want them to do it for you if there are gray areas that are open to interpretation," such as deductions, for example. To maximize write-offs, do your own return.

Where's Your Refund?

If you're due a tax refund and you're eager to know when it will arrive, you can call an automated refund information line (to find the number in your state, call the IRS help line listed in the government pages of the phone book). Have a copy of your current tax return available: You'll need to know your Social Security number, the filing status, and the exact whole-dollar amount of your refund. The IRS updates refund information every 7 days.

Help in Resolving Problems

There are an infinite number of reasons that you and other taxpayers can run into problems when completing tax forms: hard-to-decipher instructions, ambiguous tax laws, a personality clash with an IRS agent, or a dispute over an audit ruling—not to mention the overarching fact that the ultimate goals of the IRS (produce more revenue) and the taxpayer (pay less in taxes) are at odds with one another.

One goal that most taxpayers share with the IRS, however, is the desire to avoid problems. Therefore, the government has taken measures not only to reduce difficulties but also to solve them quickly and fairly. If you get into a jam with the IRS, consider the following advice.

Talk to a Counselor

If things between you and the IRS become drastic—you reach an impasse over an unresolved tax problem, say, or an agent is hounding you with aggressive tactics—the IRS will assign you a regional taxpayer advocate to help you plead your case. Although employed by the IRS, regional advocates report to the office of the National Tax-payer Advocate, who has been given a great deal of autonomy within the IRS. (In fact, the advocate is responsible for making twice-yearly status reports on the agency to Congress.)

The regional advocate's primary goal is to re-solve tax problems promptly and properly, but in the process, he also identifies broad issues that create problems for taxpayers and reports them to the IRS. You might call the taxpayer advocate your ally within the enemy camp.

"For example, let's say that you get a letter saying there is no record of an estimated tax pay-ment you made," says American Institute of Cer-tified Public Accountants taxation director Edward Karl. "Sometimes, the payments get lost or credited to another account. Then you respond to the letter, but something happens, and the re-sponse doesn't make it. You get a second letter and later a notice saying that the IRS is going to levy your account. That's when you call a taxpayer ad-vocate."

To ask for an advocate, contact the IRS Problem Resolution Office. You can get the direct number by calling the general IRS help-line number, found in the government pages of your phone book. An advocate will be assigned to you in your area if the situation calls for it.

Bringing Taxpayers Back into the Fold

There are people who, for whatever reason—per-sonal protest, carelessness, lack of funds—have not filed tax returns. Some may have skipped a year, others decades. The IRS has a carrot-and-stick way of dealing with these people. Known as the nonfiler's program, "it's a way for people to step up and say, 'I haven't filed my returns, and I need to get my life back in order,'" says Daniel J. Pilla, author of *How to Get Tax Amnesty* and *IRS, Taxes and the Beast* and a former consultant to the federal commission that helped bring about the IRS Restructuring and Reform Act of 1998.

By doing this, you avoid prosecution and put yourself in a situation where you can either pay your back taxes or work out a tax amnesty deal (see "Requesting Tax Amnesty" on page 160) with the IRS. That's the carrot. But, "if the IRS finds you be-fore you come to them, they use the stick ap-proach," says Pilla, which could result in jail time.

UNCLE SAM'S TAX SHARE GROWS

How a century can change things. Since 1890, the percentage of tax revenue going to the federal govern-ment has grown dramatically. Here is a breakdown of taxes in 1890 and 1990, indicating the percentage allocated to each major level of government.

Tax	1890 Amount Collected	1890 Percentage of Total	1990 Amount Collected	1990 Percentage of Total
Local	$405,000	46	$ 201,130,000	12
State	96,000	11	300,489,000	19
Federal	374,000	43	1,133,886,000	69
TOTAL	875,000	100	1,635,505,000	100

If you haven't filed taxes and want to get back into the system, the best thing to do is contact your taxpayer advocate.

Requesting Tax Amnesty

If your tax problems are truly desperate, you may want to turn to a service that, according to insiders, the IRS would prefer you not know about: tax amnesty. What this means is that the IRS will negotiate with you if you can't pay your back taxes and your only alternative is to declare personal bankruptcy.

These scenarios only apply if your financial situation is really bad, meaning that you cannot pay because the tax exceeds your income and assets. Knowing your rights can save you if you ever get in over your head.

The rationale on the part of the IRS is that it's better to give people a break and get them out of their financial fix and back on the tax rolls than to hound them for money they don't have. "Instead of collecting nothing from people with an unpaid tax bill, we're able to collect something," wrote IRS commissioner Charles Rossotti in a news release on the program. Here are four not so widely publicized ways that the IRS will work with taxpayers who owe more than they can pay.

1. You can request "uncollectable status," which puts a stop to attempts by the IRS to collect taxes and gives you time to get back on your feet. While it doesn't erase your tax debt, it does help stop the government from seizing your property and attaching your wages. To seek this status, file form 433A for individuals (433B for businesses), which shows the IRS that all the money you earn is needed to cover your and your family's living expenses. To obtain a copy, call the toll-free number for federal tax forms and publications, listed under "Internal Revenue Service" in the government pages of your phone book. Or you can visit the IRS's Web site at www.irs. ustreas.gov/prod/cover.html and click on "Forms and Pubs."

2. Through a program called Offer in Compromise, taxpayers who cannot pay their taxes can negotiate to pay a percentage of them. "We've settled cases for 5 to 10 cents on the dollar," says Pilla, a tax litigation consultant and author of 11 books on taxpayers' rights. "One lady owed $170,000 in taxes. We settled the case for $5,000." He says that the IRS anticipated that the taxpayer, who had large debts, was about to file for bankruptcy. So it agreed to a smaller payment, figuring that the legal fees and other charges it saved by not pursuing the case covered part of the tax debt. Their attitude was " 'We have a person whose tax liability qualifies to be discharged. If she declares bankruptcy, we get nothing,' " says Pilla.

3. If you file a Chapter 13 bankruptcy (instead of liquidating all your assets and dividing them among your creditors, this deal merely restructures and reduces your debt until you have a chance to regain financial stability), there is a chance that you can erase a portion of your tax debt. Upon filing Chapter 13, you enter into an agreement to pay back taxes in accordance with your ability to make monthly payments. Depending on your deal, you may be able to negotiate the erasure of taxes, interest, or penalties that cannot be paid within 60 months.

4. If you must file for personal bankruptcy, also known as Chapter 7 (in which your debts are forgiven once your liquidated assets have been distributed among your creditors), you're entitled to have a certain amount of tax debt completely discharged. It's the IRS's way of giving taxpayers in need a fresh start.

Don't assume that just because you declare personal bankruptcy, all of your tax liability will be discharged. There is a specific set of requirements regarding back taxes that must be met before you qualify for tax liability forgiveness. Generally speaking, the tax debt has to be more than 3 years old. Look into the matter carefully or have your lawyer and/or accountant do so.

MAXIMIZING WRITE-OFFS

Okay, let's assume that the IRS has provided all the advice and help it can, but it still looks like you'll be writing a check to Uncle Sam come April 15. What can you do? Look for little-known deductions that can reduce your bill. There are business expense write-offs for independent contractors and for those who own any business, no matter how small. Then there are itemized deductions that any taxpayer has the right to take.

Knowing what deductions you qualify for can be tricky, however. The tax laws can be convoluted and

nuanced, resulting in many legitimate but overlooked deductions, say tax experts.

Here are some ways that savvy tax insiders say you can save money by making the most of legitimate tax deductions.

Note: These deductions were in effect at the time this book was published. Since tax laws change frequently, you should check with an accountant to make sure that they are still in effect.

Business Write-Offs

Whether you're an at-home entrepreneur or you have your own small business outside of the home, maximizing business expense deductions is an essential part of achieving success. The IRS defines legitimate expenses as those that are "ordinary and necessary" for carrying on trade and business.

"Ordinary" simply means an expense that is common to your particular type of business, such

FILING YOUR RETURN ELECTRONICALLY

Since the IRS first offered online filing in the mid-1980s, this option has grown in popularity. In 1998, one out of every five taxpayers filed an electronic return. As more and more people are finding, there are real benefits to electronic filing.

"Electronic filing drastically reduces processing errors," says Edward Karl, taxation director for the American Institute of Certified Public Accountants in Washington, D.C. Even small errors on re-

turns, such as incorrect Social Security numbers or misspelled names, can result in returns being pulled for a closer look. These don't typically result in audits, he says, but anytime a return is given extra scrutiny, the chances increase. "With e-filing, you can perfect the return."

When you file electronically, you also get a verification of the filing, which means that you don't have to fret over the thought that your return got lost in the mail.

Perhaps the best reason to file electronically is that if you're due a refund, you'll get it sooner—up to twice as fast as paper filers.

One small drawback is the extra cost. As of 1999, the IRS was relying on private software developers to provide electronic filing packages, which range in price from $10 to $20.

If you want to file electronically, visit the e-file information page on the IRS Web site at www.irs.ustreas.gov/prod/elec_svs/index.html.

as movie tickets for a freelance newspaper movie critic or mileage deductions for a traveling salesman.

"Something that may be deductible for one business may not be deductible for another," says Norm Ray, a veteran certified public accountant in Windsor, California, and author of *Smart Tax Write-Offs*.

"Necessary" means anything that helps your business operate or flourish. "An expense does not have to be indispensable to be necessary," Ray says, noting that the definition is a loose one. "This is one instance where the IRS is uncharacteristically taxpayer-friendly."

Here is some advice from Ray for taking advantage of legitimate business expenses.

Make a List

Maybe you're just starting out as an independent contractor or small-business owner, or maybe you've been at it for a while. Either way, the best general advice for maximizing your business expense write-offs is to make a list of potential legitimate expenses. Take the time to look around your office, scour your budget, and analyze the expenses from a recent business trip, all the while thinking "ordinary and necessary." Compile an easy-to-reference list for yourself and any employees so that in the future, no deductible expense will slip through the cracks.

Deduct "Working Condition" Expenses

"Owners of home-based businesses or other small companies have the right to define the working conditions of their business, just like large corporations," Ray says. For example, if you buy dark French roast coffee for yourself and your employees, that's a legitimate write-off. Likewise, he says, games and recreation or background music in the form of CDs and a stereo are also legitimate.

Broaden Your View

Don't shortchange yourself because you still consider your business a mom-and-pop shop. Sure, you may only have a couple of employees working out of a room in your basement. But if you also have a network of suppliers, customers, business associates, and advisors—"anybody who helps your business succeed," Ray says—you may be able to legitimately expand the scope of your business expense deductions.

Don't Overlook Prepurchased Items

"You don't have to buy something new to deduct it from your taxes," Ray says. If you're starting up your own business, it is within your rights to deduct anything in your house or garage, such as a lamp, a sofa, or a desk, that you decide to use for business purposes.

➡◆ WHAT INSIDERS SAY:
Without cheating, you may want to push the limits of "ordinary and necessary" in order to increase the size of your deduction. The worst that can happen, say insiders, is that the IRS will question a deduction in an audit, and if it's a legitimate expense, chances are good that you can beat the audit. If you don't, you'll have to pay for the amount you deducted, plus possible late fees and underpayment penalties. You must decide if the risk is worthwhile.

Little-Known Itemized Deductions

In 1997, about 32 million taxpayers itemized deductions totaling $535 billion. The deduction for interest paid, primarily on home mortgages, accounted

FACTOID

POST OFFICES AROUND THE COUNTRY HAVE DEVELOPED SPECIAL PROGRAMS TO CHEER UP LAST-MINUTE TAXPAYERS, WHO TEND TO BE A LITTLE STRESSED WHILE WAITING IN LONG LINES TO POSTMARK THEIR FORMS BEFORE MIDNIGHT ON APRIL 15. SOME OF THE OFFERINGS INCLUDE FREE MASSAGES, LIVE CLASSICAL MUSIC, CRYING TOWELS, AND THE CHANCE TO TAKE OUT THEIR FRUSTRATIONS BY SLEDGEHAMMERING A JUNK CAR.

HOW TO AVOID
AN IRS AUDIT

If only paying taxes were as easy as agonizing over the return and forking over your hard-earned money. On top of everything else, you have to worry about being audited, meaning that an IRS agent will review your return to determine its accuracy.

Even if your return is flawless, an audit means revisiting the return, explaining income, and justifying deductions. And hiring an accountant—even if you win—will mean more money out of your pocket.

Thankfully, there are steps that you can take to reduce the chances of being picked for an audit, starting with the very basic, such as making sure everything is filled out correctly. The IRS looks for certain red flags when it processes tax returns, and even something as innocent as a missing signature or an addition error might cause scrutiny that could lead to a full-blown audit. The key to avoiding an audit, then, is to cut down on the things the IRS considers red flags.

Here are some tips from tax insiders to help your return make it through the mill without getting pulled for review.

Do it right

It may sound obvious, but "the best way to avoid an audit is to prepare an accurate return," says Edward Karl, taxation director of the American Institute of Certified Public Accountants in Wash-ington, D.C. Not only does this include accurately and honestly reporting your income and deductions, it also refers to the tax-return basics. Err on the side of caution. Double-check the math. Check to make sure everything is filled out that should be and that you have signed and dated the return properly.

Explain unusual claims

If anything you did seems questionable or involves an area of interpretation—for instance, if your travel-expense deductions were especially high this year—it's best to include a brief written explanation. "When the IRS is processing a return, they send it to an examination center if there is a red flag," Karl says. "At that point, the reviewer may use the explanatory material. It will save time in the long run."

Justify irregular deductions

One of the biggest warts on a tax return is the oddly large or inexplicable deduction. Maybe you own a home-based business and built a basketball court for your employees (a defendable deduction). Sometimes the mere inclusion of a round number, such as $1,000 for business supplies, will trigger suspicion on the grounds that it appears to be a rough estimate rather than a precise figure. Here again, a note of explanation might be in order to ease the mind of a skeptical IRS processing agent.

for the largest portion, about $207 billion. Then came deductions for taxes paid ($184 billion) and for charitable contributions ($101 billion), leaving $43 billion in other types of deductions. Taking ad-

vantage of the lesser-known types of deductions that make up the "other" category is one way to reduce your taxes. Here are ways that insiders suggest you can maximize your itemized deductions.

Power to the People

BEATING AN AUDIT

Despite your best intentions, despite your careful work, you may end up being one of the unlucky ones who are called in for a tax audit. What then? You need to build a strong case to defend your claims, say tax insiders, and that doesn't always mean that you have to provide meticulous paperwork.

If you are audited and find holes in your records, here's how you can put together a convincing argument by reconstructing the amounts spent and proving they were spent on tax-deductible items.

Locate the problem

Some taxpayers are audited at random, others because of one or more questionable deductions on their returns. If your audit was triggered by a specific expense, you may not need to spend the time (and money, if you hire an accountant) to justify everything on the return. Edward Karl, taxation director of the American Institute of Certified Public Accountants in Washington, D.C., suggests contacting the IRS agent who contacted you. Ask whether the return was picked at random or if the information on hand suggests an error. There's a chance that all you'll need to provide is an acceptable explanation of particular red flags.

Buy time, if you need it

If you receive a notice scheduling an audit, ask for a month's postponement in order to organize

your records. It's your right to have enough time to prepare your defense, and being prepared is essential for beating an audit.

Don't volunteer information

When stating your case, use only the records that the audit notice or the agent specifically requested. If the auditor asks about other records, tell him that you will have to have another extension to prepare them. This tactic will prevent the auditor from digging deeper into your tax records—and into territory that you're not prepared to defend.

Seek copies of missing receipts

Ask places of business. Look for credit card records or canceled checks that prove the expense. Proof of purchase is your best backup. If you can't find the receipt, reconstruct your expense records.

"Not only is it your right to be able to reconstruct expense records, but in certain cases it's mandatory," says tax litigation consultant Daniel J. Pilla, author of *How to Get Tax Amnesty* and *IRS, Taxes and the Beast* and a former consultant to the federal commission that helped bring about the IRS Restructuring and Reform Act of 1998.

"If you've lost records, you have an obligation to prove the expense in the best manner possible," Pilla says. Write down as many details

Note: This information is based on deductions that were eligible when this book was published; be sure to check with the IRS or your accountant to make sure they're still eligible if you claim them.

Volunteer Write-Offs

Everyone knows that dollar donations to charitable organizations are deductible. But if you volunteer your time to an official nonprofit

about the expense as you can remember. If it was a business dinner, for instance, write down the name of the restaurant, the date, who attended, and how the meal involved your business. You might also ask the other parties at the dinner to provide affidavits confirming what happened.

If an agent sends you a letter scheduling an audit date, don't ask for a "correspondence audit," because the agent might turn you down. Instead, respond with a letter of your own. "If the agent proposes April 17, say that you have a prior commitment that day," Pilla says. "In the same letter, politely ask the agent to define what issues are in question."

Most likely, the auditor will write back to reschedule and reveal that, for instance, your charitable contributions and mileage deductions are in question.

"Then you send back photocopied receipts and other records proving the validity of your deductions, along with a cover letter that says 'That date doesn't work, either, but here's everything you need regarding the questionable deduction.' There's no law that says you have to sit across the table from an IRS auditor," he says.

●◆ *WHAT INSIDERS SAY:*
Audits can be held either in person or by mail, through an exchange of letters and evidence.

Pilla's advice: Avoid a face-to-face meeting, if possible.

Appeal an adverse decision
If the audit decision goes against you, you have not only a right but also a commonsense obligation to appeal, say insiders. The goal of the IRS Appeals Office is to solve problems, whereas the goal of the auditor is to prove that you made a mistake.

To appeal the decision, simply request an appeals conference—an informal meeting with an appeals officer that can be held either on the phone, by mail, or in person (you'll find instructions on how to request the conference in the letter the auditor sends you). At this conference, you will be expected to discuss all audit issues that you don't agree with. Generally speaking, preparing for your appeal is no different from preparing for your audit. Since the appeals office is completely independent of the person who audited you, you'll have another chance to defend your case.

●◆ *WHAT INSIDERS SAY:*
"When the IRS sends a letter saying that you owe more money or else, always take the 'or else' option," says Pilla. "They may make it sound as if you're going to jail or as if they're going to seize your bank account, but 'or else' really means an appeal."

organization, you can also write off unreimbursed expenses that you incur while doing the work—telephone calls, stamps, and stationery, as well as 50 percent of meal expenses. The cost of any special uniforms or outfits that you must wear while performing the volunteer work is deductible, as well as expenses for caring for them. If you travel, you can deduct expenses such as hotel rooms and meals. If you drive your own car, you can write off 14 cents per mile.

Moving Expenses

If you move because of your job, you can write off any crating supplies, moving company charges, and even your family's lodging costs en route to your new home (excluding meals). This also applies to U.S. citizens who have been working abroad but who move back to the United States to retire.

Nursing Home Costs

Generally speaking, you can deduct any medical expenses not reimbursed by an insurance company that exceed 7.5 percent of your adjusted gross income. If you, your spouse, or a dependent is in a nursing home, some or all of those costs may be considered deductible as medical expenses, "as long as there is a medical component to the nursing home stay," says Ray.

If the primary reason for being in the home is to receive medical care, you can write off the cost of the entire package—meals, lodging, procedures, nurses, and so on. If, however, the reason is personal, only the medical expenses are deductible.

Floods, Fires, and Theft

Suppose your car was crushed by a plummeting meteorite. The IRS might give you a tax break.

Loss of property resulting from a sudden, unexpected, or unusual event may be tax deductible. This includes loss due to theft, fire, car accidents, vandalism, tornadoes, and other catastrophes, including, well, meteorites. (As improbable as it sounds, in 1938, a 4-pound meteorite crashed through the roof of a 1928 Pontiac coupe parked inside a garage in Benld, Illinois. It is unknown whether the owner took a tax deduction.)

Different rules apply if your loss took place in a zone declared a national disaster area by the President of the United States: You get even more of a break. First of all, the IRS will allow you to write off the value of the lost property in either the current tax year or the previous one, whichever is more beneficial to you. The agency will also delay the collection of taxes that you owe and eliminate any penalties and interest if the disaster caused you to file late.

Gambling Losses

Unlucky year at the races? If you itemize your deductions, you can claim your gambling losses as a miscellaneous deduction on Schedule A of Form 1040. However, you cannot deduct more in losses than the total amount of gambling income reported on your return. In fact, even if you had a good year, you'll want to keep track of your losses to offset some of the taxes you're required to pay.

To deduct losses, you must be able to provide receipts, tickets, statements, or other records that show the amounts of both your winnings and losses. "If you're a big enough high roller, the casinos should give you the proper documentation," says Ray. Be sure to ask in advance.

In addition, the IRS suggests that you keep a diary of your gambling activity, including dates and types of wagers, names and addresses of gambling establishments, and the amounts won or lost. They may even ask you to back up your claims with hotel bills, airline tickets, gasoline credit card statements, or affidavits from responsible gambling officials regarding the wagering activity.

STATE TAXES

As of 1999, all but seven states had some form of income tax. Most states follow the lead of the IRS by conforming to federal tax rules and by using the figures that taxpayers submit on their federal returns as indication of the amounts that will be taxed by the state.

While the state's bite out of your wallet is not as big as the IRS's, it can still hurt, not to mention keeping you at your desk for a few extra hours to fill out the return.

The IRS customer assistance options mentioned earlier won't help you with your state taxes. States require separate tax returns. Fortunately, similar assistance is available in most states. Because what is offered differs from state to state, it's not possible to mention all the services here, but here is some general advice to make filling out the return—and writing the check—less painful.

Search for Free Help

Most state revenue or taxation departments offer some type of free assistance, usually in the form of publications, automated phone information, telephone hotlines (with living, breathing humans on the other end), Internet sites, or walk-in assistance.

The revenue department may seem an obvious place to look, but Dianne DeLoach, public relations coordinator with the Virginia Department of Taxation, says that many people are hesitant to ask for help. "One person told me that he dreaded calling our office the way he dreaded having a root canal," DeLoach says. Still, in 1998, customer service representatives in Virginia's central and nine district tax offices fielded more than 630,000 calls and personally met with more than 47,000 taxpayers. "Once people do call, they find our services very helpful. In fact, many of our employees receive thank-you letters."

Look for the telephone number of your tax department in the government pages of your phone book.

•✜ WHAT INSIDERS SAY:

If you decide to go for a walk-in meeting with a customer service representative, call in advance to ask what documentation you should bring, advises De-Loach. Ask the person you speak to on the phone if he can pull up your records. That way, he'll know what the problem is and what you'll need to show a customer service representative in order to help solve it. Many problems can be resolved over the phone.

Avoid the Peak Season

The state filing period in Virginia—January to May 1—is just 2 weeks longer than the federal filing period, so the same advice for beating the crowds on the help lines and at the walk-in offices applies: File early. In case you don't, many states extend hours during filing season. And, since filing deadlines may vary from state to state, you should always check.

Go to the Web

The Internet has revolutionized information exchange from tax departments to taxpayers. If you have access to the Internet, you can download helpful publications and explanations of tax laws instead of ordering them by mail. You can often send specific questions via e-mail directly to trained tax advisors, who will answer in a return message. You can keep abreast of changes in the tax law. Believe it or not, you can even get money-saving tips (from the people trying to get your money). On the Virginia tax department's Web page, for instance, there's a section that advises married couples when it's most lucrative for them to file jointly.

To find your state's Internet home page, call the tax revenue department, whose number should be listed in the government pages of your phone book.

Don't Miss Out on Free Money

Because they are driven by legislation, state tax laws change regularly, sometimes in your favor. Since these changes are not as widely publicized as modifications to federal tax law, you may pay more than your fair share if you don't happen to hear about a newly established tax credit or deduction. After one state budget surplus, for example, Minnesota distributed rebates to its taxpayers in the form of 20 percent property tax discounts. "A couple hundred thousand people didn't claim them," says Lynn Reed, research director of the Minnesota Taxpayers Association, a nonprofit watchdog group. "They just had not heard the news."

Reed suggests that taxpayers visit the Web sites of their state revenue departments to find out about important tax law changes. "On its Web page, the Minnesota Department of Revenue had a blinking frog with the word 'rebate' on it," he says. Or you call and ask about changes. Look in the state government pages in your phone book for the number.

LOCAL PROPERTY TAXES

Your local government estimates the market value of your home in order to determine how much you owe in real estate taxes, which are used to pay for a wide variety of municipal services. The assessment is based on factors such as the size of your home, its location, the size of your lot, and the selling prices of other homes in your neighborhood.

Because real estate values fluctuate over time, tax assessors in most areas reassess homes every 1 to 5 years, depending on local policy. If the value of your home goes up, so do your taxes. Tax assessors are obligated by law to be fair and equitable in determining home values, but that doesn't mean that they never make mistakes.

"Market value is very subjective," says Marvin Warren, a consultant with Interstate Tax Management Services in Houston, which specializes in real estate and property taxes. "If your house hasn't been sold recently, you really don't have a market value."

If you believe that your house has been overvalued (meaning you'll be overtaxed), you may contest the assessment. "All you have to do is show proof that the value we have listed isn't what the value really is," says Donald Gentry, assessment standards specialist with the office of the real estate assessor in Richmond, Virginia.

Say that you and your next-door neighbor each live in 1960s-era ranch houses. They are similar in style and size—each is about 2,500 square feet—but you discover that he pays $1,000 in annual property taxes to your $1,500. If you can prove that your tax assessment is too high, you might save $500 a year.

Here are some tips for challenging the government's estimated value of your house and reducing the amount you pay in taxes.

Talk To the Assessor

Get the phone number for the tax assessor's office from the government pages of your phone book and make an appointment to meet directly with the person in charge of estimates in your appraisal district. If you make a good enough case, often that's all it takes. "Most issues involving houses are resolved by talking directly to the assessor," Warren says.

Take It to the Board

Disputes between taxpayers and assessors that can't be easily resolved are typically settled by an appraisal review board (or a similarly named board of citizens that's authorized to make decisions in an appraisal district). Boards and procedures differ by locality, so call your local tax office for information on making an appeal in your area.

Present Hard Evidence

According to Warren, general complaints that your taxes are too high or that you don't think you could sell your house for what the government says it's worth are likely to fall on deaf ears. You need facts and figures, photos of similar homes that are taxed at lower rates, and other evidence to back up your claims.

Check the Measurements

One way that the government appraiser may have made a mistake is by miscalculating the size of your lot and/or house. For evidence, gather blueprints, deed records, photos, and a survey, or take your own measurements.

Look For Hidden Defects

Cracked foundations, inadequate plumbing, and other problems with a house can reduce the market value and, by extension, the taxes you must pay on it. Get photographs, statements from builders, or an independent appraisal to back up your case.

Look Through Government Files

Luckily for you, real estate taxes are a matter of public record, so you don't have to rely on your neighbors for information. Finding out the assessed value of houses on your street or of similar homes in another neighborhood is as easy as visiting your local tax office with a list of addresses you want to check.

Talk To Real Estate Agents

If you feel that many houses on your street have been overvalued, you may be able to get a local real estate agent to tell you how much houses in your neighborhood have been selling for recently. You can use that information to help build a case for lowering assessments for you and your neighbors. These other houses are known as comparables, or comps—substantially equivalent properties that are used to create price comparisons. The best comps are houses that are similar in size, age, location, and type of construction. The more recent the sale, the better.

Don't Spend More Than You Save

Weigh the costs of appealing your property taxes against the potential savings. Hiring an independent appraiser can be expensive, and sometimes it's unnecessary—or worse, useless. "If the appraiser doesn't use the same comps as our office, we won't be able to use the information," says Gentry. Also, be sure that you don't start the ball rolling and end up proving that your house is worth more than the city's assessment. You'll pay more in taxes.

➊➍ WHAT INSIDERS SAY:

If you're going to contest your real estate assessment, don't wait until you receive the tax bill to act. The time to act is soon after the assessment is made. Whenever the assessment on your house changes, the assessor will send you a notice telling you the new valuation. The notice should include information on how to contest the assessment and how long you have before the new figures become effective. Warren says, "Once you get the bill, the process is over."

CHAPTER 12

BUILDING and MAINTAINING YOUR NEST EGG

Here's a secret: Uncle Sam would love to see you retire rich.

Yes, really. The government may take a fair share of your income in taxes while you're working, but it would love for you to grow a bit of what's left into a sizable next egg.

You see, the more you invest and save for retirement, the less the government has to pay to keep you afloat in your later years. And, says Nancy Granovsky, professor and family economics specialist at the Texas Agricultural Extension Service, which is part of the Texas A&M University system, having a well-designed retirement strategy also means greater productivity while you're still in the workplace. "Knowing that you have a bright future to look forward to probably makes you a better employee today," she says.

> Everyone dreams of a long, happy retirement, but realizing that dream means making smart financial choices—both now and after you retire. Here's how Uncle Sam and his friends can help.

To that end, the government provides numerous incentives to encourage you to save and invest. There are tax breaks if you save money for retirement and if you buy certain types of government bonds, to name just a couple. Both mean more money in your bank account.

The key to making the most of these offerings is knowing what incentives exist, then learning how to use them for the best tax advantage, both while you're saving and later, when you start to withdraw money during retirement.

In this chapter, we'll show you such things as:

✓ How to shelter your investments from taxes

✓ How you can use the government's own rules to avoid fees when buying U.S. treasury notes

FACTOID

THE AVERAGE WORKER SAVES $2,436 A YEAR FOR RETIREMENT. THAT'S A LITTLE LESS THAN ONE-THIRD OF THE $7,920 THAT WORKER NEEDS TO SAVE EACH YEAR TO LIVE AS COMFORTABLY AS HE WOULD LIKE.

✓ How you can avoid tax penalties on retirement accounts

✓ How you can protect your kids from paying inheritance taxes as high as 90 percent when you die

Also, any discussion of saving for the future has to include Social Security. We'll offer a government insider's advice on getting the most out of what you pay into the Social Security system.

YOUR RETIREMENT STRATEGY

According to the 1997 Retirement Confidence Survey, conducted in part by the American Savings Education Council, two-thirds of working Americans would like to retire before the age of 65. Yet, only 27 percent of workers have any idea of how much money they will need to accumulate in order to retire in the style they want. It's important to be prepared, and the best place to start is with a smart investment strategy.

"We say that retirement is going to have to provide the stability of a three-legged stool," explains Granovsky. "For many people, Social Security will be one leg." The other two will be pension income and savings/investments.

While to a large degree, others control your Social Security and pension money, you need to develop your own strategy for growing other investments. Just as there are tax-deferred company-sponsored pensions, there are also tax-deferred investment accounts that are available to individuals, such as Individual Retirement Accounts, or IRAs (see "Tax-Deferred Retirement Accounts" on page 172). Because there are countless options available for where and how to invest your money, the choices you make will depend on your financial needs and goals.

There are several ways to get sound, unbiased advice to help you plan your financial strategy. Here are three good options.

Advice from the Cooperative Extension

The government-funded agency that you most often associate with tips on tomato growing and other agricultural advice can show you how to grow your investments, too, says Granovsky. "The extension service is a comprehensive program to meet the needs of all people in all places," she says.

That includes helping you evaluate mutual funds, answer pension questions, and set up wise savings plans—and the advice is often free of charge.

Plus, "most of the people out there giving financial advice are trying to sell something—stocks or mutual funds or something else," says Alice Mills Morrow, a family economics specialist with the extension office at Oregon State University. "We're not selling anything. I don't know if that makes us smarter or not, but it takes away one set of biases."

Cooperative extension offices are located in just about every county in the United States. Although the offerings differ at each one, you may find the following types of financial help.

Publications and videos. The Oregon extension service offers such titles as "Your Saving/Spending Plan," "Paying Family Bills," and "Estate Planning for Families with Minor Children," all free of charge.

Workshops. As a tie-in with the year 2000, cooperative extension services in more than 25 states conducted a program called Money 2000, in which participants learned savings and debt-reduction techniques. The goal: to end the year with at least $2,000 in savings. Some programs are free. For others, there may be a small fee to help cover the cost of workbooks and other materials.

One-on-one counseling. Many county extension offices offer advice over the phone or in person free of charge.

Local education programming. Extension offices produce radio broadcasts, publish financial newsletters, and hold public education campaigns in communities.

If you want to take advantage of the cooperative

extension service's financial information, contact your county office. You may find the number in the white pages under the name of your state's land-grant university; in Pennsylvania, for example, you would look for Penn State Cooperative Extension. Or it may be in the government pages, listed as "Agricultural Extension" or "Cooperative Extension" under the state department of agriculture or the USDA. If none of these options pans out, call your state legislator's office, listed in the government pages.

●◆ *WHAT INSIDERS SAY:*

Many county extension offices provide family financial planning information, but if yours doesn't, contact the state cooperative extension specialist in family finances (your county office can supply the number). This spe-

TAX-DEFERRED RETIREMENT ACCOUNTS

When it comes to retirement plans, there are traditional pensions provided by employers, and then there are tax-deferred contribution plans, some of which are employer-based and others that are left up to the individual.

You benefit in several ways from these tax-deferred plans. First, with one exception, you contribute to these plans on a pretax basis, which reduces your annual income and therefore the amount of income taxes you pay each year you contribute. Second, you can buy and sell investments—stocks, bonds, and mutual funds—inside the account without tax consequences. (In normal, taxable accounts, each time you sell, you are taxed on any gain.) Third, the earnings on these investments are not taxed until you begin to withdraw the money at retirement. Then the money is taxed as income.

Here is a brief description of the most common types of individual tax-deferred accounts.

401(k) plans
Like traditional pensions, these are run by employers. But unlike pensions, you decide how much of your annual salary (up to IRS limits) you want to contribute, and typically you can pick which of the employer-designated investment options you want to invest in. Often, employers will match employee contributions as an incentive for them to save.

403(b) and 457 plans
These are comparable to 401(k) plans. The 403(b) plans are available to employees of certain nonprofit, tax-exempt organizations, while 457 plans are available to employees of states, counties, cities, and government agencies.

Individual Retirement Accounts (IRAs)
As the name implies, IRAs are not employer-based. You may contribute to an IRA in addition to an employer-based plan such as a 401(k). The maximum annual amount that you can contribute is $2,000.

Roth IRAs
Established as part of the Taxpayer Reform Act of 1998, the Roth IRA differs from traditional IRAs in two key ways. First, you contribute after-tax dollars to a Roth IRA. This means that you get no income tax deduction in the year you invest, but also you're not taxed when you withdraw funds after the age of $59\frac{1}{2}$. There are income restrictions; as of 1999, anyone who earned more than $110,000 in a year (more than $160,000 for married couples filing jointly) could not contribute to a Roth IRA.

cialist can tell you whether neighboring counties have financial services, says Morrow.

Continuing Education Courses

Most state universities and many community colleges have continuing education programs, which often offer courses in investing, saving for retirement, and other personal finance matters. At many institutions, especially the government-subsidized ones, course fees are intentionally kept to a minimum to make the classes available to everyone in the community.

The University of Georgia, for example, sponsors the University of Georgia Center for Continuing Education in Athens. Among the courses offered are "Investing Basics for Women" ($74 for four 2-hour sessions), taught by a licensed representative of the New York Stock Exchange; "Stocks and Bonds: Right Choices" ($59 for three 2-hour sessions); and "Investing with Mutual Funds" ($49 for three 1½-hour sessions).

For courses near you, check with your local community college or state university. Look for a "continuing education" heading under the college's listing in the phone book.

Free How-To Manuals

You may be familiar with the government's Consumer Information Center in Pueblo, Colorado. For years, it has published free and low-cost books and pamphlets to help Americans be better consumers. Among these publications are several on saving and investments.

Thanks to the Internet, the center's information is more accessible than ever. You can still order a catalog of publications by mail by writing to the Consumer Information Center, Pueblo, CO 81009. Or you can visit the center's Web site (www.pueblo.gsa.gov) and click on "Money." This will give you immediate access to the same information. Here's a sample list of some of the publications that the center has to offer.

✔ "Making Sense of Savings"

✔ "Planning Your Estate"

✔ "Introduction to Mutual Funds"

✔ "Invest Wisely"

✔ "Planning Financial Security"

✔ "Ten Questions to Ask When Choosing a Financial Planner"

INVESTING IN THE GOVERNMENT

Once you've developed a smart strategy for investing in tax-deferred retirement accounts, you may want to look to additional investments that have a tax advantage. Some of the soundest of these are in the U.S. government itself, usually in the form of bonds.

When you buy a bond, you become the lender. The bond is your promissory note. If it's a U.S. bond, you're lending money to the federal government, and you can rest assured that Uncle Sam will pay you back—with interest—when he says he will.

The rate of return won't be as high as it is on stocks, but, says expert Bill Bengen, a certified financial planner in El Cajon, California, "I recommend U.S. Savings Bonds as an insurance policy to offset the volatility of the stock market."

While he doesn't advise them for young investors—anyone 25 years or more away from retirement—he does suggest that his clients begin adding bonds to their portfolios at a rate of 1 percent of their total portfolio investments per year, starting at around age 45. By the time they retire, he recommends that people have about 35 percent of their total portfolio invested in bonds. "In the case of a financial crisis, the bonds will be there like steady Eddies to preserve the value of your portfolio until the stock market bounces back," he says. That's the beauty of U.S. bonds. They're about as close as you can get to risk-free investments.

State and local governments also issue bonds, called municipal bonds, and while they range in risk depending on the financial characteristics of the issuer, they can be smart investments if you're willing to accept the risk. Here are tips on investing in three different types of government bonds.

BRINGING MONEY DIRECTLY TO YOU

Yes, government tax breaks and investment advice can help you save for retirement. But there may be an even more direct way that the government can fill your bank account—by supplying cash, stock, and other valuables.

States are sitting on billions of dollars worth of precious assets that they would love to pass on to the public. The problem is, they can't find the rightful owners.

It might be money from an inactive bank account, an unclaimed insurance settlement, unused gift certificates, safety deposit box holdings, or even jewelry. Whatever the source, after a certain number of years (the time varies from state to state), the asset is turned over to the government. There, "it remains in perpetual custody until the owner comes forward to claim it," says John Baer, a spokesperson for the Pennsylvania State Treasury Department in Harrisburg.

Of course, the governments try to locate the owners through legal advertisements, notices on Web sites, and other means, but in the past few years, some states have become even more aggressive about rooting out the rightful owners. Pennsylvania, for example, has started setting up booths at fairs around the state. Armed with a laptop computer and a connection to the unclaimed property database, a treasury department representative can input your name and tell you instantly whether there are riches in your future.

Stephanie Petty, of Emporium, Pennsylvania, found out that she was several thousand dollars richer when, on a whim, her sister stopped by the booth at a Clearfield County fair. Needless to say, Petty was flabbergasted when she was told that a relative had willed her more than $8,000 in cash and stocks.

"My sister's husband wanted to stop by the booth for the fun of it," Petty says. "I won't know how to react until I actually see it." She says the whole experience has changed her perception of state government. "It's good to see there's a force out there working for the people."

If your county fair doesn't have a treasury department representative handy, or if you just can't make it to a fair, call your state's treasury department for information about unclaimed property or visit the state Web site. Just type in www.state.*(insert the two-letter state abbreviation)*.us. You'll be sure to see a link to the unclaimed property division, where you can check for money that may be due you by typing in your name. Keep in mind, though, that these sites may not list every unclaimed asset that your state is holding. If there's any doubt, contact your state treasury department's unclaimed property division.

Getting the Most From U.S. Savings Bonds

U.S. Savings Bonds, the most common of which are known as series EE Savings Bonds, are the most widely held type of security in the world. Fifty-five million Americans currently own 800 million savings bonds worth $186 billion. Available at most banks, they are easy to purchase. Yet many people underestimate the complexities of these bonds.

"There is a misconception that savings bonds are this simple thing that you buy and cash in, sort of like a CD at a bank," says Bengen, "but they're so much more complicated than that."

Here are the basics of how they work: You buy a series EE bond at half its face value (for a $100 bond, for instance, you'd pay $50). It accrues interest at rates that change every 6 months until it reaches its face value, at which time you can cash in the bond and the interest it has earned. A bond earning an average of 5 percent would reach face value in 14½ years, while the same bond earning an average of 6 percent would mature in 12 years. If you choose, you can keep a bond after it reaches its face value and let it continue to earn interest until it reaches final maturity. For newer bonds (those purchased since the 1960s), final maturity is 30 years. When you cash in a bond, you'll owe federal income taxes on the interest earned, but not state and local taxes.

To get the most from your U.S. Savings Bonds, Bengen says, you must understand how and when they pay interest, how you'll be taxed on that interest, penalties for early withdrawal, and other little-known aspects of the bonds. Here's his advice for making your savings bonds pay.

Minimize the Tax Hit

"One of the good things about savings bonds is that you don't have to pay taxes on them until you cash them in," Bengen says. "The bad news is that you do have to pay taxes." It's best to cash them in when that tax liability is not as much of an issue.

"The year after you retire, for instance, your taxes may be lower because you don't have any earned wages. That might be a good year to cash in some older savings bonds," he says.

◗◆ WHAT INSIDERS SAY:

When your series EE Savings Bonds reach final maturity, if you don't need the cash right away, you can continue deferring the majority of the earnings by rolling the bonds over into series HH bonds. These pay interest every 6 months. "Let's say you bought $1,000 worth of bonds, and they're now worth $3,000," Bengen says. "You put the $3,000 series EE bonds into HH bonds. They pay you interest on the full $3,000, and you don't have to pay the tax on the $2,000 that the original bonds gained until you sell the HH bonds." If you decide to take this route, you must roll over the bonds within 1 year of their final maturity date. Otherwise, you lose this option.

Avoid Early Withdrawal

If at all possible, don't cash in bonds before their initial maturity, or face value, date. If you do, you'll face a penalty. For any bonds bought after May 1997, for example, there's a penalty equivalent to 3 months' interest if you cash them in within 5 years of the purchase date.

Don't Let Them Lapse

When savings bonds reach their final maturity date, they stop earning interest. After that point, it's like tucking your dollars into your mattress—as time passes, you end up losing money, thanks to inflation. Plus, when a bond matures, the IRS expects you to cash it in and pay taxes on the interest earned. If you hold the bond beyond December 31 of the final maturity year, the IRS begins charging interest and penalties on the tax due.

◗◆ WHAT INSIDERS SAY:

Bonds have a great benefit for parents: The interest is exempt from federal taxes if you use it to cover college tuition for your children or yourself. There are certain income restrictions, however. Ask about this option when you buy a bond, or contact the Savings Bond Marketing Office at 999 E Street, Room 313,

Washington, DC 20226. The U.S. Treasury Department Web site is also very helpful; go to www. savingsbonds.gov.

Taking Advantage of U.S. Treasury Notes

"Treasury notes, issued by the federal government, are IOUs like any other bond," says Bengen. "You lend the government money, it pays you interest semiannually, and it returns the principal when the bond matures."

Treasury notes are considered as safe an investment as there is. The initial interest, which is locked in and is competitive with that of other bonds and bank CDs, is taxed at the federal level, but it's ex-empt from state and local taxes. At this time, for a 2-year note, a 5 percent interest rate is fairly normal, says Bengen.

Buy What Suits You

"The best advice for anyone considering notes," says Bengen, "is to buy them in small enough quantities that you're comfortable holding that note and receiving its interest for 2 or 5 years without being concerned about what happens to the market." In other words, use funds that you won't have to liquidate in an emergency. And don't panic if the bond market drops. You may end up losing some of the interest you'd hoped to accrue, but unlike investments in stocks, you're guaranteed to get your principal back.

GETTING A PEEK AT FUTURE BENEFITS

Knowing how much you can expect to receive in Social Security benefits can help you decide when it will be best for you to retire. Until recently, however, if you wanted to get an estimate of what you would receive, you had to request a form from the Social Security Administration, fill it out, and wait for a reply. Lots of people never did it. The result was that many workers knew very little about Social Security and even less about what they could expect to receive come retirement time.

Starting in October 1999, the folks at Social Security began providing an annual statement to everyone who filed a tax return—a total of more than 125 million American workers. "It's probably one of the largest customized mailings ever done by any government agency," says John Trollinger, a Social Security spokesman. Now, each year, workers learn how much they've paid into the system to date and receive an estimate of their retirement, disability, and survivor benefits.

According to Trollinger, you should expect the statement about 3 months before your birthday each year. If it doesn't arrive, you should contact the Social Security Administration, whose address and phone number are listed in the gov-ernment pages of your telephone directory. You may need to provide your most recent tax return, a W-2 form, or a pay stub from work to help the government track down your report.

●◆ *WHAT INSIDERS SAY:*

It's important to check your Social Security statement each year to be sure that it accurately reflects the amount that your W-2 tax forms shows that you paid in Social Security taxes. If your annual statement is incorrect, contact the Social Security Administration as soon as possible. To prove an error, you'll need to show a tax return, your W-2, a pay stub, or a statement from your employer.

Invest in the Short Run

Stick to 2- or 5-year notes. Anything with a longer term, such as a 10- or 30-year note, is too risky because of interest fluctuations.

Avoid Fees and Commissions

If you buy your treasury notes from a bank or brokerage firm, you'll most likely pay $25 to $50 in fees for each note. Instead, buy directly from the U.S. Federal Reserve Bank, the issuer of the notes. The Federal Reserve will link directly to your bank account, so the interest earned can be deposited directly twice a year.

For an investor's kit, which includes the address of the Federal Reserve Bank district office nearest you, write to the Bureau of Public Debt Servicing Office, Department N, Washington, DC 20239-1500. Or visit the Bureau of Public Debt's Web site at www.publicdebt.treas.gov.

Investing Tax-Free in Municipal Bonds

When used wisely (and carefully), municipal bonds, also known as munis, can be good investments for certain people. A municipal bond is a bond issued by a state or local government. Unlike U.S. bonds, which are backed by the rock-solid federal government, munis vary in stability and yield depending on the financial stability of the issuer and the maturity of the bond.

"Say you found a municipality that's on the edge of bankruptcy and has issued a 30-year bond," says Bengen. "That's going to pay a very high interest rate, but it has a low level of safety." There's a chance that you might lose the principal you put into the bond. For that reason, it's best to seek advice from a financial professional before purchasing munis. What makes them attractive is that the interest they earn is exempt from federal taxes and, in some cases, state and local taxes. Here's some advice for investing in municipal bonds safely, while maximizing your gains.

Make Sure They Make Sense for You

You'll benefit most from munis' tax-free status if you're in a high tax bracket. For example, says Bengen, "Today, a 2-year muni pays about 3.5 percent interest, while a 2-year U.S. treasury note pays about 5 percent. If you're in the 15 percent tax bracket, the treasury is much better. If you're in the 39 percent tax bracket, a treasury's 5 percent interest drops to about 3 percent after taxes, so the muni's better." The bottom line: A muni doesn't make sense for people in tax brackets of 28 percent or lower, which means most people with incomes below $62,450 or $104,050 for married couples filing jointly.

Buy Only Top-Rated Munis

Various companies, such as Standard and Poor's Securities, for instance, or Moody's Investors Services, rate bonds based on their stability as investments. The highest rating on the scale is AAA, followed by AA, A, BBB, and so on.

Anything below BBB is referred to as junk or high-yield, and while these bonds may pay a higher return, you're not as certain of getting back your principal in the end. Bengen suggests sticking to AAA or AA municipal bonds. You have to buy munis from a brokerage house (any fees are typically figured into the bond price). He suggests asking your broker what the ratings are for a particular bond.

Stick to Short Terms

Another way to increase your safety when investing in munis is to limit the maturity times of the bonds to 5 or 10 years. Bonds that take longer than that to mature—30 years, for instance—are risky, since you can't guess the state of the market or of the issuing municipality that far in the future.

Buy In-State Bonds

Bonds that are issued by municipalities within your home state or by your home state government are exempt from state and local taxes as well as federal taxes.

MAXIMIZING RETIREMENT MONEY

When you have the three legs of your retirement strategy in place and growing, you'll need to develop tactics for withdrawing your money after you retire. Your goal should be to maximize the amount you get from Social Security by using it when you need it most and minimizing the taxes you pay on your other tax-deferred withdrawals.

Maximizing Social Security means understanding the system and figuring out when it's best to start drawing benefits, based on your situation.

Minimizing the tax bite on retirement accounts is a bit trickier. Again, what you do depends on your personal financial needs and goals. The key is understanding some of the more arcane restrictions on tax-deferred retirement accounts (and the occasional exception to the rules). Here's more on both of these issues.

How to Get the Most From Social Security

Launched in 1935 by President Franklin Roosevelt, Social Security still protects more than 145 million workers and pays benefits to 44 million people. Anyone who has worked and paid Social Security taxes in this country can expect to get something back at retirement. Today, in fact, the average retiree can count on receiving Social Security benefits equal to about 40 percent of his or her pre-retirement earnings.

There are two main strategies for accessing your Social Security benefits. The one you choose will depend on your circumstances. Here's an explanation of each.

Benefiting from Early Retirement

Currently, the age at which you can receive full Social Security benefits is 65 (it will gradually increase to 67 by 2027). Nevertheless, you can retire as early as 62 if you're willing to accept lower monthly payments from Social Security. At this time, you lose $5/9$ of 1 percent for each month before the official age you retire. That adds up to a little less than 7 percent a year.

So, for example, if the Social Security Administration's official retirement age is 65, and you sign up for benefits when you are 64, you will receive $93\frac{1}{3}$ percent of your full benefit. At age 62, you would get 80 percent. But that's not necessarily a bad thing.

If you have a chronic illness or are eager to retire, and if you have sufficient funds in other accounts to supplement the reduced monthly Social Security payments, retiring early—as far as Social Security benefits go—might be economically better in the short run. Even though the monthly benefits are lower, your total payout is greater—up to a point—than if you retired later.

If your average lifetime earnings were $50,000 a year, for example, you would receive an estimated $1,269 a month from Social Security if you retired at age 65. If you retired at 62, you would receive $1,015 per month, or 80 percent of your full benefit.

Although you would lose $250 a month by retiring early, you also would receive 3 years' worth of checks that you wouldn't get by waiting until 65. This means that at the age of 75, you would have received $158,340 by retiring early, versus $152,280 by retiring on time. It's only after age 75 that your benefits from retiring on time would surpass those that you would receive by retiring early.

Benefiting from Late Retirement

If you're in good health, like your work, and want to maximize the amount you'll receive from Social Security when you eventually retire, you might want to continue working full-time and postpone filing for benefits past the official retirement age. This will increase your Social Security check for two reasons.

First, your continued contributions to the fund increase your average earnings; the higher your average earnings, the higher your Social Security benefits.

Second, the Social Security Administration

provides a bonus to those who delay collecting benefits. Currently, people receive an additional 5 percent per year for each year that they delay collecting after they reach the official retirement age. The rate will gradually increase until it reaches 8 percent per year for people who turn 65 in 2008 or later and who delay collecting past that age. That means that someone who retires today at 67 would receive 10 percent more in monthly benefits by delaying retirement beyond 65.

●◆ WHAT INSIDERS SAY:

Are you worried that Social Security and your investments won't provide enough money for your needs? Then supplement your income. You can work part-time and still collect full benefits, as long as you don't exceed certain income limits. As of 1999, retirees under the age of 65 can earn up to $9,600; those ages 65 to 69 can earn up to $15,500 and still receive full benefits; and retirees 70 and over can make as much money as they want.

Trimming Taxes on Retirement Accounts

The government gives workers a boost by providing a number of tax incentives for money that they put away for retirement. Perhaps the best-known incentives are tax-deferred retirement plans, such as the 401(k) and the Individual Retirement Account (IRA). They allow you to save pretax dollars in an investment account that can earn interest without being taxed until you begin withdrawing the money upon retirement.

How much you eventually pay in taxes depends on when and how you withdraw your money. Here is some insider advice to help you get the most from your retirement accounts.

First, Tap Non-Tax-Deferred Funds

One popular strategy that experts recommend is to draw first from those funds that have the smallest tax liability, such as mutual funds, stocks, and other investments you've made with after-tax dollars.

When you withdraw from one of these funds, you owe taxes only on the amount by which the investment has grown. And you pay taxes at the capital gains tax rate (18 percent as of December 31, 2000) rather than your income tax rate. Let's say you decide to withdraw a mutual-fund investment that you bought at $50,000 and that is now worth $75,000. You'll owe 18 percent tax on the $25,000 profit, or $4,500.

By contrast, if you withdrew $75,000 from a tax-deferred retirement account such as a 401(k), and you were in the 28 percent income tax bracket, you'd owe 28 percent tax on the entire amount, or $21,000.

Next, Dip Into Retirement Plans

After you've used up non-tax-deferred investments, you should draw from tax-deferred accounts such as IRAs and 401(k) plans. Your goal is to leave them alone as long as possible, because this will help you in two ways. As the accounts grow, the tax deferral allows for greater compounding of interest.

! FACTOID

Also, once you're retired, your yearly income will probably drop off, putting you in a lower tax bracket. Since tax-deferred retirement accounts are taxed as income in the year you draw on them, if you drop from, say, the 28 percent bracket to the 15 percent bracket, you stand to save a considerable amount in taxes.

Note: When you turn 70½, federal law requires you to withdraw a minimum amount from your retirement accounts or face a 50 percent tax penalty on anything under that minimum. For advice on doing that, see "Two Ways to Tap Those IRAs."

➥ WHAT INSIDERS SAY:

If your net worth is high enough to make estate taxes an issue, the reverse of the above strategy applies. See "Beating Estate Taxes" on page 182.

Use Your Roth IRA Last

If you've invested in a Roth IRA—one of the fairly recent options—you should make it one of the last investments you withdraw. Because there is no tax liability on the principal or interest you withdraw from a Roth IRA, the more you can allow your Roth-based investments to grow, the better.

➥ WHAT INSIDERS SAY:

The government requires that you begin withdrawing from standard IRAs when you turn 70½, but this does not apply to Roth IRAs. You can hold onto them for as long as you want. In fact, you might want to leave your Roth IRA for your children if your other retirement funds cover your cost of living. These IRAs differ from traditional IRAs in that the government doesn't dictate how and when you distribute them.

TWO WAYS TO TAP THOSE IRAS

Once you turn 70½, the federal government requires that you withdraw a minimum amount from your tax-deferred retirement accounts—401(k) plans, IRAs, and other pension plans that contain pretax contributions.

It's your right to choose one of two ways for the government to figure the minimum amount: recalculation or nonrecalculation. The choice, which is irrevocable, can make a big difference in how years of retirement savings are doled out to you and your heirs. The choice depends on many variables. Here's an explanation of each method.

Recalculation

If you choose the recalculation method—and most people do, for better or worse—the government uses mortality tables to recalculate your life expectancy each year, beginning at age 70½. The figure it comes up with is the percentage of your retirement moneys that you must withdraw each year.

If you are a 70½-year-old man, for example, and the average life expectancy of someone of your description is 17 years, you'd be required to withdraw a minimum of $1/17$ of your retirement account or face a 50 percent tax on the

balance of the $1/17$th you don't withdraw. When you turn 71, the government will recalculate and come up with a figure that is slightly less than $1/17$, such as $2/35$, for instance. That year, the minimum withdrawal would be $2/35$ of your account.

With the recalculation strategy, you're covered for the long run. As long as you go on living, the account is drawn out gradually, even if you live to the ripe old age of 95 or 100.

The downside is that when both you and your spouse die, the retirement account must be fully distributed among your children (or other heirs) within a year of the most recent

Limiting Taxes on Your Pension

Different company pension plans have different ways of distributing benefits. Some hand over one lump sum. Others pay retirees monthly payments over many years. Sometimes you have the choice between the two. There are pros and cons to each method, depending on your financial situation. Here are some tips that experts suggest for making wise choices when it comes to your pension payout.

In Most Cases, Beware the Lump Sum

Don't let visions of life on a yacht in the Caribbean dance in your head when you learn you're in line for a large, lump-sum pension payment. You face dire tax consequences if you take that money be-cause lump sums are subject to full income taxes immediately.

If your pension benefits total $100,000, for example, and you opt for a lump-sum payment, you will have to pay taxes based on your current income tax bracket. If you are in the 28 percent bracket, you'll be left with $78,000.

That said, there are instances when a lump sum can make sense—if you're starting your own business and need seed capital, for instance, or if you have to pay off large debts. Consult a financial planner for advice.

Choose a Direct Rollover

If your company requires that you receive the amount all at once instead of in monthly payments,

---

death. "Most parents don't like the idea of a large sum of money suddenly being distributed to their kids," says Jim Almond, a certified financial planner and financial columnist for the *Dallas/Fort Worth Heritage*. "It's like winning the lottery; a lot of times, after 4 or 5 years [of high living], people are no better off than before they got the money. Sometimes they're worse off."

In terms of tax planning, it's not a wise strategy either, since the children would owe taxes all at once on the lump sum.

Nonrecalculation

As the name implies, there is no recalculation of the minimum withdrawal figure using this method. Once the life expec-tancy is calculated at age $70^1/_2$, you withdraw a set amount each year. If your life expectancy starts at 17 years, then $^1/_{17}$ of the original amount is what you must withdraw each year. At the end of 17 years, you will have withdrawn all of the money in your account.

The upside to this strategy come into play if you and your spouse die sooner than your estimated life expectancy. Then, your children will be left with the same graduated with-drawal schedule. "Say there are 14 years left in the ac-count," Almond explains. "The children can continue re-ceiving distributions over that 14-year period." This reduces their tax burden.

If you live beyond the 17-year payout, however, your account will be empty, and you may be in the position of having to look for other ways to fund your retirement. The solu-tion, says Almond, is to rein-vest. "If you're pulling out more than you need to live on, you should set the extra aside for the future," he says. On these new investments, you'll owe taxes only on the amount your money appreciates, since you've already paid tax on the amount you're investing. And the earnings from the invest-ments would be subject to the capital gains tax rate (currently at 20 percent), which is less than income tax rates in most tax brackets.

BEATING ESTATE TAXES

Death and taxes, they say, are certainties. Depending on your net worth, you may also face taxation after death—at rates from 37 percent to 55 percent.

The federal government currently gives everyone a $650,000 estate-tax exemption, so you can pass on assets up to that amount without your heirs facing taxation. (The amount increases incrementally, so by the year 2006, it will be $1,000,000.) "I'll never have that much money," you might think, "so why do I have to worry about estate taxes?" Think again.

First of all, a variety of assets—cash, retirement accounts, stocks and bonds, houses, land, and other things— make up your estate. It's not as impossible as you might think to amass a net worth of a million or more, especially if you've planned well for retirement. If you die and your estate is still worth more than the exemption, the balance faces heavy taxation before it passes on to your children.

Here are some strategies for avoiding these high estate taxes and passing on more of your hard-earned money to the next generation.

Draw retirement benefits first

If you have considerable assets in non-tax-deferred investments, draw first from the tax-deferred accounts. Once you turn 70½, the government requires that you begin withdrawing a minimum amount from tax-deferred investments. When you die, your heirs must continue those withdrawals, and often the entire lump sum is dumped into their laps.

"Not only do you have an income tax liability on the retirement account, but you also may face estate taxes," says Jim Almond, a certified financial planner and financial columnist for the *Dallas/Fort Worth Heritage*. "You can literally see 70 to 90 percent of an IRA asset walk right out the door." You have more control over how the non-tax-deferred investments are passed on.

Don't leave it all to your spouse

Many couples write wills that give the surviving spouse all the assets. This is good for the survivor, since the government lets you pass an entire estate tax-free to a spouse, regardless of the cash value. However, using this strategy can cost your heirs dearly when the surviving spouse dies. Here's why.

You and your spouse each have the right to protect your heirs from taxes on the first $650,000 that you leave them. This means that combined, the two of you can shield your heirs from paying taxes on $1.3 million in assets. But if you pass all of your assets to your spouse on your death, your heirs can't claim your half of the exemption. Thus, when your spouse dies, they will have to pay Uncle Sam taxes on any amount greater than $650,000.

Instead, you and your spouse may want to consider leaving a portion of your assets directly to your heirs when the first of you dies, so they can claim the first exemption. Then, if there are considerable assets in the estate when the surviving spouse dies, the heirs can take another exemption of up to $650,000.

arrange for a direct rollover into an IRA or some other retirement account. You'll defer taxes until a later date, which allows the entire sum to accrue interest. And you may be subject to lower taxes when you finally withdraw if you wait until you've retired and have dropped to a lower tax bracket.

●◆ WHAT INSIDERS SAY:

Never let your company make out a lump-sum pension check to you or deposit it into your bank account. Even if you're planning to roll it over into a retirement account, if you receive the money—even for a short period—it will be subject to taxes. The bottom line: Make sure the rollover is done on an institution-to-institution level.

Consider a Segregated IRA

If you're leaving a company with the intention of working elsewhere before you retire, ask your company to invest your pension in a segregated IRA (also known as a conduit IRA). This is an IRA that stands apart from other existing IRAs. Since the funds in a conduit IRA are not mingled with your other investments, you may have the option of one day transferring it to another employer's pension plan.

Withdraw Money Bit by Bit

If you are under the age of 59½ and financial circumstances force you to draw from a lump-sum pension, the IRS usually will charge a 10 percent tax penalty for early withdrawal. There is one exception to this advice, say insiders. It's called Regulation 72(t), and it allows you to take more or less equal payments from your pension or other tax-deferred retirement plans prior to age 59½ without a penalty. Here's how it works.

"Let's say an individual is 50, and he wants to retire," explains Jim Almond, a certified financial planner and financial columnist for the *Dallas/Fort Worth Heritage*. "The government has mortality tables that would dictate the average mortality for a male of his age. Let's say he was expected to live another 25 years. The government would allow him to take ½₅, or 4 percent, of that account without penalty."

This might come in handy if you've been forced into early retirement due to downsizing. After, say, 30 years at one or two companies, you might not want to re-enter the job market, and you'll need the retirement money you've accrued over the years to live on.

Go to the pension manager or the company in charge of the account, Almond suggests, and say that you want to take money out of your account prior to age 59½ without penalty under Regulation 72(t). The company will be able to calculate your benefits.

FOUR

Travel and Leisure

CHAPTER 13

RELAXING
on UNCLE SAM'S
DIME

When it comes to travel destinations, the government has it all: lakes, rivers, beaches, mountain trails, volcanoes, caves, wildlife habitats, ancient ruins, historic buildings, forts, museums, monuments, and even tropical islands. You could spend the rest of your vacation days exploring federal, state, and local government sites and barely scratch the surface of what's available.

Need lodging for the night? The federal government alone has more than 15,000 shelters, cabins, and rooms—everything from fire-tower cabins perched 60 feet in the sky to a quaint lighthouse bed-and-breakfast and historic, full-service inns. If you'd prefer to rough it—or find a hookup for your RV—you'll find thousands of prime spots in national and state parks and on land owned by the National Forest Service, the Bureau

of Land Management, and other government agencies. One little-known campers' paradise, for example, overlooks the turquoise waters of the Caribbean, and $20 a night will get you and your family a site with a picnic table and barbecue grill.

Indeed, low prices are one of the best things about government destinations, and this chapter is filled with creative tips for booking bargain trips. For instance, you'll find a sample itinerary for a nearly free, activity-packed weekend in Washington, D.C., including visits to art museums, the most famous monuments, the White House, and other sites. You'll also learn how to volunteer as a park host for a week in exchange for a free week of camping. And you'll find out where to order free trail and highway maps. (For those ever-curious wayfarers who prefer back roads to

> Brilliant mountain vistas. Historic forts. White sand beaches. Quiet pine-filled forests. America is filled with inspiring travel opportunities, and Uncle Sam is there at every step to make your trip a treat.

FACTOID

ONE OF THE TOP 10 LARGEST MONEY-MAKING RESTAURANTS IN THE UNITED STATES IS IN A NATIONAL PARK. IT'S THE CLIFF HOUSE, WHICH OVERLOOKS THE BAY IN SAN FRANCISCO'S GOLDEN GATE NATIONAL RECREATION AREA AND IS FAMOUS FOR ITS CRAB LOUIS SALAD AND OTHER SEAFOOD. ITS ANNUAL TAKE: $8 TO $12 MILLION IN GROSS SALES.

interstate highways, we'll even tell you where to order county maps.)

Getting the most from your government when you vacation also means not bogging down in the information quagmire. This chapter will lead you straight to the diamonds in the rough—awe-inspiring lesser-known national and state parks, special discounts, low-cost government surplus camping gear—even unique opportunities to save on interesting vacations by volunteering. It will also explain how to get the most from your trips, whether your goal is to beat the crowds, land a prime vacation spot, or hire the most knowledgeable guide to show you around. Happy trails!

LODGING

Stephen T. Mather, the first director of the National Parks Service, understood the importance of providing for the needs and comforts of park visitors. "Scenery," he said, "is hollow enjoyment to a tourist who sets out in the morning after an indigestible breakfast and a fitful sleep on an impossible bed."

Today, when you visit the country's more than 300 national parks—as well as the national forests, state parks, and other public land—you don't need to worry about where to bed down. You'll find a mind-boggling array of campsites, cabins, and hotel rooms available in a range of styles and prices. Services abound, too: Along with restaurants, gift shops, and visitor centers, there are extras, like coin-operated laundries, day care, and even kennels, that you don't typically find in the average private hotel.

"We want to make sure that the average family can enjoy the parks no matter what their budget," says Dee Highnote, senior concessions operation analyst for National Park Service Concessions in Washington, D.C., the office that oversees the concessionaires who provide tourist services inside national parks.

Tracking Down the Perfect Retreat

To search out the best lodgings on public land, you need to learn how the system works. First, you should know that at the federal level, all the accommodations inside national parks—camping, cabins, and inns—are provided by private concessionaires under contract to the government. While prices, reservation policies, and other aspects of the concessions are regulated by the government, visitors deal directly with the park concessionaire to make reservations.

One result of this public/private partnership is that there is no central booking agent for the national parks. (The exception is the system that's in effect at 25 of the largest national parks. See "Setting Up Camp" on page 192.) It also means that overnight visitors to the national parks pay twice: In addition to the cost of lodging, there's a one-time park entrance fee, ranging from a couple of bucks to $20 in a few instances. The only way to get a break on entrance fees is to use one of the Golden Passports that are available for seniors, the disabled, or frequent park visitors (see "Golden Passports" on page 214).

Also, since there's great demand for government lodging, many federal and state spots are offered through reservation systems and, occasionally, lotteries. These often-complicated processes can be frustrating. If you're savvy about how the reservation systems work, however, you can improve your chances of finding the right place to stay (see "Getting the Spot You Want" on page 190).

The next step in finding accommodations is learning what's available on the millions of acres of federal and state land. You can get a good sense of the options by following the tips below.

●◆ *WHAT INSIDERS SAY:*

If you have a problem with a park concessionaire—a lodge has lost your reservation or has charged a higher rate than previously promised—your best bet is to contact the park superintendent. He generally has final say over matters involving concessionaires. Lodges often post signs in their lobbies with the name, address, and telephone number of the superintendent. If not, ask the lodge manager how to contact him.

Look To the Web

The National Park Service's Web site (www.nps.gov) allows you to search for national parks by name, state, or recreational theme. Once you've found a park that strikes your fancy, the site lists available lodging, activities, peak seasons, contact information, and more.

The federal government has created a centralized Web site that covers all federal land including the National Park Service, the Forest Service, Bureau of Reclamation, Bureau of Land Management, Fish and Wildlife Service, and Army Corps of Engineers. Using this extremely helpful and easy-to-navigate site, at www.recreation.gov, you can conduct a customized search—by state or the entire country—for recreation sites that have lodging and offer certain activities, such as boating, biking, fishing, or hiking.

Look To Books

The "National Parks Visitors Facilities and Services Handbook" ($3, plus $1.50 shipping) lists the names and contact information for concessionaires who run facilities inside national parks. Write to the National Park Hospitality Association, 1225 New York Avenue NW, Suite 450, Washington, DC 20005.

The Complete Guide to America's National Parks ($18), published by Fodor's and the National Park Foundation, the Park Service's nonprofit advocacy group, provides a more detailed description of the lodging available in federal parks. Write to Random House, Inc., 400 Hahn Road, Westminster, MD 21157.

It can take as long as 4 weeks for these agencies to respond to your request, so be sure to write well in advance of your planned trip.

Look in the Forest

Few people realize that there are hundreds of great vacation spots outside the national parks. The National Forest Service, for instance, oversees 155 forest sites totaling more than 191 million acres—

an area larger than the state of Texas. There are more than 4,000 campgrounds and about 500 cabins in these vast lands, and in many of the areas, crowds aren't a problem. For information, write USDA Forest Service, Office of Communications, P.O. Box 96090, Washington, DC 20090-6090.

◆○ WHAT INSIDERS SAY:

Concessionaires in the national forests offer lodging, but don't expect the amenities that are available at the national parks. Here, things tend to be more rustic, such as camping and basic cabins.

Look To the Bureau

Another agency that's flush with property is the Bureau of Land Management (BLM), the biggest U.S. landowner, with 270 million acres. The BLM manages some amazing campgrounds, including the Three Rivers petroglyph site in New Mexico, where you can camp near a basaltic ridge containing more than 20,000 petroglyphs of masks, fish, sunbursts, and other designs, drawn by the Jornada Mogollon people more than 1,000 years ago.

You can contact Three Rivers at 1800 Marquess Street, Las Cruces, NM 88005-3371. For information on other BLM sites, write the Bureau of Land Management, Office of Public Affairs, 1849 C Street NW, LS-406, Washington, DC 20240.

Look To the Water

You'll also find recreational facilities and lodging, mainly in the form of campsites, on land managed by the following agencies.

✔ The Bureau of Reclamation, which, like the BLM, is part of the U.S. Department of the Interior. It manages 310 reservoirs, rivers, and other water-based sites. Write to the BLM address given above.

✔ The U.S. Army Corps of Engineers, the country's largest provider of water-oriented recreation. Contact them at Publications Depot, 2803 52nd Avenue, Hyattsville, MD 20781-1102.

Look To the State

A wide variety of lodging is also available in state parks around the country, from camping by the coral reefs of Florida to bedding down in the former guest quarters of visiting generals at an Indiana army base turned golf resort. Tracking down information can be a little tricky because the names of the agencies that run the parks may vary from state to state, but all states have an office that oversees state parks and other recreation areas. In South Carolina, for example, the office goes by the name the Department of Parks, Recreation, and Tourism. In Texas, it's Parks and Wildlife, and in Maine, the Bureau of Parks and Lands. Check the government

GETTING THE SPOT YOU WANT

Landing a reservation at a federally or state-owned inn, cabin, or campground is not as easy as choosing dates and picking up the phone to make a reservation. Because of intense competition for these desirable sites, many of them are fully booked far in advance. For instance, the beach-front cottages at Hunting Island State Park in South Carolina are so popular that they're booked solid 18 months in advance, and all the reservations are usually taken just 3 days after the state opens its reservations line on January 1.

While the situation is challenging, it isn't hopeless. Whether the park uses a write-in or phone-in reservation system or a lottery system, in which written requests are chosen randomly from a pile, there are steps that you can take to improve your chances of finding accommodations.

Here are some tips that will give you an edge.

Learn the routine
In their attempts to deal with the onslaught of room and camping requests, government parks have devised a variety of systems for maintaining fairness. Most begin taking reservations a certain number of months (sometimes a year) in advance. The National Park Reservation System (NPRS), for example, takes camping reservations—by telephone or in writing—up to 5 months in advance for about 25 national parks.

If you're going after a really hot spot—a room at Yellowstone's Old Faithful Inn, for instance—find out from the lodge or campground exactly when it begins accepting reservations. If it accepts phone reservations, ask what day *and hour* the phone lines open. If you must write in, find out the earliest date that your letter can be postmarked. If it's a lottery, be sure you know every bit of information needed to process your request.

Book early—really early
Even if your travel plans are not firm, call or write for a reservation as far in advance as possible (how far depends on when the particular park begins accepting reservations). As long as you're allowed to cancel without a great penalty, this strategy isn't risky, and it may be your only chance at getting a spot. For example, you can book a campsite through NPRS and cancel without penalty as late as 24 hours before the date you're supposed to arrive. (If you cancel the same day, you will be charged a cancellation fee and your first night's camping fee.) And if you're willing to gamble $8.65 on a nonrefundable reservation fee, you can

pages of your phone book for numbers and addresses.

Many state-sponsored Web sites also provide tourism information. To access a particular state's site, type in www.state.*(insert the two-letter state abbreviation)*.us. Once at the site, click on "Tourism" or "Public Information."

Typically, each state can provide maps of the public lands as well as descriptions of available lodging and addresses and phone numbers. You can then make reservations with the particular park or site that interests you.

To give you a better idea of just what's available in terms of government-related lodging, here are

reserve a campsite or cabin run by the U.S. Forest Service up to a year in advance.

Keep trying
The upside of masses of people booking early is that it increases the chance that those who make reservations will have to cancel because of scheduling difficulties. If a site is full when you call, try calling again periodically (most places do not keep waiting lists). You might land a cancellation.

Do your homework
"A lot of people call and say, 'I want to go to some park in Florida,'" says Cathy Burdett, program manager for NPRS. "But you wouldn't call Holiday Inn and say, 'Give me a hotel room somewhere in Florida,' would you?" She suggests doing a little research: Request brochures and other information from the park you're interested in; call the lodge or campground where you want to stay and ask for reservations advice. "They should be

able to give you a feel for how quickly the place books up," Burdett says.

Be flexible
Have several dates in mind when you contact a reservations agent. Likewise, be willing to take a different lodge or campground within the park you want to visit.

Disabled?
Ask about special sites
Every park in the NPRS system reserves campsites for the physically disabled, which tend to be closer to restrooms and have paved areas and wheelchair-accessible picnic tables. These generally don't book up as quickly. Before calling, be sure to get a Golden Access Passport (available only in person at a national park entrance). This is a free lifetime entrance pass for persons who are blind or permanently disabled. When making the reservation, you'll be asked to provide your passport ID number.

◗◖ WHAT INSIDERS SAY:
No matter what type of lodging you choose, be sure to ask about any of a variety of discounts: seniors rate, family rate, group rate, early-season rate, off-season rate. For example, take senior citizens who have Golden Age Passports (available for $10 in person at a national park entrance). These lifetime entrance passes for anyone age 62 or older entitle you to 50 percent off camping fees at all national parks and some national forests.

Early-season and off-season discounts can be substantial as well. In 1998 during the winter off-season, rooms at the Fort Golf Resort and Convention Center in Indiana's Harrison State Park—which range in price from $49 for a double to $189 for a three-bedroom—were free every other night. If you stayed 2 nights, 1 was free; if you stayed for 4, 2 were free.

examples of campsites, cabins, inns, fire towers, and hostels around the U.S.

Setting Up Camp

For many, it's an annual tradition. You leave behind the air conditioning, television, refrigerator, and other comforts of home, pack up a sufficient amount of portable, nonperishable food, and go camping. Whether you sleep under the stars, in a tent, or beneath the pop-up roof of a car camper—or even curl up under the covers of a no-amenity-spared recreation vehicle—there is something special about fleeing your permanent address and getting closer to nature.

Hands-down, the best camping in the United States is available on government land. You can have access to the deepest wilds, the widest plains, and miles of untamed coastline, not to mention the merely secluded spots near urban centers. The National Park Service alone boasts 83 million acres of nature preserves. And government campgrounds offer a variety of camp types, from primitive back-country clearings to sites with electrical and plumbing hookups for RVs and just about everything in between.

Camping on government land is also one of the most economical ways to vacation. Fees, which are typically assessed per campsite, can be as low as $2 or $3 per person when divided among a family or group. Or, in the case of back-country camping, it can be free. Below are some examples of camping opportunities available around the country.

•◄► WHAT INSIDERS SAY:

Some campgrounds take reservations, and others offer sites on a first-come, first-served basis. If you're interested in camping on government land, the best way to ensure that you get the spot you want is to contact a particular park or other place for camping information. However, there is a central reservations office—the National Park Reservation Service—for campsites at 25 of the country's national parks, including Joshua Tree National Park, Rocky Mountain National Park, and Great Smoky Mountains National Park. Write to the National Park Reservation Service at P.O. Box 1600, Cumberland, MD 21502.

Also, the Forest Service and the U.S. Army Corps of Engineers have a joint camping reservations service, the National Recreation Reservation Service, for many of their sites. For information, write to USDA Forest Service, Office of Communications, P.O. Box 96090, Washington, DC 20090-6090.

An Island Paradise without the Crowds

Looking for a tropical paradise where the tourists aren't wall to wall? You can have it, and vacation for as little as $20 a day, at the Cinnamon Bay Campground on St. John in the U.S. Virgin Islands. This little-known campground "is on the shores of one of the finest beaches in the world," says general manager Jim Bartell. It's part of the Virgin Islands National Park, a park that many Americans don't know exists.

"Some of our visitors make over $100,000 a year, according to their guest cards, but they choose to come here instead of to one of the expensive island alternatives," Bartell says.

Campsites, tucked away in the 12,900-acre park's lush foliage, are all within a 2-minute walk of the white sands of Cinnamon Bay Beach, the longest on the island. Bare sites, which cost $20 per night, include a picnic table and charcoal grill. Semipermanent tents, 10 by 14 feet with solid floors, are $52 to $80 per night, depending on the season, and each comes with cots, a picnic table, a grill, a propane gas stove, cooking and eating utensils, an ice chest, a gas lantern, and bed linens. Cottages, 15-by-15-foot rooms with screens front and back, cost $70 to $120 per night, depending on the season. These come with four twin beds, a table, chairs, an electric fan, and all of the amenities included with the tents.

•◄► WHAT INSIDERS SAY:

Virgin Islands National Park is one of the few whose peak season is the dead of winter, December through

April. By booking your trip outside of those months, you'll save money and stand a better chance of missing the crowds. Write to Cinnamon Bay Campground, P.O. Box 720, Cruz Bay, St. John, U.S. Virgin Islands 00831.

Camping in the Majestic Mountains

One of the country's grandest natural treasures, California's 1,170-square-mile Yosemite National Park is home to well-known peaks such as Half

BEATING THE CROWDS

You wouldn't expect to run into a traffic jam in the great outdoors, but at popular national parks, like Yosemite in California, cars full of anxious visitors often sit bumper to bumper, waiting for a glimpse of Mother Nature's majesty. At these parks, vacationers stand in line at gift shops and restaurants and at first-come, first-served campgrounds. The problem is that there are too many people per park. Indeed, the number of annual visits to national parks has skyrocketed from 400,000 when the National Park Service was created in 1916 to more than 265 million today.

Here are some tips to avoid park pandemonium.

Go during the off-season
Except for Virgin Islands National Park, the Florida Everglades, Death Valley, and a few other national parks that are popular in winter, summer is the peak park season. Generally, the fall and spring months are great times to visit, not only due to fewer folks but also because of milder weather and seasonal spectacles, such as blooming wildflowers or changing leaf colors.

"People might be surprised by what there is to do in the winter," says Robert Yearout, concessions program manager for the Park Service. "There's nothing prettier than the Grand Canyon with a little snow on the ground."

Go early or late
If you must go during a peak time, stick to the early or late part of the season, when crowds are relatively smaller.

Avoid holiday weekends
Stay home during the most popular weekends, which tend to be around July 4, Labor Day, and Memorial Day for parks that are busy in the summer and around Christmas for winter parks.

Visit during the week
Avoid weekends altogether, if possible, and go while most of America is working.

Pick a lesser-known park
Though there are more than 350 different park sites in the country, most people are familiar with only the most popular ones. Some of the lesser-known parks, such as Texas's Big Bend National Park or Badlands National Park in South Dakota, are spectacular in their own right and offer lodging opportunities and more. You can contact Big Bend at P.O. Box 129, Big Bend National Park, TX 79834-0129, and Badlands at P.O. Box 6, Interior, SD 57750.

Know the park
If you know which park you want to visit, call ahead of time and ask a park official for advice. While peak days and seasons follow distinct patterns, each national park is different. Mount Rainier National Park, for example, gets extra-heavy traffic on Saturdays and Sundays, when the weekend warriors arrive from Seattle, which is only a couple of hours away by car.

Dome and El Capitan and to Yosemite Falls, the country's highest. The park offers a variety of campsites, including bare sites for tents (one to six people, $15 per night), RV sites ($15 per night), and three-walled, canvas-topped structures called housekeeping camps (one to four people, $45 per night).

You can request a Yosemite camping information brochure by writing to National Park Reservation Service, P.O. Box 1600, Cumberland, MD 21502.

➽ WHAT INSIDERS SAY

You need reservations for most Yosemite sites, especially during the summer months, which can be extremely busy. But there are spots, like the Sunnyside walk-in campground ($3 per person/per night), that have campsites available on a first-come, first-served basis.

Also, if you want to see Yosemite but can't get a spot inside the park, Cathy Burdett of the National Park Reservation Service recommends trying three underutilized campgrounds—Hodgdon Meadow, Crane Flat, and Wawona—outside of the valley but in proximity to all that Yosemite has to offer. Request a Yosemite camping information brochure by writing to the National Park Reservation Service at the address above.

In the Wilds of Remote Idaho

Home of the rugged Bitterroot Mountains, northern Idaho is a great place to camp if you want to get close to the wildlife that the pioneers experienced. And for a mere $12 a night, you can pitch your tent at Farragut State Park, which is nestled beside Lake Pend Oreille at the foot of the Coeur d'Alene Mountains in the Bitterroot Range. Campsites with RV hookups cost $16. In all, there are 108 individual sites, plus a couple of large group sites. Write to Farragut State Park, 13400 East Ranger Road, Athol, ID 83801.

➽ WHAT INSIDERS SAY:

If you'd prefer primitive—and free-of-charge—camping, the 4,000-acre state park is just the tip of the iceberg. Surrounding Farragut are the 2.5-million-acre Idaho Panhandle National Forests, where hikers can camp in the backcountry without a permit. Write to Idaho Panhandle National Forests, 3815 Schreiber Way, Coeur d'Alene, ID 83815.

Where the Appalachian Trail Begins

The Chattahoochee National Forest, home of the southernmost stretch of Appalachian Mountains and the southern terminus of the famous Ap-

PET-FRIENDLY PARKS

When you take a vacation, your pets usually have to stay at home in the care of a pet sitter or at an expensive kennel. Some national parks, however, offer inexpensive facilities for dogs and cats.

At Mammoth Cave National Park in Kentucky, for example, there is a 10-compartment kennel for dogs. "You rent the chain-link enclosures the same way you rent a hotel room," says Jim Milburn, president of National Park Concessions, Inc., the nonprofit management company that runs the hotel at Mammoth Cave. "Your pet stays there while you explore the park." There are also spaces for cats. The cost per day for either is $3.50, but if you are a guest at the hotel, they're free.

"Keeping your pets in a car is not a good idea," Milburn says. "They don't sweat like we do and can hyperventilate and perhaps die." Besides, he says, "if the park service finds your animal locked in the car, they'll fine you."

palachian Trail, has more than 25 developed campgrounds, with running water, toilets, picnic tables, lantern posts, and other camp comforts. Sites cost $4 to $15, depending on the amenities and the size of your group. More adventurous campers can sleep anywhere in the 750,000-acre national forest for free. Write to U.S. Forest Service, 1755 Cleveland Highway, Gainesville, GA 30501.

●✦ *WHAT INSIDERS SAY:*

If you want to avoid the crowds, try the Upper Chattahoochee River Campground. This is one of the more remote camp sites, located just a mile away from the river's headwaters.

Enjoying a Backwoods Cabin

There is something very American about a cabin. The early frontiersmen built them out of hand-hewn logs as they migrated west. Abe Lincoln was born in one, and in a cabin on Walden Pond, Henry David Thoreau holed up to write his famous treatise on the joys of living a simple life. Today, more and more of us work in cities and dream of buying that rustic vacation retreat—a simple beach shack or one-room cottage in the woods. To put it simply, says Jonathan Schafler, who manages eight backcountry recreation cabins for the Kodiak National Wildlife Refuge in Alaska, "cabins offer the amenity of shelter."

But why buy a cabin when there are thousands of them on public land around the country, just waiting for you and your family to arrive bearing a week's worth of groceries, paperback books, backgammon boards, bug repellent, and hiking boots?

Well, they're not exactly sitting empty. Some are so popular, in fact, that people begin booking reservations more than a year in advance. The key is to know where to look. Below are just some of the many cabins available on government land around the country.

●✦ *WHAT INSIDERS SAY:*

While many national parks and national forests provide cabins for visitors, state parks offer some of the best values around. They are typically open to all vis-itors, not just residents of the state. Out-of-state visitors usually receive equal consideration when making reservations and pay the same prices.

If you want to find a cabin in a state park, begin by deciding where you'd like to go, then simply contact the park office in that state for cabin information. In West Virginia, for example, 18 of the state's 48 parks and state forests have cabins for rent. They range from the rustic log cabins of Lost River State Park in the state's eastern panhandle to the modern ski cottages of Canaan (pronounced ku-NANE) Valley State Park in the Allegheny Mountains near Elkins. For a West Virginia state park guide, write to the West Virginia Division of Parks and Recreation, State Capitol Complex, Building 3, Room 714, Charleston, WV 25305.

Your Own Private Beach House

South Carolina's Hunting Island State Park rents 15 cottages, each built on stilts and shaded by swaying palmetto trees, a shell's toss from the surf on a pristine, semitropical barrier island.

Fully stocked, they come with bath and bed linens; kitchen utensils; a color television, microwave oven, and automatic coffee maker; central air and heat; an outside grill; a picnic table; and a screened porch. The best part? They sleep 6 to 10 people and cost a mere $66 to $105 a night. "People want to get close to the ocean," says Ray Stevens, the park's superintendent. "A woman once told me that if she couldn't come here every year, she wouldn't survive." For information, write to Hunting Island State Park, 2555 Sea Island Parkway, Hunting Island, SC 29920.

●✦ *WHAT INSIDERS SAY:*

This place books up fast, more than a year in advance for peak summer months. You stand a better chance of finding an open cottage in the fall or spring (or even winter, since the cottages have central heat).

Overnighting, Daniel Boone–Style

Staying at the Draper Cabin in Morgan-Monroe State Forest is like taking a time-trip back to the turn of the century. Tucked away in the remote hardwood forests of southern Indiana, the cabin has no running water, no bathroom, and no electricity—only two picnic tables, an indoor fireplace, and a broom.

Guests bring their own sleeping pads and bags and use Mother Nature's facilities. Despite, or maybe because of, the lack of creature comforts, the Draper Cabin is very popular. It might also be the price—$15.75 per night for up to 14 people—that makes it attractive. Write to Morgan-Monroe State Forest, 6220 Forest Road, Martinsville, IN 46151.

A Cottage by the (Finger) Lake

There are hundreds of cabins for rent in state parks around New York. You'll find 14 of them in Cayuga Lake State Park, at the northern end of the 40-mile-long "finger" lake, which like the other Finger Lakes in upstate New York, was gouged out of the earth thousands of years ago by advancing glaciers.

Built in the 1930s by the Civilian Conservation Corps, the rustic wooden cabins vary in their amenities. Some have indoor toilets; others have pit toilets. All have refrigerators and stoves. Most sleep four people, and they each rent for $122 per week. The exception is one that sleeps six, has an indoor fireplace, and rents for $239 per week. Write to Cayuga Lake State Park, 2678 Lower Lake Road, Seneca Falls, NY 13148.

Bear-Country Cabins

Although it might cost more than most cabin outings, there is no more remote an experience than staying in one of the eight rustic huts in Alaska's Kodiak National Wildlife Refuge.

The wooden cabins, which come with a kerosene heater, sleeping platforms, and a pit toilet, are available through a lottery and will set you back only $20 to $30 a night. Since the refuge has no roads, visitors must take either a private float plane or a boat to their site. The transportation costs range between $250 and $500 each way from Ko-

diak to the refuge cabins, but several passengers can share the cost. The refuge office can provide a list of boat or plane charter companies.

There are four lottery drawings each year, held on the first day of January, April, July, and September. For a lottery application package, write to Kodiak National Wildlife Refuge, 1390 Buskin River Road, Kodiak, AK 99615.

⚫❖ WHAT INSIDERS SAY:
As tempting as it might be, do not send in more than one lottery application. It's against the rules, and if you're caught, your name will be removed from consideration.

Cabins in the Canyon

Kings Canyon, in Kings Canyon National Park, California, is actually deeper than the Grand Canyon. The park is also home to some of the world's largest trees.

At Grant Grove Village—within walking distance of shops, a supermarket, and restaurants—are 52 cabins, 9 with electricity and private baths. Each has two double beds and costs either $80 or $85 per night. They're not far from the 267-foot-tall General Grant Tree, which was designated the nation's Christmas tree by President Coolidge in 1926 and is dressed with a wreath each year. For information, write to Kings Canyon Park Services, P.O. Box 909, Kings Canyon National Park, CA 93633.

Finding Room at the Inn

Don't assume that just because it's public land, the lodging is rustic.

Sure, there are pared-down campsites and cabins where travelers can rough it, get back to nature, *and* save a little money. But if you're accustomed to staying in more service-oriented accommodations, or you merely want a top-rate room, the government has something to offer. And while the prices might be higher than those for campgrounds or cabins, they're still a good value.

Indeed, some of this country's finest, most historic inns are located in national parks and other government-owned property. "At some of these lodges, not only do you have a beautiful view of the park, but you have a beautiful structure to stay in," says National Park Service senior concessions operation analyst Dee Highnote. "The Old Faithful Inn at Yellowstone National Park, one of the oldest lodges in the National Park Service, is absolutely gorgeous."

There are different types of inn-style accommodations, from old-fashioned lodges to modern

AMERICA'S MOST VISITED NATIONAL PARK SITES

Looking for a popular place to head for your next vacation? Here are 20 parks that Americans have proclaimed tops with their numerous visits.

PARK	NUMBER OF VISITORS IN 1998
1. Blue Ridge Parkway, Va.	19,026,498
2. Golden Gate National Recreation Area, Calif.	14,046,590
3. Great Smoky Mountains National Park, Tenn.	9,989,395
4. Lake Mead National Recreation Area, Nev.	8,788,055
5. Gateway National Recreation Area, N.Y.	7,124,022
6. George Washington Memorial Parkway, Va.	6,584,802
7. Natchez Trace Parkway, Miss.	5,810,094
8. Statue of Liberty National Monument, N.Y.	5,200,633
9. Delaware Water Gap National Recreation Area, Pa./N.J.	5,019,175
10. Cape Cod National Seashore, Mass.	4,804,185
11. Vietnam Veterans Memorial, Washington, D.C.	4,687,299
12. Castle Clinton National Monument, N.Y.	4,390,268
13. Lincoln Memorial, Washington, D.C.	4,368,912
14. Gulf Islands National Seashore, Miss./Fla.	4,293,301
15. Franklin Delano Roosevelt Memorial, Washington, D.C.	4,258,807
16. Grand Canyon National Park, Ariz.	4,239,682
17. Yosemite National Park, Calif.	3,657,132
18. Olympic National Park, Wash.	3,577,007
19. San Francisco Maritime National Historic Park, Calif.	3,535,081
20. Cuyahoga Valley National Recreation Area, Ohio	3,467,107

golf resorts and motels. What's available depends on the particular park. In the case of national parks, private concessionaires for each park run the accommodations.

Below are more details about the Old Faithful Inn, as well as a few others.

●◆ WHAT INSIDERS SAY:

Inns and lodges are popular, and space is limited, so many of them book up quickly—as much as a year in advance. Be sure to plan early.

Room with a View

From the terrace of the Old Faithful Inn, a 1904 log hotel in Yellowstone National Park, guests can watch the famous geyser of the same name put on its show.

Four stories high, with a broad, sloping gabled roof, the inn was built to reflect nature. "The poles and rocks actually came from inside the park," says Chad Mallo, who works in guest services. Its architect, Robert C. Reamer, was only 20 years old when he designed the building.

The inn has 327 rooms ranging in price from $52 (without bath) to $325 for a deluxe suite. It's only open from May to October and stays almost 100 percent booked the entire season. Write to Old Faithful Inn, P.O. Box 165, Yellowstone National Park, WY 82190.

●◆ WHAT INSIDERS SAY:

Ask for a room on the front side of the east wing (such as 2024, 2026, 3024, or 3026). If the trees haven't grown up and blocked the view, you'll be front and center for Old Faithful's hourly show.

Crater-Rim Inn

The Volcano House Hotel in Hawaii Volcanoes National Park offers the nearest lodging to a lava flow in any national park.

"The last eruption in our backyard was in 1983," says Cyndi Yamamoto, the hotel's reservation manager. "It's very spectacular when it happens." Located on the rim of the very active volcano Kilauea, this 42-room hotel is Hawaii's oldest. The original grass hut lodge was built in 1846, but it was replaced with a succession of larger, more permanent structures, including the two-story wooden building now perched on the volcano's edge. Room prices range from $85 to $185 per night, depending on the view. Write to P.O. Box 53, Hawaii Volcanoes National Park, HI 96718.

City-Run Resort

Every year around Christmastime, Oglebay Resort and Conference Center in Wheeling, West Virginia, puts on one of the largest light shows in America. More than 300 million bulbs light up the trees, buildings, and animated displays.

Dating back to the 1940s, Oglebay Resort—with three golf courses, 11 tennis courts, two swimming pools, and 212 rooms that range in price from $63 to $155 per night—is also special because it is part of a 1,650-acre city park. Instead of having a private owner, the resort is run by a city commission. For information, write to Oglebay Resort and Conference Center, Route 88 North, Wheeling, WV 26003.

Mountaintop Motel

A secluded and affordable getaway, the 25-room Desoto State Park Lodge in Alabama's Desoto State Park sits on top of Lookout Mountain in a park known for its waterfalls and the deepest gorge east of the Mississippi. While the rooms have cable television, most guests prefer the view from the rocking chairs on the country porch. Rooms are $55 to $65 per night. Write to Desoto State Park Lodge, 265 County Road 951, Ft. Payne, AL 35967.

A Lodge in Hiker's Paradise

The Zion Lodge in Utah's Zion National Park not only occupies one of the most spectacular settings of any national park—the base of Zion Canyon's 2,000-foot-high red sandstone cliffs—but it's also one of the best values in the national park system. Because lodging prices are based on comparable accommodations in the region, guests pay Utah prices—in this case, $85 for a double room and $116 for a suite—which are generally lower than prices in, say, California or New York. There are 121 rooms in all. Write to Zion Lodge, Zion National Park, Springdale, UT 84767.

Sleeping Sites above the Trees

One of the most interesting ways to spend the night in the woods is 60 feet off the ground in a fire tower with wraparound windows.

In the first 6 or 7 decades of the twentieth century, following the creation of the U.S. Forest Service in 1905, the government built more than 5,000 such fire towers in 49 states. Airplanes eventually took over the fire watch, making most of the towers obsolete. Today, only 1,800 of them remain, and 300 to 400 are still in working order. Some of these structures are available to rent for 1, 2, or even 7 nights.

All of the rentable lookouts are in the western United States—in Idaho, Washington, Oregon, Colorado, and a few other states. Most are not towers. "They are ground houses built on top of a precipice," says Keith Argow, chairman of the National Historic Lookout Register, whose goal is to save at least 1,000 of the country's lookouts.

The lookouts, bolted to the mountain and grounded for protection against lightning, typically sleep two to four people and cost $20 to $40 per night, but there are larger cabins that accommodate more people and cost a bit more. Some are still used by rangers during the summer and are only available during the winter months.

The best sources for information about renting fire towers are the USDA Forest Service Northern Region Office, P.O. Box 7669, Missoula, MT 59807 (ask for the guide to the region's 90 towers and ranger cabins); the Pacific Northwest Region Office, 333 Southwest First Avenue, P.O. Box 3623, Portland, OR 97208; and *How to Rent a Fire Lookout in the Pacific Northwest*, by Tom Foley and Tish Steinfeld. Below are a few examples of America's rentable historic towers.

◆ WHAT INSIDERS SAY:

The accommodations in fire towers are spartan. Few towers have electricity or running water. Some have pit toilets and fire pits. Many have some type of bed or beds but no bedding, so you should bring a sleeping bag. Anyone who is considering staying at a lookout should be reasonably fit in order to climb the stairs. While you can drive to some fire towers, you must hike 5 miles or more to reach others. Be sure to ask about access before you set out and find that a hike is too rugged. All require reservations and permits, usually arranged through the nearest ranger station.

Finally, since the purpose of a lookout is, well, looking out, take a pair of binoculars or a telescope. They'll help you spot the stars at night and wildlife, like the wild horses that live in the vicinity of Oregon's Flagtail Lookout.

A Tower Named Jersey Jim

"From Jersey Jim, you can see four states—New Mexico, Arizona, Utah, and Colorado," says Lloyd McNeil, a forest ranger and co-founder of the Jersey Jim Foundation, a nonprofit organization that maintains this historic lookout near Mancos, Colorado. The cabin sits atop a 55-foot-high tower 9,800 feet above sea level, giving you an incredible view. "People from cities like Chicago say they didn't realize how much fun it is to watch an approaching thunderstorm or to see the sunsets from up there," McNeil says.

The lookout, named after a dairy farmer who pastured his Jersey cows nearby in the early 1900s, comes with a double bed (but no linens) and costs $40 per night for a maximum of four people.

◆ WHAT INSIDERS SAY:

This extremely popular lookout usually books up within a couple of days of the first Monday in March, when the foundation begins taking reservations. You can only make reservations by phone from 1:00 to 5:00 P.M. Mountain Standard Time. For a brochure and the reservations number, write to the Jersey Jim Foundation, P.O. Box 1032, Mancos, CO 81328.

Oregon's Winter Aerie

If you like to cross-country ski, snowshoe, or snow-mobile, you'll love Flagtail Lookout in Oregon's Malheur National Forest.

Like other fire towers still used by rangers during the summer months, it's only available for rent in the fall and winter. It is accessible by a 5.5-mile road that's covered in snow most of the season, which means that you may have to ski or snowshoe in.

Perched on a 60-foot tower, the 14-by-14-foot room is surrounded by windows and a catwalk, which offer stunning vistas of the Blue Mountains. It costs $25 per night and includes a double bed, a table and chairs, closets, a propane refrigerator and

fuel, a cook stove, a heater, and lights, but no sink. It has a pit toilet, but no water source other than melted snow. For information, write to Bear Valley Ranger District, 431 Patterson Bridge Road, John Day, OR 97845.

●◆ *WHAT INSIDERS SAY:*

Tracie Houston, who works in the Bear Valley Ranger District, says that some guests rent the lookout for Thanksgiving and Christmas. "They thoroughly enjoy the solitude," she explains.

The Bitterroot River Lookout

Built in 1939, Montana's McCart Lookout sits on a ridge above the east fork of the Bitterroot River. Open from May 1 to October 30, depending on the

PANNING FOR GOLD ON PUBLIC LAND

Even though the Gold Rush is ancient history, there's still plenty of gold in America's streams and riverbeds. By knowing where to turn, you can get gold-prospecting assistance from various government agencies. If you eventually discover a gold-rich stretch of riverbed, the government will even help you stake a claim to the land.

"People are free to pan for gold on any Bureau of Land Management (BLM) or U.S. Forest Service land," says Mike York, a representative with the BLM office in California. This is generally true in all states, although regulations vary regarding dredging and other

types of prospecting. Dredging usually requires a permit. Gold mining is prohibited in national parks, except when it's part of a park-sponsored interpretive program.

"You want to be careful of prospecting in areas that are closed because of protected wildlife," says Chauncey Hood, junior past president of the Idaho Gold Prospectors Association. "Then you're dealing with the Environmental Protection Agency, and they aren't very forgiving." Here are more tips for gold prospecting on government land.

Contact the state's geology agency

These agencies usually go by

the name "Geological Survey" or "Division of Mines and Geology." Some offer free advice and even booklets. California mails out a free "gold packet" that includes a list of tips for finding and identifying gold. Write to the Division of Mines and Geology, 801 K Street, MS 14-34, Sacramento, CA 95814-3532. Alaska offers even more in its packet; contact the Alaska Public Lands Information Center, 605 West Fourth Avenue, Suite 105, Anchorage, AK 99501.

The agency can also tell you about special prospecting activities in your state. For instance, during the summer, Maine's Mt. Blue State Park of-snow conditions, it's located 20 miles east of Sula, Montana. It can sleep up to four people at a cost of $30 per night. For reservation information, write National Forest, Sula Ranger District, 7338 Highway 93 S, Sula, MT 59871.

Sharing Lodging at a Hostel

Most people associate hostels with Europe, trains, and traveling twentysomethings, but the nonprofit private organization Hostelling International (HI) has dozens of hostels around the United States—including many that it operates on government land—that offer economical accommodations to tourists of all ages. Many have private rooms in ad-

dition to the traditional hostel dorm rooms. Almost all have shared kitchens and bathrooms.

"There are a lot of opportunities for interaction among guests," says Beth Barrett, general manager of Florida's Orlando/Kissimmee Resort Hostel. "We also have volunteers from the community," she says. "One man sets up a telescope in the backyard. Another man comes by and talks about what it's like to be a cowboy."

In some cases, HI has partnered with governmental agencies to provide lodging in state and national parks. They have preserved historic homes and converted old military buildings into charming and affordable hostels. While HI is a membership organization, it welcomes nonmembers, who gen-

---

fers free half-day gold-panning trips on the Swift River. Rangers demonstrate panning technique, and then supply pans so the participants can try it themselves. You can write to the park at Rt. 1, Box 610, Weld, ME 04285.

Look for maps

In the western United States, where gold prospecting is most popular, the BLM sells color-coded Surface Management maps ($4) that show public and private land. You'll need to contact the local BLM office for the state you're interested in. Either look in the government pages of your phone book under "U.S. Department of the Interior" or write to the national BLM office at 1849 C Street NW,

Room LS-406, Washington, DC 20240.

Ask about claims

Claims are not ownership. They merely give the discoverer an exclusive right to mine for gold on that parcel of land. The BLM keeps track of mineral claims. If you provide a state BLM office with the township, range, and section of land that you're considering, it can search the records to see if there has been a claim staked on that particular location.

Of course, if you're just a weekend dabbler, you might not need to go to all this trouble. "In some areas, it's widely accepted that using a pan will never get you in trouble," Hood says. "Even if you're claim jumping, you'll just

be asked to leave, because with a pan you're not going to steal a lot of gold." And if you want to stake your own claim, the same state BLM office will assist you.

➡️ *WHAT INSIDERS SAY:*
Thanks to Mother Nature, gold-prospecting conditions in California now are probably better than they've been in a long while. "In California, up to now, gold miners have taken about 10 percent of what's out there," says Dale Stickney, a geologist with the state's division of mines and geology. "They've gotten the easiest stuff and left what's more difficult to get to." But, he says, the storms caused by El Niño in 1998 have washed out new deposits. "That gave us a boost."

erally pay $3 more per night than members for lodging.

For a map and booklet listing U.S. hostels, write to Hostelling International, 733 15th Street NW, Suite 840, Washington, DC 20005. Here's a sampling of what's available.

Civil War–Era Fort

The National Park Service acquired San Francisco's Fort Mason as part of the Golden Gate National Recreation Area in the 1970s and allowed Hostelling International to renovate it. The 150-bed hostel has a prime location in a green, hilly park that affords a sweeping view of the bay and is within walking distance of Fisherman's Wharf, Chinatown, and other attractions. For more information, write to Fort Mason, Building 240, San Francisco, CA 94123.

●❖ WHAT INSIDERS SAY:

There are no private rooms at Fort Mason, but if you're part of a family of three or four or you're traveling with a few friends, request one of the

Amazing Stories

HOME, SWEET LIGHTHOUSE

In the early 1960s, during trips to Oregon's rocky coast, Carol Korgan dreamed that one day she and her husband, Mike, might live in a historic lightkeeper's house just as the keepers had in the days before most lighthouses were automated.

Today, the Korgans are living that dream in a restored keeper's house at the often-photographed Haceta Head Lighthouse in Oregon. They serve as volunteers—at the government's request—and operate a bed-and-breakfast in the wonderful old structure.

"We were watching TV one day," says Mike, "and a news story came on about a lighthouse that needed a lightkeeper. The U.S. Forest Service was looking for volunteers." When the reporter mentioned that the house had a resident ghost, Mike and Carol, both chefs who had raised their three children in a haunted house, knew that the job was for them.

They had recently retired, so they were considering buying a motor home and hitting the road to do volunteer work. "We were looking for someplace to do some good for our country in return for the good life we've had," recalls Carol. "We thought, 'Hey, we can do volunteer work right here—and not even spend the money on the RV.'"

The Korgans beat out 500 other couples for the chance to earn $5 a day to live in the lightkeeper's house, which is part of central Oregon's Siuslaw National Forest. Then, as a way to maintain the landmark structure, the Forest Service asked them to convert the house into an inn.

Today, they have a permit for the concession. Its three guest rooms—which cost $125 to $150 per night and include the Korgans' seven-course breakfast of homemade bread, locally grown fruits, smoked fish, and other goodies—are open year-round. It's best to reserve at least 3 months in advance.

"I like to say that Europe has its castles and America has its lighthouses," says Carol. And the Korgans have their dream come true.

hostel's eight four-person rooms when you make your reservation. While the hostel does not guarantee that it will honor the request, you stand a chance of getting a "private" room for the regular $17-per-person price.

Bunking in Former Barracks

Once part of the first line of naval defense for the Puget Sound Navy Yard and the cities of Seattle, Tacoma, Olympia, and Everett, Olympic Hostel in Port Townsend now belongs to Washington's Fort Worden State Park. It houses 24 guests in either dorm-style rooms ($12 per night) or five private rooms ($32 per night).

Olympic National Park, home of glacier-capped peaks, one of the only intact rainforests in the lower 48 states, and miles of hiking trails, is an hour's drive away. Write Olympic Hostel, 272 Battery Way, Port Townsend, WA 98368.

Beating New York's High Room Rates

With New York City room rates in range of $200 a night, according to the New York Convention and Visitors Bureau, the New York Hostel is an incredible bargain. For a mere $24, you can stay at this landmark Victorian Gothic building on Manhattan's Upper West Side. Private family rooms, without bath, are $75 per night, and a private family room with a bath is $100.

"The obvious benefit is that it's a good deal," says Pam Tice, the hostel's executive director. "We also offer all sorts of activities—walking tours, evening outings, and so forth. Volunteers from the neighborhood answer questions and help you plan your time."

The colossal hostel, built in 1883 as the Association Residence for the Relief of Respectable Elderly Indigent Females (translation: a nursing home) was converted during the 1980s with federal, state, and city grants and tax-free loans. It sleeps 624 people. For more information, write New York City Hostel, 891 Amsterdam Avenue, New York, NY 10025.

GEAR

Travel, especially the rugged variety, involves a certain amount of equipment. You need a suitcase, duffel bag, or backpack to lug your things in. You need the right maps to get you to your destination. If you're camping, a sleeping bag and tent will be necessary. Then there's footwear—hiking boots, snowshoes, or skis—and other clothing appropriate for the terrain and climate, such as ponchos, windbreakers, coats, and hats. Gear is part of the fun, but it also adds to the expense.

As you may have guessed, Uncle Sam can help. Here are some tips for outfitting yourself and your family for the big adventure.

Maps for Free or on the Cheap

The United States is a big country, with endless recreational opportunities. One thing that you'll probably need to help you during your travels is some type of map. Whether it's a broad view of a national park, a historical sketch depicting the action on a particular battlefield, or a hiking map showing the contour of the land, chances are, the government will have it. And if it's not free, you can bet it'll be reasonably priced.

Detailed Views of the Parks

The country's national parks provide informational maps free of charge to those who request them. These elaborate, color-coded maps show ranger stations, camping areas, hiking trails, access areas for the disabled, and other visitor services, as well as important natural formations. Packed with information, park maps also give historical summaries of the areas they cover and ecological diagrams of different habitats.

The map of Hawaii Volcanoes National Park, for example, which includes a detailed inset of the Kilauea Caldera, shows the area's different lava flows and gives the dates they occurred as well as information on what animals and plants you might see during a trip to the park. Write to P.O. Box 52, Hawaii Volcanoes National Park, HI 96718-0052.

You can contact the park you want to visit in advance and request a free map by mail, or pick one up when you reach the park's visitors' center.

◆ WHAT INSIDERS SAY:

Not sure which park you want to visit? Save time by ordering several maps at once. The National Park Service's Public Inquiries Office, 1849 C Street NW, Room 1013, Washington, DC 20240, will send up to 10 free national park maps at a time.

The Lay of Recreation Lands

The government publishes a map of the United States called "Outdoors America," which highlights all the federal recreation lands—those managed by the National Park Service, Forest Service, Army Corps of Engineers, Bureau of Land Management, Bureau of Reclamation, Tennessee Valley Authority, and Fish and Wildlife Service. Not only is it a boon to anyone in the early stages of trip planning, it also offers a fascinating look at how much land the federal government makes available to Americans for fun and relaxation. Request a free map by writing to the Bureau of Land Management, 1849 C Street NW, Room LS-406, Washington, DC 20240.

Guides to Hiking Trails

The main source of detailed hiking maps in the country is the U.S Geological Survey, a division of the U.S. Department of the Interior. The basic map they offer is on a 1:24,000 scale (the ratio of a distance on the map to the actual distance on the ground; in this case, 1 inch equals about 2.5 miles). "It is a topographic map, which hikers use because it shows contours and elevation," says Alan Simpson, an information technician with the Geological Survey's Earth Science Information Center. The maps also include roads, railroads, trails, lakes, rivers, forests, and boundaries.

The Geological Survey has mapped every inch of the United States and its territories, and with that amount of selection, finding the map for a particular area can be tricky. Simpson suggests first ordering a free index and catalog of maps for the state or states you're interested in. Send the order to Denver–Earth

Science Information Center, P.O. Box 25286, Denver, CO 80225. Then, when you know the name of the map or maps you want, send your order to the same address. Maps cost $4 each, and there is a $3.50 shipping charge per order, no matter how large. Your maps should arrive within 6 to 12 days.

You'll find these same topographic maps at map and camping stores around the country, but the prices are often double what the government charges.

◆ WHAT INSIDERS SAY:

Still can't figure out which map covers the area you're interested in? Contact the U.S. Geological Survey at USGS-ESIC, 507 National Center, 12201 Sunrise Valley Drive, Reston, VA 20192. Says Simpson: "We have databases that we can search to help you determine what you need."

Highways and Byways

Every state receives funding from the Federal Highway Administration to print a give-away highway map. These four-color fold-outs show federal, state, and local roads; parks; forest preserves; airports; and other important sites. They give travel numbers and safety information—and on occasion a little bit of state history.

Contact your local department of transportation (look in your phone book's government pages under the state government listings). It can provide maps of your state or put you in touch with similar departments in other states. Sometimes, it's up to the state tourism office to distribute free road maps. If so, the department of transportation will direct you to the right office. Also, welcome centers near state borders keep a supply of these free maps on hand.

◆ WHAT INSIDERS SAY:

If you're the type of traveler who likes to explore the back roads, also known as farm-to-market roads, you need county maps. Most counties print them. Sometimes they're free; rarely do they cost more than a couple of dollars. Usually, county maps are available only at county offices of transportation, but sometimes state departments of transportation carry them. The Ohio Department of Transportation, for example, sells

17-by-22-inch maps of each of its counties for 35 cents each. If you go to each county office, the maps are free.

Low-Cost Recreational Gear

Whether you want to buy or rent, there are government deals to be had on outdoor equipment. Some of the best bargains come from purchasing military surplus at the source—government-run auctions—instead of Army-Navy stores, which buy the goods and mark them up.

Another good source is state universities (and some private colleges) that keep recreational equipment on hand for outing clubs and general student use. They often let others who aren't affiliated with the school borrow the gear.

Here are some of the best sources for inexpensive equipment.

Uncle Sam's Finest

With a total budget of almost $260 billion and more than 1.4 million armed forces personnel to outfit, the U.S. Defense Department is a big spender when it comes to equipment. Inevitably, as military bases close or upgrade their gear, they must get rid of lots of great stuff, including tents, sleeping bags, mess kits, boats, and other items that the average civilian can reuse for recreation.

The agency that sells military surplus is called the Defense Reutilization and Marketing Service (DRMS). The DRMS holds sealed-bid auction sales at about 70 locations around the country. The agency's Web site (www.drms.dla.mil) explains how the system works, lists catalogs of equipment (including the condition it's in), and gives dates and locations of auctions. You can also contact the service by mail at DRMS-LM, 74 North Washington Avenue, Battle Creek, MI 49017-3092.

As with any auction, prices can vary greatly, but in general, bargain hunters will find plenty to be excited about. For example, at one auction in Lakehurst, New Jersey, a pair of canvas tents listed in fair condition sold for $56. A 70-horsepower outboard motor went for $168.

However, warns Marge Akerley, the Lakehurst supervisory property disposal specialist, don't let bargain fever cloud your judgment. "We have a lot of people who bid without seeing the items," she says. "We don't recommend that."

She also points out that much of the equipment sold at auctions comes in large lots. Make sure that you don't bid on an entire truckload of sleeping bags when you want only one.

➡◆ WHAT INSIDERS SAY:

Boy Scouts and Girl Scouts can get free camping gear from the Defense Reutilization and Marketing Service before the surplus goes on the auction block. Interested troop leaders should contact their state agency for surplus property, which is often part of a state's department of general services (although agency names can vary). Look in your phone book's government pages. If you have no luck, the U.S. General Services Administration maintains a list of these agencies on its Internet site, http://pub.fss.gsa.gov/property.

College Rentals

Many state universities and other colleges around the country rent recreational equipment at extremely low prices to students and, often, to others not affiliated with the school.

The University of Tennessee, for instance, has a membership program: $40 per year for students, faculty, and staff and $55 for anyone not affiliated with the school. For no extra charge, members and nonmembers can borrow tents, backpacks, stoves, water purifiers, skis, canoes, kayaks, and more on a first-come, first-served basis. The exception is boats, which are only available to members.

"We take reservations for nonmembers," says Scott Sample, coordinator of the University of Tennessee's Outdoor Recreation Program, "so someone who is traveling to the area for a vacation can take advantage of our program and can make sure that we have what they need by making a reservation." Travelers can also check out maps, guidebooks, and videos. "With the Great Smoky Mountains and the Cherokee National Forest so near, there's plenty to do in this region," Sample says. You can contact the university at 2106 Andy Holt Avenue, Knoxville, TN 37996.

◆❖ WHAT INSIDERS SAY:

Jay Zarr, director of the experiential learning center and recreation program at the University of Southern Colorado, says that people should consider school schedules when planning to use university gear.

"We're open all year round, although in the summer, there are not many people in the office, so it's a good idea to call a week ahead," he says. You can also write to University of Southern Colorado, Occiato University Center, Room 004, 2200 Bonforte Boulevard, Pueblo, CO 81001. At this school, there are four times a year when the gear is not available because it's completely booked for classes: mid-August, mid-December, the last full week in March, and the last full week in May. Ask at the school you plan to rent from if there are similar blackout dates.

School Gear for Sale

Universities occasionally need to make room for new gear, and they can be great sources of bargain purchases at times like these.

For example, three times a year—in the spring, fall, and winter—the University of Oregon's outdoor program hosts a 1-day gear flea market. In addition to the university's no-longer-needed gear, community members bring equipment to trade and sell, typically at rock-bottom prices.

"At each event, there are more than 1,000 people," says Bruce Mason, the outdoor program director. "There are some incredible deals to be found on everything from kayaks and rafts to flash-

AN ARMCHAIR TRAVELER'S GOLD MINE

Besides maps, another way to get a handle on the incredible geographical diversity of this country is through government photos and videos. Even if you don't plan to leave the comfort of your living room, these resources will help satisfy your urge to explore. And you can always use them to prepare for a real trip. Here's a sampling of what's available.

Aerial photos

The federal government is great at documenting things. Did you know, for example, that every 5 to 7 years, the U.S. Geological Survey's National Aerial Photography Program photographs every inch of the lower 48 states in 33-square-mile blocks? (The sizes of the blocks in the photos of Hawaii, Alaska, Puerto Rico, and other territories vary.) The government sells these black-and-white photos, and because they're considered public property, you pay only for the cost of processing: $10 for a 9-by-9-inch print, $18 for an 18-by-18-inch, and $33 for a 36-by-36, plus a $3.50 shipping and handling fee.

A technician will help you choose the right map. "The U.S. Geological Survey doesn't charge for database searches," says Paula Erickson, a cartographic technician with the survey. For more information, write to U.S. Department of the Interior, U.S. Geological Survey, ESIC, Box 25046 Federal Center, Mail Stop MS504, Denver, CO 80225.

Forest Service photos

Want a poster-size, professionally snapped color photograph of Mount St. Helens before it erupted? How about one of equal size shot afterward, showing the shocking amount of earth and rock blown off the top? The U.S. Forest Service keeps these

lights and clothing." Contact the Unversity of Oregon, Erb Memorial Union, Eugene, OR 97403.

TOURS AND CLASSES

No matter how much free time you have or what you like to do with it, the government has something to offer. You can be wowed by the wonders of nature at national parks, visit sites of heroic battles, or stop at state capitols or historic federal government buildings. If you have an afternoon, you can even arrange a free tour of your local fire department.

The secret of getting the most from one of these trips is knowing how to make the system work for you: where to find up-to-date listings of activities, how to make reservations for tours, how to have a great experience with a tour guide, and where to turn for help. Here is a sampling of some of the government's best tours and attractions, along with tips on arranging the most enjoyable trip possible.

Profiting from a Park Visit

National parks are by nature big, diverse places with lots to see and do. It's easy to decide to spend a week at, say, Olympic National Park. Figuring out what to do once you arrive is another matter, and one that can overwhelm the average traveler.

Private concessionaires inside the parks organize tours, such as boat trips and horseback rides, and the national park offices sponsor activities.

---

and about 40,000 other nature photos taken on the 191 million acres of Forest Service property in its current collection, which it makes available to people for the cost of reproduction. That means a 30-by-40-inch blowup will cost $40 to $50 and an 8-by-10 will be $5 to $10. "A lot of people send letters asking for beautiful pictures," says Karl Perry, who works in the Forest Service's publishing and visual communication group. "With such a large collection, it's tough for us to select what we think would be nice for them."

He suggests that if you want to order photos, write to the Forest Service at the Office of Communications, Publishing and Visual Communication Group, 201 14th Street SW, Washington, DC 20250, and ask for a list of the photo categories. Then call one of the Forest Service visual information specialists, who will help you choose the right shot. It usually takes about a week for them to complete the order and get it in the mail.

Wilderness videos

The Forest Service also has a free video-lending service. You can borrow up to 10 videos for 2 weeks at a time by writing to Forest Service Video Library, Audience Planners, 5341 Derry Avenue, Suite Q, Agoura Hills, CA 91301. All you pay is the return postage.

The library includes about 200 titles, including videos about wildlife, environmental education, recreational opportunities, safety, and other topics. For example, you might request "Beartooth Highway," a 20-minute documentary about a stretch of Montana asphalt that CBS's Charles Kuralt called America's most beautiful roadway. Or your kids might like "Beyond the Backyard: A Practical Guide to Planning Your Outdoor Adventures," which gives pointers for beginner campers. Check out the organization's Web site at www.r5.pswfs.gov/video for a catalog of titles.

These might be ranger-led nature walks, historic home tours, or campfire lectures. One big difference is that activities sponsored by the park are often free, whereas the concessionaires charge for their events.

When visiting a national park, you want to take advantage of all that your tax dollars and/or entrance fees provide. Here are some tips from people who work for the park service on how to make the most of your visit.

Plan Well

"The first thing a person should do is write or call the park they want to visit," says Robert Huggins, an education coordinator for the National Park Service. Most parks have a variety of what are called interpretive programs, which explain the important aspects of the park. "For example," Huggins says, "a park may have a geological theme or a geyser theme, or the theme might be the natural history of trees and plants."

The bigger parks offer a publication called a trip planner, which lists concessionaires, campgrounds, and rules and regulations. But a park's trip planner doesn't include current activities. You'll find these listed in park newspapers. Yellowstone, for instance, publishes a paper four times a year, listing seasonal talks and walks. The Grand Canyon's paper publishes sunrise and sunset times, so that visitors can know when to get to the rim in time to see how the sun colors the canyon.

These newspapers are not typically included in the information packets that the parks send out. Be sure to ask for the most recent edition.

Visit the Visitors' Center

"Sometimes, there may be a new program that wasn't listed in the events information," says Huggins. When you arrive at a park, ask for an update.

Choose the Best Season

Just because summer is the most popular period at most parks doesn't mean that it's the best time to visit. "Fall is my favorite time at Yellowstone," says Cheryl Matthews, who has worked at the 2.2-million-acre park for more than a decade, most recently as assistant public affairs chief. "It's not as busy, the wildlife has moved to lower elevations, so the viewing is easier, and the temperature is good for hiking."

Make a Tour Reservation

A growing number of parks are allowing people to reserve spots on popular tours. "This is one of the fastest growing aspects of our reservation system," says Cathy Burdett, program manager for the National Park Reservation Service, which primarily books campsites at national parks around the country. "Because of budget cuts, we have fewer and fewer interpretive guides." By taking reservations, the park service is able to schedule its guides more efficiently.

In fact, at national parks that have reserved tours, you may be out of luck if you show up without a reservation. The best thing to do is contact the National Park Reservation Service well in advance of your planned visit and ask whether the park accepts reservations for a tour you want to take. If it does, you can book a spot through them. Write to P.O. Box 1600, Cumberland, MD 21502.

Katmai National Park and Preserve in Alaska, for instance, offers one of the National Park Service's most thrilling—and most popular—tours: brown bear viewing at the Brooks River. For $10, you can get a voucher that provides access to the Brooks Falls bear-viewing platforms, which put you a couple of dozen feet from the giant creatures as they fish for spawning salmon. But in July and September, the bears' peak feeding times, the passes are tough to get, and you can't buy them at the park. You have to reserve them months in advance. Get in touch with the reservation service to find out when vouchers go on sale. If you want to contact the park, write to Katmai National Park and Preserve, P.O. Box 7, King Salmon, AK 99613.

Among the other parks that accept reservations for tours are Carlsbad Caverns National Park (3225 National Parks Highway, Carlsbad, NM 88220),

Mammoth Cave National Park (P.O. Box 7, Mammoth Cave, KY 42259), and Frederick Douglass National Historic Site (1411 W Street SE, Washington, DC 20020-4813).

Summer School Outdoors

Learning has always been a part of the national park experience. These days, thanks to a growing number of national park institutes, visitors can actually enroll in environmental and cultural courses, using the park itself as the classroom.

Working in partnership with national parks, the not-for-profit institutes offer a variety of field seminars, from a class on Native American garden restoration at the Grand Canyon Field Institute to sea-otter ecology at Washington's Olympic Park Institute. Classes typically last 2 or 3 days, but there are 1-day seminars and longer backpacking trips. If you want to contact either of these programs, write to the Grand Canyon Field Institute at P.O. Box 399, Grand Canyon, AZ 86023 or the Olympic Park Institute at 111 Barnes Point Road, Port Angeles, WA 98363.

"I think it's important for people to experience nature in the purest sense," says Maitland Peet, executive director of the Olympic Park Institute. "These are lands that the public, through a democratic process, has decided to set aside for that purpose." Classes like the ones his school offers help people better understand and appreciate nature.

One of the best things about the institutes are the prices. For example, a 3-day, 2-night class in traditional plant uses at Olympic Park costs $199, including lodging and six meals at the historic Rosemary Inn, the campus's centerpiece. "It's a great deal when you compare it to the cost of the park lodges," says Lisa Eschenbach, the institute's education director. "And sometimes, when you can't get a reservation at the park, we still have openings."

There are also institutes at Glacier National Park, Great Smoky Mountains National Park, North Cascades National Park, Canyonlands National Park, Yosemite National Park, and others. Because the institutes operate independently, there is no central office to provide a comprehensive list. The best thing to do is contact the parks that interest you and ask if they are affiliated with a learning institute. You can get a park's address from the National Park Service Web site at www.nps.gov or by ordering the "National Parks Visitors Facilities and Services Handbook" ($3, plus $1.50 shipping) from the National Park Hospitality Association, 1225 New York Avenue NW, Suite 450, Washington, DC 20005.

Touring the Nation's Battlefields

For anyone interested in history, battlefields can be exciting and emotional tourist destinations. To give future generations the chance to visit them, the National Park Service has set aside 15 battlefield sites in its system. Plus, there are hundreds of others that are managed on the state and local levels.

Since battlefields are often just that—long-empty fields where two warring factions once faced off—the most important element in visiting them is having good guides. Without their detailed descriptions and dramatic stories, the visit risks being boring.

Guides at historic battlefields are usually independent contractors, although sometimes they are national or state park rangers, says Richard Kohr, a licensed freelance guide at Gettysburg National Military Park in Pennsylvania, which has had guided tours since the end of the Civil War. Not all of them have been the most reliable. "We still hear old guide stories, such as the water in the stream ran red each year on the anniversary of the battle," he says.

These days, the National Park Service does its best to ensure that guides give accurate historical accounts. Whether they're independent or employed by the Park Service, the guides should be well-trained, tested, and licensed.

Here are some tips for improving your trip.

Ask Questions

That's one of the best ways to get the most out of a tour. "The guides want to work with you," Kohr says. "Personally, I would much rather have people ask a ton of questions during my 2 hours with them than just sit there and listen to me."

Request an Interest-Specific Tour

The guides at battlefield sites usually have their own areas of interest, and many of them are willing to customize a tour for small groups that share that interest. For the Gettysburg novice, for instance, there is a general 2-hour tour. "Other visitors want something specific," says Kohr. "That might be more details about a particular day of the battle, where the cavalry fought, or things that were featured in the movie *Gettysburg*. Pickett's Charge, the climax of the battle, is always a popular topic."

If you have an area of interest, Kohr suggests letting the guide know as soon as possible. If the tour takes reservations, bring it up then.

Look for Special Events

There are many different types of historic reenactments at battlefield sites around the country, everything from living history presentations to cannon firings to full-scale battle reenactments. At the Boston National Historic Park, for instance, there are musket firings Thursdays through Sundays from 10:30 A.M. to 3:30 P.M. Knowledgeable volunteer guides lead free 4-hour hikes on certain weekends at Manassas National Battlefield Park, site of the first major Civil War battle, known as the Battle of Bull Run. For details on these specific tours, write to Boston National Historic Park, Charlestown Navy Yard, Charlestown, MA 02109 or Manassas National Battlefield Park, 12521 Lee Highway, Manassas, VA 20109.

Touring the State Capitols

Every state capitol offers some sort of tour explaining who designed it, when it was built, historic events that happened under its roof, and the famous figures that graced its halls. Usually, this means spending 30 minutes to an hour walking through the rooms with a trained interpretive guide. These tours are often free and typically don't require a reservation. Based on advice from tour guides at state capitols around the country, here are some pointers for getting the most from a capitol visit.

Request a Topical Tour

Ask about interest-specific tours, such as those that focus on art and architecture, women in government, and other topics. If you are part of a church, community, or school group, ask if a tour can be arranged expressly for your group. The department that you'll need to call differs from state to state, so ask the information operator for the general state capitol number, then call there and ask for the department that runs tours.

Look for Annual Events

State capitols sometimes hold special yearly events, usually free or for a minimal fee, that correspond with historic dates, holidays, or seasons. For instance, each October, the state capitol of Minnesota (Room B59, 75 Constitution Avenue, St. Paul, MN 55155) holds a popular tour called "Shadows and Spirits of the State Capitol." Visitors walk the dimly lit halls (only the original 1905 lighting is used) and encounter staff dressed as historic figures such as John LaFarge, who painted the murals in the supreme court wing.

Ask about Special-Needs Tours

Most state capitols should be able to provide a guide who gives sign language tours. But, says Ella Anderson, a sign language interpretive guide at the Texas State Capitol, you have to call in advance to book a reservation for this special service.

The same goes for booking a foreign-language tour guide. The folks in Texas keep trained college students with language skills on call. If your Russian aunt and uncle are visiting, for instance, and you give enough notice, you should be able to book a guide who speaks Russian—which, by the way, is the Texas capitol's most requested foreign-language tour. Less surprising is the guides' claim that the Texas capitol is the country's biggest.

Touring the Nation's Capital

Every year, 3 to 5 million people visit the U.S. Capitol building in Washington, D.C., making it one of the most popular tourist attractions in town. On a typical day, 10,000 people may pass through the building's famous rotunda. But the sight of hordes of visitors waiting in line on a hot summer day is enough to make even the most determined among us question our patriotic fervor.

According to a few Capitol Hill insiders, there are ways to beat the crowds and even to get a more in-depth and personal tour of what is fondly known as the "people's building." Here's how.

Avoid Peak Periods

Because of school breaks, spring is by far the peak season, but summer is one of the busiest times for visitors to the Capitol. Beginning September 1, the crowds dwindle, and they remain thin throughout the winter.

"Our slowest day of the week is Monday, because the White House is closed on Mondays," says Sharon Nevitt, assistant director of visitor services at the Capitol. The least crowded times of the day are midday, late afternoon, and early evening.

Call Your Congressmember

The regular, daily tours of the Capitol last 30 minutes and usually include 50 to 55 people. But every congressmember and senator is allotted a certain number of free VIP passes per week, usually 10 or 15, which any constituent can reserve in advance for no extra charge.

The benefits of the passes are many: VIP tours are by reservation only, so you don't have to wait in line; groups are smaller, usually 30 to 35 people

("I've had as few as 2 or 3 people," says Nevitt, who is trained as a guide); and the tours visit more rooms, including either the House or Senate chamber, which are not part of the standard tour. "We also give more information on the rooms, so it does take longer," Nevitt says. The VIP tours generally last approximately 45 minutes.

The trick is landing a pass. As you might imagine, they're hot commodities, despite the fact that many people don't even know that they exist.

"Send your request at least 4 months in advance," stresses Misty Merchant, case worker for California congressman Ron Packard. To get a pass during the summer months, start even earlier. During winter, you might be lucky with only a month's notice. You can always contact your congressmember's office when you arrive in Washington to see if there have been any cancellations.

◆● *WHAT INSIDERS SAY:*

To find out how to reach your congressmember and/or senator, call your local county board of elections (the number should be in the government pages of your telephone book). Give them your address, and they will tell you your congressional district, the congressmember's name, and contact information.

Use Clout at the White House

Like the Capitol tours, visits to the White House are hugely popular. They're also crowded into 2-hour slots Tuesdays through Saturdays between 10 A.M. and noon. As you might imagine, the length of the waiting line can be daunting.

"The best way to tour the White House is with a congressional pass," says Melinda Bates, special assistant to the president and director of the White House Visitors Office. You can get these by writing to your senator, who is given 15 tickets per week, or your congressmember, who gets 10. (Senate and House leaders get 17 and 12, respectively.)

A congressional pass entitles you to a guided tour as opposed to the standard 20-minute, self-guided walk-through and gives you access to rooms

(continued on page 214)

Best Bets

AMERICA'S BEST HISTORIC FORTS

Old forts are always favorite tourist attractions. Often large, impressive structures, they conjure up some of the most dramatic events in our nation's past. "They have aspects of American history, local history, and military history," says Colonel Herbert Hart, a retired Marine Corps officer and author of a book series called *Tour Guide to Old Western Forts*.

In the course of his research, Hart has visited more than 650 historic forts. His advice for making the most of a fort visit? Talk to the volunteer tour guides. "Often, the volunteer guides will know more than the paid staff," he says. "They're there because they believe in it." Here are 10 of Hart's favorites.

Fort Laramie, Wyoming

A former fur-trading post and later a U.S. Army fort dating back to 1834, Laramie was the center of U.S. military presence on the High Plains during the Indian wars. The fort's bookstore has one of the best Western history selections in the country. There are daily ranger-led tours and specialty talks. Write to HC 72, Box 389, Fort Laramie, WY 82212.

Fort Sumter National Monument, South Carolina

Located on an island in Charleston Harbor, Fort Sumter was the first Union base to fall into Confederate hands, after a historic battle on April 12, 1861. During the 35-minute boat ride to the fort, visitors listen to a taped historic summary. Write to 1214 Middle Street, Sullivan's Island, SC 29482.

Fort Davis National Historic Site, Texas

"This is the best example of a preserved Western fort," Hart says. During the summer, interpreters dressed in period clothing are stationed at the restored 1880s buildings. Write to P.O. Box 1456, Highways 17-118, Fort Davis, TX 79734.

Fort Jefferson, Dry Tortugas National Park, Florida

Built in 1846 to help protect the Florida Straits, this is the largest all-masonry fort in the Western world. Accessible only by boat, it occupies an island 70 miles west of the Florida Keys and is host to dozens of species of birds and fish. Write to P.O. Box 6208, Key West, FL 33041.

Fort McHenry, Maryland

The guardian of the Baltimore harbor, Fort McHenry is where Francis Scott Key penned the U.S. national anthem during an attack by British forces on September 13, 1814. During the Civil War, Union soldiers used it as a prison camp for Confederates. Tours are self-guided, with occasional interpretive programs. Write to End of East Fort Avenue, Baltimore, MD 21230-5393.

Fort Concho, Texas

Founded in 1867 and run by the city of San Angelo, the fort is almost completely preserved as it was in its prime, with 23 original and restored structures. On weekdays, guides wearing uniforms and other period costumes give tours every hour. Write to 630 South Oakes, San Angelo, TX 76903.

Fort Pike, Louisiana

Fort Pike is a large brick fort built between 1818 and 1827 to protect the city of New Orleans from foreign invasion. During the Civil War, it served as a Union training camp for African-American soldiers. There are self-guided tours daily. Write to Route 6, Box 194, New Orleans, LA 70129.

Fort Atkinson, Nebraska

Home to as many as 800 soldiers in its prime, Atkinson was one of the largest military outposts in the West when it was built in 1820. By 1827, the military had abandoned it in order to protect the more important Santa Fe Trail to the southwest. "The state rebuilt the fort, and it has a very active interpretive program," says Hart. Write to P.O. Box 240, Fort Calhoun, NE 68023.

Fort MacArthur, California

This former U.S. Army post guarded Los Angeles Harbor from 1914 to 1974. During the Cold War, it housed 16 missile launch sites that protected an area of about 4,000 square miles. Volunteers give tours on weekends and by appointment only during the week. Write to P.O. Box 268, San Pedro, CA 90731.

Fort Stevens, Oregon

Stevens is a coastal artillery fort constructed in 1864 at the mouth of the Columbia River. "One reason that the government built the fort was to claim Oregon for the Union during the Civil War," says Macy Yates, a park ranger at Fort Stevens State Park, which administers the fort. "There were a lot of Confederate sympathizers in the area." It was eventually upgraded, and at the start of World War II, it was fired on by the Japanese, making it the only continental U.S. fort to be fired on by foreign forces after 1812. Write to Ridge Mountain Road, Hammond, OR 97121.

◄◆ *WHAT INSIDERS SAY:*

Yates recommends taking the Fort Stevens "deuce-and-a-half" tour, a narrated drive around the site in the canvas-covered bed of a 2½-ton World War II–era Army truck. For most, this is a rare opportunity to ride in a large military vehicle. Kids love it. It's offered during only the peak season, from late spring to early fall.

not on the regular tour, such as the China Room and the Diplomatic Reception Room.

The tickets are extremely popular, though. Bates suggests requesting them from your senator or congressmember as far in advance as possible—as much as a year if you want tickets for March through August or Christmas, the busiest times at the White House, and less for a visit during fall or winter. Typically, you'll learn whether your request has been granted 1 month before the date requested, when the White House gives the congressmen's offices their allotments.

◆ WHAT INSIDERS SAY:

To improve the chances that you'll get a congressional pass, request one from both your senator and congressmember. If you're lucky enough to get both, you always can decline the second pass so someone else can get into the tour.

Fire Stations

When its members are not putting out fires, a big part of your local fire department's job is safety education. Most of this country's approximately 34,000 fire stations will accommodate just about anyone who wants to tour the firehouse. Many also hold open house cookouts, visit local schools, and attend birthday parties.

Whether it's a party or a tour of the station, the firefighters combine fire safety lessons with fun activities. "When groups tour the station," says Ed Kirtley, chief of the Guymon, Oklahoma, Fire Department, "we show them the apparatus, let them try on the gear, show them where we eat and sleep, and present at least one prevention lesson. Tours also give the community a chance to see local government in action."

Since 1986, when the Parker, Colorado, fire department began giving safety demonstrations at children's birthday parties, the total number of fire calls has dropped by 80 percent. "This is absolutely the best way to develop a rapport with the community, because citizens are requesting a service that's not an emergency," says Cheryl Poage, public edu-

cation specialist with the Parker Fire Department. "We don't just send a firefighter; we send a whole on-duty crew."

To arrange a fire station visit—whether it's for a child's party, a scouting group, a school group, or some other occasion—Poage suggests calling your community station and asking for the person in charge of public education, who is responsible for dealing with community outreach programs. If there is no educator, ask for the fire chief. And call at least 3 weeks in advance to be sure of fitting into the fire company's schedule.

◆ WHAT INSIDERS SAY:

Fire departments usually request a minimum of 10 people to book a tour. If you have fewer members in your group, ask if the department will add you to an upcoming group tour.

BUDGET VACATIONS

Compared to private hotels and tour companies, taking a vacation at a government-owned location is pretty inexpensive. You can get discounts on multiple visits, free activities, and, if you're willing to volunteer some time, maybe even free lodging and board. Topping it all off is the rewarding feeling you get from taking advantage of benefits that you have in essence already made a down payment on through your taxes. Here's the inside scoop on finding fun, relaxing, and educational activities that are affordable.

Travel Discounts and Freebies

At both the federal and state levels, there are certain programs that let you save on park entrance fees, activities, and lodging—and, with the right background, even on flights. Here are some examples of travel price breaks.

Golden Passports

These passes give you unlimited access to national parks, participating U.S. Forest Service sites, and other government recreation parks as well as certain discounts on camping fees.

There are three types of passes. The Golden Eagle Passport, which costs $50 for 1 year, is available to anyone and provides free park access to the passholder and any accompanying passengers in a private vehicle. It does not reduce camping or activity fees. If you're a frequent park visitor, this pass should pay for itself. You can buy one at any national park entrance or by mail. Write to National Park Service, 1100 Ohio Drive SW, Room 138, Washington, DC 20242, Attn: Golden Eagle.

The Golden Age Passport is a lifetime entrance pass for anyone 62 or older. It admits the holder and any accompanying passengers (or the spouse, children, and parents where entry is not by private vehicle) plus it gives a 50 percent discount on federal use fees for activities such as camping, swimming, and cave tours. You can get these passes in person only at national park entrance gates. There is a one-time charge of $10.

The Golden Access Passport is a free lifetime entrance pass for the blind or permanently disabled. Like the Golden Age Passport, you must get it in person at a national park entrance. It provides the same benefits—and it's free.

State Passes

Some state park systems offer discount passes similar to the federal government's Golden Passports. Indiana, for instance, offers a Golden Hoosier Pass for $9 to any in-state resident 62 or older. It allows unlimited entrance to all parks. For those under 62, the state offers an Annual Entrance Permit for $18 (in-state) and $25 (out-of-state), which is good for 1 year. The general entrance fees are $2 (in-state) and $5 (out-of-state), so if you're a Hoosier and you'll be using any of the state parks at least 10 times, the pass is worth the money.

Call the state park office in your state and ask about similar discount programs. You'll find the office listed in the government pages of your phone book. The names of the agencies overseeing the parks varies from state to state. Look under such names as "Department of Parks, Recreation, and Tourism"; "Parks and Wildlife"; or "Bureau of Parks and Lands."

Free Flights for Vets

All fully retired military veterans—those who hold a blue ID card—and active-duty personnel can travel for free on military flights on a space-available basis. Family members of retirees (who have proper identification to prove dependent status) can also fly free, but only to overseas destinations. To find out about flights, call your local Air Mobility Command (AMC) passenger terminal to get a schedule of departures. For the location and phone number of the nearest AMC terminal, write HQ AMC/DONP, 402 Scott Drive Unit 3A1, Scott Air Force Base, IL 62225-5302. Or you can purchase what is known as a space-available travel book at your local military base store.

"These are excellent resources," says Greg Liberto, staff sergeant at Andrews Air Force Base in Camp Springs, Maryland. "They give you everything you need to know about space-available travel."

●◆ *WHAT INSIDERS SAY:*

When taking a flight that has a layover, you have to fly stand-by on the second leg, too. You can improve your chances for getting on that second flight by registering in advance at the base where you booked the first flight.

Volunteers for America

The benefits of government-related volunteer travel are twofold: You save money while you help your country. Of course, there are plenty of other great reasons to offer your services on projects around the country, such as bonding with other volunteers on your team, learning new skills, gaining a sense of accomplishment, and discovering places that otherwise might have been off-limits. Here are some opportunities for traveling while volunteering.

National Park Host

Every year, there are about 100,000 volunteers in different national park programs. Some work as camp hosts or park hosts. If they log 30 hours a week (often for a minimum number of weeks), a few parks will offer them a free stay, either in a dorm or a campground.

"Campground hosts generally do light maintenance, welcome guests who come into the campground, and provide them with general information," says Joy Pietschmann, volunteer coordinator for the National Park Service. A park host may greet visitors, work on the office computer, or do historical research. There are also other volunteer jobs available. It depends on the park.

The National Park Service features an up-to-date opportunities list on its Web site at www.nps.gov/volunteer/opportunity.htm. Each listing gives detailed information about the particular park, the job available, its duties, and volunteer benefits. Here are a few examples of the kinds of jobs that were available during one season.

A (NEARLY) FREE WASHINGTON VACATION

There is no better place to enjoy a wide range of government travel benefits than in the nation's capital. Because many of the museums, memorials, and historic government buildings are directly funded by your tax dollars, a trip to the capital can be one of the least expensive and most activity-packed vacations you'll ever have.

If you're adventurous, you can even solve the problem of pricey lodging by camping at the little-known Greenbelt National Park, 12 miles from the city. The 174-site campground, which costs $13 a night for up to six campers (and welcomes pop-up trailers up to 30 feet long), features rest rooms and showers, tables, and grills. Best of all, a city bus that stops at the road by the campground can drop you at a nearby Metro station, where you can catch a clean, inexpensive subway car that will take you to most parts of the capital. "When people check in, we give them a Metro schedule so they can plan their travel into the city," says Bob Hansen, Greenbelt Park manager. Contact the park at 6565 Greenbelt Rd., Greenbelt, MD 20770.

Here's a sample itinerary for a 3-day trip to Washington. Everything listed is free of charge.

Day 1

✓ Visit the U.S. Capitol, seat of the legislative branch of federal government. Half-hour tours.

✓ Visit the U.S. Supreme Court, which features changing exhibits on the history of the government's judicial branch. Hourly lectures when the court is not in session.

✓ Visit the Library of Congress, the world's largest library, with more than 111 million items, including one of the world's three perfect vellum copies of the Gutenberg Bible. Daily tours.

✓ Visit the National Archives, where you can look up your family's genealogical records. Housed here are census reports from 1790 to 1920, ship passenger arrival records, federal land records, military pension information from the Revolutionary War, and other archives. Open Monday through Saturday, no appointment necessary. Go to Room 400 on the fourth floor.

✓ Visit the Smithsonian Institution, which is actually 14

✓ Cowpens National Battlefield, a Revolutionary War site in South Carolina, was looking for a couple who would be interested in helping its small staff during the summer months. In exchange for keeping the picnic areas clean, mowing grass, assisting the staff at the visitors' center desk when needed, and a few other light tasks, the couple would receive a free hookup for their RV, including a phone line.

✓ Another notice on the Web site, posted by Fort Necessity National Battlefield in Pennsylvania, sought an interpreter to present guided tours and informal talks, sometimes in period costume provided by the park. The compensation was dorm-style housing and $10 a day in out-of-pocket meal expenses.

✓ Utah's Capitol Reef National Park, a remote area of red-rock canyons, was seeking a visitors'

different museums, including the National Air and Space Museum, the National Museum of Natural History, the National Museum of Art, and the Hirshhorn Museum and Sculpture Garden. Self-guided tours. Don't try to see all the museums in one visit; choose a few, and see the rest during the next trip.

Day 2

✓ Visit the White House, home of every U.S. president except George Washington. Self-guided walk-through tours available.

✓ Tour the *Washington Post*, one of the country's most respected newspapers. On Mondays, the paper offers 45-minute guided tours of the plant and the paper's small museum, which displays old printing presses. Write in advance for reservations to Public Relations Department, 1150 15th Street NW, Washington, DC 20071.

✓ Visit the Washington Monument, one of the tallest masonry structures in the world, dedicated in 1885 to the nation's first president. Daily elevator rides to the top; self-guided tours.

✓ Visit Potomac Park, site of some of this country's most important monuments, including those commemorating Vietnam and Korean War veterans, Abraham Lincoln, Franklin Delano Roosevelt, and Thomas Jefferson. The park is also home to the famous cherry trees that bloom each spring, usually during the last week in March. Self-guided tours.

Day 3

✓ Visit the gothic-style Washington National Cathedral, one of the largest cathedrals in the world, with an observation gallery that offers great city views. Hour-and-a-half tours 7 days a week.

✓ Visit the National Museum of Health and Medicine at Walter Reed Army Hospital, which houses a small but odd collection, including the bullet removed from Abraham Lincoln's brain and an elephantiasis-swollen leg and foot in a jar of formaldehyde. Open 7 days a week.

✓ Visit the National Zoological Park, a collection of more than 3,000 different animals, including the giant panda Hsing-Hsing. Open daily for self-guided tours.

✓ Visit the Kennedy Center's Millennium Stage, offering free performances every evening at 6:00 P.M.—modern dance, classical music, drama, and other events.

center volunteer. In exchange for a 3-month, 32-hour-a-week commitment, the park would provide free dorm-style accommodations.

Assisting at State Parks

Many state parks have similar host programs. New York, for example, has a Camper Assistance Program at 35 of its parks. Volunteers in this program camp for free if they agree to serve for a minimum of 2 weeks and a maximum of 4 weeks. They're on duty 5 days a week for 2 to 5 hours each day.

Virginia's host program has 20 participating parks, natural areas, and historic sites. Volunteers can camp for free for 30 to 90 days, plus they receive a complimentary week of free off-season camping after they have worked for 30 days. After 60 days, they get 2 weeks of free camping or a week in a cabin. They can also swim, boat, and use other facilities for free. "Our volunteers might have family in the area," says Marie Coone, the Virginia State Parks operations director. "This program allows them to stay for a length of time without spending much money."

The standard duties are the same as those of most camp hosts—greeting guests, explaining rules, and cleaning—but they can vary depending on the individual. "Some of the volunteers bring wonderful skills," Coone says. "We've had people

---

Amazing Stories

FREE
STATE "PARKING"

You might say that state park volunteer programs changed Ellen and Joe Medlin's life. Once weekend RVers, they hit the road full-time soon after discovering that they could get free RV hookups in exchange for hosting at campgrounds. Now, they spend summers in Virginia, near their two sons, and winters in Texas, where the weather is more agreeable at that time of year.

They first found out about the programs when Joe, retired from the U.S. Navy, saw an advertisement for Virginia state park hosts in *Highways* magazine. He and his wife then went to the library and looked up the parks and recreation departments for all the states they hoped to visit one day. Most had park host programs.

"We decided to go for it," says Ellen, who quit her job and helped sell their house. "If it weren't for this volunteer system, we would have a very difficult time doing it on our income."

As campground hosts, they work 20 to 30 hours a week checking in other campers, passing out park literature, cleaning campsites and the occasional bathroom, and doing other light tasks—nothing, they say, that is too taxing. In return, they save $300 to $400 in campground fees per month.

The program really came in handy when the couple's two daughters-in-law were expecting babies. "The Virginia park coordinator helped us find the closest park down there," Ellen says. "We went down for a month and were nearby when the babies were born."

Next year, they're planning to hit parks in Washington state and New Mexico. You guessed it: They have family in both places.

who have been carpenters, and they've done minor renovations like building countertops and shelves."

You should contact either the particular state parks that you're interested in or the state's office of state parks for general information about volunteer programs. Check the government pages of your phone book for numbers in your state or ask the information operator for numbers in other states.

Archeological Digs

Have you ever had Indiana Jones fantasies in which you travel the globe searching for ancient ruins? Thanks to a Forest Service program called Passport in Time, you can pitch in on fascinating archeological digs—and while they may not be on foreign soil, they are in some of this country's most interesting locales.

Volunteers spend anywhere from a weekend to a month working with professional Forest Service archeologists to excavate sites, survey them, and do historic preservation and other types of work. Past projects have included stabilizing ancient cliff dwellings in New Mexico, restoring a historic lookout tower in Oregon, and excavating a nineteenth-century Chinese mining site in Hell's Canyon, Idaho.

A popular project, started in California, uses volunteers to develop and maintain relationships with Native American groups. "One way is by sending them in to help learn traditional basket weaving," says Jill Osborn, national Passport in Time coordinator. "The volunteers benefit by seeing that historic preservation is also about preserving present resources."

There is no cost to participate. Volunteers usually bring their own food and camp for free, using their own gear. While many jobs require little or no experience and provide on-site training, some call for specific skills, such as carpentry.

To find out about the 200-odd annual projects, write to Passport in Time, P.O. Box 31315, Tucson, AZ 85751, and ask to be put on the mailing list for the Passport in Time semiannual newsletter, "PIT Traveler." Projects that will take place from June through November are announced in the March issue; the September issue lists December through May projects.

Maintaining America's Hiking Trails

If you're looking for a shorter, more rigorous experience, consider volunteering for a hiking club. These nonprofit organizations usually help maintain trails inside government lands, such as the Appalachian National Scenic Trail or the Sawtooth National Forest in Idaho. While their programs vary, the clubs often provide free local transportation, meals, and camping in exchange for what can be tough but highly rewarding manual labor.

The American Hiking Society offers 50 to 75 projects to all parts of the United States as part of its annual Volunteer Vacations program. Trips, which typically last 1 to 2 weeks, cost $60 for members and $75 for nonmembers (the extra $15 buys you an annual membership). Most include either meals or a stipend to cover food expenses. Volunteers camp, often at primitive sites, and are usually given transportation from the nearest airport or train station to the work site.

The trail maintenance can be tough. Crew members rake, shovel, trim, and chop for 6 to 8 hours a day. The rest of the time, however, they're free to explore the wilderness. Most people love it. "One out of every three participants returns for another project," says Shirley Hearn, volunteer vacations coordinator. "One person went on 8 projects this year, and he's signed up for 12 for next year." For information, write to the American Hiking Society, P.O. Box 20160, Washington, DC 20041.

There are 31 regional nonprofit organizations that help maintain the Appalachian Trail. Each club offers different types of volunteer opportunities. More than just a chance for a freebie, these programs can be rewarding educational experiences. The Potomac Appalachian Trail Club, for instance, which has been in existence since the 1930s, recruits people to help update the 20 hiking maps it maintains. "Volunteers get a sense of ben-

Power to the People

GETTING A PASSPORT IN A HURRY

It used to be that if you needed a passport quickly, you'd make an appointment with one of the country's 13 passport agencies, travel to get there (if you weren't lucky enough to live in one of the 13 home cities), and plead your case. Or you'd ask your congressmember to pull strings at the passport office.

That's no longer true. Thanks to the good folks at the U.S. Department of State, anyone who needs a passport in a hurry these days can pay a $35 expediting fee (in addition to the normal $40 to $60 passport application fee) to have the application processed within 3 working days of receipt by the passport agency (plus shipping time, if you apply by mail). To qualify for the expedited process, you must be able to prove—by presenting plane tickets, itinerary, confirmed reservations, or a letter from your place of business—that you're leaving the country in less than 14 days or that you are leaving in less than 3 weeks and require foreign visas.

You can apply in person at one of the 13 passport agencies (in Boston; Chicago; Honolulu; Houston; Los Angeles; Miami; New Orleans; New York; Philadelphia; San Francisco; Seattle; Stamford, Connecticut; or Washington, D.C.) or by mail. For the address of the nearest passport agency, write to Bureau of Consular Affairs, Room 6831, Department of State, 2201 C Street NW, Washington, DC 20520.

If you apply by mail, be sure to write "Expedite" on the outside of your application envelope. If you apply by mail and want to cut down on the mailing time, you can pay in advance to have the passport shipped by overnight courier.

If you're in an even bigger hurry—if there is an emergency, for example, and you must leave right away—your best bet is to plead your case to one of the passport agencies. You can always try your congressmember as well, but it's not the congressional letter, it's the legitimacy of the emergency that's going to determine whether the passport is issued.

You can get a passport application at any of the 13 regional passport agencies or at a passport acceptance facility—either a designated post office or your county clerk or clerk of courts. You can find the appropriate numbers and addresses in your telephone book's government pages under "Passports." Or you can download applications from the State Department's Internet site at http://travel.state.gov.

●◆ WHAT INSIDERS SAY:

Beware of private expediting agents. "They're out there to prey on people who think they can get the passport faster by going through the company," says Maria Rudensky, a spokesperson for the State Department's Passport Services division. "With the government's expedite fee, these companies are actually nonessential."

efiting future hikers," says Dave Pierce, map chairman for the Potomac Club. "If they do their jobs right, hikers won't become disoriented. They also get a free copy of the map, and they can see how their recommendations turned out." For information, contact the club at 118 Park Street SE, Vienna, VA 22180.

For a complete list of Appalachian Trail clubs, contact the Appalachian Trail Conference, P.O. Box 807, Harpers Ferry, WV 25425.

•◆ WHAT INSIDERS SAY:

The American Hiking Society's most popular assignments—such as 2 weeks of building boardwalks in the waterfall-rich bamboo forests of Hawaii's Haleakala National Park or 10 days repairing cabins at Alaska's Admiralty Island National Monument—fill up quickly. The normal procedure is to list your top three choices on your mail-in application. To make sure you get a spot, says Hearn, call ahead to make a reservation.

CHAPTER 14

BUILDING the FIELD of YOUR DREAMS

Perhaps you have a vision for turning an overgrown, littered field into a playground that the neighborhood kids can enjoy. Or it could be that your goal is to convert an abandoned stretch of railroad track into a bike trail or a patch of green space that can remain forever wild. Whatever your dream, with the government's help, you may be able to make it happen.

One of the government's key roles is to provide recreation areas. While it will have the final say on where and how to build such facilities, you and your fellow community members can influence the decision greatly and in your favor. You can suggest locations and the type of recreational equipment you'd like to see. You can form a local group to lobby for community and government support. You can apply for grants to help pay for construction.

> Lush parks, friendly playgrounds, prime recreation areas: These are the things that make a community the envy of its neighbors. Here's how you—and the government—can bring them to your town.

In this chapter, we'll give you advice for working with government to make your pet project a reality, including where to find financing, how to write a grant-winning proposal, and the secrets of getting government to back you.

When it comes to government recreation grants, the bottom line is competition. There may be others fighting for the same cut of funding as you are, but with this advice, you'll be in a position to win. Good luck!

RECREATION GRANTS

No matter what type of project you have in mind, chances are much better that you'll get it built if you can attract a grant to cover part or all of the cost. The best place to start looking is your state,

FACTOID

THERE ARE MORE THAN 250,000 MILES OF RECREATIONAL EXERCISE TRAILS IN THE UNITED STATES. THAT'S SLIGHTLY MORE THAN THE DISTANCE BETWEEN EARTH AND THE MOON.

which often raises its own funds and acts as a conduit for federal block grants.

For example, "most states have some money set aside for park development," says Bryan Kellar, director of the Arkansas Department of Parks and Tourism outdoor recreation grants program in Little Rock. "We use a transfer tax on real estate; others may use some special tax or bond issue."

While it varies from state to state and from town to town, the process of landing government funds will typically follow a few important steps.

✓ Develop a detailed plan to help sell your project. Find a comparable park or playground that you can use as a model, then rough out your design on paper; this will give you something concrete to show when you approach the state for a grant or speak to people in the community to gather local support. Estimate the cost of land, material, labor, and any other expenses, and keep a portfolio of your research and sketches.

✓ Get your local government's endorsement, at least in principle if local officials aren't immediately willing to commit to your project. How do you do this? One key is to prove that your project has the backing of many people in your community by gathering names on a petition or asking neighbors to come to a council meeting (see chapter 2 for advice on creating a community group).

✓ File an application or submit a grant proposal that will wow the judges (for tips on how to do this, see "Submitting a Grant-Winning Proposal," on page 232).

✓ Follow through and complete construction in a timely manner. Government grants are often contingent on meeting a deadline.

That's the big picture on getting started. Here are some more specific tips to make the process easier.

Finding Funds

When you're ready to start hunting for money for a park or playground, the first place to go is your state conservation and recreation department, advises Jerry Cassidy, grants administrator for Virginia's Department of Conservation and Recreation in Richmond. Every state has such an office, but the names can vary. In Arkansas, it's the Department of Parks and Tourism, and in South Carolina, it's the Department of Parks, Recreation, and Tourism. Check the government pages of your phone book for the appropriate department and the phone number.

You might also try your state affiliate of the National Recreation and Park Association. This nonprofit organization works closely with communities and government agencies to facilitate recreation for healthy living, including building and improving parks. Someone there should be able to give you advice on local funding opportunities or at least tell you how to contact your state's parks and recreation department. Each state has an affiliate of the association. To find yours, write to the National Recreation and Park Association, 22377 Belmont Ridge Road, Ashburn, VA 20148, or visit the group's Web site at www.nrpa.org.

➥ *WHAT INSIDERS SAY:*

Don't expect to attract 100 percent funding from your state. Recreation grants are often matching grants, meaning that the government gives a certain percentage of the total needed—25 or 50 percent, for instance—leaving you and your community to raise the rest. The additional funds can come from corporations or private gifts, or even from materials or services donated in kind.

Also note that often, the grant money is given on a reimbursable basis, which means that your community group must pay for the work from its own funds, then submit receipts to be repaid. Governments do this to stay on top of the progress of a project. In this case, you'll need a source of capital in advance to begin the work, so local donations will come in handy. Typically, donated labor and materials are not reimbursable.

Gathering Local Support

To win a grant, you must demonstrate that your project has the backing of the community. The more people who benefit, the better, says Rosanne Boyd, who spearheaded a citizen-led campaign to modernize an unsafe playground in Cammack Village, Arkansas. The type of group that you form depends partly on the grant you are seeking. Some government agencies will give money to neighborhood groups and community associations regardless of whether they are registered nonprofit groups; others will deal only with qualified nonprofits (to find out more about types of groups, see "Should Your Group Go Nonprofit?").

Building a Network

"When you're looking for funding, the telephone is your best ally," says Bryan Kellar of the Arkansas Department of Parks and Tourism. "A lot can be learned and accomplished through networking." Contact neighboring municipalities for advice, and ask other parks departments about costs and their sources of funding.

Identifying Obstacles

Just because you think that you've developed what seems to be the perfect project, that doesn't mean it will pass government muster. The Americans

SHOULD YOUR GROUP GO NONPROFIT?

When you delve into the world of government grants, you're likely to bump up against agencies that will award money only to registered nonprofit groups—meaning that you need to complete the time-intensive process of formally applying for nonprofit status in order to qualify for a grant.

Is it worth the effort? That depends.

There are several reasons that your group might benefit as a nonprofit corporation. Corporate status protects officers and board members from personal liability in matters involving employees, services, and fundraising. It allows people to give you tax-deductible donations, and it exempts your group from paying certain taxes—federal taxes, federal unemployment insurance, and in most states, sales tax and state income tax.

But going nonprofit is no cakewalk. "The government does not let go of taxes readily," says Dan Prives, a Baltimore consultant for nonprofit groups. Here are the basic steps you'll have to take to become a nonprofit organization.

1. Establish a board of directors.

2. Create a list of bylaws governing your organization.

3. If required by your state, incorporate as a nonprofit entity, which is done by registering with the correct state office. This varies from state to state, but first try your secretary of state or state attorney general.

4. Apply for tax exemption as a 501(c)(3) nonprofit organization with the IRS. The 30-page application booklet that you'll need to fill out is number 1023. You can write to the IRS, Eastern Area Distribution Center, P.O. Box 85074, Richmond, VA 23261-5074 or download the form from the IRS Web site at www.irs.ustreas.gov. Click on "Forms and Publications" at the bottom of the page.

with Disabilities Act may require certain things, for example, or the city may want to conduct an archeological survey if the site is in a historical area.

To find out what the Americans with Disabilities Act Accessibility Guidelines require, contact the National Center on Accessibility at 5020 State Road 67 N, Martinsville, IN 46151. The center provides technical assistance to groups planning outdoor recreation projects. Someone there can provide answers to questions such as how wide a trail should be or what playground surface is universally accessible.

As for determining whether the site is of historic importance, Chris Baas, a recreation planner for the Indiana Department of Natural Resources in Indi-anapolis, recommends contacting your state office of historic preservation for advice (see chapter 18).

Okay, now you know the basics of getting funding; let's look at some specific types of projects and the insiders' advice for getting them built.

PLAYGROUNDS

All communities, no matter how large or small, need playgrounds. They're important for children's development (not to mention parents' sanity) and the general well-being of all residents. They're also among the most local recreation projects, often involving neighborhoods or even a few neighborhood blocks.

You'll probably want a lawyer and a certified public accountant knowledgeable about nonprofit tax law to review your bylaws and application before final submission. You can use qualified people from your board of directors or hire from the outside.

The standard reference for a group that is serious about starting a nonprofit organization is a book called *How to Form a Nonprofit Corporation*, by Anthony Mancuso, says Putnam Barber, president of the Evergreen State Society in Seattle, a member organization of the National Council of Nonprofit Associations. Look for it in bookstores or at your library. For more information, contact your state attorney general's office or ask your state council of nonprofit associations for advice. Most states have one. For a state-by-state list, contact the National Council of Nonprofit Associations at 1900 L Street NW, Washington, DC 20036 or visit the group's Web site at www.ncna.org.

An easier route
You may decide that your group's project doesn't merit nonprofit status. Don't give up. There's still hope for landing that grant by finding a nonprofit sponsor to act as a fiscal partner. This type of situation is perfect for short-term projects such as playgrounds.

Bill Conkle is president of the Richmond Recreation and Parks Foundation in Virginia. "We were created because there are a lot of grant agen-cies that can't designate funds to groups that don't have non-profit tax status," he explains. "We work with local groups to develop a proposal, then serve as their fiscal agent." The foundation is involved in about 40 projects a year.

To find a sponsor, ask around. Talk to any lawyers you know. Ask larger organizations that share your common interest. "For example," says Barber, "if your group is trying to create a nature preserve, I'd say the first place to look is the nearest office of the Nature Conservancy. If they can't help, ask if they can recommend an association that can." He also suggests the book *Fiscal Sponsorship: Six Ways to Do It Right*, by Gregory L. Colvin.

This small size is both good and bad if you're trying to attract community support: It's good because you can sell neighbors on the benefits of having a safe place for kids—and adults—to play and socialize. It's bad because it can be tough to convince people who don't live in your neighborhood to back your project. Still, there are ways to build a case for a playground you want built. Here's what experts suggest.

Think Locally

If you're looking for funding or verbal support, talk to the members of your school board, city council, and board of commissioners. These governing bodies are typically responsible for providing areas for children to play, and they're among the first places people turn for answers when children are injured on old equipment or when there's a shortage of play space. It's in their best interests to promote new and well-maintained playgrounds.

Bring Educators Into the Fold

Teachers and school administrators are important additions to your advisory board. They often serve as the point of contact between children and parents. "You really need them on your team," says Bill Conkle, parks and recreation consultant for the Department of Conservation and Recreation in Richmond, Virginia. "If you don't have them on your team, you will miss the resources they can bring to the table." Physical education teachers can also offer technical expertise during the design phase.

Involve the Kids

The kids who will use the equipment should be involved in planning the playground. Not only do they make persuasive fundraisers by holding car washes, exhibition games, or other events, the younger set can also provide input on what equipment or playing fields they prefer.

YOU GOTTA HAVE PARK

Of course, your community needs some green acres and playgrounds set aside for fun, exercise, relaxation, and fresh air. But how much is enough? The American Public Health Association, the National Recreation and Parks Association, and other groups have estimated minimum amounts of outdoor space needed based on population. Here are their figures.

POPULATION	RECREATION LAND (ACRES)
50,000 +	500 +
25,000–50,000	250–500
10,000–25,000	100–250
5,000–10,000	50–100
2,500–5,000	25–50
1,000–2,500	10–25

Stress Safety

Each year in this country, more than 200,000 children—94 percent of them under the age of 15—are injured on playgrounds. According to studies conducted by the Consumer Product Safety Commission, about 70 percent of the injuries are associated with public equipment, sometimes equipment that is worn out or faulty.

To help back up your playground proposal, compile data on the number of playground-related accidents in your area. Ask school nurses and local pediatricians to help with the statistics. If you feel that a playground in your area has outdated equipment, contact the Consumer Product Safety Commission at 4330 East West Highway, Bethesda, MD 20814, Attn: Freedom of Information Officer, and ask for data on injuries caused by this type of equipment. Be as specific as possible, sending the name of the manufacturer, model number, and age of your local equipment. Ask for a copy of the commission's free, 31-page brochure, "Handbook for Public Playground Safety." It will help you demonstrate how building a new facility will be safer and might reduce the number of accidents. If you have access to the Internet, you can also find information and order the safety handbook at the commission's Web site, www.cpsc.gov.

Break Down the Costs

If you're looking for matching donations from the private sector (a prerequisite for many government grants), make it easier for people to give by being specific about what you need. "A $10,000 rocket ship might be in someone's range," Conkle says, "while someone else might be able to afford a $50

NOW, THAT'S PARK SERVICE

If the standard swings and seesaws seem a little tame for the park you'd like to create, you might want to check out Adventure Playground in Berkeley, California, for inspiration. The unusual public park aims to satisfy children's building urges by providing plywood, old carpeting, hammers, nails, paint, and brushes in a fully supervised *This Old House*–like environment. (In fact, because of the constant supervision, for a fee, children older than 7 can be dropped off for as long as 3 hours at a time.) Shacks, clubhouses, forts, and rocket ships built by the kids constantly appear and disappear over the course of a week.

There are lots of more conventional features as well, including a giant cargo net to play in, a tire wall, and plenty of rope swings. The favorite activity may well be what's called the zipline. From a high wooden platform, children can ride a rope attached to a pulley and cable down into a big pile of sand. Then they walk the rope back uphill to the next child waiting in line.

If your child has any energy left over, there's also a beach, a kite park, a pier, and a marina within walking distance.

Run by the city of Berkeley, Adventure Playground is open on weekends during the school year and all week during summer vacation. For more information on how the park was conceived and built, write the Adventure Playground at 160 University Avenue, Berkeley, CA 94710.

swing." People like to know exactly what their money will be used for.

Want some experienced advice on creating a playground? Talk to KaBOOM! This national nonprofit group's sole purpose is to facilitate playground development, mainly as a way to revitalize low- to moderate-income neighborhoods, says Kimberley Rudd, the group's director of marketing and development. Since it was founded in 1996, the group has helped build more than 150 playgrounds in 15 different states and Canada.

KaBOOM! can locate corporate sponsors and foundations that are interested in funding playgrounds. It

Amazing Stories

THE PARK THAT ROSANNE BUILT

In 1994, when Rosanne Boyd initiated a plan to improve Cammack Village's only park, she had no idea what she was in for. After all, here was a small but relatively wealthy Arkansas community (pop. 800) whose children, including Boyd's 3- and 5-year-old, were forced to play on equipment built in 1949, much of it broken, rusty, and unsafe. It would be easy to have that replaced, Boyd thought. She would propose it to the town council, and the city would pay for it.

In her dreams.

What began as a simple plan turned into a project that lasted more than 4 years. In the end, Boyd and her allies were victorious. Through a combination of city and state grants, private gifts, and donations of labor, materials, and technical expertise, they built a state-of-the-art, $250,000 park. "Rosanne raised a lot of money, twisted a lot of arms, and did everything right along the way," says Bryan Kellar, who, as director of the Arkansas Department of Parks and Tourism outdoor recreation grants program, awarded Cammack Village two grants.

Early on, Boyd decided to run for town council. Cammack Village was a small town, and she figured that she had a better chance of making things happen as an insider. Elected on the promise that she would one day build a new park, she began by writing down the manufacturers' names and model numbers of the park's outdated slide, monkey bars, and other equipment and sending them to the Consumer Products Safety Commission, which responded by mailing her a 60-page book listing the numbers of injuries those products had caused. It was graphic, including amputations and deaths.

"I slapped the book down at a city council meeting and said, 'This is what we're dealing with,'" she recalls. There was only one problem: The town didn't have the budget for a new park.

Meanwhile, she and her husband, Bob, set up Friends of Cammack, Inc., a nonprofit citizens' group with a committee devoted to fixing the park. Instead of soliciting support with letters, she knocked on doors and explained her cause.

With input from parents and children, Boyd and a designer, who donated more than $1,000 in services, created sketches of the proposed park. "I didn't ask for donations until I had a picture to show people," she says. She then applied

can help citizens' groups identify the government offices they need to work with and can even offer sample letters that the groups might send to request funding.

If you're interested in having KaBOOM! help you develop a playground, Rudd suggests registering with its Playground Pool, a database of community groups. The pool keeps on file the name of your group, a con-

tact person, and a little about your particular situation in order to match communities with corporate sponsors when they become available. You might also be interested in attending one of KaBOOM's Playground Institutes, which are how-to conferences that are open to community group representatives, who learn to put together playground equipment and organize volunteer

for and won a $50,000, dollar-for-dollar matching grant from the state. But where to get the matching money? The town pitched in $3,000, and individuals donated $12,000.

One day, Boyd visited the Baker family, who owned the lot adjacent to the park, to ask if they would sell or lease the lot. They said no. "My heart sank," she remembers. "But in the next breath, they explained that they wanted to donate it in their parents' name." The value of the land, $35,000, met the match.

Soon, however, the park committee needed more money. Costs had far exceeded earlier estimates. Boyd applied for another state grant and this time got $30,000, which again had to be matched with cash, land, donations, or in-kind labor.

In her friendly but insistent way, she began asking for things, and she got them. One person gave picnic tables worth $8,400. Another installed $17,000 in lighting. A drainage problem arose, and someone donated $3,500 worth of stone to help fix it. More gifts followed: $1,000 in plumbing work, $2,000 in water fountains, a $10,000 basketball court. Boyd was on a roll. She donated her $1,800 annual alderman salary

to the cause and helped organize a community-wide garage sale (publicized, of course, with free ad space) that raised $3,000. The community was behind her all the way.

The secret of Boyd's success is simple: Make your neighbors feel that they're part of the process. "Then, they'll fight for it, they'll sacrifice, they'll volunteer their time and labor," she says. She invited children to the public hearings and town council meetings. Even if they didn't speak, their presence showed people that they cared. When the time came to choose playground equipment, she recruited a committee of mothers to help conduct research. They took their children to other parks and watched them play. "That's how we discovered the Thunderbolt slide," she says, referring to the one now standing in Baker Park. "You can have salesmen show you products all day. What really sold us was that all the children would get off that particular slide and then get right back on it."

Says Boyd: "When I go out there and look at the park, I think 'How did we ever do that?' The community built that park regardless of the obstacles. I don't think there's a better park in Arkansas."

building teams. For more information about either the pool or the institutes, write to KaBOOM!, 2213 M Street NW, Suite 200, Washington, DC 20037.

BIKE PATHS

If your goal is to create a bike trail where you and your neighbors can exercise and enjoy the country-side, you're in luck. Between the federal government and the nonprofit world, you can get both money and technical assistance to make your wish come true.

The money comes from the Transportation Equity Act for the 21st Century (TEA-21). This act authorizes funding for all sorts of trans-portation-related projects, with more than $1 billion to be spent over 6 years on trails, in-cluding bicycle paths. The advice comes from the Rails-to-Trails Conservancy, a Washington, D.C.–based nonprofit organization that was founded in 1987 to help people convert unused railroad corridors into trails for recreation and transportation.

Both resources are available to community groups, provided that you can convince the people in charge that your project deserves their support. How can you do that? Here's what the experts advise.

Brewing a TEA Grant

Now that the government is catching on to the idea of bicycling as a source of exercise as well as a fuel- and pollution-free transportation alternative, there's an upward trend in funding for nonmotorized trans-portation, and TEA-21 is the most visible sign.

Getting TEA-21 funds is not easy, however. "It's a huge piece of legislation divided into lots of programs that are managed either at the state or local level," says Andy Clarke, a transporta-tion specialist with the Federal Highway Ad-ministration in Washington. "It can be difficult to find the one person you need to talk to in each state."

As a member of the Highway Administration's bicycle and pedestrian team, Clarke suggests tar-geting two areas of funding under TEA-21: the Transportation Enhancement Program and the Recreational Trails Program.

Transportation Enhancement

Part of the money in TEA-21's Transportation En-hancement pool pays for infrastructure related to automobile alternatives, such as bike paths. Typi-cally, once the states receive federal funds, they work with city or county agencies, often requiring the local government partner to match, say, 20 percent of the total cost of a project. Many states also will work directly with nongovernment orga-nizations such as community groups, as long as the local government signs a resolution supporting the project.

If you want to be involved in developing a local bike path, "go to the mayor first," advises John Bettis, former programs and contracts engineer for the Arkansas Highway and Trans-portation Department in Little Rock. "Your com-munity group can say, 'We know there is this pool of funding available, and with your support, we can apply for funds for this project.' On the ap-plication, there is a spot for the government spon-sorship contact, and I'd say 99 percent of the time, it is either the mayor or county judge." (In rural, unincorporated areas, where there are no mayors, judges typically act as the point people for state grants.)

To find out exactly how the TEA-21 proposal process works in your state, contact your state de-partment of transportation (listed in the govern-ment pages of your phone book) and ask how you can reach your state's enhancement coordinator. You also can contact the National Transportation Enhancement Clearinghouse. The mailing address is 1100 17th Street NW, 10th Floor, Washington, DC 20036, and it also has a site on the Internet at www.railtrails.org/ntec. Also ask the clearinghouse for a copy of the "Citizens' Guidebook to Trans-portation Enhancements," which, like all of the group's publications, is free.

The key to landing Transportation Enhancement funding, says Clarke, is to pitch your project as one whose primary function is transportation, even if recreation is one of your goals. That means that if you want to build a bike route, "it must be a trail that goes somewhere, as opposed to a circular path around a lake," he says.

Recreational Trails

Another good TEA-21 funding category is the Recreational Trails Program, under which $270 million will be spent by 2003 on trails for biking, motorcycling, horseback riding, hiking, and other activities. Grants, which vary from state to state, generally range from $2,000 to $50,000 per project. Among other things, they can be used for:

✓ Constructing new trails

✓ Acquiring property for trails

✓ Maintaining and restoring trails

✓ Construction and maintenance equipment

✓ Safety and environmental education

Many states offer funding directly to private community groups for these projects. For information about applying for a grant, contact the recreational trails coordinator in your state. To get the name of this person, call your state department of transportation or request the Recreational Trails Program brochure (which includes a list of state coordinators) by writing to the Federal Highway Administration, Office of Human Environment, 400 Seventh Street SW, Washington, DC 20590. If you have access to the Internet, you also can read the brochure online at the agency's Web site at www.fhwa.dot.gov/environment/rtbroch.htm. (For tips on improving your chances of winning funding, see "Submitting a Grant-Winning Proposal," on page 232.)

There's one key qualification for a Recreational Trails Grant: "All projects must be open for public access," says Steve Weston, who handles the program's funding for the Arkansas Highway and Transportation Department in Little Rock. "For example, the University of Arkansas has a cooperative extension homemakers program with clubs in each county. One club was able to build a trail around its clubhouse, but only because the trail is open to the public."

New Uses for Old Railroad Tracks

Each year, 3,000 to 4,000 miles of railroad track are abandoned in the United States. Yet, thanks to the efforts of the Rails-to-Trails Conservancy, more than 1,000 miles of this forgotten track is converted annually into bike and recreation trails. "Our vision is to build a coast-to-coast network," says David Burwell, conservancy president. "At one time, the country had more than 300,000 miles of regulated rail lines. We now have about 140,000 miles. That leaves about 160,000 miles of unused rail corridors that are available for rail-to-trail projects."

One of the conservancy's main goals is to offer technical assistance to community members like you who want to create rail trails. Along with keeping tabs on government funding procedures in all 50 states, the conservancy can help you locate unused rails in your area, negotiate with landowners for rights of way across their property, and support your efforts by providing data that prove the various benefits that a trail can bring to a community.

For more information on the group or to get a copy of the conservancy guide, *Acquiring Rail Corridors: A How-To Manual* ($17.95, plus $4.50 shipping), write Rails-to-Trails Conservancy, 1100 17th Street NW, 10th Floor, Washington, DC 20036.

In the meantime, here are some tips from the folks at the Rails-to-Trails Conservancy on creating your own rail trail.

Look for Unused Rail Corridors

Contact the Surface Transportation Board (STB), part of the U.S. Department of Transportation, if you know that a rail line is being abandoned and you are interested in making it into a trail. The board can help you through the process. For information, write to Surface Transportation Board, Office of Congressional and Public Services, 1925 K Street NW, Washington, DC 20423. To learn more about the abandonment process and how to make a trail, visit their Web site at www.stb.dot.gov. Click on "Publications" and download the brochure

Power to the People

SUBMITTING A GRANT-WINNING PROPOSAL

Tracking down available funding for worthy community recreation projects—parks, trails, or playgrounds—is only part of the battle. The biggest challenge is beating the competition to actually win the grant. "I know of a lot of situations in which a great project was not funded because something went wrong in the grant process," says Susanna Barricklow-Arvin, recreation planner for the Indiana Department of Natural Resources in Indianapolis. Here are tips from experts for wowing the awards committee.

Read and study the application

It can be complicated. Ask questions of the granting agency or committee *before* filling yours out.

Address all grant criteria

Don't leave any boxes empty, and "if anything, overdocument," advises Barricklow-Arvin. "If it asks for one letter of support, give two or three."

Keep score

In order to judge proposals fairly, many agencies have adopted a scoring system in which each criterion earns points. The highest score wins. Ask how your application will be scored, and do your best to earn more points. For in-stance, the Arkansas Department of Parks and Tourism gives points for applicants who prepare a local recreation plan that lists which facilities and programs are available, which are not, whose needs are being served, and whose needs are yet to be met. It also gives points for proactive involvement with minority groups such as including their opinions in the project's planning.

◀◆ WHAT INSIDERS SAY:

To test your project's competitiveness, take a rough draft to the granting agency early on and ask for feedback, advises Chris Baas, a recreation planner for the Indiana Department of Natural Resources. "Ask them directly, 'Are we as competitive as we can be?'" If the response is no, ask the grantor to suggest how you might increase your score.

Document community support

Conduct a survey to show that community members, especially young people, endorse your recreation plan.

Take advantage of free advice

Many agencies offer free workshops explaining the application procedure. Some even agree to meet one-on-one with groups. Ask your granting

"Overview: Abandonments and Alternatives to Abandonments."

Almost every state department of transportation has a railway division, which periodically publishes an updated state rail plan. These plans include rail maps, which often show abandoned corridors. Ask the railway division to send you a copy, or look for it at your public library.

Start a "Friends of the Trail" Group

In most cases, a government agency will end up owning and managing the rail trail you want es-

---

agency if an advice session exists. "If they say no, request one," says Baas. "Then continue to check back to see if your request is granted. People come and go, programs change. One person might think workshops are a great idea and establish one."

Ask your cooperative extension for help

Almost every county has one. They're great sources of technical assistance in planning a project or demonstrating how it fits in with the surrounding environment.

●◆ *WHAT INSIDERS SAY:*

Cooperative extension offices aren't always easy to find because they're affiliated with different parts of government in different states. You may find your local office listed in the white pages of your phone book under the name of your state's land-grant university; in Pennsylvania, for example, you would look for Penn State Cooperative Extension. If the number isn't there, go to the government pages and look for "Agricultural Extension" or "Cooperative Extension" under the state department of agriculture or the USDA. If none of these options pans out, call your state legislator's office, listed in the government pages.

Seek help from college students

Students in parks and recreation or forestry classes are often hungry for live projects to help plan as class exercises. Likewise, students studying grant-writing typically may be willing to take on your project to get experience in writing real proposals.

Use matching gifts as leverage

Most government grants cover only a percentage of a project's costs and require the community to raise the balance, be it in cash, volunteer labor, or donated materials. Having a matching grant in hand can help convince the government to pick your project. "A community applying for a grant from us went to Levi Strauss, which had a factory in the community, and the company said it would match any grant the government gave," says Bryan Kellar, director of the Arkansas Department of Parks and Tourism's outdoor recreation grants program. "We gave them the grant."

Deliver the proposal in person

That way, you know it arrived on time. If you can't do it personally, be sure to mail it well before the deadline. It won't be considered if it's late.

tablished. Nevertheless, private "friends" groups are essential for fundraising, gaining the support of the community, and what Burwell calls "sweat equity"—rolling up their sleeves to help design, build, and maintain the trail. Consider applying to the IRS for 501(c)(3) status to make your group a nonprofit organization; people can then claim a tax deduction for donating to your cause (see "Should Your Group Go Nonprofit?" on page 224).

Lobby the Public and Private Sectors

On the public side, talk to your town planner or park director to find out if your local government has plans to develop an unused rail corridor. If so, great. Urge your organization to pitch in and help as volunteers to publicize, build, and maintain the trail.

If not, convince the government to create a plan. "An agency is better-equipped to convert and maintain a trail than a community group," says Steve Emmett-Mattox, director of the Rails-to-Trails Conservancy's Trails and Greenways Program. "They have the experience, the equipment, and the manpower." But, he says, unless the citizens are involved in design and long-term planning, the trail will not achieve its potential. "What works best is when there's an agency and a community group working together."

In the private sector, seek support from the chamber of commerce, bicycle clubs, environmental organizations, and historic preservation groups.

Ease the Fears of Adjacent Landowners

Explain that the trail won't attract noisy crowds or vandals to the area and that on the contrary, it has the potential to increase property values, improve safety, and beautify the area. The conservancy can provide success stories to prove that trails won't attract trouble.

Promote the Public Use Angle

"If the land is put to public use, it can be exempt from property taxes," says Burwell. This can be attractive to landowners, particularly private corpo-

rations that own large parcels through which a rail corridor runs. "If a big company, for example, owns part of the land, it stands to benefit if it allows public access."

◖◗ WHAT INSIDERS SAY:

If you want to develop a local railroad corridor, act while a railroad still owns it. Once a railroad company officially "abandons" a corridor, it becomes the property of the many landholders whose lots it borders. That makes gaining access complicated and downright contentious. But thanks to a 1983 amendment to the National Trails System Act, unused railroad corridors that are still under the authority of a railway company can be preserved for future rail use through interim conversion to a trail. Known as "rail banking," this process is a way for the federal government to save the country's many miles of established rail corridor, even though chances are good that the lines will never be used again for tracks.

NATURE TRAILS

When it comes to public recreation projects, one of the most popular types these days is nature trails. "The focus of the funding programs changes from time to time as the trends change," says Susanna Barricklow-Arvin, recreation planner for the Indiana Department of Natural Resources in Indianapolis. "Right now, swimming pools aren't on the hip list for funding, but trails are."

Nevertheless, creating recreation trails can be tricky. Because they are linear corridors, they cross multiple jurisdictions, meaning that "you frequently have to deal with a variety of citizens' groups and lots of private property owners," says Tom Ross, assistant director of recreation and conservation for the National Park Service, in Washington, D.C.

Ross administers a program of the National Park Service called the Rivers, Trails, and Conservation Assistance Program (RTCA), which provides technical assistance to community groups and public agencies that are looking to establish trails. This program can help you overcome the challenges associated with establishing trails, including raising the money needed to fund them. Here's more about the RTCA, plus other tips on creating trails.

Free Advice from Ranger Rick

Not all lands worth protecting can be national parks. Recognizing this, the National Park Service created the RTCA to help communities protect natural areas and provide close-to-home recreational opportunities outside the federal domain and without federal ownership.

If you are interested in protecting a green space—in particular, a trail, greenway, open space, or river—the RTCA can lend a hand with building support for your plan (including helping residents understand the area's ecology and explaining why it's important) and helping to iden-

tify sources of funding. It offers conservation workshops and consultations. "We bring the expertise of the National Park Service from around the country to help community groups envision ways to protect land and provide recreation opportunities," says Ross.

For more information, write to Rivers, Trails, and Conservation Assistance Program, National Park Service, 1849 C Street NW, Washington, DC 20240. Ask how to get in touch with your regional RTCA office. Or visit the group's Web site at www.ncrc.nps.gov/rtca/index.htm.

Because the demand for the RTCA's consulting services exceeds their resources, your group might have to file a formal application for help.

Trails as Alternative Transportation

The federal government's Transportation Equity Act for the 21st Century (TEA-21), which pro-

A GRANT RESEARCHER'S PARADISE

Based in New York City, the Foundation Center is one of the best single resources for finding out about available grants. The center has libraries open to the public in New York, Atlanta, Cleveland, San Francisco, and Washington, D.C., as well as more than 200 cooperating collections around the country, with at least one in every state. (Cooperating collections are public libraries, university libraries, and nonprofit

organizations that keep a core collection of foundation-related books on hand.) Each of these sources can provide information about establishing a nonprofit organization, lists of government and private grants, how-to manuals for writing winning proposals, and more. The Foundation Center also publishes the *National Guide to Funding for Community Development*, an 808-page book that it keeps on hand in its libraries.

And if you have access to the Internet, the center's Web site, at www.fdncenter.org, is particularly helpful. "On the site, we give the basic elements of a good proposal," says Suzanne Scarola, an online librarian with the center. Or you can look up the location of the cooperating collection nearest you. You can even send the group e-mail questions about funding issues.

vides grants for bike trails, also makes money available for walking trails—which is only fair, since feet are man's oldest form of transportation. As with bike trails, your best bet for getting some of the grant money set aside for pedestrian trails is by contacting your state or local government and asking about TEA-21's Recreational Trails Program or Transportation Enhancement Program.

If your state allows it, private organizations can apply for funding under the Recreational Trails Program, and the money can be used for any type of recreational trail. The enhancement program, on the other hand, is meant strictly for transportation alternatives; thus, as with bike trails, you'll have to prove that a walking path leads from one point to another and doesn't just circle your community or the local lake. Many states will also work with non-government organizations such as community groups, as long as the local government has approved the project.

For more information about either program, contact your state department of transportation (listed in the government pages of your phone book) and ask how you can reach your state's enhancement coordinator. You also can contact the National Transportation Enhancement Clearinghouse at 1100 17th Street NW, 10th Floor, Washington, DC 20036.

◗◆ WHAT INSIDERS SAY:

Generally speaking, a good proposal will answer questions such as "What will a trail do?" "Who will the trail serve?" and "How close will the trail be to populated areas?" A longer trail usually scores better because more people have access to it.

WATER RECREATION

Some of the most creative community recreation projects relate to bodies of water. But funding them is not as straightforward as obtaining a grant to build a playground. Pardon the pun, but the logistics of some of these deals can be downright murky, mostly because of things like ambiguous land rights and tricky engineering. Still, opportunities abound for government gimmies. Here are some ideas—and examples—to help get you started.

Fire Ponds

In rural areas where there are no fire hydrants, fire departments will sometimes use freshwater ponds as water sources in case of fire. These are known as fire ponds or dry hydrants. If you live in a rural area and there aren't any fire ponds nearby, you might be able to convince your local department to build one for your community at no cost or at least to provide free technical assistance. Then, when the pond isn't being tapped for fires, it might be used for recreation or community beautification, says R. Wayne Powell, program chair for fire prevention management at the National Fire Academy in Emmitsburg, Maryland.

Raymond Faith, deputy chief at the Howard County Department of Fire and Rescue in Columbia, Maryland, says that his department builds dry hydrants. "A lot of times, it's part of the development of a whole community," he says. His department works in conjunction with the county department of parks, which manages the ponds after they're built to ensure year-round access. Roads to fire ponds must be paved or made of gravel (not dirt, which will turn to mud during periods of heavy rain), and they must feed into major thoroughfares.

For more information on having a pond built, contact your local fire department or your county cooperative extension service, which in some counties is involved in building fire ponds.

◗◆ WHAT INSIDERS SAY:

Emphasize the versatility of your pond for fire department use, and you'll increase your chances of having it built. "We try to look for projects that have multiple uses," says Faith. "We use them as water sources. We've put in boat ramps so we can use the ponds for boat training. In winter, we use them for ice rescue training."

Rivers and Dams

More and more, communities are realizing the recreational potential of the rivers that pass through them. They build scenic trails, overlooks, and ramps and slips for boats. If they build dams, they often include picnic areas and playing fields. This means that you may find an enthusiastic audience if you approach your local government with a plan to develop a river recreation area.

Still, getting your government to back a large-scale recreational project will take some effort. Your role may be limited to lobbying local officials to support the project and applying for grant money to help them pay for the work.

If this type of project interests you, start by contacting the appropriate government agency (the local soil and water conservation district, planning office, public works office, and so on). Ask about possible government grant money, follow the procedures necessary to apply for the grant, and finally, bolster your efforts with as much community enthusiasm as possible.

One example of a successful large-scale project are Nebraska's Papio dam sites, sponsored by the city of Omaha and the Papio–Missouri River Natural Resources District in Omaha. These five areas, totaling 4,800 acres, include picnic spots, trails, fishing sites, and other recreational areas, with an emphasis on preserving urban wildlife, such as gophers, skunks, raccoons, opossums, and turtles. "We worked with the U.S. Army Corps of Engineers and the Environmental Protection Agency," says Gerry Bowen, a planner for the district. "But I'd say it's best to work through the local government like the city or our district, because we have a vested interest."

●◆ *WHAT INSIDERS SAY:*

Want local government to support your recreation project? Stress the multiple-use angle—that it will have more than one function. For instance, says Bowen, his district is also helping to build 80 miles of recreational trails on top of the city's levees. Flood control is his agency's number one priority, but it also saw an opportunity to give people a place to exercise. You want government officials (especially those looking for votes) to recognize a chance to make more people happy by including parks and trails in an otherwise utilitarian project.

FIVE

Arts and Education

CHAPTER 15

CULTURAL DELIGHTS at a DISCOUNT

When it comes to showcasing our nation's artistic and cultural treasures, the government, along with universities and many nonprofit groups, offers a diverse—and inexpensive—mix. From Shakespeare's plays to orchestra performances under the summer stars, from public art and architecture to Internet concerts, you can take advantage of thousands of free or low-cost opportunities to enjoy the arts—if you know where to look.

Interested in visiting a major museum? Many offer free admission once a week. Want to take in a play or concert? There are hundreds of performances for which you can leave your wallet at home and enjoy the show from a blanket or lawn chair.

> Concerts, plays, art shows, dance recitals: Events like these are both inspiring and entertaining. Here's how the government, universities, and nonprofit groups can help you enjoy the arts without emptying your wallet.

In this chapter, we'll give you an insider's view of some of the best arts opportunities available. Whether you're a refined patron of the arts or a cultural neophyte, chances are good that there is a program here that will delight you.

THEATER

A night at the theater may sound like a costly proposition, and with ticket prices reaching $90 for some professional shows, it certainly can be. But if you play your cards right, you can snag a plum seat to a great production for a fraction of the full cost. You can get half-price tickets to top shows, pay what you wish for admission to certain nonprofit theaters, or even see some shows for free. Here are the options that insiders recommend.

FACTOID

THERE ARE MORE THAN 1,500 ART MUSEUMS NATIONWIDE, INCLUDING UNUSUAL PLACES SUCH AS THE MUSEUM OF BARBED WIRE IN LACROSSE, KANSAS; THE MUSEUM OF BATHROOM TISSUE IN MADISON, WISCONSIN; AND THE MUSEUM OF BAD ART, OUTSIDE BOSTON.

Half-Price Tickets

All you need to succeed at the half-price ticket game is a little patience and a lot of flexibility. And, of course, you have to be in a city that has a non-profit discount ticket program.

There are 14 major discount programs around the nation, with the oldest being in the heart of the nation's theater world—New York City (for a full list of programs, see "Where to Find Discount Tickets").

Most half-price ticket booths have an information line that you can call to find out what's available that day. Some maintain lists on their Web sites. Atlanta's Atlantix program goes a step further and broadcasts its daily offerings on a local radio station. Times Tix in Los Angeles will even e-mail you a daily update of shows for which tickets are available at its booth. A few of the booths accept credit cards, but many are cash-only operations.

The best tactic for any of these discount programs is to have several choices of what you'd like to see. In New York, "sometimes changes in availability occur almost hourly as cooperating theaters supply or withdraw tickets, depending on box office demand," says David LeShay, communications director for the Theatre Development Fund, the nonprofit group that runs the city's program, called TKTS.

➥ *WHAT INSIDERS SAY:*

Want to see a Broadway show? At the Times Square location, the lines are longest from 3:00 to 4:00 P.M. for

WHERE TO FIND DISCOUNT TICKETS

Interested in seeing Broadway-quality shows without paying Broadway prices? Here's a list of cities that currently offer half-price and discount ticket programs, along with the locations of their ticket booths and their Web addresses, where applicable.

✓ Atlanta—Atlantix: Underground Atlanta; www.atlantatheatres.org

✓ Austin, Texas—AusTix: 603 North Lamar; www.austix.com

✓ Boston—Bos/Tix: Copley Square, Faneuil Hall Marketplace, Harvard Square; www.boston.com/artsboston

✓ Chicago—Hot Tix: Various locations; www.theater-chicago.org/hot-tix.html

✓ Cincinnati—PNC Bank Tower Tix: Tower Place Mall

✓ Cleveland—Mailtix: Cleveland Cultural Coalition; www.clevelandculture.org/culture/html/marketing_programs.html

✓ Los Angeles—Times Tix: Beverly Center; www.theatrela.org/WebTix.html

✓ New York City—TKTS: Times Square at 47th and Broadway, Lower Manhattan at 2 World Trade Center; www.metrobeat.com/E/V/NYCNY/0011/48/79/

✓ San Diego—Times Arts Tix: Broadway Circle at Horton Plaza; www.sandiego-online.com/sdpal/artstix.stm

✓ San Francisco—Tix Bay Area (and Tix by Mail)—Union Square at Stockton Street; www.theatrebayarea.org

✓ Santa Barbara—Hot Spots: 36 West State Street

✓ Seattle—Ticket/Ticket: 401 Broadway East and Pike Place Market

✓ Washington, D.C.—Ticket-Place: 1100 Penn Avenue NW (Old Post Office Pavilion)

*evening shows and from 10:00 to 11:00 A.M. for mati-
nees, says LeShay. There is usually only a short wait—
or no wait at all—he says, around 6:00 P.M. for
evening performances and from noon to 1:00 P.M. on
matinee days.*

*Also note that the TKTS booth at 2 World Trade
Center often has shorter lines than the one at Times
Square, and it's indoors. It's open Monday through
Friday from 11:00 A.M. to 5:30 P.M. and on Saturday from 11:00 A.M. to 3:30 P.M. At this booth,
you can buy matinee tickets the day before a performance.*

Pay-What-You-Can Shows

The next best thing to a free performance is one
where you get to decide how much to pay. Many
nonprofit theaters have at least one night during the
run of a play or concert where people pay whatever
they can afford or deem appropriate.

"Generally speaking, it won't be on a Friday or
Saturday night," says Kim Larsen, director of theater services for Theatre Bay Area, a nonprofit organization that serves the theatrical community in
and around San Francisco. "Some theaters do it
once a week. Others have just one pay-what-you-
can night for the entire run of a show," she says.
"Some theaters in San Francisco coordinate it with
a food drive, so if you bring a can of food to the theater, you can get in for free."

The government-run John F. Kennedy Center
for the Performing Arts in Washington, D.C., regularly sells pay-what-you-can tickets as part of its
Performing Arts for Everyone initiative. And the
Shakespeare Theater, also in Washington, includes
them as part of its commitment to accessibility.
"We have pay-what-you-will nights once or twice
during every performance run," says Roberto
Aguirre-Sacasa, the theater's publicist.

To find out about these opportunities and any
that may be available in your community, call the
theater box office. The Washington, D.C., information operator can supply the numbers for the

Kennedy Center and the Shakespeare Theater.
Local theater groups are listed in the yellow pages
under "Theaters."

◗◆ WHAT INSIDERS SAY:

*If you want to take advantage of a pay-what-you-
can night, get to the theater early. These shows can
sell out fast. You can imagine the lines that formed
outside the Shakespeare Theater in Washington
when it offered a pay-what-you-can-night during a
production of* Othello *starring Star Trek's Patrick
Stewart!*

Free Plays in Central Park

Back in 1957, Public Theater founder Joseph Papp
parked his Mobile Theater in Central Park and invited the public in for free. The Delacorte Theater,
an open-air amphitheater near the turtle pond in
Central Park, was erected 5 years later as the
group's permanent summertime home, and it's
been host to more than 60,000 theatergoers every
year since.

In June, July, and August, you can watch free
performances of a variety of plays, including at least
one Shakespeare production each season. Free
tickets are available on the day of the performance,
beginning at 1:00 P.M. at the Delacorte Theater in
Central Park and from 1:00 to 3:00 P.M. at the
Public Theater at 425 Lafayette Street. You can also
pick up tickets at locations in the Bronx, Queens,
Staten Island, Harlem, and Brooklyn.

To contact the theater, ask the New York City
information operator for the number for the Delacorte Theater, or visit the Public Theater's Web site
at www.publictheater.org.

Shakespeare for a Song

It seems we can't get enough of the Bard. Every
summer, across the United States, actors stamp
the boards, breathing new life into words written
half a millennium ago. There are 50 to 60 active
Shakespeare festivals in the United States, says

Charles McCue, producing director of the San Francisco Shakespeare Festival, and many are inexpensive or free. Here are some of the best-regarded festivals.

Shakespeare Theatre Free for All

This festival, now in its 9th year, happens every June for about 2 weeks at the Carter Barron Amphitheater in Rock Creek Park, Washington, D.C. "It's a very beautiful, lush park with trees and creeks that cut through the city," says publicist Roberto Aguirre-Sacasa.

Each play is a full production that has been performed earlier in the season before paying crowds at the Shakespeare Theatre in downtown Washington. Although festival performances are free, tickets are required. For information, write the Shakespeare Theatre, 516 Eighth Street SE, Washington, DC 20003, or visit the group's Web site at www.shakespearedc.org/.

Kentucky Shakespeare Festival

In existence since 1960, the Kentucky Shakespeare Festival takes place in a park in the historic district of Old Louisville. With more than 100 productions under its belt, this is the king of Shakespeare festivals.

"We try to do an equal number of comedies and tragedies," says Holly Johnson, assistant to the producing director, "but there are some, like *Macbeth* and *The Taming of the Shrew*, that we keep coming back to." Contact the festival at 1114 South Third

---

Amazing Stories

DISCOUNT TICKETS FOR TEENS

When Rebecca Ann Neuwirth, a student at New York's Stuyvesant High School, spent a semester abroad in Vienna, it wasn't just the great pastries and Old World ambiance that impressed her. A budding culture maven, what dazzled her most was the discount student ticket program that made theater and musical performances affordable to those who were living off parental allowances rather than paychecks.

On her return to New York City, Neuwirth dashed off a letter to the mayor, telling him that there should be a similar program in the Big Apple. Her impassioned request didn't fall on deaf ears, and before long, a volunteer effort called High 5 had sprung up, involving staff at the American Symphony Orchestra.

Now a full-fledged nonprofit organization, High 5 has sold more than 16,000 tickets to middle school and high school students since 1993. The $5 discount tickets are available at Ticketmaster outlets, and students have a choice of more 100 arts events.

"Anything by Shakespeare is insanely popular," says executive director Ada Ciniglio. "So are performances at Lincoln Center, Carnegie Hall, the Brooklyn Academy of Music, and the Apollo Theater." Over time though, Ciniglio finds, students start experimenting more, checking out events such as Bargemusic, a chamber music performance on an old coffee barge in Brooklyn.

Similar programs have been started in Cleveland and Columbus, Ohio, and Hartford, Connecticut.

Street, Louisville, KY, 40203, or visit the group's Web site at http://kyshakes.org.

Shakespeare Goes West

This free outdoor festival takes place in three locations: San Francisco, Oakland, and Cupertino, California. While there's some seating at the Cupertino venue, the others are just big, open meadows. Historically, says producing director Charles McCue, the festival has tended to feature comedies rather than tragedies. "There's something about a warm day and picnicking that doesn't really jibe with tragedies," notes McCue. Since evening performances have now been added to the roster, though, it's likely that some of the historical plays will be included. Contact the Shakespeare Festival at P.O. Box 590479, San Francisco, CA 94159, or visit the group's Web site at www.sfshakes.org.

The Nebraska Shakespeare Festival

Through its Shakespeare on the Green series, this festival produces two Shakespeare plays each summer in Omaha's Elmwood park. For more information, contact the festival office at Nebraska Shakespeare Festival, Department of Fine Arts, Creighton University, Omaha, NE 68178, or check out the festival Web site at http://neshakespeare.creighton.edu.

◆ WHAT INSIDERS SAY:

If you live near Omaha, take advantage of the theater company's speakers bureau, a free program through which you can have a speaker visit your community group and present a slide lecture about the plays, Shakespeare's life and times, Shakespearean language, or any other Bard-related topic that interests you.

Sit In on a Reading

The most active way to get involved in the theater without acting is to sit in on a live reading of a new play. In Chicago, the nonprofit Chicago Dramatists Workshop hosts a reading every Saturday night at which, for a suggested $3 donation, you can see a performance of the first or second draft of a play.

Sometimes, a reading will be a sit-down affair, with the actors just reading from the script. Other times, it might include limited staging, so you can get a sense of the physical life of the play. "Usually, the playwright is there, so you can offer your feedback," says Rob Chambers, marketing director of the League of Chicago Theaters, a nonprofit organization that supports the city's theatrical community. "It's pretty darned exciting if you've gone to a reading and then you see the full production. It helps you understand how the whole process works." To find out more about this program, write the Chicago Dramatists Workshop, 1105 West Chicago Avenue, Chicago, IL 60610.

If you're interested in sitting in on a reading in your area, call the box offices to find out which theaters in your community focus on producing new plays. You can find the theater numbers in the yellow pages under "Theaters."

Free Access for Volunteers

Most theater groups couldn't get by without the dozens of volunteers who work the box office, act as ushers, and otherwise help out. To show their appreciation, the groups give volunteers free tickets to their shows.

"There's always a big call for volunteer ushers," says Rob Chambers of the League of Chicago Theaters. "Just call the theater company you're interested in and say, 'I'd like to usher,'" he advises. Normally, it's the house manager who coordinates volunteer ushers.

Behind-the-Scenes Theater Tours

If you yearn to stand on the stage and see what the actors and musicians see, or if you're just curious about what's behind the curtain, call a theater or concert hall and ask about behind-the-scenes tours. Many places offer them, although they tend not to be heavily advertised.

In Philadelphia, for example, you can tour the

splendid turn-of-the-century Academy of Music building, the oldest opera house in the United States. During a 3-month period (usually sometime between October and May), the tours are often given on chosen days of the week at 2:00 P.M. twice a month. The architectural and historical tour costs $5 and lasts about an hour.

To find out about dates for the upcoming year and to make a reservation, ask the Philadelphia information operator for the phone number, then call the company and ask for the manager. You can also find the company manager's number as well as get some historical background on the Academy of Music by logging on to the Web site at www.philorch.org. When you're at the site, click "Meet the Orchestra," then "Academy of Music." At the bottom of this window, you'll find the manager's office number.

You also can tour the Boston Ballet's building, one of only two studio buildings in the world built specifically for dance. The tours are free of charge, says public relations director John Michael Kennedy, and you'll see each of the ballet's seven state-of-the-art studios. "We try to coordinate it so people can see working rehearsals," says Kennedy. "We also do tours of the wardrobe department, where you get to see people sewing and fitting costumes." To find out more, check out their Web site at www.boston.com/bostonballet.

◗◆ *WHAT INSIDERS SAY:*

If you want to take a bunch of friends on a tour, the Boston Ballet can accommodate moderate-size groups, although you'll need to call a few weeks ahead of time.

MUSIC

"Music is critical to life," says Pat Page, executive director of the American Music Conference, based in Carlsbad, California. "It surrounds us—in the car, on the computer, in the supermarket. It is an integral part of our being."

Apparently, many government agencies and university and nonprofit groups agree, for they go out of their way to provide low-cost or free opportunities to hear a wide variety of good music. If your tastes tend to the classics, free concerts abound. And there's a good mix of rock, jazz, and popular concerts available as well. Here are some of the best.

Performances in the Capital

For arts lovers, Washington, D.C., is a dream come true. In addition to all the free museums and historical sites, the capital also plays host to the greatest music bargain around: the John F. Kennedy Center for the Performing Arts.

As part of its Performing Arts for Everyone initiative, the Kennedy Center presents free performances every night of the year. At 6:00 P.M., you can catch the concert on the group's Millennium Stage. "It's actually three stages," says Lawrence J. Wilker, president of the Kennedy Center. "There's one in front of the Eisenhower Theater, one in front of the Concert Hall Theater, and a third stage on Capitol Hill that presents performances every Tuesday and Thursday at noon throughout the summer."

The range of performances is mind-boggling. One night, you might be treated to a musical trio from Madagascar. Another night, legendary trumpeter Donald Byrd could be the featured performer.

For information on coming shows, write Millennium Stage, The John F. Kennedy Center for the Performing Arts, Washington, DC 20566.

Free Shows on the Web

Even if you can't get to the capital in person, you can keep up with the music there. The Kennedy Center offers past and current performances on its Web site at www.kennedy-center.org. To see and hear parts of recent shows, connect to the site, click on "Millennium Stage" and then on "Highlights." To hear and see that day's show, broadcast each evening at 6:00 P.M. Eastern Standard Time, connect to the site, click on "Millennium Stage" and then on "Broadcast."

Last-Minute Tickets for a Song

Managers of concert halls hate to have empty seats, and they'll go to great lengths to ensure the fullest house possible. That's where rush tickets come in. The rules vary, but the basic idea is that just before the performance is about to begin, the staff will rush you into a seat for a minimal charge.

Some groups will accommodate you anywhere that there's an empty seat. These programs tend to cost more, but you could end up with one of the best seats in the house. The nonprofit Chicago Symphony Orchestra, for example, runs an Orchestra Rush Club that makes it possible to purchase a ticket to most concerts for $25.

"Right before curtain, we'll rush you into the hall to take any seat that's open," explains Synneve Carlino, associate director of media relations for the orchestra. "You may end up with a $90 seat on the main floor." On the other hand, you could end up with a seat in the back row.

Other areas have programs that are even less expensive. The Philadelphia Orchestra offers a limited number of unreserved seats for $5 apiece 1 hour before the Friday matinee and Friday and Saturday evening subscription concerts. If you happen to be in St. Louis, you can take advantage of the cheapest rush tickets of all—they're free. Show up an hour before one of the regular Friday night subscription concerts, and you can pick up one of 50 tickets that are set aside on a first-come, first-served basis. To find out about these programs and any similar opportunities in your area, call the appropriate box office.

◗❖ WHAT INSIDERS SAY:
There's no guarantee of a seat with rush tickets, and you may have to get to the concert hall earlier than you normally would to beat out the competition. The concept appeals to those who are gamblers at heart, says Carlino.

Inexpensive Summer Shows

For many orchestras and ballet companies, the summer months bring a change of venue. With the lengthening of the days, musicians, vocalists, and ballerinas emerge from darkened concert halls across the nation to perform outdoors on stages in parks.

If you have kids in tow, or you just like a more relaxed atmosphere than the typical concert hall offers, summer concerts are great alternatives, with programming that's every bit as high in quality as that offered during the rest of the season.

There are bargains to be had, too. While regular seats for these shows can cost $70 or more, if you're willing to sit on a blanket on the grass, you'll pay just a fraction of that. Many venues allow you to bring a picnic meal and lawn chairs, so you can relax under the stars and nibble on chicken salad while the stirring melodies of Beethoven's *Ninth Symphony* wash away your workday worries.

A few of the better-known summer concert venues are described below. In addition to these programs, many smaller cities also host summer concerts. Check with your local convention and visitors bureau or the parks department to see what's offered in your area.

Tanglewood

Probably the most famous summer concert series, Tanglewood, in the Berkshire Mountains of western Massachusetts, is the summer home of the Boston Symphony Orchestra. The orchestra performs each July and August, with guests such as the Philadelphia Orchestra as well as jazz, opera, folk, and popular music acts. Past performers have included Bob Dylan, Bonnie Raitt, the Dave Brubeck Quartet, and the Lincoln Center Jazz Orchestra.

Lawn seats at Tanglewood cost $13.50. (You can also attend concerts given by Tanglewood's summer music academy—a training academy for musicians—for a suggested donation.) Seats are unreserved and are available 1 hour before concert time.

If you're curious about the conductor/musician relationship, check out the open rehearsals that take place most Saturday mornings at Tanglewood. For $15, you can sit in on the rehearsal as well as a 30-minute prerehearsal lecture.

For more information, write the Boston Symphony Orchestra at Symphony Hall, 301 Massachusetts Avenue, Boston, MA 02115, or take a look at the group's Web site at www.bso.org.

Mann Center for the Performing Arts

When it's not on tour, the Philadelphia Orchestra makes regular summer appearances at the Mann Center for the Performing Arts in Philadelphia's Fairmount Park. You can show up with your lawn chair the day of a performance and get in for $8. Or, if you live in the area, you can look for ads in the *Philadelphia Inquirer* and the *Philadelphia Daily News* a couple of weeks before the concert you're interested in, call the number in the ad, and pay just a $2 processing fee for tickets. To find out more, visit the Philadelphia Orchestra Web site at www.philorch.org.

Wolf Trap

Run by the National Park Service, Virginia's Wolf Trap Foundation for the Performing Arts, near Washington, D.C., annually brings together popular and classical music, ballet, and a special jazz and blues festival. Past headliners have included Judy Collins, the National Symphony Orchestra, Bobby McFerrin, the Joffrey Ballet, and Broadway hits such as *Riverdance* and *Rent*.

Lawn tickets range from $7 to $20. For a nominal extra charge, you can attend a master class, where you'll get a behind-the-curtain view of what goes into creating a professional music, opera, or dance performance.

PLAYING ALONG WITH THE BAND

There's nothing quite as stirring as the crisp, lively rhythms of a military march played by a military brass band. It's possible to get one of the military's many bands to play in your community, but there's an even better option for the musically inclined: Join the group for the night.

The U.S. Army Band hosts an Eastern Trombone Workshop each March at its base in Fort Myers, Virginia. There are no registration fees for the workshop, and all events are free and open to the public.

As well as concerts, master classes, recitals, scholarly lectures, and clinics by leading guest artists, there are also recitals by invited guests. And you could be one of them! If you play the trombone and know a composition that you feel is worthy but rarely performed, submit your suggestion, with a résumé, description, and the approximate length of the piece to Sergeant First Class George Allen, U.S. Army Band, 204 Lee Avenue, Fort Myers, VA 22211-1199 by early January.

"It's the only workshop of its kind in the country," says Sergeant First Class Greg Corcoran. "Musicians from all around the country sign up for the chance to perform."

The band sponsors a tuba-euphonium conference, too. That one's in January, and again, there's no registration fee and events on all 4 days are free and open to the public. Tuba and euphonium players (and we know there are lots of you out there) are invited to bring their horns and participate in reading sessions. For information about that event, write to the band at the same address.

For information, write Wolf Trap Foundation for the Performing Arts, 1624 Trap Road, Vienna, VA 22182. Or check the group's Web site at www.wolf-trap.org.

Saratoga

The Philadelphia Orchestra (along with the New York City Ballet and Miami City Ballet) makes a summer pit stop at the famous Saratoga Performing Arts Center in upstate New York. Saratoga now has a state-of-the-art video system that enhances visibility from the lawn, where tickets are usually around $12. For more information, write to Saratoga Performing Arts Center, Saratoga Springs, NY 12866-0826, or visit the group's Web site at www.spac.org.

●◆ *WHAT INSIDERS SAY:*

The lawn area at Saratoga is huge—around 15 acres—so if seeing the performers live on the stage is important to you, be sure to seat yourself in the area called the bowl, where you'll be assured a decent view.

Ravinia Festival

In the Chicago area, the place to enjoy jazz, pop, classical, and chamber music all summer long is the Ravinia Festival, 25 miles north of the city in Highland Park. The big names here are resident companies such as the Chicago Symphony Orchestra and Hubbard Street Dance Chicago, along with guests from all over the performing arts spectrum, such as the Doobie Brothers, Tony Bennett, and Natalie Cole. It's an eclectic mix.

A lawn ticket will cost you $8 to $10, and with that ticket, you'll get free access to master classes during the 4-day "Jazz at Ravinia" festival as well as 1-hour mini-concerts before and after the main shows. Tickets are sold on a first-come, first-served basis starting a half-hour before the performance.

Note: If you go through the Chicago Public Library's program, Words and Music, you can get lawn passes for free. You must be over 18 and have a Chicago Public Library card to access this free deal. The individual passes are for selected jazz and classical concerts.

Concerts by the Steans Institute, Ravinia's professional study program for young classical musicians, are free (no lawn ticket required), and so are the weekly Steans Institute master classes that take place in the afternoons before the park opens. To find out more about Ravinia, write the festival at 400 Iris Lane, Highland Park, IL 60035, or visit the group's Web site at www.ravinia.org.

Miller Outdoor Theatre

In Houston, the Miller Outdoor Theatre offers full-production performances by the Houston Ballet and the Houston Grand Opera as well as major Broadway touring shows and various ethnic festivals. Although they're all free, you have to pick up tickets between 11:30 A.M. and 1:00 P.M. on the day of performance for seating in the sheltered area, a preferred spot if you're planning to see a play or a dance performance. For more information, write the Miller Outdoor Theatre at 100 Concert Drive, Houston, TX 77030.

●◆ *WHAT INSIDERS SAY:*

Be warned! Outdoor shows in Houston can be mighty buggy on a hot summer night, so take plenty of repellent.

Stern Grove

Summer visitors to San Francisco's Sunset/Parkside district can hear a lively mixture of concerts—from San Francisco's Symphony and Ballet to the Preservation Hall Jazz Band to Cuba's Chucho Valdés Quintet—at the free Stern Grove Festival. No tickets or advance reservations are required, and the performances are enriched with preconcert talks and "musical conversations" with the performers. To find out more, write to Stern Grove Festival Association, 44 Page Street, Suite 600, San Francisco, CA 94102, or check the festival Web site at www.sterngrove.org.

Musikfest

The largest music festival of its kind, Musikfest is a 10-day extravaganza that takes place every August in the historic Pennsylvania city of Bethlehem. There are more than 650 acts in all, and the vast majority are free. This is how it works: Visitors stroll around the streets of the old Moravian city and stop by numerous stages to hear music that ranges from polka to reggae to rock to folk to ethnic specialties such as Andean mountain music. "It's based on the concept of a German festival," says Sharon McCarthy, the festival's director of communications.

Along with the free performances all over town, Musikfest hosts a major act each night at an outdoor amphitheater. Past stars have included Kenny Rogers, Tony Bennett, Wayne Newton, and Hootie and the Blowfish. Tickets are in the $8 to $35 range, but if you're willing to sit away from the stage on the grass, it's free. You can't see a lot of the stage from that distance, but the sound is good, and three massive video screens do simulcasts of each performance.

A million-and-a-half people visit Musikfest each year. If you'd like to be one of them, write for more information to Bethlehem Musikfest Association, 211 Plymouth Street, Suite 300, Bethlehem, PA 18015, or visit the group's Web site at www.fest.org.

Music School Concerts

Attending concerts at music schools instead of pricey symphony orchestra performances is one of those win-win situations. You hear high-quality music-making, plus you're doing a great service to the young musicians just by being there.

"It's part of the educational and academic mission of the school for our students to perform in front of a live audience," explains Carrie Throm, director of public relations for the College-Conservatory of Music at the University of Cincinnati. "In fact, they have to perform in order to graduate."

Rarely will you have to pay anything to attend a music school concert, although some faculty concerts do come with small price tags. And we're not talking about just a handful of concerts a year. "We offer more than 700 concerts a year," says Allison Duffey, director of public relations at the University of Rochester's Eastman School of Music. "Most of them are free, and they range from early music to the most recent contemporary compositions."

Some of the best-known programs are described below. Note, though, that most colleges and universities that have music programs offer live performances. Call the general number at a local campus to find out what's offered there.

Eastman School of Music

You never know what stars-to-be will turn up on the stage at this prestigious school. Alumni include soprano Renee Fleming and jazz great Chuck Mangione, as well as principal players in all the major orchestras in the nation. You can see free student recitals on campus, plus free noontime recitals by Eastman faculty and notable musicians from the Rochester community, at the First Unitarian-Universalist Church on Washington Square in downtown Rochester.

A summer concert series of chamber music, solo, jazz, and other musical performances is also free. For information, write to the Eastman School of Music at 26 Gibbs Street, Rochester, NY 14604-2599, or visit the school's Web site at www.rochester.edu/Eastman.

Curtis Institute of Music

In Philadelphia, this renowned school, whose graduates include Leonard Bernstein, Gian Carlo Menotti, and Samuel Barber, invites the public to attend recitals on most Monday, Wednesday, and Friday evenings. The bill of fare is varied: single-instrument recitals, new compositions by Curtis students, and eclectic presentations of several compositions and multiple instruments.

When Curtis brings in national artists to work with students in master classes, it often lets the public in on the creative dialogue as well. For free! Also, three times a year, the Curtis Symphony Orchestra plays at the prestigious Academy of Music, which is the home of the Philadelphia Orchestra. Ticket prices are very low in the reserved areas, and seating in the amphitheater is free. Plus, you get to see world-class conductors like Andre Previn, Leonard Slatkin, and Wolfgang Sawallisch.

To find out more, write to Curtis at 1726 Locust Street, Philadelphia, PA 19103.

Civic Orchestra of Chicago

All performances of the Civic Orchestra of Chicago, the training orchestra affiliated with the Chicago Symphony Orchestra, are free to the public. The group is led by distinguished conductor Daniel Barenboim, and performances are broadcast nationwide through syndicated radio broadcasts on more than 90 radio stations. If you live in Chicago or are planning a visit, check out the current concert season on the Civic Orchestra's Web site, which you'll find at www.chicagosymphony.org. Once you get to the site, click on "Performances" and then on "Civic Orchestra." Although the concerts are free, you need to have tickets. To order them, write Civic Orchestra Tickets, Orchestra Hall, 220 South Michigan Avenue, Chicago, IL 60604.

A Day Full of Bargain Arts

In San Diego, concerts and much more are available at a discount once a year. On Bargain Arts Day, concert halls, theaters, ballet companies, and museums all over town donate hundreds of tickets (6,000 in all) that then go on sale for 1 day at San Diego's discount ticket booth, Times Arts Tix. You pay whatever you want.

"People line up for up to 4 hours to get tickets on that one day," says Toni Robin, marketing director for San Diego's Performing Arts League.

Some people pay 50 cents, says Robin. Some pay $5. It averages out to around a dollar a ticket. "No offer is refused," she says.

To find out about the next San Diego Bargain Arts Day, contact San Diego Performing Arts League, 625 Broadway, San Diego, CA 92101-5403 or check out the league Web site at www.sandiego-online.com/sdpal.

VISUAL ARTS

With admission to many art museums hovering at the $7 to $8 mark (and up to $10 at some places), taking the family out for a day of culture can quickly add up to be an expensive proposition.

That's the bad news. The good news is that many nonprofit art museums offer low-price incentives to get you in the door. Plus, outside the museum walls, there's a whole world of free or nearly free visual arts delights to discover. Here are some of your best choices.

Open Days and Festivals

Most museums open their doors for a few free hours at least 1 day a month. As with many art bargains, the policy varies widely, depending on the museum. The Walker Art Center gallery in Minneapolis, for example, is free on the first Saturday of each month. "The entire museum is open to the public," says associate director of public relations Karen Gysin. "We have a sort of arts sampler, with film screenings, hands-on studio workshops, performances, guided tours of the sculpture garden, or special exhibits." The Walker also has free Thursdays once a week just for the exhibition galleries.

The Art Institute of Chicago has 1 free day a week—on Tuesdays. For the Seattle Art Museum, mark your calendar for the first Thursday of each month; at the Los Angeles County Museum of Art, it's the second Tuesday; and at San Francisco's Asian Art Museum, it's the first Wednesday.

At some museums, you have to sneak your free visit into a rather small time slot. Boston's Museum of Fine Arts, for example, allows visitors to pay a voluntary contribution on Wednesday evenings from 4:00 to 9:45 P.M. At New York's Museum of Modern Art, the same policy applies on Fridays between 4:30 and 8:15 P.M., and just a few blocks away at the Whitney Museum of American Art, the pay-what-you-wish night is Thursday between 6:00 and 8:00 P.M. Still others, like the San Francisco Museum of Modern Art, limit the offer to half-price admission on Thursday evenings from 6:00 to 9:00 P.M. Call your area museums to see if they offer similar bargains.

➡◆ *WHAT INSIDERS SAY:*
You should be aware that when a museum has a special exhibition with a ticket price above and beyond the admission fee, you'll generally still have to pay that fee even if admission to the museum is free.

The Benefits of Volunteering

Behind-the-scenes access to great art. Insider information on the great artists. Both of these things can be yours for free if you're willing to volunteer at a nearby museum.

The qualifications for volunteers vary from museum to museum. At the Philadelphia Museum of Art, docent candidates (docents are volunteers who lead tours of the museum collections) "are selected from a large pool of applicants who reflect diverse ethnic backgrounds and skills," says Kaki Gladstone, manager of volunteer services. More important than an art history major are qualities such as enthusiasm, commitment to the institution, and good communication skills, she says.

AUDITIONS AS ENTERTAINMENT

You may think of auditions as nerve-wracking events, filled with tense performers waiting anxiously for a thumbs-up or thumbs-down from the director. Actually, though, they can be great entertainment, says David Roche, artistic director of the annual San Francisco Ethnic Dance Festival.

Five months in advance of this 3-day festival, more than 100 dance groups gather for auditions, and Roche says that the tryouts, for which admission is $5 at the door, draw just as loyal a crowd as the main event.

"There's a German couple who plan their business trips to San Francisco every year to coincide with the auditions," Roche says. "They say there's nowhere else in the world that you can experience such ethnic diversity."

In 1999, that diverse group included Scottish sword dancers, American tribal-style belly dancers, Andalusian flamenco, and a Korean Buddhist monk's solo dance. Each dance company performs a 10-minute piece in front of the selection committee, and about 30 are chosen to perform in the festival itself.

To make the auditions even more palatable for the audience, ethnic foods are offered in the lobby. "There's a party atmosphere that spills over," says Roche.

To find out when the next open audition will be held, write to World Arts West, Fort Mason Center, Landmark Building D, San Francisco, CA 94123 or log on to www. worldartswest.org.

The rewards are great, but make no mistake, being a museum volunteer is a big commitment, too, especially if you want to be a docent.

Docent training at the Philadelphia Museum of Art lasts 2 years. Trainees learn general art history as well as detailed information about the museum's collections, attend education classes, and learn how to lead school and special-audience tours. Then they develop their own thematic tours. The commitment to the 12-month program, which includes both desk and tour duty, requires a minimum of 8 hours a month of active duty.

If you're interested in being a volunteer or a docent, get in touch with a local museum's volunteer coordinator.

Art on the Streets

Public art is such an integral part of a city that it's easy to take it for granted. For seekers of arts bargains, though, it could be the all-time greatest value, because it comes with absolutely no price tag attached.

Many of these works—from the neon tubing atop Manhattan's 59th Street Marine Transfer Station to the 36-foot, hammered-copper Portlandia sculpture that graces Portland's city center—have been funded through Percent for Art programs.

Although the details of the program vary from city to city and from state to state, the concept is basically the same. Through the program, a percentage (usually 1 percent) of the total construction costs of courthouses, schools, police precincts, and such must be dedicated to artwork for those facilities. Competition among artists is fierce, and the resulting works of art are often of very high quality.

The government agencies that administer the programs (usually the arts commission or office of cultural affairs) make it their business to inform the public about the various artworks on display. If you take advantage of the brochures and self-guided tours that they have to offer, you'll enjoy a rich experience. Here are some examples of notable public arts programs.

Miami

Established in 1973, Miami's public arts program is one of the oldest in the country, and it's also one of the most generous, allocating 1.5 percent of construction costs for all county buildings to the creation of complementary artwork. Some of the most spectacular public art is in the Metromover (the city's public transportation system) stations and at Miami International Airport.

Connecting the main airport terminal with Concourse A is a moving walkway that's a work of art in itself. The 180-foot-long space is enlivened with 132 sheets of vividly colored glass—an interactive art installation created by artist/composer Christopher Janney. As travelers move through the artwork, they activate photoelectric cells that in turn trigger sounds that the artist has recorded from the Everglades and blended with harmonic tones recorded on a synthesizer.

To find out more about the Miami-Dade arts program, write to Art in Public Places, 111 NW 1 Street, Suite 610, Miami, FL 33128. Or, if you have access to the Internet, visit the city's Web site at www.co.miami-dade.fl.us. Click on "Culture and Entertainment," then on "Art in Public Places."

Toledo

The Arts Commission of Greater Toledo administers a public art program that is remarkable for its commitment to educating the public. The commission will mail you a brochure with annotated photographs of the works (nearly all sculptures), along with maps of the three self-guided tours and such handy advice as where to park your car and additional sights (such as the Toledo Museum of Art) that you might want to visit if you have time. Write to the commission at 521 West Woodriff Avenue, Toledo, OH 43624.

Alternately, you can preview the tour by visiting the group's Web site at www.acgt.org.

Clicking on "Sculpture Tour" leads you to a page that neatly divides the works into three tours: downtown, the botanical gardens, and a neighborhoods tour.

Phoenix

In Phoenix's busy Civic Plaza, there's a quiet monument to Arizona's most regional icon—the bola tie. The Official State Neckwear of Arizona is glorified in a series of 59 bronze sculptures set into the columns of the plaza's colonnade.

Justly proud of this and the other public art it administers, the Phoenix Arts Commission has produced a beautiful, spiral-bound book with black-and-white photographs of some of the city's finest public artworks. You can get a copy of the book, as well as a map of locations of projects, by writing to the Phoenix Arts Commission, 200 West Washington Street, 10th Floor, Phoenix, AZ 85003.

New York City

The Percent for Art Program run by the New York City Department of Cultural Affairs doesn't produce a printed guide or maps, but if you have access to the Internet, you'll want to check out the agency's information-packed Web site. Go to www.ci.nyc.ny.us, then use the site's search function to search for "Percent for Art." There you'll find the lowdown on 117 Percent for Art projects that have been completed since the program was begun in 1984 as well as information about 80 more works that are still in progress.

It's well worth browsing through this site, since you'll learn about the art, the artists, and a whole lot about the Big Apple in the process. You'll find out, for example, how Greek artist Stephen Antonakos responded to the challenge of adorning a building on the West Side Highway where garbage trucks dump their contents onto Hudson River barges: He gave it stately neoclassical arches framed in neon. And that's just the tip of the iceberg.

America's Murals

Painting on walls is hardly a new idea. Ever since cavemen drew galloping horses on cave walls with sticks, man has had the urge to make his mark on his surroundings. Murals have been undergoing a bit of a renaissance of late, though, and in some cities, they number in the hundreds or thousands. Coming to grips with this most expressive artistic medium requires a little guidance, and thankfully, it's there for the asking. Here's what's available in some of the best places to view mural art.

Philadelphia

In the world of murals, the City of Brotherly Love leads the pack, producing more each year than any other city in the nation. According to Jane Golden, executive director of the city's Mural Arts Program (housed in the city's Department of Recreation), there are 1,826 murals on Philadelphia walls, and that number is growing by the day. The subjects are as varied as the city's neighborhoods and include homages to basketball star Julius Erving and actor/singer/activist Paul Robeson as well as historical murals and bold, bright celebrations of community spirit.

You can get a brochure that lists Philadelphia murals and provides directions for a self-guided tour by sending $3 to the Mural Arts Program, 1515 Arch Street, 10th Floor, Philadelphia, PA 19102. If you get a group together, Golden will organize a trolley tour on which you'll see 15 or 20 murals and benefit from her lively information- and anecdote-filled commentary. The cost for those tours runs from about $20 a person (with coffee and muffins) to $35 (with lunch).

Los Angeles

Los Angeles is another mural mecca. Mural expert Robin Dunitz estimates that there are more than 1,500 murals in the city, with the largest concentration in East L.A. For $5, you can get a map and guide to 225 of the murals in five Los Angeles neighborhoods. Write the Mural Conservancy of Los Angeles, P.O. Box 5483, Sherman Oaks, CA

91413. The group also maintains a Web site at www.lamurals.org that provides the same information for free.

If you're in that area, you have another option: Take one of the tours that the conservancy offers. They cost $25 ($20 for students and seniors), but they're all-day affairs during which you'll visit muralists' studios, explore the murals of South L.A. and Echo Park with mural artists as your guides, and find out more about the city's New Deal murals from the 1920s, 1930s, and 1940s.

San Francisco

With around 500 murals, many located in the city's historic Mission District, San Francisco offers plenty for the mural lover, and—unlike in L.A. or Philadelphia—it's possible to do many of the tours on foot or bicycle. Precita Eyes Mural Art Center, a nonprofit organization in the Mission District, offers numerous walking and bicycle tours that range in price from $5 to $10. You don't need reservations, but to learn the times of the tours and find out where to meet, write to the center at 2981 24th Street, San Francisco, CA 94110, or log on to their Web site at www.precitaeyes.org.

Free Art Viewing Online

An innovative program called Open Studio: The Arts Online has been developed by the National Endowment for the Arts and the Benton Foundation. It was set up to help artists get on the Internet, increase the arts presence there, and provide public Internet access at arts and community cultural organizations.

What this means for you, the arts consumer, is that you can get free access to the Internet at a growing number of local theaters, libraries, art centers, and museums. You'll also get hands-on training in using the Internet effectively to access cultural resources.

Depending on the host institution, the details of the program may differ. At the Mid-Atlantic Arts Foundation in Baltimore, for example, visitors can reserve a 1-hour time slot at the foundation's computer workstations. They can use that time to check out an art exhibit in London, England, look up a recent arts-education study, or find out when the Boston Ballet will perform *The Nutcracker.* The foundation's staff is on hand to help visitors plumb the depths of the Web's artistic resources without drowning.

Current access sites for the general public include Ketchikan Area Arts and Humanities Council in Alaska; Prichard Art Gallery in Moscow, Idaho; the South Carolina State Library in Columbia; the Mattress Factory in Pittsburgh; and the Vermont Arts Exchange in North Bennington. To find out if there's an Open Studio access site in your community, write to Open Studio: The Arts Online, 1634 Eye Street NW, Washington, DC 20006, or visit the group's Web site at www.openstudio.org.

ARCHITECTURE

Mention the word *architecture*, and people have a tendency to lose interest, assuming that you're talking about something rather dry and abstract. On the contrary, however, it can be fascinating to take a walk through your city with an expert guide who can tell you the stories behind the buildings that surround.

Many cities with rich architectural resources have architectural foundations, and many of them offer walking tours. Sometimes, tours are offered by the local historical society or in conjunction with the public library. A call to the convention and visitors bureau in your city may help put you in contact with the right organization. Here are a few examples of some architectural strolls to whet your appetite.

The History behind Chicago's Sights

With more than 50 downtown and neighborhood tours, the Chicago Architectural Foundation (CAF) probably has the most comprehensive tour program in the nation. Although most of the tours aren't free (you can expect to pay $5 to $10 for walking tours and up to $25 for bus tours), you get a wealth of information. You'll learn about Frank Lloyd Wright, early skyscrapers, the Chicago theater district, and much more.

Through a partnership with the Chicago Transit Authority and the Chicago Office of Tourism, CAF offers a free tour of the downtown business district from the lofty perspective of the elevated train. A series of Wednesday lunchtime lectures, which focus on a different architectural theme each week, is also offered free of charge. Topics may include current building construction, architectural historians discussing famous Chicago architects, and city planners talking about new parks.

For a brochure, write to the CAF at 224 South Michigan Avenue, Chicago, IL 60604.

San Francisco's Alluring Side

If you're curious about life in San Francisco in the days of the Gold Rush or are intrigued by the elaborate gingerbread of the Victorian era, take a free City Guides walking tour that will enlighten you about the culture, history, art, architecture, legend, and allure of San Francisco.

Sponsored by the San Francisco Public Library, the free tours have been offered since 1978. You can also learn about Art Deco San Francisco, the landmark Victorians of Alamo Square, Japantown, and more than two dozen other topics. Two hundred volunteers (and one staff member) make the program possible. For a printed schedule, write City Guides, c/o San Francisco Public Library, Main Library, San Francisco, CA 94102. Be sure to send a self-addressed, stamped envelope.

Touring the Streets of Philadelphia

When the Foundation for Architecture first started offering guided tours of Philadelphia's architecture, "people would say, 'I can't go on your tours; I'm not

an architect,'" recalls tour director Ken Hind. So the group now stays away from the word *architecture*. Instead, "we tell a story about a neighborhood—its past, present, and future," Hind says. Popular choices among the 45 tours offered include Littlest Streets (residential alleys in a Bohemian neighborhood populated by artists and their clubs in the late nineteenth century), Architectural Terra Cotta, and Beaux-Arts Philadelphia. The tours, which last 1½ to 2 hours, cost $7. For a brochure, write to the foundation at 1737 Chestnut Street, 2nd Floor, Philadelphia, PA 19103.

READING

You have one of the best reading resources right there in your own community—your public library. Chances are, it offers a wealth of books, plus compact discs, videos, and free access to the Internet. Some libraries take the idea of lending a step further (see "Libraries That Lend More Than Books," opposite).

Beyond the walls of the library, however, you'll find exceptional opportunities for free or one-of-a-kind books and other interesting offerings. Here are some of the best.

Free Books from the NEA

The National Endowment for the Arts (NEA) has several publications that are available free of charge. The books aren't exactly of the coffee table variety, but the content is informative and thought-provoking. And, that's right, they're free. Here's a sampling.

✓ *Lifelong Journey: An Education in the Arts.* Written by Gary O. Larson, this book focuses on the NEA's principles for lifelong learning in the arts and features articles on nine exceptional programs in various parts of the United States that exemplify the ideal of the lifelong learning environment.

LIBRARIES THAT LEND MORE THAN BOOKS

Do you think libraries are simply places to pick up the latest Patricia Cornwell mystery or track down your ancestors? Well, think again. At select libraries around the country, you can check out free passes to local museums, cultural attractions, and historic sites.

In Chicago, the Check-Us-Out program—started by the Chicago Public Library and Museums in the Park—lets Chicago residents over the age of 18 who have Chicago Public Library cards borrow a special laminated museum pass. The pass provides 2 weeks' free admission to any of nine Chicago museums, including the Art Institute of Chicago, the Chicago Historical Society, the Field Museum of Natural History, and the Mexican Fine Arts Center Museum. Each pass is good for a family or group of up to eight people.

The thinking behind the program, says Gerry Keane, special projects coordinator at the Chicago Public Library, was to encourage people to use the resources of the library to enhance their cultural experiences. To that end, the library has prepared a bibliography for each of the institutions.

Similar programs now exist for the Children's Museum of Chicago (Imagination on Loan) and the Museum of Contemporary Art (Art Access). The program has been such a phenomenal success, says Keane, that they can hardly keep the cards in the library.

On the north shore of Massachusetts, libraries have created a similar program. Local volunteer groups known as Friends of the Public Library have raised money to purchase annual passes to local museums, cultural attractions, and historic sites. They then make the passes available free of charge to anyone with a library card.

The Hamilton Public Library, for example, has eight passes that allow people to visit some of Boston's top attractions, including the Museum of Fine Arts, the Boston Children's Museum, the Kennedy Library and Museum, and the Peabody/Essex Museum, which is one of the country's oldest, featuring maritime art and history, early American furniture, and other collections.

Sometimes, the museums charge minimal fees for the passes. Still, a family of four can get into the Boston Museum of Science for $4 instead of $32. "It gives people a little bit of culture for not an awful lot of money," says Annette Janes, the Hamilton Public Library's director.

If your local library does not have a similar program, Janes suggests starting one. "It's just ordinary folks getting together and calling themselves a friends group," she says. "Sometimes, they incorporate, and then they can raise money." For more information on starting a group and a new members' kit, contact Friends of Libraries U.S.A. at 1420 Walnut Street, Suite 450, Philadelphia, PA 19102.

✓ *The Changing Faces of Tradition: A Report on the Folk and Traditional Arts in the United States.* This book by Elizabeth Peterson reports on two surveys of folk and traditional arts organizations, complete with case studies that highlight the full spectrum of folk activity in the United States.

✓ *Arts in America.* This 10-minute video narrated by Walter Cronkite is essentially an advertisement for the NEA and the impact of its programs on American culture. But the production values are superb, and the range of art it covers is quite spectacular.

To find out more about what's available from the NEA, write the National Endowment for the Arts, 1100 Pennsylvania Avenue NW, Room 614, Washington, DC 20506. You can order any of these items or browse through the entire list of available materials by visiting the NEA Web site at www.arts.endow.gov/pub/General.html.

Government Bookstores

The U.S. Government Printing Office (GPO) produces an array of books, posters, and pamphlets on subjects ranging from economic policy to pest and weed control. Among the 10,000 publications, there are hundreds that fall into the arts category, including many high-quality books of art prints.

Soldiers Serving the Nation, for example, contains color reproductions of works from the Army art collection, while *Eye for History: The Paintings of William Henry Jackson* has reproductions of some of the artist's best works gathered into a 112-page book. Books from the GPO can cost from $6 for a National Endowment for the Arts report to about $40 for a coffee table book on Native American art. In addition, there are reproductions of World War I posters available for $9.

Instead of listing all of its offerings in one catalog, the GPO produces subject bibliographies that are devoted to particular areas of interest. You can order them by writing to Superintendent of Documents, U.S. Government Printing Office, Washington, DC 20402. For books on art and artists, you should ask for subject bibliography 107, while buildings, landmarks, and historic sites are covered in subject bibliography 140.

You can also request the bibliographies or search for books on specific topics at the GPO Web site at www.access.gpo.gov/su_docs.

Moreover, the government maintains regional bookstores in more than 20 cities around the country where you can see some of the more popular titles. You'll find these bookstores in Atlanta; Birmingham, Alabama; Boston; Chicago; Cleveland; Columbus, Ohio; Dallas; Denver; Detroit; Houston; Jacksonville, Florida; Kansas City, Missouri; Laurel, Maryland; Los Angeles; Milwaukee; New York City; Philadelphia; Pittsburgh; Portland, Oregon; Pueblo, Colorado; San Francisco; Seattle; and Washington, D.C.

Viewing Treasures Online

You probably know that the Library of Congress in Washington, D.C., is a rich storehouse of specialty and one-of-a-kind books and documents that you can review when you're in the capital. But did you know that it's also becoming a great Internet resource?

Go to the library's Web site at http://lcweb.loc.gov and click on "Exhibitions." From there, you can read the text and view art or photos from library exhibits or learn the complete history behind Lincoln's Gettysburg Address.

Do films and music interest you more? From the home page, click on "American Memory," and you can watch short film clips and listen to sound recordings from among the more than 50 collections in the National Digital Library.

CHAPTER 16

SUBSIDIES
for YOUR ABC'S

Paying for college in the 1960s and 1970s was a simpler job than it is now. You saved up a thousand dollars or so by bagging groceries at the A&P or tossing burgers under the golden arches. You hit up Mom and Dad for a contribution. Then *maybe* you still needed to take out a small student loan. But that was in the days when State U cost just a couple of thousand dollars a year, and even private colleges seemed reasonable.

In the past 20 years alone, the price of college has risen nearly twice as fast as inflation. Today, private universities can have price tags upwards of $30,000 for room, board, and tuition, and some public universities cost as much as $13,000 a year. In a high-dollar world like this, finding financial aid for your child's education has become almost more important than getting into a school.

> The high cost of education may seem daunting, but if you know how and where to look, you can find grants, scholarships, and even free programs that will cut your out-of-pocket expenses by thousands of dollars.

Fortunately, there are many ways to reduce the out-of-pocket costs of education. If you know where to look—and how—you can find good deals on government-supported loans, grants, scholarships, work-study programs, and more. You can cut the costs of college to the bone by having your child attend a tuition-free school. Or your child could tap into free education by auditing classes or studying over the Internet. In fact, the opportunities to save money on education extend right down to the secondary level, where some states are now looking at funding for private secondary schools.

Yes, learning is more expensive these days, but if you educate yourself about all the opportunities available, you'll find that there are clever ways to keep the costs manageable.

FACTOID

IF YOUR TWO KIDS PAID YOU 50 CENTS AN HOUR TO RAISE THEM UNTIL AGE 18, YOU'D SOCK AWAY $157,680—A GOOD PART OF WHAT IT COSTS TO PAY FOR THEIR COLLEGE EDUCATION.

FINANCING HIGHER EDUCATION

When you start your hunt for educational aid, one of the best weapons you can bring to bear is an open mind. The way in which aid is parceled out often goes against what seems like common sense, and if you start with preconceptions about whether your child is eligible for certain types of grants, you can lose out on thousands of dollars of support. Specifically, keep the following myth-busting rules about financial aid in mind.

Your best chance for aid lies at the public trough. With heavy competition for public grants and scholarships, you might think that you'd have a better change of getting aid by ignoring federal and state money and trying to locate some little-known private scholarship that few people compete for. The truth is, you're better off applying for public money first because the pile of aid is much bigger. In fact, the overwhelming majority of all financial aid comes from federal, state, and collegiate sources. Unfortunately, many parents and students ignore this fact, says Anna Leider, financial aid expert and author of *Don't Miss Out: The Ambitious Student's Guide to Financial Aid*. "They make the search for crumbs—that small percentage of the student-aid pie that represents private scholarships—their number one priority. Not smart!" she says.

Even the well-to-do can get support. While in theory, student aid should go to those who need it most, in practice, it goes to those who best know how, when, and where to apply. While 90 percent of all financial aid is need-based, says Patrick Bellantoni, author of *College Financial Aid Made Easy*, "families with six-figure incomes can—and do—snag generous financial aid packages, depending on circumstances, while those who earn half that may not."

For example, a few years ago, Kalman A. Chany, author of *Paying for College without Going Broke* and president of Campus Consultants in New York City, had a client "who owned a $1 million apartment in New York and a stock portfolio with a value in excess of $2 million." Her daughter attended college "with a $4,000-a-year need-based grant."

The reason? Different aid programs have different eligibility criteria. In this case, the family was awarded a New York state grant for residents attending an in-state school; the eligibility was based on net taxable income, not assets. Therefore, don't assume that your child won't qualify for aid because you make too much money or have too many assets. Indeed, at the majority of colleges, more than 50 percent of students qualify for some form of aid, says Chany.

Expensive private schools can actually cost you less. If your combined income and assets are around $20,000, a pricey private school may seem out of the question. In reality, though, that private school may offer a better financial aid package than a state college would, Chany says.

Most of all, as you apply for financial aid, keep in mind that the more you know about how the system works, the more you'll earn in aid. How do you develop the knowledge? Read on.

Getting Your Fair Share

No matter which school your child plans to attend, the process of applying for financial aid starts with a single form that the federal government processes. This form, called the free application for federal student aid (FAFSA), helps determine your expected family contribution (EFC), which is the amount that the government thinks your family can pay toward your child's education. The lower your EFC, the larger the package of work-study help, grants, and subsidized loans you can get.

There are many ways to reduce your EFC legally so that you can qualify for more aid (see "Looking Poor Can Earn You Aid" on page 264). But even if your EFC shows that you have to pay full freight for the $30,000-a-year private college your child wants to attend, you may be able to trim the bill.

Each college or university financial aid officer has the discretion to allow for special circumstances. If there are any unusual family financial situations, such as an expected layoff, unusual medical bills, or anything else out of the ordinary, ask for a special-circumstances review. Provide the counselor with as much documentation as possible. Appeals are worth the effort, especially if you as parents can document special circumstances like these:

✓ Unusually high unreimbursed medical or dental expenses

✓ Natural disasters that caused you to make expensive repairs to your home

✓ The impending retirement of a parent

✓ One or more children in private schools

✓ Repayment of student loans for you or for another of your children

✓ Recent past unemployment that resulted in a large debt

What Is It?

COLLEGES VS. UNIVERSITIES; PUBLIC VS. PRIVATE

Underneath the umbrella of higher education, there are the smaller parasols of individual schools. Some are universities, and some are colleges. Some are privately owned; some are operated by the state or federal government. Before beginning a search for a school, it's good to know the differences between them.

Junior colleges: Also known as community colleges, these are state-owned schools that offer 2-year associate degrees and vocational diplomas. Tax dollars help subsidize tuition. Students can do 2 years toward a 4-year degree at a junior college, then transfer to another school.

Private colleges: Privately owned, these schools depend on endowments and tuition to operate. Tuition is often triple that of a state college. Four-year bachelor's degrees are offered. In the past, colleges did not grant postgraduate degrees, such as M.B.A.'s, but that line has blurred, and some now do.

Private universities: Privately owned and generally larger than colleges, universities always offer postgraduate degrees. This means that a student who earns a bachelor's degree can stay at the same school and continue work for a master's or Ph.D. Universities often have research facilities as well.

State colleges: As the name implies, these schools are state-owned, with subsidized tuition. Generally, they do not offer advanced degrees. Students who want a master's or Ph.D. have to go elsewhere after completing a bachelor's program.

State universities: These are similar to private universities, only less expensive. A state university is generally larger than a college and offers postgraduate degrees. Tuition is still subsidized but is usually not as low as that at a state 4-year or junior college.

Even if you get a favorable financial aid package, you may want to appeal the school's offer if your circumstances change or if another school offers you more. Be prepared to go back to the school's financial aid officer two or three times. And be creative in your bargaining. If you can't get the financial aid officer to increase the total amount of aid, try to negotiate for a larger portion of aid as grants and scholarships—which won't have to be paid back—rather than as loans.

●❖ *WHAT INSIDERS SAY:*

What's your best strategy when asking for a better aid package? It depends on your personality, says Bonnie Hepburn, a certified financial planner with Moneysense Financial Planning, a fee-only practice in Acton, Massachusetts, that has expertise in financial aid. "I counsel parents with endearing personalities to make personal pleas for more aid; with others, I suggest that they send letters."

When making your plea, keep it brief, respectful, memorable, and factually and grammatically sound. Also, Hepburn suggests, be persistent without being a pest. You want the aid officer to know that you're still there, waiting patiently for an acceptable answer.

Low-Interest Loans

Okay, your expected family contribution shows that you're eligible for some financial aid. Now the question is what form it will take. Loans are most likely, and the choices are low-interest and no-interest and subsidized and unsubsidized loans (see "The Alphabet Soup of Financial Aid"). Given a choice, you want no-interest and subsidized.

The financial aid office will determine your eligibility for loans based on the information that you provided in the free application for federal student aid. Loans come from both private companies and the federal government, and they often vary in terms of interest rates and repayment terms.

With any loan, you should shop for the lowest interest rate and the best terms. Usually, you can get the best deals through the federal government's loan programs, thus making credit union or bank loans unnecessary, experts say. A rundown of the most common types of government loans follows.

●❖ *WHAT INSIDERS SAY:*

Often, if your family has a good credit rating, you'll get an offer of unsubsidized loans to defray part of your child's school costs. Be forewarned: Unlike subsidized loans, which typically don't have to be paid back until after your child has graduated, unsubsidized loans often come due 60 days after you've secured them, meaning while your child is still in school. Also, the interest rates are often higher than for subsidized loans.

Federal Stafford Loans

Formerly known as Guaranteed Student Loans, Stafford Loans come from a federally funded program and are available to graduate and undergraduate students. Depending on your family's income, these low-interest loans are either subsidized or unsubsidized. If you have financial need, your child will qualify for a subsidized loan, meaning that the government pays the interest while your child is in school. Repayment usually begins 6 months after your child graduates or leaves school, which is also when interest begins accumulating.

Unsubsidized Stafford Loans are available to most students and usually carry a lower interest rate than other unsubsidized loans. But interest starts accruing from the day the loan is made, rather than after graduation.

Federal PLUS Loans

The Parent Loan for Undergraduate Students, or PLUS loan, is a federally subsidized loan that allows parents to borrow up to the total cost of their child's college education, minus any financial aid. It has a variable interest rate, but it is almost always higher than that of a Stafford Loan. Repayment begins 60 days after the loan is granted.

Federal Perkins Loans

These federal loans help the neediest students. They carry a low interest rate, and interest doesn't start accruing until 9 months after graduation. Repayment also begins at that time. Each school makes its own determination of who is needy, based on the average income of its student population.

Educational Grants and Scholarships

Obviously, when it comes to college aid, there's nothing like getting money that you don't have to repay. This money is usually available in two

---

THE ALPHABET SOUP OF FINANCIAL AID

EFCs. FAFSAs. FAAs. All of the acronyms government and college officials use can make the world of financial aid seem like an impenetrable maze. Fortunately, there is only a handful of terms that you need to know, and there are easy explanations for each one.

FAFSA (free application for federal student aid): Analyzes the ability to pay for college and is required for just about every student who applies for financial aid.

SAR (student aid report): Issued to those who have filed a federal application for student aid. Shows the amount the student or his family will be expected to pay.

FAA (financial aid administrator): Also known as a financial aid officer or FAO.

EFC (expected family contribution): The amount of money that a family is expected to contribute annually to defray the cost of tuition and room and board.

PFS (parents' financial statement): Required by many secondary schools to determine financial aid. Administered by the School and Student Service (SSS) for Financial Aid in Princeton, New Jersey.

Grant: Free money, usually awarded by the federal or state government or the institution of higher learning, that doesn't have to be repaid.

Scholarship: Also free money, but often with strings attached, such as a requirement that the student maintain a certain grade point average, participate in a sport, or pursue a talent or hobby.

Subsidized student loan: Usually secured by the student rather than parents. Loans are frequently guaranteed by the state or federal government, which provides low interest rates and generous payback allowances. Often, no interest is charged on the loan while the student is in school, and no repayment is expected until after graduation.

Unsubsidized loan: A loan on which the student begins paying interest while still in college and may have to start repaying the principal as well. If not, repayment must begin immediately after graduation.

forms: need-based grants and scholarships that are offered by the government, and merit-based grants and scholarships that are offered by schools. As you'd expect, need-based aid usually goes to students whose families can least afford to pay for college, and merit-based aid usually goes to students with good high school records. Here's a look at both types.

Need-Based Aid

Free money for students with exceptional need comes in the form of federal Pell Grants of up to $4,500 and federal Supplemental Educational Opportunity Grants of up to $4,000. The actual amount of each grant is left to the discretion of the college or university's financial aid officer, who awards the grants based on the expected family

Power to the People

LOOKING POOR CAN EARN YOU AID

Want to improve your chances of getting financial aid for your child's education? Consider the following tips offered by Kalman A. Chany, author of *Paying for College without Going Broke* and president of Campus Consultants in New York City, and Mark Kantrowitz, research scientist and author of *The Prentice Hall Guide to Scholarships and Fellowships for Math and Science Students*.

1. Paint as bleak a financial picture as you can. The single most important step is to reduce your adjusted gross income—line 33 on your 1040 federal income tax return— as much as possible. Some strategies: Minimize capital gains, avoid cashing in U.S. Savings Bonds, and avoid premature withdrawals from pension plans and IRAs. Do whatever you can legally to pay less taxes, short of refusing salary increases or lottery winnings. You don't want to turn down money, but you want to give the appearance of earning less.

   Beware, too, of accountant-recommended strategies that can lead to decreased, in-

stead of increased, financial aid. One of the most common mistakes is saving for college in an account set up in your child's name, says Bonnie Hepburn, a certified financial planner with Moneysense Financial Planning in Acton, Massachusetts. Student assets, in particular, are counted at a very high rate when determining financial need. When calculating your expected family contribution, the federal government will expect parents to use no more than 5.64 percent of their total assets to pay for college. Students, however, are expected to contribute up to 50 percent of their incomes and 35 percent of their assets to defray college costs. If you have already saved in your child's name, consult an accountant about shifting the money into the account in the name of a parent or younger sibling.

2. Max out contributions to retirement plans. Not only is this good financial advice, it will also help whittle down the savings that you would report on the federal financial aid form, especially if you begin contributing well before

contribution (EFC) as calculated from the information provided in the free application for federal student aid. Usually, students must have an EFC of $2,270 or less to qualify.

In addition, each state has its own financial aid office that administers state grants for students with exceptional need. These are almost always based on the EFC.

●◆ *WHAT INSIDERS SAY:*

The best way to help your child get a need-based grant is to reduce your EFC through strategies like investments. See "Looking Poor Can Earn You Aid."

Merit-Based Grants

The competition among colleges for top students with 4.0-plus grade point averages and soaring

your child enters college. When calculating your expected family contribution, the federal financial aid formula considers only what you contributed in the most recent tax year, not what you've already saved, says Kantrowitz.

3. Realize capital gains on stocks at least 2 years before your child starts college, advises Kantrowitz. That way, your income won't show a huge bump in the year that you apply for financial aid.

Also, you can remove assets from consideration for financial aid purposes by putting them in retirement plans, suggests Hepburn. Note, too, that if you've been saving for college all along, you should begin shifting money out of the stock market and into liquid assets several years before your child starts school. That way, you have the luxury of selling high, rather than risking having to sell low if the market turns down the summer before school starts.

4. Have more than one child in college. The more children you have in college at one

time, the better a financial aid package you'll receive, says Kantrowitz.

5. Take advantage of a divorce. Divorcing or separated parents are allowed to split income for financial aid purposes. The custodial parent—the one with whom the child lived more than 50 percent of the time, as determined by the divorce decree—should file the federal application for student aid. Remember, too, that the income considered for the expected family contribution is the combined amount earned by the custodial parent and the step-parent, if there is one. The other biological parent is not considered in the equation, regardless of income level, says Kantrowitz.

6. Pay off debts with savings, then accelerate necessary spending in order to improve your financial aid position. Reduce cash assets by paying off credit cards, car loan payments, and even mortgages. If you're still awash in cash, consider preparing your child for college by buying a computer, car, or clothes.

SAT scores can be fierce, allowing the most sought-after students to secure hefty merit-based grants and scholarships regardless of need. But even B students with special affiliations (such as religion) or talents or interests (such as music or journalism) are able to secure partial or full scholarships or grants. Both mean free money that's awarded on the basis of merit, without regard to the family's financial status. While that doesn't mean that your child has to be a budding Beethoven, Diane Sawyer, or Martin Luther King, having that level of expertise would make a prospective student quite attractive to financial aid officers at top-tier schools such as the Ivy League universities or Stanford.

A student who has potential but an uneven track record in a particular field of interest should try applying to less well known colleges and universities that want to grow programs in the areas in which he may want to participate. Southern California's Chapman University, for example, has a host of merit-based grants and scholarships for students who don't have extremely high grade point averages but who show potential.

Chapman student Will Matthews was awarded 85 percent of Chapman's $19,000 tuition, plus subsidized loans for room and board, in a combination of grants and scholarships. He received the aid even though his family's income was very nearly six figures and he graduated from high school with a 3.2 grade point average. How did he do it?

Matthews had worked for his high school newspaper and is the son of a United Church of Christ minister, a church he attended but in which he was not particularly active. Even so, he was able to parlay his newspaper experience and church affiliation into $16,000 in aid, since Chapman awards merit-based religious and journalism scholarships. Although his first-choice schools were Syracuse University in New York and Emerson University in Boston, both gave Matthews financial aid offers below Chapman's.

He says he has no regrets about attending a second-choice school. "My Chapman experience has been fabulous every step of the way," he says. "I've gotten opportunities here that I know I wouldn't have had at the East Coast schools."

Had Matthews not carefully read a footnote in a recruiting brochure that Chapman sent him, he would have never known about the programs. "It was just dumb luck," he says. You don't have to leave it to dumb luck, but you do have to investigate what's available.

Dollars for Scholars Program

Another source of aid that is often omitted from the financial aid books is Dollars for Scholars. This nonprofit, publicly supported organization helped provide more than $11 million in aid to 22,000 students in 1998, says Beth Holcomb, the group's program manager. Based in St. Peter, Minnesota, with 806 chapters across the nation, Dollars for Scholars helps community groups set up scholarship funds, including advising them on dealing with the IRS and forming a board of trustees. Each chapter sets its own qualifications for making awards, but they tend to be merit-based.

The group also has developed a partnership with more than 100 colleges and universities that have agreed to match Dollars for Scholars scholarships with their own funds. And, while many colleges and universities will reduce financial aid by the amount received in private grants and scholarships, schools that participate in Dollars for Scholars will not. Checking out what's available could result in an award of several thousand dollars or more, offered under the most favorable terms.

Sometimes, finding a scholarship that's a good match for your child can take patience and persistence. Start by writing the national Dollars for Scholars office at P.O. Box 297, St. Peter, MN 56082, and ask for the name, phone number, and contact person for the chapters in your area. They'll also provide you with a directory that lists their collegiate partners and indicates which ones provide matching grants.

Specialty Grants and Scholarships

Once you've exhausted the public sources of financial aid, it's time to look into private grants, where an amazing variety of opportunities awaits you. How unusual are they? Well, if your ancestors fought for Robert E. Lee, your child can qualify for one grant. If family time at your house includes har-

nessing up the horses and going to the races, he qualifies for another. And if your prospective student has an interest in death and dying, there's even scholarship aid there. How can you find such grants?

Start with a high school guidance counselor, then contact the schools that your child wants to attend and ask for lists of unusual or unpublicized scholarships. You can also try writing to the National Research Scholarship Service, 1200 K Street, Washington, DC 10022, a clearinghouse that compiles an annual list of unusual awards. Or, if you

---

DIGGING FOR DOLLARS

To find the best sources for merit-based financial aid, consult the following sources.

High school guidance counselors

A good counselor is one of the best people to consult to find out about the latest scholarships available, both locally and nationally. The counselor can also help you plan a strategy for nailing down the best aid package.

Financial aid books

Many, though not all, of the institutional merit-based aid programs are listed in books on college financing. (One in particular, Anna Leider's *The As and Bs of Academic Scholarships*, lists merit scholarships school by school.)

Books on scholarships can cost as much as $30, so whenever possible, try to find them in the library or through a high school guidance counselor. Be sure that the books you consult are the most recent available—no more than 3 years old for scholarship listings and 1 year old for general information on financial aid. Many books also list a host of private scholarships, which account for only about 10 percent of the available financial aid money.

The Internet

If you have access to the Internet, a great way to find scholarships tailored to individual talents and abilities is by using a free online search service such as Fastweb (www.fastweb.com) or the one

provided by the U.S. Department of Education (www.ed.gov).

"There's no need to pay to search a scholarship database, since the best services are available for free," says Mark Kantrowitz, research scientist and author of *The Prentice Hall Guide to Scholarships and Fellowships for Math and Science Students*. Fastweb, for example, asks a series of questions about who the student is and what he likes (the survey takes about 10 minutes), searches its database for grants and scholarships that best fit the student's personality profile, and e-mails the results: an up-to-date list of scholarships and grants.

have access to the Internet, use your browser's search function to look for "special scholarships."

There are also myriad grants and scholarships available for women, people of alternate sexual orientation, and students of various ethnic and minority groups. Here are a few samples of the unusual support money that is available out there.

Dollars for Descendants of Confederate Soldiers

Students who can trace their ancestry to soldiers who fought for the South in the Civil War are eligible to win scholarships worth anywhere from $400 to $1,500. For information, write the United Daughters of the Confederacy Business Office (Scholarship Request), Memorial Building, 328 North Boulevard, Richmond, VA 23220-4057.

Help for Harness Racers

If your family is actively involved in harness racing, your child can apply for post-secondary-school scholarships worth $5,000. Contact Harness Tracks of America, 4640 East Sunrise, Suite 200, Tucson, AZ 85718.

Scholarships for the Shoemakers' Children

Scholarships worth up to $2,500 are available to students who are employed in the footwear industry as well as dependents of footwear industry workers. Contact Two/Ten International Footwear Foundation, 56 Main Street, Watertown, MA 02172.

Support for People with Special Names

Many colleges offer grants to people who can trace their ancestry to donors of specific scholarships. The University of California, for example, awards schol-arships to descendants of Arthur Arlett, Charles Cole, Violet E. Wilson, William James Gray, Adolph Braese, Alice Mara Tibbits, Elede Prince Morris, Rose Humann Rogers, and blood relatives of Mildred L. Muller, among others. Contact the school that your child wants to attend for information on possible programs.

Money for Mortuary Education

Students interested in pursuing careers in funeral service or funeral education may apply for scholarships from the Hilgenfeld Foundation for Mortuary Education. Write the foundation at P.O. Box 4311, Fullerton, CA 92634.

Scholarships for Bat Lovers

Adults tend to loathe bats, but kids are more open-minded. If your child is fascinated by these beneficial bug-eating denizens of the dark, that interest just might help send him through graduate school. Bat Conservation International grants a total of $40,000 or more annually to students doing research in fields dealing with bat conservation. Awards average about $2,000. For information on the application process, write Bat Conservation International Scholarship Program, P.O. Box 162603, Austin TX 78716-2603.

Aid for Nurses in Need

Grants are available at selected institutions for economically disadvantaged students who want to pursue nursing. For more information and a list of participating schools, write Division of Nursing, Bureau of Health Professions, Health Resources and Services Administration, Public Health Service, U.S. Department of Health and Human Services, Parklawn Building, 5600 Fishers Lane, Room 9-36, Rockville, MD 20857.

FACTOID

MORE THAN 1,200 COLLEGES OFFER ACADEMIC SCHOLARSHIPS TO STUDENTS WITH B AVERAGES OR BETTER AND SAT SCORES OF 900 OR MORE.

Support for Doctors-to-Be

Scholarships are available for doctors, certified nurse practitioners, physician assistants, or certified nurse midwives if they are willing to serve as doctors in disadvantaged communities. A year of service is required for each year of financial assistance; minimum service is 2 years. Write to the National Health Service Corps, Health Resources Development Branch, NCHSC Scholarship Program, Public Health Service, 4350 East-West Highway, 10th Floor, Bethesda, MD 20814.

●◆ *WHAT INSIDERS SAY:*

In your search for aid, beware of the scholarship scam game. Around college campuses, you'll see brochures and coupons from companies that offer to find scholarship money—for a fee. Ignore them, especially those that require you to provide tax returns or private financial information, says financial aid authority Mark Kantrowitz. In recent years, the government has begun investigating these companies and cracking down on the many that are fraudulent, he says.

GETTING THEM TO SHOW YOU THE MONEY

How can you get the most financial aid from a school? Here are tips from Anna Leider, financial aid expert and author of *Don't Miss Out: The Ambitious Student's Guide to Financial Aid*.

1. Along with the normal search criteria, make financial aid a consideration when selecting a college or university. Find out if the school has matching scholarships, sibling scholarships, installment plans, middle-income assistance programs, or tuition remission for high grades. Then compare to see which will give you the best deal.

2. Choose an institution most likely to offer a financial aid package heavy on grants and scholarships that you won't have to repay. Your best bet is any school in which your child's academic record places him in the upper 25 percent of the profile of the incoming freshman class.

3. Send two applications to two colleges of equal merit. If your child is accepted by both, try playing one against the other to secure the best financial aid package.

4. Ask your child to consider public service after graduation. Individual colleges and universities—as well as most states—have loan-forgiveness programs for prospective teachers, nurses, medical technicians, law enforcement officers, Head Start workers, and Peace Corps or VISTA volunteers, for example. To find out about eligibility, talk to your child's guidance counselor or the financial aid officer at the school your child wants to attend.

Note that participants selected for AmeriCorps, part of the Corporation for National Service, receive a minimum-wage stipend and almost $5,000 a year for 2 years to help pay tuition or repay educational loans. Contact AmeriCorps at their Web site, www.cns.gov.

Work-Study Programs

When filling out the free application for federal student aid, be sure to mark the box that says your child wants work-study. Students who qualify may land on-campus jobs—anything from slinging hash in the cafeteria to checking library cards to assisting professors in research projects—that pay anywhere from minimum wage to $8 an hour or more.

Universities love hiring work-study students, since the government helps subsidize their salaries. The students usually must work a maximum number of hours per semester, and often, because the jobs are supervised by on-campus bosses who have sympathy for students' busy schedules, the hours are flexible. Some jobs are so downright cushy—being a security guard in the library or answering phones in the dorms late at night, for example—that the students can study while they're working. Paychecks are usually credited to students' accounts to help defray tuition and room and board fees.

Of course, there's a catch: Work-study is need-based and is awarded by federal and state governments according to the expected family contribution as calculated on the student aid form. The lower your family's expected contribution, the greater the chance that your child will qualify for a job (see "Looking Poor Can Earn You Aid" on page 264 for specific tips on lowering your expected family contribution to increase the chances of getting work-study aid).

Veterans' Benefits

One of the best ways your child can pay for college is by serving in the armed forces, although the tradeoff isn't for everyone. Under the current program, known as the Montgomery GI Bill, active-duty military personnel can contribute $100 a month to an educational fund for the first year of their service. At the end of a 2-year enlistment, the Department of Veterans Affairs contributes more than $12,000 toward education costs; at the end of 3 years, it contributes more than $15,000. The money is paid on a monthly basis.

Some dependents are also eligible for educational benefits. "Wives and children of veterans who died or were totally disabled as a result of service qualify," says financial counselor and author Anna Leider. Dependents of former prisoners of war or soldiers classified as missing in action are also eligible, she adds, as, of course, are dependents of those on active duty.

For more information on these programs, you can contact your regional office of the Depart-

SHOULD YOU PREPAY TUITION?

Over the past few years, some state and private colleges and universities have tried to reduce the burden of higher education costs by offering families the option of paying tuition years before their children enroll. The benefits, they say, are lower tuition costs (you pay current rates instead of the rates 15 years down the line) and peace of mind.

Experts warn against falling into this trap. "Such prepaid plans are a disaster for families who would otherwise qualify for need-based aid, since withdrawals for tuition reduce aid eligibility dollar for dollar," says Kalman A. Chany, author of *Paying for College without Going Broke* and president of Campus Consultants in New York City. "Why lock up the money when you're not getting that big a benefit?"

ment of Veterans Affairs, listed in the government pages of the phone book. Or, if you have access to the Internet, visit the Veterans Affairs benefits Web site at www.va.gov/benefits.htm. From there, you can click on "Education and Training" and download the veterans benefits booklet.

◆ *WHAT INSIDERS SAY:*

Looking for a way to maximize veterans education benefits? Leider offers one strategy for students: "Go on active duty for 3 or 4 years. While on active duty, take off-duty courses (the military will pay up to 75 percent of the tuition costs) and make sure that the courses add up to an associate degree. At the same time, participate in the Montgomery GI Bill. When you're ready for discharge, you'll have credit for 2 years of college and a tuition kitty of at least $17,000."

ROTC Scholarships

If your child intends to pursue a military career after college, he may want to apply for an Reserve Officer Training Corps (ROTC) scholarship. Coordinated at many (although not all) college and university campuses nationwide, ROTC scholarships pay for tuition, books, and fees and will usually allow a small monthly living stipend of $100 or so. In exchange, your child must serve in the military upon graduation (the length of service depends on the military branch).

To find out how to apply for an ROTC scholarship, inquire at the financial aid office of the college or university that your child would like to attend. Information is also available on the armed services Web sites: Army ROTC at www.goarmy.com, Navy ROTC at www.navyjobs.com, Marine Corps at www.militarycareers.com, and Air Force ROTC at www.airforce.com.

Aid for Returning Students

What if you're seeking aid for yourself instead of your child? You're in luck. There are a number of ways to qualify for aid if you're planning to return to college to finish your degree, extend your education, or gather skills for a new career.

For one thing, the federal government has no age restrictions on eligibility for federal student financial aid, so you can apply just as a high school student would. Also, although colleges often limit their own financial aid programs to students who are pursuing their first bachelors' degrees, some schools will waive the restrictions for adults who are returning to school to prepare for career changes.

Some organizations also earmark money specifically for returning students. The Business and Professional Women's Foundation, for example, provides scholarships and fellowships for women over 30 who are returning to school to upgrade their skills, build knowledge for new career fields, or prepare to reenter the job market. For more information on this group's offerings, write to Scholarships, Business and Professional Women's Foundation, 2012 Massachusetts Avenue NW, Washington, DC 20036.

The Internet also has special pages of grants and scholarships for older students. To access the information, use your browser's search function to search for terms like "financial aid and older students."

GETTING A FREE EDUCATION

Almost everyone knows that the U.S. military academies offer exceptional education that's 100 percent free. And most people also know that it's extremely tough to be accepted; students must be nominated by a member of Congress, plus have top grades and other talents. But free educational opportunities don't stop with the academies. A handful of colleges and universities offer 100 percent tuition scholarships to all accepted students. Although admission to these institutions of higher learning is extremely competitive, being accepted isn't as hard as winning the lottery. Here are a few schools that are worth checking out.

Cooper Union

Located in New York City, this college is well-known for its emphasis on art, architecture, and engineering. Art school candidates must submit a portfolio of work, while architectural candidates are required to take home tests. Those accepted into the engineering school must have exceptional academic records and SAT scores. For information, write Cooper Union, 30 Cooper Square, New York, NY 10003.

Webb Institute

This extremely small school enrolls fewer than 90 students and trains them to become marine engineers and naval architects. To get in, prospective students must demonstrate an interest in engineering and score a minimum of 500 on the verbal portion and 650 on the math portion of the SAT. For information, write to the Webb Institute, Crescent Beach Road, Glen Cove, NY 11542.

AN IVY LEAGUE DEGREE AT A BUSH LEAGUE PRICE

In 1999, undergraduate tuition at Stanford was $22,110. At Yale, it was $23,780. Harvard was a relative bargain at $22,028.

Compare that to Miami-Dade Community College in Florida, which is widely considered to be one of the better community colleges in the country, says Edward B. Fiske, former education editor of the *New York Times* and author of the popular *Fiske Guide to Colleges* series. For the same year, tuition at Miami-Dade was $1,075 per year for Florida residents.

Sure, there's a big savings, you say, but your child has his heart set on that Ivy League degree.

Well, Junior can have it and save you a fortune, too, if he's willing to attend a 2-year community college for an associate degree, then transfer to an Ivy League school for the final 2 years. He'll end up with a bachelor's degree bearing a prestigious name, and you'll save nearly half the cost of his education.

Lots of savvy people use this strategy, says Fiske, but putting it into practice takes some real work. The Ivy League schools are highly selective and always turn down far more applicants than they accept. It's a given that your child will have to be at or near the top of the community college class to stand a decent chance of acceptance.

Nevertheless, students who use this strategy have something going for them that kids right out of high school don't. "They'll be 2 years older than if they applied to Ivy League schools right out of high school," says Fiske. That's 2 years to make themselves more attractive to the scrutiny of an admissions board. "They'll have time to become more interesting people," Fiske adds.

Yes, grades are important to an admissions board, but so is the idea of a student who will bring diverse and in-depth experiences to the campus. Ivy League admissions boards look for life experiences like summers abroad, working and learning in a foreign country—ideally, a non-English-speaking one. They also look for things like volunteerism or political involvement—"anything that shows that you will bring interesting perspectives to the university," says Fiske. "There are no set rules. The main thing is to follow your interests and get passionate about something."

Berea College

Set in the hills of Kentucky, Berea accepts students with both high financial need and exceptional potential. The college is well-known for its programs in the arts, especially crafts and drama, but it also offers a wide variety of liberal arts majors. The approximate income cap for those accepted is $44,000 for a family of four. For information, write Berea College, CPO 2344, Berea, KY 40404.

Deep Springs College

This tiny 2-year college near the Nevada border is open to men only, most of whom transfer to elite private institutions to finish their schooling. The school aims to prepare students for a life of service; the enrollment is approximately 26 students, whose average combined SAT score is 1500. Students spend nearly half their time tending the on-campus cattle ranch; the other half is devoted to liberal arts courses. For information, write Deep Springs College, Student Body Applications Committee, HC72, Box 45001, Dyer, NV 89010.

College of the Ozarks

This liberal arts college is truly student-run. The 1,500 students have built many of the buildings; they staff the campus fire department, airport, and restaurant; and they tend the animals in the college-owned beef and dairy farm. Ninety percent of the students enrolled there must come from low-income families and qualify for a Pell Grant, meaning that their family's expected college contribution is $2,270 or less. The remaining 10 percent of the student body come from alumni families, friends of the college, and exceptionally qualified applicants. The enrolled students have scored an average 21 on the ACT test. For information, write College of the Ozarks, Point Lookout, MO 65726.

Learning by Just Showing Up

If you or your child is after skills, not college credits or a degree, one way to get them is to audit classes at a local college or university. The definition of auditing varies from school to school, but generally it means that auditing students are allowed to attend lectures, participate in labs, complete assignments, take exams, and do just about everything a regularly enrolled student can do—except receive academic credit for the course. It's also possible to just sit in on lectures and learn for the joy of it. In this case, the professor and the auditing student usually work out an arrangement ahead of time to determine what level of work the auditor will complete.

Each institution has its own policy about auditing; some have no auditing provisions, others charge full fare, still others charge a nominal fee, and a large number allow students to audit classes for free. To find out if the school you or your child is interested in allows free auditing, call the admissions office.

●◆ WHAT INSIDERS SAY:

Even if a school has no provisions for auditing, or if it wants to charge for taking the course, a student can appeal directly to the professor. Professors often will allow students to sit in on classes informally.

Tapping Into Government Research

If you or your child is already attending college or is looking for access to information without paying the cost of attending school, the Internet is an incredible resource. From a computer hooked to the Internet, it's possible to tap into hundreds of free sources of current government information from around the world. The World Wide Web provides a wealth of federal and state research and studies and statistics that students can use to write research papers or theses or conduct experiments.

Many of these sites are available on university library Web pages under "government documents." The Federal Government General Information Resources page provides links to hundreds of documents on various topics, including higher education research grants and opportunities, embassies, federal courts, federally funded research, and the University of Michigan's government documents library. The address is http://lcweb.loc.gov/global/executive/general_resources.html.

Although the easiest way to gain access to government documents is through the Web, selected libraries also provide student researchers with massive numbers of printed documents. Large research universities generally have the most comprehensive government documents databases, although some public libraries, especially in large urban areas, have huge document collections as well. To find out what's available in your area, call your local library's reference librarian and ask for the address or phone number of the best government documents collection in your area. Since much of what's available is for in-library use only (in the library's reference collection), you should have no trouble getting access to use whatever you need.

Amazing Stories

THE MILLION-DOLLAR (SCHOLARSHIP) MAN

Imagine being offered a total of nearly a million dollars in scholarships. Impossible? Not for Chris Vuturo. He received $885,000 in offers from colleges and other sources, then wrote the book on how you can find the money you need to fund your child's educational dream. Vuturo's book *The Scholarship Advisor* lists hundreds of thousands of scholarships totaling more than $1 billion.

When he was preparing for college, Vuturo was in the same boat as thousands of other students who had great ambitions but limited funds. He maintained an A average at his small Catholic high school in Louisville, Kentucky, volunteered at a local hospice for the mentally retarded, and earned money during the summer and on weekends taking the tops off radishes at the produce factory where his father worked.

In his junior year of high school, Vuturo decided he wanted to go to a top-notch, preferably private, university. But his father's annual income was barely as much as Harvard's $20,000-a-year tuition. The summer before his senior year, Vuturo started applying for every scholarship he thought he could land, doing all the research himself. He also applied for financial aid at eight colleges and universities.

He wound up with about $12,000 in portable scholarships—money that could be used at whatever college or university he chose to attend—and offers of near full tuition at the other places he wanted to go, including a full ride at the Air Force Academy and a $40,000 ROTC scholarship.

In the end, he turned down most of the money and accepted a generous offer from Harvard. After acquiring an $80,000 Ivy League education, Vuturo says he was left with only about $10,000 in loans to pay back—and those were subsidized loans at 5 percent interest.

"There are a lot of myths out there about what it takes to win scholarships," says Vuturo, who has continued his studies with graduate work at Duke University. Students "think they have to

FINANCING SECONDARY EDUCATION

Even if your child hasn't yet reached college age, you may be struggling to pay tuition—for a private secondary school. With costs for private elementary schools and high schools ranging from a few thousand dollars for many parochial schools to medians of $9,000 to $12,000 for independent private schools, the average middle-class family can be squeezed. And although government offers generous support to students attending private colleges, it doesn't make money available for secondary education, says Mark Mitchell, director of financial aid services at the National Association of Independent Schools.

Most of the 1,100 schools that belong to the association dedicate a significant portion of their budgets to providing need-based aid to students who have been accepted for admission. About 16 percent of students in independent schools receive some aid, ranging from grants of a few hundred dollars to full tuition.

have a 4.0 or be the all-state quarterback or be on the all-state band. You can tell from my experience that isn't true.

"I worked hard, I read a lot, and I tried to be as well-rounded as possible. Admissions committees really value well-rounded success; they want to give money to someone they believe will contribute to the community. They're looking for maturity and a connection to the community as a whole, and that comes out in the activities that you participate in and the service you do."

Vuturo believes that he benefited from Harvard's commitment to having a diverse student population. "I came from a limited academic pool," he says. "I was a southerner from a blue-collar family, a working-class kid."

Here's Vuturo's advice for those who'd like to win big at the scholarship game.

1. Don't sell yourself short. "The biggest mistake you can make is not to try."

2. Don't start too late. "The summer of your junior year is the best time to get started applying for aid. The minute you hit your senior year, it all starts going too fast. You have the SATs, the last football game, the senior prom, your classes, your college applications." Scholarship applications require "quite a bit of time," he says. "It's really easy to put them aside, but don't."

3. Apply for scholarships the same way you would prepare for a test. "You have to have a strategy," says Vuturo. He says that at the time he was applying, "I didn't have a strategy. That's why I wrote the (scholarship) book."

The advance from his book paid his room and board while he spent a year studying at the London School of Economics before going to Duke. And who paid his tuition? "I got a full scholarship," he says.

Happily, there is a wide range of private grants and loans, from a few thousand dollars to $15,000 at the most exclusive day schools.

●◆ *WHAT INSIDERS SAY:*

With government support unlikely, snagging a good aid package at a private high school can be tricky—but not impossible. According to Mitchell, the needs analysis system has been revised with an eye to helping more middle-income families qualify for assistance. When trying to secure aid, follow the same steps suggested for reducing your expected family contribution for college aid (see "Looking Poor Can Earn You Aid" on page 264).

Tuition Vouchers

A recent development in private school funding is the use of tuition vouchers, which are usually reserved for poor families who don't want their children to attend public schools. It works like this:

Parents who aren't satisfied with the education their children are getting in public schools can apply for vouchers for a specific amount of money that they can use to pay for private or parochial education.

So far, the majority of funding comes from private sources, although some public financing does exist in the state of Florida and in the cities of Milwaukee and Cleveland.

While some funds exist for high school students, the bulk of the money is reserved for the most economically disadvantaged students in kindergarten through eighth grade, according to Troy Williamson of Children's Educational Opportunity Foundation (CEO America), one of the largest supporters of private tuition vouchers.

"Philanthropists are trying to use their money most effectively, getting it to the students who need it most as quickly as possible," he says. For information on how to apply for private tuition

Amazing Stories

LIFELONG LEARNER

It may be that you lose the ability to easily master foreign languages as you grow older, but your ability to learn other academic subjects doesn't wane in the slightest. Just ask Janet Hammond, who has maintained a 3.82 grade point average as an English major at the University of Maine in Fort Kent despite the fact that she is past her 80th birthday.

Hammond, a member of the class of 2000, takes classes through a state program that allows anyone over the age of 65 to attend college for free.

"It's a shame that many people don't realize this is out there for them, because it's a won-

derful opportunity," she says. Hammond is determined to seize the opportunity to its fullest. In addition to her full course schedule (12 hours of class time and 15 to 20 hours of study time a week), she's involved in a number of extracurricular activities, including the French Club and Alpha Chi, an honors club open only to upperclassmen in the top 10 percent of their class. She's also taken a number of courses with her daughter, who graduated in 1998 with a degree in nursing. "I'm not so sure the professor was thrilled," says Hammond. "We were always laughing about something or other."

vouchers or for information on how to start your own privately funded voucher program, write the national office of CEO America, P.O. Box 1543, Bentonville, AR 72712-1543.

BRINGING UNCLE SAM TO SCHOOLS

If you're looking for ways to enhance the education experience at your child's elementary or secondary school, Uncle Sam and his friends are ready to oblige.

The federal government provides dozens of programs for schools, as do many nonprofit organizations. In most cases, they are available to both public and private schools. Here are examples of some of the more innovative programs.

Musical Performances

Are you hankering for a Sousa march or perhaps the *1812 Overture*? Or maybe you'd enjoy a free rock concert or jazz or chamber music show. Military bands have been known to offer all of these at local schools, although the chances of getting a concert depend on the bands' schedules. The fastest way to request a performance is to call the public information officer at a military base in your region that has a band. If there are none, you can make a request to the military branch's band office in Washington, D.C. Officials will tell you how to

PAYING FOR SECONDARY SCHOOL

If the price of a private secondary school seems daunting, you can try some of these strategies to hold down costs.

1. **Leave no stone unturned.** Waivers of the fee for processing the parents' financial statement are available to families who can demonstrate extreme hardship, so be sure to ask your school's financial aid officer if you qualify and how to obtain one.

2. **Explore the possibility of** getting aid from local organizations, civic and church groups, philanthropies, or local employers.

3. **Ask about payment plans.** Some schools will allow you to pay tuition, interest-free, over a period of 8 to 10 months.

4. **Look into loans.** The National Association of Independent Schools urges parents to work with the school's financial aid administrator to help secure the best financing arrangements possible. Some schools have their own plans, and others will suggest outside sources. When comparing loan options, ask the following questions: Is the interest rate fixed or variable? What is the repayment term? How is the interest rate calculated? Are there any fees charged in addition to interest?

Note: Tuition Management Systems has a program called BorrowSmart, which reduces student debt burden by 50 percent on average. The program considers what the family can afford to pay each month, then determines the least costly loan to cover the balance. To find out more, write to 127 John Clarke Road, Newport, RI 02842-5641.

contact the nearest military band. Many bands tour and may be willing to make a stop at your school when they're in the area.

To inquire about Air Force bands, write Programs (SAF/PAB), 1690 Air Force Pentagon, Washington, DC 20330. For Army bands, the address is Office of the Chief of Public Affairs, Attn: Community Relations Team, 1500 Army Pentagon, Washington, DC 20310-1500. For Marine Corps bands, write to the Commandant of the Marine Corps, Headquarters, United States Marine Corps, Code: PAC, Washington, DC 20380-1775.

Aerial Art

If your taste in entertainment runs more to the visual than the aural, you can contact the military for an in-the-air performance. The Blue Angels and Thunderbirds precision flying teams are available for flyovers, while the Golden Knights parachute team may perform jumps. There may be costs involved with bringing these groups to your town. To request a group, write the office of the assistant secretary of defense at OASD (PA) DCR, Pentagon, Room 1E776, Washington, DC 20301-1400.

LOW-COST WAYS TO BUILD YOUR SKILLS

The government and various nonprofit agencies have Web sites, brochures, and booklets for secondary school students and adults who are interested in expanding their intellectual horizons. Although most printed materials are free, a few have nominal costs—up to about $2. Here are some of the best resources.

✓ Better understand banking by borrowing a variety of films, filmstrips, and videos for free from the Federal Reserve Bank. These materials explore such topics as the monetary system, electronic fund transfers, free enterprise, and the history of money. For a catalog, write to the Federal Bank, 230 South La Salle Street, Chicago, IL 60690.

✓ Study American history during a virtual visit to the Smithsonian Institution. Its Web site features information on most of the museum's collections, plus First Ladies' gowns, biographies, and documentary photographs, with links to the White House, the Senate, the House of Representatives, and the Library of Congress. Log on to www.si.edu/resource/faq/nmah/political.htm.

✓ Take a trip to outer space. The Johnson Space Center, part of NASA, provides access to its archives of photos, software, and links to NASA's myriad research sites at www.jsc.nasa.gov.

✓ Explore America's library. The Library of Congress has

placed much of its huge collection of information on the Web. You can view photos of current and recent exhibits, read about famous Americans and key events from our history, or look through Congressional information, White House documents, crime statistics, State Department reports, and more. Go to www.lcweb.loc.gov.

✓ Check the pulse of America's health at the National Institutes of Health (NIH) archive. The site features the NIH's own health reports and links to consumer health publications put out by the agencies that make up the NIH. Go to www.nih.gov.

History Lessons

The Bureau of Land Management's Adventures in the Past has a variety of programs to promote public education and awareness of archeological and historical resources. The Heritage Education Program's Project Archaeology provides teachers and youth group leaders with hands-on classroom activities. Write to the Bureau of Land Management, Anasazi Heritage Center, 27501 Highway 184, Dolores, CO 81323.

Space in School

NASA will send speakers to schools to conduct hands-on assemblies on NASA history, rockets, space, and aeronautics, among other topics. The program is coordinated by NASA's field centers; you can find the one closest to your school by writing NASA FEO2, NASA Publications, Washington, DC 20546, or checking NASA's Web site at www.hq.nasa.gov/education.

Hands-On Rocket Instruction

NASA also provides activities for classroom projects on rockets, including building and launching models. For "Rockets: A Teaching Guide for an Elementary Science Unit on Rocketry," write to NASA Publication Center, 300 E Street SW, Washington, DC 20546.

Lectures on Defense

The U.S. Department of Defense sends speakers to schools to discuss a wide range of topics, from national missile defense to prisoners of war or related current events.

To find out what's available, call the public affairs office of the nearest military installation or write OASD, Community Relations, Speakers Bureau, Pentagon, Room 1E776, Washington, DC 20301-1400.

Best Bets

RECOMMENDED BOOKS

As you'd expect in an area that generates intense interest, many authors have written books to advise readers on how to cover the high cost of college. Here are four that are recommended by financial aid expert Mark Kantrowitz, a research scientist and author of the book *The Prentice Hall Guide to Scholarships and Fellowships for Math and Science Students.* Kantrowitz also is author of one of the best financial aid Web pages on the Internet (www.finaid.org), a site that is sponsored by the National Association of Student Financial Aid Administrators. All the books listed here are available in bookstores. You also may find them at your local library.

You Can Afford College: The Family Guide to Meeting College Costs by Bart Astor

The Princeton Review Student Access Guide to Paying for College by Kalman A. Chany

Internet Guide for College Bound Students by Kenneth E. Hartman

Don't Miss Out: The Ambitious Student's Guide to Financial Aid by Anna Leider

Wildlife Programs

National wildlife refuges across the country have educational programs and will send rangers with animals to schools or invite classes for trips through the refuge. A free booklet, "National Wildlife Refuges—A Visitor's Guide," will tell you what's available in your area. You can request it from the U.S. Fish and Wildlife Service, Publications Unit, Route 1, Box 166, Shepherd Grade Road, Shepherdstown, WV 25443.

Bringing Archeology Alive

The Heritage Education program, a hands-on learning project aimed at teaching students what life was like for the earliest North American inhabitants, takes traveling exhibits to schools and community groups. For a free brochure, write the Imagination Team, Bureau of Land Management, Anasazi Heritage Center, 27501 Highway 184, P.O. Box 758, Dolores, CO 81323.

➥ *WHAT INSIDERS SAY:*

Many nonprofit groups operating under government grants also offer special programs for elementary and secondary students. They may invite children to subsidized, low-cost performances, provide teacher training or assemblies at nominal cost, or even bring artists into the schools. To find out if there are groups in your area that offer opportunities like these, call the education and events program coordinator at your local museum, performing arts center, or regional theater.

SIX

Environment

CHAPTER 17

PUTTING
the GOVERNMENT'S
GREEN THUMB to WORK

Pretty much from the day it was founded, the United States has been a nation of gardeners. And growing right alongside the people who till the earth have been government agencies devoted to helping them keep their harvests healthy. Today, dozens of federal and state departments and many more nonprofit organizations offer assistance to beautify, renew, or improve your garden and yard. They'll offer you free or low-cost seeds, plants, pest controls, and advice on everything from growing old-time varieties of trees to building a pond. In fact, these agencies stop just short of digging your garden for you.

Why are they so interested in what goes on in your backyard? More than just about anywhere else in the world, we are a nation of homeowners. That means that the way we care for our properties has a big effect on the health of the United States. When several million people become involved in composting, recycling, gardening, conserving water, preventing soil erosion, and such, people in government and nonprofit groups pay attention.

As you'll see, the government and these groups have their hearts in the right place. And the people you contact—county extension agents, forestry experts, plant pathologists, entomologists, and volunteer Master Gardeners, for example—are almost all eager to help you.

> Do you want to turn your little plot into a piece of America the beautiful? Look to the government. From free advice and compost to low-cost trees and seeds, it offers help in hundreds of ways.

ADVICE

It's common to think of agencies like the USDA as consultants to America's big farmers. These days,

---

FACTOID

GORDON GRAHAM OF EDMUND, OKLAHOMA, IS THE WIZARD OF TOMATO GROWERS. HE ONCE GREW THE WORLD'S LARGEST TOMATO, A 7-POUND 12-OUNCE BEAST THAT WAS AS LARGE AS A CAULIFLOWER, AND HE HAS HAD TOMATO PLANTS AS BIG AS 28 FEET TALL AND 53½ FEET WIDE.

however, they are increasingly responsive to the needs of homeowners, even those whose "acreage" is nothing more than a few pots on a sunny windowsill. In fact, many programs are aimed specifically at helping individuals with their lawns and gardens.

As with much of what the government does, help for gardeners begins at the federal level and trickles down through state and local programs. The USDA generates most of the action through its many arms: the Forest Service, the Farm Service Agency, and the Natural Resources Conservation Service, among others.

At the state level, the USDA has established agricultural experiment stations at land-grant universities. At these special schools, scientists and teachers carry out research and education in farming, horticulture, and forestry. This isn't theoretical work; it's intended to have practical benefits for you, the taxpayer. To make sure that the information reaches you, it is available through cooperative extension agents who work in county offices throughout the United States. These experts are trained to help with all sorts of projects on the local level, from farm-scale problems to choosing plants for a patio. Here's how they and others can help you. For details on how to locate your local extension office, see "Tracking Down the Elusive Extension."

A Little-Known Treasure

Question: Who's the least-known but best source of advice on your yard and garden?

Answer: Your county cooperative extension agent.

Extension agents can offer advice on most aspects of your yard, from identifying bugs to helping you improve the yield from your apple tree. And they're great first contacts if you have trouble tracking down other programs in the maze of overlapping government agencies that offer services and goods for gardeners. Yet, they're so anonymous that when asked to name his office's least-appreciated service for homeowners, Dave Suchanic, a Pennsylvania extension agent in the ornamental horticulture program, answers, "Almost all of them."

If you have a question on any aspect of gardening, contact your extension office first. Ask if the extension has experts in the area in which you need advice. Many offices have agents who specialize in various home gardening fields—vegetables, ornamentals, fruit trees, pest control, and so on. Since each office reflects the needs of its county,

TRACKING DOWN THE ELUSIVE EXTENSION

Finding cooperative extension agents in the phone book can sometimes be a challenge. It's not that they're playing hard to get. The difficulty arises because their offices are typically supported by a combination of county, state, and federal funding, so there's no one logical place to list the number. You may find it in the white pages under the name of your state's land-grant university; in Pennsylvania, for example, you would look for the Penn State Cooperative Extension. Or check the government pages for "Agricultural Extension" or "Cooperative Extension" under the state department of agriculture or the USDA. If none of these options pans out, call your state legislator's office, listed in the government pages.

services vary. Offices in rural areas focus more on agriculture than horticulture. But even if your county office doesn't have a staff horticulturist, it will have fact sheets to help with your questions.

Free Help from Master Gardeners

Do you have the shabbiest lawn on the block? Are your shrubs refusing to flower? Help is a phone call away in the states that have Master Gardeners on staff to handle questions. These horticultural good angels, who volunteer their time, work under the direction of state agricultural extension offices.

First and foremost, these Master Gardeners are enthusiastic hobbyists. They have more than enthusiasm to offer, however, since each has completed the state extension's training program and an internship in gardening, and they keep up-to-date through annual in-service education sessions.

You can ask Master Gardeners for help with lawns, trees and shrubs, flowers, and vegetables— just about anything that grows. They may visit your property and chat with you in person, especially in more rural areas, and they may even pick up tools and give a hands-on demonstration. Chances are, there will be no charge for these services.

"Think of them as an extension of your county extension," says agent Deborah Van Arkel, formerly coordinator of Iowa's Master Gardener program. At last count, 45 states sponsored the program; to find out if the services of a Master Gardener are available to you, call your county's cooperative extension agent.

Landscape Designs on the Cheap

Just as barber schools offer bargain haircuts to give their students real-life experience, some landscape design schools offer design discounts so students

TOP STATE WEB SITES FOR GARDENERS

These days, the fastest way to get to a government expert or service may be to log on to the Internet rather than paging through the phone book or driving down to the local field office.

Just as public agencies once handed out pamphlets by the ream, they now have embraced cyberspace, and you are the beneficiary. A case in point is the illustrated online guide to more than two dozen problems afflicting tomatoes that's posted at a University of California Web page, http://vric. ucdavis.edu. Type in this address, follow the prompts to vegetable crops, and you can access a full-color gallery of tomato woes.

Most states now have Web sites that home gardeners will love. Here are five of the best in terms of information, ease of use, and just plain fun.

✓ Arizona:
http://ag.arizona.edu/
extension

✓ California:
www.uccencmr.ucdavis.edu

✓ Minnesota:
www.extension.umn.edu

✓ New Jersey:
www.rce.rutgers.edu

✓ New York:
www.cce.cornell.edu

can try out their stuff. A professor may be willing to take on your property as a class project. Or you can independently hire a student to come up with a design. You stand to pay less (probably less than half of the going price, according one college department's estimate) because the student needs the experience and is not yet registered or certified.

To find an undergraduate or graduate landscape design department in your area, contact the local branch of your state university or your county extension agent. Then call the landscape design department and speak to a professor about having a class work on your property in an upcoming term.

To hire a fledgling landscaper, ask the department to post a notice outlining what you have in mind. In the University of Pennsylvania's graduate program, the design department publicizes these requests in a "job book," which students can look through for opportunities.

●➔ *WHAT INSIDERS SAY:*

Want to improve your chances of getting a professor or student to take on your yard? Explain what makes it unique and play up the features that might make an interesting challenge for designers, like water on the property or a rock outcropping.

Rx for Sick Trees

If you're faced with a sickly maple in your front yard, you might not think to dial the state forestry department for help. Don't they have their hands full with forests, after all? In fact, foresters have a growing appreciation for the problems of suburban, and even urban, landowners.

Many agencies are staffed with specialists who are trained to help treat the ailments of lawn trees that are bothered by insects, disease, drought, or environmental stress. Their concern goes beyond the appearance of your yard and street; healthy trees can help everyone by helping to cool and filter the air and even cut down on noise pollution. To contact your state forestry experts, look in the government pages of the phone book under terms like "Parks and Forestry" and "Conservation and Natural Resources."

On a local level, many towns offer the services of an "urban arborist." Check with the parks bureau or public services department in your city or town. The number is listed in the local government pages of your phone book.

●➔ *WHAT INSIDERS SAY:*

Before you call for advice, be prepared with specifics: the tree's history, estimated size, species, and location. That information will give the expert on the other end of the line a better chance of telling you what's wrong.

Restarting "Stuck" Compost

Is your compost pile "stuck," refusing to digest its meals of yard litter? If you have Internet access, you can get practical advice to get your pile churning again by contacting the Compost Connection at

GET YOUR EARLY FROST WARNINGS HERE

Are you worried that a frost might blacken your basil or ruin your petunias? You don't need to buy a weather radio to find the answer. If you can access the Internet, you can visit Pennsylvania State University's Department of Meteorology's Web site and get extended forecasts for many parts of the country. Maintained as a public service by Penn State and other universities and organizations around the country, the site also offers current weather observations, satellite and radar weather images, and severe and tropical storm warnings. The Web address is www.ems.psu.edu/wx.

http://csanr.wsu.edu/compost. Click on "The Compost Connection Newsletter," an online publication of the Washington State University Center for Sustainable Agriculture and Natural Resources.

How to Put a Pond Together

A pond can be the centerpiece of a property, but pond construction and maintenance are involved matters. You need a reliable source of water, and that big hole in the ground has to do a good job of holding it. Plus, ponds are catchalls for fertilizer runoff, which can lead to problems with algae blooms and fish kills.

If you are considering building a new pond, contact your county's office of the federal Natural Resources Conservation Service for advice. The level of help will vary, since some offices are strapped for staff and funding. In some offices, however, agents can advise you about costs, perform a soil analysis to determine if your site will hold water, offer tips on planning and constructing the pond, and help you select species of fish with which to stock it. Some even make on-site visits to survey the area and supervise construction.

The conservation agency should be listed in the government pages under the USDA or possibly under its former name, the Soil Conservation Service. You can also check with your state's department of natural resources. Names vary by state, so check the government section of your phone book.

TESTS

Often, when things go wrong with plants, you end up stymied. You're not sure whether your plants' ill health is caused by insects, disease, soil imbalance, or just plain bad care—overwatering has killed many an otherwise healthy plant.

If you're puzzling over a plant, your county cooperative extension office is a good place to consult first (for details on how to locate your local extension office, see "Tracking Down the Elusive Extension" on page 284). Although in the past these offices concentrated on doing tests for commercial growers, they now offer gardeners many of the same services. And even when your local office can't help directly, it often can refer you to other agencies that can. Here are some of the best services you'll find at the local, state, and federal levels.

Getting the Dirt On Your Dirt

As the title of one gardening book says, it all starts with the soil, for down in the dirt is where the health, size, and vibrancy of everything you grow begins. Even small imbalances—either too much or too little of the right ingredients—can cause problems, so it's important to test the levels of nutrients and pH (acidity) every 3 years, or even more often if what you're growing is a heavy feeder.

Fortunately, agricultural extension offices in many states offer low-cost soil-test kits. The price covers the cost of tests in a state laboratory, along with recommendations on how to improve your soil. Simpler tests deal with pH, phosphorus, potassium, calcium, and magnesium, but some states offer a broader analysis. For example, for just $7 (in state) and $10.50 (out of state), the Virginia Tech Soil-Testing Lab will check for the above components plus zinc, manganese, copper, iron, and boron. You can contact the lab at 145 Smyth Hall, Blacksburg, VA 24061.

The more items included in a test, the better the portrait you get of your soil. Give your cooperative extension a call to find if it will mail you a test kit; in some states, you have to pick them up at either the extension office or a garden supply store that stocks them as a convenience for customers.

Typically, after collecting a soil sample, you mail the soil to a central laboratory. Results should reach you in from 1 to 3 weeks; to speed replies, some states now will notify you via e-mail or fax or post your results on their Web sites. The instructions that come with the kit will tell you how your state makes findings available.

◆ WHAT INSIDERS SAY:

Like gardeners themselves, soil-test labs are busy in the spring. You stand to get faster service if you send off soil samples in the fall. Another advantage to fall testing is that you'll have time to adjust the soil's pH for spring planting if the test suggests adding lime to correct a problem with acidity.

Also, if your state doesn't offer the tests you want, check with neighboring states; they may handle tests for nonresidents, but you can expect to pay roughly double for the service.

Maybe Your Whole Yard Is Sick

If your plants and trees aren't growing well, and you suspect that the problem may be bigger than a few missing minerals, there is another approach

you can take: Zoom in on your neighborhood with the U.S. Environmental Protection Agency's remarkable maps of environmental messes. Log on to the Internet at www.epa.gov/enviro/html/mod/index.html and you can check your area for Superfund cleanup sites, discharges into streams, toxic releases, hazardous waste handlers, and other good reasons that you might want to look elsewhere to grow.

Putting a Name On That Crawler

Are your plants being bugged by an unfamiliar insect, disease, or weed? The county extension office may be able to identify it for you. Depending on the type of problem, agents may ask to see anything from a leaf to the entire plant, with the roots and soil ball included. If they're stumped, they may refer you to the state's testing facilities. The service is free of charge in some states; elsewhere, charges range

Amazing Stories

A WAY TO GET YOUR GOAT

Clearing weeds is usually an unpleasant task, but the city of Denver has come up with a novel approach: Hire goats to do the dirty work.

Each year, 50 to 100 Kashmir goats are brought in during early spring, midsummer, and fall to clear harmful weeds from the banks of Denver's rivers. "The noxious weeds are the ones that the goats like best, so they do the job pretty quickly," says Judy Montero, spokeswoman for the Denver Parks and Recreation Department.

It's all part of a program designed to restore and protect the wilderness adjacent to the

rivers. Because the animals graze in a way similar to that of the bison that were once native to the area (and because once the area is reseeded with native seeds, the foot action of the goats helps to drive them into the ground), the weed-clearing program encourages more desirable plant growth while cutting down on the need for high-tech weed management.

"This is a weed-management strategy that allows us to stop using pesticides and mechanical lawn mowers," says Montero, "and it's a chance for parents and kids to see working animals in the heart of a city."

from $5 and up. Contact your local extension office to find out about potential charges in your area.

●◆ WHAT INSIDERS SAY:

Mailing bugs can be a challenge because they're delicate, and identifying them depends on getting them to the experts in one piece. To make sure that a larger insect gets where you want it to go, seal it in a small, sturdy cardboard box, such as a gift box for jewelry. To mail small, fragile insects (such as aphids, mites, and caterpillars), put them in a small, well-sealed bottle of rubbing (isopropyl) alcohol. Then place the bottle in a sturdy cardboard box with enough padding to keep it from shifting around.

Diagnosing a Sick Lawn

For most homeowners, their biggest crops are their lawns. When it gets sick, the whole neighborhood knows, making a cure all the more urgent. In some states, you can get the county cooperative extension to analyze your lawn and recommend a cure. The procedure typically involves cutting out sample plugs from the area where the good grass turns strange and mailing in the samples. Check with your extension agent to see if this service is available.

Inspections for Your Beehive

Honeybees are notoriously vulnerable to diseases and parasites, and some states offer free inspections of hives to keep problems from spreading from one site to another. Ask your cooperative extension agent whether your state offers inspections and whom you should contact if it does.

Keeping the Old Pond Healthy

If you have a pond on your property, it may be picking up polluting agricultural chemicals from runoff, depending on what it's downstream from. Fertilizers, in particular, can come cascading off fields and cause excessive growth of algae, harming fish and making the pond unattractive as well. If you suspect that runoff is causing a problem, contact your county agriculture board or cooperative extension agent. They sometimes offer free water tests to landowners.

PEST CONTROL

Mosquitoes and dandelions aren't just backyard nuisances. When insects and seeds get out of hand, it may take a community-level response to control them.

In some parts of the country, bugs can make it all but impossible to enjoy the outdoors during certain times of the year. And these humming pests do more than make you itch. Mosquitoes, for example, may be carriers of diseases, including encephalitis, some forms of which can be fatal.

As for weeds, they cause problems by reproducing themselves so enthusiastically that they displace native plants and elevate pollen counts. If you're concerned about pests in your yard, here are some places to look for aid.

Help With Bloodsucking Bugs

The standard fix for mosquitoes is to spray insecticides. In heavily settled areas, however, nonchemical methods are increasingly popular, including biological control by fish.

Attacking Bugs Where They Breed

If you live near the water, you have one constant in your life: bugs that bite. Fortunately, your county or state may have programs to help you control mosquitoes without spraying. In Connecticut, the Wetlands Habitat and Mosquito Management Program of the state's department of environmental protection encourages native killifish to eat the pests' waterborne larvae. Workers provide habitat for the killifish by digging shallow ponds in tidal marshlands or plugging old ditches so they hold water. The fish arrive with the next flooding tide and complete their work.

For more information about Connecticut's programs, write to Franklin WMA, 391 Route 32, North Franklin, CT 06254, and ask for a free copy of their brochure, "Connecticut Mosquito Management Program." You can also contact the environmental protection agency in your state to see if it offers a similar service; the number is in the government pages of your phone book.

New Jersey's Cape May County Mosquito Commission will visit county homeowners' properties and monitor for the pests, using water samples to check for larvae and light traps to snare adults on the wing. If the commission confirms a problem, it can drain stagnant water and fill in breeding ponds on your property for no charge. Contact the commission at P.O. Box 66, Cape May Courthouse, NJ 08210.

In several areas of the country, public agencies distribute free mosquitofish (*Gambusia affinis*) to landowners. This is an exotic species that has a particularly keen appetite for the pests' wriggling larvae and pupae, which live in water. A single fish may eat more than 100 larvae a day. The Mosquito Abatement District in Alameda County, California, uses the fish and also goes a step further. The staff visits county residents who are beleaguered by mosquitoes and offers to knock drain holes in ornamental concrete pools to prevent the pests from breeding; the holes are made as small as possible so that the pools can someday be repaired for future use. To find out more about the program, contact the Alameda County Mosquito Abatement District, 23187 Connecticut Street, Haward, CA, 94545.

How to Get Rid of Gators

Landowners who build ponds for fish and wildlife can be surprised by the wild things that move in. In the Southeast, alligators often find family ponds to their liking—and their numbers are increasing, thanks in part to strict federal and state protection. Their range is growing, too, with the big reptiles now living as far north as Virginia.

Alligators won't affect the catch of fish from your pond, but they may eat turtles, frogs, snakes, birds, and mammals that venture into the water—including small dogs, according to Walt Rhodes, alligator project supervisor at the South Carolina Department of Natural Resources. If you are concerned about a gator guest, contact your state's department of natural resources.

Don't be surprised if you seem to have a return visit, though. Alligators have a knack for finding their way to ponds. Once the original occupant is gone, a new gator may take its place.

Amazing Stories

AIRBORNE FISH?

Imagine it—a fish for backyard pools that snaps mosquitoes right out of the air before they can spoil your cookouts. That was the good news reported by a California newspaper not long ago, but unfortunately, it stretched the truth.

As helpful as mosquitofish have proved to be, they can do nothing about adult pests on the wing, according to John Rusmisel, manager of the Mosquito Abatement District in Alameda County. That was the bad news that he had to tell the 600 mosquito-slapping homeowners who called about the remarkable fish. Stocking a pool with the fish is only a preventive measure that is useful for controlling the earlier life stages of mosquitoes.

Putting Bees in All the Right Places

Honeybees may be a nuisance at certain times and in certain places. Nevertheless, they are beneficial insects, responsible for pollinating many essential crops. Some municipalities will go out of their way to remove swarms or hives and release them in the countryside. In Los Angeles County, for example, workers suck up these good bees with a "bee vacuum" and carry them off in a small cage. And across the country, you can call police departments or extension agents for the phone numbers of beekeepers who will gather swarms free of charge. In southern states, extension agents themselves may pick up a swarm on the chance that it is a gang of infamous "killer bees" (see "Attack of the Killer Bees" on page 292). Ask your cooperative extension agent whether your area offers bee control and whom to call if it does (for details on how to locate your local extension office, see "Tracking Down the Elusive Extension" on page 284).

How to Whip Those Weeds

Ever since the first weed ordinance was passed (against Canadian thistle in Connecticut, back in the 1830s), weeds have been treated as public enemies. Some, like purple loosestrife, are lovely but invasive. Others can make you itch or sneeze. And a few, marijuana among them, have druglike properties that have led to their control by the government. If you have trouble with wild weeds, here are some places to for help.

Zap Your Neighbor's Weed Patch

Both municipal and state agencies may come to your rescue if the guy next door is raising a luxuriant crop of weeds, because it doesn't take many weed seeds to infiltrate a street of lovely lawns. Not just any weed will interest the government, however; it must be a species named in an official list of noxious plants. Your first step is to identify the plants in question, using a field guide; if you don't own one, check a copy out of the public library.

Your county extension agent may be able to help you name a weed that doesn't seem to match any of the pictures (for details on how to locate your local extension office, see "Tracking Down the Elusive Extension" on page 284).

Your next step is to ask either your town zoning officer or county extension agent for an official list of noxious weeds. If the weeds that you've identified are on the list, talk with your neighbor and discuss your concern. If the neighborly approach doesn't work, contact your municipality and ask it to enforce its laws. Typically, the weeds must be mowed or sprayed within a certain period of time. If they are not, the authority may levy a fine or do the job itself and bill the offender.

◆❖ WHAT INSIDERS SAY:

Your municipality may not consider your weed complaint serious enough to pursue with the neighbor. If you find this is the case, try going over their heads by contacting the state's noxious weed program. This is usually part of the state department of agriculture, which is listed in the government pages in the phone book.

Battling Invading Plants

In some parts of the country, invasive plants—meaning those that force out other, more desirable plants—may grow so enthusiastically that it is all but impossible for tree seedlings that you plant to survive. If your young trees are threatened, check with your county and state foresters. They may subsidize your expenses for spraying to control invasive ferns, barberry, multiflora rose, and other troublesome plants, typically reimbursing you on a per-acre basis. Contact the district forester, listed in the government pages of your phone book under the state department of forestry.

Put a Damper On Waterborne Weeds

Weeds don't just grow on land, as most pond owners can tell you. Because you can't very well go into your pond with a mower and weed whacker, aquatic weeds are apt to grow lavishly. A first step in controlling a pond weed is to identify it, and wildflower guides may not be of much help. Consult your county extension office. Its agents may be able to provide just the advice you need to identify and control your pest. If they can't, they may suggest sending a sample of the weed to a state laboratory for identification and suggestions on how to control it (see "Tracking Down the Elusive Extension" on page 284 for details on locating your local extension office).

ATTACK OF THE KILLER BEES

It may sound like something from a bad science fiction movie, but africanized honeybees are attacking people and animals in the United States, forcing municipalities and states in the southern part of the country to control these pests and alert the public.

The africanized bee is a highly defensive species that has been working its way northward from Brazil since the 1950s. Texas was the pest's first beachhead in the United States, and it is now found in Deep Southern states, including Arizona, New Mexico, California, and Nevada.

"Killer" may be an exaggeration, but not by much. A grim fact about this species dates to 1984, when a University of Miami graduate student in Puerto Rico died after being stung 8,000 times. Contrary to rumor, the stings of an africanized bee aren't any worse than those from a honeybee in your backyard. But the africanized species is very defensive about its colonies, so hordes of them will attack repeatedly for seemingly small insults.

If you think that these bees may be in your area, Eric Erickson, Ph.D., director of the USDA's Carl Hayden Bee Research Center in Tucson, suggests the following strategies.

✓ Avoid wearing either fuzzy or dark-colored clothing so you don't look like the furry animals that are the bees' natural enemies.

✓ Refrain from using perfume and any other scented products.

✓ Wear long-sleeved shirts and long pants.

✓ If you are attacked, run for a shelter, such as a building or a car. Bees may follow you for up to $\frac{1}{2}$ mile. Cover your head and try not to swat at them (this just angers them further). Don't jump into the water; they'll just be waiting when you come up for air.

If someone is being attacked, call 911 before offering assistance. Actually, it's better if you forget about going to the aid of someone who is being stung, because you could become a victim yourself. Encourage the victim to run from the area. If you must help (if, for instance, the victim is very young or infirm), cover yourself with a blanket, go to the victim, cover him with a blanket, and escort him to shelter.

Your best bet is prevention. If you live in the southern tier of states where the bees have been reported, inspect your property for colonies. As yet, there is no single government agency to deal with the bees. Depending on where you live, you may have to try the city health, emergency medical, and fire departments. Private pest control operators are also valuable sources of assistance.

GARDENING GIVEAWAYS

As gardening insiders will tell you, people who love plants also love to give them away or sell them at low cost. Both government forestry departments and nonprofit gardening groups offer a wealth of vegetation—from marigolds to sugar maples—that you can grow to provide food, landscaping, wildlife habitat, and shelter from the elements. Often, government groups will charge modest prices—just enough to keep from putting commercial growers out of business—while with nonprofit gardening groups, you'll often have to pay just enough to cover postage and handling.

The largesse doesn't stop there. Many local governments and utilities offer mulch and manure free for the asking. Gardening doesn't have to be an expensive hobby if you follow the following tips.

Unique Plants and Seeds for Less

Chances are, you have houseplants that friends gave you for nothing. In the same way, you can get free or inexpensive seeds and plants from gardeners around the world. Nonprofit networks bring thousands of backyard growers together to share the plants—vegetables, herbs, flowers, and fruits—that they love best. In some cases, you may have to pay a membership fee and join the organization to get great deals on plants, but usually your dues buy you catalogs, newsletters, and free advice in addition to the plants. That's a good deal for one small price of admission.

On top of that, through your membership and the exchanges you make, you help to preserve hundreds of quirky, distinctive plants that might otherwise become extinct, such as Cherokee Trail of Tears beans and the pinkish Brandywine tomatoes said to be the finest variety anywhere. Here are some of the choicest deals available.

Antique Vegetable Seeds

Do you have memories of great-tasting tomatoes and salad greens and carrots from your youth? Or maybe you've heard a parent or grandparent rave about vegetables as they used to be, before seed conglomerates and supermarkets dictated the varieties we eat. If so, you'll be intrigued by the *Seed Savers Yearbook*, an annual compendium of seeds for more than 10,000 unusual, obscure, and just plain odd vegetables. These plants are grown in backyards around the world by members of the nonprofit Seed Savers Exchange and kept alive from year to year by their efforts.

To get a yearbook, sign up by sending $30 for a year's membership to Seed Savers Exchange, 3076 North Winn Road, Decorah, IA 52101. Then order away. Selections have included Hermit horseradish, found on the site of an upstate New York hermit's cabin; Mostoller Wild Goose bean, supposedly pried out of a goose's innards and then planted and grown for more than a century by the Mostoller family of western Pennsylvania; and Aunt Ruby's German Green, a tomato that is actually green when ripe.

The prices of seeds vary and are set by the members.

Flower and Herb Exchange

Seeds for more than 2,000 unusual flowers and herbs are available through the Flower and Herb Exchange, 3076 North Winn Road, Decorah, IA 52101. Its yearbook is distributed to members, who pay $10 a year. Again, the prices of seed packets vary. Interesting items include Poor Man's Weather Glass (with "scarlet flowers which open with sun, shut when cloudy") and black cumin ("blue flowers, aromatic black seeds have fennel odor with peppery nutmeg flavor, used in Russian rye bread").

You can get a free 40-page catalog from either Seed Savers (see above) or the Flower and Herb Exchange even if you don't want to become a member. Your selections will be far fewer, and seed packets will cost more, but it is a good introduction to what's available. Both catalogs will give you membership information.

Easy Access to Affordable Fruit

If you're one of the fruit and nut lovers in this country, you're caught in a bit of a quandary. There are almost limitless varieties of your favorite foods—more than 1,000 varieties of apples alone are grown around the United States—but you'll sample only a few types unless you go beyond the meager offerings of standard supermarkets. What to do? Grow your own, with the help of government and nonprofit groups. Here are several sources.

Low-Cost Apple Cuttings

You can make your own multiflavored apple tree by adding short sections of living branches (called scions) to an existing tree. Once they mature, each new branch will grow a different variety. Scions of more than 100 old-time apples are available each spring from the Worcester County Horticultural Society, Tower Hill Botanic Garden, 11 French Drive, P.O. Box 598, Boylston, MA 01505-0598.

This nonprofit society goes to the trouble of cutting all those little sticks because of a mission. It wants to help ensure that antique apple varieties— a number of them natives of New England—will survive well into the new millennium. Scions are just $2.50 each, including postage, with a minimum order of $10; all orders must be received before March 15 each year. You can find instructions for grafting scions onto a tree in any good book on orcharding, or contact your extension agent (for details on how to locate your local extension office, see "Tracking Down the Elusive Extension" on page 284).

Fruit and Nut Tree Exchanges

Like gardeners, home fruit growers love to trade advice, opinions, and plants. North American Fruit Explorers, Inc., is a nonprofit group of passionate growers who share their know-how and offer trees and bushes for sale in a friendly, informative quarterly called *Pomona*. Some examples of members' offerings: nut trees for less than $1 each and highly unusual pear varieties that are grown for making perry, as hard pear cider is known. Membership in the group costs $10; a subscription to the magazine is included. Write to 1716 Apples Road, Chapin, IL 62628.

Taste the Fruit before Buying the Tree

It takes a half-hour to plant an apple tree and then at least another 5 years until you get to taste the fruit. Thus, it's smart to make sure that you like the taste and texture of a variety before committing yourself. Fall tastings are held around the country at events sponsored by nonprofit organizations. Here are two of the best; write for more information on their programs.

What Is It?

"SCIONS"

Apple trees don't grow true to seed, the way a tomato or zinnia does. Plant a seed from a great-tasting apple, and there's no telling what sort of fruit the offspring tree will produce. Chances are, it will be inferior. Because of this, apple trees are reproduced by taking a small section of living branch—called a scion—from one species of apple tree and attaching, or grafting, it to the base of a tree of another species. The scion determines what the apples will look like; the base regulates the tree's size.

✓ Midwest Fruit Explorers, P.O. Box 93, Markham, IL 60426

✓ Monticello, P.O. Box 217, Charlottesville, VA 22902 (preregistration is required for this very popular program)

Finding Trees for a Song

Wouldn't it be nice if someone paid you to care for your lawn? Dream on. But a number of state and federal agencies *will* underwrite the planting and care of trees on your property, even if you have only a modest suburban lot.

The reason for this generosity is simple. Public agencies have found that by offering incentives to families across the country—free or inexpensive seedlings, free consultation, and all sorts of cost-sharing programs—they can do a lot to keep America's forested acres healthy, productive, and in their natural, undeveloped state.

Most of the government's support begins with the USDA, then goes through the U.S. Forest Service to forestry departments in each of the 50 states. From the state level, funds may be further channeled through local and nonprofit organizations.

Your best contact is the state's district forester, who is a member of the forestry department. This agency may be part of a larger one such as the state's department of environmental conservation, so you may have to check several places in the government pages of your phone book to get the right number. If you have trouble tracking it down, ask your county extension agent for help (for details on how to locate your local extension office, see "Tracking Down the Elusive Extension" on page 284). The district forester can be something of a nature-appreciation guide, happy to introduce you to the many pleasures of living with trees, whether you have just a few or a real forest.

➽ WHAT INSIDERS SAY:
Inexpensive government trees not only provide shelter for wildlife, they can keep your family warm as well. "Trees have dozens of real, practical uses," says Kevin

Keys, state service forester for Stephens County, Oklahoma, "including windbreaks. Windbreaks are especially important here to lower heating expenses for homeowners." A living barrier to winter winds can cut heating costs by up to 30 percent. Before you order seedlings for a windbreak, ask your district forester's help in planning its location and shape for best effect.

Seedlings from Your State Forest

Are you the patient type who's willing to wait a few years for regal trees to fill your lot or the woodland you'd like to grow? If so, your state forestry department has a deal for you in the form of inexpensive tree seedlings.

While some states concentrate on just a few of the most popular species, others offer an intriguing selection of nut- and fruit-bearing trees and shrubs. Ohio's nurseries sell pawpaw, an unsung native American fruit tree; Oklahoma lists wild plum and Osage orange, which, in spite of their names, don't produce suitable fruit for humans but are excellent sources of food and habitat for wildlife.

Although costs typically are kept low to encourage you to get out there and plant seedlings, the little trees may not be available at giveaway prices. Some states have made their offers less generous in order to avoid undercutting (and angering) commercial nurseries. As examples of what you can expect to pay, Montana sells 1- and 2-year-old conifers in containers for $33 to $120 per 100 seedlings; most are from 6 to 12 inches tall. In Indiana, all 1-year-old, bareroot deciduous tree seedlings are $20 per 100 trees; they range from 6 to 20 inches tall. Kentuckians can order 50 seedlings for $15.

How many you'll have to buy depends on your state's rules. In Oklahoma, the minimum buy is 200 seedlings. If that is far too many for your needs, consider finding neighbors who will split a big order with you.

States vary in delivery policies. Kentucky will ship trees to residents' homes at the residents' cost, while other states require that you pick up the trees in person.

Some states have a minimum property size to qualify for a seedling buy. In Colorado, you need to have at least 2 acres, while in Montana, you'll get first pick from the nursery if you have at least 10 acres; people with less land can't place orders until after February 28.

Some states place other restrictions on their sales, perhaps requiring that you use the trees to grow a woodland, not landscape your yard. As with pricing, the idea is to avoid competing with private nurseries. "We try to keep the commercial nursery people happy," explains John Justin of Montana's Conservation Seedling Nursery in Missoula.

◆◇ WHAT INSIDERS SAY:

Does your state have a meager variety of trees available? Check with nurseries of neighboring states. You may find one that offers an interesting selection and will ship to out-of-state customers. Nursery officials caution, however, that their trees are selected to do well in a specific area and may not flourish out of state. Also note that your order may be filled only after state residents have gotten first pick.

County Seedling Sales

A good source for just a few inexpensive trees is the spring seedling sale that many county conservation districts conduct. You may even find that your local district will let you preorder in small quantities, reserving trees before the date of the sale. For details, check with your conservation district; you can find the number in the government pages of your phone book under the county office listings.

Free Trees for Members

If you join the nonprofit National Arbor Day Foundation for $10, it will send you 10 complimentary trees selected to do well in your area. The seedlings average 6 to 12 inches tall and will arrive in either spring or fall, at the proper time for planting depending on the species. Write the National Arbor Day Foundation, 100 Arbor Avenue, Nebraska City, NE 68410.

◆◇ WHAT INSIDERS SAY:

Not all trees take to transplanting equally well, says Randy Moench, nursery manager at the state of Colorado's Nursery and Conservation Tree-Planting Program. Evergreen seedlings are more prone to drying out, and they stand a better chance of surviving if you get them in containers, with soil around the roots. Deciduous trees—those that drop their broad leaves each fall—don't have to be pampered in the same way, which is why they're often sold bareroot.

Forest Transplants

The Forest Service has come up with a great idea— to let park visitors in the Northwest dig up and remove trees along power line rights of way and in stands where a species is becoming too crowded.

At Oregon's Willamette National Forest, for example, you can pick up a free permit and take a maximum of 12 transplants, as long as they are less than 2 feet tall. Choices include the wild, pink-flowering rhododendrons that grow in these lush woods. At Sawtooth National Forest in Idaho, a $10 permit allows you to dig five of the aspen that spring up so plentifully there.

The most popular transplants in Washington's Gifford Pinchot National Forest are mountain hemlock, lodgepole pine, subalpine fir, noble fir, and vine maple. These native species are desirable because they have adapted naturally to the local climate and thrive better than commercially grown trees trucked into a garden center. A free permit allows you to collect up to $20 worth of seedlings per year. Harvesting seedlings or young trees in early spring or late fall increases the chances that the trees will survive. Check with the office of the particular forest where you'd like to harvest to see if public digging is allowed.

A Fir for Christmas

For many families who live within driving distance of our state and national forests, harvesting their own low-cost Christmas trees is an annual event. Trees taken from the wild not only cost less but also have an informal, natural look that's missing in commercial evergreens that have been pruned into geometrically perfect cones.

Another plus for saw-wielding families is that wild specimens were grown without the benefit of herbicides, fertilizers, and mechanical cultivation. Also, the forest may offer interesting species that aren't available commercially. At Idaho's Sawtooth National Forest, Ed Waldapfel says a regional favorite is the juniper. It grows like a weed and puts off a substance that discourages the growth of surrounding plants, but families like its distinctive scent and come back to cut a tree every year. If the snow flies early, some even come for their tree on cross-country skis.

Contact the nearest Forest Service ranger district office or your state forest department to check on cutting periods and permits in your area. Your state agency may be listed as a bureau or division under the department of natural resources, environmental protection, conservation, or agriculture. If you can't find the listing, contact your county extension agent (for details on how to locate your local extension office, see "Tracking Down the Elusive Extension" on page 284).

Cost generally ranges from $5 to $10 per tree. In some parks, that buys you an 8-footer; if you have a high ceiling and want a taller tree, there may be a surcharge for each additional foot.

◗◗ WHAT INSIDERS SAY:

Considering harvesting your own tree? Rangers caution that you should dress warmly and make sure that your vehicle can handle the back roads that lead to the best trees. When harvesting a tree, cut it close to the ground, rather than taking the top half of a nice specimen and leaving a tall stump to disfigure the forest.

Free Plants and Rocks

State and national forests yield many items that are free for the taking. Remember to check in with a ranger when you arrive. Describe your plans and inquire about limits, areas that are restricted, and maximum amounts that you can take. Fill out and pay for permits if necessary. Here are some examples of what's available.

✓ You can gather enough evergreen boughs to deck the house, within limits, at many national forests. If you are interested in amounts that would be considered commercial— at Willamette National Forest in Oregon, that means 25 pounds or more—ask about purchasing a special permit.

✓ At Oregon's Mount Hood National Forest, you can harvest such perennial plants as ferns, Oregon grape, and beargrass in modest amounts for floral arrangements for free, but you will need to get a permit.

✓ Some parks allow you to quarry shale for walkways or patios—up to 300 pounds a year—for no charge.

✓ You also can harvest berries, nuts, mushrooms, and much more (see "Foraging in the Forest" on page 39 for more information on these items).

To find out if there are national forests in your area, look in the government pages of the phone book under the USDA listings for "Forest Service" or "National Parks." If you can't find anything there, you can write to USDA, Forest Service, Office of Communications, P.O. Box 96090, Washington, DC 20090-6090, and ask for a free copy of "A Guide to Your National Forests." For nearby state forests, look in the government pages of your phone book under the state listings for the department of forestry or natural resources.

Your Own Wildlife Refuge

Wetlands are valuable—and vulnerable—parts of the landscape. They are home to a great variety of plants and animals and tend to lose soil to erosion if it is not anchored by vegetation. The U.S. Fish and Wildlife Service works with landowners to restore these special areas by providing technical assistance and, in many cases, paying for at least a portion of the improvements through their Partners for Fish and Wildlife Program. To date, the service has helped some 17,000 landowners. A staff biologist in each state is responsible for running this program. To contact the nearest office, look in the government pages under the U.S. Department of the Interior. If you have trouble finding the listing, ask your county extension agent for help (for details on how to locate your local extension office, see "Tracking Down the Elusive Extension" on page 284).

Mulch and Compost for the Taking

Many counties and municipalities perform the double service of hauling away grass clippings, leaves, and brush and then making them available to the public as compost and mulch. The advantage for them is that it reduces the amount of solid waste that ends up in local landfills.

That amount can be substantial. The city of Fort Worth, Texas, estimates that its solid waste volume jumps 20 to 50 percent during lawn-mowing season.

Local government isn't the only source of free nutrients for your garden, however, and your choices aren't limited to just compost and mulch. Here's a look at some of the offerings.

Power Line Mulch

Electric utilities are always cutting back trees that threaten to overtake their rights of way, and the trimmings are reduced to a coarse mulch—mountains of the stuff. Some companies will take your name and notify you when a crew is scheduled to work in your area. For the customer service number of your local utility, look in the yellow pages under "Electric Companies."

●◆ *WHAT INSIDERS SAY:*

You can't argue with the price of free wood-chip mulch from electric company trimmings, but it might not be an ideal product for all uses. You are apt to get a mix of both coniferous and deciduous material; it is coarse, and coniferous mulch is on the acid side, which favors some plants and discourages others. Check with your county extension agent if you're unsure how the mulch will affect your plants (for details on how to locate your local extension office, see "Tracking Down the Elusive Extension" on page 284).

Police Horse Manure

If your community has a mounted police unit, it has a source of rich manure. "People don't realize it's there and that it would be great in the garden," says Sergeant Mike Wilske of the Seattle Mounted Police. If you are interested and your police department has a mounted unit, call the department's general information number and ask whether it offers free manure.

On the other coast, the New York City Police Department has a mounted unit of 100 horses, and although there's no program for giving the manure away, residents are allowed to stop by the city's six stables and take what they need.

●◆ *WHAT INSIDERS SAY:*

Zoos produce a lot of manure, and you'd think that they'd be a gold mine of free fertilizer for gardeners. But along came someone with a stroke of marketing genius—boutique manure. The stuff has been transformed from a nuisance to a gift shop item. The Philadelphia Zoo, with 1,800 animals, packages its exotic manure in little 2.2-pound bags and sells them in its shop for $2.95 each. It's enough to make a cow jealous.

FACTOID

LOS ANGELES IS NO LONGER THE WILD WEST, BUT A SURPRISING NUMBER OF HORSES ARE STILL CORRALLED THERE—1,500 BY OFFICIAL COUNT—AND THEY GENERATE AN IMPRESSIVE AMOUNT OF MANURE (L.A CONTENDS WITH 10 TONS DAILY). THE CITY HAS RESPONDED BY DROPPING OFF SPECIAL 30-GALLON MANURE CONT.AINERS AT STABLES SO IT CAN COLLECT THE MANURE AT NOMINAL CHARGE TO THE HORSE OWNERS.

Tree Mulch

Some municipalities collect and mulch discarded trees. Most that do require residents to pick up the finished mulch themselves, but your town might be one of the few to deliver right to your door for a small charge. Citizens of Chatham Township, New Jersey, can have a pickup-truckload dropped off for $25.

Discounted Compost Bins

Before you spend a lot of money on a good compost bin, find out whether your waste authority sells them at a deep discount. San Jose, California does this as a way to reduce the amount of waste it has to process or bury in a landfill. The city offers citizens a heavy-duty Smith and Hawken bin for $43. That's $37 less than retail. And if you want to enlist worms to speed up the process, the city will sell you a Can-O-Worms Vermicomposting Bin ("the Cadillac of worm bins," says the city Web site) at half price—$60.

Seattle residents are eligible for low-cost bins through the free workshops sponsored by Seattle Public Utilities, Dexter Horton Building, 710 Second Avenue, 10th Floor, Seattle, WA 98104-1717.

Dumpsters on Loan

Here is an idea that's worth testing around the country. In Lexington and surrounding Fayette County, Kentucky, the waste authority is so eager to encourage recycling that it will drop off 10-cubic-yard boxes in front of residents' homes if they have yard debris to dispose of. Homeowners fill the box over the weekend with leaves, tree limbs, and other waste, then the authority drives it away to a landfill. The charge is just $38 per load. To find out more, contact the Division of Solid Waste at 675 Byrd Thurman Drive, Lexington, KY 40510.

Grow Your Own Animals

You can think of bird eggs as large (and fragile) seeds that produce either meat or pets. The eggs themselves may be free or very inexpensive, but the birds will be more demanding of your time and money than, say, a row of radishes. Still, if you have the land, either wild or domestic fowl are fascinating for kids to have around. Here is one way to get bird eggs at a bargain.

Quail Eggs, Free for the Hatching

Many state game and wildlife departments raise quail and pheasants and then release them into the wild to give hunters something to shoot. Eggs are sold in quantity to game clubs, but you may be able to pick up a half-dozen or so free, for educational use. Hatch them at home or send them off to school with your child for a science project. Look in the state listings in the government pages of the phone book for "Game Commission" or "Fish, Game, and Wildlife Commission," then call to see if it offers this service.

Fish for Your Pond

A pond can be a self-contained ecosystem: Little organisms are eaten by little fish, and big fish eat the little fish. Then, presumably, you eat the big fish, with some help from blue herons, kingfishers, ospreys, or other birds. A standard little fish/big fish combo is bluegills and bass, and some states will sell you 1-inch-long fingerlings of both species for a modest cost. In South Carolina, for example, the Freshwater Fisheries Section of the Department of Natural Resources provides residents with enough bass and bluegill fingerlings to stock a 1-acre pond for as little as $38.50. To find out if your state offers this service, call the state fish and wildlife agency, listed with the state numbers in the government pages of the phone book.

CHAPTER 18

PROTECTING YOUR FAVORITE TURF

Managing million-acre parks. Restoring priceless historic sites. Protecting one-of-a-kind landmarks. It's big jobs like these that usually come to mind when you think of government in its role as America's caretaker.

Yet, in collaboration with nonprofit groups, the federal, state, and local branches of government also can play a huge role in preserving or protecting the smaller things around you, from historic buildings to vacant land to neighborhood woods and more. In fact, if you dig deep enough, you'll find that they provide support whether you're reviving a choked pond or converting your century-old barn to a home office.

All told, government and nonprofit groups invest more than $3 billion a year in programs to protect, renew, or restore land and valuable buildings.

> Yes, Uncle Sam spends millions to save special forests and restore priceless buildings, but here's a secret: He offers that same generosity to protect your land, your building, or your woods.

Included in those funds are tax credits, grants, and direct payments that you may be able to tap. Valuable advice is also available. If you want to save the family farm from development, get a little financial help with restoring an old building, or find funds to remove a leaking underground oil tank in your yard, you can use these resources directly. They're also a great benefit if you're trying to encourage a large landowner in your community to keep his land pristine or lobbying your town to give new life to an old industrial site.

RESTORING OLD BUILDINGS

It can be inspiring to bring a weary old building back to life, but more than that, the government

! FACTOID

SINCE 1970, THE UNITED STATES HAS LOST AN AVERAGE OF 1 MILLION ACRES OF RURAL LAND EACH YEAR TO URBAN SPRAWL. THAT'S ROUGHLY 1⅓ TIMES THE SIZE OF RHODE ISLAND.

can make it worth your while to do it. Combined, federal and state governments devote more than $52 million each year in tax incentives and grants to help people save historic properties.

Why do they do it? It's simple, says Curtis Johnson, coordinator of the Rehabilitation Investment Tax Credit Program for the Vermont Division for Historic Preservation in Montpelier. Restoration helps protect significant parts of our national heritage, and, just as important, it attracts business and jobs, which builds a community's tax base.

Here's a look at some of the best programs available.

Federal Tax Credits

Looking for a way to trim the cost of renovating an older property? Check with the federal government. You may qualify for a tax credit if the building is a "certified historic structure." That is, it must be listed individually on the National Register of Historic Places, or it must contribute to the historic significance of a registered historic district. You also must be willing to put the property to commercial, industrial, agricultural, or residential rental use. But that can mean something as simple as turning it into a bed-and-breakfast, rental housing, or a store for your small business.

HOW TO QUALIFY FOR THE NATIONAL REGISTER

To earn a spot on the National Register of Historic Places, a building, site, district, structure, or object must be historically significant and must have enough of its historic character preserved to illustrate its importance.

To qualify as historically significant, a property must meet one of four tests: It must have been associated with a historical event or pattern of events that contributed to American history, have been associated with the life of a significant historical person, have a distinctive design or construction features, or have yielded or possess the potential to yield important information about the past. The last standard usually applies to archeological sites.

Normally, religious properties, properties that have been moved from their original locations, birthplaces, properties that are reproductions of vanished buildings, or properties that have achieved significance in the past 50 years are not eligible for the National Register. They may be eligible, however, if they meet other criteria, such as being an integral part of an eligible district.

For more information about applying to the National Register or for free bulletins on historic preservation, write to the Keeper of the National Register, National Park Service, 1849 C Street NW, Washington, DC 20240, or visit the group's Web site at www.cr.nps.gov/nr.

●◆ *WHAT INSIDERS SAY:*

If your nomination is going to be turned down, it will usually happen early, when the state historic review board refuses to send it to the National Register. Should that happen, you can submit the nomination directly to the Keeper of the National Register for review. If the staff there thinks that the nomination does meet the National Register's criteria for significance and documentation standards, they will ask the state office to complete the nomination process.

The credit comes from the Federal Historic Preservation Tax Incentives Program, which is jointly run by the National Park Service and the IRS and administered in partnership with the historic preservation officer in each state.

How big a tax break can you get? If, in the view of the National Park Service, your building is a certified historic structure, you will be eligible for a 20 percent rehabilitation tax credit. But to be certified means that you will face some restrictions. You can't just lop off the porch, add skylights that are visible from the street, and replace those drafty old windows with vinyl-clad Andersens.

Even if your property is not certifiable, however, you still may be able to get help under a program that provides a 10 percent tax credit for nonhistoric, nonresidential structures built prior to 1936. In either case, if you qualify for a credit, it means that you can deduct part of the cost of the restoration from your federal income taxes. If you're eligible for a 20 percent credit and you spend $10,000 on renovations, that means the government will let you deduct $2,000 from your taxes. To qualify for the deduction, you must meet these criteria.

✓ You must spend at least $5,000 on the renovations.

✓ You must agree to keep the building for at least 5 years after you get the tax credit.

✓ You must agree to refrain from making unapproved alterations during that time.

If you violate either of the last two qualifications, you'll have to pay back at least part of the tax credit.

REAL-LIFE PRESERVATION LESSONS

The government can take some of the sting out of the cost of renovating a historic building, but there also can be drawbacks to participating in the Federal Historic Preservation Tax Incentives program, as two building owners in Montpelier, Vermont, learned.

Jane and Alan Lendway earned a $3,200 tax credit when they rehabbed the top floor of their barn for use as an office for Alan's property-management business. Jane, who is a preservation professional, estimates that she spent 15 to 20 hours filling out the paperwork, and the construction project lasted 2 months. The approval for the tax credit came just as the project was completed.

She says the rehabilitation guidelines are stringent for façades that face public ways, but they are "practical and reasonable, assuming that you have the desire to preserve the building's historic nature."

Sandy Vitzthum, an architect, earned a $26,000 tax credit when she rehabilitated a barn for use as office space.

Still, she hesitates when asked if she'd use the program again. "It would depend on the building and how easy it would be to qualify it as historic," she says. "It would depend on how 'positive' and supportive the preservation officer is. There are so many variables."

Vitzthum spent about 100 hours on her application. She made drawings of the existing building and the proposed changes, and she photographed the barn. She researched tax maps in the state

➥ WHAT INSIDERS SAY:

To get the 20 percent tax credit, you must have approval from the National Park Service for all rehabilitation projects to make sure that they suit the historical character of your property. Don't start any renovations until you get your application approved; doing so could threaten your chance for the tax break.

Restoration Advice

In addition to money, the federal government provides restoration do's and don'ts in two booklets, "The Secretary of the Interior's Standards for Rehabilitation" and "Illustrated Guidelines for Rehabilitating Historic Buildings." The first is available from Federal Historic Preservation Tax Incentives, Heritage Preservation Services, National Park Service, 1849 C Street NW, Washington, DC 20240. You'll also find it at the group's Web site at www2.cr.nps.gov.

You can get the second booklet from the U.S. Government Printing Office. Write to the Superintendent of Documents, P.O. Box 371954, Pittsburgh, PA 15250-7954, or view the guidelines on the Internet. Go to www2.cr.nps.gov and click on "Historic Buildings" to get to the guidelines link.

State Breaks for Renovations

Some states offer their own tax incentives for preserving historic buildings, and you can earn the state tax break in addition to any federal tax credit for which you may be eligible. Georgia, for example, encourages owners of historic buildings to rehabilitate them by freezing the assessed value of

archives and scoured city maps and deeds to trace the barn's evolution. Her house and carriage barn were built before 1850, she explains, but the barn was converted into a three-car garage when cars became available. The roof line was also changed, and those changes had to be documented. It was a lot of work, she says.

The tax credit also requires concessions. Vitzthum has a strong interest in historic authenticity, but she had to let go of several design elements. South-facing skylights were a no-no because they would have been visible from the street. The larger porch that she wanted would have expanded the structure's volume, which is also prohibited. "I was faced with building the way I wanted to or doing what I thought would get me the tax credit," Vitzthum says. "You compromise."

Jane Lendway suggests these tips to smooth the process of getting a historic preservation tax credit.

✓ Don't skimp on the time you spend on the application. Be as descriptive as possible of the existing conditions and your proposed changes, and justify the proposed changes. A staffer at the U.S. Department of the Interior will read your application, and the fewer questions it raises in his mind, the better.

✓ Be respectful of the building's history. Don't expect to put a convenience store into an old church.

✓ Ask your state's historic preservation officer to put you in touch with others in your community who have earned the tax credit. It helps to talk to people who know the ropes.

the property for 8 years, holding down property taxes for that period of time. The deal can save a property owner thousands of dollars in taxes, especially in cities like Atlanta, Savannah, and Macon, where rates are high, says Lee Webb, the state's tax incentives coordinator.

North Carolina offers state incentives, too—a 20 percent credit on state income taxes for people who own income-producing buildings that meet the federal qualifications for historic preservation. Your state may have similar incentives. The person to ask is your state historic preservation officer.

Money for the Status Quo

If you're willing to make a permanent commitment to preserving the appearance of your historic building, you may qualify for a preservation easement tax break. Under a preservation easement, you retain the title, but you give up control over part of the structure—the façade, the foyer, the gardens, or maybe the whole building, depending on what qualifies. In exchange, you are entitled to a hefty charitable deduction on your federal income taxes—up to 30 percent of your adjusted gross income per year for as long as it takes to write off the assessed value of the easement.

For example, say your historic home is assessed at $150,000, and the easement, which covers the façade visible from the street, is assessed at $15,000. If your adjusted gross income is $30,000 a year, you'd be able to excuse $9,000 of your income from taxes in the first year and $6,000 the next year.

You also may reap reductions in property taxes if the local government agrees that the value of your property has dropped because of the easement. And your heirs may see an estate-tax break if they inherit the building.

Note: This agreement is binding on future owners, too, so it could affect your ability to sell the property. Also, if you live at the site, you may lose a bit of privacy, since the easement carries a requirement that the public have some degree of access to the structure. However, a clear view of the historic façade from the road may suffice, or you may have to open the building to the public for just a few hours per year. For more information, contact your state historic preservation officer (see "History's—And Your—Best Friend").

HISTORY'S—AND YOUR—BEST FRIEND

Your state historic preservation officer is a person you'll want to get to know well if you're after historic preservation money. It's the preservation officer who nominates properties for the National Register and selects the properties that receive financial assistance. If you are not certain whether your property is registered, the preservation officer can help you find out. Once your building is registered, the officer also will be able to point you to the preservation programs that suit your needs and provide you with the application forms. And if you need help restoring your property, the officer can give you technical assistance on how to do it properly.

For a list of preservation officers throughout the United States, write to Heritage Preservation Services, National Park Service, 1849 C Street NW, Washington, DC 20240. Or, if you have access to the Internet, you can visit their Web site at http://grants.cr.nps.gov/shpos/shpo_search.cfm.

PRESERVING VACANT LAND

Picture an ideal world where government and nonprofit groups work hand-in-glove to save valuable land. Where they labor together to create tax breaks for the property owners. Where they quickly acquire the most exceptional sites to protect them from the threat of development. No, it isn't just a wish. That's the way things often operate when it comes to land preservation, one of the great public-private success stories.

In this partnership, government usually plays the moneyman, providing funds to purchase land or granting tax breaks to landowners who keep their land pristine. The nonprofit groups, such as the Nature Conservancy or local land trusts, offer a combination of advice, tax advantages, and short-term financing. When they lay out money, their goal is to do it on an interim basis. That is, they offer financing to quickly buy and protect a piece of land from development with the understanding that the local government will repay them.

The Little Traverse Conservancy in Harbor Springs, Michigan, for example, bought the 200-acre Miller's Marsh on Beaver Island in Lake Michigan on behalf of the Central Michigan University Biological Station. The marsh has been a valuable outdoor laboratory for the university for years, but when the owner was ready to sell, the university wasn't prepared to buy. The conservancy stepped in and bought the land and will hold it until the university can pay for it. The conservancy has even sent out flyers to help the school raise money for the purchase.

Nonprofit groups can also provide tax benefits to people who want to donate land. When a landowner donates development rights to a nonprofit organization, he gives up a certain value of the property. This is considered a donation, which qualifies the landowner for a tax deduction. Here are some of the ways that you can work with these groups to save your property or the land around you.

Selling Development Rights

You can think of it as the best of both worlds: You get to hold on to a valuable piece of vacant land, but you may still get a one-time cash payment from the government and possible tax breaks, too. That's what may be possible if you sell development rights to a property that a nonprofit group or the federal, state, or local government wants to conserve. You retain title to the land, but you agree to use it in a way that protects its conservation value.

If, for example, you sell the development rights to the state's agricultural protection program, you may give up the right to build certain structures, like houses or commercial buildings, on it, but you may still be able to farm the land. Selling the development rights also may reduce inheritance and property taxes and yield a one-time "bargain sale" charitable contribution deduction on federal and state income taxes.

Farmers in Pennsylvania sell development rights to the commonwealth under the Pennsylvania Agricultural Conservation Easement Program, which buys rights to preserve the character of the countryside, says Jeff Zehr of Allentown, farmland preservation specialist for Lehigh County. The commonwealth and the county fund the program.

A farmer usually has to own 50 acres to qualify, but if the soil is of unusually high quality, the farm adjoins an already preserved farm, or it produces an unusual crop, exceptions can be made, Zehr says—sometimes for farms as small as 10 acres. Payments for the land vary from county to county, but in Lehigh County in eastern Pennsylvania, the going rate is currently $1,300 to $3,000 per acre.

Many states have similar programs. Contact your state department of agriculture for information; the number is in the government pages of your phone book.

➥ WHAT INSIDERS SAY:

The pool of money available for buying development rights is limited, so states are picky about the land they'll accept for the program. To enhance the value of a piece of land, try to build a case for its uniqueness. Zehr recalls one farmer in Lehigh County who convinced the authorities to buy the development rights to his 19-acre farm by pointing out that his operation is unusual enough to warrant preservation: He sells

bags of organic produce and recipes to a group of regular customers.

Designating Land as "Open Space"

If you own undeveloped land—farmland or even an oversize residential lot—your state might give you a short-term property tax break for leaving it as it is.

What Is It?

"LAND TRUSTS"

If you're interested in preserving land, either your own or a large tract in your town, your first contact should be with the most common form of nonprofit conservation group: the land trust.

Land trusts are nonprofit, volunteer-run groups dedicated to preserving natural areas by buying them outright, receiving them as donations, or receiving donated conservation easements that reduce the owner's taxes while restricting his right to build on the land. In addition to providing financial help, the members know how your local land preservation system and tax laws work, and their advice can save you hours of calls to track down information from various government agencies.

The first land trust was formed in Massachusetts more than a century ago, and New England is still a hotbed, with Connecticut alone having 113 active land trusts.

As of 1998, 4.7 million acres nationwide were preserved by land trusts. Of that total, 1,385,000 acres were protected by conservation easements, 828,000 acres were owned outright by land trusts, and 2,487,000 acres had been donated to land trusts to provide tax breaks for the donors, then transferred from the trusts to the government.

Biggest holdings: California, with 119 active land trusts, protects 536,922 acres.

Smallest holdings: Seven acres of land are protected in Hawaii, which has four active land trusts.

How do you find a land trust? Call your town planner or planning and zoning official. These people are likely to have regular contact with citizens involved in land trust projects. If no one in your local government knows of a land trust, write to the Land Trust Alliance, a national, nonprofit network of land trusts. It can put you in touch with people in your area, plus provide contacts through Expert Link, its directory of tax lawyers, estate planners, land managers, and a host of other professionals around the nation who specialize in land preservation issues. The address is 1319 F Street NW, Suite 501, Washington, DC 20004.

Several states have laws on the books that allow towns to reduce your property taxes if you formally classify your land as "open space" and agree to preserve it for a specific period of time.

While the amount you'll save varies from town to town and may change over time, it can be substantial. In Guilford, Connecticut, for example, state statutes allow the assessor to reduce the assessable value of land from about $6,000 per acre to about $500 per acre. This type of reduction may lower your tax obligation if the land is classified as open space and you don't sell or develop it for 10 years.

The land doesn't have to have any particular conservation value to be eligible, but you must own more than twice the acreage required for a residential lot in your area, and the land can't be part of a subdivision. Thus, if the zone you live in requires 1-acre building lots, anything that you own above 2 acres can be classified as open space, and you may be able to reduce the taxes on it. This program is perfect if you have a big yard, most of which is a pond that can't be built upon or a stand of trees that you have no intention of cutting down.

Granting a Conservation Easement

You may save a considerable amount on your income, estate, and property taxes by granting a permanent conservation easement to the government or to a nonprofit conservation group, such as a land trust.

Income tax reductions can be substantial. Also known as a conservation restriction in some places, this legal agreement lets you keep the title to the land, but you or subsequent landowners must permanently give up certain rights regarding its use. Typically, the easement prohibits building and requires that you safeguard a specific asset, such as wetlands, a wildlife population, or a scenic vista.

If you follow IRS guidelines, says Rene Wiesner, information services manager for the Land Trust Alliance, a nonprofit group that promotes land conservation, "you may significantly reduce estate taxes if the easement restricts future development." If development is restricted, the fair market value of the land will be reduced, along with taxes based on that value.

In some states and localities, laws dictate how much of a property tax break you'll get by placing an easement on your property. However, local assessment practices vary, so ask your assessor if a reduction is available or if you need to apply for a reduction in the assessment, advises Wiesner.

Note that only properties that are deemed to have conservation value will qualify for easements. There could also be other factors that make a donation unacceptable to a particular recipient. Martha Nudel, director of communication for the Land Trust Alliance, recalls one landowner who wanted to donate a sizable tract, including a significant wetlands area, to the local land trust. From the road, it looked pristine, she says. But when the land trust did an aerial survey as part of its investigation of the property, it discovered what looked like an old railroad dump—piles of scrap steel, bricks, and railroad ties—in an area that was virtually inaccessible from the road. Nudel says the red flag of potential toxic waste went up, and the land trust said no thanks.

●◆ *WHAT INSIDERS SAY:*

Interested in protecting your open-space land and learning about all the tax benefits that can accrue? Contact the Land Trust Alliance at 1319 F Street NW, Suite 501, Washington, DC 20004. It can put you in touch with land trusts in your area that have helped landowners successfully reduce their taxes while preserving their land, so you can benefit from the first-hand insider information.

Recycling "Used" Land

Say a factory near you closes, and it looks like a perfect location for an exercise park that you'd like your town to build or perhaps an alternate spot that you could suggest to a developer who wants to put a commercial building on pristine farmland. You could be in luck: There are special funds available to revive old industrial sites.

Called brownfields, these abandoned, idle, or underused properties are places where redevelopment is complicated by real or perceived contamination, says Karl Alvarez, a program specialist at the U.S. Environmental Protection Agency (EPA) in Washington, D.C. They are considered "lightly contaminated" and will not appear on a list of the most highly contaminated sites in the country.

To encourage their reuse, the federal government offers a tax incentive that allows the owners of property within the targeted area to deduct the full costs of any cleanup in the year that the costs are incurred, rather than requiring that the costs be depreciated over the life of the property. The incentive is currently scheduled to "sunset" on January 1, 2001.

In addition, the EPA has developed a number of tools to help potential buyers understand, manage, and minimize legal and financial liability concerns. Bankers, too, are being reassured under the Lender Liability Law that they won't be held liable if they lend money to developers of brownfields but don't take an active role in managing the new business. For more information on brownfields, go to the program's Web site at www.epa.gov/brownfields.

Some states, such as Maryland, also offer grants and low-interest loans to developers of brownfields. Call your state department of environmental protection to find out about local incentives. The number should be listed in the government pages of your phone book.

●❖ *WHAT INSIDERS SAY:*

How can you encourage your city to turn an industrial eyesore into an asset? Your first call should be to the nearest office of the federal Rivers, Trails, and Conservation Assistance Program (RTCA). A division of the National Park Service, this program helps community groups organize to restore parks, riverfronts, bike and foot trails, and other natural assets. Steve Golden, program leader in the Boston office, says RTCA staff members provide skilled people to support your community development projects. They'll help brainstorm ideas for funding, act as liaisons between citizens' groups and community leaders, and help generate public support for the project.

Even if the RTCA doesn't get actively involved in your project, it can offer advice and direction. There are 25 RTCA offices. To find the one nearest you, write to Rivers, Trails, and Conservation Assistance, National Park Service, 1849 C Street NW, MS-3622, Washington, DC 20240. Or visit their Web site at www.ncrc.nps.gov/rtca.

SAVING FORESTS

Maybe it's the smell of damp leaves or the look of lush moss that makes a forest so inviting. Or maybe it's just the feeling of pleasant isolation that you get when a thick stand of trees cuts off your sight of anything human-made.

Whatever's responsible for the allure, the government recognizes that forests are valuable and is willing to help you preserve them. Here are some of the programs available to you.

Federal Money for Reforesting

Through the USDA Forestry Incentives Program, you can earn up to 65 percent of the total cost of reforesting or improving forest land, or up to a maximum of $10,000 a year. The program is open to people who own nonindustrial, private forest land, meaning that the land is owned by an individual and is not managed full-time for profit. It must produce at least 50 cubic feet of wood per acre per year. That's roughly the amount in two 50-foot-tall oak trees that are 2 feet in diameter at the base.

The government will share the cost of planting new trees and managing the existing stand. And participating in the program doesn't mean that you have to leave the forest untouched. To the government, "managing" means either removing dead trees or selectively harvesting mature ones so that smaller or more valuable trees can get more light.

The Forestry Incentive Program is customized to

fit each state's needs, so the criteria, and your chances of being accepted into the program, differ depending on where you live. Contact your state forester for information. You may find the number listed in the state government pages of your phone book under "Department of Forestry" or "Conservation and Natural Resources Department." If you can't locate the number there, write the National Association of State Foresters, Hall of the States, 444 North Capitol Street, Suite 540, Washington, DC 20001, or visit the group's Web site at www.stateforesters.org.

Advice from Your State

Some states also have reforestation programs designed to help landowners create windbreaks, provide wildlife habitats, or simply add shade or beauty to their property. South Carolina, for example, will send a forester to assess your trees and land, advise you on what to plant and what to cut, order seedlings, and even help you find state and federal cost-sharing programs. There is no minimum or maximum acreage requirement to qualify, and the state will cost-share a maximum of 100 acres per year. You must let the trees grow for 10 years, but there are no restrictions on how you use them after that time.

To learn whether your state offers such a pro-

gram, check with your state forestry or environmental protection department. You should find the number listed in the state government pages of your phone book. If you can't locate the number there, write the National Association of State Foresters, Hall of the States, 444 North Capitol Street, Suite 540, Washington, DC 20001, or visit the group's Web site at www.stateforesters.org.

Be a Forest Steward

Several programs are available to help you manage your private forest, even if you don't own a huge, Ponderosa-size tract. The Forest Stewardship Program and the Stewardship Incentive Program (SIP) are federal programs that are managed cooperatively with state forestry departments. In some states, people who own as few as 10 acres can get reimbursement for improving their woods.

Your first step is to develop a forest stewardship plan for improving your woods. You can do this with the assistance of a forestry professional or consultant designated by your state's forester's office. Once you have completed the plan, you can apply for cost-share assistance through the SIP. There are nine different forest management activities that can be cost-shared. After you do the work, you are eli-

Amazing Stories

LEAF PEEPER HOTLINE

In addition to helping you preserve forests, the government maintains one program that helps you enjoy looking at them. Each fall, when millions of Americans pile into their cars for foliage tours, the USDA Forest Service sets up a Fall Color Hotline on the Internet (www.fs.fed.us/news/fall.shtml).

At this site, there are links to specific areas of the country so you can get updates on which states are ready to bloom with color and where you'll find the most spectacular leaves. Reports usually begin around Labor Day and run until the second week in November.

gible for compensation for up to 75 percent of your expenses.

Some state forestry departments have staff foresters who will develop this plan for you at no charge. In other states, a district forester may pay you an initial visit but then direct you to hire a commercial forester. Each state manages these programs somewhat differently, so contact your state forester's office for more details. You may find the number listed in the state government pages of your phone book. If you can't find the number there, visit the Web page of the National Association of State Foresters at www.stateforesters.org. You can also write to the USDA Forest Service, Cooperative Forestry Staff, P.O. Box 96090, Washington, DC 20090. Here are some examples of specific stewardship incentive programs.

Making Trails

In some states, the Stewardship Incentive Program will reimburse part of your costs for designing and constructing trails through your woods. The trails can have any of a variety of purposes, including bicycling, cross-country skiing, snowmobiling, or even just walking. Note, however, that you can't just stick trails anywhere to qualify: They have to be placed with sensitivity to plants, animal habitats, and soil conservation. The idea is that the public will be welcome to use the trails for certain activities.

Planting Trees and Shrubs

Native trees and shrubs can make a woods more inviting to a range of wildlife species, and in some states, the Stewardship Incentive Program may help pay for both purchasing and planting recommended species.

Keeping a Well-Groomed Woodlot

Even a woodlot needs an occasional trim to look its best. In some states, this program compensates you for bringing in a consulting forester to mark which trees should be cut, or "released," to avoid competing with the best specimens. Reimbursement is also available for pruning. Note that trees may not qualify if they are within 250 feet of your house—close enough to be considered part of the home landscape. Nor does the program cover improvements to Christmas or orchard trees.

Creating a Scenic Vista

Yes, you may qualify for incentive program funds to carve out a great view. Cost-sharing covers the expense of designing and carrying out the job. This is an artful process, with an eye to leaving just enough trees to frame the view. The area may be limited to a maximum of 1 acre, and you are expected to maintain that window on the landscape for at least a decade.

Making Wildlife Happy

You can receive aid for establishing wildlife food plots. Think of this program as putting seed in a bird feeder, only on a large scale. To qualify, you must select a woodland clearing or a field bordering a woods and plant vegetation that favors wildlife. Compensation helps to cover the costs of preparing the site and applying lime, fertilizer, and seed.

•◆ WHAT INSIDERS SAY:
Curiously, incentives cover not only making clearings but also just the opposite—making enormous heaps of branches. Brush heaps may be unsightly to us, but they are havens for wildlife. For certain species, a brush pile makes a perfect household.

Planting a Woodlot

In some states, all you need is an acre of land for this one. You plant seeds or seedlings, then protect them in their youth from weeds and gnawing animals. The government may subsidize the costs of purchasing and planting. Christmas, orchard, and ornamental trees don't qualify.

Tax Breaks and Cash from Uncle Sam

If you own forest land that is being threatened by development, and it is considered important to the health of a watershed or has the potential to produce forest products, the federal Forest Legacy Program may be willing to help you protect it from development and other nonforest uses.

Much like the farmland easement process, the Forest Legacy Program purchases conservation easements from private landowners. You maintain ownership of the land, but you are required to restrict development and practice sustainable forestry practices. Cash payments have ranged from thousands of dollars to more than a million. There may be tax advantages as well. And you, the landowner, get to hold on to every green, birdsong-graced acre.

A Forest Legacy easement will apply to any future owners as well, which can lower the value of your land if you attempt to sell it. Also, an appointed group, often a nonprofit land trust, will keep an eye on the property to make sure that you follow the terms of the easement. Nevertheless, many landowners take satisfaction in knowing that their decisions will live on long after the property changes hands. "An easement allows you to pass on to your heirs land that will remain in perpetuity as you managed it during your lifetime," says Jim Geiger, manager of California's Forest Stewardship Program, based in Sacramento.

At this point, fewer than half of the states are participating in the Forest Legacy Program. To find out if it is an option for you, contact your state's forestry department. You may find the number listed in the state government pages of your phone book under "Department of Forestry" or "Conservation and Natural Resources Department." If you can't locate the number there, write the National Association of State Foresters, Hall of the States, 444 North Capitol Street, Suite 540, Washington, DC

Amazing Stories

COMPENSATION FOR LETTING TREES ROT

It may seem odd, but in Connecticut, the Forest Stewardship Program, which is managed cooperatively by the USDA Forest Service and the state, will compensate you for *not* chopping down old decaying forest and fruit trees.

Why? Gnarled old apple trees produce small, unsightly fruit that people wouldn't think of biting into but that browsing animals love. This program encourages landowners to maintain vintage trees with an occasional pruning rather than sawing them down. There is a limit of 10 trees.

Animals are also attracted to the trunks of run-down forest trees for nesting and for the wood-eating bugs that thrive there. The stewardship program in some states also may share your costs for creating "snags," or dead or dying trees, if your property now has fewer than three of them per acre. Snags are made by using a chain saw to girdle the bark around trees that are at least 9 inches in diameter. If this sacrifice sounds odd, consider that more than 85 wildlife species use snags for housing and dining.

For more information on this program, contact the USDA Forest Service, Cooperative Forestry Staff, P.O. Box 96090, Washington, DC 20090.

20001, or visit the state foresters' association Web site at www.stateforesters.org.

Creating a Wildlife Habitat

If you don't want to tie up your land's development rights for the long term, you may still find government support through the USDA Wildlife Habitat Incentives Program. Here's how it works: In consultation with the Natural Resources Conservation Service, you draw up a plan to protect or develop a wildlife habitat. Those groups will then pay up to 75 percent of the costs for carrying out your plan, up to a maximum of $10,000.

In exchange, you enter into a 5- to 10-year agreement to maintain the land's viability as a fish or wildlife habitat. You must also provide access to your land so the conservation service or its agent can monitor how effective your improvements have been. In addition, certain activities may be restricted. For instance, haying may have to be delayed until birds have ended their nesting season.

Each state sets its own priorities for local habitat improvement programs, determining which species and habitats it wants to protect and how large your property must be to qualify for the program. For more information, contact your local conservation district. You may find the number in the government pages of your phone book under "Conservation District" or "Conservation and Natural Resources Department." You can also visit the Web site maintained by the National Association of Conservation Districts at www.nacdnet.org.

Attracting Birds and Butterflies

Interested in turning your barren backyard into a wildlife habitat? Your state's Cooperative Extension Service can tell you how. Dana Belshe, agriculture agent for the extension service located on the campus of Kansas State University in Goodland, says that extension agents will explain what to plant and what to provide to attract butterflies, birds, and other creatures. And if you send them a sample of an insect that's chewing holes in your plantings, they can identify it and tell you how to control it.

You can contact your local cooperative exten-

TRADING TRASH

In our modern-day consumer society, garbage accumulates in landfills at a rapid pace. But an innovative program run by the state of California, called the California Materials Exchange (CalMAX), aims to slow down the process.

Here's how the program works: When a company has something that it no longer wants (ranging from containers, electronics, and organics to paint, plastic, and wood), it notifies CalMAX. The item is listed on an Internet site (www.ciwmb.ca.gov/calmax) and in a quarterly catalog. If businesses or individuals see something they want in either of these sources, there's contact information on where and how to pick up the items.

CalMAX charges absolutely nothing for these services. "Not only does the program enable businesses to save on disposal costs, it also encourages the reuse and recycling of discarded materials," says Sarah Weimer, CalMAX program student assistant/intern. "We don't have to pay for a storage site or deal with the material at all," she says. "We're just the facilitators."

sion office by calling the number listed in the phone book. It may be listed in the white pages under the name of your state's land-grant university; in Pennsylvania, for example, you would look for Penn State Cooperative Extension. Or it may be in the government pages, listed as "Agricultural Extension" or "Cooperative Extension" under the state department of agriculture or the USDA. If none of these options pans out, call your state legislator's office, listed in the government pages.

If you have access to the Internet, you also can track down extension information on the Web. Use your browser's search function to look for "cooperative extension." This will take you to a list of a wide variety of sites around the nation, many of which have publications that are available free for printing or downloading.

Preserving Wetlands

They may look like nothing more than boggy mosquito breeding grounds to some, but wetlands have great value in the government's eye—so much so that the government funds a program to help landowners preserve them.

Through the USDA Wetlands Reserve Program, you can get financial incentives to restore and protect your wetland. First, you must work with a government agent to develop a plan. Then you can commit to one of three options: a permanent easement on the land; a 30-year, long-term easement; or a 10-year restoration cost-share agreement. If you opt for the permanent easement, in addition to paying you for the easement, the USDA will cover up to 100 percent of the cost of restoring the wetland. If you grant a 30-year easement, you will be paid up to 75 percent of the value of a permanent easement plus 75 percent of restoration costs. In exchange for the 10-year agreement, you will be paid up to 75 percent of the restoration costs.

Under all these agreements, you still will control access to the land, and you'll be allowed to hunt and fish there. Under certain conditions, you may also be allowed to grow hay and graze the land or produce timber if it is decided that these practices are compatible with the functions and values of the wetland.

Whether your land will qualify for the program is up to your state. For information on this program, contact your local conservation district. You may find the number in the government pages of your phone book under "Conservation District" or "Conservation and Natural Resources Department." Or visit the Web site maintained by the National Association of Conservation Districts at www.nacdnet.org.

◆ WHAT INSIDERS SAY:

For a complete list of all the incentives available for preserving open space, wetlands, historic structures, and more, see the Government Assistance Almanac, *which lists every federally funded program and explains them in layperson's terms. It's also profusely indexed. The book is expensive, but many public libraries carry it.*

PROTECTING THE ENVIRONMENT

Protecting the land in your community can mean more than just safeguarding what's on the surface. A leaking oil tank in your backyard or the cans of paint that you may have inherited when you bought your old house can threaten the groundwater if you dispose of them improperly. And there are dozens of other toxic and hazardous objects that you may come in contact with. How can you safely get rid of them? Your government might have the answer.

Some states and local municipalities offer advice on disposing of household toxics and other potentially hazardous substances. Some states and counties also fund permanent disposal sites for household waste that doesn't belong in landfills.

One source of advice that's free to all is the Cooperative Extension Service of your state university. You can contact your local office by calling the number in the phone book. It may be listed in the white pages under the name of your state's land-grant university; in Pennsylvania, for example, you would look for Penn State Cooperative Extension. Or it may be in the government pages, listed as "Agricultural Extension" or "Cooperative Extension" under the state department of agriculture or the USDA. If none of these options pans out, call your state legislator's office, listed in the government pages.

You also can track down extension information on the Internet. Use your browser's search function to look for "cooperative extension." This will take you to a list of many sites around the country. Here are some other ways to get help.

Household Toxics

Household products can pollute a well or the stream that runs through your subdivision just as easily as industrial waste can. It's important to get rid of leftover household products properly, but there are no federal rules governing their disposal. Your local or state government, however, may provide guidelines or even disposal sites.

Some states help fund regional programs to collect remnants of paint thinner, paint, insecticides, fertilizers, and other household products. The programs tend to be very local; for example, several towns may band together to organize waste collections twice a year. Since those towns are paying for the proper disposal of the chemicals that people bring in, workers will turn you and your station wagon full of paint cans away unless you can prove that you're a resident.

The city of Tacoma, Washington, operates a permanent collection site that's open to all county residents, says John Sherman, environmental health specialist with the Tacoma–Pierce County Health Department. After city employees sort the wastes by category—paint and solvents, used oil, antifreeze, and so on—hired contractors dispose of them.

Dare County, North Carolina, recycles paint, too, but in an even more environmentally friendly way: It encourages residents to swap paints. On certain dates, residents can drop off latex paints and

GETTING RID OF TOXICS AROUND THE HOUSE

If you take a careful look around your house, you'll see that you're surrounded by toxics.

The leftover paint and solvents in the basement, the insecticide in the garage, and the can of silver cleaner under the sink are all considered household hazardous waste. Each one can damage the environment if you dispose of it improperly by throwing it in the trash or dumping it down the drain.

How should you handle these toxics? The best policy

with all of them is to buy only as much as you need and use it up (or give it to someone who will). If you have leftovers and your community runs a collection program, drop them off there. If the community doesn't organize collections, here's how to safely dispose of them.

✓ A general rule: Read the labels so you know what's in the products—acids, chlorine bleach, and so on. Never combine products in

one container for disposal, and never dump them down the drain at the same time, even in diluted form. Some chemicals (like bleach and ammonia, bleach and acidic drain openers, and bleach and caustic cleaning products) combine to form lethal gases. Pouring these down the drain could produce poison gas that will boil up into your home.

✓ For latex paint, leave the can open until the leftover paint

stains at the county's Solid Waste Management Authority, then pick up other people's leftovers on the way out, if they see a color they like.

To find out if your town regularly collects household hazardous wastes, call the town hall or the state environmental protection department. You'll find the numbers in the government pages of your phone book.

●❖ WHAT INSIDERS SAY:

If you don't have a local collection site for household waste, and you're sure what you're dealing with, try the do-it-yourself disposal advice in "Getting Rid of Toxics around the House."

Bombs and Explosives

Maybe it's a piece of war memorabilia that you're just not sure is safe. Maybe it's a suspicious package that you found lying at the edge of your backyard. Or maybe it's some mysterious liquid that you found in the house and that you suspect may be hazardous or even explosive. How do you deal with it, whatever it is?

First of all, don't touch it. Contact your local waste disposal collection site. If your area doesn't have a site, call your state department of environmental protection for advice. The number is listed in the government pages of your phone book.

●❖ WHAT INSIDERS SAY:

Sometimes, what you may find around your home can be a serious hazard. Tom Metzner, environmental analyst with the Connecticut Department of Environmental Protection in Hartford, recalls one woman who discovered a mayonnaise jar full of a liquid that her grandfather had used years earlier to clean gun barrels. She didn't know what it was, so she put it in the trunk of her car and drove to a collection site.

It turned out to be picric acid, a highly shock-sensitive explosive. "When the firefighters saw it, they nearly passed out," Metzner says. They evacuated the area and detonated the jar. Metzner says that he shudders to think what might have happened to the woman's trash

---

hardens, then put it in the regular trash. You also can paint it onto old newspaper and let it harden. This will be faster than waiting for a half-gallon of latex paint to dry in the can. Never put oil-based paints in the trash.

✓ Use up or give away unused portions of paint thinners, turpentine, and varnish. To dispose of used paint solvents, wait until the paint residue settles to the bottom of the container, then pour off the "clean" solvent and reuse it. Do not dump the solid paint residue down the drain or toilet or on the ground.

✓ Dilute antifreeze well with water and pour it down the drain. Do not pour it on the ground or into a storm sewer. Antifreeze has a sweet odor and taste, so keep it away from children and pets! Wild animals are also known to be attracted by the smell and taste.

✓ Use up bleach, drain openers, toilet-bowl cleaners, and other caustics. They don't go bad.

✓ Empty aerosol cans completely by spraying until nothing comes out, then put them in the regular trash.

✓ Use up oven cleaners, rug cleaners, furniture polish, and the like, then reseal the containers and put them in the regular trash.

✓ Put plastics and foam insulation into the regular trash. Never burn them, as they could produce toxic fumes.

✓ Use up insecticides, then follow the directions on the label for disposing of the containers.

hauler if she'd simply placed the jar at the curb with her trash and the hauler had compacted it in his truck.

Handling an Oil Tank Leak

If you have an underground oil tank that is leaking, it can be a nasty and expensive job to remove it and clean the site. Government won't cure the problem for you, but it may be able to help.

"Recognizing that some people might just walk away from the problem or try to hide the tank, some states have established programs to help homeowners deal with tanks properly," says Bill Torrey, manager of the Underground Storage Tank Program for the U.S. Environmental Protection Agency's regional office in Boston. States may, for example, provide low-interest loans for proper disposal or designate emergency response funds to deal with the tank, then place a lien on the property to recover the cost of the work.

To find out if your state has a program, write to the U.S. Environmental Protection Agency, Hazardous Waste Ombudsman Program, MC 5101, 401 M Street SW, Washington, DC 20460. Ask whom to contact in your region for underground storage tank information.

●◆ WHAT INSIDERS SAY:

How do you know if an underground oil tank is leaking? The first alert often comes from a furnace technician after water that has seeped into the tank fouls the furnace jets. "There's only one way for water to get in there unless you pour it in," says George Gdovin, hazardous waste coordinator in Guilford, Connecticut, "and that's through a hole in the tank. If groundwater is seeping into the tank, oil is leaking out."

If you decide to stop using an underground storage tank, you should abandon it properly. Either hire a licensed contractor or unearth enough of the tank yourself to enable you to cut it open. Then mop it out and fill it with an inert material such as sand, Styrofoam, or cement, says Gdovin. That will prevent it from caving in as it rusts underground. To locate a contractor, contact your state department of environmental protection for advice; you can find the number in the government pages of your phone book.

SEVEN

Law and Politics

CHAPTER 19

TAKING YOUR PROBLEMS to the LOCAL BAR

Whether you were raised on Perry Mason, Ben Matlock, or Ally McBeal, you came away with the distinct impression that a courthouse is the last place you want to spend a chunk of your time or lay out a chunk of your money. But even if you're the model citizen—the one whose life is always lived on the straight side of the law—society is so complex that in all likelihood, there will still be times when you'll need to hack your way through the thicket of our nation's legal jungle.

You might need legal help to sue someone for damaging your car or to dispute a home repair bill. Perhaps you'll just want to file a will. In any case, you'll find opportunities to use the government and nonprofit legal groups to smooth your path. With a little investigation, you'll see that there are numerous ways they can help you

> A day in court doesn't have to be something you dread. With the help and resources of the government and nonprofit groups, you can prepare a successful case or perhaps avoid court altogether.

handle legal matters, some of which stop well short of the courtroom and this side of breaking your bank.

That benefits not only you but the groups as well. Because of an enormous backlog of litigation and the snail-like pace at which that litigation can sometimes move, organizations such as the American Bar Association and the American Arbitration Association and government offices such as your state's attorney general, supreme court, and office of consumer protection consider it in their best interests to help you resolve your legal entanglements as swiftly, simply, and inexpensively as possible.

From your point of view, if they can help you move quickly through court, they've done you a service, says Jeffrey Liebling, a political consultant and tutor of attorneys in Carson City, Nevada. If

FACTOID

ABOUT 70 PERCENT OF THE CASES ADJUDICATED IN VERMONT FAMILY COURTS OCCUR WITHOUT THE PARTICIPATION OF ATTORNEYS.

they can help you avoid court, they've done you a bigger service. And if they can help you dispose of your legal matter without your even needing a paid attorney, they may have done you the biggest service of all.

HIRING A LAWYER

If you're like most people, your first contact with an attorney will come when you're forced to go to court to handle a dispute, a lawsuit, an accident claim, or some other unforeseen problem. At a time like this, your first inclination may be to rush to choose someone to defend you. Don't, say insiders; you may end up choosing someone who doesn't fit your needs. Picking an attorney isn't like buying a pair of stretch socks; one size most definitely does not fit all.

"When you're looking to hire a lawyer, you need to answer a number of questions," says Bill Savage, a personal injury lawyer in Portland, Oregon, and member of the Association of Trial Lawyers of America and Who's Who in American Law. Foremost are how much you can afford to spend, what exactly you want the lawyer to do for you, and whether the lawyer you contact is someone with whom you can feel comfortable. The nonprofit American Bar Association and the government can help you address many of these issues.

Finding the Right Rep

The first question you'll want to answer before hiring an attorney is, "What kind of lawyer do you need?" If, for instance, you haven't been able to resolve an honest dispute over the $300 plumbing bill you received for installing your new water heater, you don't want to settle the problem by hiring a $400 attorney. Nor do you want to retain someone who's an expert in divorce and child custody but knows little or nothing about contract law or someone whose pit-bull legal tactics are going to

---

DO YOU REALLY NEED A LAWYER?

Obviously, it's not worth hiring an attorney to handle every dispute. If, for example, you're disputing a car repair bill, a property line, or the work of a dry cleaner who ruined your favorite suit, you may well be able to manage it yourself because these are simple transactions with little monetary risk in the outcome, according to Bill Savage, a personal injury lawyer in Portland, Oregon,

and member of the Association of Trial Lawyers of America and Who's Who in American Law.

But if the issue is serious—there's a question of medical negligence, for instance, or of whether your mortgage is in arrears and you could lose your home—you usually should hire an attorney.

"The Rules of Evidence (protocol and restrictions on how to present a case in civil

court) alone can cover an entire year of law school, so when the stakes are high, you either want to know what you're doing or have someone who does," says Savage.

There's one other clear indicator that it's time to haul in a hired gun: "When the other side hires a lawyer, it's time for you to hire one, too," says Karen Predom, chief clerk for the district and family court in Rutland, Vermont.

ensure that you'll never be able to use that plumber again. So how can you make a decision?

Ask the bar association for help. Your state bar association—the organization that oversees the licensing and conduct of all attorneys—is a gold mine of information on legal questions. Each state bar association has a lawyer referral service, says John Ventura, a consumer attorney in Brownsville, Texas, and author of 11 books on the legal profession. "The service doesn't offer legal advice or legal services," he says, "but it will help direct you to attorneys who will determine whether you have a case and what attorneys in your area have expertise in your particular matter."

Each state has a bar association office, and most have several. To find the location nearest you, look first in your phone book. The number may be in the government pages under "Legal Services," or it may be in the white pages under terms such as "Attorney Referral and Information Service," or "Lawyer Referral Service." If you don't see the number there, call the office of administration for your local court. Or, if you have access to the Internet, you can visit the American Bar Association's (ABA) Web site at www.abanet.org.

➥ *WHAT INSIDERS SAY:*

It pays in more ways than one to ask the ABA for a referral. If it refers you to an attorney, you're entitled to a half-hour consultation at no charge or for a nominal fee that goes to fund the lawyer referral service's operation.

Quizzing the Candidates

Once you've been referred to a lawyer or several lawyers, insiders say that you should determine the person's specific qualifications for your case by asking questions like these.

What are his areas of expertise? Most states certify lawyers in certain areas, such as real estate law, malpractice, consumer law, and the like, and attorneys normally have to take entrance exams and maintain annual education credits in order to be certified.

How long has he been in practice? Because of the great complexities of law as well as the constant flow of new legislation, it can be useful to hire someone who has a long record of knowledge about the matter you're taking to him.

What is his success record? Because so many case resolutions are negotiated, it's not always possible to define a "winner" or "loser," but what you can do by talking to him about his record is find out whether he has a sizable number of satisfied clients.

How will he charge? Some lawyers will agree to work on a contingency basis, which means that the only payment they'll accept will be a portion of your settlement with the other party, no matter how long a case may take. Others require a flat fee, meaning that you agree to pay a specific amount no matter how much or how little time it takes to resolve your case.

➥ *WHAT INSIDERS SAY:*

Even if a lawyer insists on a flat fee, ask if it's a negotiable amount. An attorney who normally charges, say, $100 an hour may be willing to work for much less if yours is a simple case that can be handled with a minimum amount of effort.

Am I comfortable with him? "Make sure this is someone you think you can trust, someone whose ethics and values seem to fit with yours, and someone whose expertise in your area of concern is well-established," says Savage.

➥ *WHAT INSIDERS SAY:*

"Hiring a lawyer is a little like hiring a babysitter," says John Thirkield, chief clerk for the Nassau County Supreme Court in Mineola, New York. "Price does matter, expertise matters more, but confidence in their abilities matters the most."

Has he ever had a client file a complaint against him? While this needn't be a disqualifier, especially if the complaint was never substantiated, you would certainly think twice about hiring someone who has a history of complaints, especially if they show a pattern of, say, negligence, underhandedness, or inefficiency.

Making a Background Check

If you find an attorney you like but who's reluctant to talk about past complaints, you can look elsewhere for information. Each state also has some kind of disciplinary board, usually financed by the state bar association and the state government, which receives complaints and grievances brought against attorneys, says Vivian Berg, disciplinary counsel to the disciplinary board of the supreme court of North Dakota in Bismarck. "If you're thinking of hiring an attorney," she says, "you can call the state board and find out if any complaints have resulted in public discipline."

Disciplinary boards have different names in different states, and the way to find out the exact name and phone number of your state's board is to call the clerk's office in your state supreme court. The number is listed in the government pages of your phone book. Or, if you have access to the Internet, you can find a list for all 50 states at the ABA Web site at www.abanet.org.

You can also call your local office of the Better Business Bureau, which accepts complaints about local attorneys and supplies information on member attorneys, ranging from how long they've been practicing to what their areas of specialization include, says Jeanine Carlevato, director of financial affairs for the Central Washington office of the Better Business Bureau in Yakima.

➥ *WHAT INSIDERS SAY:*

If you research an attorney's record with a disciplinary board, beware. These checks aren't foolproof: You won't get information about any unsubstantiated grievances or grievances that are resolved through private discipline, which is governed by rules of confidentiality.

REPRESENTING YOURSELF

When you take a close look at your dispute, you may find that there's no justification for hiring a lawyer; the case just may not be complex enough or financially rewarding enough to warrant a lawyer's time. In cases like these, it may be best to take matters into your own hands, which is something the government has made easy to do.

"With a little bit of research and effort, there are any number of matters that you can handle yourself and any number of ways to handle them," says

THE ABA: NOT FOR LAWYERS ONLY

"The American Bar Association (ABA) is not just a professional organization for lawyers," says John Newhouse, an attorney in New York City. "For the average consumer, the ABA offers a wide array of services and programs, including publications and videotapes covering topics such as dealing with debt, mediation, the right to privacy, and even the Bill of Rights."

Moreover, the ABA publishes literature for teachers who want to teach students about nonviolent conflict resolution, the basics of the Constitution and the Bill of Rights, and the legal dimensions of racial and cultural diversity.

And in addition to media materials, the association offers assistance in helping people locate low-cost legal services, legal specialists, nontraditional legal service plans, and even lawyer disciplinary agencies.

Nevada consultant Jeffrey Liebling, "including issues like disputed home repairs, simple zoning variances, uncontested divorces, and the like."

Pro Se Representation

If your case is fairly simple, you may want to represent yourself, using what the legal profession calls *pro se* representation. In this type of legal matter, you fill out a set of forms and submit them to the court. The court then issues its ruling and informs you by mail.

"A good many issues, such as an uncontested divorce, settlement of an estate, repayment of a small sum of borrowed money, or the writing and filing of a will," can be processed this way, depending on the rules of your state and the local court, says Liebling.

In fact, if it's a simple family matter, such as a request to modify child support or custody arrangements, courts often look kindly on litigants handling the matter pro se, says Karen Predom, chief clerk for the district and family court in Rutland, Vermont.

To determine whether you can handle your case this simply, consult your bar association's lawyer referral service or go to the courthouse directly, says Predom. Court clerks or assistant clerks can't advise you on legal tactics or strategies, but they can informally tell you if your case is the kind that can be handled pro se, and they can walk you through the paperwork necessary to take your case before the judge.

In Vermont, the courts will even show you copies of completed forms to guide you, says Larry Robinson, a county clerk for the Windham County (Vermont) superior court in New Fane. In addition, some states make their forms available over the Internet. You can learn how to file for an uncontested divorce in New York state, for example, by going to www.nylj.com/guide and clicking on "Uniform Uncontested Divorce Packet."

Classroom Advice

A large metropolitan area might offer information about pro se litigation in some of its court systems. You can speak with lawyers, ask questions about procedure and terminology (although you can't solicit or accept legal advice or strategy), and pick up brochures about how to represent yourself, says Mai Yee, assistant director of communications for the New York office of court administration in New York City.

To find out if this information is available in your area, contact your local civil court and ask if it has an office of pro se litigation, or what some states call the office of self-represented cases. You can find the number for your civil court in the government pages of the phone book.

Even if you're in a small jurisdiction that doesn't have classes, chances are good that the courts will have brochures available to guide you, says Robinson.

SETTLING OUT OF COURT

While most people assume that disputes have to be worked out in a court of law, insiders say that there are other, lower-cost alternatives, including arbitration and mediation.

Disputes that arise over different points of view or different interpretations of a contract often can be resolved in a manner satisfactory to both parties by an outside arbitrator, whose decision is quick, final, and fair. These disputes might include such things as the length of the warranty on a new dishwasher, the amount of time it's supposed to have taken to complete a car repair, or the repayment of a security deposit from the rental of an apartment.

If the parties want to work it out themselves and broker their own resolution but need guidance in doing so, a mediator may be invited in to help them steer themselves to a point of common ground. In addition to simple cases such as those involving private contracts or warranties, disputes such as noise from a neighbor's stereo or the glare from an intrusive floodlight could go to mediation, where the involved parties are empowered to solve their own problem with a mutually forged compromise. Here's how each process works.

Arbitration

Arbitration lets you draw on some of the benefits of the judicial system without having to deal with some of the hassles. In arbitration, you submit your dispute to a panel of one or more impartial persons who make a final and binding decision, says Janet Denunzio, corporate communications director of the nonprofit American Arbitration Association in New York City. For any number of reasons, it can be preferable to an appearance in court.

For starters, it's a highly private procedure. Unlike contesting a problem in a public courthouse, arbitration takes place behind closed doors, so no one needs to know the details of your personal business.

Moreover, the rules are more flexible than those in a courtroom. You can hold your hearings anywhere that's mutually convenient, at any hour of the day or evening. And instead of following the arcane rules of the courtroom, in arbitration, each party simply states his side of the story to the arbitrator and introduces any evidence he thinks is useful to his case.

In addition, arbitration is generally much quicker than court litigation. You have no protracted waiting time before your case is heard, there's no backlog of cases in front of you, and no appeals process can hold up the final verdict. "It's difficult to say precisely how much time is saved in arbitration," says Denunzio, "but we found that in 1996, the average commercial dispute in which no more than $15,000 was at stake took about 140 days from the time the parties agreed to arbitration to the time the arbitrators rendered their verdict. That's almost certain to be quicker than the courts, which, in extreme cases, can take years to adjudicate the same types of cases."

And finally, it's cheaper. "Again, although it's an estimate," says Denunzio, "our research shows that an arbitration case—say, in the field of commercial

HOW TO BUILD AN AIRTIGHT ARBITRATION CASE

Even though you won't be in a court of law when you meet with an arbitrator, you need to prepare just as seriously.

Insiders suggest that you accept the possibility of real discrepancies in the facts that you and the other party present and that you build as strong a case as you can. This can mean having copies of contracts you've signed, receipts, canceled checks, a log of telephone calls, a clear chronology of events, personal witnesses, and perhaps even a brief narrative summary of how you remember the dispute starting.

So if you're disputing your contractor's right to charge you more than you initially agreed upon to build a home and you're taking your case to arbitration, you would do well to be able to show the arbitrator the agree-upon price in the body of a contract or a letter of agreement. You might also be able to provide receipts for the overages or even show—perhaps with copies of complaint letters that you wrote—that the contractor made no effort to consult you about them ahead of time or explain them to you after the fact. And finally, you might be able to obtain the opinion of a third party, such as a contractor or professional building assessor, who disagrees with your contractor's facts and figures.

construction—that costs between $2,000 and $3,000 to arbitrate could run as high as $50,000 to $100,000 in a court of law."

So how do you take a dispute to arbitration? That's easy, too. Here are the steps you'll need to take, say insiders.

Strike a Deal with the Other Party

Say, for instance, that a contractor is building a home for you. His bills are coming in higher than you expected because he's run into some unanticipated expenses and delays, but you think he's shaking you down, and you want an independent expert to come in and resolve the problem. First, approach your contractor with your beef and ask if he would rather work it out in arbitration or in court.

➥ *WHAT INSIDERS SAY:*

In many cases, professionals such as builders and repairmen have arbitration clauses built into their contracts, and in many other instances, court judges will insist that the parties go to an arbitrator instead of court.

Choose an Arbitrator

Unlike a court, where you are assigned a judge, in arbitration, it's up to you and your contractor to pick someone to review your case—and both of you have to agree on the person. One way to do this, says Denunzio, is to have each party compile a list of local arbitrators or arbitration agencies, interview them separately, and see how many you would both be satisfied with. After you've compiled a short list of finalists, chances are good that you can find one candidate who receives high ratings from both of you.

So how do you begin looking for arbitrators? You may find listings in the white pages or yellow pages of your phone book, of course, but you can often use your government. Many state courts have lists of alternative dispute resolution (ADR) attorneys who work as arbitrators, and although regulations vary from state to state and from court to court within a state, in most states, those attorneys will have had some specific, court-sanctioned training. (In New York City, for instance, ADR attorneys registered with the courts have had at least 7 years of practice as attorneys and at least 24 hours of ADR training, according to Mai Yee of the office of court administration.) You should find the number for your state courts in the government pages of your phone book under "Courts" or "Judiciary."

In addition, you can get in touch with the nonprofit Society of Professionals in Dispute Resolution (SPIDR) at 1527 New Hampshire Avenue NW, Washington, DC 20036, and ask for the address or phone number of their regional office nearest you.

Once you've developed your list of prospective arbitrators, you'll want to look into the following issues.

Check credentials. There is no national organization similar to the American Bar Association that has oversight of arbitrators, but each state has its own set of regulations governing who may hear arbitration cases and what credentials they must hold. Although a great many arbitrators are attorneys by training, some arbitration specialists in construction might have experience as contractors or builders, while physicians and nurses might work on medical cases and social workers might adjudicate disputes over social welfare benefits.

Check experience. When you're interviewing prospective arbitrators, ask how long they've been in the business, how many cases they've handled that are similar to yours, and how those cases turned out. You might also ask them for references.

Check for conflict of interest. Make sure your arbitrator is neutral. It might be good to have a professional contractor as part of your arbitration team to decide whether your electrician owes you a reimbursement for shoddy workmanship, but not if the arbitrator and the electrician happen to be old buddies who used to work together.

Ask about specific expertise. If you have complaints with your tree surgeon, you probably want someone who has a working knowledge of tree care and/or complaints directed at the industry.

Ask about fees. As with attorneys, you'll find that fees vary widely, and while you don't want cost to be a deciding factor in whom you hire, you're also not going to want the cost to be such that it's not worth your while to adjudicate your dispute.

●◆ *WHAT INSIDERS SAY:*

More is sometimes better when it comes to arbitration. If, for example, you fear that the arbitrator your auto mechanic suggests is such an industry insider that you won't be treated fairly, you can request a panel of arbitrators that would also include at least one person with no connections to the mechanic's industry.

Mediation

Like arbitration, mediation offers a way to settle disputes more simply than through the court system. Unlike arbitration, however, there is no single person or panel to render a binding judgment for you. "In mediation, the parties are sitting down at a table and negotiating with one another, trying to find a common solution—often a compromise— that they can both live with," says Sharon Press, a veteran mediator with the Neighborhood Justice Center in Tallahassee, Florida. "The mediator's role is more that of a facilitator and counselor than a judge; the resolution of the dispute rests with the parties themselves."

"A key difference between mediation and arbitration is that in mediation the power really lies with the constituents," says John Doggette, director of the Community Mediation Center in Knoxville, Tennessee. "Mediators aren't necessarily interested in the facts of the case, the evidence, or even what they themselves might consider to be a fair and equitable resolution. Their interest is in helping people to arrive at what *they* consider to be fair and equitable."

How can you find the right mediator? Here are two suggestions.

Check with the courts. Just as if you were looking for the right lawyer or arbitrator, finding the right mediator is a matter of studying candidates' credentials, expertise, personality, and fees. One way to begin is by calling the clerk's office of the local branch of your state supreme court and asking if it has a list of qualified mediators. In addition, the clerk is likely to know if there are licensing requirements for mediators in your state and if statewide mediation associations exist that can offer referrals (some states have these nonprofit organizations, and some don't).

Ask an association. Although there are few national organizations for mediators, the National Association for Community Mediation (NACM) at 1726 M Street NW, Suite 500, Washington, DC 20036, and the American Arbitration Association (AAA) at 335 Madison Avenue, New York, NY 10017, both have directories that list thousands of affiliated members throughout the country.

●◆ *WHAT INSIDERS SAY:*

When is the best time to turn to mediation? When you and the person you're arguing with have a relationship that's worth preserving, says Press. "In arbitration, one person wins and the other loses, which can be damaging to a relationship. So if, for instance, you're talking about two neighbors who have a dispute over the placement of the satellite dish that one of them just installed in their front yard, an arbitrator might declare one of the neighbors victorious, but at great cost to the relationship. In mediation, however, the two of them will eventually walk away from the table satisfied that they have a resolution they can both live with."

Judging a Mediator's Skills

Once you have established a list of prospective mediators, you'll want to interview each one to make sure the person you pick has the attitude and skills that will help you reach a successful settlement. Here are specific points that insiders suggest you explore.

Look for a license. Credentials of mediators vary from state to state, but if your state qualifies mediators, you'll want to know if the ones you interview are licensed and/or certified. Also, check whether they have taken any licensing exams, received any specific training, or are affiliated with any state or national organizations. (Most private mediation organizations, such as NACM and AAA, have qualification requirements, codes of ethics, and continuing education programs.) While these factors don't guarantee a mediator's expertise, they are measures of their professionalism.

Look for experience. In addition to paper credentials, you should ask how long the person has been doing mediation and whether he has ever handled a dispute such as yours. Find out what the person knows about your specific type of problem.

It may or may not be to your advantage to work with someone who has a working knowledge of your particular issue, says Press. If, for instance, you're trying to resolve a dispute with an auto repairman, it might be helpful for the mechanic to have a mediator who knows something about cars, while it would benefit you to have someone with a working knowledge of consumers' rights. In such a case, you may opt for a team of mediators, which many mediation services offer, instead of an individual.

Get an estimate. What you're likely to find is that mediators' fees are commensurate with their training. If a mediator is a lawyer by training, you'll

THE KEYS TO SUCCESSFUL MEDIATION

Let's say that you and your neighbor are arguing over his willow tree, which is weeping its buds all over your yard. Your lawn's littered, your grass is drying out, and your kids are tracking buds into the house on the soles of their sneakers. How do the two of you work it out when talking it out hasn't gotten you anywhere?

"It's best to prepare for mediation by giving serious consideration to two fundamental questions," says Sharon Press, a veteran mediator with the Neighborhood Justice Center in Tallahassee, Florida. "First, what do you want to achieve? Do you want the problem solved to your satisfaction? Do

you want to find a compromise? Or do you want above all else to preserve the relationship you have with your neighbor?

"Second, what are the other person's needs? What is it that's important to him that they will be wanting to defend and protect in these negotiations?"

By doing this, Press notes, both parties gain clarity and agreement as to the ultimate aims of mediation; you're able to go in knowing where you want to come out.

Insiders also recommend that you and your neighbor agree on ground rules for settling your dispute, including such things as how much time you're

willing to give to the process (although you can certainly leave it open-ended), whether or not you'll discuss the proceedings with outside parties, where and when the proceedings will be held, and how payment will be made. It is also good to have a general agreement to treat one another with respect, courtesy, and consideration.

●◆ WHAT INSIDERS SAY:
When you're in mediation, always leave yourself an escape hatch in the event that it's just not working out. "If need be, spell out in the contract that if you can't negotiate a resolution, you just may have to litigate one," says John Doggette, director of the Community Mediation Center in Knoxville, Tennessee.

probably be charged at a rate comparable to a typical attorney's fees in your part of the country. The benefit, though, is that you'll be billed for fewer hours than if you took the case to court. You'll pay only for a limited amount of preparation time and the time spent at the mediation table.

"If, for instance, your mediator makes a 5-minute phone call inquiring about some specific piece of your case before you have a first session, you won't be charged for an hour's worth of time, as some attorneys will do," says Doggette. "And once the mediation starts, you're billed only for the sessions themselves."

You also may agree to a flat rate for services, regardless of how many sessions are required, and many mediation organizations have sliding fee scales based on their clients' ability to pay.

Study them. "Beyond questions of professional expertise, credentials, and cost," says Doggette, you "must feel confident that this is a person or team of people capable of getting you successfully through this process." Your best bet is to look for someone who listens attentively, actively, and accurately.

"An attentive listener establishes eye contact with me when I'm talking, is not distracted by external intrusions, and wears a facial expression that indicates that he cares about what I'm saying, that he's neither bored nor impatient," says Doggette. "An active listener lets me talk but demonstrates that he's listening, perhaps by nodding in agreement, leaning toward me ever so slightly when I'm making a point, or reiterating what I say in a concise sentence. And an accurate listener gives me feedback that shows he has a thorough understanding of what I'm thinking and feeling."

TAKING A CASE TO SMALL CLAIMS COURT

Each state has a court in which financial disputes over relatively small sums of money can be argued without the need for attorneys or a working knowledge of the intricacies of courtroom procedure. They call it small claims court, and it may be just what you need to straighten out minor financial disputes such as questionable bills, unpaid loans, bounced checks, fender benders by uninsured motorists, or limited property damage to your home.

Some small claims rules vary from state to state, so when you need to know what the rules are where you live, you should contact the clerk's office in your local court. (The number is in the government pages of your phone book.) Most clerks' offices have written information that they can send to you.

Each state, for instance, sets a dollar maximum beyond which you may not use small claims court, and it varies from state to state. Oregon requires that disputes of up to $750 be handled in small claims court, those between $751 and $3,500 can go to either small claims or circuit court, and any dispute over $3,500 must be taken to circuit court. In Vermont, the maximum for small claims is $3,500, and in Texas it's $5,000.

In addition, while all states will allow you to represent yourself, some will not allow you to appear in small claims court with an attorney. And while many states allow for an appeals process if you're dissatisfied with the ruling, some, such as Oregon, do not, so both parties have to live with the judge's decision. Despite the variations in the particulars from state to state, however, most small claims courts follow the same general filing procedures, such as those that are used in Vermont.

1. You contact the clerk of the court and ask to receive the necessary complaint forms, which you can either pick up at the courthouse or receive by mail.

2. You fill out the forms, which will ask you for your name and address, the names and addresses of the person(s) you're suing, and the nature of your complaint.

3. You submit the completed forms and pay court costs, which range from $25 to $50. When you file these papers, you will receive a docket number, which identifies your case,

and copies of your complaint will be mailed to your defendant(s).

After a judge has a chance to review your complaint, you will receive one of three rulings. If the other party hasn't answered your complaint, the judge will rule in your favor by default and award your requested amount. If the other party agrees to your charges, the judge will compel him to pay you the money in question in a settlement. And if the other party challenges your claim, the judge will set a hearing date for your case.

Pleading Your Case

If the case goes to trial, on the date of your hearing, the judge will call you before the bench, listen to your side of the story, examine your evidence, and listen to your witnesses (if you have any), then do the same with the defendant. The entire hearing might last no more than 10 to 15 minutes, after which the judge may either render an immediate decision or take more time to consider your claim, in which case you will be notified of the decision by mail.

As simple as this sounds, however, insiders warn that you'll want to be fully prepared for those 15 minutes, and that means doing the necessary legwork and prep work from the time you decide to sue (or receive notice that you're being sued) to the time the judge has heard your case.

Suppose two parties are in dispute over property damage; suppose Sam hired Willie to trim his hedges, and in the process of doing this, Willie damaged some of Sam's flower beds. Now Sam refuses to pay Willie until he either repairs the beds or reimburses Sam for the cost of replacing them. What do they need to know?

Be Organized and Brief

Both parties should come to court equipped with all the evidence they need to make their case but without anything that isn't immediately relevant.

"One great way to get on the wrong side of judges," says Oregon personal injury lawyer Bill Savage, "is to waste their time."

The one who makes a good impression, according to Vermont superior court clerk Larry Robinson, is the one who comes with his evidence in clear, concise, chronological order, perhaps even in the form of an outline.

On their day in court, then, Sam might stand before the judge and say "On June 4, I planted 30 begonia plants at a cost of $75. Here are my receipts. On July 13, I hired Willie to trim the hedges surrounding the flowers for $50. Here is a photocopy of my calendar for that day and a dated copy of the contract. On July 14, when he finished the job, the beds were ruined. Here is a photo of the beds that afternoon."

In turn, Willie might go before the judge and reply, "When I went to work on Sam's hedges, I noticed that the flowers clearly hadn't been watered in some time, as they were dry and wilting. Here is a copy of a statement from his neighbor attesting to this. That same day, I suggested that he take better care of them. When I finished my work and noticed that I had bruised about half of them, I offered to deduct $20 from my bill. Sam refused. Here is a copy of the letter I wrote with this offer, along with a copy of his reply."

Don't Act Like a Lawyer

Remember that small claims court is an informal setting designed specifically to get away from the arcane procedures and peculiar language of civil court. Sam shouldn't refer to the photo of his flowers as "people's exhibit A," and Willie should avoid a line like "I proffered the plaintiff a conditional plea of nolo contendere, Your Honor."

Be Polite

As informal as small claims courts are, judges want their courtrooms and themselves respected. Don't interrupt the other party, and be sure to treat the judge with deference.

Anticipate Your Opponent's Argument

Think in terms of how the other party is going to try to make his case. Knowing that Sam was going to charge him with trampling his begonias, Willie was quick to point out that the flowers were already in poor condition. Sam, on the other hand, anticipating Willie's assertion, used his opening argument to impress upon the judge that they were newly planted.

Don't Be Stubborn

If a judge renders a decision that affects both parties equally, don't be quick to dismiss it, even if you do have access to an appeal. "The judge suggests a compromise when he sees merit in both sides," says Texas consumer attorney John Ventura, "and that may be the best you can do." Thus, when the judge decides that the cost of the flowers should be shared and instructs Sam to pay Willie, say, $25, it's probably wise for both men to walk out of court with their respective half-loaves of bread.

●◆ WHAT INSIDERS SAY:

Ideally, you should always be preparing for a trip to small claims court, says Ventura. "Create and maintain written records. Keep a log of every day's activities. Certify anything that you mail. And be prepared to demonstrate to a judge that you tried to broker a settlement out of court."

Power to the People

HOW TO (LEGALLY) BEAT A SPEEDING TICKET

It's extremely difficult but not impossible to beat a speeding ticket, according to Bill Savage, a personal injury attorney in Portland, Oregon. "When a speeding ticket puts you in court, the judge finds in favor of the police officer in about 98 percent of cases." Still, there are some things that might help you.

Pay attention

Listen carefully to what the police officer says and see if there's anything in the testimony that you disagree with. Then, when you get your chance to talk, present your case carefully and cogently. For instance, if you've been cited for exceeding a posted speed and the police officer tells the judge where he was stationed when he tagged you, you might be able to point out that there was no posted speed limit sign anywhere in the vicinity. Or, if he claims to have clocked you with a radar gun, you can question the reliability of the reading and its admissibility in court.

Ask for a jury trial

In some states, you can request a jury trial. In some cases, because of the time it would require and the overall inconvenience, there's a chance that the police officer won't bother to show up and the charges will be dismissed, according to Anthony Carrabba, a Texas attorney who handled nothing but traffic tickets in Houston for more than 6 years.

Plea bargain

Some states also offer what in Texas is called deferred adjudication, whereby you agree to pay a fine, accept a period of probation, and perhaps attend driving school. This means that although you accept responsibility for the ticket, it will not go on your driving record, and your insurance company won't be able to raise your rates as a result of it if you successfully complete the terms of your probation.

GETTING UNCLE SAM'S BACKING

Whether the case you're taking to court is simple or complex, whether you're representing yourself, using an arbitrator or mediator, or hiring counsel, there are a number of ways to get Uncle Sam involved in your pursuit of justice.

Perhaps you're taking a big corporation to task in a kind of David versus Goliath lawsuit. Or maybe you've actually won the suit, but now you're having trouble getting Goliath to pay up. Smart citizens are the ones who know how to gather the full force of their government to fight on their behalf, say insiders. On the other hand, maybe it's Uncle Sam himself with whom you have your beef, in which case there's even a government office that can help you make your case.

Whether government's your ally or your adversary, here are some ways that your taxpayer dollars can come back to you in the form of legal assistance.

Letting the Government Plead Your Case

Let's say that you have a complaint against Mammoth Electronics about a television set that you purchased at a local department store. Ever since you bought it, you've had problems: The color is all screwed up, the speakers sound tinny, and some channels don't come in clearly, if at all. You've had it checked at the store where you bought it, you've shipped it back to the company for inspection, and you've even had your own electrician look at it, yet each time, Mammoth refuses to take responsibility for the problem.

Well, now you've just plain had it. Four months and a half-dozen angry letters later, you decide to take action: Either Mammoth is going to refund you the cost of the set, or you're going to take the company to court. But when you make this threat, Mammoth dismisses you as little more than a gnat on an elephant's nose. Where do you turn? Your state's attorney general, who is part of the state justice department.

"Most state attorney generals' offices house a division of consumer protection, which is charged with looking out for negligent or unscrupulous companies doing business in the state," says Mary Horsch, director of communications for the Kansas attorney general in Topeka. "Any complaint called to our attention is going to be investigated by our offices if we have jurisdiction." You can find your state's office of consumer protection by looking in the government section of your phone book; it may be listed under its own name or as part of the attorney general's office.

So how would your consumer protection office protect you in your complaint against Mammoth? Well, there are a few things it might do for you. Here's how it could work.

Register a Threat

The first thing you want to do is inform Mammoth that you're going to bring your complaint to the attention of the state's attorney general. Because the company's not interested in paying its attorneys to go to court or its public relations people to put a good spin on a potential P.R. disaster, says Texas consumer attorney John Ventura, this will let it know that you are serious.

Register a Complaint

If the threat doesn't get results, make good on it by calling the office of consumer protection to ask what steps you have to follow to lodge a complaint against a private company. In most instances, notes Horsch, you'll be asked to fill out a form and include copies of any documentation—receipts, letters, warranties, and so on—that substantiate your case. "Kansas, like many states, also makes the form available on the Internet," says Horsch, "and while ours is not yet interactive (that is, you can't simply submit it electronically), you can download the form from our site and mail it to us."

WHAT INSIDERS SAY:

When filing a complaint against a company, ask whether other people have also registered complaints.

In some states, if consumer protection does have a completed file on the company, that file is available to the public.

Let Them Do Their Work

After you've supplied consumer protection with the information they need, they will investigate the allegations, during which time your best bet is to remain quiet. If, when they've completed their work, they find that your case has merit, they may try to mediate an agreement between you and Mammoth or perhaps get the company to sign what's called a consent decree, in which it agrees to abide by certain rules and practices in the future with respect to the sale and service of its products.

If the company agrees to this, says Horsch, it might agree to reimburse you as well. But if for some reason it doesn't, you may use the decree and all other information gathered by consumer protection as evidence if you sue the company.

Asking the Government to Be Your Friend

Even if the state justice department doesn't find grounds to pursue your case directly, it can provide help through what's called an *amicus curae*, or "friend of the court" statement. This is a brief that it files on your behalf in a lawsuit or appeal that says it agrees that your position has merit. Having the government make that claim can be powerful.

"Cases of consumer fraud, securities fraud, and the like can often be bolstered when you get the weight of your government behind you," says John Newhouse, an attorney in New York City. "The government can add both knowledge and the credentials of its officials to bolster your case."

Newhouse warns, however, that you're not likely to get "friend of the court" backing in a case that the government deems relatively small or insignificant. "An attorney general isn't going to get his office involved in a rent squabble between a tenant and a landlord," he says. "On the other hand,

if there's a widespread problem affecting public safety or welfare, such as asbestos or lead abatement, the attorney general may join your cause by filing a 'friend of the court' brief. In general, if your case is representative of a pervasive and deeply entrenched problem that the attorney general is trying to attack, you stand a better shot."

To request a "friend of the court" brief, contact the state attorney general's office. "Simply call the local branch and ask to speak with one of the staff attorneys. Be prepared to make a compelling case for why your situation is representative of a larger problem or why it's in the state's best interest to be involved in it. Then, if it's a matter they're interested in, they may write the brief and submit it to the judge who's hearing your case," says Newhouse.

Using Your Government against Your Government

There may be times when the government is your adversary, but that needn't stop it from being your ally as well. Let's say, for instance, that you're unhappy with the state-certified nursing home your father is living in, because it doesn't appear to be properly maintained. Can you get one agency of your government to help take on another? It's not so easy, but it can be done. Here are several ways that the government might help you.

Dig Up Information

The office of consumer protection in your state attorney general's office can't act as a co-plaintiff in your case against the nursing home (in this case, the state department of aging) because both agencies serve under the aegis of the state's executive branch, and a lawsuit would then amount to the executive branch of the government suing itself. But it can ask for information from the department with regard to who has been inspecting the home, how often it's been inspected and on what dates, what violations it was cited for, and whether and when there was follow-up to see if those violations were corrected.

Cut Red Tape

If your attorney has been appealing directly to the department of aging for the reasons that this substandard home has passed inspection and no information is forthcoming, the attorney general can intercede on your behalf and force the agency to comply.

Use an Ombudsman

An ombudsman is a government official whose sole job is to help you eliminate red tape and get satisfaction from the government agency with which he is associated.

You can usually find out whether ombudsmen are available to you by calling the state attorney general's office or your local state legislator. Both numbers are in the government pages of your phone book.

"Ombudsmen will not help you in a lawsuit against the government per se," says Texas consumer attorney John Ventura, "but they will help you cut through the bureaucracy and get what you need." If, for instance, you want to consider bringing charges against your city department of transportation because the sidewalk in front of your home has been broken for 3 or 4 months and you can't get any information from the department about when it will be repaired, the ombudsman could step in. In addition, if the ombudsman's efforts fail to produce results, you can present that in a court of law as an example of the government's unresponsiveness.

Collect Your Attorney's Fees

Although it's not common, it is possible for you to be reimbursed for the fees you incur when you hire a licensed attorney. A federal statute known as the Equal Access to Justice Act allows you reimbursement from a government agency that you've sued if it is determined that the government's position was not substantially justified, says John Rao, staff attorney with Boston's Consumer Law Center.

For example, Rao notes, "the Social Security Administration was demanding repayment from a citizen whom they had inadvertently overpaid, but the citizen in question had declared bankruptcy and should therefore have been protected from debts he could not pay. Social Security took the position that it was immune from bankruptcy laws, but the judge disagreed and ruled that a debt to them is no different from, say, a credit card debt to a department store. Not only was the individual absolved of the debt, but the government had to pick up the tab for what it cost him to sue them."

●◆ WHAT INSIDERS SAY:

It can be very difficult to successfully sue the government. "Some government agencies and personnel do have immunity from prosecution," says Ventura, "and it's not always easy to figure out who you can go after and who you can't. Judges, for instance, are immune from civil suits, even if you think the one who heard your case was partial. And in suing the IRS, if you are successful, you might collect your attorney fees, but you won't collect damages or interest."

The best way to find out if you have a case against the government? "The litmus test is to find a lawyer who's familiar with government law who will agree to take your case on a contingency basis (meaning that the fee is established as a portion of your settlement and is payable only if you win the case)," says Ventura.

Receiving Your Just Rewards

Suppose someone owed you money, you took them to court, and the judge ruled in your favor. Now what? Most people presume that once they've proven their case in a court of law, their rewards will be served up to them in no time and with no hassle. Actually, it sometimes takes time, perseverance, and a little government intervention to guarantee that you get your due.

While the particulars of how government can help collect a judgment may differ slightly from state to state, the general services are pretty similar. Most often, you have to fill out forms (and in some cases, even deliver them), and for the most part, the office of the court clerk will handle your matter. Here's what the clerk can do—in conjunction with you—to help you collect your debt.

Go After Personal Property

If you can locate and identify the debtor's personal property—automobiles, savings bonds, bank accounts, or jewelry, for example—you can ask for an "execution on goods and property," which empowers the court to impound those assets and apply them to the debt. In addition, if you don't know where the debtor has savings or checking accounts or what personal property he owns, you may obtain an information subpoena from the clerk's office, which you can serve by certified mail and to which the debtor must respond or face prosecution.

Go After Wages

Courts can also seize a portion of the debtor's wages for you, provided you fill out your state's equivalent of an application for wage execution, which man-

---

Power to the People

HOW TO (LEGALLY) BEAT A PARKING TICKET

Only at a parking meter could being 30 seconds late cost you $50. But there are things you can do other than simply gritting your teeth and paying up, say insiders.

"The first step is to look very carefully at your ticket," says Louis Camporeale, author of *The New York City Motorist's Parking Survival Guide* and founder of the Parking Pal Company, which has been teaching motorists their rights for several years.

Unlike the situation with a traffic ticket, where the accusing officer has to show up in court to testify about your violation, a parking ticket itself serves as sworn testimony. Thus, a significant mistake can cause a parking bureau judge to rip up the ticket. (Camporeale says that some studies estimate as many as 25 percent of all tickets have some sort of error.) Here's the information to check.

The time, date, and address

"This is critically important information, because parking regulations differ on different days," Camporeale says. If it's been left blank, is incor-

rect, or is scrawled illegibly, you have a defective summons—and a case to have it dismissed.

References to your license number, car model, or registration

Once again, if any of these areas are incorrect or left blank, you can argue that the ticket wasn't meant for your car.

Information about the statute

"The ticket has to state clearly exactly what regulation you violated; otherwise, you've been given a fine for some unknown reason," Camporeale says.

Even if the ticket seems to be valid, don't give in quite yet. Parking judges have been known to reduce fines or dismiss them outright if someone can prove that the parking signs were misleading—if, for instance, there are two conflicting signs in close proximity, making it difficult to tell which one is in force. If you plan to use this defense, take plenty of photographs, then take them to court with you. "Being prepared is a way to treat the judge and the system with respect," Camporeale says, "and when you do that, you have a better chance to win your case."

dates that the debtor's employer (or the debtor himself, if self-employed) withhold a portion of each paycheck and pay it directly to you. If the debtor agrees to the execution, the court notifies the employer, who will immediately withhold money for you. If he wants to fight it, however, and the court allows him to, a hearing will be scheduled by the court.

Go After Future Revenue

Finally, if you still haven't collected all that is due you, the court can issue a judgment that forbids the debtor from selling any real estate holdings until such time as the debt is paid.

●◆ WHAT INSIDERS SAY:

Once you have a judgment in hand, sometimes a threat is all it takes to force a settlement. If you want to try this angle first, contact the court or the local sheriff and ask him to issue what is called a writ of garnishment if the defendant doesn't pay you what you're owed. This is legal action that will be taken against the defendant to collect the judgment. It includes having a portion of all future earnings set aside for repayment. As Oregon personal injury lawyer Bill Savage notes, the writ itself shows that you're serious, which can often scare the person into making good on the debt.

CHAPTER 20

GETTING YOUR REPS to VOTE YOUR WAY

The United States has a long and grand tradition of letting citizens coax their representatives into political change. It's one of the benefits inherent in the rights to free speech and assembly guaranteed by the Constitution.

Nevertheless, there's a huge difference between making a plea to a legislator and getting him to vote your way. That's where effective lobbying comes in.

Few terms in politics have a slipperier and less savory sound than *lobbying*. The word suggests backroom deals and payoffs for self-serving purposes. Yet, in its basic sense, lobbying is merely the process of working to change people's minds. "Think of it as informing a member of Congress on your views so that you might move his thought process," says Tim Smith, director of Congressman Tim Holden's (D-Pennsylvania) district office in Reading. "Lobbying only becomes an awkward word when it describes an organization that spends a lot of money."

You can lobby effectively on your own, or you can hire a pro to do the job for you. In this chapter, we'll offer insider advice that will help you get the best results from either option.

> You can play a major role in shaping the laws that your state and the federal governments enact. The keys: the power of your words, the passion of your views, and some good old-fashioned lobbying.

LOBBYING ON YOUR OWN

Perhaps you want a legislator to support a tax increase to fund a new program. Or maybe your goal is the opposite—to get your congressmember and senator to stop spending so much and cut your taxes instead. Regardless of which side of an issue you come down on, you can be sure that there will be hun-

FACTOID

OF THE 20,512 LOBBYISTS REGISTERED TO DO BUSINESS BEFORE THE U.S. CONGRESS IN 1999, 138 WERE FORMER SENATORS OR CONGRESSMEN.

dreds, if not thousands, of people on the opposite side, too. And they'll be pressing that same elected official to take their position instead of yours.

That doesn't mean that your plea will get lost in the din, and it doesn't mean that you need to hire a professional lobbyist to get your message across. While being a good lobbyist takes a certain savvy and smart timing, these are skills that you can learn, say insiders. Also, it's sometimes more effective if you do your own lobbying. Because professional lobbyists are such fixtures around seats of government, you, as an earnest individual, can make more of an impression than a hired gun.

However, to be successful on your own, you need to do two things: Time your plea so that it lands on your legislator's desk when he is most open to persuasion, and build a rational, convincing, politically smart case. Here's how insiders suggest that you work.

Start Your Crusade at the Right Place

It's not widely known, but in recent years, much of the government's business has shifted from Washington to the state capitals, says Steve Perkins, associate director of the Center for Neighborhood Technology in Chicago, a nonprofit organization that fosters ecologically sound community development. That's a major plus if you're attempting to get government to do your bidding: State legislators often represent smaller districts than federal officials and may be more dependent on—and responsive—to individual voters like you.

Therefore, if you have a concern, your best bet is to check first to see if your state representatives can help you. Then, if necessary, you can turn to your federal representatives. To contact either state or federal officials, look in the government pages of your phone book.

HOW THE LEGISLATIVE PROCESS WORKS

We all have at least a rough idea of what a law is—something that, when broken, gets someone in trouble. But that law has gone through a number of steps to reach the point where it's ready to be enforced.

Before an idea can become a law, it exists as a bill, a written description that is intended to be molded (often many times) until it is polished enough to be voted on by lawmakers. This polishing stage is where you have the first opportunity as a lobbyist to shape the legislation. You can point out potential flaws and suggest that changes be made, for example.

If a bill survives this initial shaping, it is voted on by both chambers of a legislature, and there is a second opportunity for you to get involved. You can push to have the bill passed into law or to have it killed.

Only elected officials have votes, although occasionally a controversial issue is presented to voters as a referendum at election time, allowing the public to determine its fate.

If both houses pass a bill, it faces a final hurdle; it goes on to the president (at the federal level) or governor (for state legislation). That person may sign the bill into law, allow it to become law by not acting on it, or veto it. A vetoed bill has a last chance if the legislators feel strongly enough about it to override the veto by a specific majority.

Start at the Right Time

If the laws of our land just popped out of legislators' heads, there would be no way for ordinary citizens to get involved. But every law begins as an idea, or bill (see "How the Legislative Process Works" on page 337). This is something that you can shape if you act at the right time—when legislators are shaping the bill. This means that you have to keep track of the bill as it passes through hearings and other legislative processes.

How can you do this? You can phone your representative's local office to find out about upcoming hearings or committee meetings. Also, if you have access to the Internet, you can check Web sites. At the federal level, you can access the public hearing schedules of the House and the Senate by going to www.congress.gov. This will take you to an extensive site maintained by the Library of Congress.

Many states have Web sites as well. Maine's site, at www.state.me.us, for example, posts a weekly legislative calendar. You can locate other state sites by typing www.state.*(insert the two-letter state abbreviation)*.us. Then search the site for a legislative agenda.

◆ WHAT INSIDERS SAY:

In addition to tracking the progress of a bill through written information, you may want to contact the committee that is considering it or individual committee members, suggests Jenette Nagy, a staff member of the Work Group on Health Promotion and Community Development, a nonprofit group based at the University of Kansas in Lawrence that helps communities plan their futures. "If legislators know a citizens' group is watching them, and the group makes its mission very clear, it's more likely that the legislators will follow that path," she says.

Know Your Legislator

Before you appeal to officials for their votes, it's essential to know where they stand. This sounds obvious, but it's a step that many people skip, say congressional insiders.

You can learn an official's stance by consulting the weekly records in some newspapers, checking government Web sites for recent committee votes or transcripts of debates, or visiting a legislator's own Web page. These personal pages can be informative, with transcripts of speeches, press releases, and bills.

You can access your federal representatives' Web sites by going to either www.senate.gov or www.house.gov. State legislators' sites are more difficult to find, since each state's site is set up differently. But you can locate the general state site by typing www.state.*(insert the two-letter state abbreviation)*.us. Once there, you can search for recent votes or look for information on individual legislators' Web sites.

You also can call your area representative's office and ask for his positions on recent votes. If a legislator knows that you are sophisticated and committed enough to follow each pertinent vote, he's apt to take your cause more seriously, insiders say.

Check With Special Interest Groups

Private and nonprofit groups often tally legislators' positions on specific bills. Taxpayers for Common Sense, for instance, a special interest group that wants to reduce spending at the federal level, maintains a Common Sense Taxpayer Scorecard on the Web (www.taxpayer.net) that lists votes on tax-related issues. Enter the last name of a congressmember or senator (or your zip code if you don't know the name), and in a few nanoseconds, you'll see a list of that person's votes.

FACTOID

LEGISLATIVE WEB SITES CAN BE BOTH INFORMATIVE AND ENTERTAINING. IN ADDITION TO HIS STANCE ON POLITICAL ISSUES, SENATOR TED KENNEDY'S (D-MASSACHUSETTS) SITE ONCE OFFERED HIS RECIPE FOR CAPE COD FISH CHOWDER.

Other special interest groups provide similar records. To access them, use your Internet browser's search function to look for the phrase "congressional voting records."

Send a Personal Letter

Insiders say it's important to send a personal letter rather than a form letter supplied by a group that shares your cause. Form letters just don't have the impact that your own words do.

Use the Phone When Appropriate

The phone is a quick and convenient way to reach your representative's office, but don't expect a busy legislator to pick up at the other end. Most likely, you will get an office assistant or aide. If the message you want to leave is involved, there's a chance that the person you speak to won't relay all your points to the legislator. That said, if you urgently want to voice concern over a pending vote on a bill, the telephone is useful.

In this case, clearly and briefly state your position on the issue, citing the name and number of the bill. Then your opinion will be added to a tally of voter opinions that is passed to your representative.

For the phone numbers of state and federal officials' home offices, consult the government pages of your phone book. To contact a federal representative's Washington office, get the number from the local office.

Amazing Stories

A STATE THAT LOVES CITIZEN LOBBYISTS

Is it fair for you to exert more influence than your neighbor down the street? Yes, and in fact, lawmakers in some states welcome citizen lobbying, noting that voters become apathetic when they feel that they have little influence on the government's decisions.

Hawaii may set the standard for this form of participatory government, going as far as to encourage public lobbying in a variety of ways. First is the state's Internet guide to lobbying. The site (go to www.capitol.hawaii.gov and look for "Citizen's Guide" in the site map) lists a number of measures that were passed with the nudging of active citizens, including stricter standards for drunken driving and improved housing options for the elderly and disabled.

Then there is the public access room at the capitol in Honolulu, which provides citizens with computer terminals, a copier, fax machines, and a television for viewing videos of hundreds of proceedings. To round out citizens' education, the access room offers workshops on giving testimony and understanding how laws are made.

The room is a busy place, says Kimo Brown, public access coordinator, and it draws a broad cross-section of the public. Brown says that you can find everyone from the down-and-out to well-heeled executives, all working to become their own lobbyists.

The address for the access room is Hawaii State Capitol, 415 South Beretania Street, Room 401, Honolulu, HI 96813.

Send an E-Mail

With the growth of the Internet, electronic mail has become a popular way to quickly contact elected officials. Some activists feel that e-mail has less impact than a personal letter sent by mail, both because it takes relatively little effort to send and because it is so easily deleted from the legislator's electronic mailbox. Still, if your legislator receives enough e-mails supporting your position, it will give him a sense of popular support for the issue.

To find your representative's e-mail address, check newsletters mailed to your home, or call the legislator's local office and request it. You can look up e-mail addresses for federal representatives at www.senate.gov for the Senate or www.house.gov for the House.

Since your representative may prefer to respond by conventional mail, be sure to include your postal address in any e-mail communication, however.

10 KEYS TO WRITING AN EFFECTIVE LETTER

When you want to write a letter that will get a busy legislator's attention, your best bet is to follow the example of advertising copywriters and keep it short and simple, say insiders. As with the long-running "swoosh" ad campaign for Nike, when you do it right, less really can communicate better than more. Here are some specific insider tips for writing a effective letter.

1. State the purpose of your letter in the first paragraph, and if the letter relates to a particular bill, identify it by number and subject and remind the legislator where it is in the legislative process.

2. Address only one issue and keep the letter to a single page.

3. Include key information, using examples to support your position. Specifically, tell the legislator how the bill will affect you.

4. Stick to the point rather than including nonessential material that a speed-reading legislator or aide may be tempted to skim over.

5. Be courteous, but let some emotion show. Tell the legislator that you're deeply committed to your position.

6. Make your personal letter truly personal, mentioning any local connections or personal contact that you may have had with the lawmaker.

7. Thank the legislator for reading your views and request a response.

8. Follow up. If you get a response that's vague or unclear, write and ask for clarification of the legislator's stance on your issue.

9. Know when to say "when." If you and/or your group have been writing frequently and don't really have new information to offer, then stop. Have some other sympathetic group deliver your message or begin writing to another lawmaker.

10. How's your handwriting? There's an untested theory shared by some insiders that handwritten letters are the first to snare the attention of busy legislators.

Use Statistics as a Tool

The right statistic, clearly presented, can stick in a person's mind far longer than an argument on a position. To lobby effectively, try to come up with a selection of remarkable facts or even a "top 10" list to support your point of view. One group, TV-Free America, based in Washington, D.C., has gathered an impressive list of statistics on television viewing habits, including the fact that by age 65, the average American will have spent nearly 9 years glued to the tube.

Lobby the Whole Committee

On their way to becoming laws, bills are discussed, torn apart, and reassembled by a committee of legislators. If you want to increase the chances of influencing a bill, communicate with each member of the committee. You can determine who is on a committee by contacting your legislator's office or, at the federal level, by looking up the committee by name on Congress's Web site at www.congress.gov.

Committee members will be most responsive to voters in their district or state, so if you can, enlist the help of any contacts that you may have in those areas to lobby their representatives on your behalf.

VISITING YOUR LAWMAKERS

Even in this age of sophisticated communication, there is no substitute for face-to-face meetings. Politicians continue to make public appearances for that reason, and in turn, your physical presence can help get your message across to these officials.

The basic rules for personal meetings with local officials (detailed in chapters 1 and 2) still apply at this level: You want to be polite, prepared, concise, clear about your needs, and assertive. But there are additional tips that you'll want to keep in mind when meeting with state or federal representatives to ask for their vote.

Amazing Stories

LOBBYING WITH A PERSONAL WEB SITE

Increasingly, citizens with a point of view are climbing onto the virtual soapbox of a personal Internet page. One example is the Web site maintained by 89-year-old Doris Haddock, who calls herself Granny D. In 1999, the site offered periodic updates when Haddock conducted a cross-country protest march, the purpose of which was to send out the message that "soft money is a cancer on our society."

Haddock's site included a map of her progress and offered an e-mail listing of U.S. Senators to encourage others to express their opinions on the issue of campaign financing. Foremost, though, the site stirred up publicity. Within days of the start of her walk, she had been featured on National Public Radio and CNN.

Be Prepared to Sell Yourself

Lawmakers tend to be workaholics (the job demands it), yet they still don't have time to see all of the constituents who'd like to schedule face-to-face meetings. You can expect to be screened by office personnel—from the chief of staff down to the person assigned to answer the phones—to see if your visit is worth a piece of the boss's time. To improve your chances of getting through this sieve, be prepared with a clear explanation of what you're after. For example, "I'd like 30 minutes of the congressman's time to discuss bill HR-234, which my 200-member group and I support."

➥ WHAT INSIDERS SAY:

When you call to schedule a meeting with a legislator, you may be encouraged to meet with a legislative aide instead. Don't assume that you're being stuck with a second-string player. In many offices, aides specialize in certain areas, such as veterans' affairs or Social Security benefits, and they are your representative's key source of information on those issues.

Be Flexible about Timing

Because much of a legislator's time is split between a home office and the capital and meetings can be arranged only during certain periods in each loca-

tion, be prepared to work your request into the available time slots. For members of Congress, local meetings are restricted to "district work periods" when they will be in their home districts. Ask the person in your representative's office who schedules appointments when the legislator will be available.

➥ WHAT INSIDERS SAY:

Before meeting with a member of Congress, mail a written statement of your position. Not only will you give the lawmaker a chance to get acquainted with your views, says Tim Smith, director of Pennsylvania congressman Tim Holden's district office, but "it's a courtesy sort of thing."

Do Your Homework

You could storm into a representative's office and vent on a dozen favorite subjects, but that's not going to get the results you want. Your goal should be to present a logical argument that will convince your rep that you're right.

Yes, this sounds obvious, but it's a step that many people skip, says Jim Hart, chief of staff for Congressman James Maloney (D-Connecticut) at his Waterbury office. Instead, he says, people sometimes come into a meeting

THE BENEFITS OF COMPROMISE

You could be like the hero of the movie *Mr. Smith Goes to Washington* and take on the political machine all by yourself, but there are excellent reasons for working with a coalition of groups that share your position. Foremost among them is the fact that this can help you develop a well-rounded and rea-

sonable-sounding platform that will impress lawmakers with its seriousness.

The members of a coalition don't have to agree on all issues. In fact, it might be more credible if they don't. The more diverse the backing for your issue, the less likely that legislators will dismiss it as just an-

other "special interest."

Activists have formed all sorts of surprising alliances with groups that, on the surface, appeared to be on the opposite side of the fence. The matter of school vouchers, for example, has brought together political conservatives, church officials, and welfare advocates.

with surprisingly little preparation and waste the short time that they have with their representatives.

You may even want to make an outline, just as if you were about to deliver a talk in front of a class. "Have your argument laid out well," advises Tim Smith, director of Pennsylvania congressman Tim Holden's district office, "so that you don't jump from point A to point B."

Also, be prepared to answer questions that your representative may raise about your position or that of the opposing side. You want to come across as an expert, not just another in an unending stream of irate citizens.

➡ WHAT INSIDERS SAY:

It never hurts to be political when presenting your case. If you can show an official how supporting your cause will help keep him in office or how your group can help him in other ways, you improve your chances for success.

Learn the Lingo

Politics is like any other business—it bristles with workplace jargon. Unless you learn at least a few of these unfamiliar words and speak in the same terms the legislators use, you'll have a hard time communicating.

If you want to discuss a piece of legislation, for example, you should refer to it by its prefix and number: S.942 is the 942nd bill introduced in the Senate. And you shouldn't talk about a "law" when you're really referring to a "bill" (see "How the Legislative Process Works" on page 337). To learn other jargon, look to legislative aides, lobbyists, and fellow activists. Each time one of them mentions a term you don't know, ask for an explanation.

Stay Calm

Are you passionate about your cause? Of course you are, or you wouldn't be lobbying for it. That doesn't mean, though, that you should let your emotions rip when you meet with government officials.

"If you feel strongly about something, it is very easy to become emotional, whereas politicians are much more pragmatic," says Kimo Brown, public access coordinator at the Hawaii state capitol in Honolulu.

LOBBYING 101

If you don't feel that you're adequately prepared to be an effective lobbyist, you can get schooling and advice that will improve your pitch.

The Advocacy Institute, a Washington-based nonprofit organization, offers training to help "underrepresented" people influence decision makers. It typically works with groups of one or two dozen participants over a period of a few days to a month. Topics in a typical program include defining your message, taking advantage of the media, and influencing elections. Participants may also visit with graduates of the program to see how they are putting these practices to work. To date, leaders from more than 2,500 nonprofit groups have benefited from this training.

You should note, however, that the workshops aren't cheap. A 2- to 5-day session can cost several thousand dollars. Typically, participants are leaders in public interest organizations rather than private individuals. For information on the program, contact the institute at 1707 L Street NW, Washington, DC 20036.

That stands to reason. Politicians deal in issues like yours day after day, and consequently, they take a relatively detached, logical approach. Thus, when talking to your representative, you may want to alter your tone to suit the situation. Or take along a calm friend who can help moderate your visit.

➥ WHAT INSIDERS SAY:

Even if you can't get a legislator to agree with your view, you're better off leaving on cordial terms. "We try to stress that you never consider anybody your enemy," says Brown. "The person you're fighting today may be your ally tomorrow."

HIRING A LOBBYIST

Sometimes, you can derive satisfaction just from getting the chance to plead your case directly to your elected officials. But what if you feel a particular urgency to get action on a cause? Let's say a busy stretch of highway through town has been claiming a life each year, and the bill for a bypass that you think is needed is bottled up in the state legislature. Then you may want to bring in all the guns—including a professional lobbyist.

Not all lobbyists work in the same way. The best-known stereotype is the big-spending schmoozer who walks the halls of the capitol with plenty of political action committee money to toss around. Others work more quietly—and affordably—and have a level of expertise in both the workings of government and the technical side of certain issues.

Chances are, you'll be looking for a lobbyist of the second sort. You'll also want the lobbyist to have certain specific qualities, suggests Vicki Spencer, executive director of the Wyoming Audubon in Casper. The person should be an excellent researcher, have good speaking skills, and be able to get along well with people. It also helps if the lobbyist can put on a "performance," with a show of sincerity and conviction, Spencer says. Here are tips on finding the perfect lobbyist.

DO CAMPAIGN CONTRIBUTIONS OPEN DOORS?

With even basic statewide and federal campaigns costing millions of dollars, candidates are forced to search constantly for funding. The unspoken promise that goes with each generous contribution they solicit is access—if the lawmaker is elected.

Do contributions really buy you some of a legislator's time? Some insiders aren't so sure. They say that the most generous contributors can ex-pect to have a better chance of getting a politician's attention, but the definition of *generous* is rising with the cost of getting elected.

These days, unless you're well off enough to hand over an amount that will probably be noticed—say, at least $500 for a congressional election—you might be better off giving your money to an organization that is working to promote your cause, says Steve Perkins, associate director of the Center for Neighborhood Technology in Chicago, a nonprofit organization that fosters ecologically sound community development.

And one congressional insider says that even if you can afford a substantial donation, it may not automatically open doors for you. As this aide points out, the legislator's staff won't necessarily associate your name with that generous lump of cash when you call.

Let Your Fingers Do the Walking

Start by calling an established organization that has something in common with your interest and ask who it uses. Also, if you live in a major city, you may find entries under "Lobbyists" in the yellow pages of your phone book. If you have access to the Internet, use the search function on your browser to look for "lobbyist." This will direct you to a number of Web sites.

Search For Specialists

To find a lobbyist who concentrates on a certain issue, consult the Selected Subjects index of the guide "Washington Representatives," which is available in some libraries and bookstores. Also, some Web sites, including the Online Pennsylvania Lobbyist Directory, let you search their member listings by specialty. Use your Internet browser's search function to look for "lobbyist," then click on specific Web sites to see if they offer this service.

Look for Relevant Experience

If you want your presence known in the District of Columbia, don't assume that a lobbyist at the state level will know the ropes (and the names and faces) there. Make it clear to a potential lobbyist just what levels of government you're concerned with and ask whether the person is qualified to help you.

Check References

Ask for the names of some of the lobbyist's clients who can serve as references, then call each one. You want to get a reading on whether the lobbyist was effective for them and responsive to their needs. Also, speaking to previous clients will give you a sense of whether the lobbyist is a good fit for your cause.

Put a Cap On Your Costs

Don't have much money to spend on a lobbyist? Say so up front, and detail the length of time for which you wish to be represented. Or state that you want to retain the lobbyist only for a particular issue. You may be able to sign someone on for as little as $2,000.

●◆ *WHAT INSIDERS SAY:*

You may be able to save money and increase your influence by joining lobbying forces with a large corporation or organization. Be careful, though; rather than working for your benefit, a big player may want to be associated with you or your small advocacy group solely for the sake of favorable public relations.

EIGHT

Work

CHAPTER 21

GROWING YOUR BUSINESS on a BUDGET

Being your own boss.
Bringing *your* ideas to life.
Making a fortune the old-fashioned American way—by doing it yourself.

Dreams like these inspire Americans to start more than 150,000 small businesses each year. But for every owner whose small-business dream succeeds, four others will fail, often due to a lack of planning, financing, advice, and training.

How can you improve the chances that your business will be among the ones that prosper? Turn to Uncle Sam.

While you may not automatically think of the government as a business owner's best friend, in reality, one of its key roles is helping small businesses succeed. The reason for its interest is simple: New businesses help drive the economy. They are the sources of most new jobs, they generate tax revenue, and they help local communities prosper and grow. All of these things strengthen the nation.

In fact, Aida Alvarez, administrator for the U.S. Small Business Administration, views small businesses as the source of "most of the innovation in the economy."

Government help comes in many forms. Through federal and state programs, you can tap the expertise of an experienced management consultant, borrow money, buy a file cabinet for a pittance, and even get free recommendations for cutting your company's electric bills.

Furthermore, if your brand-new venture needs a few square feet to start, some clerical help, management guidance, and room to grow, many areas

> It's the great American dream: Turn the seed of an idea into your own giant sequoia of a company. And the government can help you make it happen, with financing, training, and advice every step of the way.

FACTOID

WHEN PEOPLE TALK ABOUT LAS VEGAS BEING HOT, THEY AREN'T TALKING ONLY ABOUT THE SUMMER TEMPERATURES. THE CITY OF 740,000 HAS MORE BUSINESS STARTUPS PER CAPITA—2.38 NEW FIRMS FOR EVERY 100 RESIDENTS IN 1997—THAN ANY OTHER METRO AREA IN THE UNITED STATES, ACCORDING TO *INC.* MAGAZINE. IN ADDITION, *ENTREPRENEUR* MAGAZINE CALLS LAS VEGAS ONE OF THE "BEST BETS FOR ENTREPRENEURIAL ACTIVITY."

of the country have business incubators to match your need and pocketbook.

The government can be your teacher, landlord, overseas business-development guide, financial partner, or customer. And if you have access to the Internet, it can even deliver much of its services and documents directly to your home or office. Ready to launch your business? Read on.

STARTING A BUSINESS

When ice cream moguls Ben and Jerry decided to set up their own business, they knew exactly what their product would be and where they would open their first store. When Jeff Bezos, president of Amazon.com, the world's largest online bookstore, began looking into business, he had no idea what he'd sell; he just knew that he wanted to take advantage of this incredible new medium, the World Wide Web.

What these two examples show is that there is no single path to success in business. In many ways, conceiving a business is a make-it-up-as-you-go-along adventure. There are some common keys, however. The first is a formal business plan. Every business needs a plan that provides things such as:

✔ A description of the business and your plan for making it successful

✔ A marketing plan

✔ An analysis of the competition

✔ An estimate of how much money you'll need to get started

✔ Revenue projections for the first several years

This means doing some footwork, but thankfully, the government can help you with every step.

Through the U.S. Small Business Administration (SBA), the Service Corps of Retired Executives (SCORE), and a half-dozen other groups, you can get everything from written advice to one-on-one counseling. And much of the help is available free or at low cost. Here are some of the best of the services you'll find.

Savvy Advice in a Booklet

The SBA publishes more than 50 brochures that can give you an overview of what lies ahead. Many, such as "Checklist for Going Into Business," "How to Buy or Sell a Business," "Business Plan for Small Service Firms," and "Business Plan for Retailers," are written especially for first-time owners. They are inexpensive—just $2 to $4 apiece—and they can answer many of your basic questions.

For a complete list and order form, contact your nearest SBA district office, which is listed in the government pages of your phone book, or write SBA Publications, P.O. Box 46521, Denver, CO 80201-46521. Also, if you have access to the Internet, you can get much of this information for free on the SBA's Web site at www.sba.gov. From the site's home page, click on "Starting" to access "Your First Steps," "Startup Kit," and more.

➡◆ *WHAT INSIDERS SAY:*

These booklets and the information online are too brief to answer every question you'll have. However, the "Profit Costing and Pricing" and "Pricing Your Products and Services Profitably" booklets cover all the bases on these important topics in just five pages each. Also, the business plan tutorial on the Web site is as good as many books on the subject.

Hands-On Help from the Experts

If you want some personal business advice from owners who have been there before, turn to one of the 389 chapters of SCORE. Although it's not a government agency, SCORE is a nonprofit resource that partners with the SBA to help fledgling business owners. It now has more than 12,000 volunteer retirees nationwide who share the expertise they developed during their own long, successful careers in business.

SCORE offers in-person counseling at its chapter offices (the number is listed in the white pages of your phone book), but like many government small-business resources, it is providing more and more of its services via the Internet. Its Web site at www.score.org gets an estimated 10,000 to 16,000 visitors a month, and 15 percent of the group's counseling is now done online.

Cyber counseling is similar to face-to-face meetings, says Betty Otte, chair of the SCORE chapter in Santa Ana, California, who enjoys working with business owners in both venues. "As with counseling in the office, if clients like me and the help I provide, they e-mail me time and again," Otte explains. "If they don't, or I answer their questions in one message, we have just one cyber meeting."

➥ WHAT INSIDERS SAY:
Some SCORE counselors are more experienced than others, and some are more knowledgeable about certain types of businesses than others. If you're not satisfied with the advice you get from the first counselor you meet, don't feel obligated to stay with that person. Make an appointment with a different counselor.

Startup Workshops

If you'd like to have someone walk you through the steps in starting a business, SCORE can help there, too, with small group workshops. Most sessions are 3 to 7 hours long and teach you how to write a business plan, handle financial basics like keeping the books, create a marketing plan, and launch into direct-mail advertising. Chapters usually charge a modest fee of around $20 to $40 per workshop.

THE DO'S AND DON'TS OF STARTING A BUSINESS

Whether you're planning to open a business that's high-tech or low, flush with employees or just you, experts say you should consider these six basic principles before making the plunge.

Do your research
Find out what your competitors are doing, who your customers are likely to be and what they want, where you can get financing, and more, advises Patricia O'Rourke, director of the Rhode Island Business Information Center in Providence.

Don't take shortcuts
A lot of work will go into opening your shop, and dodging tasks you don't like will hurt your long-term success.

Do spend time picking the right location
An easy-to-see shop on a busy street is more important in retailing than in just about any other business.

Don't expect to get rich
Retailing means long hours for relatively low income. You'll have to grow to a chain of shops before you'll start beefing up your bank account.

Do find a buddy or mentor
The first year is the loneliest of your business life. You'll second-guess every decision. Someone who has already been through it can provide reassurance, guidance, and a swift kick when needed, says Betty Otte, chair of the Service Corps of Retired Executives chapter in Santa Ana, California.

Don't give up
All business owners hit plenty of uncertainty and difficult times in the beginning. The successful ones persevere through everything.

A One-Stop Source for Marketing Facts

It's tough to succeed without a business plan, but it's also tough to write a plan without a clear understanding of your market. That's where Business Information Centers, or BICs, can help. Established by the SBA with help from SCORE chapters, chambers of commerce, or other education and business-related groups, these centers are resource libraries for business owners. They can provide the data, statistics, and other information you need to produce a business plan, understand your industry and competition, and even identify your customers.

The BIC libraries are well-stocked, thanks to companies like Microsoft and Apple, publishers like Upstart Publishing and Entrepreneur Media, and government agencies like the U.S. Census Bureau, which have provided high-speed, Internet-capable computers, suites of office software, CD-ROM disks, reference books, and videotapes, says Patricia O'Rourke, director of the Rhode Island BIC in Providence.

Suppose you want to start a bookkeeping service for the elderly in your community. You can go to a BIC and search the census data to find out how many potential clients live in town. You can use the American Yellow Pages on CD-ROM to find out how many bookkeepers are already in the community. You can write your business plan using "Automate Your Business Plan" software. You can even design your own business cards using Biz Form software and clip art, O'Rourke says.

Most BICs also have SCORE counselors on hand so you don't have to go to another office for in-person advice. "We'll even give your business plan to an SBA loan officer to prequalify you for a loan," O'Rourke adds

To find the nearest BIC, contact your local SBA district office, which is listed in the government pages of your phone book, or visit the SBA Web site at www.sba.gov and click on "Offices and Services." You also can request the brochure "The Facts about Business Information Centers" from

FROM CLIENT TO ADVISOR

Even before Michael Brinda started a computer-training school in Laguna Hills, California, in 1982, he made an appointment with the Service Corps of Retired Executives, better known as SCORE. But like many fledgling entrepreneurs, Brinda quickly discovered that he had gone to SCORE for the wrong reason: He wanted startup capital, but SCORE doesn't make loans.

Instead, Brinda got a dose of reality and invaluable instruction in how to set up and manage a business from John Spalding, then a SCORE counselor and previously an employee of the California state government.

Brinda knew what he wanted to do: use the skills he'd developed as a computer instructor at Sperry Univac to create a private center where computer neophytes could

learn skills. What he didn't know was how to run a business. "I needed to hear the truth, and John gave it to me," Brinda says.

Brinda's first loan application for New Horizon Learning Centers was rejected because it lacked good financial record-keeping and forecasts. Spalding helped Brinda correct that. He did the work by hand because low-cost financial software was not available in those days.

the SBA at 409 Third Street SW, Washington, DC 20416.

●◆ *WHAT INSIDERS SAY:*

Even if you've already attended businesses workshops and sought advice from a SCORE counselor, a trip to your regional Business Information Center is essential. Before committing to start a business, you should have a clear understanding of your market and your industry. Plan on spending at least 2 to 3 days at your local BIC, O'Rourke says.

A Clearinghouse for Rules and Regulations

Often, one of the most frustrating experiences for novice entrepreneurs is trying to figure out what local, state, and federal rules and licenses apply to their businesses. To help handle this problem, some states have set up central locations where business owners can get all the information they need. Following are examples of some of the best programs. Ask your state department of commerce or economic development if it has similar offerings. You can find the number in the government pages of your phone book.

Arizona Department of Commerce

The state of Arizona has found a way to do individual hand-holding for people who are just starting a business with a unique computer program that assists a representative in customizing a business startup, expansion, or relocation package for each caller, says Joe Dean, the state's small-business advocate. The package includes a helpful booklet with names, addresses, and phone numbers of public agencies and nonprofit groups that assist businesses; worksheets for business and marketing plans, personal financial statements, and business startup costs; and startup checklists. Plus, you can get applications for most of the forms you'll need to file, names of business-owners' groups that can provide advice, and a list of SCORE and small-business development center programs and workshops. Write to 3800 North Central Avenue, Suite 1650, Phoenix, AZ 85012.

Spalding's help didn't stop there. When Brinda opened his school—initially a one-man operation with an answering machine and a 1,800-square-foot leased shop financed with a mortgage on Brinda's house—Spalding, who lived a mile away, came in to answer the phones and talk business concepts with Brinda between calls.

"Sometimes you just need someone to talk to about how business is run, and John was there," Brinda says.

The help that SCORE and Spalding provided paid off. Twelve years after Brinda started his business, it had grown to a 60-franchise company that he was able to sell for $14 million.

After the sale, Brinda became a SCORE volunteer, counseling other would-be business owners 3 days a month. At 40, he was the youngest SCORE member in the chapter.

And like Spalding before him, he's given prospective business owners a taste of reality. Sometimes, he has to tell them that the idea they're so enthused about needs a lot of work. Too often, Brinda laments, they leave discouraged and never return instead of rolling up their sleeves and working to correct the flaws.

Such people are unwilling to risk their own money and too unsure of themselves to start their own businesses, Brinda says. "I give them my card and say, 'Keep in touch,' and they never call back."

Connecticut Economic Resource Center

The center provides free booklets, such as "Starting a Business? Start with Our Help" and offers the SmartStart Program, which helps business owners file the correct paperwork and obtain the right licenses and permits. If you visit the center, the staff will even help you fill out the forms, and you can pay all fees with one check, says Beth Wallace, SmartStart business registration specialist. The address is 805 Brook Street, Rocky Hill, CT 06067.

Ohio One-Stop Business Permit Center

When you contact the center and answer a series of questions about your business, the staff will send you a startup kit plus information that you might need about specific industries, such as state laws about producing frozen dairy products. Everyone receives the "Start Your Own Business" kit with all the necessary legal forms, tips on writing a business plan, and advice on setting up your financial systems. The state sends out about 35,000 kits a year. For information, write the Ohio Department of Development, P.O. Box 1001, Columbus, OH 43216-1001.

Cheap Real Estate

If you can't start your business in your garage, and you don't want to be tied down to a long-term lease in a building that can't accommodate growth, look around your area for a business incubator. Much like their mechanical counterparts on the farm, business incubators nurture fledgling companies until they can thrive on their own. They typically provide shared office services such as receptionists and secretaries, for example, plus access to office equipment such as copiers and fax machines.

Many also offer below-market rents for newcomers, flexible leases, and room to expand without moving, which is a great benefit for a beginning business. You can start in a small office that you can afford and move to larger quarters as soon as you need them.

There are more than 600 incubators in North America, according to Dinah Adkins, executive director of the National Business Incubation Association in Athens, Ohio. Ninety percent are nonprofit and most are operated by cities, economic development agencies, or universities. Some specialize in specific industries, such as high technology. Others accept a variety of companies, from x-ray equipment repair services to business consultants to silk screeners. Note, though, that many don't allow retailers or real estate agents.

To find out if your community has an incubator, contact your local university or the town or city agency that oversees business development. They will usually be listed in the government pages of your phone book under listings for "Commerce" or "Economic Development." You can also get a list of incubators in your state by sending your request, along with a stamped, self-addressed envelope, to the National Business Incubation Association, 20 East Circle Drive, Suite 190, Athens, OH 45701-3751. The information is also available on the group's Web site at www.nbia.org.

➥ *WHAT INSIDERS SAY:*

Acceptance into an incubator isn't based on your business's financing or lack of it. If you want to get in, you need to convince the center that you have a good product or business idea and a willingness and understanding of what it takes to build a successful enterprise, says Sally Hayhow, director of publications at the National Business Incubation Association.

Starting with Someone Else's Idea

Franchising as a way to grow a business (for the franchiser) or get into business for yourself (for the franchisee), has been around since the 1850s, but the modern concept of business format franchising really boomed in the 1960s and later. Today, the United States has more than 600,000 franchises for everything from fast-food restaurants and muffler shops to personnel services, candle stores, and janitorial services. Together, they generate more than $800 billion in annual sales.

There are many pluses to starting your small-business career by purchasing a franchise. If you deal with a reputable company, you can expect help with much of the up-front work of owning a business. Some franchises, for example, include a system for operating your business, a trademark, a logo, and help with startup, site selection, training, and product supply. Of course, you, as the franchisee, pay for all of this with up-front franchise fees and ongoing royalties and advertising fees.

Nevertheless, franchising can be chancy. You could buy into a company that offers poor support or delivers inferior supplies. Before you consider

GROWING BUSINESSES IN BIRMINGHAM

Often, when government wants to stimulate business growth, it offers tax incentives or grants, but Birmingham, Alabama, decided to take a more hands-on approach in the 1980s and create a business incubator to nurture new businesses.

The brainchild of top business executives and the mayor, the Birmingham Business Assistance Network's Entrepreneurial Center launched in 1988 in a 10,000-square-foot space. It was a quick success, growing fivefold in size in its first 10 years, says Susan Matlock, who has been the center's executive director since it opened. Now occupying a 50,000-square-foot site, the center has helped a mix of tenants, from publishers and food distributors to software developers and health care services.

Tenant John Williams, chief executive officer of Group 8760, a company that develops software for computer networks and derives its name from the number of minutes in a year, says that benefits to the business owners are many, but a key one is the opportunity to network with other tenants. "There are also necessary services that we'd rather not mess with, such as trash pickup and a cafeteria," he adds. "And we get a chance to meet a lot of business investors who come through here."

Tenants can use the incubator's office equipment, receptionist, clerical and security services, business library, and business training. The early assistance helps the startups later on, too. Up to 70 percent of tenants succeed after moving out of the incubator,

usually after 3 to 5 years, Matlock says.

Group 8760 has been in the incubator for 2 years, growing from three separate rooms to one of the largest spaces. Williams figures that the company will outgrow the incubator and have to move soon.

Although rent at the center is lower than at other commercial locations, when all the services and amenities are considered, low rent is not the biggest benefit for startups, Matlock says. "The space flexibility and shorter-term leases are most important. And we do a lot of training."

Two-thirds of the incubator's $550,000 annual budget comes from rent paid by 25 business tenants; the rest is from local banks and a contract with the city to teach business startup seminars.

buying a franchise, experts suggest that you investigate carefully. The Federal Trade Commission (FTC) can help. It requires franchisers to provide at least a minimum amount of information to potential franchisees. This includes the identity and experience of top executives, any lawsuits or bankruptcies involving the company or its executives, and any restrictions that the company might place on the way the franchisee is allowed to run the business. In addition, more than a dozen states require a more detailed disclosure, known as the Uniform Franchise Offering Circular. A reputable franchising company will provide this disclosure information.

You can also ask the FTC for a free booklet entitled "A Consumer Guide to Buying a Franchise" by writing the commission at Sixth and Pennsylvania Avenue NW, Room 240, Washington, DC 20580.

➬ WHAT INSIDERS SAY:

What's the best way to find out how reputable and professional a franchiser is? Ask current and former franchisees, says Don DeBolt, president of the International Franchise Association. The franchiser must give you a list. Talk to at least 20 to 25 franchisees before making your decision, he advises.

RUNNING A BUSINESS

Your company's need for help doesn't end with the startup phase; in fact, your needs may be even greater once you've been in business for a while.

You may need advice on refining your business plan to address competitors or costs that you didn't foresee. You may want help in figuring out how to expand because things are going so well, or perhaps just the opposite—you may need help controlling the costs that are threatening to put your business under.

Thankfully, the government is there for you at these times, too. Free and low-cost counseling, seminars, and publications abound to help you run your business. Here are some sources that experts recommend.

Workshops and Counseling

With more than 1,000 locations across the country, some of the most abundant and useful sources of assistance for existing businesses are the Small Business Development Centers. Staffed by counselors and local professionals from education, financial institutions, and businesses, these centers provide group workshops on such topics as revising a business plan and developing loan packages. They'll also provide personal assistance with everything from finding a new location for your business to establishing yourself with a bank that will give you a business loan.

The U.S. Small Business Administration (SBA) provides as much as half of the funding for these centers, with the rest of the money coming from states, chambers of commerce, economic development agencies, and public and private colleges and universities.

You can find the nearest Small Business Development Center by calling your local SBA district office; look in the government pages of your phone book or go to the SBA Web site at www.sba.gov and click on "Offices and Services." For a written list of centers in your area, write the Small Business Development Center National Information Clearinghouse, 1222 North Main, #712, San Antonio, TX 78212. If you have access to the Internet, you can obtain the list at http://sbdcnet.utsa.edu.

Help for Struggling Companies

The Small Business Development Centers help businesses that are thriving, but they also provide sound advice when companies flounder and seem headed toward bankruptcy. "That's one of our most important services, to get small businesses back on the right track," says Gregory F. Kishel, director of the Orange County Small Business Development Center in Santa Ana, California.

Counselors can work with a financially struggling business owner to find ways to cut costs and increase revenues. They can show the owner how to live on a budget and save cash from busy months to help survive lean months. In some cases, counselors even help negotiate lower rents or work with the business owner and creditors to set up more manageable payment plans.

A Business Study on the Cheap

Are you looking for low-cost, comprehensive advice on improving your business? Check with a nearby university to see if it has a small-business institute (about 200 schools nationwide do). As part of the curriculum at these institutes, students conduct in-depth case studies of existing businesses.

If your business is chosen, teams of students, under the guidance of a business professor, will analyze your business and offer well-researched recommendations on finance, operations, marketing, and management. Some student teams have developed marketing campaigns or written custom software for their clients. They often do a financial analysis, recommending products or services that should be discontinued or other ways to trim costs. Teams sometimes write entire business plans for their clients. Most programs are either free or charge a small fee.

For a list of small-business institutes, write Small Business Institute Directors' Association, Ronald Cook, Associate Professor of Small Business and Entrepreneurship, Rider University, 2083 Lawrenceville Road, Lawrenceville, NJ 08648. The information is also available at the group's Web site at www.sbida.org.

•❖ WHAT INSIDERS SAY:
What's the secret to being chosen for an in-depth study? Approach an institute when your company is facing an interesting challenge. You might be a good candidate if you're introducing a new product, for example, dealing with intense new competition in your industry, or facing a major shift in your industry that means you need to develop a new strategy for success. Even very small businesses may be chosen for studies, but the owners must be willing to share hours of time and private company information with students.

"Write" Advice for Established Businesses

The SBA library of booklets and other written material isn't just for startups. It includes plenty of material for established businesses, too, including titles such as "Transferring Management/Family Business," "Management Issues for Growing Business," "Computerizing Your Business," and "Employees: How to Find and Pay Them." The booklets cost $2 to $4. The SBA also sells four videotapes—"Promotion: Solving the Puzzle," "Marketing: Winning Customers with a Workable Plan," "Home-Based Business: A Winning Blueprint," and "The Business Plan: Your Roadmap to Success"—for $27 each. For an order form, write to SBA Publications, P.O. Box 46521, Denver, CO 80201-46521.

The SBA also maintains an extensive Web site with information about its various loan, grant, and assistance programs and advice for growing businesses. You can also get worldwide exposure by posting your business information in the "Business Card" section on the site. The Web address is www.sba.gov.

•❖ WHAT INSIDERS SAY:
One of the most useful publications available is free. Small Business Success is an annual magazine, sponsored by the SBA and Pacific Bell Directory in California, which offers information that will be useful no matter where you live. Articles in past issues included how to avoid fraud, marketing through trade shows, using barter in business, and managing diversity in the workplace. Each issue has a directory of useful resources. More than 600,000 copies are distributed nationwide each year. For a free copy, write Pacific Bell Directory, 2375 Northside Drive, San Diego, CA 92108.

Tips on Taxes from the IRS

The IRS provides so much information for business owners that it offers a whole catalog of products. The "Guide to Free Tax Services" (Publication 910) lists publications, videotapes, tax assistance phone numbers, and programs. For a copy of the catalog, call your nearest IRS office or write IRS Central Area Distribution Center, P.O. Box 8903, Bloomington, IL 61702-8903.

The IRS's most popular booklet for businesses is "Tax Guide for Small Business" (Publication 334), which explains federal tax laws that apply to one-owner businesses. The agency will also provide a wall calendar (Publication 1518) with the dates that business owners must remember to make payroll deposits, pay estimated taxes, and file major business tax forms.

Paring Your Postage Costs

With 95 percent of the 276 billion pieces of mail it delivers coming from businesses each year, the U.S. Postal Service has a clear interest in helping companies do things right. Thus, it offers free assistance and publications to save both you and the post office time and money.

The Postal Service has set up about 100 postal business centers nationwide where you can find out if your business mailings will qualify for lower prices, update your mailing lists and ZIP+4 codes, and more. Call your local post office to find the nearest center or search the Postal Service Web site at www.usps.gov/ncsc/locators.

You also can ask the Postal Service for printed advice on ways to save money on your business mailings. It publishes dozens of booklets, such as "Designing Business Letter Mail." For copies, contact your nearest postal business center or download the publications from the Web site, www.usps.gov/cpim/pubsbus2.htm.

"Designing Business Letter Mail" tends to use a lot of postal jargon, such as "single-piece rate mail" for individual letters. But it includes every detail on business mail, such as acceptable inks and papers to use. It even includes diagrams. It's worth the time to decipher this booklet, because you can save as much as 28 percent on large mailings such as ad-

vertisements. Talk to your local post office staff if you need help figuring out any terms. Other booklets, such as "How to Find Financing for Your Business," are quite easy to understand.

➡ WHAT INSIDERS SAY:

If you intend to sell products through the mail or by phone or even advertise in these ways, be sure to thoroughly learn the government's rules. Otherwise, you may end up facing thousands of dollars in fines for violating them. "A Business Guide to the Federal Trade Commission's Mail or Telephone Order Merchandise Rule," prepared jointly by the commission and the Direct Marketing Association, will tell you everything you need to know. For a copy, write the Federal Trade Commission at Sixth and Pennsylvania Avenue NW, Room 240, Washington, DC 20580.

The commission also answers frequently asked questions about all types of advertising, including mail order, in a free booklet called "Advertising Practices: Frequently Asked Questions: A Guide for Small Business." For a copy, write to the above address.

Reducing Your Electric Bill

Experts say that there's one clear and easy way to improve the profits from a small business: Use less energy. Energy is a significant expense for the average small business, so much so that if all U.S. small businesses cut their energy costs by 30 percent, "$10 to 15 billion a year would go straight to their bottom lines," says Jerry Lawson, director of the Energy Star Small Business program of the U.S. Environmental Protection Agency (EPA) in Washington, D.C. Here are two sources of advice.

Energy Star

This program will help you find some of those savings in your business in ways that will fit your budget. Just replacing some incandescent security lights with high-pressure sodium fixtures, for example, could save 80 percent on lighting costs while providing more light. That's just one of the tips in a 100-page book, *Putting Energy into Profits:*

Energy Star Small Business Guide, which is available by writing EPA, Energy Star Small Business 6202J, 401 M Street SW, Washington, DC 20278-1663. The information is also available at the agency's Web site at www.epa.gov/smallbiz.

◗◆ *WHAT INSIDERS SAY:*

If you're looking for the least expensive ways to reduce energy use, stick to things like replacing incandescent lights with fluorescents and repairing leaky ductwork and faulty machinery. These measures should cut use by at least 10 percent, and the first 10 percent of energy savings is easy and relatively cheap, according to Lawson. After that, you may have to make substantial and costly changes to cut energy use further.

"Straight Talk Energy"

The EPA and the California Energy Commission offer this booklet, which can help you no matter where your business is located. Although most of the resources mentioned are in California, "Straight Talk Energy" also features success stories, energy-saving tips, and resources available nationwide. One feature is a Monopoly-like board game that rewards efficiencies such as turning off office equipment on the weekends (receive one gold coin) and penalizes wasteful habits like ignoring broken windows (lose one gold coin). For a copy, write the California Energy Commission, 1516 Ninth Street, MS-29, Sacramento, CA 95814-5504.

◗◆ *WHAT INSIDERS SAY:*

Some local utility companies offer free or low-cost energy audits that will help you pinpoint ways to reduce costs. For example, an audit saved a small newsletter publisher $800 a year after energy auditors advised her to switch to energy-efficient lighting in her 2,000-square-foot office. Ask your local utilities.

Special Advice for Minorities

The Minority Business Development Agency, part of the U.S. Department of Commerce, helps millions of minority entrepreneurs start, operate, and grow small businesses. It does so through a nationwide string of business development and resource centers and business opportunity committees run by private firms, state and local government agencies, Native American tribes, and educational institutions.

Through these groups, you can get personalized help with writing a business plan, marketing, and seeking loans and grants. Counselors usually charge modest fees for these services. The Corpus Christi center in Texas, for example, gives 1 hour of consultation free. Later fees depend on the amount of work that must be done and the time involved, but they are lower than market rates. To find the minority center or committee nearest you, write the U.S. Department of Commerce, Minority Business Development Agency, 14th and Constitution Avenue NW, Room 5055, Washington, DC 20230, or visit the agency's Web site at www.mbda.gov.

The SBA provides business development assistance to minorities and other economically or socially disadvantaged business owners through the 8(a) Business Development Program, named for a section of the federal Small Business Act. If you qualify and your company is at least 2 years old, you can receive guidance in growing your business and access to small government contracts without competitive bidding. Southern California business/technology consultant Martha V. Daniel, for example, an African-American from Costa Mesa, has supplied technology consulting services to numerous government agencies. More than $75 billion in federal contracts has gone to 8(a) firms since the program started in 1969. For more information, contact your nearest SBA district office; look in the government pages of your telephone directory or go to the SBA Web site at www.sba.gov and click on "Offices and Services."

Help With Paying the Bills

The federal government and many states offer programs that can help you reduce the cost of training and staffing your business. In many cases, both you and the employees must meet specific criteria, but

(continued on page 362)

Best Bets

TOP STATES FOR SMALL BUSINESS INFORMATION

Some states do an especially good job of providing information to new, existing, and relocating businesses about the requirements and resources for doing business within their boundaries. Here are the top 10, in alphabetical order, and some of the material they offer to businesses.

Alaska

The Alaska state Web site at www.state.ak.us contains the full text of publications on doing business in Alaska, financial and business assistance programs, advice on establishing a business, and laws relating to business. Whether you're an acupuncturist or a midwife, a fisherman looking for a commercial loan, or a business owner seeking new employees, you'll find the information you need here.

Colorado

This state offers the "Colorado Business Resource Guide," a comprehensive booklet of good advice, much of which is useful regardless of which state you set up your business in. You'll find a checklist for starting a business, descriptions of the legal structures under which you can operate, and the basics of business recordkeeping. For a copy, write to the Colorado Office of Business Development, 1625 Broadway, Suite 1710, Denver, CO 80202, or order it from the Web site at www.state.co.us.gov_dir/oed/guide.html.

Connecticut

A new or relocating business can get informative booklets from the Connecticut Department of Economic and Community Development in partnership with the Connecticut Economic Resource Center. Need an environmental permit? Look in "Starting a Business? Start with Our Help." Need a distributor for your exports? Check "Help Is Here" or "Port Connecticut: Transportation and International Trade Resource Directory." For a packet, write the Connecticut Economic Resource Center, 805 Brook Street, Building 4, Rocky Hill, CT 06067-3405. Its Web address is www.state.ct.us.

Kentucky

Kentucky provides a thorough packet that opens with a step-by-step contact list for starting a business in that state. You'll also get information on obtaining a business loan and a how-to article on writing a business plan. Write the Kentucky Cabinet for Economic Development, Small and Minority Business Division, 67 Wilkinson Boulevard, Frankfort, KY 40601, for information. Its Web site is www.state.ky.us.

Nebraska

The Nebraska Department of Economic Development packs its Web site at www.ded.state.ne.us with startup, finance, and tax information. If you need to find a factory for your Nebraska business, this site has a list of available buildings. For just about every question, the site provides a link to a source. You can even e-mail business tax questions to the taxpayer assistance office. For information, write the Nebraska Department of

Economic Development, Existing Business Assistance Division, P.O. Box 94666, 301 Centennial Mall South, Lincoln, NE 68509-4666.

New Hampshire

The three-ring business binder offered by this state starts with the fact that "New Hampshire is one of only two states in the nation that does not have either a general sales or an income tax"—an immediate benefit for new business owners. Extra brochures tell about services such as job training and a matching grant program through which the state will provide funds to help new owners establish businesses. For a packet, write the New Hampshire Department of Resources and Economic Development, Division of Economic Development, 172 Pembroke Road, P.O. Box 1856, Concord, NH 03302-1856, or check the state's Web site at http://econdevelop.state.nh.us/obid.

New Jersey

Doing Business in New Jersey is a comprehensive 96-page magazine with a sample balance sheet for fledgling business owners, maps of state enterprise zones, and easy-to-read charts of the pros and cons of operating your business as a sole proprietorship, partnership, or corporation. Every assistance program and chamber of commerce is listed. For a copy, write New Jersey Department of Commerce and Economic Development, Division of Development for Small Businesses, Women, and Minority Businesses, 20 West State Street, Trenton, NJ 08625-0835.

New Mexico

New Mexico's three-ring binder for people looking to start new businesses is packed with advice. It lists utilities, Navajo Nation contacts, and every business tax. For information, write the New Mexico Economic Development Division, Joseph M. Montoya Building, 1100 St. Francis Drive, Santa Fe, NM 87505-4147.

Pennsylvania

Beginning business owners can find suggestions for assessing their ideas. The owners of growing businesses can find recommendations for planning growth and conducting a growth audit. These helpful touches are just the beginning at the Doing Business in Pennsylvania Web site: www.dced.state.pa.us. Other useful information includes who's eligible for job-creation tax credits and where to apply for the capital access loans.

South Dakota

A four-page resource list of agencies that help startup and established businesses is one essential item in the South Dakota business packet. The packet also tells you that the state has no income or business inventory taxes. For a copy, write the South Dakota Governor's Office, Economic Development, 711 East Wells Avenue, Pierre, SD 57501-3369. The information is also on the state's Web site at www.state.sd.us/goed.

if you qualify, you can save thousands of dollars a year. Here are the most popular programs.

Job Training for New Employees

Suppose that you run a machine shop and you're having trouble finding skilled lathe operators. The Job Training Partnership Act (to be replaced by the Workforce Investment Act in 2000) may be willing to pay part of your training costs. This federal program provides money to train teenagers and other people who have a tough time getting work because they lack the right skills.

The federal money is given to states, which then parcel it out to Private Industry Councils in local communities. The councils decide the type of job training that they want to promote in their own towns, then approach local businesses to set up training programs. A participating shop is reimbursed for part of the new worker's wages during the training period. The dollar amount depends on the job and the training needed.

Ask the office that oversees your city or town's economic development about the nearest Private Industry Council. There are councils in every part of the country; in some cases, such as in Rhode Island, one council covers the entire state.

Hire a Worker and Trim Your Taxes

If you're willing to hire a person who was formerly on welfare, the federal government may make it worth your while. Under the rules of the federal welfare reform approved in 1996, you may claim tax deductions for each former welfare recipient you hire. For example, the original act let you deduct up to $8,500 from your business's income taxes over 2 years, and up to half of the employee's wages could be subsidized if your company provided on-the-job training. Plus, you could cut your federal tax bill by an additional $2,400 for each new employee who was a welfare recipient or was from another targeted group such as military veterans who receive food stamps or disabled people in government rehabilitation programs.

For more information, contact the local branch of your state employment office, listed in the government pages of the phone book. (*Note:* You need to fill out significant paperwork to earn the deduction.)

Colorado Customized Training

If your business is in Colorado or you are planning to expand into that state, you may be able to receive a short-term customized training grant through either the Colorado FIRST or Existing Industries program. Local community colleges or vocational schools provide the training, are the points of contact, and work with applying companies to create effective, customized training programs.

Furthermore, participants in these programs may be eligible to recoup 60 percent of their direct costs for training, up to $400 per worker. More than 47,000 workers at nearly 600 companies have been the recipients of grants used to train employees in computer software, machinery operation, and more. Due to the competitive nature of the grant, applicants are chosen on a case-by-case basis.

Both programs are intended to offset the costs of technological changes and to retrain workers in order to remain competitive and increase the state's labor pool. Not only does this help to attract more businesses and increase tax revenue, it also decreases turnover rates and keeps the economy strong.

Contact the Office of Economic Development, 1635 Broadway, Suite 1710, Denver, CO 80202, to learn more about either program. To find out if your state offers similar programs, contact the local office of your state employment department, listed in the government pages of your phone book.

Tax Breaks for Urban Businesses

Locating their businesses in certain inner cities will earn the owners grants and/or tax incentives under a program run by the U.S. Department of Housing and Urban Development (HUD). If you open your shop in one of the cities that HUD has designated as "empowerment zones," you can get tax credits for hiring people who live in the zone. You might take advantage of other benefits, too. For example, GD Laminates, located in Baltimore's empowerment zone, earned $250,000 to train 10 people how to do cabinetry. The company hired some of the trainees and persuaded other shops in the area to hire the others. Businesses also receive tax credits for creating new jobs, especially in high-poverty areas, and for hiring welfare recipients.

Among the cities designated as empowerment zones are Atlanta, Baltimore, Chicago, Detroit, New York, and Philadelphia-Camden. There are also 66 other cities that HUD has designated as "enterprise communities," meaning that they qualify for some of the same benefits. To find out if your business is in a federal empowerment zone or enterprise community, and thus eligible for tax incentives, contact your city's economic development department. Look for the number in the government pages of your phone book.

State Enterprise Zones

Forty states have established programs to encourage private business investment in low-income areas called enterprise zones. The details of the programs vary, but their basic goals are to create jobs and revitalize economically distressed communities, according to Dick Cowden, executive director of the American Association of Enterprise Zones in Washington, D.C.

If you start a small print shop in an enterprise zone in California, for example, you can earn $23,400 in state tax credits for hiring workers who live in targeted employment areas. You can earn sales tax credits for purchasing up to $20 million worth of qualified machinery. The city may waive your fees for permits and construction and even lower the utility rates for your business inside the zone. To find out where the enterprise zones are in your state and get more information about specific tax breaks and other benefits, contact your local or state economic development office, listed in the government pages of your phone book.

FINANCING A BUSINESS

While the government isn't a sugar daddy for entrepreneurs, it does offer multiple avenues of financial help for new and growing small companies.

Generally, neither the federal nor state governments make direct business loans. Instead, they let local banks write the loans and then help business owners in other ways. A common federal tactic, for example, is to guarantee loans, pledging to reimburse the lender for a portion of the money you borrow if you are unable to repay the loan. This makes it somewhat easier for you to qualify for financing. Some states, on the other hand, accept lower returns on deposits from banks that will offer lower rates to business owners.

Whatever the route, the important thing is that government can help make your financial chase a little easier. Here are some specific programs that you should check.

SBA Guaranteed Loans

Under the umbrella of its guaranteed loan program, the U.S. Small Business Administration (SBA) takes the lead in many of the federal government's efforts to assist businesses financially. The largest part of this program is 7(a), through which private financial institutions made more than 42,000 loans totaling more than $9 billion in the 1997–98 fiscal year.

Here's how it works: You apply directly to a bank that participates in the program. If the bank approves you, the SBA agrees to guarantee as much as 75 percent of a business loan up to $750,000. The total amount of the loan depends on the lender. Federal money is on the line only if the borrower defaults on the loan, which happens less than 5 percent of the time.

The interest rates on this and the other types of SBA-guaranteed loans vary with the type of industry, current economic conditions, and your company's credit-worthiness. While the interest rates aren't below market rates, the repayment period is usually longer, so monthly payments are lower.

Keep in mind, though, that if you can't show a good record of paying your bills, either personally (if you're applying for a loan for a new business) or professionally (if you're seeking funds for an estab- lished company), bankers and the SBA won't give you a loan. These loan programs aren't charity; you are expected to make repayment. If you want to improve your chances of getting a loan, strengthen your financial track record by reducing expenses and boosting sales to show stronger profits and cash flow. Or, if your company has lost money in the past, demonstrate ways that you have corrected the problem so it won't recur.

PROMOTING BUSINESS BUFFALO BILL'S WAY

Some communities seem to have friendly attitudes toward business that go right down to their roots. That's the case in Cody, Wyoming, a town of 8,700 established in the 1890s by frontier showman Colonel William "Buffalo Bill" Cody and some of his friends as a business venture.

Buffalo Bill's early efforts set a strong foundation for the town, located 52 miles east of Yellowstone National Park, and continue to pay benefits today. He induced the Burlington Railroad to build a spur into town and persuaded his friend, President Teddy Roosevelt, to build the Shoshone Dam and Reservoir, which gave the town plenty of water and electricity. And Buffalo Bill established a newspaper for the community, the *Cody Enterprise*.

Today, Cody's businesses pay some of the lowest utility rates in the nation. For example, the town operates its own electric utility, which in spring of 1999 charged less than 7 cents per kilowatt hour, even for firms with low electricity use. That's less than half of what Consolidated Edison in New York City charges small businesses. Cody's housing and health care costs are also below the national average.

Buffalo Bill's fame also laid the foundation for one of Cody's most important industries: tourism. More than a quarter-million people visit the Buffalo Bill Historical Center in Cody each year, making it the state's second largest tourist destination.

But Buffalo Bill and his buddies gave Cody something even more valuable in attracting business. "For the most part, Cody has a friendly attitude toward business," says Paul Hoffman, executive director of the Cody Country Chamber of Commerce. "People here are conservative by nature and don't support excessive government regulation."

Cody and all of Wyoming have tax rates that are among the lowest in the nation, with no personal or corporate state income tax, no inventory tax, and no franchise tax. In fact, Wyoming has the lowest cost of doing business of any state, according to *Financial World Magazine*.

Although farming and ranching, oil and gas industries, and tourism are Cody's economic mainstays, "we have been successful in attracting some manufacturers and software development companies because of all our benefits," Hoffman says.

For a list of participating lenders in your area, contact your nearest SBA district office; look in the government pages of your telephone directory or go to the SBA Web site at www.sba.gov and click on "Offices and Services." Or you can write to Public Affairs Office, U.S. Small Business Administration, 409 Third Street SW, Washington, DC 20406.

A smaller program for long-term, fixed-rate financing of buildings, equipment, and land is the Certified Development Company (CDC) 504 Loan Program. A private lender puts up half the loan, the SBA guarantees a loan from the CDC for up to 40 percent (usually a maximum of $750,000), and the borrower covers the remaining 10 percent. This project also requires the borrower to create or keep jobs, generally one for every $35,000 borrowed.

•❖ WHAT INSIDERS SAY:

If you're interested in running a seasonal business like a Christmas tree lot, or you own a small construction company and must pay your workers before you collect payment for a job, ask your lender about a CAPLines loan. CAP is short for Capital Access Program, part of the SBA's loan program. It provides short-term lines of credit and working capital.

Nontraditional Loans

Say that you've got a great idea for a service to repair computers for large corporations or make umbrellas for outdoor furniture, but the business won't grow fast enough to attract venture capitalists and needs more money than an SBA loan will bring. Are you out of luck? Not at all, thanks to Small Business Investment Companies (SBICs).

These private investment firms, which are licensed by the SBA, provide so-called patient money, offering either loans or financing in exchange for a piece of the company to help people develop promising ideas that could take 5 to 20 years to return the investment. The average SBIC investment is $770,000. To find an SBIC in your area, contact your nearest SBA district office;

look in the government pages of your telephone directory or go to the SBA Web site at www.sba.gov and click on "Offices and Services." Or you can write SBA Associate Administrator for Investment, 409 Third Street SW, Washington, DC 20416.

Financial Aid from the State

To give small-business owners a break on financing, some states deposit state funds in area banks and accept below-market interest rates if the bank will pass its savings on to borrowers. Some states require borrowing firms to create jobs, which boosts the local economy. Following are examples of some of the best programs. If you live in a state other than the ones mentioned, ask your local lender or state economic development agency if it has similar programs. You can find the number in the government pages of your phone book.

Alaska

There are several small-business loan programs in Alaska, including a guarantee of as much as 80 percent for financing and working capital loans up to $1 million for Alaskan companies that have already qualified for commercial loans. Write Alaska Industrial Development and Export Authority, 480 West Tudor Road, Anchorage, AK 99503-6690, or visit its Web site at www.aidea.org.

The Alaska Division of Investments will lend up to $300,000 to buy permits and upgrade fishing vessels and gear. You can direct inquiries to the Division of Investments, P.O. Box 34159, Juneau, AK 99803-4159, or visit the Web site at www.dced.state.ak.us/investments.

Kentucky

Kentucky provides loans for 25 percent of the cost of land, building, and equipment up to $250,000 to companies that create jobs. Small businesses whose projects cost less than $100,000 can borrow up to 45 percent of the cost. For information, contact the Kentucky Department of Financial Incentives, Capital Plaza Tower, 24th Floor, Frankfort, KY 40601, or check the state Web site at www.commerce.state.ky.us/edc/edchome.htm.

Texas

This state has a program to help businesses owned by minorities and women, businesses in enterprise zones, and child-care facilities. Through this program, banks pay the state interest equal to the Treasury note rate minus two points. Then the banks lend at a variable rate that's usually less than that for most conventional loans. For more information on a loan for a Texas business, contact the Texas Department of Economic Development, Office of Business Services, P.O. Box 12728, Austin, TX 78711.

Marketing Information from the Web

If you're applying for financing for a new or existing business, you'll need to develop a comprehensive business plan that provides, among other things, information about your market, community, and industry. That means investing time in research.

In the past, you might have spent days sifting through paper piles for the facts you needed, but the federal government's decision to embrace the

BEN AND JERRY'S: A SMALL-BUSINESS SUCCESS

The world might have been deprived of ice cream flavors such as Cherry Garcia, Chunky Monkey, and Wavy Gravy if Ben Cohen and Jerry Greenfield hadn't received a $30,800 loan guaranteed by the U.S. Small Business Administration (SBA) in the early years of forming Ben & Jerry's Homemade, Inc., of South Burlington, Vermont.

These boyhood buddies pooled $8,000 of their own money and $4,000 borrowed from family to open an ice cream shop in a renovated gas station in downtown Burlington, in 1978. They just needed a bit more financing to get their business going.

Fred Burgess at Merchants Bank liked their idea and spunk, so he was ready to lend them money to get started if the SBA would guarantee the loan. Sure, the SBA said, if Ben & Jerry's could find a "suitable" location. A gas station that they'd planned to use as a shop wouldn't do, not because of its past life but because the pair could get only a year's lease. They decided to stick with the gas station and forgo the loan.

They made their ice cream in small batches, but a year later, they wanted to open a separate manufacturing plant. This time, Burgess got the SBA guarantee on the loan because the company had a track record. They opened the 750-square-foot facility, and the rest is history.

By 1998, Ben & Jerry's had three manufacturing plants in Vermont, plus licensees in Israel and Canada, and 700 employees, each of whom is entitled to 3 pints of ice cream daily. The company sold $209 million in ice cream, frozen yogurt, and sorbets in 1998.

By the way, Cherry Garcia is named for the late Jerry Garcia, guitarist for the rock band Grateful Dead, and Wavy Gravy for the counterculture hero from the 1969 Woodstock festival.

Internet has changed all that. Now, much of what you want is available at the click of a button on a federal or state Web site. Here are several good sources of information on the Internet.

U.S. Census Bureau

Say that you want to open a women's clothing shop, and you need to provide your banker with data showing that sales in this segment of retailing are on the rise. You can turn to the U.S. Census Bureau. Every 10 years, it counts and gathers this information and mountains more. Some of the data are updated annually. Retail information is updated monthly.

You can search for the exact information you want at the Census Bureau Web site at www. census.gov. Most Census Bureau publications are also available from the U.S. Government Printing Office by writing Superintendent of Documents, P.O. Box 371954, Pittsburgh, PA 15250-7954. Your local library may also have census reports, especially if it is a public or university library that has agreed to be a depository of federal documents.

On the Web, you can search by location or subject. If your shop will cater to Asians, for example, you can learn how many Asian people live in your county. If you're a plumbing contractor, you can find out the number of toilets there are in your zip code area. With more than 162 tables to choose for your geographic area, this is one of the most comprehensive Web sites for business research.

◗◖ WHAT INSIDERS SAY:
While you can easily find your way around the Census Bureau site, you will need special software such as Adobe Acrobat Reader to open some files.

Bureau of Labor Statistics

Perhaps you need to know the wages being paid in your area. Maybe the rate of inflation impacts the prices you charge or pay raises that you plan on giving to employees. Perhaps you think that an area

of low unemployment is the best location for your firm. You can find such information at the Web site for the Bureau of Labor Statistics, a division of the Department of Labor, at http://stats.bls.gov. Many of the bureau's reports are also available at federal depository libraries, or you can order them from the bureau's Publications Sales Center, P.O. Box 2145, Chicago, IL 60690.

Bureau of Economic Analysis

If you want to know what the future may hold for your business and industry, check with the Bureau of Economic Analysis, part of the U.S. Department of Commerce, which is responsible for preparing estimates of various aspects of the economy. Perhaps you're trying to decide where to sell your products. This site can tell you which states are prime targets because their economies are growing the fastest. At the bureau's Web site at www.bea.doc.gov, you can find out the amount of product your industry has produced in the past and where the bureau estimates that production is headed. What are employment trends for your industry? How has inflation impacted the amount of product your industry is manufacturing? It's all here.

State Web Sites

Several states also provide research on the Web. Here are some of the best.

✓ Colorado has set up a direct computer link to 1,800 national and international database files. The program is called the Business Research and Information Network, or BRAIN for short. Do you want to find new technology to reduce your business costs or increase production? How about a market that you haven't thought of for your new product? If you live in Colorado, you can ask the BRAIN specialists to find the research project or market opportunity to match your need. You can request help online at www.colorado.edu/cubac or write the CU Business Advancement Center at 5353 Manhattan Circle, Suite 202, Boulder, CO 80303.

✓ Hawaii's Department of Business, Economic Development, and Tourism gives visitors to its Web site at www. hawaii.gov/dbedt 50 reports on the people of the island state. You can look up the number of people who speak native Hawaiian, the number of divorced men in Hawaii, or the population density of Oahu.

✓ Texas has set up a comprehensive Web site for all data and analyses of the state's economy at www.bidc.state.tx.us. The site is maintained by the Texas Business and Industry Data Center, an ongoing effort by the Census Bureau, the Texas Department of Economic Development, and Texas A&M University to make economic data more widely available. You can look up the most recent economic forecasts and population projections or find out how much apparel Texas companies exported to India in the second quarter of 1998.

CONTRACTING WITH THE GOVERNMENT

The federal government is the world's largest consumer, spending more than $248 billion a year on everything from paper clips to space shuttles, according to the Office of Management and Budget. Wouldn't it be nice to get a slice of that huge pie for your company?

Maybe you can. The government will certainly do its part to make sure that you are considered. Its brochures and Web sites will put you in touch with dozens of purchasing programs. Its Small Business Administration (SBA) offices will help you negotiate the contracting maze. And its special clearinghouse on the Web will help you locate state and local purchasing needs. Here are your best sources of help.

◗◗ *WHAT INSIDERS SAY:*

If you're serious about doing business with the government, you must be wired to the Internet. Increasingly, federal agencies are posting their purchasing needs at their Web sites and requiring vendors to respond by e-mail with their proposals and bids.

Special Breaks for Little Businesses

To make sure that small-business owners get a fair chance to bid on government contracts, the SBA has created Offices of Government Contracting. These offices monitor the largest federal agencies, such as the U.S. Department of Defense, and private companies that are prime contractors with the government to make sure that they give you opportunities to bid on work or subcontracts.

The SBA agency also has a program in 10 districts that gives firms with fewer than 15 employees and less than $1 million in annual receipts first shot at federal contracts under $50,000.

Call the SBA district office to find the nearest Office of Government Contracting. Look for the SBA number in the government pages of your phone book, or go to the Web site at www.sba.gov and click on "Offices and Services."

◗◗ *WHAT INSIDERS SAY:*

These contracting offices can't be advocates for a specific business or person. You have to find your own opportunities. Nevertheless, each agency and prime contractor handles purchasing differently, and the people in these offices can tell you whom to contact and how to get through the bureaucracy.

Programs to Help Women and Minorities

To help women and minorities obtain government contracts, the SBA also certifies small businesses that are run by members of these groups so they can get preferential treatment when they bid for government projects. They also reward large companies that use these certified firms as subcontractors on government work.

Revisions in the small disadvantaged business certification process have opened this opportunity to a wider array of businesses and made it simpler to prove eligibility, says D. J. Caulfield, SBA program and policy analyst in Washington, D.C. "The owners most likely to benefit from these changes are nonminority females, the physically challenged, and minorities other than African-Americans, Hispanics, Asians, and Na-

tive Americans." Again, to learn more about this program, call the SBA district office and ask for the location of the nearest Office of Government Contracting.

Daily News on the Government's Needs

Commerce Business Daily, the bible of federal purchasing, is issued by the U.S. Department of Commerce Monday through Friday, except on federal legal holidays. It lists many proposed government

FREE ACCESS TO THE FEDERAL BRAIN TRUST

How would you like to make use of some of the more than $75 billion in research conducted in the name of the federal government each year?

It's all available to you through the National Technology Transfer Center (NTTC), a semigovernment agency that puts research financed by the federal government into the hands of U.S. companies.

The center plays matchmaker between companies and the 100,000 scientists doing government research at federal laboratories and universities. And "much of it has commercial potential," says Joseph Allen, president of the center, which is located in Wheeling, West Virginia.

Using technology employed in the solid rocket boosters

that power the Space Shuttle, for example, a company named Hi-Shear Technology Corp. in Torrance, California, created a low-cost, lightweight rescue tool named Lifeshear. That tool was used by rescue workers to free trapped victims after the bombing of the Oklahoma City federal building, and it's also employed in auto accidents. The transfer center connected Hi-Shear with NASA scientists.

Sometimes the process works in reverse, with the center reviewing federal research for work that has commercial potential and then looking for private companies to participate in taking the product to market.

"We have to do a lot of hand-holding to make these

partnerships work, because researchers and business have different cultures," Allen says. "We also do management training for the companies, business-plan development, and investor searches."

The transfer center will do basic database searches for free. More extensive and specific searches and work locating research contacts costs $100 an hour. It also will provide other expert services for a negotiable fee. Companies can also subscribe to the center's databases to do their own searches for $100 a month or $1,000 a year.

To find out how the center can help your business, write NTTC, 316 Washington Avenue, Wheeling, WV, 26003, or visit the Web site at www.nttc.edu.

purchases, contract awards, and leads for subcontracts and foreign business. When the federal Jet Propulsion Laboratory in California needed a secretarial service and the Veterans Affairs hospital in Delaware needed laundry service, they published the specifics in *Commerce Business Daily*.

You can find copies of *Commerce Business Daily* in district offices of the Department of Commerce and the SBA. Federal depository libraries also carry this publication, which can be viewed on a computer, or you can write to the Superintendent of Documents, U.S. Government Printing Office, P.O. Box 371954, Pittsburgh, PA 15250-7954, for a subscription at a cost of $275 a year. A free electronic version is available on the Internet at www.access.gpo.gov. Click on "Access to Government Information Products."

●◆ *WHAT INSIDERS SAY:*

Read the contract notices carefully. While the descriptions of the goods or services being sought usually are easy to understand, many notices also include the information that small businesses won't be given special consideration for the contract.

A Free Way to Advertise for Work

Increasingly, the federal government is moving its information and buying activities onto computers for efficiency and cost savings. That can actually be a benefit to you: One of these moves created the free Procurement Marketing and Access Network, or PRO-Net. This Internet database lists 171,000 small businesses that government buyers and prime contractors can search when looking for subcontractors or partners. PRO-Net is also linked to *Commerce Business Daily* and other places where the government seeks suppliers. If you want to let the government know that you'd like its business, register for PRO-Net at www. pro-net.sba.gov.

State and Local Contracts

Hundreds of state and local agencies also buy from private businesses. You can contact the purchasing departments of the city or state in which you're interested, if you're patient, or you can find thousands of opportunities at one time by visiting the Federal Marketplace. This Web site serves as a gateway to federal, state, and local government agencies that post their product and service needs on the Internet. The basic Web site is www.fedmarket.com. From there, you can search federal categories such as military specifications or state and local procurement or search your own state directly.

●◆ *WHAT INSIDERS SAY:*

You can make it easier to find opportunities that are specific to your field of business by searching the site by Standard Industrial Classification (SIC) code. If you are a member of a trade association, contact the association to learn the code. You can also look up the code for your industry at a public library that carries the SIC Manual published by the Office of Management and Budget, along with the North American Industry Classification System (NAICS) Manual, which is replacing the old classification system. The books can also be ordered from the National Technical Information Service, Springfield, VA 22161. The SIC Manual costs $30, and the NAICS Manual is $28.50 (softcover), plus $5 shipping and handling for each order.

DOING BUSINESS WORLDWIDE

Maybe you have an idea for a product that's so revolutionary that you just know it will attract consumers in Japan. Maybe you're a farmer with a large crop surplus that you'd like to sell in South America. Or maybe you've made a line of dresses that you're sure will be a hit in Paris.

Whatever drives your ambition to sell overseas, you can be sure that the government is in your corner. Through agencies as diverse as the U.S. Department of Commerce and the U.S. Small Business Administration (SBA), the government can provide advice, information, training, and promotion to help you succeed. Here are several programs that the experts recommend.

Facts on Foreign Markets

Part of the Department of Commerce, the Trade Information Center (TIC) is the single comprehensive resource for information about government help with exporting. If you want to know which countries buy pens or how much tariff India places on cows, a TIC specialist will assist you Monday through Friday from 8:30 A.M. to 5:30 P.M. Eastern Standard Time. Write the Trade Information Center, Department of Commerce, 14th Street and Constitution Avenue NW, M800 Ronald Reagan Building, Washington, DC 20230, or go to www.ita.doc.gov/tic for a toll-free number to call.

➡◆ WHAT INSIDERS SAY:
Your best bet for getting trade information from the federal government is by phone, but if you can't call during the available hours on weekdays, a more reliable way to reach the agency is to send an electronic message via TIC's Web site at www.ita.doc.gov/tic.

Advice on Selling Overseas

If you own a small or midsize company, another Department of Commerce agency, the International Trade Administration, can be a valuable contact for you. Its U.S. and Foreign Commercial Service maintains offices in 80 U.S. cities and 69

Odd Lots

STOCKING YOUR FIRM FOR A SONG

Imagine buying a desk for your new business for $75, a chair for $25, a copier for $75, copier paper for $31 a case, and a dot matrix printer for $35. Those are the kinds of bargains that Californians can pick up at warehouses for the state Agency for Surplus Property in Sacramento and Fullerton.

Even better, the warehouses occasionally have sales at which shoppers can get 50 to 75 percent off the marked prices, says program administrator Jim Curran.

The warehouses are part of California's program to sell surplus government property instead of dumping it into landfills. The Fullerton warehouse gets three 40-foot truckloads of surplus material every week. The Sacramento warehouse gets as many as five truckloads weekly. And everything is sold a piece at a time.

Some of the merchandise is in bad shape or obsolete, so it's hard to image anyone buying it, Curran acknowledges. Nevertheless, small business owners say that they sometimes find great bargains on quality goods.

Curran, who used to own laundromats, says, "As a former small-business owner, I know this surplus program is a dream come true for the small business working on a limited budget."

The warehouses are open to California residents and nonresidents alike. You can write for information about upcoming special sales to State Agency for Surplus Property, 701 Burning Tree Road, Fullerton, CA 92833, or 1700 National Drive, Sacramento, CA 95834.

other nations especially to help smaller companies increase their exports. For the office nearest you, write the Department of Commerce at 14th Street and Constitution Avenue NW, M800 Ronald Reagan Building, Washington, DC 20230.

A Step-by-Step Guide to Exporting

If you'd like an overview of the export business, contact the SBA for a copy of "Breaking into the Trade Game." This free publication explains the export process step-by-step. You'll learn how to develop an export strategy and do market research to identify buyers and financing. Check the government pages of your phone book for the nearest SBA office, or visit the Web site at www.sba.gov/oit.

Export Seminars

Some states and private organizations offer "new-to-export" seminars to help you understand overseas markets. You can get a full list of seminars by contacting the Trade Information Center, listed above, or by visiting the center's Web site at www.ita.doc.gov/tic. Click on "Tradebase—Export Education Events."

Free Legal Tips

If you need some quick help with legal questions about exporting your products, the Export Legal Assistance Network, a program of the SBA, can help. The network is made up of attorneys who have experience in international trade and who are willing to offer small-business owners free initial consultations of 30 minutes or so. They can help you plan the legal aspects of your export business, explain basic agree-

ments, and so forth. You can get a list of participating attorneys by contact your nearest SBA district office, which is listed in the government pages of your phone book, or by going to the agency's special legal advice Web site at www.fita.org/elan.

Counseling and Financial Advice

In cooperation with other government agencies such as the SBA and the Export-Import Bank, the Commerce Department has established a network of Export Assistance Centers to help small firms do business in foreign countries. If your company is ready to jump across international borders, these centers will provide business counseling and financial services under one roof. For the center nearest you, contact your nearest SBA district office, which is listed in the government pages of your telephone directory. Or go to the SBA Web site at www.sba.gov and click on "Offices and Services."

Help for Farmers

Farmers and companies involved in agricultural products can get help selling to foreign countries from the USDA's U.S. Trade Assistance and Promotion Office, Stop 1052, Room 4939 South, 1400 Independence Avenue SW, Washington, DC 20250-1052. The department's Foreign Agricultural Service has targeted programs, such as one to boost overseas sales of certain dairy products and another that helps farmers compete in nations that subsidize their native farmers, especially in the European Union.

CHAPTER 22

HELP for US HIRED HANDS

Whether you are looking for your first job, have just lost your last one, or find yourself in a rut with your current one, the government can help put you on track toward the career in private business that you want and deserve.

With money or supervision from the government, you can get training for jobs that you may not even have thought of. You could become a theater stagehand, a computer graphics designer, a commercial aircraft builder, or even a cook in one of the best Creole kitchens in New Orleans.

If you're looking for work under special circumstances, the available support is even greater. At last count, there were 163 federal programs providing $20 billion annually in employment training services for low-income adults, veterans, Native Americans, the elderly, the young, the disabled, the incarcerated, and workers who have lost their jobs due to plant closings, company relocations, or cheap imports.

Still need help? You can turn to America's best tool for job searches. The federal government, in collaboration with the states, maintains a giant information network that links job seekers with potential employers and training programs.

But why is the government providing employment training, career counseling, and labor market information for the private sector? In the preamble to the Constitution, the founding fathers said that their fledgling government would "promote the general welfare." And in this age of fierce global economic competition,

> With the economy humming and government help at a peak, there's never been a better time to look for that high-paying job you want. Here's how the government can help you get the position you deserve.

FACTOID

IT'S PROBABLY NO SURPRISE TO MOST PEOPLE THAT HIGHER EDUCATION MEANS HIGHER EARNINGS. BUT THE NUMBERS PUT IT IN STARK RELIEF: HIGH SCHOOL DROPOUTS EARNED, ON AVERAGE, JUST $15,000 A YEAR IN 1996 COMPARED WITH $22,000 FOR HIGH SCHOOL GRADUATES, $25,000 FOR WORKERS WITH ASSOCIATE DEGREES, $38,000 FOR COLLEGE GRADUATES, AND $61,000 FOR THOSE WITH ADVANCED DEGREES.

there are few things more important to the welfare of our country than well-trained workers.

"Quite frankly, the government has been involved in job training since the birth of the nation," says Bob Knight, president of the Washington, D.C.–based National Association of Private Industry Councils, which provides information and advocacy for some 580 such councils nationwide. "The reason they're involved is that economic growth and prosperity and democratic inclusiveness have always required a well-prepared workforce."

At the local government level, having a skilled workforce is simply a matter of dollars and cents. "Seventy percent of city government revenues come from business-generated taxes of some sort or another," says Patti Nunn, the economic development manager for Santa Ana, California. "The most important thing you can do is grow your business base, or at the very least, maintain it. If businesses can't get workers who are trained, skilled, and have a good work ethic, they're not going to stay here."

Ready to learn how government can help you get the skills you need to succeed at work in the twenty-first century? Just keep reading.

SEARCHING FOR A JOB

When you turn to the government for help in finding a job in the private sector, the first thing you'll realize is that there's a maze of overlapping federal and state government employment programs to navigate. Even the experts say that the system is complicated: One official at the U.S. Department of Labor likens it to the federal tax code.

There's the bad news. The good news is that there are several ways to get help in accessing the wealth of government-sponsored information and advice. And once you get to the right agency, you'll find that the government's help is available to you at no or low cost. Here are your best options.

America's Job Clearinghouses

While most of the public money for job training and advice comes from the federal government, the actual services are supplied by nearly 2,000 local employment offices across the United States. These local centers, part of a new trend to provide "one-stop" job advice, provide job counseling and act as information clearinghouses for a large number of public and private job programs. Thus, they are good places to start your search.

At a minimum, most of these centers can help you sign up for unemployment benefits, if you need them; view job postings; consult lists of available training programs; get basic advice from job counselors; and find out whether you are eligible for government-funded training. But some go even further.

Free Workshops, Faxes, and Phones

Job seekers at the one-stop centers in Orange County, California, can use computers and printers, fax machines, and telephones to aid in their job hunts.

Nancy Madey, who visited the center in Costa Mesa, California, after losing her job with the high-tech firm Ingram Micro, says, "It's a wonderful center. I received assistance with writing my résumé as well as having access to computers, fax and copy machines, and telephones to set up interviews—all free of charge."

In nearby Santa Ana, the Work Center offers workshops on interviewing techniques and résumé writing, and it has separate staff for veterans' and youth employment services.

Rapid Response to Layoffs

Some job centers also offer employment triage when large numbers of workers are displaced. When the Detroit Medical Center announced in early 1999 that it was laying off nearly 700 employees because of a $100 million deficit, the Michigan Department of Career Development sent in a "rapid-response team" to provide job counseling for affected employees—everyone from administrators and midlevel managers to orderlies, janitors, and food service personnel.

The department helped stage a job fair in downtown Detroit exclusively for the medical center workers, and nearly 40 employers set up booths there. It also applied for a $1.5-million grant from the Labor Department to help provide extensive retraining for the workers and began publishing a newsletter for them with the latest news and tips on job opportunities in the area.

Local job centers go by different names around the country; in Michigan, they're called Michigan Works! Service Centers; in Wisconsin, they're known as Workforce Centers; and in Indiana, it's the Customer Self-Service System. Increasingly, they're also referred to as one-stop centers (see "One-Stop Job Shopping").

To find a center near you, look under the state listings in the government section of the phone book. The number may be under "Employment Service" or "Job Service." If you don't see a direct listing, call your local department of labor office and ask for the number of the job center or one-stop nearest you.

ONE-STOP JOB SHOPPING

Because they were well aware that the government's employment training system had become a web of hard-to-decipher programs, federal lawmakers developed one-stop job shopping centers, where everyone from welfare moms to laid-off corporate execs can find a wide range of interconnected services all under one roof.

Run by states but funded mostly by federal money, these centers can supply career counseling; information on job vacancies, required skills, and available training; help with writing résumés and developing interview skills; assistance in filing unemployment claims; and advice on eligibility for government-funded training or student financial aid. These centers act like the hub of a wheel, providing a venue where job seekers, employers, and trainers can find each other.

"The hope is that, for the first time, you won't have to go to 40 places to get information," says one congressional insider who helped write the new law.

Also under the new system, local authorities and businesses will have greater latitude in setting program parameters and deciding who's eligible for government training funds. "Our message is 'look, we're getting out of the way,'" says Ray Bramucci, assistant secretary of labor for employment and training in Washington, D.C. As an example, dislocated workers who lose their jobs because of company shutdowns, foreign competition, and so on, will get individual retirement accounts on which they can draw to pay for the training that best meets their needs.

Employment officials at the state and local levels are still trying to figure out how best to adapt to this new system. "I think the job training world is going to be in flux for a few years as the states figure out how they want to restructure," says Sigurd Nilsen, assistant director for education, workforce, and income security issues at the General Accounting Office in Washington. "But in general, it should make it easier for people using the system," he adds, "because there are fewer categorical programs."

If you have access to the Internet, you also can find a list of state employment agencies on the Web site of the Department of Labor's Employment and Training Administration, which oversees the lion's share of federal job programs. The address is www.doleta.gov.

◗◆ WHAT INSIDERS SAY:

Often, when people lose jobs, one of the biggest mistakes they make is waiting too long before going to a job center. "Unfortunately, people won't go into a center right away, and by the time they get to us, they're a couple of months behind on their mortgage payments," says Peter Kaiser, an employment consultant whose firm co-manages YWR Works, a workforce center in Milwaukee.

Not only can a job center help you find work more quickly than you can on your own, some—including Kaiser's—will even act as credit referees to help you negotiate with your debtors. If you lose your job, go to your local job center the next day.

Networking for Professionals

If you're a professional searching for work, government may be able to offer you special help. In California, for example, the employment development department sponsors networking clubs called Experience Unlimited for professionals such as engineers, accountants, human resource executives, and others, who have lost their jobs. The groups—about 20 statewide—have access to office space at their local job centers where members can receive training in job searching, make phone calls, share job leads, and exchange war stories.

Ask your state employment agency if it sponsors a similar group. Also check with your local chamber of commerce to see if it sponsors events such as luncheons and speakers' forums, which are good networking opportunities for business professionals.

Searching at the Library

Libraries can be rich sources of information on finding a private-sector job. There's a staggering number of self-help job-hunting books available,

and your local public library is likely to carry many of them.

Also, be sure to visit the library of your local state college or university, which probably has a wealth of information that can help you get started in your job search. At the University of California at Irvine, for example, the library provides a four-page career-planning reference guide. It lists titles and call numbers of numerous handbooks, guides, and directories in its collection that are related to finding a job.

Government-Sponsored Job Fairs

Cities and states, desperate for quality workers to fill openings at local companies, are increasingly in the business of sponsoring another excellent source of career information—job fairs.

The state of Nebraska, for example, held a fair in Anaheim, California, hoping to woo back Cornhusker expatriates to fill more than 13,000 open positions statewide. Patty Wood, director of Nebraska Works in Lincoln, the state agency that put on the fair, says that her counterparts in other states have since called to ask for advice on doing job fairs of their own. Check your local newspaper and radio as well as community and college bulletin boards for job fairs near you.

Job-Hunting Information Online

Whether in a job center or at the local library, you cannot miss the fact that job searching is increasingly done on the Internet. At Indiana's Customer Self-Service Centers, job seekers can enter their résumés into a big database, then wait at home to be notified when something that fits their description comes up.

Indiana's computers will also scan in licenses, certificates, or other relevant materials that might be called for in a job and attach them to the job seeker's profile.

"It's true that fewer people come into our offices now," says Larry Less, a labor market economist at the Ohio Bureau of Employment Services in Columbus. "Everything has become more electronic, and there's less need to make a visit to a local office." If you don't have an Internet-linked computer at home, chances are good that there's one you can use at the local library.

There are a number of government-run Web sites that can help spur your job search. Here are two of the best offered by the federal government.

The Million-Listing Job Bank

America's Job Bank (www.ajb.dni.us), with nearly 1 million job listings, is now the largest job site on the Internet. It allows you to search for job openings, create and submit your résumé to a pool of

---

GETTING THE MOST FROM A JOB CENTER

Before you walk into a job center, there are a few simple steps you can take to help make your visit as fruitful as possible.

First, you should show up looking like you're ready to work. That means, for starters, being clean and well-groomed. You should also have a résumé, or at least some written version of your work history, ready to show to one of the job center staff. Experts say that you will also benefit more from your time at the job center if you heed the following advice.

Act like a customer

When you enter a one-stop, think of yourself as a customer shopping for the product that is right for you. Be sure to ask your counselor about the full range of services available to you, and once you know the direction you're heading, shop around for the training com-

pany or school that has the best record. Don't be afraid to let your wishes be known.

Dress for success

When you enter a job center, you should look professional. Think of the center as a business environment. The labor market experts there are probably well plugged into the local business community, so you want to make a good impression on them. Besides, you never know whom you might run into there. Many job centers provide space for employers to conduct interviews on site, so you may end up interviewing sooner than you imagined.

Stay open to new opportunities

Seasoned job counselors and trainers like to see people come to them with open minds about their next career moves. If you've just lost a job, try to view your circumstances as an

opportunity to do something you've always dreamed of. "For people who have to make changes in their lives, the most important thing is to listen to what's inside themselves, not what other people tell them they should be doing," says Carol Pough, administrator of the Wolden Multimedia Institute in Anaheim, California, which trains people for new careers in multimedia arts and computer graphics.

Be persistent

Once you begin looking for a job, stick with it. "If you commit as much time to your job search as you committed to your (previous) job, you will find a job you want," says employment consultant Peter Kaiser of Milwaukee. He says that his rule of thumb is that finding the right new position can take as long as 1 week for every $1,000 of salary you made in your last job—up to about 40 weeks.

potential employers, and launch customized job searches. It also links you directly to the Web sites maintained by the states, by companies, and by private employment agencies.

America's Job Bank is a free service, but to submit a résumé or request a customized search, you have to register and obtain a password and user identification. Just connect to the site and click on the section you want. There are clear instructions to guide you through each step. The site is also referred to as America's Talent Bank, because employers can log on to it and draw from the résumés that job seekers submit.

Electronic Job Forecasts

Another useful site sponsored by the federal government is America's Career InfoNet (www.acinet.org), which offers information on the job outlook and prevailing pay scales for virtually all occupations, anywhere in the United States. If you want to know how much you can make or where your best prospects are in the industry of your choice, check out this site.

Printed Advice on Finding a Job

If you prefer to get advice from a brochure or booklet, there is a huge volume of job information available in print from the government at low or no cost. The U.S. Government Printing Office offers numerous pamphlets and books related to career development. Here are several that insiders recommend.

✓ "Tips for Finding the Right Job," a 27-page government booklet with information on all aspects of job searching.

✓ "High-Earning Workers Who Don't Have a Bachelor's Degree," an eight-page pamphlet full of tips on jobs paying over $700 a week that don't require a 4-year college degree. Workers in these positions include computer programmers, food service and hotel managers, police and firefighters, registered nurses, insurance claims adjusters, carpenters, electricians, and corrections officers.

✓ "Job Search Guide: Strategies for Professionals," which discusses how to get back on your feet after losing your job.

✓ "Occupational Outlook Quarterly," a colorful periodical filled with articles on all the latest employment trends, primarily for young people.

You can get many of these publications for free at your local public or university library. The library may also have a Government Printing Office list, with prices and stock numbers of all publications related to employment and occupations.

You can also order copies directly from the government. Write to Superintendent of Documents, P.O. Box 371954, Pittsburgh, PA 15250-7954. Or you can get information on publications and order them from the printing office's Web site at www.access.gpo.gov/su_docs.

TRAINING FOR A JOB

Once you know what kind of work you want to do, there's a good chance that you will need some training. To get government funding for training, you must meet certain eligibility criteria. In general, that means that you must fall below a certain income level or have recently lost

FACTOID

THE U.S. ECONOMY MAY BE CREATING JOBS AT A RECORD CLIP, BUT APPARENTLY PEOPLE DON'T STAY IN THEM FOR VERY LONG. MORE THAN ONE-QUARTER OF ALL PEOPLE EMPLOYED IN THE UNITED STATES HAVE BEEN AT THEIR CURRENT JOBS A YEAR OR LESS, ACCORDING TO THE BUREAU OF LABOR STATISTICS. NEARLY 40 PERCENT HAVE HELD THEIR JOBS LESS THAN 2 YEARS.

your job. There are also training funds available for veterans, people with disabilities, and certain minority groups. Set up an appointment at your local employment office or one-stop center to find out if you are eligible.

If you already have a job with decent pay but are just looking for a new challenge, you probably won't get financial support from the federal government. "If you're not happy, we don't send psychologists to your house," says Ray Bramucci, assistant secretary of labor for employment and training in Washington, D.C.

Even if you can't get free training, there probably are several low-cost options for you. The staff at your local job center can refer you to a wide range of training providers, including community colleges, vocational-technical schools, nonprofit organizations, apprenticeship programs, or even employers who are willing to train you on the job. You can also inquire at those places on your own.

●◆ WHAT INSIDERS SAY:

Although job centers typically provide comprehensive services, it wouldn't hurt to look into some private staffing agencies, which can train and place you with a wide range of employers, especially those looking for administrative support staff. You may even be able to get some government money for private training and placement. Many states have what's known as grant diversion, in which government money goes to a company, or in some cases, even a temp agency, that hires and trains job seekers who are eligible for funding.

UNCOVERING ARTISTIC TALENTS

At the Wolden Multimedia Institute in Anaheim, California, people who have lost their jobs in downsized industries can get a whole new lease on life by training for careers in the up-and-coming fields of computer graphics and multimedia arts.

Many students at the institute discover a passion inside themselves that they didn't know existed or that they never took the time to develop. "I take artists, writers, storytellers, and other dreamers and teach them how to do what they love for the rest of their lives," says Freida Wolden, who founded the school in 1992. "I do it by combining art and business,"

she says. "It's not just the skills but also how people market themselves." Every student, for example, is enrolled in Wolden Multimedia Presenters, a Toastmasters club, for public speaking skills.

Carol Pough, Wolden's administrator, estimates that as many as 40 percent of the students at the institute are using the government's money to attend, either because they are low-income adults or because they were laid off from jobs in other industries.

Students can study for 3 months and get a certificate in computer graphics or attend for 6 months for the multimedia package, which

includes animation, sound, and 3-D. Graduates of the institute get jobs in advertising, television production, Web design, video games, publishing, and even the movie business.

One engineer who lost his aerospace job attended the institute on federal money, and he now owns his own business designing Web sites for local companies. Another, a graphic artist who was laid off, went through Wolden's multimedia course. After he graduated, the institute found him a job that paid $25 an hour, but he didn't accept it: He was already making $50 an hour freelancing.

If You've Been Laid Off

Generally speaking, you can get federally funded job counseling, retraining, and in some cases even a living allowance if you have lost your job in a mass layoff or plant closing, if you're working in a dying industry, or if your company is slashing its workforce because of competition from foreign trade.

You also qualify if you are self-employed and have been hit by a natural disaster or poor local economic conditions. Also, there is money for divorced or widowed homemakers who are suddenly thrust into the labor force, for laid-off workers in the defense industry, and for those who lose their jobs as a result of employers' efforts to comply with the federal Clean Air Act.

Retraining Funds

There's no set dollar amount for retraining funds. It depends on the field you are preparing for and who's doing the training. But changes in the law in July 2000 give laid-off workers more control over their own training through "individual retirement accounts" from which they can pay—with vouchers or direct transfers—for the courses that they decide are best for them (see "One-Stop Job Shopping" on page 375).

Living Allowances

The government offers financial support for people who are out of work, but this money usually is available only to workers who were laid off due to foreign trade competition or whose total family income is below a certain level. For those who meet the income requirement, the allowance kicks in only after unemployment benefits have stopped—usually about 6 months after they lose their jobs.

The amount of the living allowance is typically the same as your unemployment benefits, which

---

Best Bets

TOP BOOKS
ON JOBS AND CAREERS

Want to find a few good books on the subject of jobs and careers? Here are some that the experts recommend. You should be able to find them in a public library or at your local bookstore.

✓ *Job-Hunting on the Internet.* By Richard Nelson Bolles, this is a supplement to *What Color Is Your Parachute?*.

✓ *Peterson's Hidden Job Market: 2,000 High-Growth Companies That Are Hiring at Four Times the National Average*, edited by Karen Hansen. One of Peterson's numerous guides on all aspects of career development and education, this book is updated annually.

✓ *The Complete Job-Search Handbook*, by Howard Figler, Ph.D. The cover of this handbook boasts that it will give you "all the skills you need to get any job and have a good time doing it."

✓ *Best Answers to the 201 Most Frequently Asked Interview Questions*, by Matthew J. DeLuca. As the cover explains, this thin volume teaches you "how to answer awkward or illegal questions, personal questions, curve-ball questions, and trick questions and still get the job."

✓ *The Very Quick Job Search: Get a Better Job in Half the Time*, by J. Michael Farr. This is one in a series of job-search books written by Farr.

vary from state to state and depend on how much you were making and how long you were on the job. To qualify for the allowance, you must apply for eligibility for re-employment training assistance within 13 weeks of signing up for unemployment. Therefore, if you think you may need the money, apply quickly for these benefits.

To determine whether you're eligible, check with your local one-stop center, which in most places is the local administrator of these funds.

◆ WHAT INSIDERS SAY:

Even though the federal programs for laid-off workers have some pretty specific guidelines, the rules aren't necessarily as hard and fast as they seem. Frequently, if you argue your case convincingly, you can get funding even if your local job center told you no at first.

"One-stops have so many different funding sources that they can generally find a way to work with you," says employment consultant Peter Kaiser of Milwaukee. Another thing to consider is that even if there's no federal funding for you, there may be a state-funded training program that you could enter (see "State Training Programs" on page 383).

When Foreign Trade Kills Your Job

Retraining programs for people displaced by foreign trade have pretty generous support benefits, but in order to get them, your company must be certified for group eligibility by the U.S. Department of Labor.

If you belong to a union, your union leaders can file a petition for certification. Otherwise, any group of three or more workers or an official of your company may file one. You can print out a petition form from the Employment Training Administration's Web site. The form will be in the section on layoff retraining at www.wdsc.org/layoff/trade.htm. You can also get one at your local job center.

There are two trade-related assistance programs that you can petition for. One, known as Trade Adjustment Assistance, is for job losses due to general trade competition. The other, North American Free Trade Agreement Transitional Adjustment Assistance, is for those who lose jobs because of increased imports from, or company relocation to, Canada and Mexico.

Address the petition to U.S. Department of Labor, Employment and Training Administration, Office of Trade Adjustment Assistance, 200 Constitution Avenue NW, Room C-4318, Washington, DC 20210.

Filling out a petition for trade-related job assistance is straightforward. You need to supply the names, phone numbers, and signatures of the people affected and the name and location of the company. You don't have to argue the case at all. Just give the basic information, and the Labor Department will follow up. But be aware that 39 percent of petitions filed are rejected because the job losses aren't associated with the criteria mentioned above.

If your petition isn't accepted, you can always apply for assistance under other dislocated-worker programs. Here are some of the best.

Careers in the Trades

Tradeswomen of Purpose/Women in Non-Traditional Work, Inc., in Philadelphia is a private non-profit group that gets federal money to train women—usually single mothers—for careers in blue-collar and nontraditional jobs (see "From Welfare to High Pay" on page 382). The women often enter the program from jobs at which they make $6 an hour, at best, and when they graduate in a matter of months, they average $11 an hour plus benefits. Some make much more than that.

A larger organization that does similar things is Wider Opportunities for Women, with offices around the United States. Check with local community organizations or with a nearby one-stop center for information on such programs close to you, or write to 815 15th Street NW, Suite 916, Washington, DC 20005.

Nontraditional Jobs for Women

The Labor Department's Women's Bureau administers its own nontraditional training programs under the Nontraditional Employment for Women Act and the Women in Apprenticeship and Nontraditional Occupations Act.

The bureau also offers a variety of publications on the subject of women and work, and it holds workshops around the country on issues of concern to women in the workplace. It maintains a Fair Pay Clearinghouse, which offers a range of data on women's pay, including a list of employers committed to the principle of equal pay for women.

For information on the bureau's programs and publications, you can write the Women's Bureau, U.S. Department of Labor, 200 Constitution Avenue NW, Washington, DC 20210. Or you can reach it via the Internet at www.dol.gov. Once you connect to the Web site, click on "DOL Agencies" in the site directory, then look for "Women's Bureau."

Employment Incentives

If you are a veteran and your income falls below a certain threshold or you're overcoming a disability, you may be able to get a new job and secure a tax credit for the employer who hires you.

Under the federal Work Opportunity Tax

Amazing Stories

FROM WELFARE TO HIGH PAY

Dinetta Walton, a resident of Philadelphia, was a single mother on welfare until she decided one day that enough was enough.

Prompted by a friend, she went to a job center run by the local private industry council, met with a counselor, and took some tests. She discovered that she qualified for federal training money, and soon she enrolled in Tradeswomen of Purpose/Women in Non-Traditional Work, a local blue-collar training program exclusively for women.

Aside from reading and math, Walton learned about carpentry, plumbing, and electricity. It was tough, both physically and mentally, but her instructors were always on her side, she says. "They said, 'You can do it. Don't give up.' They taught me how to deal with workplace issues, how to deal with pressure."

Not only that: The private industry council paid for Walton's transportation, her work boots, and child care. And she continued receiving public assistance checks during the 3 months of her course.

When it was over, she got a union job with the gas company, reading meters and working on heaters. She started out grossing $478 a week, nearly five times what she received on welfare. On the first day, she sat on the stoop outside her rented house in her new gas company uniform until she fell asleep.

"I wanted everybody to know I had a job," Walton says. "And the welfare card—I set it on fire, because I didn't need it anymore."

Today, Walton makes $659 a week, plus full medical benefits. She is married and has just bought her first house. "When I think about it, sometimes it brings tears to my eyes," she says. "They work you hard, but oh, goodness, it's a blessing."

Credit, employers can cut their tax burden by up to $2,400 for each eligible new hire. For more information, contact your local employment center or IRS office or visit the Department of Labor Employment and Training Administration Web site at www.doleta.gov. Use the site's search function to look for "work opportunity tax credit." There's also a federal tax credit of up to $8,500 for employers who hire long-term welfare recipients. For more information, contact the sources just mentioned.

State Training Programs

Another source of potentially valuable job training is state-funded workforce development programs.

Many states, in fierce competition to lure and retain employers, are investing heavily in worker training that's tailored to meet the needs of specific companies.

Oklahoma's Training for Industry Program, for example, has paid to "custom-train" workers for companies such as Boeing, Lucent Technologies, Oracle, and many others.

"Businesses are actually screaming—not yelling, screaming—for skilled workers. There simply aren't enough bodies to go around," says Ron Wilkerson, public affairs coordinator for the Oklahoma Department of Vocational Technical Education in Stillwater.

In 1998, Oklahoma placed 15,341 workers

STATE TRAINING PAYS OFF

When Jessica Jackson applied for a program that promised to teach her to build Boeing airplanes, she never realized that it was the state of Oklahoma that was paying for the training. All she knew was that she would learn skills that would earn her much higher pay than the near-minimum wage she had received working in the collections department of a company in Baton Rouge, Louisiana.

The training was part of a Oklahoma's innovative Training for Industry Program, through which the state custom-trains workers for companies that can't find enough skilled labor.

In Jackson's case, the program was a godsend for her and Boeing.

She had left her former employer and returned to her native Tulsa when the Louisiana company moved its corporate headquarters to Mississippi. Within a week of her arrival, she attended a job fair where she learned that Boeing, the giant aerospace company, was looking for people to train as commercial aircraft builders. Two weeks later, she entered the Boeing course at Tulsa Technologies, a local vocational-technical school that provided free training, thanks to funding from the state.

Jackson performed well in the program, and Boeing hired her full-time. She started at $9 an hour as a metal bonder, building door panels for Boeing's 747 jetliners. Now she is training to build slats, which are part of the wings, for 737s. The company also paid for her to study accounting at Tulsa Community College, and she now attends Oklahoma State University, also financed by Boeing.

"I feel like I'm able to stand alone and to accomplish dreams like owning a house and raising my daughter and putting her through school," Jackson says.

through its Training for Industry program. They earned wages averaging $10 an hour and as high as $85,000 a year. These programs are particularly strong in states in the South and Southwest, where populations are growing rapidly and there is increasing demand for skilled workers.

Contact your state employment agency, listed in the government pages of your phone book, or check newspapers and local job fairs for opportunities.

Training the Old-Fashioned Way

If you want to be paid while receiving on-the-job training, consider an apprenticeship. In general, apprenticeship programs are geared toward the building trades and manufacturing, but if you look hard enough, you may be surprised at what you find.

There are registered programs in beekeeping, acting, accordion making, baking, cheese making, and a wide range of other not-so-common occupations. Apprentices usually start at half the full journeyman wage and gradually work their way up. After all program requirements are satisfied, an apprentice receives a certificate that is widely recognized as a license in the chosen field.

Apprenticeships can be a good way to get your foot in the door. They also hold some promise for people who are looking for changes in their working lives.

"If you don't like sitting at a desk and just want to get your hands dirty and change your line of work, there are some great opportunities out there," says Stephen Simms, director of the Oregon State Apprenticeship and Training Division in Portland.

Apprenticeship programs are usually administered—and workers paid—by labor unions, private companies, or both operating jointly. They are over-

THE FASTEST-GROWING OCCUPATIONS

Are you looking for a new career path that will have employers pounding your door with job offers? Think "computers" and "health care." Experts predict that these two professions—already among the hottest today—are going to be even hotter. Here are their predictions for the top 10 occupations through the beginning of the new millennium.

OCCUPATION	INCREASE (%)	JOBS ADDED
Database administrators and computer support specialists	118	249,000
Computer engineers	109	235,000
Systems analysts	103	520,000
Personal and home care aides	85	171,000
Physical and corrective therapy aides	79	66,000
Home health aides	76	378,000
Medical assistants	74	166,000
Desktop publishing specialists	74	22,000
Physical therapists	71	81,000
Occupational therapy assistants	69	11,000

NOTE: Percentages and total number of jobs added reflect estimates between 1998 and 2006.

seen by the federal Bureau of Apprenticeship and Training (BAT) or associated state apprenticeship councils.

For general information on apprenticeships, write to the Bureau of Apprenticeship and Training, U.S. Department of Labor, 200 Constitution Avenue NW, Washington, DC 20210.

For information on specific programs, contact the local office of your state apprenticeship council or of the BAT. You should find the number in the government pages of your phone book. You can also find a list of state apprenticeship councils and regional BAT offices on the Internet at www.doleta.gov. Click on "Contacts." Examples of some of the best programs follow.

◗◆ WHAT INSIDERS SAY:

Apprenticeships in some of the construction and building trades can lead to jobs paying well over $20 an hour, but if you're looking for a really lucrative field, you might want to be an elevator builder. "They must be cresting at $50 an hour," says Mike Potts, a representative of the Los Angeles and Orange Counties Building and Construction Trades Council.

Cajun and Creole Cookin'

Delgado Community College in New Orleans has a 3-year culinary apprenticeship in which participants are paid while training at the city's fanciest restaurants. They must do six semesters at the college; the tuition is $650 a semester for in-state residents and $2,000 for out-of-state students. One-quarter to one-third of the students get government grants or guaranteed loans to cover the tuition. For more information, write Iva Bergeron, Director, Culinary Arts Department, Delgado Community College, 615 City Park Avenue, New Orleans, LA 70119-4399.

There are nearly 90 other registered cooking apprenticeships in the United States that are recognized by the American Culinary Federation. For information on these programs, contact Arlene Weber, the federation's apprenticeship

program coordinator, at 10 San Bartola Drive, St. Augustine, FL 32086. You can also inquire at your local state apprenticeship council or BAT office.

Training in the Theater

The state of Oregon offers an apprenticeship program that trains people to be wardrobe dressers, stage technicians, and film and video electricians. These jobs pay nearly $15 an hour after training is completed. Related coursework at Portland Community College is required, but tuition is paid by the local theater and stagehands' union, which apprentices must join.

For more information, contact the Oregon State Apprenticeship and Training Division, 800 Northeast Oregon Street, Portland, OR 97232, or check with your local apprenticeship council or BAT office to see if there is a similar program near you.

◗◆ WHAT INSIDERS SAY:

If you're interested in apprenticing in a traditional manufacturing industry, contact a European firm with a branch in this country. National Association of Private Industry Councils president Bob Knight says that they tend to put more value on apprenticeship training than American manufacturing companies.

One good prospect is Siemens, a German company that values apprenticeships and has been expanding its presence in the United States because labor costs are cheaper here. Or look for an old-line manufacturing firm that's unionized. Apprenticeships for skilled machinists can still be had, and if you get one, "you can probably name your price" when you finish, Knight says.

Learning to Be a Shipbuilder

The South Louisiana Economic Council in Thibodaux, Louisiana, operates an apprenticeship program for high school students age 16 and older who want to become welders. They get high school course credit while doing paid work for shipbuilding companies along the Louisiana coast.

The apprenticeship takes about 3½ years to complete, and the students are usually finished with high school before that. They make as much as $14 an hour when they're finished. Check with your local apprenticeship council, BAT office, or high school counselor for similar school-linked apprenticeships.

➥ WHAT INSIDERS SAY:

If you have a tax incentive to dangle in front of an employer, you may find it easier to convince him to take you on as an apprentice. The state of Michigan, for example, offers a credit of $2,000 per apprentice to employers who train high school students through registered apprenticeship programs. You may want to check with your apprenticeship council or local one-stop job center to see if your state offers a similar tax credit.

UPGRADING YOUR SKILLS

With technological advances constantly changing the way business is done, it is increasingly important to stay on the leading edge of the job skills that are most in demand. Being familiar with the hottest new software or hardware, handy with the latest tools, or fluent in some strategic foreign language can only enhance your value to your current employer or boost your future employability should you decide to look for greener pastures.

The federal government, cognizant of the need to constantly upgrade the U.S. workforce, has made the training of "incumbent workers" an important part of the new Workforce Investment Act. Under that law, up to 15 percent of the funds set aside for dislocated workers may be used to train those who are already employed.

Numerous states, including Texas, California, and New Jersey, invest in incumbent worker training. Here are some of the programs available.

State-Sanctioned Training

In their efforts to retain employers in their states, the workforce development programs mentioned earlier also frequently do incumbent worker training for existing companies.

The Oklahoma Training for Industry program, for example, has taught computer skills to thousands of General Motors workers. It has also helped the Goodyear Tire and Rubber plant in Lawton, Oklahoma, upgrade the job skills of its workers. These programs are usually instituted at the request of the company, so check with your human resources department to see what kinds of training opportunities are on tap. You might also inquire at your local job center or state employment agency.

College and Tech-School Training

Community colleges and vocational-technical schools are becoming increasingly important in the skills equation. National Association of Private Industry Councils president Bob Knight says that community colleges are one of the more knowledgeable places to go for middle-class people who are rethinking their careers.

Many occupations—such as bank clerk, tailor, and funeral director—that were once learned primarily in apprenticeship programs are now taught at community colleges. Morgan Lewis, a research scientist at the Center on Education and Training for Employment at Ohio State University in Columbus, says that many of the adults who are being trained in Ohio are enrolled in community colleges or adult vocational programs.

His wife, Maureen, had spent 25 years taking care of their children while the whole technological revolution passed by, so she enrolled in Columbus State Community College. She spent a year learning such common office computer programs as WordPerfect, Microsoft Word, and Excel. Now she works as the office manager for

IMI International, a joint-venture manufacturing company.

"The time I took to do that coursework was absolutely invaluable," she says. "I could not possibly have presented myself to an employer without those skills. I would recommend it to anyone."

Courses for Incumbent Workers

Some community colleges are also offering incumbent worker training to local employers. The Marketplace Education Center, part of the Rancho Santiago Community College District in Orange County, California, tries to woo existing workers from local companies into its training programs. The center offers free training to the public in the areas of computers, health services, retail sales, and food services. Check with your company's human resources office or your local community college to see if there are similar opportunities available near you.

Paying for Your Retraining

Going back to school for additional career training will not only bolster your future earnings, it can also save you money right now because current government programs will cover some costs. Here are two ways.

Federal Tax Credits

If you go back to school to change careers or upgrade your skills, you may be able to reduce your taxes through the federal Lifetime Learning tax credit. Each year through 2002, you can take a 20 percent credit for the first $5,000 of tuition you or your dependents pay to a community college, technical school, or 4-year university. After 2002, the yearly credit is 20 percent on up to $10,000 of tuition.

You qualify for the credit regardless of whether you're a full-time student or just taking a course or two. For more information, check with your local office of the IRS or U.S. Department of Education, listed in the government pages of your phone book.

Special Scholarships

Another program, the Hope Scholarship tax credit, can put as much as $1,500 a year back into the pockets of college or vocational school students for the first 2 years of school. In each of the 2 years, you get a 100 percent tax credit on the first $1,000 in tuition and 50 percent on the next $1,000. To qualify, you must be enrolled at least half-time in a degree or certificate program for any portion of the year.

The Hope Scholarship is intended to make the first 2 years of college more affordable, but it can also help adults who are going back to school for some career retraining. For information, check with your local IRS or U.S. Department of Education office, listed in the government pages of your phone book.

Nonprofit Programs

There are numerous nonprofit and labor-management partnerships around the United States that offer workers in various industries a chance to improve their workplace skills. Here are two of the best.

The Alliance for Employee Growth and Development

This nonprofit group, funded by AT&T, Lucent Technologies, the Communications Workers of America, and the International Brotherhood of Electrical Workers, provides training for telecommunications and other high-tech workers employed by those companies. The program, with more than 200 local committees run jointly by labor and management, helps employees evaluate their skills, interests, and professional objectives. Then it helps them get the training they need to meet those objectives. For example, it helps workers prepare for high-tech certification programs, upgrade their technical skills as their jobs evolve, improve their basic business skills, and train for new assignments within their companies. For more information, write to the Alliance for Employee Growth and

Development, 8201 Corporate Drive, Suite 20, Landover, MD 20785.

The Auto Industry Partnership

The United Auto Workers (UAW) union has negotiated a similar partnership with Ford, General Motors, and DaimlerChrysler, which offers a wide range of programs to nearly 400,000 UAW members working at the three companies nationwide. At the heart of the partnership are specific, on-the-job training courses to help incumbent workers stay on top of the latest job skills. Workers learn to operate the computers that now control so much of the production and parts distribution.

For more information on this partnership, contact the United Auto Workers, Public Relations Department, 8000 East Jefferson Avenue, Detroit, MI 48214.

For other similar training programs, get the booklet "21st Century Skills for 21st Century Jobs." You can order it from the U.S. Government Printing Office by writing to Superintendent of Documents, P.O. Box 371954, Pittsburgh, PA 15250-7954, or view it online at www.vpskillsummit.org.

NINE

Making a Living Off Government

CHAPTER 23

LANDING a GOVERNMENT JOB

When you're prospecting for a new job, there are few places richer to mine than that mother lode of opportunities: the government.

Federal, state, and local offices combined employ nearly 20 million people—nearly one out of every six people in the total U.S. workforce. And they hire more than a half-million workers a year just to fill vacant positions.

Moreover, with jobs in 2,000 occupations, government offers a wider selection of positions than any private company. Whether your interest lies in art, computer science, sports, economics, forestry, laser technology, or nuclear physics, chances are good that the government has a job to meet your description—and possibly an opening somewhere between Hawaii and Maine, Spain and Bahrain.

> Good pay, good benefits, exotic jobs, security—you can get all this and much more when you work for the government. But to qualify, you first need to learn how to get your foot in the door.

If you don't have special qualifications and you're at an entry-level stage in your career, government has opportunities with competitive salaries, sound benefits packages, and room for advancement. If you're an executive or skilled professional with years of experience and advanced education, government jobs can provide challenging career opportunities. There are job programs designed for students. There are seasonal jobs and part-time jobs. And there are job programs for special groups like veterans, disabled people, and minorities.

There are government jobs that you won't find anywhere else in fields such as foreign affairs, national security, and air traffic control. There are opportunities in some of the most beautiful and historic places in the world—the national parks and monuments.

FACTOID

DOWNSIZED GOVERNMENT? FAR FROM IT. THE U.S. BUREAU OF LABOR STATISTICS PROJECTS THAT FROM 1996 TO 2006, THE NUMBER OF JOBS IN FEDERAL GOVERNMENT WILL DECLINE A BIT FROM 2.76 MILLION TO 2.67 MILLION. AT THE SAME TIME, HOWEVER, STATE AND LOCAL JOBS WILL JUMP FROM 16.7 MILLION TO ALMOST 18.5 MILLION.

All you have to do is figure out where in this world you want to go and then follow our insider tips to get there.

HOW THE SYSTEM WORKS

When people talk about government jobs, they often use the term *Civil Service*, thinking of the central office that used to perform most government hiring. Today, much of the old Civil Service system, with its "cattle-call" tests and tortuous hiring processes, has been dismantled. Instead, in the federal government as well as in many states, hiring has been turned over to individual departments, which set their own standards and screen candidates for themselves. In most cases, this has streamlined the process.

Testing for jobs is much less common these days. Instead, the department that is doing the hiring will use a résumé or application as the primary tool to locate the most qualified candidates. Often, the person who conducts the interviews is the person who will supervise the successful candidate.

Despite these major changes, when you start looking for a government job, you'll want to begin your hunt with one of the central employment services that government maintains. At the federal level, this agency is the Office of Personnel Management (OPM).

The Three-Step Job Search

The OPM has developed a job search process that boils down to three steps.

1. Consult the automated federal job bank for listings, applications, résumé formats, and necessary forms.

2. Obtain job listing announcements from the automated system or the agency that will be hiring. (Most of your questions about qualifications, testing, applications, pay, and job duties will be dealt with in these announcements.)

3. Follow the instructions and submit your application. Usually this boils down to writing and presenting a precise, detailed résumé or using government form OF-612 to guide you.

Depending on the job or jobs you're applying for, you also may be required to take a test, and you may be called for an interview.

Job Classifications

Jobs at the federal level are classified as either competitive or excepted, and the classification affects hiring practices. Most civilian federal jobs are competitive, which means, as the word indicates, that the application process is open and applicants compete for each spot. Most government jobs that

REAL JOBS: COIN CHECKER

Want to put your hands on some money? If you combine manual and visual dexterity with the ability to focus on a task, you may be a good candidate for a job inspecting newly minted coins for the U.S. Department of the Treasury. This job at the U.S. Mint in San Francisco is for U.S. citizens only and requires an awareness of safe practices around machinery. The pay range is $11.11 to $12.96 an hour.

don't fall within that category are classified as excepted service. These jobs often involve policy-making or sensitive areas. Positions include attorneys, foreign language specialists, chaplains, CIA and FBI staff, and federal court staff. Also in the category are patronage jobs, such as aides and other staff members who are hired by members of Congress.

The advantage of excepted service is that the hiring process is often streamlined. The person doing the hiring frequently goes after an individual with whom he is familiar, and openings may not be posted or advertised to the general public.

◗◀ WHAT INSIDERS SAY:

There may be less paperwork and competition for excepted jobs, but there are also some downsides: Jobs in this category don't offer all the benefits and protections that are among the attractions of government service. And jobs that are considered patronage positions can change with a change in administration.

STARTING YOUR HUNT

If you're interested in a position with the federal government, there is a variety of ways that you can learn about open jobs, but for the most current and accurate information, you should rely on the Office of Personnel Management. Here's how you can find the information you need.

Visit the Internet

The Internet has become a prime source of information about jobs at the federal level as well as at state and local levels of government, in part because it can be updated and read easily and often. From a computer at home or at your local library, you can connect to hundreds of thousands of current listings, and, at any time of day, you can get information and advice on applying for a job (see "Your Fast Track to Government Jobs" on page 394). It's such a valuable source that private and government personnel professionals point job seekers there first.

In searching the Internet, your first stop should be USAJobs at www.usajobs.opm.gov. This Web site is sponsored by the OPM. It carries listings of jobs in federal, state, and local government as well as information on special hiring programs for veterans and others.

USAJobs also offers online applications. There's a feature called "What's Hot," which lists positions that the government wants to fill right away. And there are links to other valuable Web job sites. Touch a button and you're in the U.S Department of Labor's guide to planning your future as a federal employee. Touch another and you're in America's Job Bank at www.ajb.dni.us.

The OPM also offers timely information on openings through its central data center at www.fedworld.gov/jobs/jobsearch.html. You can search for specific jobs that interest you by typing in keywords such as "engineer" or "postal worker." The site even lists jobs appropriate to students who have specific college majors.

Call for Listings

You also can access the OPM's job listings by telephone. Available 24 hours a day, 7 days a week, this service offers specific information on current job openings worldwide, plus how to get applications and forms. When you call from a touch-tone phone, a computer-generated voice takes you through a menu of options. To get the national number for the OPM, call your local congressmember's office or write OPM Employment Services, 1900 E Street NW, Washington, DC 20425.

There are also 17 OPM service centers located throughout the country. To get the job-line phone number for one of these centers, look in the government pages of your phone book for "Office of Personnel Management Jobs" or "Federal Job Information" or write to the OPM at the above address.

◖◗ WHAT INSIDERS SAY:

Keep paper and pencil at the ready while on the phone, because the job titles and numbers can be lengthy. At the end of each job description, you're given the option of requesting a job description and application form by mail. Remember, hunting for jobs this way can take a while, and due to budget cuts, these are not toll-free numbers.

Go to a College Placement Office

Job placement centers at colleges and universities will have information on positions for which students finishing school may qualify. They also can provide tips on government jobs for students who are still in school. These can be a foot in the door to a career with the government. As in the private sector, workers who are close to the people doing the hiring often have an advantage in the competition for better jobs. And the government uses entry-level jobs to bring in some of the nation's best and brightest.

If you are enrolled in even one course at a college or university, you should be able to take advantage of career-guidance staff and publications. To qualify for special government job programs for students, though, you generally must be on track toward a degree.

Visit a Computer Kiosk

The OPM also maintains computer kiosks in federal office buildings and at some colleges and universities nationwide. With a touch of a finger, the computers give you access to current job announcements that list vacancies worldwide as well as application forms.

Tap the *Federal Jobs Digest*

Another outstanding and long-standing source of government job information is the biweekly newspaper *Federal Jobs Digest*. Many libraries carry this

YOUR FAST TRACK TO GOVERNMENT JOBS

There's no doubt about it, insiders say: While the government still advertises job openings in traditional print media, the best way to learn about a job and to land it is to turn to the Internet. With its speed, currency, and thorough coverage of job offerings and issues, it is almost indispensable.

The Internet is so important that Rick Brown, personnel assistant with the Grand Teton National Park Service in Moose, Wyoming, says that "chances of landing a job without it these days are reduced."

If you have access to an Internet-connected computer, you can find out about jobs the instant they are advertised. You can search for jobs by keyword instead of wading through pages and pages of notices. You can even get help creating a résumé, then apply online.

"People talk about government not being innovative," says Don Myers, human resources management professor at Virginia Commonwealth University in Richmond. "With the Internet, government has changed dramatically." Internet job boards and related Web services are getting millions of contacts daily, he says, "and it's working. I do 90 percent of my job research over the Web."

publication, or you can subscribe by writing to *Federal Jobs Digest*, 310 North Highland Avenue, Ossining, NY 10562. A subscription to six biweekly issues costs $34. This publication carries extensive classified ads placed by government agencies as well as articles on improving résumés, preparing for tests, and special programs for job seekers. It also promotes numerous books, brochures, and training programs you can buy that may help your job search. The digest generally gets high marks from government sources as a tool for savvy job seekers.

APPLYING FOR A JOB

In the private sector, whether you're granted an interview for the job you want often depends on the effort you put into your written application. If anything, this is even more true for government jobs, which can draw large numbers of applicants.

Thus, if you want to make it past the reject pile, you'll need to build an extensive case for your experience, talent, and skills. What can you do to improve your application? Here's what insiders say.

The Perfect Application

The federal government uses a two-stage screening process in selecting candidates to interview. In the first stage, the government reviews the federal résumé (known as OF-612) that you fill out to be sure that you meet the basic qualifications for the job. If you get through this review, a screening panel will check your knowledge, skill, and ability factors (KSAs). These are the specific criteria for the job.

KSAs: The Keys to Being Noticed

You must respond in writing to these KSAs in order to be selected for an interview, says Gabriel Heilig, founder of Action Résumés in Washington, D.C., and director of the only résumé service inside the Pentagon. As a general rule, if you are applying for a position at the GS-5 level or below, a half-page response to each job criterion is usually sufficient. If you're applying at the GS-7 level or above, however, you should submit a full-page written response for each factor, detailing examples of situations in which you used the type of knowledge, skill, or ability referred to in the vacancy announcement.

To make your KSA stand out, use a separate page for each job you've held previously. Use paper that's the same size as the application form and type the information or use a computer and print it out. Consult old résumés or even tax records if you need to refresh your memory about details such as former employers' addresses. Number or letter the

REAL JOBS: ECOLOGIST IN HAWAII

Call Hawaii home. Travel to island nations throughout the Pacific. Spend your workdays studying the invasion of forests by nonindigenous plants and see how the plants in these forests interact with bugs. The goal of this job is to do research that will lead to an understanding of how these invaders affect an ecosystem and how they might be controlled. The position requires at least a bachelor's degree in biology or a related field, along with at least a year's experience doing research in ecology. The pay range is $61,862 to $73,102 yearly.

sheets sequentially, beginning with your current or most recent job.

Thoroughly describe your duties, responsibilities, and accomplishments. Duties include numerous specific chores you performed, such as reconciling bank statements, welding seams in steel plants, or conducting personnel interviews. Responsibilities are the things for which you were held accountable by your employer. If things went well, you got credit for these. If things went wrong, you were blamed. They could include items like maintaining accurate ledgers, keeping faults in welds to less than 2 percent, or overseeing the performance of 20 engineers. Accomplishments are specific tasks that you completed with positive results.

Be accurate. Ask yourself what you did well on the job and why you can say that you did it well. Again, be expansive and specific. Don't just say you saved the company money; say you saved the company $10,000 by initiating competitive bidding on a maintenance contract.

●◆ *WHAT INSIDERS SAY:*

"The KSAs are very important in the final selection process," says Heilig. "Don't ignore them or give them short shrift. They are usually the difference between a merely acceptable application and a winning one."

The Power of Recommendations

Your application and KSAs also should contain performance appraisals from current or former employers or a letter of recommendation from someone familiar with your work. These should include the length of time that you worked with the company, the title of your last position, basic duties and responsibilities, and how well you carried them out. If you're including a letter of recommendation from a respected industry peer, college professor (if you are a recent graduate), or former employer, it should comment on your qualifica-

THE BENEFITS OF GOVERNMENT WORK

The federal government was always known for providing better worker benefits than private industry. In these days of low unemployment and competitive hiring, however, the consensus among employment counselors is that the packages provided by government and private employers are comparable, with many bigger corporations today offering more frills than Uncle Sam.

Still, when it comes to the basics, government can be a great place to work. Here's a look at its standard benefits.

Holidays
Ten yearly, including New Year's Day, Martin Luther King Day, Washington's Birthday, Memorial Day, Independence Day, Labor Day, Columbus Day, Veterans Day, Thanksgiving Day, and Christmas.

Vacation
Thirteen days a year for full-time employees with less than 3 years' service, 20 days for those with 3 to 15 years, and 26 days after 15 years on the job.

Family leave
Workers can take up to 12 weeks unpaid time off for the birth or adoption of a child, to care for a sick family member, or for their own extended illnesses. Those who qualify under the Federal Employees Family Friendly Leave Act of 1994 may take an additional 13 days off for reasons other than their own illness, such as caring for an ailing family

tions for the job you seek as well as on responsibilities you've handled and achievements that they are familiar with.

Final Advice

Be sure to be thorough and be careful. Sometimes clerks help sort through the mass of applications and "deselect" candidates who fail to fill in all the blanks or who make obvious errors.

The *Federal Jobs Digest*, with the OPM's cooperation, has produced a book, *Working for Uncle Sam* ($19.95 plus shipping and handling from Breakthrough Publications, 2050 Elmwood Avenue #5, Sharon Hill, PA 19079). It contains sample KSAs and a complete list of federal job categories, along with a wealth of relevant information on the federal job hunt. Personnel professionals like Heilig also will help you fill out the forms or can review your form for a fee. If you want to try this route, check the yellow pages of your phone book for em-

ployment agencies, and when you call, ask whether they handle federal job searches.

●◆ WHAT INSIDERS SAY:

Personnel specialists are impressed by computer-generated, laser-printed applications. That said, sometimes in this high-tech age, applications and résumés are scanned into computers, and scanners may not pick up words that are italicized or underlined, so you should avoid trying to stand out typographically.

Acing the Test

A written test, or Civil Service exam, was once about the only method used to examine candidates for federal service, but these "cattle-call" exams have become so unpopular that few agencies require them.

Still, some city and state governments and some federal agencies rely on tests in certain circumstances. If you're applying for an entry-level job, where there are a large number of new hires, you probably will be

---

member or arranging for or attending a family funeral.

Pay

Most federal workers are paid on a scale that's determined by what is paid locally for similar work. If they work on Sundays, they earn time-and-a-quarter; for overtime, they're paid time-and-a-half; and for holidays or night work (from 6:00 P.M. to 6:00 A.M.), they get double-time. Employees who work in places where the cost of living is especially high or where there is extraordinary demand for their skills may also receive extra pay.

Life insurance

Workers also are automatically covered by group life insurance. Employees usually pay two-thirds of the cost. They may extend coverage to family for an additional cost.

Health insurance

Employees and their families can use either standard fee-for-service plans or comprehensive medical plans/HMOs. The government picks up 60 to 75 percent of the cost, depending on the plan. No dental coverage is available.

Retirement

Workers hired after December 31, 1983, are on a three-tier plan that combines Social Security, a basic annuity, and a thrift savings plan, which is similar to a 401(k) plan. All are adjusted to the cost of living as protection against inflation. Employees may also directly fund Individual Retirement Accounts (IRAs).

Education

Federal employees and their children are eligible for grants and scholarships through the Federal Employee Education and Assistance Fund.

required to take a written test. You're also likely to be tested if you apply for a job when there is an oversupply of candidates. Some excepted service jobs—including those in the Postal Service, FBI and other law enforcement agencies, and Foreign Service; federal apprenticeships; and air traffic control positions—also require tests. Job vacancy announcements will spell out whether a test is required.

●◆ WHAT INSIDERS SAY:

Want to speed up the testing process? Stay away from major metropolitan test sites. Busy government centers like Washington, D.C., see so many job applicants that it may take weeks to get a reservation for the test you need. Instead, file for a reservation at a nearby site (for Washington, sites would be Reston, Virginia, or Bethesda, Maryland), where the wait is likely to be much shorter. The trip to a nearby town for the test can save you weeks.

Practice, Practice

Brochures with sample questions may be provided for some tests, with materials supplied by the agency when you request an application. Private publications like *Federal Jobs Digest* also offer samples and guides. One thorough one, published by *Federal Jobs Digest* with the OPM's cooperation, is "Working for Uncle Sam" ($19.95 plus shipping and handling from Breakthrough Publications, 2050 Elmwood Avenue #5, Sharon Hill, PA 19079). Sometimes these guidebooks are available at well-stocked libraries or bookstores. The books can be helpful and probably are worth a look, although you can spend a bundle for what becomes information overload, say experts. But some exams are difficult, and preparation is helpful.

You also may be tempted to take one of the preparatory courses that are available from some private services. Government personnel experts say that these can be helpful but in most cases are unnecessary because the essential material that you'll need is available through the OPM or the agencies that are doing the hiring.

Government tests are tailored to jobs. Postal Service applicants, for example, are asked to place addresses in the correct locations. Foreign Service applicants are questioned about history, economics, and language. Applicants for clerical work must alphabetize names and work math problems. Treasury agent prospects read facts about a crime and answer questions such as "Which statement would be least likely to be used in proving the case?"

●◆ WHAT INSIDERS SAY:

Don't pay for something that you can get for free, say insiders. There are people out there (the government calls them scam artists) who will advertise in newspapers and on the Internet to help you locate and land government jobs for a fee. You can get all the job information you need from the OPM's Federal Employment Information System. It's free except for phone charges.

REAL JOBS: WRITER, EDITOR

Traveling to interesting places to observe noteworthy events is part of the appeal of this position offered by the U.S. Information Agency. The job requires an understanding of the Internet and the ability to design, create, and maintain Web pages. In some positions, these workers assist translators. Jobs may involve travel out of town (or out of the country) and possible weekend and night work. You'll need to be able to work well in a team environment with highly skilled professionals. The ability to communicate effectively and to use technology in communication are musts. The pay range is $33,650 to $63,436 yearly.

Making Your Case in Person

If you've reached the point where you've been called for an interview, you are competing only with people who have been judged to be qualified for the job. Now, in a face-to-face meeting, you must distinguish yourself. Frequently, these job interviews are conducted at federal offices by a panel that includes people from the office where you hope to work.

Sally Brown, a career counselor in Richmond, Virginia, says that before you go for an interview, you should research the particular job and the agency that's doing the hiring. Read the job announcement thoroughly. It will describe duties, expectations, and qualifications. Also, contact the agency that will do the hiring so that you can ask about the work. If possible, speak to someone there who has a similar job and ask for a description of the duties and responsibilities. Then, when you ask or answer questions during your interview, point out experience or training that may be relevant to the job, Brown says.

You are likely to be given an opportunity to question the panel, so be prepared to demonstrate that you are thoughtful and that you have done some research to get this job.

Special Ways to Improve Your Chances

You can make yourself more attractive to the government than the next person in line, even if that person's in front of you. How? By making use of the special opportunities for employment that the government offers to members of certain groups. Here are the most commonly used ones.

Credit for Veterans

Ever since thousands of veterans marched home from the Civil War, Congress has given some preferential treatment to veterans looking for government jobs. Time spent in the military counts heavily in your favor in most federal job searches. There are also a limited number of jobs set aside for veterans exclusively through what are called readjustment appointments. These jobs are filled noncompetitively by people who fall into specific categories: veterans of the Vietnam era who have service-related disabilities, veterans who served on active duty during the Vietnam era in any campaign or expedition for which a campaign badge or expeditionary medal has been authorized, and vets who served after the Vietnam era (May 7, 1975) for more than 180 days of active duty and who were discharged other than dishonorably.

Mothers and spouses of some disabled and deceased vets also may be eligible for favorable treatment. For example, they may file applications outside the time limits set for nonveteran applicants. Moreover, in some jobs, such as custodian, guard, and messenger, veterans move to the front of the line in hiring. In jobs in which military experience is useful, such as military pay clerk or aircraft mechanic, veterans also are hired before comparably qualified nonvets. Always let it be known if you are a veteran.

Minorities and Women

The government requires agencies to have affirmative action plans to encourage the hiring of minorities and women. In fact, each employment field office should have a counselor available to assist applicants who qualify for special assistance on the basis of race, color, religion, gender, or national origin. And government agencies that serve certain groups such as Native Americans or Hispanics are required to have programs designed to hire members of those groups themselves. If you think you might qualify, talk to the minority employment counselor in the agency where you are seeking work.

Outstanding Scholars

The government makes some entry-level positions available to recent college graduates based on academic achievement. A grade-point average of 3.5 or better or a class rank in the top 10 percent or higher can exempt applicants from testing requirements.

Applicants in this pool still need to file a government employment application, along with a form applying for the outstanding scholar exemption. Write or call the agency you are interested in or talk to career counselors at your college to obtain forms and information.

Using an Insider's Clout

As in the private sector, there is always an advantage to knowing someone inside an agency who's willing to go to bat for you. This is more of an advantage in high-level excepted service jobs than in those that are filled by open competition.

Can your congressmember or senator smooth your path toward government employment? That depends. Over the years, several legislative attempts have been made to keep patronage out of the competitive hiring process. But if one of your elected representatives knows you and can speak favorably about your work, you might benefit from a letter of recommendation. The weight that's given to this kind of recommendation by the person doing the hiring certainly will vary, depending on factors such as the political affiliations of the prospective employer and your endorser, one senatorial aide points out. This kind of reference may be more valuable if you are seeking an excepted service job, for which agencies have more latitude in hiring.

Start at the Bottom

You also may want to consider taking a low-level job in the place where you want to work, just to get onto the track. Or, if you're willing to go anywhere for the job of choice, that improves your chances, because market conditions vary from place to place. For example, one search showed some openings for part-time mail carriers in rural Virginia, while there were no openings at all in Washington, D.C. Once you pile up some experience, you can highlight it in your application for a better job, which will improve your chances of moving up.

Furthermore, if you will work in a field where there is an undersupply of applicants for jobs such as clerk, secretary, or computer technician, your chances are obviously better than if you'll accept nothing less than a post as an economist in Paris.

OTHER JOBS WITH UNCLE SAM

Your options for work with the federal government aren't limited to standard, on-the-books jobs. If you're willing to be a little creative about what you do, you may find opportunities in the vast world of secondary positions, ranging from full-time contractors to short-term interns.

Some of these jobs pay extremely well; all are

REAL JOBS: SUPERCAR DESIGNER

Can you make a car that can go 80 miles on a gallon of gas? In Ann Arbor, Michigan, the U.S. Environmental Protection Agency's National Vehicle Fuel and Emissions Laboratory is involved in programs that are aimed at reducing air pollution from motor vehicles. They're hiring creative, highly competent people—mostly engineers—to work in the SuperCar Program. The government and domestic car manufacturers are working together on the project. They are not looking for trainees but for people with at least a college education and experience. The pay range is $42,776 to $77,014 yearly.

rich in experiences and contacts that you can use to build a case for long-term employment.

Internships

Are you interested in Asian-Pacific American affairs? Do you come from a Hispanic, Chinese, African-American, or Native-American background? Are you looking for that first job, and you'd like to start on Capitol Hill? Maybe an internship would be right for you.

Almost all federal agencies offer some paid internship program that can lead to a career. Internships benefit the government as well: They are viewed as one way that government can land some of the best and brightest right out of school. To find out about internship opportunities, either contact the agency for which you'd like to work (it will have its own personnel or employment office) directly or go through your school's career placement office, which should be able to put you in touch with the Office of Personnel Management and other agencies.

The USAJobs Web site at www.usajobs. opm.gov also carries a list of internships. Most provide transportation to and from Washington, health insurance, and a stipend. Some provide housing and meals.

Students who have distinguished themselves and who earn nominations from their colleges or universities also may be selected for highly competitive appointments in the Presidential Management Intern Program. These service appointments are for 2 years, and interns are placed throughout the government. At the end of the internship period, those who have performed well and who desire to do so may have their positions converted to competitive service positions, which come with job security and enhanced benefits.

The White House also grants about a dozen fellowships each year to people who are starting careers who have an interest and aptitude for leadership. The White House Fellows Program provides a year of experience in the White House to a select few after an intensive application process.

Contract Work

As the largest buyer and employer in the nation, the government increasingly relies on good temporary help. Government agencies hire people on a contract basis, whether as cleaning crews or computer wizards. Sometimes these jobs can be quite lucrative.

Most contract work provided by the government is in the form of temporary or term appointments. These are used to fill positions when there is not a continuing need for a job or when the agency believes that the work can be done more efficiently

REAL JOBS: HOLOCAUST MUSEUM TECHNICIAN

Spend your workday digging into history at the U.S. Holocaust Memorial Museum. The U.S. Holocaust Memorial Council in Washington, D.C., recently needed someone to assist the curator of the permanent exhibits at the museum. The job calls for enhancing the exhibits, completing exhibit projects, performing research, preparing records, and answering questions that may be asked by interested people. Applicants for such jobs should have both an understanding of museum operations and a knowledge of the Holocaust. They also need to be able to communicate effectively orally and in writing. The pay range is $33,650 to $43,747 yearly.

by an outside vendor. Still, some contractors, once they have a foot in the door, have found that they can move from job to job, in effect creating full-time work for themselves.

Temporary Appointments

Temporary appointments last a year or less and come with specific expiration dates. These jobs are filled by the agency that needs the worker. They should be posted on the USAJobs Web site (www.usajobs.opm.gov) or included in the OPM phone listings, with their temporary status specified. Information on contract work and on meetings where such opportunities may be discussed can be found in print in the *Commerce Business Daily*. This paper, published Monday through Friday, is available at federal depository libraries and on the Internet at www.cbdnet.access.gpo.gov. You can subscribe to the print version at a cost of $275 a year by writing to the Superintendent of Documents, U.S. Government Printing Office, P.O. Box 371954, Pittsburgh, PA 15250-7954.

Temporary appointments may be extended by the agency for up to another year. Most of these jobs are filled competitively, although agencies may give priority to veterans, former Peace Corps workers, or other special individuals.

Many of these jobs are seasonal, such as those with the Postal Service around Christmas. These workers are covered by Social Security and unemployment compensation but do not receive other fringe benefits. They may buy health insurance after a year of temporary service if the work is extended or if they land another appointment, but they pay the full cost. Also, they are not eligible for the federal life insurance program or retirement benefits.

Term Appointments

Term appointments are given to contractors for jobs that are expected to last from 1 to 4 years. Usually, these jobs are tied to a specific project, such as preparing computers for Y2K, or they may be designed to fill positions that are slated to be abolished or reassigned after a department's expected reorganization. The government, like private business, also provides term appointments to hire outside contractors for services for which it believes that subcontracting will be more efficient than doing the work in-house.

Term employees are eligible to earn vacation time and holidays and have most of the same benefits as permanent employees, including life and health insurance, coverage for retirement, and a thrift savings plan, which is similar to a 401(k).

Jay Torg of Washington, D.C., is one term employee who has developed a lucrative business working from assignment to assignment on technology with the Postal Service in Washington. He got there from humble beginnings, starting as a temporary employee on a 90-day assignment. Hired as a temporary worker by first one post office subcontractor and then another, Torg says he realized that he had skills that were in demand. He incorporated and began hiring himself directly to the government at a considerably higher rate.

Once he's working inside, Torg says, a contractor can anticipate what projects will be coming next and be on the spot, ready to do the work when a new job is available. He also is in a position to meet and team up with other successful contractors to bid on larger projects.

Once you get inside, you can start tasking here and there, developing peripheral staffs to do work that you may not do yourself, he says.

BEYOND THE FEDS

Although the federal government is a major employer, it's actually small potatoes compared with state and local governments, which in total employ six times as many workers. And there's a major world of pseudo-government jobs beyond that in community associations.

The hiring system at these levels varies from place to place, but there are some common elements that can help you search out a job.

State and Local Jobs

State and local governments provide plenty of employment opportunities, and their pay and benefits packages compare to those of many private employers. In many states and localities, upper-level managers, from school superintendents and health care administrators to county managers, planners, and engineers, earn six-figure salaries. Increasingly, in states as in the federal government, these agencies and organizations are doing their own hiring. To find out how to proceed, you must contact their personnel or human resources offices for the jurisdiction you're interested in. The telephone number should be listed in the government pages of your phone book.

Local Job Ads on the Internet

One Internet site that can link you to state and local governments throughout the United States is the Public Service Employees Network at www.pse-net.com. You can search for jobs by state, city, town, or county, and you can obtain study guides, career advice, and information on interviews, résumés and applications. Did you know, for example, that Anchorage, Alaska, is continually looking for lifeguards? You'll find that information and more like it at this Web site.

Also, even some smaller jurisdictions today have Web sites through which you can obtain information on jobs. These are usually linked to a state site that you can reach by typing in www.state.*(insert the two-letter state abbreviation)*.us.

COMPARING PUBLIC AND PRIVATE WAGES

Government work used to be known for great benefits and so-so pay, and pay at the state and local level was usually lower than that in federal government. Those times are gone. Nowadays, you're likely to find that wages are fairly similar in both camps. The figures here show how they stacked up for some selected jobs in 1999.

Note: These numbers are guidelines only. Salaries vary broadly from company to company and from place to place. Even the government adjusts salaries based on the cost of living and the supply and demand for candidates.

POSITION	PRIVATE SECTOR PAY	STATE/LOCAL PAY	FEDERAL PAY
Accountant I	$ 523/wk	$ 535/wk	$ 532/wk
Budget analyst II	656/wk	680/wk	656/wk
Clerk	289/wk	313/wk	372/wk
Computer operator I	357/wk	381/wk	442/wk
Corrections officer	–	547/wk	623/wk
Drafter I	409/wk	380/wk	571/wk
Personnel supervisor I	1,180/wk	1,058/wk	1,151/wk
Secretary	395/wk	371/wk	500/wk
Tool-and-die maker	19.04/hr	–	19.57/hr
Truck driver (heavy trucks)	13.29/hr	13.74/hr	13.79/hr
Word processor II	493/wk	498/wk	469/wk

Recruitment Newsletters

Most states operate employment or personnel offices that help recruit people. In Virginia, for example, the state department of personnel and training publishes a newsletter called "Recruit" in both print and Internet formats with links to federal and local job banks. Visit www.dpt.state.va.us or write the department at the Monroe Building, 101 North 14th Street, 12th Floor, Richmond, VA 23129. You can link to other states by typing in www.state.*(insert the two-letter state abbreviation)*.us.

Furthermore, if you are a police officer or work in most medical fields or with computers—or are willing to undertake training in these areas on your own initiative—you open doors to government employment. These jobs are continuously under recruitment, and qualified applicants are in demand.

All state jobs must be posted, usually in newspapers and on agencies' Web pages. The job posting will specify if the position is open to agency employees only, state employees only, or the general public. It's helpful to contact the particular office or facility where you want to work to find out who's likely to do the hiring and who's likely to know when jobs open up. Stay in touch with that person to keep abreast of opportunities and to show your interest.

Community Associations

While they don't fall directly into the classification of *government*, community associations, which have many governmental functions, are alternative sources of employment that may be worth investigating. There are 205,000 of these associations in the United States providing services to communi-

Amazing Stories

BLOWING YOUR WHISTLE ALL THE WAY TO THE BANK

One of the most lucrative ways to make money from the government may be the most offbeat: Thanks to a law known as the False Claims Act, turning in companies who are attempting to defraud Uncle Sam can earn you a multimillion-dollar bonanza.

Here's how it works: First, you need to provide government investigators with credible evidence of a company's misdeeds—if the company overcharged the government for goods and services, for instance, or attempted to hide earnings. The investigators examine your statement, and if they feel there's enough evidence to go forward, they'll investigate and seek damages from the company to-

taling three times the amount of the government's loss.

Here's the good part: Under what's known as *qui tam* (a Latin term that means someone who represents his own interests as well as the government's), if the government wins its case, you receive between 15 and 25 percent of the penalty assessed against the offending company. If the company settles before the case reaches court, you receive the same percentage.

When company fraud is widespread, this can result in a jaw-dropping payday. "In one case, a whistle blower received more than $60 million," says William J. Hardy, a leading qui tam lawyer in the Washington, D.C. area.

ties where 42 million Americans live, according to Donna Reichle, vice president of communications for the Community Associations Institute in Alexandria, Virginia.

Reichle describes associations as "definitely a growth field" for job hunters. In places like Sun City, Arizona, and Columbia, Maryland, associations are very similar to town offices, with salaries and benefits packages that are competitive, she says. Columbia's association has about 400 employees.

An association may have a professional manager, a maintenance staff, accountants, clerks, human resources personnel, architectural review staff, lifeguards, and recreation planners. Some publish newspapers and run cable TV channels. Community associations offer alternatives to government work where that work is hard to get, and the experience you gain working at association jobs can improve your chance of landing the city, county, state, or federal government job you want later in your career.

The Community Associations Institute keeps a list of associations around the country. The institute's address is 1630 Duke Street, Alexandria, VA 22314.

CHAPTER 24

RUNNING for OFFICE

By now, you've learned a lot about how to get more out of government. You've discovered the "for the people" part of Lincoln's Gettysburg Address. Perhaps now, you'd like to learn about the "of the people" part. That's where this chapter comes in.

Here, we'll show you how to give a lot back through the political system while helping friends and neighbors, developing valuable programs, and dealing with issues that have real impact on your life and that of your community. In short, how to run for office.

Although climbing the ladder—by working as a volunteer, then running for a local position to pay dues on the way to higher office—is still a common path to political success, there are other routes to office these days. Demographic shifts, suburban-ization, and the increase in influence of minorities and women have all shaken the old political structures that once groomed and promoted candidates. These shifts have also created opportunities that didn't exist a few decades ago. You don't necessarily have to play the political party game to be elected these days. There are now even schools that teach prospective candidates to run successful campaigns for everything from school boards to city councils to the U.S. Congress.

Running for office can be an extraordinarily rewarding process whether you win or lose. But, like anything worth having, it doesn't come easily—so take a hard look inside, survey the electoral landscape where you wish to serve, prepare yourself, and enjoy the run. This can be one of life's great experiences.

> Who's in charge here? It could be you! Dramatic changes in the way voters pick candidates are making it easier to be elected, even if you don't have party connections and years of practice in the political machine.

! FACTOID

THE UNITED STATES HAS MORE THAN 501,900 ELECTED OFFICIALS IN FEDERAL, STATE, LOCAL, AND SCHOOL DISTRICT GOVERNMENT. THAT'S AN AVERAGE OF ROUGHLY ONE ELECTED OFFICIAL FOR EVERY 54 PEOPLE.

WHERE DO YOU START?

In her highly recommended book *Political Campaigning: A New Decade*, Seattle political consultant Cathy Allen points out that there is no single correct way to run a winning campaign. There are some common steps to take, however, and decisions to make that will improve your chances. (Allen's classic book is out of print, but your librarian or bookseller may be able to order it for you.) Here is what Allen and others recommend.

Follow the Golden Rules

For Allen, there are a handful of "golden rules" that will improve your chances of winning. The first is simple: Don't try to do too much and what you do, do as well as possible, she recommends. Focus on just two or three issues, for example. Concentrate on getting your message to the people who are likely to vote, not the population at large. Don't overschedule so that you wear yourself out or miss engagements. Not showing up at a planned event leaves a bad taste in voters' mouths.

Her other recommendations?

✓ Despite the pressure that comes with any campaign, don't hurry. Take time to think things through. Make decisions as though you are running a small business—shop around for everything from stationery to office space to the professional staff that you'll probably bring into your campaign.

✓ If you're a newcomer to this process, you have a lot to learn, so ask questions about everything. Ask people in your district about their concerns. Ask people with political experience for advice on running your campaign. Ask vendors for ways to save money on supplies that you'll need.

✓ Be careful who you bring into your campaign. No matter how well-intentioned they are, keep an eye on friends, supporters, and staff to be sure they don't take off with their own strategies "to save you." They may raise issues that deflect attention or distract you from those you've investigated and developed, or they may lead you to waste time dealing with constituencies that are not likely to turn out to vote.

✓ Above all, don't take the whole process too seriously. Keep your sense of humor. You'll make mistakes, so you should be able to laugh at them and move on.

Ask Yourself Why

Many people get an urge "to save the world" or at least make a positive contribution to their own little corners of it. If you're reading this, you've probably felt that way. Good for you. Feelings like that are a big part of what makes democracy work.

You may be motivated by a particular issue, such as cuts in education funding or plans to put a highway through the old neighborhood. Sometimes, the reasons aren't quite so noble. Political pros also hear from people who want to run for office to promote themselves or their businesses or even to meet members of the opposite sex.

When Chris LaCivita, executive director of the Republican Party of Virginia in Richmond, hears people voice reasons like the last two, "I tell them, 'Out of here,'" he says. "They have to be able to give us a good reason for putting themselves through the hell that a campaign is."

In addition to having a good reason, you'll need to know that you have a core following. "I have a prospective candidate make a list of 25 people in the community, then call all 25 and ask if they'll support him in his campaign," LaCivita says. "That usually gives a pretty realistic picture of whether you have a chance for success."

More bluntly, "if you can't find five people who'll lie down and die for you, don't run," says Diane Waltrip, a political consultant who has taught at the Women's Campaign School, a program for women who are considering running for office or who are interested in politics. It is offered annually or biannually at Yale University.

What does it take to win that kind of support? S. J. Guzzetta, of Washington, D.C., who has run campaigns for dozens of candidates in races at all levels of government across the nation over the past 25 years, says he looks for "fire in the belly"—desire and commitment—when he considers offers to work for candidates.

He wants to see "someone I would be proud to have represent me," he says. That means someone who is serious (about running, not necessarily in demeanor), reasonable, not an extremist, honest, and willing to talk over issues and compromise. He also likes to talk to the prospective candidate's family and inner circle to be sure that everyone there is committed and that they are coming into the campaign with their eyes wide open. "I don't want to face an elderly lady who gave $10 from her Social Security check and tell her the candidate lost because he didn't want it enough," Guzzetta says. "This is an incredibly tough business."

●◆ WHAT INSIDERS SAY:
Are you comfortable in large groups? Can you handle attention, including TV lights and protruding microphones? More than one promising candidate has frozen and failed when confronted with an audience and media attention. Attending and participating in public meetings, whether they're for the school board, Kiwanis Club, PTA, or church committees, can give you a feel for your ability in this area, and they help make you known in the community.

Check the Closet

Be honest with yourself. Brutally honest. Get together a group of trusted advisors and talk over anything from your past that is negative. If it's out there, you can figure that the opposition or the media will find it.

Have you had tax problems? A drunk driving charge? A messy divorce? A close relative with se-

rious problems? It's all fair game. Remember, though, that virtually everyone has something in their past that they're not proud of. A blemish doesn't necessarily rule you out, but you must be willing to have it brought to public attention, and you must be able to explain something that may seem personal and embarrassing to you and your family.

Be accurate and honest in your publications. A little omission or enhancement that might seem slight at first can look huge on the front page of the newspaper.

Talk to your family members about what a campaign will mean to them. They'll probably be picking up some of the load at home while you are away, and they may have to make sacrifices in their own lives to join your campaign.

●◆ WHAT INSIDERS SAY:
If you smoke, try to quit, or at least smoke in private. These days, an unflattering picture of you with a cigarette will turn away voters who are offended by the habit.

GATHERING FINANCIAL SUPPORT

Call it dialing for dollars.

Your ability to raise money to pay for starting your campaign is the first hurdle you'll face, and it will come at you again and again. Things like telephones, mailings, gasoline for travel, and time away from work will cost money, even in the barest of campaigns.

An office, a paid staffer, a copier, and other necessities will cost more. Advertising, which will almost certainly be necessary to get your name before the electorate, can run the budget up quickly.

"If you don't have the guts to raise money, you have no business running for office," says Nancy Finch of Richmond, who lost her first race for Virginia's state legislature in 1995. For her race to represent a suburban county, she went so far as to take out a home equity loan.

"Anyone who doesn't think fund-raising is the key is dreaming," says John A. Cosgrove, who has run both losing and winning campaigns for city offices in Chesapeake, Virginia.

"It's the beans and bullets in this war," says LaCivita of the Republican Party of Virginia.

So what are some strategies for raising money?

Pay Your Own Way

While only a few candidates have the wherewithal to write themselves all the checks they'll need to pay for a campaign, the first place that most first-time candidates for office are going to have to find seed money is in their own bank accounts. Home equity loans, credit cards, retirement funds, and the family business all may be tapped to show your commitment and to get the campaign off the ground.

When interviewing potential candidates, "one of the first questions we ask is 'What are your financial resources?'" says Robin Winston, chairman of the Indiana Democratic Party in Indianapolis. "Your personal resources and your ability to garner resources are directly related to your ability to build a name among voters," she says. Without name recognition, your campaign isn't likely to go anywhere.

Raising Funds in the Community

Where should you look for money after sowing seeds yourself? You can try "the usual suspects" in your community—people who are known to be wealthy and philanthropic. Since they probably are hearing from every fund-raiser in town, however, you should frame your pitch around a specific issue that you think might open purse strings. If you're going to focus your campaign on improving county schools or the public library, for example, look for people who have been active in parent-teacher groups or who have patronized and contributed to the library.

Lobbyists (the people who represent specific industries and interests) back candidates generously and often. They lean heavily toward incumbents and sure things, but they may back a candidate who clearly will represent their interests. The pharmacy association's lobbyist, for example, may provide support to a pharmacist who's running for the state legislature. The Realtors' association may back a developer running for the county commission. In most states, lobbyists are required to register with the state government, so you should be able to get a list of who represents whom by contacting your state elections office or attorney general's office. Look for the numbers in the government pages of your phone book.

For newcomers, veteran campaign manager S. J. Guzzetta suggests first looking at your natural constituencies. This includes people in your business who will be glad to have one of their own in government, like the pharmacist in the example above. Funeral directors would like a fellow director in the state legislature where regulations affecting them may be written. Education associations are known for political activism and are likely to back one of their own—a teacher or principal or parent who's been active in school—in a political contest by providing money and volunteers.

Look at political action committees (PACs) and interest groups that fit your message. There are pro-gun PACs, pro-environment PACs, Christian PACs, and liberal and conservative PACs. Approach committees to which you'd consider contributing. Political parties maintain PAC directories and can provide you with a PAC kit that contains detailed information. Call your local board of elections to find out how to contact a committee; the number should be in the government pages of your phone book.

Check your Christmas card list, relatives and friends, your Rolodex at work, and members of clubs, your religious community, or civic organizations in which you serve. College friends and racquetball buddies are likely sources, as are people whom you may have supported financially in various endeavors. Now is the time to cash in any outstanding chips.

Fundraising events as common as barbecues and auctions still work. Check for professional associations, from bar associations to "friends of the parks," that will be comfortable with your message; such groups often back candidates. And, with the graying of America, you may find concentrations of the area's most politically active people in retirement communities and senior centers. They vote, they volunteer, and they give.

●◆ WHAT INSIDERS SAY:

Sitting down to call a list of people whom you know well or hardly know at all to ask for money can be the toughest part of getting your campaign off the ground. You may need the equivalent of someone putting a gun to your head. How to do it? Have a trusted volunteer sit with you and even dial the numbers for you, and have him promise to keep you there until the business is done.

When requesting money, as with other campaign matters, pitch the two or three issues that will be your message. To personalize the calls, be aware of who you are calling ("How's Uncle Ed?") and to mention an issue that may be particularly important to them ("Ed's farm is right on the site of that sewage treatment plant, and I oppose that location.") You might even "practice" with calls first to a few close friends and relatives to get comfortable.

WHERE TO GET TRAINING

Nancy Finch thought that she was pretty savvy when she went into her first campaign for public office. She had worked as a volunteer in several campaigns. She had served as legislative liaison for colleges and universities. She had watched the political process as a news reporter.

When the campaign began, though, Finch found that she was naive. "I didn't know anything," she says. But she turned to successful politicians and campaign operatives she knew and set out to get an education. Today, she looks at that education as a lasting, valuable result of her run for office. "It was wonderful to learn about politics and how it works," she says.

Here are some of her key discoveries.

✓ Fund-raising is vital, and you never stop doing it.

✓ Even seeking a low-level office, you need a professional campaign manager whom you can trust with the details while you're knocking on doors. While volunteers are great, they tend to work on their own schedule, not yours.

✓ Computers are essential in reaching voters these days, via e-mail or the Internet, as well as in getting access to records you'll need.

✓ Polls and voter data are valuable to help you focus on a few key issues of importance to you and people in your district and to identify where votes will come from.

✓ Campaign institutes can give you both the knowledge of the process that you'll need and credentials that attract political leaders and workers to your side (more on them later).

✓ If you're running against an incumbent, you're going to have a tough time getting money—and winning. Start early, at least a year before the election. Note that many areas allow active campaigning only within a certain time frame, but you can begin working behind the scenes well in advance.

Political Parties

As mentioned above, people who are running for office have traditionally worked their way through the party ranks, beginning as volunteers for various candidates, then moving on to lower-level elected positions and finally up the ladder to bigger things. Doing it this way helps you learn the machinery and the people behind the scenes while they learn about you.

Politics is still an inside game, and the parties control much of the board. Knowing the right people on the inside and having them know you is a giant first step. You should understand that more than 90 percent of incumbents win when they run for reelection, largely because of the party support behind them.

The support can be varied and creative. Like political parties in most states, the Florida Republican Party holds "campaign schools" for prospective candidates who align themselves with the party. Here, candidates get lessons on challenges that they will confront, such as campaign laws, strategies, fund-raising, and dealing with the media.

These programs also offer new candidates a chance to meet party leaders and campaign professionals, says Todd Schnick, director of party development in Tallahassee. The introductions can mean the difference between active and not-so-active party support in the race, and that in turn can be the difference between winning and losing. Call the state office of your political party and ask about their schools or similar programs. The parties run these regularly for people who are willing to invest the time. You can get the number from the information operator in your state capital or by checking with a local elected representative who's a member of the party.

If a candidate is running for a seat that the party sees as attainable and important, and it also sees the candidate as worthy, the party may throw money and professional staff, including a campaign manager, pollsters, and media experts, into the race. More likely, the party will offer a talent bank to draw from, voter lists, and pamphlets and videos that can be helpful. If nothing else, a professional party leader will offer frank advice about the campaign's chances of success that a paid consultant or starry-eyed supporter might be unwilling to offer.

Both the Republican and Democratic parties offer extensive campaign training manuals, and even videos, that are full of detail. These and other materials should be available from your local or state party office, free or at a modest cost, or from the Democratic National Committee, 430 South Capitol Street SE, Washington, DC 20003, or the Republican National Committee, 310 First Street SE, Washington, DC 20003.

The Government

State and local elections officials are not in the business of running campaigns, so don't expect them to tell you what to do, but they can provide extremely valuable information. If you are running for town or county office, go to the elections or registrar's office at that level. If you are running for state office, check with the state elections board. Do this early in the process. They will provide a packet of information, including the forms you need to fill out as well as information on steps you need to take, such as having petitions signed, and deadlines that you must meet. Look in the government pages of your phone book for the number of the local board of elections, which may be able to put you in touch with the state board. Or you can call the information operator in your state capital.

Registrars, elections commissioners, and similar government professionals do hold the key to a wealth of information that will be valuable. David Ellis, director of elections in Bradley County, Tennessee, says his office can provide names and addresses of registered voters in local districts. He can break them down by age (older people vote in much higher percentages than the young) or according to participation in party primaries. He can point out new subdivisions where there may be new voters. With this information, you can direct your door-to-door canvassing and mailers.

In addition, studying these demographics can show you which politicians are popular in a district. That can provide insight into which issues and positions are important to the voters there.

●◆ *WHAT INSIDERS SAY:*

Remember that if you have even one person on your campaign's payroll, you must register with the IRS and state tax officials and perform necessary withholding and other paperwork, just as any business must. This means forms to file. And if you still have a manual typewriter, you might want to put in a new ribbon. In some localities, forms are still on paper, not computer.

The Professionals

Although there are many aspects of a campaign that you can run with volunteers, if you want to succeed in a run for political office, you're almost

---

RUNNING FOR OFFICE 101

Wayne Kuipers' first exposure to political campaigning came in 1991, when a friend asked him to work on his campaign for Congress. The campaign resulted in an upset: They beat an incumbent. Kuipers found himself in demand. He was called on to serve with various civic groups and committees.

"Suddenly, I found myself chairing these committees," he says. Then people started asking if he might like to run for office himself. Up until then, the only thing he'd run was a landscape business.

Bitten by the bug and encouraged by friends, Kuipers turned for his real education to one of a growing number of nonpartisan programs across the nation that are designed specifically to train and develop community leaders. He enrolled in the Michigan Political Leadership Program. Shortly after graduation, he ran for the Michigan House of Representatives and won.

Kuipers says that there were three significant lessons to be drawn from his success.

✓ You do not have to come through the traditional party structure to be successful in seeking office. In fact, status as an outsider can help if the electorate in your area is dissatisfied with both main parties.

✓ You can learn how to run a campaign and, more important, how to be an effective elected official through leadership programs that are popping up around the nation that focus on building consensus and on working with others despite differences.

✓ You can win if you apply good business principles to your campaign and make an issue of your desire to serve in a businesslike manner. "This was the route I took, not as an insider but as someone who could apply what he knew about business to government," Kuipers says.

Depending on where you live, you may want to contact one of the following programs. If you don't qualify to enroll, you still may be able to get materials or suggestions for sources of advice in your state.

✓ North Carolina Institute of Political Leadership, 106 Westside Hall, 601 South College Road, Wilmington, NC 28403. Run by Dr. Walter De Vries, this is the granddaddy of the programs and a good source for advice on such programs in general.

✓ Snelling Center for Government, 460 South Prospect Street, Burlington, VT 05401.

✓ Thomas C. Sorensen Institute for Political Leadership, 918 Emmet Street, Suite 300, Charlottesville, VA 22903.

✓ Michigan Political Leadership Program, 321 Berkey Hall, Michigan State University, East Lansing, MI 48824.

certain to need professional help at some point—even if it's only to provide a few days of specialized advice. "Woe to the candidate who thinks he can run his campaign on his own," says Chris LaCivita,

executive director of the Virginia Republican Party. "It's hard for a person running even for school board to spend all the time he needs meeting and speaking with people without paying someone to

What you can expect to learn

While individual programs differ somewhat, nonpartisan programs for candidates generally are nonprofit and are located on or near college campuses in order to tap resources there. They provide training for emerging candidates, often in several weekend sessions spread over periods of up to a year and taught by political pros, journalists, and college professors.

Some of the programs also offer intensive weeklong sessions. The curriculum often has a practical orientation. You write speeches, tape commercials, face interviewers, and learn fund-raising techniques. The programs also emphasize public policy and ethics and attempt to have students solve problems through compromise with people who have different points of view. Classes sometimes move around to expose students to places that they may not know.

Who gets in

Most of the programs running today are open only to residents of the states they serve. That enables them to focus on state and local issues and to keep the institute "family" to a reasonable size so that graduates and those who teach there know one another. People who have already demonstrated some interest in community involvement—through schools, churches, or chambers of commerce—are most likely to be accepted by public leadership programs.

"This is not just an intellectual enterprise," says Bill Wood, executive director of the Sorensen Institute. "You have to want it to give up a Saturday to talk transportation issues."

The Michigan program usually has about 100 applicants for 20 to 25 slots. About one-quarter of those enrolled already have held public office.

Most programs have written applications and an interview stage that will focus on how applicants intend to use their experiences. The participants range in age from twenties to seventies. There are high

school graduates, Ph.D.'s, veterinarians, housewives, and business people. Most of the programs do cost money—as much as a couple of thousand dollars when room and board are included—but most also have growing endowments that enable them to provide discounts or free tuition to qualified people in need.

Promising results

How helpful are the schools? Graduates have been elected to the North Carolina Supreme Court, state legislatures, numerous city and county governing boards and councils, and even to the Chippewa Indian council.

"The biggest benefit comes from people who have different philosophies and views dealing with one another over a long period of time," says Wood. "I don't think people necessarily change their minds on issues, but they learn that someone from a different background might have a totally different point of view, and they learn how to craft compromises without acrimony."

handle all the daily grind that's important."

Consultants, a professional campaign manager, and a pollster are all virtually essential to most campaigns today. The pollster will determine your election chances by polling your district to see if the incumbent or other candidates are beatable. Polls should tell you what issues voters see as most important. (Some of this information can be obtained from local elections offices, usually at a modest cost, but the data will come without analysis, which a pollster will provide.)

Consultants will help develop your message based on the polls and design a plan for delivering that message, again and again, with force. The campaign manager handles details that can overwhelm a candidate, such as coordinating volunteers, and scheduling and getting out the vote. There are consultants who work in 15 to 20 specific fields, such as media, finance, mail, and phones.

There are also general consultants who have experience in all aspects of campaigning who can coordinate all the activities for you. Money (again) and the experience of volunteers will affect which you hire. Some consultants are driven by issues or party affiliation, while others are "hired guns" who work for individual candidates at their discretion. Some will work for you by the hour or week if your budget is severely limited. Sometimes, political science departments at colleges and universities can be sources of help in the form of students and faculty who are interested in practical experience.

●◆ *WHAT INSIDERS SAY:*

If the name-brand polling companies are too expensive for your campaign, try local media outlets such as newspapers and television stations. Often, they have their own polling operations that feed news and advertising divisions. They may be available, for a competitive fee, to conduct polls for candidates.

Finding the Right Pro

Where can you find good consultants? The political parties keep talent banks that candidates can draw from. *Campaigns and Elections* magazine at 1414 22nd Street NW, Washington, DC 20037, and its Web site (www.camelect.com) contain directories of consultants as well. Word of mouth is important, too, so ask people who have run successfully which consultants they used.

Veteran campaign manager S. J. Guzzetta suggests that you avoid professionals you know by name. The best consultants are unseen. It's the candidate, not the consultant, that the public should recognize. A consultant with a "name" can be a detriment to a campaign because people may have preconceived notions about them.

●◆ *WHAT INSIDERS SAY:*

When you begin planning your race, consider running in an off-year election, when there is no presidential or gubernatorial race to compete for hired help. Consultants use off-year elections to hone their skills and build their résumés, and they may be available for less than premium prices.

Also, consider hiring the young and eager—the less experienced professionals. They can make up for inexperience with enthusiasm. Running a winning campaign is the quickest route into the big time for them.

CAMPAIGNING ON THE INTERNET

When Jesse "the Body" Ventura won the election and became Jesse "the Governor of Minnesota" Ventura, people started looking at his campaign to see what he had done to pull such an upset.

What they found was a great Web site and a solid ring of supporters who were kept involved via e-mail. In fact, the Ventura campaign was so effective that it won a special award from the consultants' association for best use of technology.

In an article in *Campaigns and Elections* magazine on how campaigns are using this inexpensive, proliferating medium, it was reported that 63 percent of the campaigns said they were using the Internet.

Editor Ron Faucheux stated that the Internet is "rapidly taking its place as a full-fledged component of the political campaign mix." It is "a new method of leveraging the most valuable currency in the modern world of political campaigns—information."

Planning Your Web Site

Jesse Ventura was lucky to be running as the Reform Party candidate. The party's unorthodox founder is Phil Madsen, a self-described Internet enthusiast who has parallel passions for antiestablishment politics and the Web. He developed Ventura's technological attack from scratch, and now he is being courted by other campaigns interested in learning just how he did it. Here are Madsen's tips for developing an effective Web site.

✓ Since the domain name is the address that Internet visitors use to find your Web site, start by registering a name that is as straightforward as possible. For Ventura, the choice was www.jesseventura.com. Madsen recommends using your own name, with no cute or clever additions.

✓ For ideas on designing your site, survey those that states have set up. They are easy to understand and use, and they contain content and features that you might adopt. State sites are at www.state.*(two-letter state abbreviation)*.us. For example, the Pennsylvania site is www.state.pa.us. Another simply designed, user-friendly site is www.webwhiteblue.com. Its purpose is to be a democracy portal for information on elections, campaigning, issues, and election-oriented sites. And the award-winning Ventura site will continue to run at www.jesseventura.com. Don't miss it.

✓ Create a focus group to survey sites and suggest what they like and don't like.

✓ For content, start with an accurate biography and information on public policy positions. "If I had to choose between content and whizbang features, I'd go for content," Madsen says. Put in all press releases, position papers, a current schedule, copies of brochures, and even TV commercials.

✓ Keep the site changing and current. Madsen says that the Web community will be watching you and the opposition over the Internet, and what they see will influence their votes. A static site means a dull candidate.

✓ Place your Web master in the campaign hierarchy just below the campaign manager. This person should be involved in policy decisions and may end up working closely with your most dedicated volunteers and supporters. Check the yellow pages under "Internet" or "Computers" for experts in this area; check state or local party talent banks, or look at *Campaigns and Elections* magazine or its Web site (www.camelect.com), all of which may carry lists of companies and individuals who do this. If you're willing to take a chance on a novice who may be enthusiastic, ask around the political science or computer science departments of a local college or university.

✓ Promote your Web site. Put the domain name on everything from T-shirts and billboards to press releases. Go to the media, almost all of which now have Web sites, and make sure that your site can be accessed from theirs. That way, people who read the newspaper's site can click over to yours. Sometimes, these links are provided as a public service and are free; if you want a prominent display, there probably will be a charge, although it should be relatively low.

✓ Place a box on your site where people can sign up to receive e-mail from the campaign. Ventura's "Jessenet" became a legion of committed followers who were kept up-to-date with sometimes-daily messages about how they might help. They also used e-mail to notify the campaign of opportunities or issues that needed to be addressed. Keep these contacts meaningful, Madsen says, and be aware that the opposition will see the information, too.

•➔ WHAT INSIDERS SAY:

Never send unsolicited e-mail. (If you encourage people to sign up for a mailing list, you will know that they welcome your e-mail.) In increasing numbers, states are passing laws against this form of junk mail. And, like telephone solicitations and traditional junk mail, it angers people or just ends up in the trash can.

Setting Up Your Site

Depending on your technology comfort level and that of your campaign staff, you may want professional help in registering your domain name and setting up your Web site. For help, you can work through Internet providers such as America Online or go to professionals listed in the yellow pages under "Internet" or "Computers."

If you decide to do it yourself, visit www. internic.net. This site is operated by Network Solutions, the company that used to register *all* domain names. (Their exclusive contract expired in spring of 1999, and others have entered this marketplace.) There you will find detailed application forms and instructions for registering domain names.

Be aware that the opposition, whether in competitive business or in politics, has begun locking up domain names that their competitors might want to use. It's a good idea to register as early as possible and to consider registering more than one name that logically leads to you, in case you find that you need a second site later. Internic charges just $70 to register a name for 2 years.

•➔ WHAT INSIDERS SAY:

You may find that it's surprisingly inexpensive to hire a smaller local Internet company to help with the technical work you'll need. It can register your domain name, help design the site to your specifications, make sure that it's operating properly, and get you linked to other sites for a monthly cost that's close to that of a phone line. In addition, you'll have a clear relationship with the Web master. "I'll know you and you'll know me when you call with a question," says Wayne Clevenger, director of marketing at ALC Communications in Richmond, Virginia. "Try that with AOL."

CAMPAIGNING ON A TIGHT BUDGET

While all this talk of Web sites and paid consultants may seem daunting, keep in mind that thousands of candidates run for office each year on budgets of $5,000 or less. Usually, they are running for school board, county commissioner, a judgeship, or another relatively low-level job in the political hierarchy.

To be successful in such a no-frills campaign, or even in campaigns that cost thousands more, you'll have to find the right media to get your name out to the public and to spread your message. In addition, it's more important to target your efforts toward the people who are most likely to vote.

You'll also be heavily dependent on volunteers. Any campaign is, but the smaller the budget, the more you'll have to rely on the donated efforts of friends and supporters. Also, say insiders, you'll need to run a very focused campaign that concentrates on these points.

The Message

It's crucial to keep the key building block of any campaign—your message—foremost in your mind. Mixed messages send your supporters in different directions.

Look for your likely constituency, find two or

three major issues, use them to mold the message, then "stick to it and repeat it," says veteran campaign consultant Diane Waltrip. "If you and everyone else can't recite your message off the tip of your tongue, you're going to fail."

The Target

There are a lot of methods that you can use in a low-budget campaign to make yourself aware of where your likely voters—those who will respond to your message—are in your district and what in-

---

POLITICS, THE OLD-FASHIONED WAY

Michael Coleman was raised in a family that valued community service. His father, a doctor, made house calls. Coleman lived in an old-fashioned neighborhood where everyone looked out for each other.

That family, that neighborhood, and a deep-rooted sense of commitment to it drove Coleman to a successful, rewarding life in politics done the old-fashioned way. Now in his forties, he has climbed the ladder: Today, he is president of the Columbus, Ohio, City Council, and he is mentioned prominently as mayoral material. Thirty-two years ago, he was pleased to be sweeping the floor at Democratic Party headquarters.

As a child, Coleman, an African-American, volunteered to work for then-rare candidates of his race in Toledo, his hometown. He cleaned up and took out trash. Still, he never considered it demeaning.

"I felt like I was doing something worthy," he says. Among other things, he was seeing campaigns from the inside. In college, Coleman ran for freshman class vice president. He lost, but it was a great experience, he says. He worked as a reporter for the school paper, keeping an eye on political issues. He went on to law school and joined the Democratic Voters League in Dayton, where he passed out literature, went door-to-door for candidates, and got involved in the community.

One day, he wrote a letter to President Carter asking for a job at the White House, and to his surprise, he was hired for an internship as a law clerk there. After that heady experience, he returned to Columbus and worked as a lawyer, only to find himself wanting to do more for his community.

With some party support and a lot of door-to-door cam-

paigning, Coleman ran for city council, stressing his "abiding commitment to community service" as his message. Specifically, he pressed public transportation initiatives, neighborhood revitalization, and housing initiatives that were the concerns of many in his district. His campaign attracted a broad-based constituency, he says. That constituency has remained with him, supporting him with time, money, and, most important, votes.

Asked what lessons his career might provide for others, Coleman cites just one: Hold firm to your commitment to serve the community, and the community will return its support.

"In the real world of politics, you have to find resources," which often means money, he says. "I've succeeded because I can bring a lot of people to the table who will each contribute something to get things done."

terests them. Drive around the district and see how people live, carefully examine census data and voting records (available from your voting registrar or commissioner), and sit in on every meeting you can find in your community.

You should develop a clear mental picture of where your potential voters are. "Don't spend your few dollars to send direct mail to areas where people probably won't vote for someone of your party persuasion," says John Cosgrove of Chesapeake, Virginia, who won his last race for city council. "Target your material where it will be most effective."

Since many low-budget elections also tend to be free from party involvement, you need to focus first on the people in the district whom you know are going to vote. Political parties, elected officials whose districts include yours, and even local voter registration offices are likely to have this information. Check newspapers for published returns by precinct in previous elections. If you can't knock on the doors of individuals who always vote, you should at least be able to spend most of your time in neighborhoods that have higher voter turnouts than others.

The Media

One of the most important people in a small-scale campaign can be the yard sign coordinator. The coordinator should be a hardworking supporter who is willing to scout out busy locations, solicit space there, and then have colorful signs (with your name and message printed clearly) made up and posted.

Because paid advertising can quickly bust a campaign budget, low-budget candidates need to be comfortable with news reporters who will cover (or ignore) the race and editors who will coordinate that coverage. It can be helpful to fax them weekly schedules, along with making occasional phone calls to remind them of special events. Just remember to stick to the message and not overwhelm reporters with insignificant information. Always get back to those two or three issues.

A casual meeting over lunch, at which you introduce yourself and ask how to approach the paper effectively, can be helpful as well. Be aware that news reporters and editors are separate from editorial page writers and editors who are likely to endorse candidates. You'll need to approach the editorial people separately, probably by setting up a meeting with the editorial board at which you will be questioned about issues. If you read editorials carefully over time, you should have a picture of where the paper stands on issues. Be prepared to agree or disagree intelligently on the issues.

Network TV time is probably out of the question for most small-budget campaigns, especially if your district falls inside a major market. Look into cable and local public access channels, which can be substantially cheaper. Never turn down a chance to go on a news or local talk show, and be aware that you'll be lucky to get a few minutes' time. Deliver the message.

➠◆ WHAT INSIDERS SAY:

Consider buying a spot or two on CNN. Through your local cable franchise, you can target a relatively small geographical area that includes the county in which you are seeking that school board or council seat. Ads on cable cost a fraction of those on broadcast TV. You can buy spots on cable networks like CNN, whose viewers are likely to be politically active, which will give you extra bang for your buck. Or you may find your voters on The Golf Channel, Black Entertainment Television, or The Nashville Network. Cable can focus on specific audiences cheaply, and if you're lucky, your CNN ad will run during a major international incident or sensational trial and everyone will see it.

APPENDIX

Benefits for Residents, State by State

TAX ADVANTAGES FOR RETIREES

Ready to head for the hills when you finally retire? Or maybe you want to move closer to the kids. Before you decide where to relocate, check this chart for some of the possible tax advantages (or disadvantages) that each state offers retirees. States are ranked from the lowest percentage of personal income that

STATE	MAX INCOME TAX RATE (%)	TAX BREAK FOR AGE 65+	SALES TAX (%)	SOCIAL SECURITY EXEMPTION
1. New Hampshire	5 (dividends and interest only)	Yes	None	NA
2. Texas	None	NA	6.25	NA
3. South Dakota	None	NA	4	NA
4. Colorado	5	Yes	3	Based on income
5. Tennessee	6 (dividends and interest only)	Yes	6	NA
6. Illinois	3	Yes	6.25	Full
7. New Jersey	6.37	Yes	6	Full
8. Virginia	5.75	Yes	3.5	Full
9. Florida	None	NA	6	NA
10. Maryland	4.88	Yes	5	Full
11. Alabama	5	No	4	Full
12. Missouri	6	Yes	4.225	Based on income
13. Oregon	9	Yes	None	Full
14. Georgia	6	Yes	4	Full
15. Ohio	6.8	No	5	Full
16. New York	6.85	No	4	Full
17. Pennsylvania	2.8	No	6	Full
18. Nebraska	6.68	Yes	5	Based on income
19. Louisiana	6	Yes	4	Full
20. Arizona	5.01	Yes	5	Full
21. Rhode Island	27% of federal tax; max of 10.67%	Yes	7	Based on income
22. Vermont	25% of federal tax; max of 9.9%	Yes	5	Based on income
23. Indiana	3.4	Yes	5	Full

goes toward state taxes (New Hampshire) to the highest (New Mexico).

Please note that this chart provides only a simple breakdown of some common tax considerations, and all are subject to change. Also note that all states have estate taxes, but exemptions may be available. Check with your accountant, the state's tax bureau, or the American Association of Retired Persons (AARP) for help in doing a complete analysis.

INHERITANCE TAX (EXEMPTIONS AVAILABLE)	MILITARY OR GOVT PENSION EXEMPTION	PRIVATE PENSION EXEMPTION	HOMESTEAD EXEMPTION (RESTRICTIONS MAY APPLY)
Yes	NA	NA	Yes
No	NA	NA	Yes
Yes	NA	NA	Yes
No	Some	Some	No
Yes	NA	NA	Yes
No	Full	Full	Yes
Yes	Some	Some	Yes
No	Some	Some	Yes
No	NA	NA	Yes
Yes	Some	Some	Yes
No	Full	Some	Yes
No	Some	Some	No
No	Tax credits	Tax credits	Yes
No	Some	Some	Yes
No	Tax credits	Tax credits	Yes
No	Full	Some	Yes
Yes	Full	Full	Yes
Yes	None	None	No
Yes	Full	Some	Yes
No	Some	None	Yes
No	None	None	Yes
No	None	None	Yes
Yes	Some	None	Yes

(continued)

STATE	MAX INCOME TAX RATE (%)	TAX BREAK FOR AGE 65+	SALES TAX (%)	SOCIAL SECURITY EXEMPTION
24. Nevada	None	NA	6.5	NA
25. Iowa	8.98	No	5	Based on income
26. South Carolina	7	Yes	5	Full
27. Kansas	6.45	Yes	4.9	Based on income
28. Massachusetts	5.95 (12% on interest, dividends, capital gains)	Yes	5	Full
29. Montana	11	Yes	None	Based on income
30. Alaska	None	NA	None	NA
31. Oklahoma	7	Yes	4.5	Full
32. Wyoming	None	NA	4	NA
33. Washington	None	NA	6.5	NA
34. California	9.3	No	6	Full
35. Connecticut	4.5	No	6	Based on income
36. North Carolina	7.75	Yes	4	Full
37. Arkansas	7	Yes	4.625	Full
38. Utah	7	Yes	4.75	Based on income
39. Idaho	8.2	Yes	5	Full
40. North Dakota	12	Yes	5	Based on income
41. Maine	8.5	Yes	5.5	Full
42. Mississippi	5	Yes	7	Full
43. Kentucky	6	Yes	6	Full
44. West Virginia	6.5	No	6	Based on income
45. Michigan	4.4	Yes	6	Full
46. Wisconsin	6.77	Yes	5	Based on income
47. Minnesota	8.5	Yes	6.5	Based on income
48. Delaware	6.9	Yes	None	Full
49. Hawaii	10	Yes	4	Full
50. New Mexico	8.2	Yes	5	Based on income
District of Columbia (not ranked)	9.5	Yes	5.75	Full

INHERITANCE TAX (EXEMPTIONS AVAILABLE)	MILITARY OR GOVT PENSION EXEMPTION	PRIVATE PENSION EXEMPTION	HOMESTEAD EXEMPTION (RESTRICTIONS MAY APPLY)
No	NA	NA	Yes
Yes	Some	Some	Yes
No	Some	Some	Yes
No	Full	None	No
No	Full	None	Yes
Yes	Some	Some	Yes
No	NA	NA	Yes
No	Some	Some	Yes
No	NA	NA	Yes
No	NA	NA	Yes
No	None	None	Yes
Yes	None	None	Local option
No	Some	Some	Yes
No	Some	Some	No
No	Some	Some	Yes
No	Some	None	Yes
No	Some	None	No
No	None	None	Yes
No	Full	Full	Yes
Yes	Some	Some	Yes
No	Some	None	Yes
No	Full	Some	Yes
No	Some	None	No
No	Some	Some	Yes
No	Some	Some	Local option
No	Full	Full	Yes
No	Some	Some	Yes
No	Some	None	Yes

SUPPORT FOR COLLEGE TUITION

Other than the cost of buying a home, putting your kids through college could be the greatest expense you'll face in life. Some states appreciate this burden more than others and dedicate a larger portion of state aid to their university systems. This helps lower your out-of-pocket expenses. To give you a reading of how your state and others fare, this chart, alphabetical by state, compares 1999 tuition rates for a full-time liberal arts major taking 30 credit hours per year. The figures include mandatory fees but not room, board, books, or incidental expenses.

Note: A number of states offer a little-known feature called

SCHOOL	LOCATION	RESIDENT TUITION AND/OR FEES	NONRESIDENT TUITION AND/OR FEES	RECIPROCITY
University of Alabama	Birmingham	$3,090	$5,820	No
University of Alaska	All	2,250	7,020	Yes
University of Arizona	Tucson	1,132	4,708	No
University of Arkansas	Fayetteville	3,532	8,872	Yes
Arkansas State University	Jonesboro	2,972	6,826	Yes
University of California	Los Angeles	3,678	13,851	No
California State University	Sacramento	1,917	9,297	No
University of Colorado	Boulder	1,559	7,949	No
Colorado State University	Fort Collins	1,531	5,374	Yes
University of Connecticut	Storrs	5,398	13,916	No
Connecticut State University	New Britain	3,772	9,312	No
University of Delaware	Newark	4,978	13,348	No
Delaware State University	Dover	3,096	7,088	No
University of Florida	Gainesville	2,140	9,130	No
Florida State University	Tallahassee	2,196	9,184	No
University of Georgia	Athens	1,517	5,138	Yes
Georgia State University	Atlanta	2,414	9,656	No
University of Hawaii	Manoa	3,141	9,621	Yes
University of Idaho	Moscow	2,348	8,348	Yes
Idaho State University	Pocatello	2,398	8,638	Yes
University of Illinois	Chicago	4,628	10,904	No
Illinois State University	Normal	4,210	10,466	No
Indiana University	Bloomington	4,244	12,900	Yes
Indiana State University	Terre Haute	3,426	8,554	No

reciprocity, which means that they reduce out-of-state tuition rates for select students from neighboring states. If your child has a craving for a new locale or a major that isn't offered in your state, this feature could save you thousands of dollars. States may give tuition breaks for one or more of the following reasons: student exchanges with other states in their region, student merit, residence in specified regions or counties, student connection as a child of an alumnus, and membership in the Academic Common Market (some states trim tuition for students who can't take a specific major in their own state systems). Reciprocity responses are based only on the campuses listed and are subject to change; satellite or branch campuses nearer state borders may have their own reciprocity programs.

SCHOOL	LOCATION	RESIDENT TUITION AND/OR FEES	NONRESIDENT TUITION AND/OR FEES	RECIPROCITY
University of Iowa	Iowa City	$2,786	$10,228	No
Iowa State University	Ames	2,786	9,346	No
University of Kansas	Lawrence	2,313	8,907	Yes
Kansas State University	Manhattan	2,341	8,944	Yes
University of Kentucky	Lexington	3,296	9,216	Yes
Kentucky State University	Frankfort	2,270	6,310	No
Louisiana State University	Baton Rouge	2,888	7,084	Yes
University of Maine	Orono	3,090	7,560	Yes
University of Maryland	College Park	4,939	11,827	No
University of Massachusetts	Amherst	5,212	13,365	Yes
University of Michigan	Ann Arbor	6,342	19,792	No
Michigan State University	East Lansing	5,320	12,684	No
University of Minnesota	Minneapolis	4,649	12,790	Yes
University of Mississippi	Oxford	3,054	6,156	Yes
Mississippi State University	Mississippi State	3,017	6,119	Yes
University of Missouri	Columbia	4,580	12,495	No
University of Montana	Missoula	2,967	8,077	Yes
Montana State University	Bozeman	2,976	8,725	Yes
University of Nebraska	Lincoln	3,338	7,845	Yes
University of Nevada	Reno	2,145	8,492	Yes
University of New Hampshire	Durham	6,939	15,829	Yes
Rutgers (State University of New Jersey)	New Brunswick	4,762	9,692	No
The College of New Jersey	Ewing	5,685	9,002	No

(continued)

SCHOOL	LOCATION	RESIDENT TUITION AND/OR FEES	NONRESIDENT TUITION AND/OR FEES	RECIPROCITY
University of New Mexico	Albuquerque	$2,430	$9,172	Yes
New Mexico State University	Las Cruces	2,502	8,166	Yes
State University of New York	Buffalo	4,510	9,410	No
University of North Carolina	Chapel Hill	2,262	11,428	No
North Carolina State University	Raleigh	2,414	11,580	No
University of North Dakota	Grand Forks	2,956	7,098	Yes
North Dakota State University	Fargo	3,089	7,231	Yes
Ohio University	Athens	4,800	10,101	No
Ohio State University	Columbus	4,137	12,087	No
University of Oklahoma	Norman	2,210	6,290	Yes
Oklahoma State University	Stillwater	2,340*	6,400*	Yes
University of Oregon	Eugene	3,700	12,800	Yes
Oregon State University	Corvallis	3,549	12,393	Yes
Pennsylvania State University	University Park	6,162	13,278	No
Rhode Island College	Providence	4,082	10,082	Yes
University of South Carolina	Columbia	3,618	9,473	No
South Carolina State University	Orangeburg	3,410	6,702	No

*Tuition and fees for both residents and nonresidents are based on 28 credit hours per year.

SCHOOL	LOCATION	RESIDENT TUITION AND/OR FEES	NONRESIDENT TUITION AND/OR FEES	RECIPROCITY
University of South Dakota	Vermillion	$3,243	$7,062	Yes
South Dakota State University	Brookings	3,148	6,967	Yes
University of Tennessee	Knoxville	2,858	4,586	Yes
Tennessee State University	Nashville	2,442	7,558	No
University of Texas	Austin	2,280	8,760	No
Texas A&M University	College Station	1,350	8,970	No
University of Utah	Salt Lake City	2,412	7,609	Yes
Utah State University	Logan	1,928	6,207	Yes
University of Vermont	Burlington	8,046	19,254	Yes
University of Virginia	Charlottesville	4,300	16,775	No
Virginia State University	Petersburg	3,086	8,630	No
University of Washington	Seattle	3,638	12,029	No
Washington State University	Pullman	4,340	11,374	Yes
West Virginia University	Morgantown	2,568	7,920	Yes
West Virginia State College	Institute	2,836	5,588	No
University of Wisconsin	Madison	3,735	13,049	Yes
University of Wyoming	Laramie	2,326	7,414	Yes

COSTS AND INCENTIVES FOR SMALL BUSINESS

There's an old adage about starting a business that says there are three major keys to success: location, location, location. Well, location doesn't mean just the part of town where you settle down; it also can refer to the state. Some states are more supportive of business than others, offering everything from low corporate income tax rates to special incentives for small-business startups. They put more money in your pocket and increase the chances that your new

STATE	MAX CORP INCOME TAX RATE (%)	FRANCHISE TAX/ ANNUAL REPORT FEE
Alabama	5	$10/$1,000 of capital stock; $50 minimum; $10 annual report fee
Alaska	9.4	$100 biennially
Arizona	8	$45/year
Arkansas	6.5	27% of capital stock; $50 minimum
California	8.84	Same as corporate income tax; $5 annual report fee
Colorado	5	$25 biennially
Connecticut	9.5	Same as income tax
Delaware	8.7	Generally $30–$90, depending on level of capital stock
District of Columbia	9.98	$200 biannually
Florida	5.5	$150/year
Georgia	6	$10 minimum; up to $250 for corporations with capital of $500,000; rates increase for capital above $500,000
Hawaii	6.4	$25/year
Idaho	8	NA
Illinois	4.8	1% of capital investment; $25 minimum

business will succeed. Here are the benefits that you'll find in the state-by-state table below.

Maximum corporate income tax rate: Some states' maximums are lower than others'.

Lower franchise taxes and annual report fees: These are assessed on all corporations as payment for the right to do business in a state.

S corporation tax incentives: These policies let small-business owners claim business profits on their personal income returns, which may be taxed at a lower rate.

Other common corporate tax incentives: Some states give tax credits or exemptions to encourage location in low-income areas called enterprise, renaissance, opportunity, or development zones. They may also offer credits for small-business startups and for certain employee-friendly business practices.

S CORP TAX INCENTIVE	COMMON CORP TAX INCENTIVES
Yes	Tax credits for enterprise zones and basic skills training
Yes	Industrial business credit
Yes	Tax credits for enterprise zones, research and development, hiring of welfare recipients
Yes	Tax credits for enterprise zones, youth apprenticeship programs, child care facilities
Yes, but franchise tax imposed at 1.5% of net income	Tax credits for enterprise zones, child care expenses
Yes	Tax credits for enterprise zones, contributions to promote child care; school-to-career investment tax credit
Yes, but 9.5% corporate income tax imposed; to end after 2000	Tax credits for enterprise zones, various worker training programs
Yes	Tax credits for neighborhood assistance programs, including job training or education
No; taxed like other corporations	Tax credits for enterprise zones
Yes	Tax credits for enterprise zones, child care expenses, youth employment programs
Yes	Tax credits for job creation, basic skills education programs, retraining programs, child care
Yes	Tax credits for enterprise zones, hiring vocational rehabilitation referrals
Yes	Tax credit for investment in depreciable property and machinery and equipment
Yes, but subject to 1.5% tax on net income	Tax credits for enterprise zones, training expenses, job creation, dependent care programs

(continued)

STATE	MAX CORP INCOME TAX RATE (%)	FRANCHISE TAX/ ANNUAL REPORT FEE
Indiana	3.4	$30 biennially
Iowa	12	$30/year
Kansas	4	0.1% of shareholder equity; $20 minimum
Kentucky	8.25	0.21% of capital; $30 minimum
Louisiana	8	0.3% of capital stock; $10 minimum; additional $25 annual filing fee
Maine	8.93	$60/year
Maryland	7	$100/year
Massachusetts	9.5	$85/year
Michigan	2.2	$15/year
Minnesota	9.8	NA
Mississippi	5	0.25% of capital stock; minimum $25; additional $25 annual filing fee
Missouri	6.25	0.05% of capital stock; additional $40 annual filing fee
Montana	6.75	$10/year
Nebraska	7.81	Rates vary; examples: $13/year for corporations with less than $10,000 capital stock, $400 for $500,000 of capital stock
Nevada	NA	$85/year
New Hampshire	7	$100/year
New Jersey	9	$40/year

S CORP TAX INCENTIVE	COMMON CORP TAX INCENTIVES
Yes	Tax credits for enterprise zones, economically disadvantaged areas, teacher summer employment
Yes	Tax credits for enterprise zones, new jobs and income
Yes	Tax credit for small employer health benefit plan
Yes	Tax credits for enterprise zones, hiring unemployed, health insurance premiums
No; taxed like other corporations	Tax credits for new business, new jobs, reentrant jobs, employer donations, hiring unemployed residents
Yes	Tax credits for investment in new equipment, subsidizing child care, high-tech investment, low-income health plan contributions, subsidizing long-term care insurance
Yes	Tax credits for enterprise zones, hiring recipients of Federal Aid to Families with Dependent Children, employee (or child of employee) with disability, providing long-term care insurance, paid work-based learning programs for students
Yes	Tax credits for economic opportunity areas, locating in poverty areas
No; taxed like other corporations	Tax credits for enterprise zones, small businesses, unincorporated taxpayers and S corporations, investment in minority-owned business, high-technology businesses, apprentice training, renaissance zones
Yes	None
Yes	Tax credits for new jobs, providing child care, hiring recipients of Federal Aid to Families with Dependent Children, ad valorem property taxes (for new businesses)
Yes	Tax credits for enterprise zones; restoring abandoned property; contributions to higher education, youth opportunity and violence prevention programs, domestic violence shelters and maternity homes, adoption expenses
Yes	Tax credits for first 3 years of corporation existence or a corporate expansion, investment in wind-power equipment, conversion of a licensed vehicle to alternative fuel, investments in property to collect or utilize reclaimable property, disability insurance, S corporation investment
Yes	None
No	Tax credits during first 4 years of operation and for hiring students in work-study programs
No; taxed like other corporations	Tax credit for job creation
Yes	Tax credits for enterprise zones, new jobs, high-technology businesses, partnerships, commuter transportation benefits

(continued)

STATE	MAX CORP INCOME TAX RATE (%)	FRANCHISE TAX/ ANNUAL REPORT FEE
New Mexico	7.6	$50/year; $25 biannual report fee
New York	9	$9/year
North Carolina	7.25	15% of capital stock; $35 minimum; $10 annual report fee
North Dakota	10.5	$25/year
Ohio	8.5	$10 annual filing fee
Oklahoma	6	0.125% of capital stock; $10 minimum
Oregon	6.6	$30/year
Pennsylvania	9.99	0.119% of capital stock; $300 minimum
Rhode Island	9	0.025% of capital stock; $250 minimum
South Carolina	5	1% of capital stock plus $15; $25 minimum
South Dakota	NA	$10/year
Tennessee	6	0.25% of capital stock
Texas	NA	0.25% of capital plus 4.5% of net taxable earned surplus; additional $20 annual fee
Utah	5	$10 annual fee
Vermont	9.75	$15 annual fee
Virginia	6	$50/year if less than 5,000 shares are authorized
Washington	NA	$50/year
West Virginia	9	Rates vary; most common is 0.7% of apportioned equity, or $50, whichever is greater
Wisconsin	7.9	$25/year
Wyoming	NA	$25/year if corporate assets are $50,000 or less

SOURCE: Martin Geller CPA and Associates, 1999.

S CORP TAX INCENTIVE	COMMON CORP TAX INCENTIVES
Yes	Tax credits for enterprise zones, child care, qualified diversifying businesses, new business located on Native American land, hiring youth in school-to-career program
Yes; but fixed annual filing fee; $100 minimum	Tax credits for economic development zones
Yes	Tax credits for residential dwellings made handicapped accessible, solar and alternative energy
Yes	Credits or exemptions for qualified new businesses for first 5 years, renaissance zone investment, comprehensive health insurance
Yes	Tax credits for creation of new jobs, day care
Yes	Tax credits for Small Business Administration fees, alternative energy, inventions, health benefits, child care benefits, new jobs in specific industries
Yes	Tax credits for enterprise zones, programs qualified by state department of education, youth apprenticeship programs, child care benefits
Yes	Tax credits for Keystone Opportunity zones, employing recipients of Federal Aid to Families with Dependent Children, new jobs
Yes	Tax credits for enterprise zone investments during first year of operation, wages paid to juvenile offenders, cash bonus program, child care benefits, Small Business Administration fees, disabled access costs
Yes	Tax credits for economic impact zones, conservation tillage systems, new jobs, hiring recipients of Federal Aid to Families with Dependent Children, hiring terminated employees of military installations, child care benefits
No	None
No; taxed like other corporations	Tax credits for enterprise zones
No	None
Yes	Tax credits for new jobs, hiring disabled employees
Yes	Tax credits for job development zones, new jobs
Yes	Tax credits for enterprise zones, hiring disabled
Yes	None
Yes	Tax credits for hiring veterans, loans to retain jobs, business expansion
Yes	Tax credits for development zones, day care benefits
No	None

CONSUMER TAXES

A fair portion of your annual cost of living results from the taxes and fees your state collects. In some cases, these costs are clear—for example, your state sales tax rate is displayed virtually everyplace where you do business. But other taxes and

STATE	CIGARETTE TAX (PER PACK)	ALCOHOL TAX	MAX INCOME TAX RATE (%)	GAS TAX (PER GAL)
Alabama	16.5¢	5¢/12 fl oz of malt or brewed beverage, plus statewide local tax of 16.25¢/4 fl oz	5	16¢
Alaska	$1	35¢/gal of malt beverage	9.4	8¢
Arizona	58¢	16¢/gal of malt liquor	5.01	18¢
Arkansas	32¢	24¢/gal of beer (less than 5% alcohol)	7	19¢
California	87¢	20¢/gal of beer	9.3	18¢
Colorado	20¢	8¢/gal of malt liquor	5	22¢
Connecticut	50¢	19¢/gal of beer	4.5	32¢
Delaware	24¢	15.6¢/gal of beer	6.9	23¢
District of Columbia	65¢	9¢/gal of beer	9.5	20¢
Florida	68¢	48¢/gal of malt beverage	NA	4¢
Georgia	12¢	32.25¢/gal of malt beverage	6	7.5¢ plus 3% on sales price
Hawaii	80¢	93¢/gal of beer; 58¢/gal of draft beer	10	Varies by county; maximum of 32.5¢
Idaho	28¢	15¢/gal of beer	8.2	25¢
Illinois	58¢	7¢/gal of beer	3	19¢
Indiana	20.6¢	11.5¢/gal of beer	3.4	15¢
Iowa	36¢	18¢/gal of beer	8.98	20¢
Kansas	24¢	18¢/gal of beer	6.45	18¢

fees are less distinct, often hidden in the base price of the goods or services you buy.

Here's a breakdown of the major taxes and fees each state collects, along with some common tax exemptions. Note that municipalities may charge additional sales tax. Also, property tax rates vary by locality and may change annually.

SALES TAX (%)	SALES TAX EXEMPTIONS			PROPERTY TAX
	FOOD	PRESCRIPTION DRUGS	MEDICAL SERVICES	
4	No	Yes	Yes	Tax based on 20% of full market value, 15% of full market value of autos
NA	NA	NA	NA	Tax based on 100% of full market value
5	Yes	Yes	Yes	Maximum for residence is 1%; tax based on 100% of full market value
4.625	Yes	Yes	Yes	No statewide tax; tax based on 100% of full market value
6	Yes	Yes	Yes	Tax based on 100% of full market value
3	Yes	Yes	Yes	Tax based on 21% of full market value of residence, 29% of full market value of all other property
6	Yes	Yes	Yes	Tax based on 100% of full market value
NA	NA	NA	NA	No statewide tax; tax based on 100% of full market value; personal property exempt
5.75	Yes	Yes	Yes	Tax based on 96% of full market value
6	Yes	Yes	Yes	No statewide tax on real or tangible property; state tax on intangibles (e.g., stocks and bonds) at a rate of 0.2%; tax based on 100% of full market value
4	Yes	Yes	Yes	Tax based on 40% of full market value
4	No	No	No	Tax based on 100% of full market value of real estate
5	No	Yes	Yes	Tax based on 20% of full market value
6.25	No	Yes	Yes	Tax based on 33.33% of full market value
5	Yes	Yes	Yes	Tax based on 33.33% of full market value
5	Yes	Yes	Yes	Tax based on 100% of full market value; personal property exempt
4.9	No	Yes	Yes	0.175% statewide rate; tax based on 30% of full market value

(continued)

STATE	CIGARETTE TAX (PER PACK)	ALCOHOL TAX	MAX INCOME TAX RATE (%)	GAS TAX (PER GAL)
Kentucky	3¢	8¢/gal of beer	6	9% of wholesale price
Louisiana	20¢	32.25¢/gal of malt beverage	6	20¢
Maine	74¢	35¢/gal of malt liquor	8.5	19¢
Maryland	66¢	2.378¢/gal of beer	4.88	24¢
Massachusetts	76¢	10.645¢/gal of malt beverage	5.95 (12% on interest, dividends, capital gains)	19.1% of average price
Michigan	75¢	20.32¢/gal of beer	4.4	19¢
Minnesota	48¢	14.8¢/gal of beer	8.5	20¢
Mississippi	18¢	42.68¢/gal of beer	5	18¢
Missouri	17¢	6¢/gal of malt beverage	6	17¢
Montana	18¢	13.9¢/gal of beer	11	27¢
Nebraska	34¢	23¢/gal of beer	6.68	13¢
Nevada	35¢	9¢/gal of malt beverage	NA	18¢
New Hampshire	52¢	30¢/gal of malt beverage	5 (dividends and interest only)	18¢
New Jersey	80¢	12¢/gal of beer	6.37	11¢
New Mexico	21¢	41¢/gal of beer	8.2	17¢
New York	56¢	16¢/gal of beer	6.85	8¢
North Carolina	5¢	53.376¢/gal of malt beverage	7.75	18¢
North Dakota	11¢	16¢/gal of beer	12	20¢
Ohio	24¢	18¢/gal of beer	6.8	22¢
Oklahoma	23¢	40.32¢/gal of beer	7	16¢
Oregon	58¢	6.45¢/gal of malt beverage	9	24¢
Pennsylvania	31¢	8¢/gal of beer	2.8	12¢

SALES TAX (%)	SALES TAX EXEMPTIONS			PROPERTY TAX
	FOOD	PRESCRIPTION DRUGS	MEDICAL SERVICES	
6	Yes	Yes	Yes	0.153% statewide tax on real property, 0.25% statewide tax on intangibles (e.g., stocks and bonds); tax based on 100% of full market value
4	Yes	Yes	Yes	Real estate tax based on between 10% and 15% of full market value
5.5	Yes	Yes	Yes	Tax based on between 33.33% and 75% of full market value
5	Yes	Yes	Yes	Tax based on 40% of full market value of real estate, 100% of full market value of personal property
5	Yes	Yes	Yes	Maximum on real and personal property of 2.5%; tax based on 100% of full market value
6	Yes	Yes	Yes	Maximum of 1.5%; tax based on 50% of full market value
6.5	Yes	Yes	Yes	Tax based on 50% of full market value
7	No	Yes	Yes	Tax based on 100% of full market value
4.225	No	Yes	Yes	Tax based on 33.33% of property value, generally; 19% of full market value of residential property
NA	NA	NA	NA	Tax based on 100% of full market value
5	Yes	Yes	Yes	Tax based on 100% of full market value
6.5	Yes	Yes	Yes	Maximum of 3.64%; tax based on 100% of full market value
NA	NA	NA	NA	Tax based on 100% of full market value
6	Yes	Yes	Yes	Real estate tax based on between 20% and 100% of full market value
5	No	No	No	Tax based on 33.33% of full market value
4	Yes	Yes	Yes	Tax based on 100% of full market value
4	No	Yes	Yes	Tax based on 100% of full market value
5	Yes	Yes	Yes	Tax based on 9% of full market value of residential property
5	Yes	Yes	Yes	Tax based on percentage not to exceed 35% of full market value
4.5	No	Yes	Yes	Real estate tax based on percentage not to exceed 13.5% of full market value
NA	NA	NA	NA	Tax based on 100% of full market value
6	Yes	Yes	Yes	Tax based on 100% of full market value

(continued)

STATE	CIGARETTE TAX (PER PACK)	ALCOHOL TAX	MAX INCOME TAX RATE (%)	GAS TAX (PER GAL)
Rhode Island	71¢	9.67¢/gal of beer	27% of federal income tax; maximum of 10.67%	28¢
South Carolina	7¢	0.6¢/oz of beer	7	16¢
South Dakota	3.4¢	27.4¢/gal of malt beverage	NA	21¢
Tennessee	13¢	$1.10/gal (less than 5% alcohol)	6	17¢
Texas	45¢	19.35¢/gal of beer	NA	20¢
Utah	63.5¢	35¢/gal of beer	7	25¢
Vermont	44¢	26.5¢/gal (less than 6% alcohol); 55¢/gal (6–8% alcohol)	25% of federal tax; maximum of 9.9%	19¢
Virginia	3¢	0.827¢/gal of beer plus 2.65¢/bottle	5.75	18¢
Washington	82.5¢	19.6¢/gal of beer	NA	23¢
West Virginia	17¢	17.7¢/gal of beer (less than 4.2% alcohol)	6.5	21¢
Wisconsin	12¢	6.25¢/gal of beer	6.77	25.8¢ in 1999; rate changes annually
Wyoming	12¢	0.5¢/l of malt beverage	NA	14¢

SOURCE: Martin Geller CPA and Associates, 1999.

SALES TAX (%)	SALES TAX EXEMPTIONS			PROPERTY TAX
	FOOD	PRESCRIPTION DRUGS	MEDICAL SERVICES	
7	Yes	Yes	Yes	Tax based on 100% of full market value
5	No	Yes	Yes	Primary residence tax based on 4% of full market value
4	No	Yes	Yes	Tax based on 100% of full market value
6	No	Yes	Yes	Residential property tax based on 25% of full market value
6.25	Yes	Yes	Yes	Tax based on 100% of full market value
4.75	No	Yes	Yes	Tax based on 100% of full market value
5	Yes	Yes	Yes	Real estate tax is 1%; tax based on 100% of full market value
3.5	No	Yes	Yes	Tax based on 100% of full market value
6.5	Yes	Yes	Yes	Tax based on 100% of full market value
6	No	Yes	Yes	Maximum of 1% for real property; tax based on 60% of full market value
5	Yes	Yes	Yes	Tax based on 100% of full market value
4	No	Yes	Yes	Tax based on 100% of full market value

INDEX

Underscored page references indicate sidebars and tables.

H

Handicapped persons. *See* Disabled persons

Hanover, New Hampshire, food cooperative in, 41–42

Hawaii
lobbying in, 339
marketing information from, 368

Hawaii Volcanoes National Park
lodgings in, 198
map of, 203

Hazardous waste disposal, 313–15, 314–15

Health care
books on, 86
cost of, 79
dental care, 80–83
emotional care, 83–86
medical care, 86–92
patient rights in, 84–85

Health insurance, 86–87

Hearings, community, for persuading government, 18

High schools
financial aid for, 275–77, 277
government programs brought to, 277–80

Highway maps, 204

Hiking clubs, volunteer work in, 219, 221

Hiking maps, 204

Historical societies, as resource, 7–8

Historic preservation officers, 304

Historic properties
on National Register of Historic Places, 71, 73, 301
restoring, 300–304
contacting preservation officer about, 304
preservation easement for, 304

publications on, 303
standards for, 74–75
tax credits for, 301–3, 302–3, 303–4

History, school programs on, 279

Home building
inspections of, 62–63
permits for, 61
planning phase of, 60–61
zoning variance for, 62

Home buying
classroom training on, 68
mortgages for
FHA-backed loans, 63–64
from Rural Housing Service, 65–66
state loans, 66–67
Veterans Affairs loans, 64
publications on, 67–68

Home care, for elderly, 90

Home management
advice on, 109–11
classes in, 110
saving money on, 113–19

Homeowners' associations, 9

Home restorations
of historic properties, 74–75
National Register listing for, 71, 73
private organizations aiding, 76–78
publications on, 74
tax credits for, 74–76

Home safety
air quality, 70–71, 70, 123–24
for children, 120, 122, 122–23
fire safety, 120
health and safety advice, 119–20
warnings on unsafe products, 119

Home security
do-it-yourself, 94–95
for empty homes, 97–98

engraving possessions, 97
evaluating, 94–97
for mail, 98–99, 98–99
for new construction, 96

Honeybees. *See* Bees

Horses, adopting, 25–27

Hostels, 201–2

Hotlines
air-quality, 70–71
fall foliage, 309
IRS, 156–57
meat and poultry, 113
radon, 71

Household toxics, disposing of, 313–15, 314–15

Hunting Island State Park, cabins in, 195

I

Idaho, camping in, 194

Identity theft, preventing, 150–51

Immigration records, 23–24

Incubators, business, 354, 355

Indianapolis
community gardens in, 38–39
free seeds in, 39

Individual Retirement Accounts (IRAs), 172
pension rollovers to, 183
Roth, 172, 180
segregated, 183
withdrawing from, 179–80, 180–81

Inns, in national parks, 196–99

Inspections
fire safety, 120
home-building, 62–63
home energy, 48–49

Insurance, health, 86–87

Internal Revenue Service (IRS)
audits by
avoiding, 163
handling, 164–65